Date Due

Pushkin

Also by Henri Troyat
(Published in English)

Fiction

ONE MINUS TWO
JUDITH MADRIER
MOUNTAIN
WHILE THE EARTH ENDURES
- MY FATHER'S HOUSE
- THE RED AND THE WHITE
- STRANGERS ON THE EARTH

THE SEED AND THE FRUIT
- AMELIE IN LOVE
- AMELIE AND PIERRE
- ELIZABETH
- TENDER AND VIOLENT ELIZABETH
- THE ENCOUNTER

THE LIGHT OF THE JUST
- BROTHERHOOD OF THE RED POPPY
- THE BARONESS

EXTREME FRIENDSHIP

Non-fiction

FIREBRAND: THE LIFE OF DOSTOYEVSKY
TOLSTOY
DAILY LIFE IN RUSSIA UNDER THE LAST TSAR

1. (Frontispiece) Alexander Sergeyevich Pushkin (1799–1837)

There are the solemn names of emperors, generals, inventors of instruments of death, torturers and martyrs; and alongside them this one bright sound: Pushkin.

—Alexander Blok

Contents

PART FOUR

PART FIVE

PART SIX

PART SEVEN

PART EIGHT

APPENDICES

List of Illustrations

Author's Note

My feelings about this new English version of my *Pushkin* are two: there is the joy of seeing a personality I love and admire in the limelight again; and then relief, for it is now possible to clear up a misunderstanding which has been prejudicial to both myself and the author whose life I aspire to present.

The first edition of the work, published in the United States some years ago, was so truncated, presumably for commercial reasons which escape me, that—even though I was forewarned—I could hardly recognize my work when the book was in print. Large portions of chapters had been amputated; important general considerations remained in the translator's inkwell; almost everything relating to Pushkin's working methods and the analysis of his creations was cut. His personality emerged shorn of that dense tissue of thoughts and dreams which anyone weaves around the exercise of his profession, whatever it may be. What the American reader had was the abridged, amputated and impoverished text of the adapter, not my book. This new edition contains the whole of the original by a trusted translator.

One word more: Few authors have been more thoroughly studied in Soviet Russia than Pushkin. Every time a specialist unearths some scrap of paper embellished with his signature, a national holiday is declared. The slightest initial, the most insignificant recollection becomes material for exegesis. After so much research it need hardly be added that new material on Pushkin is extremely rare. Almost all the information in this book has been taken from previously published Russian sources. However, the last section of the volume includes excerpts from a few essential documents which should help to explain the duel and the poet's death.

H.T.

Notes on the Translation

1.

Although the Russians of Pushkin's class and day spoke as much if not more French than Russian, they did so with varying degrees of felicity, and French remained an artificial language for them. It did not quite evolve on its own as in, say, the French-colonized West Indies; but as an instrument of written expression, especially for those who spent most of their lives in the provinces, it suffered somewhat the same deformities and eccentricities as did Vatican Latin, for instance, at the hands of a monk in medieval Bohemia.

For this reason, Troyat indicates every instance in the book in which the text he is quoting was originally written in French—if only to make it clear that he is not responsible for some of the idiosyncrasies. The English translator has followed suit, because where the tone of a passage is in doubt, as it sometimes is, there was no alternative but to stay very close to the constructions used by the Russians, at the expense of fluency.

2.

Readers are reminded that although the book is translated from the French, that French is a mixture of four things: Troyat's own French, the Russians' own French (as in most official letters and many private ones), Troyat's translations from Russian into French (as in the poems) and, in some cases, Troyat's translations from Russian into French of texts (often official) which were first written in French but are now accessible only in Russian!

3.

Spellings will be found to be unbelievably inconsistent (e.g. Tsarskoye Selo but Griboedov and Dostoevsky; Turgenev but Guryev and so forth), depending on usage, ease of pronunciation and arbitrary choice

(Vulf/Wulf/Wolfe are all found in English books, as are Fikelmon/Ficquelmont and Pletnev/Pletnyev/Pletnyov). An attempt has been made, at least, to spell each name the same throughout. The same possibilities for confusion reign with respect to first names: a tsar, for example, is always called Alexander, whereas a man's first name nowadays is often written Aleksandr. For Vasily there exists the English counterpart Basil, which is used here, although Vasily would have done just as well; for Ivan we have, of course, John, but no one thinks of using it; for Sergey we have nothing. Marya is perhaps unnecessary, but we tend to think of Marya and not Mary when we think of Russian women; Yekaterina, on the other hand, seems a little forced, while Katerina is acceptable—although the name was invariably spelled and pronounced Catherine by the French-speaking upper classes. The translator can only offer apologies to any readers who are (justifiably) partial to a consistent scheme of transliteration.

4.

All quotations from the poetry and prose of Pushkin appearing in this book are fairly literal renderings of Troyat's translations into French —which are themselves unrhymed, straightforward versions in which he has attempted no more than to retain the approximate length and shape of the Russian line, and to avoid all decorative or exotic expressions other than those used by Pushkin himself. One must conclude that the experts are right, and that Pushkin's poetry is so embedded in the very marrow of the Russian language that it will not tolerate transplant or grafting onto any other organism. In other words, these texts can claim no kinship whatever with the original, but it is hoped that they do not contradict it. As Troyat wrote: "Translation of Pushkin is treason."

5.

The structure of the Russian ruling class may help to explain the forces combining to exterminate Pushkin. It was composed of two groups: the old boyars and their relations down to the lowliest country squire, who had existed long before the consolidation of the imperial dynasty and continued to thrive, to a considerable extent, apart from it; and the court and ambassadorial circle, containing a significant proportion of non-Russians. Pushkin belonged to the former, by blood and heart; circumstances forced him to live in the latter. There is not much tangible evidence of conflict between them, but the great and consistent difference between Moscow and St. Petersburg, in manner and attitude and style, certainly implies grounds for conflict. It is likely, for example, that Pushkin could not have come to grief so easily in Moscow; he would have been less isolated.

6.

Much that the Western layman finds strange and reprehensible in post-Revolutionary events becomes at least partially comprehensible when one thinks that a totally independent secret police, subject to no authority—not even that of the tsar—was set up and began functioning *by 1825*, and was presumably, at the time of the Revolution, more stable and ingrained than any other force in the country.

Pushkin

PART I

1. *Moscow*

It was not so much a city as a cluster of villages. Old, sprawling rural manses lurked beneath a tangle of bushes and weeds alongside gleaming, brand-new patrician town houses with neoclassical façades. The variegated cupolas of churches rose above lines of hovels built of overlapping boards covered with milky whitewash. The streets were rivers of dust. The squares resembled vacant lots. Scattered everywhere, for the benefit of all, miracle-working ikons surveyed the scene from beneath their dark peaked roofs. The sky was shattered by great peals of bells. Flocks of pigeons cut across the sun and were engulfed by a hole in a wall, or disappeared beneath the cabbage-green portico of some monastery.

In the city's center, above the bend in the Moskva, rose the massive red walls of the Kremlin with their swallow-tail crenellations. Behind the fortifications lay an imposing chaos, of gilded bulbs like pleated turbans, watchtowers ringed with bands of emerald-green tiles, aerial promenades, gingerbread cathedrals, two-headed eagles and perforated Orthodox crucifixes caparisoned with dangling chains. Outside the walls stretched the markets, milling crowds, cavernous shops and chapels with domes that looked as though they had been screwed on. People sauntered past booths displaying apples and watermelons—the men in loose blouses and high boots or bast* sandals, the women in wide-skirted, bright-colored gowns whose hems slapped the dust, their faces round as dolls' in the red or blue kerchiefs tied beneath their chins. Everyone shouted and gesticulated, or nibbled sunflower seeds or loitered at the corner of a booth.

Moving away from the center, the bustle faded, fewer people were seen about, and the houses nodded off into a dignified and cozy slumber.

Patriarchal, opulent and barbarous, the second capital of Russia had

* Bast is the inner bark of the lime or linden, and is made into rope, mats, etc.

just been colonized, at the end of the eighteenth century, by an invasion of aristocratic families fleeing the ostentation—and the perils—of St. Petersburg: St. Petersburg, home of the government, the court and the emperor, Paul I. And "the further you are from Paul I, the better," for the inhabitants of St. Petersburg lived in terror of their lives, the victims of a series of wildly arbitrary regulations adopted without warning, overnight. One edict made it illegal to wear Western-style trousers and fitted coats. Another forbade professors to use the word "revolution" in reference to the movements of celestial bodies. A police order required pedestrians to remove their hats, and horsemen to dismount, upon sight of the emperor.[1] At nine o'clock every evening, after curfew, the main thoroughfares were closed off by posts and chains, and only doctors and midwives allowed to pass. Officers carried their money with them on parade, as they were in perpetual fear of being arrested for some trifling misdemeanor and packed off to Siberia on the spot. "Even the weather is out of sorts," a contemporary wrote. "It is always dark, weeks go by and we never see the sun, one has no desire to go out of doors, apart from the fact that it is dangerous to do so. One is tempted to say that God has forsaken us."

In Moscow, however, far from the emperor's whims and tantrums, the rich could relax in a happy alliance of the libertine influences of eighteenth-century France and the rustic and openhearted customs of Old Russia. Every house of note harbored its French tutor, its émigré with powdered wig and elegant manners. It was positively uncouth to be without a Frenchman in the house. The demand for foreign instructors was so great that "governors" were snapped up on the street as they came out of mass. Seven Parisian footmen in the service of Count Shuvalov deserted their benefactor and set themselves up as teachers in other distinguished households. In the reign of Alexander I, one Moscow newspaper printed the following advertisement: "Dog keeper, German-born, seeks situation in kennel, or as tutor."[2]

In every home of consequence, the backbone of the family library was formed by the works of Voltaire, Jean-Baptiste Rousseau and Montesquieu. But the fine young ladies who spoke French better than their native tongue and the swaggering young bloods who wrote poetry in the style of the divine Parny but could hardly draft a thank-you note in Russian heard mass in the same church as the shopkeepers and artisans; their faith and tastes and fears and dearest hopes were all the same (although they did not know it) as those of the people whose ignorance they sneered at. Often, at dawn, a coach emblazoned with gilded coat of arms, drawn by six horses with braided, flower-strewn manes, would pull up at the door of some old chapel drowsing at the back of a cul-de-sac. Three curious characters were perched up behind:

a Heyduck in scarlet kaftan, a footman in white hose and snowy wig and a little blackamoor in pistachio-green turban. The Heyduck leaped down and lowered the velvet-upholstered carriage steps, and a young woman in a "Parisian gown" adorned with diamonds, pearls and plumes glided furtively into the church. She was on her way home from the ball; but, faithful to the rites of her childhood, she would hear matins before collapsing into bed.[3]

Although these young people were all brought up to worship Western ideas, their distractions had very little in common with those of their contemporaries in France, England or Germany. Despite the unflagging efforts of Empresses Elizabeth and Catherine, the theater in Moscow was still a costly divertissement patronized by a few of the idle rich in their own homes. Cock- and goose-fights were more popular. The geese, urged on by the spectators, only pecked at each other's wings and uttered demented shrieks that made everyone laugh; but the roosters were partly plucked before the fight and, with bare necks and rumps and iron claws fastened to their spurs, would hurl themselves at each other and tear each other to bits. A winning cock would fetch two or three hundred rubles.

On "Christian feast days," many merchants set up impromptu booths and kiosks in the fields around Moscow. Servants spread carpets on the ground and stood holding the flaps of the magnificent tents inside which their masters and their masters' guests disported themselves. Crowds surged and eddied around the stalls, and vehicles of every description threaded their way through the sea of idlers—from the shabby barouches of the *petite bourgeoisie* to the nobles' coaches with gilded doors, plumed trotters and bawling urchin astride the lead horse. Zhikharev, a government official, recorded his impressions of a drive he took on May 1, 1805: "Such a crowd! Such carefree, boisterous joy, such noise and shouting, music, singing and dancing! There are sumptuous Turkish and Chinese tents with tables laid for the guests and excellent orchestras, and simple branch huts half covered with rags, whose sole embellishment is a steaming samovar. The followers of Bacchus sing and dance to the accompaniment of a shepherd's horn."

It was a strange time, colorful, wild and simple: Houses were huge, with stables and barns and rows of outbuildings, and ancestral chambers filled with precious antique furniture; families were equally huge, and boisterous; guests were always welcome; people set out on a seven-day trek in a lurching, jolting carriage, just to say hello to a friend and admire his country estate. Blood was hot, appetites keen, cupboards bulging with mouth-watering provender—enough to victual a ship for a voyage around the world. One of the gastronomical proverbs of the day gives the measure fairly enough: "The goose is a useless fowl, for there is not enough meat on it for two, but almost too much for one."

The lady of the house was surrounded by a swarm of domestics: coachmen, laundresses, cooks, kitchenmaids and chambermaids. Her hospitable roof also sheltered an assortment of singular little old women taken in out of charity or curiosity, a great-uncle who was losing his hearing, a son's friend who had dropped in from Kiev and a few tutors who spent their time complaining about each other. There were never fewer than fifteen at table. At a dinner given by Count Sheremetyev, "only sixteen were invited," observed Zhikharev, "but the table was set for thirty, in case anyone should drop in unannounced." Mme. de Staël wrote that Count Orlov "was not acquainted with half the people dining in his home." She also said that "Mr. Naryshkin's door is always open, and when there are only twenty guests in his country house he groans at the tedium of his 'philosopher's retreat.'" She also mentioned a certain merchant who "practiced hospitality 'Russian-style'; that is to say, he flies a banner from his rooftop to announce that he is dining in, and that is invitation enough for his friends."

According to contemporary accounts, the model housewife rose at seven. She then proceeded to say her prayers and drink a cup of tea in the drawing room.[4] The steward soon appeared, bearing his accounts for her approval. The lady raged and fumed: The income from her estate would not begin to cover her expenses, which were enormous. Here it was the end of January, and the buckwheat had not been threshed, the rye was still unsold; an overseer would have to be sent to the village. The steward was succeeded by the coachman, come for his orders for the day; then it was the cook's turn, followed by the chambermaid in charge of the young ladies' wardrobes. The lady of the house added up her columns with a frown; despite her considerable fortune as the owner of more than 2500 souls in the governments of Ryazan, Tambov and Penza, she was perpetually in debt and could see no way of either cutting down her establishment or augmenting the income from her property. Besides, everyone in Moscow lived beyond his means.

After a luncheon of many and richly sauced courses, the lady drove out for her afternoon calls. Her evenings were taken up with balls, masquerades and amateur theatricals. Balls began at nine or ten, and none but the lions of fashion came late.

Thursday was Count Razumovsky's day "at home," Friday was the Apraxins', Sunday the Arkharovs received. The "dandies" contrived to attend two balls in an evening. The lighting in the ballrooms was so dim that it was impossible to make out the faces of people at the far end; but gowns were elegant, coiffures daring, and young and old alike burned with the desire to laugh, dance and drink. There were waltzes, quadrilles and frenzied mazurkas, with much clinking of spurs and flouncing of diaphanous skirts, and gentlemen dropping on one knee to kiss their ladies' hands as they tripped in a circle around them. The ball would end *à la grecque,* with all the dancers following the head couple through a maze of figures and on in a mad race through every room in the house. "On Saturday," wrote one of Mrs. Rimsky-Korsakov's daughters, "we danced at the Obolenskys' until five in the morning, and on Monday at the Golitsyns' until three; Thursday there is a fancy-dress ball at Mrs. Ryabin's, Saturday evening there is a party at the Obolenskys', Sunday we are invited to lunch at Count Tolstoy's and there will be dancing afterward, and the same evening there will be dancing at F. Golitsyn's. And so it will go all winter long, with never a pause. And yet the balls are all so lively, you dance until you drop . . . and then you have to lie in bed half the next day, paralyzed with exhaustion."

In another letter she wrote: "This year many have paid a high price for their love of dancing. Poor Princess Shakovskaya is seriously ill, and the little Countess Bobrynskaya caught cold at a ball, and now she is dying."

"In Moscow," Viegel wrote in his memoirs, "the winter is one long carnival." Bulgakov found the season of 1805 particularly insane: "There is one ball after another, and I can't understand how it is they do not all drop dead from exhaustion. If this madness goes on all winter, every single one of them will expire and the next season will have to open with a mass funeral for all the dancers."

But when the nobility abandoned their Muscovite drawing rooms and buried themselves in their country estates some thirty or forty verstst† from the city, it was a very different world they found: a world of impenetrable forests haunted by famished wolf packs, fierce bears and authentic highwaymen. This upper-class exodus from Moscow drained off a good half of the city's population, too, for when the gentry went to the country they took along the serfs attached to their persons (as distinct from those attached to the land)—men and women who performed every conceivable function in the household, from cooking to carpentry to shoeing horses to playing musical instruments and acting in amateur theatricals. Mme. de Staël speaks of Naryshkin's serf orchestra: "Each of the twenty players has his own note to play—always the same—every time it occurs in the music, and so they are all known by the note they play. When people see them they say, 'There goes Mr. Naryshkin's *do, re,* or *fa.*'"

† 1 verst = 0.66 miles.

In 1825 the population of Russia was forty-nine million souls, thirty-six million of whom were peasant serfs. A proposal had been made to give them some distinguishing form of dress, but the Senate rejected the bill, "fearing they might learn to recognize each other and so realize how numerous they were."

In Europe the traditions of serfdom had worn thin with time, but in Russia they were gathering strength with the rise of a national culture. The Russian serf had more freedom in the Middle Ages than he did in 1800, and the reason for this was that the state had required unremitting co-operation from the nobles, throughout the eighteenth century and, in exchange for services rendered, had ceded increasingly large tracts of land to them, all farmed by peasants. Catherine II distributed 800,000 souls during her reign; Paul I disposed of 500,000. Gradually, the peasants became attached to the master's land, then to his person; they were sold both with the land and without it. Newspapers carried such piquant advertisements as: "For sale, one hairdresser plus four beds, eiderdowns, and other utensils." Or, "For sale, girl of sixteen, excellent conduct, and a barouche, in fair condition." Or, "For sale, one cook, one coachman, and a parrot." "For sale, boy capable of grooming horses, and one milch cow." "For sale, by Panteleymon across from the market, a girl of thirty and one young stallion."

Nor were serfs particularly expensive. A gentleman would pay two thousand rubles for a purebred hound, but only three or four hundred for a male peasant, and one hundred or one hundred and fifty for a female. Those were the prices in the capital, of course; in the country you could buy a serf girl for five rubles in the 1800s, and a nursling for a few kopecks. Those with special skills, however, fetched a good price: A cook or musician would be worth at least eight hundred rubles.‡

This human livestock was totally subject to the master's whim. He judged all civil disputes between his peasants, deported and married them off at will, and if they showed any signs of resistance, had their heads shaved and sent them to the army for twenty-five years. A Russian serf owned nothing outright, and his credit was limited to five rubles by law.

The serf population of the greatest families was so large that the master could not even begin to know their names. The Sheremetyev household had a staff of three hundred, the Stroganovs had six hundred, the Razumovskys, nine hundred. Under the orders of a maître d'hôtel, who was identified by the fine cambric handkerchief in his hand, a vast flock of valets and footmen hurried and scurried about. The cook was surrounded by scullery maids and kitchen boys and dish-

‡ In the French colonies during the same period, a Negro was worth between two and three thousand francs.

washers. The head coachman directed a whole tribe of grooms and Vorreiters. The laundress in chief presided over a battalion of apprentices. One servant had sole responsibility for pharmaceutical matters, applying leeches impartially to his masters and his masters' horses. Others did nothing but polish the floors. There were especially trustworthy men to wind the clocks, and chauffeurs to light the fires before the family arose. A stripling was posted in every room to act as messenger, for the corridors were endless and the sound of a bell could never carry from one end to the other of these vast residences.

Even minor civil servants kept a full domestic panoply, and would have considered themselves dishonored had they been forced to pay a visit unattended by a footman with faded livery and vacant stare.

Many of the nobles, intoxicated by their own omnipotence, treated the serfs abominably. Beatings were common, and so was sexual abuse. General Izmailov kept a harem for his guests' delectation: Girls thirteen to sixteen years old were torn away from their parents "to suffer their common shame." According to police archives of the period, another "baryna" subjected his serfs to a full gamut of tortures ranging from the commonplace tearing off of toenails to more ingenious and scandalous devices. Alexis Pashkov sentenced wayward servants to "one or two pipes"; that is, the culprit was flogged uninterruptedly for as long as it took his master, seated in the courtyard, to smoke one pipe or two—depending on the gravity of the offense—while he enjoyed the spectacle. Princess Kozlovskaya is said to have struck her peasants on the sexual organs and had them hunted with dogs. Countess Saltykov kept her hairdresser in a cage, to prevent him from working for anyone else in her absence. The iron collar was not abolished until February 9, 1827, by imperial edict.

To be sure, these were exceptions, and it would be absurd to regard every member of the landed gentry of the period as a concupiscent monster of ultrarefined cruelty. The Comte de Ségur, for example, wrote in his memoirs: "I have already remarked upon the moderation with which Russian landowners exercise the virtually absolute powers they possess over their peasants, whose devotion to their masters, of which I observed many instances during my visit to Russia, proves I was not mistaken." Like American Negroes before the Civil War, Russian serfs were ill- or well-treated according to their master's temperament. Very often, they would refuse freedom when it was offered to them. "The way we are now, little father, we belong to you, but the land belongs to us. We want to stay as we are now," the liberal Yakushkin's serfs told him when he tried to emancipate them.

Most of the serfs knew that the hardships of their condition were offset by their lord's obligation to house and feed them, and they preferred the security of slavery to the uncertainties of independence.

The truth is that most of their owners—urbane, unconcerned, bored—scarcely knew their peasants, were indifferent to their fate, and delegated their authority to a crafty steward. There were a few sensitive souls, who dreamed of a constitution and some utopian future for the country; but it was such an effort to stir up Russia, with all her weight of land, forests and rivers, and her ignorant and wretched muzhiks. So they read Voltaire, Montesquieu and La Harpe, chatted about the social advantages of an ideal republic, thought vaguely of emancipating a few peasants, gave their valet a present, even contemplated joining a Masonic order, and, in the end, enjoined their stewards to keep a closer watch over the harvest.

During the reign of Paul I, for example, his son, the Grand Duke Alexander, apparently could hardly wait to put into practice the liberal precepts of his tutor, La Harpe. Alexander said, "Everything I have learned, and whatever virtue I may possess, I owe to M. de La Harpe"; and M. de La Harpe wrote of Alexander: "Even the most skeptical have been forced to admit that he was one of those rare products that appear only once in a thousand years." In his memoirs, Czartorysky tells of a conversation he had with the tsarevich in 1796: "The Grand Duke told me he detested despotism wherever and in whatever form it existed, that he loved freedom, that it was the right of all men equally, that he had been most keenly interested in the French Revolution; that, while deploring its dreadful excesses, he wished the Republic every success and rejoiced to see it created. . . . I left, I confess, quite beside myself, profoundly stirred, not knowing whether I was dreaming or awake. Really! A prince of Russia, disclaiming Russia's hateful policies, a passionate lover of justice and liberty, sympathizing with Poland and desiring her happiness? Was this not a miracle?"

At last, the long-awaited reign of that "mystic" and "liberal" Alexander I arrived. During the night of March 11, 1801, Paul I was assassinated in his bedroom by a group led by Count von Pahlen and General Bennigson. Grand Duke Alexander had refused to take an open part in the conspiracy, but he had told the men which regiments of the guards they could rely upon. When Count von Pahlen entered Alexander's rooms after the murder, he found him stretched on his camp bed fully dressed and in his boots, feigning the sleep of the innocent. Upon hearing the great and terrible news, Alexander burst into tears. "Stop behaving like a child," said Von Pahlen. "Come outside and show yourself to the troops. The welfare of millions depends upon your conduct and firmness in this moment." He pushed him into the palace courtyard, where the guards were already assembled. At the sight of their uniforms, Alexander squared his shoulders and declaimed in ringing tones: "My father has died of an attack of apoplexy. Everything shall be done in my reign as it was done in the reign of my beloved grandmother, Empress Catherine."

His words were drowned in a roar of cheers.

The country went mad with joy. The people's love for Alexander I verged upon idolatry; he was acclaimed wherever he went, followed in the street; people looked for his footprints in the sand and deposited fervent kisses in them. Forthwith, the new emperor gave permission for people to keep their hats on when he passed if it were raining, and also in the vicinity of the Winter Palace. The gibbets that had been erected in the public squares were dismantled. He flatly repealed his father's regulations regarding dress, and on the seventh day of his reign he allowed the importation of foreign books and the operation of private printing presses.

On the stength of these first gestures, hopes of a complete liberal reform began to rise. There was even talk of the emancipation of the serfs, freedom of the press, and revision of the entire code of laws then in force.

But philosophy was only Alexander's fancy; by instinct, he was a despot. La Ferronays wrote: "He talks about human rights, the rights of the people, and the duties of a sovereign as the pupil of a philosopher can and should talk; but at the same time he makes certain that his every wish, however arbitrary, is carried out with more despotism and severity even than was exercised by the late Peter I."[5]

From promise to retraction to postponement, every concession being immediately withdrawn, Alexander I contrived to maintain the country exactly as he had found it upon his accession. The dream of freedom faded, the French authors came back into fashion, and people spent their time being madly gay in order to forget all the reasons they had not to be.

During the reign of Paul I, Moscow had become the center of intellectual and artistic activity. True, Russian literature was but a pale copy of the French literature of the period, and the upper class preferred Racine, Corneille and Voltaire to their imitators, Lomonosov and Sumarokov. True too, the products of the Moscow and Petersburg poets could not compare with Parny's elegies or the epigrams of Jean-Baptiste Rousseau; and the grand, glorious and dull Russian poet Derzhavin, bard of the reign of Catherine the Great, was not the man to fan the flame of enthusiasm in rising generations. But young ladies were already shedding tears over Karamzin's sentimental stories and making pilgrimages to the pond where poor Liza drowned herself after being abandoned by the heartless Erasmus. And in boarding school and university and family library, young men sat dreaming of the sublime upheavals of German romanticism.

One of the most "literary" homes in Moscow, beyond any doubt, was that of Sergey Lvovich Pushkin, where the minor poets of the day often foregathered. Sergey Lvovich, formerly a young officer of the guards, had resigned his commission in 1798 and moved to Moscow from St. Petersburg. Two years earlier, he had married a distant cousin of his, Nadezhda Osipovna Hannibal, the granddaughter of the famous Negro of Peter the Great.

Upon their arrival in Moscow, the young couple moved into a house on German Street, and then into another house on the same street—an unpretentious wooden structure at the back of a courtyard. It and all those like it were consumed in the fire of 1812, and nothing remains of it today. But the neighborhood has retained something of the imperial epoch, with its *ci-devant* mansions, their façades garnished with lions' heads, upended torches and stone garlands. One such palatial residence has become the Academy of Military Chemistry; the others will soon disappear in the redevelopment of Moscow. The Soviets changed the name of German Street; now it is called Baumann Street, after a revolutionary killed in 1905. A new school has been built at No. 10; in 1927 a commemorative tablet was fixed to one of its walls, bearing the following inscription in eighteenth-century characters: "On this ground stood the house in which Alexander Sergeyevich Pushkin was born, on May 26, 1799."

2. *Ancestry*

"In the house of ministerial steward Ivan Vasilyevich Skvartsov; to his tenant Sergey Lvovich Pushkin, was born a son, Alexander, baptized on the eighth day of the month of June." The words are written in the parish registry by an unknown sacristan, in a round, awkward, uneven hand. Other names have been carefully inscribed in the same narrow column on the same yellow page. The notation relating to Pushkin is preceded by a record of the birth of an obscure scion whose godfather was a servant named Yofimov and whose godmother was a "Muscovite working woman," the widow Marfa Gerasimov, and it is followed by a record of the birth of the child of one Marya Vladimirovna Ilin, of whom nothing further is known. The writing is the same, but the scribe began a new line for each entry—because that was the rule. All men's children are the same—a date, a number, a name; here they are, catalogued for life, now they can breathe, marry, procreate and die, legally.

Stretching back from the cradle of the child who had just been born in the wooden house on German Street—little Alexander Pushkin, baptized in 1799 "on the eighth day of the month of June"—was a genealogy worthy of legend. In him meet and mingle the great lords who built Russia and the characters of African saga. Through his father, he was the last of the violent and noble line of the Pushkins; on his mother's side he was descended from the "Abyssinian Negro," Abraham Hannibal, favorite of Peter the Great.

A portrait of Abraham Hannibal has been found: a strange-looking fellow with a chocolate-colored face, flattened lips and round eyes with yellowish corneas. His slightly frizzled hair is tied back, and he is dressed in a court costume resplendent with decorations.

Abraham—originally Ibrahim—was the son of an Abyssinian princeling whose stronghold was a town on the Mareb River in what is now Eritrea. When the child was a few years old, his father's army waged and lost a fierce battle with the Turks, who were invading the country.

After a palace conspiracy, Ibrahim was chosen and sent to Constantinople as a hostage. One of his sisters bravely threw herself into the sea in the wake of his ship, and drowned; and Ibrahim, as befitted a child of noble birth, was inducted into the sultan's seraglio.

Shortly before this, Peter the Great had instructed his ambassador in Turkey to procure him a few of those adorable, clever little blackamoors who were the rage just then: Every court in Europe had its pet pickaninnies, and Peter the Great could not live without one. The ambassador must have bribed one of the sultan's viziers, and so it was that Ibrahim, now eight years old, came to be abducted from the seraglio and spirited away to Russia, where Peter the Great greeted his latest acquisition with signs of delight. The child was baptized at Vilno; the Emperor of Russia was his godfather and the Queen of Poland his godmother. He was christened Peter, like his august protector, but the African never would adopt the name, and called himself Abraham Petrovich until his death; around 1730 he took the family name of Hannibal.

Other than this, Abraham's beginnings at the emperor's court were inauspicious; he was just another lackey. But Peter the Great soon became aware of his blackamoor's potential, and admitted him to his inner circle. Abraham became first his chamber valet, then his stable valet, then his personal secretary, and in 1717, when Peter the Great made his second trip to Europe, he took his godson along and deposited him in Paris with instructions to study the profession of military engineer. For a while, Abraham attended classes at the Military Academy, but then he decided to volunteer for service in the war with Spain, where he received a head injury and was taken prisoner; upon his release, he returned to France and applied for admission to the new artillery school founded by Maréchal Vauban at Metz. His scholastic prowess led him from promotion to promotion, until he reached the rank of captain in the French army.

The young man, relatively penurious and cast adrift in an unfamiliar world, bombarded the emperor with pleas and complaints. He had "nothing to put on his back, so to speak, neither kaftan nor shirt . . ."; he could neither "feed himself nor pay his debts"; the "professors had to give him lessons on credit"; and he would "die of starvation with the French paper money." He demanded that his allowance be paid regularly, and if he had to go back to Russia, he pleaded to be spared the sea voyage. "I am not a good sailor. You know yourself how brave I was at sea. But I'm not used to it any more. I implore you, in the name of Christ and the Virgin, do not force me to travel by sea."

At the beginning of 1723, after five or six years abroad, the turbulent and tearful Abraham returned to St. Petersburg. With him came a library of four hundred volumes, in which Bossuet's sermons were packed alongside the *Lettres d'amour d'une religieuse portugaise,* and a thorough technical background which was much appreciated by the emperor. However, his promising career was cut short by the death of Peter the Great, and as a result of the ensuing court intrigues he was sent first to Kazan and thence to the Chinese frontier, where he was abandoned, ostensibly to build essential fortifications but actually to languish in a harsh exile. Abraham wrote interminable letters to everyone he knew, begged, threatened, plotted, wasted his time and hatched furious schemes. He was not recalled until 1730, when Empress Anna Ivanovna came to the throne; then he was appointed to a post "befitting his rank" at the fortress of Pernau (Parnu). Later that year Abraham became friendly with a Greek named Dioper, who was the captain of a galley and the father of a very pretty and marriageable daughter. Abraham determined to wed the fair Eudoxia, obtained her father's consent, and paid no heed to the young woman's protests.

Eudoxia complained that her fiancé was "an Arab by birth and of a different race from ours," but the plain truth is that she was in love with a naval officer. Obedient to her father's will, she married Abraham; but before doing so, out of spite or perversity, she slept with her chosen one. Later, another lover was to console her for the aversion she felt toward her husband. When Abraham learned of his wife's misdemeanors he fell into a towering rage and decided to use the incident as a pretext for divorce—for he too had a mistress: Christine Scheberg, the daughter of a captain of German origin; and as soon as he was free, Abraham planned to marry his paramour. Divorce laws were very strict, however, and it was virtually impossible to put asunder two beings united by the sacraments of the Church. To improve his chances, therefore, Abraham conceived the idea of suing his wife on two counts. In his declaration to the chancellery of Pernau he accused Eudoxia not only of failing to keep her altar vows but also of attempting to poison her husband with the active assistance of her lover. Pending the court's decision, he locked his wife in a room and tortured her daily in an attempt to persuade her to confirm his allegations: He enclosed his victim's hands in rings which he had fixed to the wall at a height calculated to prevent her feet from touching the ground, and there she hung, while he beat her with rods or a whip, in the hope that she would eventually agree to testify in court as he directed. If she did, he would spare her life; if she denounced him, he would kill her. Eudoxia yielded, and was put in prison to suffer cold and hunger for almost five years—the period during which the case was being prepared for hearing. Meanwhile, Abraham decided to go ahead and marry his mistress. A succession of priests were consulted, none of whom would oblige by sanctifying their union; but at last one was found who agreed to be a party to the travesty.

From his marriage with Christine Scheberg, Abraham had eleven children. The prolific Christine was also a redoubtable termagant, who held her own in every quarrel and would proclaim with compelling authority, in her thick German accent: "This black defil begets on me black children and giffs to them defils' names." For Abraham wanted to baptize his third son Januarius; but Christine would not hear of it, and called him Osip until her death.

Meanwhile, Eudoxia had appealed to the Holy Synod and was conditionally released, whereupon she immediately took another lover. A few months later, she became pregnant. There was no time to lose. On the advice of her confessor, she filed a countersuit against Abraham, accusing him of bigamy. The case dragged on for years, while Abraham fought like a caged lion, invoked his past achievements, and called upon every influential person he knew for help. From Synod to bishopric to consistory and back to Synod again, the case slowly sank under a great sea of paper. Abraham's initial application for divorce was filed on February 28, 1732; the consistory's final judgment was not pronounced until September 9, 1753. It solemnly legalized Abraham's second marriage, on condition that he pay a fine and impose some penance upon himself. The hapless Eudoxia, convicted of double adultery, was condemned to end her days in the monastery of Staraya Ladoga, "in perpetual travail."

Abraham's matrimonial imbroglios did not prevent him from pursuing a successful career. On April 25, 1752, he became chief of the Russian engineer corps, with the rank of major general. His colleagues dreaded the Ethiopian's stormy, quarrelsome, whining, deceitful and obstinate temper, but his technical skill was universally esteemed, and so the authorities contrived to employ him on specific tasks while keeping him, insofar as possible, out of the way of subalterns.

In 1762 Abraham retired to his estate at Suyda, where, for the first time in his life, he had nothing to do; his only amusement was to torment everyone around him with his senile greed and selfishness. He died on May 13, 1781, at eighty-four years of age. In 1746 Empress Elizabeth Petrovna had given him a large estate in the province of Pskov, and the Mikhailovskoye farm was part of this holding.

Abraham was survived by eleven children, at least two of whom were destined for some form of renown. Ivan Abramovich, the eldest son, was an inspector in the naval artillery; he commanded courageously at Navarino, distinguished himself at the Battle of Chesme (Cesme), and built the fortress of Kherson, where a monument was erected to his memory.

His brother Osip Abramovich, alias Januarius, had a less brilliant official career; his sentimental life, on the other hand, was correspondingly agitated. In 1773, after attaining the rank of major in the naval artillery, he was sent to the Lipetsk cannon foundries. Twenty-two versts away, there lived a landowner named Pushkin with his daughter Marya Alexeyevna. Now, Osip Abramovich was a fine figure of a man, a good talker, witty, effervescent and determined, and he made short work of the young country girl. He married her in 1773, gave her one child—Nadezhda—and abandoned her three years later, after committing various minor infidelities with local farm girls.

On May 18, 1776, Marya Alexeyevna wrote to him: "Since your indifference to me has grown so great that you no longer wish to share my life, I have decided not to be a burden to you and to be separated from you forever, relinquishing every claim I might have upon you on the sole condition that you leave me my daughter. . . ." Osip's reply: "I wish you joy of your gilded freedom, and I sign myself, for the last time, your husband. . . ."

Having dealt with the matter by this rather summary piece of correspondence, and with no thought of applying for a divorce, Osip Abramovich proceeded to Pskov, where he found a position as assessor and a young woman to his liking: Justine Tolstoy, daughter of a small landowner. He decided to marry her. After all, his father, that general nuisance Abraham, had been a bigamist and could not be said to have suffered unduly from the irregularity of his position; his example was enough to silence any qualms of conscience his son might have had. With breathtaking cheek, Osip asked for the young lady's hand, declaring that he knew on certain authority that his first wife was dead and he was free of all obligation. A village priest believed him, and the wedding took place. Prior to it, at his fiancée's behest, Osip signed an accommodation paper certifying that he had received from her, in addition to the dowry, a sum of 27,000 rubles.

A few months later, Osip's second marriage was denounced by his first wife and annulled by the Archbishop of Pskov, whereupon Osip appealed to the Holy Synod, and then to Empress Catherine II, accusing his first wife of desertion, swearing he was not the father of the child in her care, and offering, in support of his claims, documents which were falsified from beginning to end.

On January 17, 1784, Catherine II signed a judgment declaring Osip's second marriage null and void. His first wife retained the title and all the rights of a lawful spouse. Osip himself was sent "on a long voyage in the North Sea, to atone by service and penitence for the crime he had committed." One fourth of his estate, including the Kobrino farm, was placed in trust for his daughter's maintenance. Osip, shattered by his misfortunes, left the country and sailed the high seas for four years; but his troubles were not over. A few years after his return, his second wife demanded the 27,000 rubles he had allegedly received from her and spent. The case went through court after court. "I admit," Osip wrote to Emperor Paul I, "that the paper was signed by me, but I never received a particle of a dowry in exchange. . . ." The case was still pending when Osip Abramovich died, at Mikhailovskoye, on October 12, 1806, "from the consequences of a dissolute life." He had not seen his first wife, Marya Alexeyevna, since their separation in 1776.

Marya Alexeyevna lived alone with her daughter Nadezhda, wintering in St. Petersburg and summering at her farm at Kobrino. Intelligent, thrifty and energetic, she was an excellent housewife, and after her husband's desertion transferred all her affection to her daughter. Great pains were taken with Nadezhda's education; she was spoiled and over-indulged by her mother, and soon grew into a willful, capricious and vain person. At twenty-one she married an officer in the guards who had been courting her for some time: He was a distant relative of Marya Alexeyevna's, and his name was Sergey Pushkin—by curious coincidence, upon her marriage Nadezhda resumed her own mother's maiden name. The newlyweds were made for each other: Both were worldly, irresponsible, superficial and cultivated. Both came from old families of the middle nobility: In Karamzin's *History of the Russian Empire* the name of Pushkin is mentioned twenty-one times. The earliest known ancestor appears to be one Radsha, who in A.D. 1146 "took our city of Kiev." Of the lives of Radsha's descendants nothing is known until we reach a certain Gregory Pushka, who lived at the end of the sixteenth century and whose offspring, members of the lesser nobility, did little to distinguish themselves. One Gabriel Pushkin, sent into exile by Boris Godunov, defected to the false Dmitry and tried to foment a rebellion in Moscow. His son Gregory "served courageously" in 1607 in the Nizhny Novgorod militia. Four Pushkins signed the Romanov election charter. Alexander Petrovich Pushkin, grandfather of Sergey Lvovich, owned a vast estate in the government of Nizhny Novgorod, and married Eudoxia Golovin, daughter of the favorite of Peter the Great, in 1720 or 1721. The marriage was not a success: In 1725, in a fit of rage, Pushkin cut his pregnant wife's throat. He was imprisoned and died the same year.*

The father of Sergey Lvovich, too, was "a cruel and violent man." He was married twice: the first time to a woman who—or so the poet alleges in his genealogy—"died on a straw pallet, locked by her husband

* His brother Theodor had a son, Alexis, who married Sarah Yuryevna Rzhevsky in 1742, and it was their daughter, Marya Alexeyevna, who married Osip Abramovich in 1773 and gave birth to the little Nadezhda Hannibal who was to become Sergey Lvovich's wife.

in a dungeon on the estate for having an affair, real or pretended, with his sons' French tutor, who was hanged in the courtyard by his order."[1]

However ill-tempered and criminal he may have been, this Pushkin educated his children *à la française*. His sons Sergey Lvovich and Basil Lvovich read all the right books, learned French, English and Italian, and were enrolled from early childhood in a regiment of the imperial guards. But neither of them could tolerate the discipline of army life.

Marriage only aggravated Sergey Lvovich's frivolity and idleness. He remained in the guards for two years after his wedding to Nadezhda Osipovna Hannibal, and then resigned, perhaps in alarm at the emperor's latest excesses, and came to live in Moscow in 1798. There the young couple plunged body and soul into the social whirl.

Sergey Lvovich was a well-groomed, chubby, busy little man with darting eyes and the bony, prominent nose of a Roman emperor. Through his brother Basil, who had published a few lines of insignificant verse, he was in touch with all the authors of the day. He also wrote "incidental" poetry himself, in Russian and French, and could amuse the ladies with a pun, organize an evening's entertainment in the drawing room and reel off whole scenes from Molière and Racine, by heart and with fervor.

It always seemed to everyone who spoke to Sergey Lvovich that he was playing a part, for his own benefit as well as that of his audience; everything was a pretext for attitudinizing, epigrams, grimaces and exclamations. He wept and laughed at the drop of a hat. He was an overgrown, selfish, spoiled, sentimental, sensual baby, who spent his life flitting from drawing room to drawing room and theater to theater, scorched by the lights, dizzied by the laughter, buzzing with anecdotes and bons mots. He never set foot on his estate, which he entrusted to the care of a German steward over whom he assiduously avoided exercising the slightest supervision. The property went to rack and ruin, while the steward throve and prospered, sending his master a few hundred assignation rubles every year and a cartload or two of fowl and butter pickled in brine. One day a delegation of peasants arrived to complain to their lord of their ill-treatment; Sergey Lvovich shooed them away without a hearing.

He so abhorred having to think about money that he handed over the entire responsibility for the household to his wife; but Nadezhda Osipovna was no better equipped for the arduous task of manager than he. In the drawing rooms, she was known as an attractive young woman with soft shoulders and a fine bosom. She had a sallow complexion, thin lips and large, dark eyes. The palms of her hands were yellow. Her friends called her *la belle créole* and liked her because she was gay and clever and good at repartee. But when the door of her own house closed behind her, Nadezhda Osipovna was transformed. Authoritarian, selfish and inconsistent, she could only add to the natural disorder within. Sometimes she nagged the servants unmercifully, and sometimes she ignored them completely. If she were in a bad mood she could remain silent for days on end; then she would explode into a frenzy of activity, and rearrange every stick of furniture in the apartment. "When she could not change houses," her grandson Pavlishchev wrote, "she would transform Sergey Lvovich's study into a drawing room or the bedroom into a dining room and vice versa, moving all the hangings and furniture, etc., without consulting a soul. She differed fundamentally from Sergey Lvovich in that she never lost her temper and never raised her voice, but she would sulk for days, weeks, even months at a time."

Under Nadezhda Osipovna's administration, the Pushkin home became a gypsy encampment. "One room," a contemporary wrote, "was filled with beautiful antique furniture; in another there was nothing but the walls, not so much as a chair; quantities of servants roamed about, all shabby and drunken; bony old nags were harnessed to ancient carriages; there were masses of expensive gowns, yet there was never enough of anything, from money to wineglasses. If they invited two or three people in to dinner, they had to send to our house for dishes."[2]

The Pushkins hated their home and were bored to extinction in each other's company. Their chilly, soulless rooms, in which everything looked broken-down, abandoned and artificial, were the wings in which the young couple dressed, made up and rehearsed before going onstage. Convenience, comfort, even cleanliness were sacrificed to appearances.

In running the household, Nadezhda Osipovna was assisted by her mother, who lived with them. But with all her common sense and orderliness, Marya Alexeyevna was unable to dominate the chaos perpetually renewed by her daughter and son-in-law.

First the Pushkins lived in German Street, then in Volkov's house on the Chisto-Prudny Boulevard, then in Santi's house in the same street, then in Hospital Street. . . . In all, an average of one move a year between 1799 and 1807.

One document states that in November 1801 the Pushkins paid half their year's rent in advance—five hundred rubles; but the balance was a long time coming.

At that time the Pushkins had only six servants living in, but there were twelve hundred muzhiks on their estate at Boldino, in Nizhny Novgorod.

In 1799 Marya Alexeyevna sold her farm at Kobrino and emancipated, among others, a serf woman named Arina Rodionovna, who refused her freedom and elected to remain with her mistress. She was a mild-tempered, garrulous body of forty-five, who knew all the old country tales, folk songs and sayings by heart, and she became the "nanny" of the new baby of the household, Alexander Pushkin.

3. *Childhood*

He was a graceless, morose infant. His face was a sallow, soft globe, with thick lips that were too bright a red and glittering, dreamy eyes. His hair, the color of horse chestnuts, grew in tight, curly shavings from brow to nape. The nose, with flaring nostrils, was slightly flattened between well-filled cheeks. Alexander never laughed. He never ran. He let his toys drop from his hands. He dragged listlessly from room to room. The child's silence, his ponderous immobility, irritated his mother exceedingly. She would have liked a high-spirited, mettlesome, laughing son, and preferred her daughter Olga, two years his senior, and was later to prefer her other son Leo as well. She even felt a kind of resentful loathing for him; she could not believe she could have produced such a lumpish creature. Besides, he looked like an ill-bleached blackamoor. She wanted to shake him, wake him up, give him some energy, some muscle, a sense of repartee, a love of outdoor games and new songs and new faces. She grimly ordered him to run and leap about, strained to catch the sound of his laughter, coldly observed his lethargic breathing. Often, the harassed child took to his heels and sought refuge in some back room or inside his grandmother's workbasket. Nadezhda Osipovna was *offended* by her son, and would not speak to him for days on end. She complained to Sergey Lvovich, she wept; he grew angry, shouted and waved his arms, and made it clear that she was to come to him no more with her tales of little Alexander. For him, children were like estates, like Boldino and Mikhailovskoye: It was nice to know they were there, he liked to imagine them thriving and prospering somewhere far away; but the thought of actually having to do anything about them was intolerable to him.

Alexander had two habits which his mother found particularly exasperating: He was forever rubbing the palms of his hands together, and he was always losing his handkerchiefs. To cure him of the former vice, Nadezhda Osipovna "tied his hands behind his back and made him go without food for a whole day."[1] The latter was corrected in the following manner: Nadezhda Osipovna had a handkerchief sewn to the front of the child's jacket and gave instructions that it was not to be changed more than twice a week. And, to humiliate him, she never failed to send for him when there were visitors in the house; she would point a stern finger at the immovable handkerchief, no doubt, and give a full explanation of how it came to be there, while the child stood with his eyes fixed on the floor, burning with shame.

Nadezhda Osipovna administered similar corrections to her daughter Olga. To punish her one day, her mother struck her in the face, dressed her in a worn, dirty frock, forbade her to come to table, and gave orders that she was to be fed on bread and water. The little girl whimpered, "I won't say I'm sorry, I'll hang myself first." At this, Alexander seized a nail and tried ineffectually to drive it into the wall. "What are you doing?" cried his nanny. "My sister wants to hang herself," he answered, "so I'm getting a nail ready for her."[2]

When he could get away from his vociferous, gesticulating father and his cold, irritable and everlastingly hurried mother, Alexander buried himself in a warm, cozy inner world. From this remote vantage point he proceeded to observe his parents with curiosity. From the sparse clues that have come down to us, we can imagine what he saw: Maman would rise very late and drag herself, yawning, from room to room, her complexion tinged with yellow, her skull covered with curlpapers. She nagged the servants, smacked the children, chewed at her nails. She was bored. And Papa was clearly afraid to go near her and hid in his study behind an unread book. Suddenly Maman would look at the clock, utter an exclamation and spring to life. The guests would be arriving any minute and she was still not dressed. Orders went flying, doors slammed right and left, scarlet-cheeked girls staggered along with great buckets of hot water from which clouds of steam rose to the ceiling. The splash of water, the thud of galloping bare feet, and the clink of innumerable vials and flacons could be heard from Maman's room. Occasionally the sharp report of a slap cut through the background noises, and a servant girl would come running out of the room with tears streaming down her cheeks. She sniffled, vanished and was back in a flash bearing a silken gown, oh, so fine! like some grand bird slain in the forest in a fairy tale. Sergey Lvovich would pace back and forth outside his wife's room. He was scented like a fruitcake; his gleaming hair looked as though it had been painted onto his head. At last Nadezhda Osipovna would emerge, with all the majesty of a great ship turning out to sea. She was beautiful, serene, suave; Sergey Lvovich kissed the tips of her fingers. The candles were lit. The guests arrived. Maman and Papa were unrecognizable. Papa was the real head of a real family, his voice resonant with self-confidence. Maman, instead of contradicting him, would give a little laugh like the coo of a dove at every witticism he uttered. She even stroked her children's heads and called them "My little Sasha, my little Leo," as though she had not thumped them soundly two hours earlier after lunch. And indeed, it was a different family and different parents Alexander now observed, better, younger and more handsome than the real ones.

But the charm did not last. As soon as the guests were gone, the other parents came back, squabbling, bored, distant, losing their tempers, shoving the chairs about, looking down at their son with worn, hard faces. They were so far away: surrounded by a ring of ice. And Alexander so desperately needed to be understood, petted, forgiven, entertained, until he could float away into the delicious numbness of sleep.[3]

The moment his parents' backs were turned, he would run off to his grandmother, a teller of old tales. She would be busy with some piece of embroidery from her workbasket filled with scraps of multicolored materials and soft, slippery skeins of silk. As her needle moved in and out, she would talk of the past, of that famous Negro of Peter the Great who was born in some far-off land of desert and blazing sun, or of another ancestor, the one who was so brave at the Battle of Navarino, or of herself and her own childhood. Little Alexander half listened, half grasped what she said, but he felt himself momentarily free from his scolding mother and imposing father and the whole hostile world in which there was no room for him. He could breathe. He uncoiled. His eyes closed in calm and exquisite pleasure.

Sometimes it was to the old nanny, Arina Rodionovna, that the boy went, still reeling from his mother's scolding. She had a pink, plump, creased face, with a minute nose turned up trumpetlike at the tip. The ends of her fichu were knotted on her forehead. A single tooth wobbled in her wrinkled mouth. She was jolly; she knew bawdy legends, old songs and velvety, sonorous Russian words one could never tire of hearing. Her room was a little niche draped in night and mystery, a thoroughfare and meeting place for wizards with beards as long as the snow-covered country roads, wasp-waisted, mournful-eyed princesses, knights-errant in soft-topped boots flashing scimitars in front of their sweeping, bejeweled collars and elves swift as sparks. The moment she opened her mouth it was plain that the only things that really mattered were outside the house and outside the city, and that the grownups were simply wasting their time scolding children. And he would drift away into a world of semidarkness through which fresh springs bubbled eternally, witches flew and tall castles loomed, light seeping from their windows and chalky bone heaps and steel-blue lances piled at their feet. Truth was not in the drawing room, it was in Arina Rodionovna's room, where it was dark and people spoke in hushed tones with the Russian accent of olden days. She lived, and lives on, in every Russian family: Arina Rodionovna, the nanny, the faithful and loving *nyanya*. How could they manage without her? In all the wealthier families the father was occupied by business, hunting and cards, and imagined he was quite above reproach because he had delegated the responsibility for bringing up and educating his heirs to high-priced foreign tutors. The mother read novels, and lived them, with feverish determination. The child was alone. So he turned to his nanny, some emancipated serf woman who had nothing to expect from the world. She knew that the household was her destiny, that she would have no joys or sorrows but those of that house, no children but those of that family. The master's children were her children. With total abnegation she replaced their mother who had no time to fondle and play with them, and their learned and elusive father too. She brought them up in the traditions of their country, in the melody of their language. Then, when they grew older, they would be taken over by the tutors, they would leave her and marry and have children of their own. And she would lean gratefully over the cradles of her children's children, and joyfully begin all over again the process of bringing up those who would leave her one day like the others, giving them the same love, the same dreams, the same caresses, until her very substance was consumed and there was nothing left of her but a gray phantom that bumped into the furniture and was allowed to remain out of pity in the house filled with the men and women whose first dreams she had cradled in her arms.

Alexander's nanny was his most generous and steadfast companion; it was thanks to her, and to his grandmother Marya Alexeyevna, that he had any knowledge at all of woman's tenderness, of pampering and cuddling and comfort, in his early years. He never forgot the nights of feverish sleeplessness when his nanny sat up with him:

> Before the ikon a pottery vigil light
> Threw the furrows of her wrinkled face into dim relief,
> And her quaint old granny's nightcap,
> And her cavern of a mouth in which two teeth collided.

Later, trying to fix the far-off images of his childhood, Pushkin scribbled these few words: "First impressions. The Yusupov garden. The earthquake. Nanny . . ."

Out of the general calamity of his infancy, the rushing river of sounds and colors on which faces bobbed like big corks, what Alexander remembered was his nanny's baked-apple countenance, the ferns and statues and artificial grottoes of the Yusupov garden where she used to take him for walks, and the great earthquake that shook Moscow on

October 14, 1802. "The tremors," a contemporary wrote, "rocked even the tallest houses; everywhere lamps, tables, and chairs were dancing about. Many people couldn't believe their eyes and thought they were suffering an attack of vertigo. . . ."

In St. Petersburg, where the Pushkins were living in 1800, there was another Yusupov garden, whose memory was bound up in Alexander's mind with the dreaded mask of Paul I. He was only a little over a year old at the time, and his nurse used to take him into the park. One day the emperor happened to pass; the nurse stopped, but forgot to remove the child's bonnet. The emperor, who had ordered all his subjects to uncover their heads upon sight of him, reprimanded the woman sharply and commanded her to rectify the baby's attire at once. "I have seen three emperors in my life," Pushkin later wrote. "The first, Paul, ordered me to take off my hat and, as I was too young to be scolded, he scolded my nurse instead."

It was after this incident, and perhaps because of it, that the Pushkins left St. Petersburg and returned to Moscow.

In the meantime, Grandmother Hannibal had sold her farm at Kobrino at her daughter's behest and bought a property at Zakharovo, thirty-eight versts from Moscow. All the "best" people had a country home near Moscow, and Nadezhda Osipovna would have felt a social outcast if hers were any farther away. The Pushkins spent their summers at Zakharovo until Napoleon's invasion of Russia in 1812.

Alexander Pushkin was deeply attached to the little country house hidden in a grove of slender, shimmering birch trees. In a clearing stood a wooden table with a bench running around it; here the Pushkin family ate and drank tea on the hot summer days humming with the flight of bees. Beyond lay a pond darkened by a ring of black, pointed pines. A single ancient linden stood at the water's edge, and beneath it Pushkin used to conceal himself with his toys and dreams.

The Zakharovo peasants were independent and gay. In the evenings they could be heard singing on their way home from the fields. On feast days they formed circles in the meadows and danced and shouted until they dropped. Pushkin would elude his parents' watchful eyes and slip away, to listen to their ballads and chatter with their youngsters, who were the same age as he, but whose feet were caked with mud and whose hair grew in tousled manes.

It was more than a different landscape they found when they left their Moscow drawing rooms for this pastoral retreat; it was a whole new world. Two versts from Zakharovo lay the town of Vyazma, which had belonged to Boris Godunov. Grandmother Hannibal must have told the boy all about the dreadful tsar who had murdered a child to gain the throne and then died, haunted by blood-filled visions; about the months of famine and plague in Moscow, and the arrival of the false Dmitry, a monk escaped from the Chudov monastery; about the omens in the sky and the battles on the ground; and about the death of Boris Godunov, jeered and hooted by the crowds, to the tolling of the inexorable bells. Later, when Pushkin wrote his barbarous and noble tragedy of *Boris Godunov,* he may have been remembering that church at Vyazma and old Grandmother Hannibal's tales; in any event, it was at Zakharovo that Alexander learned to love the land and language of his country.

It may also have been at Zakharovo that he first experienced the sensation of love, at about the age of seven; he mentions it in his notes, but we shall never know any more about it. Was this some little serf girl with heavy braids down her back, or a guest of his mother's, or the silhouette of a peasant woman glimpsed at the edge of a field? And how long did this childhood passion endure? Pushkin's notes contain only the words of two entries: "Death of Nicholas—First love." His brother Nicholas died in 1807, aged five. Once during his illness, Alexander leaned over his bed to look at him, and Nicholas had just strength enough to stick his tongue out at his brother, to make him laugh; then he died. That is all anyone knows of the event.

Pushkin's parents could have told us more about the poet's childhood, but they took no interest in this boy who was forever underfoot and in the way. The only observation Pushkin's father ever troubled to make was recorded in a biographical note: "One day, N. M. Karamzin came to see me and stayed for a long time; Alexander, seated opposite him, listened attentively to all he said and never took his eyes from his face."

However, as the years passed and the child grew, his nature imperceptibly changed. From the sluggish and somnolent infant emerged a new being, stubborn, impetuous and full of mischief. At eight, Alexander Pushkin's adult personality was already visible. An old lady who was a friend of the Pushkins in Moscow has left us a portrait of the child at this time: "Sasha [Alexander]," she wrote, "was an awkward, uncontrollable child with curly hair and dark skin; homely perhaps, but this was offset by his amazingly animated eyes, in which the sparks seemed positively to leap. Sometimes when we came to call, he would be sitting in a corner of the room behind a barricade of chairs, no doubt in punishment for some misdemeanor. Another time he would begin dancing about with the others, but they used to tease him because he was so clumsy, and then he would blush, pout, and retire to his corner, and could not be budged for the rest of the evening, because he was offended and wished to sulk and be left alone. Marya Alexeyevna [his grandmother] often used to say, 'I do not know, my dear, whatever will become of my grandson. The boy is clever and loves books, but he is a poor student, he can hardly ever recite his lesson properly. Sometimes it is impossible to make him stir at all or play with the other children, and sometimes he becomes overexcited and wild and then it is impossible to calm him. He rushes from one extreme to the other, he is never moderate. God knows how it will end, if he does not learn to control himself.' "[4]

The emergence of the boy's personality coincided with his first formal schooling—a loathed time, summarized by Pushkin in these terms: "First troubles—the governesses. Bleak memories . . . Montfort—Rousseleau—unbearable situation."

Later, in a report on public education which Pushkin wrote in 1826, he said: "In Russia, private instruction is worse than inadequate and worse than immoral. The child associates exclusively with fools, sees nothing but bad examples, becomes spoiled and cunning, and receives absolutely no notion of what justice, honor, and human relations should be. His education is confined to an acquaintance with two or three foreign languages and a smattering of elementary science, taught by vague hired instructors. . . . There must be no hesitation, private tutoring must at all costs be abolished."

Pushkin's grudge against it is understandable: As soon as he was old enough to read, a flood of tutors, governesses and instructors hailing from the four corners of Europe poured into the house. After the fashion of the time, Pushkin's parents hired them quite haphazardly, more concerned with quantity that ability. Alexander's one authentic teacher was the Comte de Montfort, a French émigré of whom we know only that he was a painter and musician. He was succeeded by one Rousseleau, who laughed at the child's first literary endeavors and wrote execrable verse himself. One day, coming upon a poem entitled *La Tolyade* which his pupil had written in French, he burst out laughing and began to tear it apart, word by word. True enough, the poem—an imitation of *La Henriade* in six stanzas, telling of a war between male and female dwarfs in the time of King Dagobert—was not much good. But the boy began to cry, and Rousseleau crossly complained to Nadezhda Osipovna, who sided with the tutor, increased his wages and punished the young poet severely for wasting his time writing verse instead of learning what other people had written. Rousseleau's successor, a man named Schedel, was an unprincipled rogue who disliked teaching and was far happier playing cards with the servants. Caught at this occupation, he was soon sent packing. Then there was another German —a Fräulein Laerm, who could hardly speak her own mother tongue; and an Englishwoman named Miss Belly, who never succeeded in teaching her pupil anything; and a Russian teacher named Schiller; and a priest, Father Belyakov, who was a sworn enemy of the French émigrés—he called them "apostles of the devil"—and the author of a book, *L'Âme de Massillon.* He undertook to instruct the Pushkin children in the history of religion, history, geography and elementary arithmetic.

Dancing and lessons in deportment completed the young socialite's curriculum. Alexander was a poor student. Relying on his memory, he could repeat the lessons after his sister if she were questioned first, but could not say a word when the recitation began with him. He wept over arithmetic, which he had considerable difficulty in mastering; and long division was his daily Calvary.

Abandoned to this continually changing procession of foreign tutors, alternately hounded to death and left to his own devices, Alexander became increasingly disobedient, lazy, capricious and scatterbrained, learning only what it pleased him to learn, and nothing out of textbooks. His true education was acquired in the drawing room, where he would crouch in a corner for hours, listening to the grownups chattering in French; or in his nanny's room or that of his grandmother; or in the front hall where some little Cossack boy squatted, knitting a woolen stocking; or, more than any of these, in his father's library. At the age of eight, Pushkin knew as much French as Russian, and the French authors were the first to catch his eye on his father's shelves. "Passion for reading," he wrote in the notes for his memoirs. The word "passion" is not too strong. The child literally threw himself into the world of books.

What did he find there? From the tales of nanny and Grandmother Hannibal he progressed to Plutarch, Bitaubé's translations of the *Iliad* and *Odyssey*, La Fontaine, Molière, Corneille, Racine, Beaumarchais, Diderot, Voltaire, Parny. Philosophy, eighteenth-century libertine tracts, classical tragedies, political pamphlets, erotic fables, the *Encyclopédie*—he swallowed them all pell-mell, amazed and alarmed by his new learning. He did not fully understand what these great morocco-bound figures were saying; they all talked about liberty, the social contract, the rights of man and citizens; but also about immoral love affairs, frolicking shepherdesses, flirtatious marquises, abhorrent tyrants, and the Church—source of all evil and superstition. And of course they were right. And of course one had to believe them. With reference to Voltaire, he later wrote, in a draft of a poem:

Long ago, in my defenseless youth
I knew that bare-browed old man,
His darting eyes, his lips compressed
Into a crooked smirk.[5]

Soon *La Pucelle d'Orléans, La Henriade, Candide, Zadig,* and *Micromégas* held no more secrets for him. And the more he read, the more he wanted to read. "My father's library," wrote Pushkin's younger brother Leo, "contained nothing but French books. In his childhood, if he could not sleep at night, Pushkin would creep into the paternal study and devour his books one after the other. He had a prodigious memory and by the age of eleven he knew the whole of French literature by heart."

Gone were the bearded wizards and the knights in embroidered doublets, forgotten the princesses whose hair flowed like honey. Alexander's new model was irony; he wanted to be a liberal, a sensual atheist like the French authors he so admired. He would write like them: that is, in French. After burning *La Tolyade*, he composed a comedy in imitation of Molière entitled *L'Escamoteur*. His sister Olga, two years older than he, was his confidante, audience and critic. He acted out his play for her, and she booed him off the stage, whereupon he improvised the following rather feeble quatrain in French:

Dis-moi, pourquoi *L'Escamoteur*
Fut sifflé par le parterre?
Hélas, c'est que son pauvre auteur
L'escamota de Molière.

Tell me, why was *The Filcher*
Hooted throughout the house?
The reason, alas, was: Its author
Had filched it from Molière.

Alexander was now old enough to go out with his parents, and on one occasion he accompanied them to a grandiose reception given by the multimillionaire Buturlin, a lover and collector of books, paintings, flowers and autographs. "At his home," a contemporary wrote,[6] "I danced and paid court to the delightful, pale, and delicate Countess B——. Young Pushkin was whirling about underfoot, but neither I nor any of the other dancers took the slightest notice of him."

But he took notice of everybody. He had already made up his mind: He would be a writer, a poet. Already, a few little girls had offered him their albums,* in which he blushingly inscribed French verses copied from Parny or Voltaire. And his Uncle Basil had already begun to beam benignly down upon him.

Basil was the poet of the family. He was a round little man with a protruding paunch and frail legs. His sharp, crooked nose hung over a moist mouth in which a few discolored stumps wobbled pitifully, and he spluttered when he spoke, but this did not deter him from being as vain as a debutante. In 1801, when it was announced that the elegant

* Autograph books.

Duroc, Bonaparte's ambassador and future Maréchal of the Empire, was to visit St. Petersburg, Basil made a special trip to the capital to study the Frenchman's style, and when he returned his friends hardly recognized him: He was wearing a monumental jabot and an excessively short frock coat, and his hair had been curled *à la Duroc*—that is, like a sheep's fleece. In 1802 Basil took a long trip abroad, through France, Germany and England. In Paris he requested the honor of being presented to the First Consul, inspected the Panthéon, and took lessons in diction from Talma.

"When he returned," wrote Vyazemsky, "the air of Paris still clung to him. He was dressed from head to foot in the latest Paris mode, his hair was worn *à la Titus*, and his head was smoothed and greased with Roman oil. With serene conceit, he extended his pate to the ladies so that they might admire the scent."

Alexander looked up to his uncle. He learned all his trivial poems by heart, and read his long poem, *The Dangerous Neighbor*,[7] in which Basil recounted a bawdyhouse brawl.

One day, Uncle Basil was preparing to recite some improper composition of his to the poet Dmitryev and asked young Alexander to leave the room.

"Why chase me away?" the boy complained. "I know it already, I've already heard it all."

And indeed he had; by virtue of his indiscriminate reading and constant eavesdropping on the adults' drawing-room conversation, little Alexander did know it all, had heard it all already. Be it politics, love, theater or religion, he knew what to say. He was a precocious sophisticate, a cool Voltairian octogenarian with pink cheeks and a child's face. He was fascinated by women, he drank in their perfume as they passed by, and sighed as he dreamed of the exotic caresses known to him by allusion only. The awakening of his senses was hastened, it is true, by his incursions into the field of erotic literature, but also by the constant movement all around him of the swarm of servant girls, the healthy, easygoing lasses who ran from room to room, laughed boisterously, darted provocative glances on all sides and left something of their warm scent behind them in the halls. Alexander spied on them, coveted them and must have fumed to think he was too young and bashful to embrace them. However, he was no longer the insignificant dolt of his babyhood. He was ten, and had already been transferred from the pampering hands of his nanny to the care of a manservant, Nikita Kozlov.

This Nikita was a stalwart muzhik with a face framed in blond side whiskers. In his company the young Pushkin roamed all over Moscow, toured the most obscure back alleys of the city, climbed the tower of

Ivan the Great, and, in 1809, stood on the steps of the Myaznitskaya Church to watch the inaugural procession of Alexander I. Nikita also took him to the places frequented by the common people, where strolling players acted out the tale of Petrushka in the open air, with false noses, wigs of tow, much booting of behinds and squealing of Jews whose beards were torn off, and, all around, the hearty, innocent guffaw of the crowd. One day, this Russian slapstick must surely mingle in the child's heart with the memory of Molière's farces. During these outings Pushkin renewed his acquaintance with the Russian life and language he had begun to forget in the company of his father and uncle. In him, Slavic culture and the civilization of the West must ultimately collide and fuse, but he had no idea of this as yet. Oscillating from the overrefined atmosphere of the drawing room to the commoners' world of kitchen and street, how could he have guessed that this dualism, this conflict, would engender in him a voice that had never been heard before?

"In the past," he wrote in his *Pensées de Voyage*, "Moscow was the rallying point of the Russian aristocracy, when it abandoned the provinces for the winter months. The glamorous young guardsmen also left St. Petersburg and came flocking into Moscow. Music resounded, the crowd pushed and shoved into every nook and cranny of the old capital. In the hall of the Society of the Nobility over five thousand souls assembled twice weekly. Young people met there, marriages were arranged. Moscow was renowned for its fiancées, like Vyazma for its gingerbread; Moscow dinners were famous. The innocent eccentricities of the Muscovites were the sign of their independence. They had their own way of life, they amused themselves as they pleased, with no thought for their neighbor's opinion. Some rich madman would build himself a Chinese palace on one of the main streets, covered with green dragons and wooden mandarins beneath gilded parasols. Another would drive through the Marya Park in a coach made of 840-fine silver. A third would seat five little Negro errand boys at the back of his sledge, and drive it through the streets in midsummer."

Beyond any doubt, Alexander Pushkin loved this Moscow—a little mad, a little drunken—which Voltaire would certainly have damned; and he was to love it even more when he learned, from his parents' conversations, of Russia's first political reverses.

In the Pushkin salon, parlor games and the reading of epigrams were often interrupted by anxious speculation about the country's future. After one or two attempts to form an alliance with Bonaparte, in whom Alexander I had hoped to find "the sincere and disinterested son of the Revolution," the tsar realized his error and wrote to La Harpe, "The mask has fallen. By his own hand, Bonaparte has refused the purest glory a mortal can aspire to, the only glory he had still to conquer: that is, to relinquish, after ten years and according to the Constitution to which he had sworn obedience, the power invested in him, as proof that he was acting without ulterior motives for his country's honor and prosperity. Instead of that, he has preferred to imitate the aristocrats and violate his country's Constitution. Henceforth he will be the foremost among all the tyrants known to history."[8]

In 1804, after the assassination of the Duc d'Enghien, which was seen in Europe as an act of defiance directed at all supporters of legitimate authority, Alexander I sent a note of protest to Paris. Shortly afterward, France recalled her ambassador, and the next day, General Bonaparte became Emperor Napoleon I.

Thereupon, Alexander I rushed to join the coalition.† This commitment of Russia to a quarrel in which she had no part could bring the country nothing but trouble. The war was not national, or popular, or desired. One people were fighting—God alone knew why—another people whose language they still spoke and whose culture they deeply admired. The disaster at Austerlitz in 1805, after one and a half hours of battle, and the defeats at Eylau and Friedland in 1807, forced Alexander I to sign the ignominious treaty of Tilsit.

Under its terms, Alexander I accepted Napoleon's blockade of England—a measure which directly threatened the Russian economy. The educated class rose in fury against this alliance, which would cut off Russia's traditional markets. The religious were shocked to see the "very pious" sovereign of Russia in the arms of that "Antichrist," that "base, contemptible creature," in the words of the appeal of the Holy Synod. Even at court, Alexander was surrounded by mute hostility, led by the dowager empress. Count Steding wrote to King Gustav IV that "discontent with the emperor grows apace; things appalling to hear are now being said openly."

The Pushkin family, too, was affected by the economic repercussions of the defeat. After Tilsit, the value of the ruble dropped to sixteen kopecks and the family's income shrank accordingly. To the deep chagrin of young Pushkin, Marya Alexeyevna was forced to sell their summer home at Zakharovo.

But even national humiliation and hatred of the French emperor combined did not deter Russian high society from using the conqueror's language in preference to its own. "Russia," wrote Count Vorontsov, the chancellor, in 1805, "is the only country in which the mother tongue

† Based on Great Britain's alliances with the Netherlands, Sardinia, Spain, Naples, Prussia, Austria and Portugal, eventually leaguing all of Europe except Switzerland and Scandinavia against Napoleon.

is ignored and the younger generation has no knowledge of anything relating to the fatherland."

In St. Petersburg, the children of the best families were sent to the Jesuit school founded by Father Nicholas. The instruction dispensed there was exclusively French, Latin and Catholic—hardly an ideal basis for a clear grasp of the problems of Russia. The pupils wore black velvet tunics with lace-frilled cuffs, held their elbows tight against their ribs, and spoke in monotones.

It was to this establishment that Pushkin's parents intended to send him when he was twelve. But an imperial order instituting a *lycée* at Tsarskoye Selo was issued in 1811, and the Pushkins changed their minds at the last minute and decided to enroll their son in the new institution. The school was to be housed in the Tsarskoye Selo palace, and would train "young men destined for high office in the state, chosen from among the best which the foremost families had to offer." The emperor was donating his personal library, the teaching staff would include professors of universal repute, and tuition was free. According to the imperial charter, there would be between twenty and fifty pupils, among whom were to be the Grand Dukes Nicholas and Michael; but the dowager empress would not hear of her grandsons being educated in the company of boys of lesser rank.

It was not easy to gain admission to this privileged institution: Recommendations, attestations and skillful maneuvering were required. The Pushkins could count on their friend A. I. Turgenev, who held an influential position in the Ministry of Religious Affairs.‡ On March 1, 1811, Sergey Lvovich submitted an application for admission on behalf of his son Alexander Pushkin, who, the letter said, "had mastered the elements of Russian and French grammar, arithmetic, geography, history, and drawing at home." On June 2, the future headmaster of the school was appointed by imperial order—a man named Malinovsky, who also happened to be an old friend of the Pushkins; so they could forget any apprehensions they might have had about their son's admission. Sergey Lvovich had to obtain a certificate of birth and baptism for his son; this was issued on July 15, 1811, and with all Alexander's papers now in order, plans could be made for departure. It was decided that Uncle Basil should accompany Alexander to St. Petersburg and act as his guardian until he entered the school. His grandmother's sister gave him a little capital, one hundred assignation rubles, but Uncle Basil stuffed the purse into his own pocket for safekeeping, and never remembered to return it to his nephew.

Alexander Pushkin was glad to leave home; he had judged his parents,

‡ Not to be confused with the author I. S. Turgenev (1818–83).

he knew the extreme triviality of their minds, the awful barrenness of their hearts. And then, the thought of living at Tsarskoye Selo, far from his family, in a wing of the imperial palace, and wearing a uniform, was rather exciting.

The only person he was sorry to leave was his sister Olga, who sniffled forlornly in the background all the time he was preparing to go. His younger brother Leo was too much of a baby to interest him; besides, Leo was Nadezhda Osipovna's favorite. True, there was Grandmother, and Nanny. . . . but with St. Petersburg and its glamor, its legendary mist and fog, lying ahead, who could stop to weep over grandmothers and nannies?

At last the great day arrived. Alexander and Basil were to leave by the Tverskaya road. According to custom, the entire family accompanied the travelers to the gate. Also according to custom, the hired coach was strongly criticized and the agent berated. Then came the tears, the exhortations, the play of handkerchiefs, streaming eyes and promises. Alexander alone shed no tear. His wolf-cub eyes gleamed with impatience, he gnawed at his fingernails, and when the coachman cracked his whip, he could not repress a smile. Looking at him, Uncle Basil must have wondered whether it was not some young spirit of malice he had seated beside him in the coach.

In St. Petersburg, Alexander and Uncle Basil rented rooms on the Moyka Canal, probably at the famous Hotel Demuth, host to "German tailors and English grooms as well as ambassadors and eccentric lords." Uncle Basil was accompanied by an extremely pretty and amiable young woman named Annette Vorozheykin. She was a freed serf who (Uncle Basil having been abandoned by his wife) was consoling him in his matrimonial distress. Little Alexander knew all this and was, of course, highly amused by his uncle's efforts to hide his game. But what were the charms of an Annette Vorozheykin compared to the majestic allure of St. Petersburg!

Everything in St. Petersburg was different—the streets and great homes, the people, the sky, even the air. Here there were no broad avenues, peaceful and provincial; no country houses choked with dusty greenery; no alleyways ending in gray stake fences crowned with lilacs and trilling birds; no tiny churches sleeping beneath their golden bulbs. Here it was all new façades, granite-paved quays, canals, bridges and squares. And all of it huge, glacial, impersonal and administrative. A city in uniform. Stone and water. The streets were all straight, and the people strode along straight, and the sun shone down straight and hard on their heads. It seemed as though no one ever had time to pause and stare into a shopwindow. The very beggars in the streets wore a solemn, official air, unknown to those of Moscow. At the edge of the gray, shifting sky shone the needle of the Admiralty Palace; along the Nevsky Prospect strolled guards armed with glittering little hatchets. Light European coaches swung past. And at every corner one expected to meet the emperor.

The moment he reached St. Petersburg, Uncle Basil began looking up his old literary cronies. Their little world was in a turmoil, split into two irreconcilable factions over an argument of style. One group, led by Admiral Shishkov, had risen in protest against the dominant Gallomania and preached a return to the ancient Slavonic language of the Church. The other claimed that it was absurd to banish essential words like "pantalon" (trousers) and "paradox" from the vocabulary merely because they did not have Russian roots. Basil attached himself to the progressives, wrote two *Messages Against the Illiterate Slavs,* and defended Karamzin, Zhukovsky, Turgenev and Dashkov against the attacking Admiral. Alexander Pushkin accompanied his uncle to meetings of the men of letters, listened, stared hungrily at these famous figures, became a passionate partisan of their cause, and longed to grow up in their shadow and, one day, become worthy of their esteem and friendship.

The entrance examinations for the Tsarskoye Selo school were held on August 12, 1811, at the residence of Razumovsky, the Minister of Education. In a vast pillared hall, a crowd of parents and children stood waiting. The parents wore uniforms or frock coats studded with decorations. The children eyed one another with curiosity, or exchanged signs of recognition. Alexander Pushkin was escorted by his uncle, in a black frock coat and foaming, scented jabot. His fat little face exuded self-importance and satisfaction. He bowed right and left. One of the applicants, young Pushchin, related his impressions of the day as follows: "I didn't know what to do; I do not believe I was particularly timid as a boy; but there, I was lost; I looked at everyone and saw no one. Some civil servant came in with a paper in his hand and began to read off a list of names. I heard: Alexander Pushkin. And I saw a quick, frizzly-headed boy with flickering eyes come forward with a rather bewildered expression on his face. I don't know whether it was the similarity between our names or some other thing that unconsciously drew me to him; in any event, I noticed him from the very first. I also noticed Gorchakov, who was then a very pretty boy. This diversion seemed to bolster our courage and we began walking up and down while we waited to be presented to the minister, after which the examination would commence. Someone—very probably Basil Pushkin, who had brought Alexander—called me over and introduced me to his nephew, who told me he was living with his uncle on the Moyka, not far from us. We agreed to meet often. . . . Soon we were called, one at a time, into another room, where, in the presence of the minister, the examination finally began. . . ."[9]

What questions did young Alexander Pushkin have to answer as he stood in the minister's office? Behind the table sat His Excellency, fat, curled, pomaded, his chest bristling with decorations. A tall, gaunt man stood beside him: Malinovsky, the headmaster. Malinovsky questioned his future pupil, who replied in a voice strained by nerves and oncoming adolescence. He received the following marks: "Russian grammar—very good; French grammar—good; German grammar—has not studied German; arithmetic—has learned up to the rule of three; properties of physical bodies—good; basic knowledge of geography and history—some rudiments."

On September 22, 1811, Tsar Alexander I approved the list of pupils admitted to the school. Thirty of the thirty-eight candidates had passed the examination, and both Pushkin and Pushchin were among them.

The conversion of the palace wing into a school was not yet completed, and in the period before classes began Pushkin and Pushchin lost no opportunity to meet. Pushchin was a chubby, gray-eyed boy with a glowing, calm expression. He too was unhappy at home. His father, head of the naval quartermaster general's office, was a hot-tempered, sensual man who lived with a girl of "low estate." His mother was insane and had been committed; his sisters ran the house. Pushchin shared his new friend's tastes in literature, knew French perfectly, and was interested in the literary quarrel of the day. He was good-natured, sympathetic and obliging. The turbulent Pushkin amazed and fascinated him.

"Whenever I could," wrote Pushchin, "I went to find Pushkin, and sometimes we would go for walks in the Summer Garden. . . . The other boys we used to meet were Lomonosov and Guryev; occasionally Mrs. Guryev would invite us home. We all realized that Pushkin was far ahead of us, he had already read lots of things we knew absolutely nothing about, and he remembered everything he read; but—this has to be said to his credit—he never tried to show off or brag to us, which would have been natural in boys of our age (we were then twelve). . . . He cared nothing for his erudition; the only things he seemed to want to excel at were racing, jumping over chairs and ball-throwing. We were amazed at his changes of mood: One moment we would see him deep in daydreams or reading something far in advance of his age, and the next, he would drop whatever he was doing and fall into a sort of mad rage, simply because some other boy had outrun him or knocked over all the pins with one bowl. I saw an instance of this on Krestovsky Island, where Basil Lvovich often used to take us in a boat."

Alexander Pushkin met the rest of his class when he went for fittings in the headmaster's home. In a big, bare room, the boys had to stand and have their measurements taken by a tailor, a bootmaker and a haberdasher. The tailor was a bearded bumpkin with a peasant's face and a growl of a voice, and the boys must have had a laugh or two at his expense until they learned that his name was Malgin and that he was no less a person than His Majesty's own chief tailor.

The school uniform consisted of a blue serge jacket piped in red, with red collar and gilt buttons; a white piqué vest; a gray overcoat with red buttonholes; close-fitting white trousers; boots; and a plumed, three-cornered hat. The young pupils laughed as they stripped, and a few hung back in embarrassment at their darned underclothes or dirty cuffs. Some looked fine and dashing in the belted tunic with the mandarin collar and tights outlining their thighs from hipbone to pointed knee. Pushkin, spare, stiff-necked, with slim thighs and straight shoulders, looked like an arrogant little French drummer boy. Pushchin was chubbier, pink and babyish beneath his plumed hat. The two friends were very pleased with their appearance, and took off their uniforms with regret; they went home yearning after gilt buttons, patent-leather boots and white vests. Pushkin often asked his friend in for tea, when Annette Vorozheykin, Uncle Basil's *amie,* would serve the boys refreshments and parry their teasing and jokes. Both Pushkin and Pushchin were vaguely in love with her.

"She made certain that our caresses never exceeded the bounds of propriety, yet she liked to tease and play with us," wrote Pushchin. "As for us—need I say that we were utterly entranced by the lack of constraint, the freedom established between ourselves and this amiable young woman."

On October 13, 1811, the pupils were to arrive at the Tsarskoye Selo school, and on the appointed day young Pushchin left St. Petersburg for his new home. An inspector led him up to the third floor of the building and stopped in front of the room that was to be his; over the door, a little black plate bore the inscription: "No. 13. Ivan Pushchin." Pushchin looked at the door on the left and read: "No. 14. Alexander Pushkin."

4. School—The Teachers

The official opening of the Tsarskoye Selo school was to take place on October 19, 1811. There were no regular classes in the intervening days, but the teachers came to chat with their future disciples, questioning them about their likes and dislikes and reading aloud to entertain them.

On the eve of the ceremony, the Minister of Education inspected the thirty pupils, who had all donned their dress uniforms for the occasion. "We were made to march into the room in order," wrote Pushchin, "we were halted each in his special place, our names were called in turn, and we were taught how to bow, facing the spot where the emperor and imperial family would be standing."

The great day came. At dawn the boys began to scrub and dress and inspect themselves in the mirrors. The warden and governors were pale, flustered, elated, unrecognizable. They ran to the windows, checked every detail of the boys' uniforms, arranged them in threes, divided them up again, regrouped them and scurried back to the window once more.

At last the august presences were announced. The emperor, the two empresses, representatives of the imperial family, court dignitaries, ministers and members of the Council, all flowed into the school. The ceremony began with a mass and Te Deum, celebrated in the palace church in the presence of the sovereigns. The pupils sat together in the galleries. After the service, the clergy made a tour of the school, sprinkling all thirty pupils and the walls with holy water. Then they assembled in the school's reception hall, a huge room all in gold and white. Doric pillars supported a coffered ceiling. The walls were decorated with Roman-style frescoes of laurel wreaths, Roman eagles and war banners. Down the center stretched a long table covered with a gold-fringed scarlet cloth. To the right of the table the pupils were arranged in three rows, and in front of them, standing at attention, were the governors, warden and headmaster of the school; to the left was a compact crowd of teachers and lesser officials. The remainder of the hall was occupied by armchairs for the spectators. When the boys' parents and sundry guests of note had been installed in their respective places, Minister Razumovsky, curled, portly and pallid, commanded the doors to be opened for the entrance of the sovereigns. The emperor appeared. He looked very tall. His heavy shoulders were squeezed to bursting point inside his blue uniform. Beneath his bald, white forehead, clear eyes shone in a doll's mask. The little, cherry-shaped mouth betrayed a rather appealing expression of feminine vanity.

Alexander I was accompanied by the reigning empress, the dowager empress, Grand Duchess Anna Pavlovna and Grand Duke Constantine, sleepy, slouching and disgruntled.

The emperor sat at the red table and the imperial family in the first row of armchairs. Behind them sat lines of wrinkled and dignified old ladies, young women with diamond monograms on their shoulders, gentlemen in frock coats, parents, Uncle Basil . . .

In the center of the table lay the school's founding charter, written on parchment, illuminated and bound in gold brocade, with dangling seals and tassels.

The pupils stared in a stupor at this glittering array of uniforms, decorations, gold braid, lorgnettes and illustrious faces. Was it really for them that the most eminent personages of the realm had come all this way? What did they have to deserve all this attention? How could they believe they were not still lost in some collective dream? Meanwhile, two of the teachers were unrolling the charter under the eyes of Martynov, secretary-general of the ministry of education; and Martynov was reading out the text, in a weak and quavering voice:

"Having received our scepter from the hands of Him, possessor of all Wisdom, we are certain that our Reign will not shine with deathless Light until our Land has been rid of the Obscurity of Ignorance."

Malinovsky, the headmaster, was next to speak. He sidled up on his long, skinny legs, leaning forward, his face unbelievably pale. The kindly, unassuming man seemed quite overwhelmed by the eminence of his audience. The sheets of paper containing his speech rattled in his hands. His desperate eyes sought out the emperor's motionless blue gaze. And suddenly the pupils realized that he was speaking, because his lips were moving determinedly; but it was impossible to make any sense out of the confused murmur. They heard "Your Majesty," and another "Your Majesty," and then "the school will give wings to the talents of the young so that they may achieve glory as true sons of their fatherland and worthy servants of the throne," and then "Your Majesty" again, and "Your Majesty."

"The guests in the back rows," wrote Pushchin, "began whispering among themselves and leaning back in their chairs. Having concluded his speech, the orator bowed, more dead than alive, and returned to his place."

The audience was numb with boredom and immobility. Old gentlemen were coughing and inhaling vials of perfume, ladies were gossiping behind mother-of-pearl fans. It looked as though the occasion was going to be a fiasco. The emperor himself, of course, must be sorry he ever came. Overzealous attendance at artillery practice had made him rather hard of hearing anyway, and all these professors with their choirgirl's voices were quite incapable of penetrating his private silence.

Then came Kunitsyn, the professor of philosophy, ethics, natural law and political economy. He was a young man of average height, with square shoulders and an open face framed by a thin line of side whiskers. Dominating the hubbub, he began to speak in ringing tones that awoke his audience and even the emperor. Unlike his predecessor, Kunitsyn addressed himself to the boys, not to the tsar, and somehow contrived not to make a single allusion to the sovereign's presence in the room. "Love of glory and the fatherland," he cried, "such should be your commandment." Alexander I was delighted with this little impertinence. He felt dangerously liberal, more liberal than his own best enemy Napoleon! He beamed.

When Kunitsyn had finished and withdrawn after a deep bow, Alexander I leaned toward the minister and spoke a few words in his ear. By imperial order, Kunitsyn was decorated then and there with the Cross of Vladimir, Fourth Class.

Now the pupils filed past the emperor, who gravely returned each of their awkward bows. They were eager for the ceremony to end, for a huge lunch was awaiting them in the dining room. The moment they were set free, they made a dash for the tables. "After inspecting the building," wrote Pushchin, "the guests joined us in the dining room and found us busy on our soup and piroshki. The emperor chatted with the minister. Empress Marya Fyodorovna wanted to sample our fare. She came over to Kornilov, leaned on his shoulder so he should not rise and asked, in Russian, if the soup were 'goot.' Like a little bear, he answered, 'Oui, monsieur!' I don't know whether it was because of embarrassment, or because he hadn't realized who was speaking to him, or because of the empress' dreadful accent, but whatever it was he gave his answer, God only knows why, in French and as though he were speaking to a man. The empress smiled and proceeded on her way, asking no further questions of anyone." The boys pointed at Kornilov and giggled under their breath, calling him "Monsieur! Monsieur!" while he choked on his soup.

In a corner of the room by the window, Grand Duke Constantine

Pavlovich was tickling and pinching his sister, Grand Duchess Anna Pavlovna. It was the end of the ceremony, the dignitaries were unbending; suddenly it felt like a family reunion. At last, the imperial guests left to dine with Count Razumovsky. The boys' supper was also worthy of note: "That evening," wrote Pushchin, "instead of our usual meal we were given dessert, *as much as we wanted.*"

The school building was illuminated; multicolored lanterns hung everywhere. The balcony was resplendent with the gleam of a shield bearing the emperor's monogram. At the end of their meal, the boys flung off their dress uniforms and raced out into the snow-covered gardens in their everyday clothes. It was cold. The lanterns' reflections fluttered like wings of fire on the white ground and weighted branches of the pines. Laughing and pushing, the same boys whom Professor Kunitsyn had called the "pillars of the fatherland" a few hours before now began to wage a snowball fight beneath the emperor's monogram.

A dormitory welcomed the flock to sleep—thirty exhausted, solitary children murmuring indistinct names beneath their blankets. Their parents were so far away. The school was so big. It was like some great ship, setting out to sea on a voyage that was to last six years.

Pushchin has left a full description of life at Tsarskoye Selo. "One wing of the imperial palace at Tsarskoye Selo, four stories high, and all the outbuildings were redecorated to house the school. In the reign of Catherine II that part of the palace had been occupied by the grand duchesses, but by 1811 they were all married, with the exception of Anna Pavlovna. The bursar's office and the rooms of the warden, governors, and some other members of the staff were on the ground floor; the dining room, infirmary, lecture room, and offices were on the first floor; the recreation room, classrooms (two with rostrums and one for individual study), a physics laboratory, a reading room for newspapers and periodicals, and the library—in the vaulted hall that led to the main body of the palace through the jube of the imperial chapel—were on the second; and the dormitories were on the top floor."

The sleeping quarters were composed of fifty cubicles in two rows separated by a corridor. Each room contained an iron bedstead, dresser, desk, mirror, chair and washstand; on the desk were an inkstand and candleholder with its snuffer. Pushkin's room, No. 14, was the last of the row, so he had only one neighbor, his friend Pushchin in No. 13; often, at night, they would hold whispered conversations with their cheeks pressed against the partition. There were hanging lamps on all the floors, parquet flooring on the first and second, and wall mirrors and damask-upholstered furniture in the main hall. The gardens of Tsarskoye Selo stretched out on all sides full of shivering statuary, raw, new monuments, cunning little grottoes and frail fountains. In this de luxe school, unique in Russia and probably in the world, it seemed as though, in Pushchin's words, an attempt had been made "to combine all the comforts of home with the necessities of a public school."

The boys rose to the peal of a bell every morning at six, washed hurriedly, donned their everyday uniforms—blue trousers and a fitted blue coat with red collar—and went down to the main hall for morning prayers. Classes began at seven and continued until nine. From nine to ten the students had their tea and went out for a collective walk. At ten, back to the classroom. At noon, second walk; at one, lunch. From two to three, calligraphy or drawing. From three to five, lessons. From five to six, tea and a walk, followed by homework or supplementary classes. Wednesday and Saturday were devoted wholly to dancing and fencing. Every Saturday all thirty pupils took a compulsory bath. The dinner bell rang at 8:30 P.M.; after dinner and until lights-out, which was at ten, they were free to run and play ball in the gymnasium on the second floor.

Ilichevsky, one of the pupils, wrote a somewhat exaggerated account, no doubt, to a friend: "In all, we work seven hours a day, and with breaks too, each one lasting over an hour. We are always doing something. Whoever wants to study studies, and whoever wants to go out for a walk, goes. To tell the truth, the lessons are not very long, and the rest of the time we are outdoors. Summer will soon be here and then we are in the gardens from morning to night, gardens more beautiful than any in St. Petersburg."[1]

At night, vigil lamps were lighted in the corridors, and a felt-slippered supervisor padded slowly up and down, scolding any boys who were still awake.

There was a woman whose only duty was to take care of the boys' underclothes, on all of which the owner's number and name were printed. They were changed twice a week, and the table and bed linen once a week. There were three courses (four on feast days) for lunch. In his memoirs Pushchin wrote: "The food was good, but that did not stop us, occasionally, from throwing our piroshki at the bewhiskered face of Zolotarev [the bursar]. For morning tea each boy received a whole loaf of white bread, and half a loaf at evening tea. On Monday the week's menus were posted in the dining room, and the boys arranged exchanges according to their preferences. In the beginning a half glass of 'porter' was served at lunch, but later this English custom was abandoned and we had to content ourselves with kvass and plain water."

In this ideal establishment the pupils did not even have to brush their clothes or polish their shoes or clean their rooms: There were servants to relieve the young elite of all such humdrum chores. One of these menials, Leonty Kemersky, set up shop in a corner somewhere and secretly sold chocolate, candy, hot coffee and even spirits, which were expressly forbidden.

A few days after the school opened, an announcement was made which plunged Pushkin and his young friends into despair. At tea one afternoon, the headmaster dryly informed them that he had received an order from the minister forbidding the pupils to leave the school, but authorizing their close relatives to visit them on holidays. "This categorical order, which must have been prepared in advance and then carefully kept secret, was so unexpected that it threw us all into a turmoil," wrote Pushchin. When the headmaster left the dining room, an ominous murmur spread from table to table. The boys were indignant; there was talk of imprisonment; the legality of the ruling, which had been concealed from them before they entered, was contested. The Tsarskoye Selo boarders suddenly found themselves cut off from the outside world, placed in a hermetically sealed jar to undergo nobody knew what artificial and horrible form of growth. "During our six years at school," wrote Baron Korf, another pupil, "we were never allowed to leave Tsarskoye Selo, not even for a trip to St. Petersburg. . . . And even at Tsarskoye Selo we were not allowed outside the walls of the school for the first three or four years; when our parents or relatives came to see us, they had to sit with us in the common room or go trotting along behind us through the gardens."

Classes began on October 23, 1811. According to the imperial decree, the course was to last six years, and was divided into lower and upper schools. The curriculum in the lower school included the following subjects: "1. grammar: instruction in the Russian, Latin, French, and German languages; 2. moral sciences: introduction to religion, philosophy, ethics, and logic; 3. mathematics and physical sciences: arithmetic, beginning with the rule of three, elementary algebra, physics, and trigonometry; 4. historical sciences: history of Russia and foreign countries, geography, and chronology; 5. basic knowledge of literature: excerpts from the best authors, analyses, rules of rhetoric; 6. fine arts and gymnastics: calligraphy, drawing, dancing, fencing, horsemanship, and swimming."

In addition, there were lessons in psychology, military strategy, political economy, aesthetics, law, "French and German rhetoric, and, if possible, architecture."

This curriculum was so broad and so disorganized that a lifetime would not have sufficed to cover it all, and the teachers accordingly adopted the wise plan of ignoring the whole elaborate edifice and educating the boys as best they could, following their personal inclinations and special fields of knowledge.

The method might have been disastrous; it proved excellent, because the teachers were, by happy accident, a well-chosen lot. For that period this was something of a feat, for the Russian nation was basically illiterate. There were virtually no good secondary schools and the universities were mere talking-shops. In 1822 the entire student body at the University of Kazan numbered some forty individuals; at the University of St. Petersburg there were thirty-eight professors and fifty-odd students—seventeen in the law school, six reading philosophy, and four in mathematics. Most of the faculty were recruited in Germany. It was only eight years prior to the opening of the Tsarskoye Selo school that an imperial decree ordered "both foreign and Russian" professors to give their lectures in Russian. On this subject, A. I. Turgenev wrote, in naïve jubilation: "At the Pedagogical Institute there is not a single course any more that is not given in Russian. Even political economy is taught in Russian!"[2]

Truly, Russia was just beginning to wake from her long slumber. There was no scientific or literary language. Culture was entangled in a web of French, English and German affectations. It was a period of imitation, plagiarism, antipatriotism; of intellectual subjugation to the outworn fashions of Europe. It was the negation of the Russian genius by the Russians themselves.

By what miracle were teachers found for these thirty youngsters at Tsarskoye Selo who were able to cultivate in them an awareness of a rich, new Russian culture? What would have become of Pushkin if he had been sent to the Jesuit boarding school?

Two of Pushkin's more noteworthy instructors were Kaydanov, author of a number of historical works, and Kunitsyn, the philosophy teacher who was decorated by the emperor for his inaugural address. Kunitsyn was a fanatic liberal who did not hesitate to condemn serfdom openly to his pupils. He preached "natural law" and later wrote a book on the subject, in which the authorities seized upon this sacrilegious statement: "Every individual is completely free and subject only to the laws of his own reason." He was forced to resign in 1821.

The boys loved Kunitsyn's exalted generosity and could easily follow his reasoning. Unconsciously, they began to absorb his ideas; later, this love of independence and horror of social injustice were to lead a few of them into conspiracy, revolt and exile. In 1822, outraged by Kunitsyn's gun-point resignation, Pushkin wrote his *First Epistle to the Censor:*

As your fancy pleases, you call black what's white,
Satire is calumny to you,

> The voice of reason: a call to revolution,
> Poetry a vice, and Kunitsyn–Marat!*

In his poem *October 19, 1825* he also wrote:

> To Kunitsyn, our hearts and glasses raise,
> He modeled us, he breathed upon our coals.

Pushkin had two teachers of Russian literature. Koshansky, the first, was a young man (thirty-six) who posed as a dandy, pursued the ladies, was happiest speaking French and perpetrated ponderous and execrable elegies. A partisan of the old school of writers and author of a treatise on rhetoric and a collection of excerpts entitled *The Flower of Greek Poetry,* Koshansky encouraged his pupils' literary endeavors, while the boys listened to his lessons but ignored his advice. He preached a pompous lyricism, padded out his lines with mythological allusion, and forbade the boys to employ such trivial locutions in their poems as "dig a well" or "cross the square." They, however, continued to admire Zhukovsky, Karamzin and the other innovators, the lovers of free inspiration and simplicity. They wrote satiric couplets about Koshansky, and sneered at the poems he submitted to the *European Herald.* Koshansky's instruction was beneficial because of the opposition it aroused in his pupils. Where his own work was concerned, he awoke only their resistance; but elsewhere, he awakened their interest in poetry as an art; he provoked their sarcasm, but also their emulation.

"I can still recall," wrote Pushchin, "that afternoon class when Koshansky, having finished his lecture early, announced, 'Now, gentlemen, we shall try our pens: Describe for me, if you please, a rose, in verse.' Our rhymes, as usual, came with difficulty, but Pushkin finished in a twinkling and read us out two quatrains which were unanimously applauded. Koshansky took the manuscript away with him."

Koshansky acknowledged Pushkin's talent, but judged him superficial. The young man's verse was facile, his rhymes farfetched, and his vocabulary too prosaic for his teacher's taste. To hear him talk, the child's attempts were play, not art. Pushkin responded to this with a poem entitled *To My Aristarchus,* mocking his teacher's poetical efforts and divulging the secret of his own inspiration:

> I think, then lift my arm, and the lines are born in a flash.

In 1814 the unfortunate Koshansky, who drank like a fish, fell ill and was replaced by Galich, a philosopher.

Galich was a fervent admirer of Kant and Schelling, and the author of a *History of Philosophical Systems* and an *Essay on the Science of*

* Jean-Paul Marat, the extremist Revolutionary figure. See below for references to his brother, who was one of Pushkin's teachers at the school.

the Beautiful—a young idealist, ardent, upright, likable and learned. Too learned, in fact, for his disciples. He would have made a good university professor, and it was hard for him to descend to the elementary level of Tsarskoye Selo. He decided to ignore his erudition and treat his students as equals. He soon became their friend, and his lessons were transformed into rambling and enthusiastic discussions. The boys liked him, joked with him, read him their clandestine verse. He was occasionally reminded of his pedagogical duties and, brandishing a volume of Cornelius Nepos, would announce, "Now, then, gentlemen, shall we have a little go at this old fellow?" And the class gleefully sat down to translate Nepos' *Lives*.

"This scatterbrain, the best and most comical of men," wrote Baron Korf, "taught Latin and Russian at the school; we made fun of him sometimes, but we loved him dearly for his companionship and almost childlike simplicity."

Long afterward, on March 17, 1834, Pushkin wrote these few words in his diary: "Chance meeting with dear old Galich, was delighted. He used to be my teacher, and encouraged me in my chosen path. It was he who insisted that I write my memories of Tsarskoye Selo for the examination of 1814."

Galich was not a poet, but he liked poets and could claim some understanding of them. Pushkin dedicated poems of fervent friendship to him, in which he called him the "faithful companion of the bottle," "apostle of all sloth," "lover of pleasures" and "chairman of the boys' banquet table."

These student banquet tables, tankards and bottles and piles of wreaths and tons of wine were, of course, mere poetical stage props, and the debauchery to which Pushkin alluded took place around a cup of tea in the student common room or Galich's room. But its influence on Pushkin was incontestable. In his pupils' eyes, the young Galich personified a sort of epicurean ideal that appealed strongly to their imaginations. His later life, however, was star-crossed. In 1821 he was accused of propounding anti-Christian theories in his *History of Philosophical Systems*. "Mr. Galich," his accuser said, "you openly prefer paganism to Christianity, the decadence of philosophy to the pure doctrine of the Christian Church, the atheist Kant to Christ, and Schelling to the Holy Ghost." Galich apologized and his enemies triumphantly led him off to church to be sprinkled with holy water. In 1837 he was permanently debarred from the faculty of the university. Finding no consolation in his wife, a corrosive, thick-headed and graceless woman, he immersed himself in two enormous studies, *General Law* and *The Philosophy of the History of Mankind*. But his house caught fire one day and the manuscripts were destroyed. In despair, he gave up, turned to drink and died in acute physical and moral distress.

Another teacher worth mentioning was the French professor, M. de Boudry, who was none other than the younger brother of Marat. After completing his studies at the Academy of Geneva, young David Marat was engaged as tutor to a Russian family. When his brother Jean-Paul became embarrassingly well-known, David applied to Catherine II for permission to change his name to de Boudry.† Later, he opened a little shop, where he wove and sold gold and silver cloth, greatly prized by Catherine II's circle. It went out of fashion, however, when Paul I came to the throne, whereupon Boudry was ruined, lost his shop and returned to private tutoring. Engaged to teach French at the Tsarskoye Selo school, he proved an energetic and exacting master. He was a funny little old man, wizened and pear-shaped, with a greasy, scantily powdered wig. He seldom washed, and only changed his underclothes once a month. His passion was the art of diction in general, and in the theater in particular. Under his direction the class rehearsed and performed French plays from which he excised all the women's parts, replacing lovers by friends. Pushkin relates how Boudry venerated his brother's memory. One day, telling the boys about Robespierre, he is alleged to have said, "It was he who secretly supplied the weapon for Charlotte Corday and made of this young girl a second Ravaillac."‡

"Apart from that," Pushkin continues, "and in spite of his family, his democratic ideas, his stained waistcoat, and his expression, so reminiscent of a Jacobin, Boudry, with his stubby little legs, was a very astute courtier." Pushkin was one of his best pupils; his fellow students nicknamed him "the Frenchman."

Kartsov, the science teacher, was a thickset, yellow-skinned man who moved heavily and was contemptuous of his pupils' ignorance. One day he called Pushkin to the blackboard and set him a problem in algebra.

Pushkin rocked from one foot to the other for some time, and then scribbled a few figures on the board. At length, Kartsov demanded: "Well? And the answer? What is the value of *x*?"

With a vague smile, Pushkin replied, "Zero."

"That's just fine!" roared Kartsov. "With you, Pushkin, everything in my class always equals zero. Go back to your seat and write poems."

All of these teachers, so dissimilar in background, temperament, ability and fortune, played their part in Pushkin's intellectual development.

† Marat was born at Boudry in the canton of Neufchâtel.

‡ Robespierre, the most powerful figure in the French Revolution; Charlotte Corday, the girl who stabbed Marat (an "extremist" colleague of Robespierre's) in his bathtub in 1793; Ravaillac, the assassin of Henry IV of France (the first Bourbon king) in 1610.

Above them stood the headmaster, the tenderhearted, pensive Malinovsky. Author of a book entitled *War and Peace,* he advocated, over a century before Woodrow Wilson, the formation of a great league of nations to settle disputes between European states. He also wrote an essay on *The Emancipation of the Slaves,* translated the Bible from Hebrew into Russian, and published a periodical, *Autumn Evenings.* He was responsible for the recruitment of teachers, wrote the school's rules and regulations and defined its educational policy. Malinovsky was opposed to learning by coercion, physical punishment and overwork for the young. He thought education should be a happy process, and encouraged the teachers to converse with their pupils, give them entertaining books to read and cultivate a competitive spirit among them by organizing literary contests; he often invited the boys to his own apartment. They came to regard him as a sort of older brother, indulgent, rather weak, but infinitely good-natured, and they were stunned by his death after barely three years as headmaster.

The school then entered upon a troubled "interregnum," as Pushkin called it. A succession of teachers without authority tried to run it, such as Koshansky, or the Austrian Hauenschild, or retired Lieutenant Colonel Frolov, an insensitive ignoramus who thought Rousseau was the last name of a woman called Emilie; he made the boys stand in rows for morning prayers and sit in the dining room according to their rank in class, and he punished them by making them kneel on the stone floor. He was replaced at the beginning of 1816 by a new headmaster, the good, kindhearted Engelhardt, who once wrote in his diary: "It is only by participating wholeheartedly in the pupils' joys and sorrows that one can win their affections. The trust of the young can only be gained by acts, not words. Education without any punishment at all is a chimera, but if the child is punished too often and for no visible reason, he will come to regard his tutor as an executioner who is trying in some obscure way to take revenge upon him."

Englehardt had no difficulty in restoring an informal discipline among the boys. After the uncertainties of the "interregnum," he gave them a sense of direction, of being guided, watched over and cared for as they had been while Malinovsky was alive. Continuing the tradition established by his predecessor, he drank tea with them, talked poetry and ethics to them and invited them to his home, so that they might learn how to conduct themselves correctly in the presence of ladies.

Finally, in 1816, Engelhardt lifted the old ban and allowed the boys to visit the homes of some of the residents of Tsarskoye Selo. They were so grateful for his kindness and understanding that some of them, like Pushchin and Volkhovsky, kept up a correspondence with the headmaster for the rest of their lives.

Pushkin alone remained insensitive to Engelhardt's charm. The headmaster disliked Pushkin, and their animosity was mutual; but the reasons for it have never been fully elucidated. "I personally," Pushchin wrote, "was never able to understand why Pushkin repelled all the overtures of Engelhardt and his wife. He refused to see the headmaster as he really was, and avoided all contact with him. His attitude concealed something, but what it was he would never tell me."

Engelhardt had a chubby face, with large, melancholy eyes and fleshy lips. Most of the time he wore a blue serge frock coat with gilt buttons and a broad black velvet collar, black silk hose and buckle pumps; and he had a winning voice. But Pushkin, more perceptive than his fellows, detected something objectionable and false behind his face, gestures, words. He sensed that Engelhardt was playing at being an admirable man, that all his kindness and patience were feigned, and that he was complacently deceiving both himself and everyone else. This headmaster was too perfect to be true. What was wrong with him, as far as Pushkin was concerned, was that there was nothing wrong with him.

One day Engelhardt came over to Pushkin's desk, sat down and softly inquired, "Why are you angry with me?" Pushkin was embarrassed and replied that he had no grievance against the headmaster. "Then it's just that you don't like me?" pursued the gentle Engelhardt. At these words the boy burst into tears and cried, "I feel guilty because I haven't been able to appreciate you!" Engelhardt also shed a tear or two, patted Pushkin on the shoulder and left, sighing with joy: He had overcome the last of the rebels. A few minutes later, passing by Pushkin's seat again, he saw the boy blush and slip a piece of paper into the desk.

"Poetry, I presume?" asked Engelhardt, with an ingratiating smile.

Raising the desk top, he picked up the sheet of paper between his fingertips, and his eyes beheld, not some idyllic lines of verse, but a hideous caricature of himself adorned with a few scurrilous rhymes. Engelhardt replaced the sheet of paper and murmured sorrowfully, "Now I know why you always refuse my invitations. But I still don't understand what I have done to antagonize you."[3]

Engelhardt, who had won the unqualified approval of all the other boys, was literally confounded by Pushkin's obstinate resistance, and the only thing that could arouse this mild man's rancor was a refusal to believe how good he was. Having failed to win Pushkin's affection, his reports on the boy became distinctly vindictive. "Pushkin's supreme and ultimate ambition," he wrote on March 22, 1816, "is to excel in the field of poetry; but it seems unlikely that this ambition will ever be fulfilled, for he has an aversion to serious study and his intelligence, being neither profound nor penetrating, is superficial and, one might say, French. And this is the most indulgent judgment that can be passed upon him. His heart is cold and empty. There is neither love nor religious conviction in him. Never, it may well be, was a young man's heart as devoid of feeling as his. The tender sentiments characteristic of adolescence are cheapened and debased in his imagination by his reading of erotic works of French literature—which he knew almost by heart when he first entered the school, as though they were the proper content of a primary education."

Other evaluations of Pushkin as a schoolboy have been preserved, and some of the reports from the year 1812 are worth quoting. For example, Russian: "Alexander Pushkin has more understanding than memory, more taste than perseverance. . . . That is why the smallest obstacle is enough to stop him." Philosophy: "Pushkin understands quickly, grasps subtleties and has considerable wit. But he is incapable of applying himself and makes absolutely no progress." Drawing: "Considerable ability, but works too quickly and carelessly. Progress negligible." German literature: "No progress, no aptitude, perseverance, or willingness to learn. Corrupted by education." Mathematics: "Intelligent, superficial, extremely lazy, conduct in class poor. Achievement poor." Lastly, character: "Inconsistent and lacking in perseverance, talkative, witty, good-natured, but scatterbrained and violently hot-tempered."

Also in 1812, Piletsky, the head proctor, wrote the following comment on Pushkin: "Pushkin (Alexander), thirteen years. His nature inclines to brilliance rather than thoroughness; his mind is keen and intense, rather than profound. Lacks perseverance as a student, for love of work has not yet become his chief quality. Having read many French books, not all of which are suitable for his age, he has filled his memory with a great number of fine passages culled from famous authors. Equally advanced in Russian literature, knows a large number of fables and poems. Although he is learning to reflect more deeply, his knowledge is on the whole superficial. Personal features: hypersensitivity and pride, resulting sometimes in shyness; good-natured, perceptive, but subject to fits of violent rage; frivolous, talkative, witty. Apart from this, there is considerable goodness in him: admitting his weaknesses, he accepts advice readily, and heeds it, with good results. . . ."

"Frivolous," "hypersensitive," "talkative," "superficial," "hot-tempered" —the same words recur in report after report, defining Pushkin's behavior at Tsarskoye Selo.

His teachers all agree. No good can ever come of this unfeeling, untidy, fiery-eyed youngster with the cannibal lips. Oh yes, he has read quantities of Russian and French books, classical and modern, and he writes poetry with dazzling ease, and if he will only fix his mind on any problem for five minutes he can outstrip all his fellows. But there is something elusive, unstable, even dangerous about him that inhibits wholehearted approval. His very talent will be his undoing. Relying on his exceptional gifts, his inspiration, his luck, he will never have the determination to tackle and complete a major work. He will continue to dissipate himself in charming little incidental pieces, he will become an entertainer like his Uncle Basil, a sensualist, a butterfly, a mischief-maker, a "Frenchman."

When the calligraphy master was asked to remember his former pupil, he replied, "What is all this fuss about Pushkin? He was a useless scamp, and nothing more!"

5. *Friends—A Vocation*

The school doors had closed behind a wild and timid child. Having only just escaped from his family, Pushkin looked at this second universe imposed upon him by his parents' will with deep suspicion. He saw a palace, gardens, sympathetic teachers and other boys, moving about him and staring at him boldly. The boys all seemed alike. Their faces and voices formed a single face and a single, monotonous voice. They were the others. He was alone. Alone with his dear Pushchin, his dormitory neighbor and confidant. Fiercely, he rejected all new attachments. He intended to be sufficient unto himself, and to live for six years on his own store of hope, learning and high spirits. But little by little, lesson by lesson, night by night, the monolithic features of "the others" began to crack and crumble. Individual faces detached themselves from the mass. Personalities suddenly emerged. Some were mysterious, fascinating, absurd. Some made him want to laugh, others seemed as though they might, perhaps, be worthy of admiration. Names ceased to drift about and fastened themselves to eyes, noses, shocks of hair and changing voices. There was the inert Delvig, lost in his dreams and lies and poetry. (He was nearsighted, and since it was forbidden to wear spectacles, every female he looked at seemed a raving beauty to him.) There was the headmaster's son, little Malinovsky, playful, quarrelsome, raucous, insufferable and delightful; Korsakov, curly-headed and pretty as a girl; Volkhovsky, studious and calm, but so frail that in order to strengthen his spine, he forced himself to carry both weighty volumes of the lexicon on his back (his indomitable will earned him the nickname of Suvorov, after the redoubtable field marshal of Catherine II, known for his martial bearing); young Prince Gorchakov, graceful and voluble; Danzas, so thick and mulish; little Yakovlev, who began to mimic the teachers' mannerisms on the first day of school and knew how to make two hundred different faces (he was called "the comedian"); Ilichevsky, so oddly shaped, "broad on top and narrow at the bottom," but with moments of great drollery; Baron Modest Korf, wary, bigoted and sniveling; Kornilov, the one who said "Oui, Monsieur" to the empress and was not as stupid as he looked; the mischief-maker Broglio, forever being punished and forever laughing; Guryev, who was strangely sweet to the other boys (and was expelled two years later for "Greek instincts"); and others. And finally, there was the scrawny, tall, doltish, impossible Wilhelm Küchelbecker. Küchelbecker was half deaf. His face was askew, his mouth crooked, his eyes protruded like a broiled trout's. His movements were jerky. He seemed utterly absorbed in some higher realm of thought, which made him stumble when he walked and stammer when he spoke. He was nervous, sentimental and softhearted. Everyone found him hysterically funny, and this made him very indignant.

There were so many of them, and now they were all so different, these boys among whom Alexander Pushkin must find a place for himself. Cautiously, he began to emerge from his shell, he edged forward to take a closer look at these strangers, and, silently, he weighed them up and judged them. He was afraid they would make fun of him and call him a monkey: He looked like a little monkey, and he knew it. And then, he was not as strong as Danzas or Broglio, not as likable as Korsakov, and he was neither baron nor prince, like some of his fellow students. Therefore, he must attack first, and win, at all costs. Absurdly oversensitive, Pushkin detected mute hostility, veiled sarcasm, ulterior motives, allusions and secret intrigues on all sides. Mortified at the thought that anyone might laugh at him, he answered an inoffensive jest with a sneer of insult. He was clever, and he knew how to annihilate his adversary with a few piercing words. Deliberately, he went too far, delivering his flayed, humiliated victim up to the general mirth and then withdrawing, afire with gleeful wrath. At night, however, he was invariably seized by remorse. He realized that he had been unfair and wicked and that nobody liked him. He wanted to be forgiven by the boy he had publicly humiliated; but in order to be forgiven he would have to apologize, and he would never stoop to that. Hostility toward him mounted steadily. He was feared for his sarcastic tongue, he was avoided; and he suffered. Tormented, miserable, lost, he wept into his pillow, then turned to the partition and called out to his friend, his only friend, Pushchin. He told him everything, asked him what to do. And the other boy answered as best he could, encouraged, comforted, scolded, his voice dropping to a whisper at the sound of the night supervisor's regular footfall down the icy corridor.

"Most often," wrote Pushchin, "after some ill-timed joke or tactless needling, he would find he had put himself in a false position and could not get out of it. This made him commit more blunders, which never go unnoticed in a boarding school. . . . I realized that his excessive sensitivity caused him to attach too much importance to every little thing he did, and he would become dreadfully upset afterward. Together, we would do our best to smooth out some of the difficulties. He was a mixture of extreme boldness and extreme timidity—both unjustified—and that was what got him into all the trouble. Sometimes we would play some prank together; I always got away with it, but he never knew how to smooth things over. What he was most lacking was what is called tact. . . . The result of all this was that no one, in the group of boys to whom he was originally drawn, could respond spontaneously to his overtures."

Some of his schoolmates nourished a long-standing grudge against him on account of his scathing tongue. The popish and spiteful Baron Korf wrote: "There was no religion in him, either outwardly or in his soul; no noble sense of virtue; and he even affected an obtrusive cynicism about such matters, cruelly—often obscenely—mocking the commandments and rites of the Church, respect for parents, family affections, social relationships; all that was nothing to him, and I am sure he often said more than he meant, for the sheer pleasure of making a funny remark."

Baron Korf was not the only boy to detest Pushkin during their first months at Tsarskoye Selo; but he was his only detractor in later years. The miracle occurred, as slowly as a plant's leaves unfold. Links were formed, masks dissolved and affection grew, in the isolated little universe of the school. One day Pushkin learned that Ilichevsky wrote poetry in his spare time, and even recited his poems to his friends, and they applauded. He was enchanted by this discovery, particularly as it now transpired that Ilichevsky was not the only poet in school. Other talents began to emerge on all sides. Delvig, Yakovlev, Korsakov, Rzhevsky—even the impossible Küchelbecker, who could scarcely speak Russian—all became rabid rhymesters. A brotherhood immediately sprang up among the budding poets of Tsarskoye Selo. They were united by their passion for literature; they read each other their work, encouraged and vied with each other. Professor Koshansky fed the boys' ambition, suggested themes to them and declaimed the best examples to the class. At the headmaster's suggestion, Piletsky, the head proctor, even proposed the creation of a kind of Academy, to be composed of "all young people whom the members deemed fitted for the profession of author."

At this, the boys could not contain themselves for joy. They never left the library, neglected their studies, rhymed day and night, struggled and strove and flooded the school with epigrams and fables and idylls and patriotic hymns. The headmaster, alarmed by this epidemic of inspiration which was taking the boys away from their work, was forced to dissolve the Academy he had originally promoted and forbade the writing of verse in the institution. But can the muse of poetry be stilled? The boys wrote on in secret and read their efforts in whispers behind the supervisors' backs. On March 25, 1812, Ilichevsky solemnly announced to a friend: "As far as my work in poetry is concerned, I must say I have made great strides; in fact, one of my good friends is a young man who, having lived among the best poets of our time, has acquired great knowledge and skill at versemaking. Even though we have actually been forbidden to write, we are still composing, in secret."

The "young man" in question was Pushkin, then aged twelve. He and Ilichevsky soon left the rest of the field behind. Their friends compared the merits of the two rivals, and, at first, opted in favor of Ilichevsky. At length, the headmaster's injunction was lifted and they could compete openly. Ilichevsky's efforts were pompous and resounding. The boys said:

> Immortal Ilichevsky,
> You wear the crown among our poets,

and compared him to the glorious Derzhavin; Pushkin, they said, was like Dmitryev.

The school opened on October 19, 1811; by December of that year the pupils had already decided to print two papers: the *Tsarskoye Selo School Gazette* and the *Tsarskoye Selo Imperial School Herald.* These were unprepossessing periodicals, handwritten on dingy paper, childish in content and limited in appeal. But beginning in 1812, literature made so many new recruits at the school that the poets split into two camps: Pushkin, Delvig and Korsakov published *The Inexperienced Pen,* while Ilichevsky, Volkhovsky, Küchelbecker and Yakovlev produced *For Pleasure and Profit.* In 1813 the two merged into a new review, entitled *Novice Swimmers.* This was followed by a periodical, *The Schoolboy Philosopher*, of which four copies have survived, bound in red leather with a gold vignette stamped on the cover. The first page bears the inscription: "Typography by Danzas," for it was written entirely in his hand; and below that, "Imprimatur, the censor: Delvig."

The first issue of *The Schoolboy Philosopher* contained the traditional statement of editorial policy: "In this periodical we shall publish jokes and new songs and any other thing, in short, that does or might entertain our honorable readers."

Its pages are filled with anecdotes, comic letters and caricatures. The jests are aimed impartially at teachers and students, but their young authors have certain pet victims. Their wit is unfailingly tickled by the good Wilhelm Küchelbecker and his bad verse:

May God forget his sins
As the world has done his poems,*

wrote Pushkin. And Ilichevsky:

Come forth, O Wilhelm, that all may see:
Perfect specimens of monsterdom are made
In mind as well as limb.

Another time, Pushkin was bedridden in the infirmary; Küchelbecker and a few friends came to visit, and asked him to read out his latest composition. Pushchin describes the scene:

"The reading began:

'Friends, the hour of release has come,
Peace and silence everywhere . . .'

"Everyone was listening intently, the quiet broken only by enthusiastic exclamations. Küchelbecker, enthralled, dazzled, enraptured, begged the others not to disturb the reader. We reached the final stanza, and we heard:

'Where are you all; where am I, too?
By Bacchus, answer, do!
You're fast asleep, dear friends,
Your noses in your copybooks.
You, poet, for your precious crimes,
You alone remain alert.
Now, Wilhelm, come, read me your verse,
That I may sleep in turn!'"

Küchelbecker admired Pushkin and forgave him every jibe; and Pushkin teased Küchelbecker unmercifully, but loved him like a brother.

"Rennenkampf speaks very well of you," Mrs. Küchelbecker wrote her son, "but he asked me to remind you that it is not right for you to spend too much of your time on exercises in poetry, and I agree that you must not make that your sole occupation. . . . Without a thorough knowledge of the language, and with no serious artistic training, versifying is merely a waste of good paper."[1]

Pushkin advised Küchelbecker to write in German, as the good Wilhelm spoke that language better than Russian. But Küchelbecker solemnly replied that Germany already had a large number of poets, whereas in Russia, "even he would not be too many."

One day the boys' teasing went beyond the usual limits. One of

* The central section of Shostakovich's Fourteenth Symphony is a setting for voice of a poem by Küchelbecker.

them, Myasoedov, emptied his plate of soup onto Küchelbecker's head, and Wilhelm, overcome with shame, fell into a sort of fever-fit and had to be hospitalized. But the moment he was put to bed, he escaped from the infirmary, ran down to the garden and threw himself into a pond which, alas, was too shallow to drown a baby. The supervisors came running and fished out the wretched youth, shivering and sobbing with rage, and *The Schoolboy Philosopher* promptly published a caricature by Ilichevsky, showing a group of teachers struggling to beach poor Wilhelm after harpooning his cravat with a grappling hook.

Cruel, fierce, fickle and witty, the little band of poets had to be closely watched by the authorities, for some of their pranks demanded instant punishment. The ringleader of these mischievous rascals was, always, Pushkin—the elusive, the satanic, the dread Pushkin. Piletsky, the head proctor, wrote in a report in 1812:

"On November 6 Pushkin announced, on the subject of the logic class: 'I must confess that I do not understand anything about logic and, moreover, many men more learned than I do not understand it either, for the simple reason that there is nothing to understand in a syllogism. . . .'

"On the sixteenth, he spoke insultingly of the fourth department. . . . On the twentieth, in his drawing class, he called Gorchakov a Polish prostitute. . . . On the thirteenth, when I tried to confiscate one of Delvig's poems which alluded to the warden in disrespectful terms, Pushkin flew into a rage and said, quite loudly, 'You have no right to take our papers away. If you keep on like that, you'll soon be stealing letters out of our drawers. . . .' On the thirtieth, in the evening, he was telling Mr. Koshansky heaven only knows what scandalous tales of dress shops in St. Petersburg, and the goings on among those women they call *marchandes à la toilette*. . . ."

This proctor, loathed and feared by all the boys, was a dangerous fanatic, a rigid disciplinarian, torn between sexual lusts and sudden outbursts of asceticism. Piletsky pursued the boys' sisters and cousins when their families came to visit Tsarskoye Selo, and some of the students claimed they had heard him maligning their own parents; so the rebels closed up ranks behind Pushkin, and much nocturnal plotting ensued. Then, in the dining room, Pushkin openly denounced the proctor's conduct. His colleagues were incensed by his allegations and summoned Piletsky to the lecture hall, where they told him they would leave school in a body if he did not resign forthwith. Fearing a scandal, Piletsky preferred to lose his job. In his draft memoirs, Pushkin jotted down the following note: "Philosophical thoughts—martinism—we expel Piletsky."

One day Pushkin, Pushchin and Malinovsky, the late headmaster's son, decided to sample a beverage called "goggle-moggle," composed of rum, sugar and beaten eggs. "We had determined, I, Pushkin, and Malinovsky," wrote Pushchin, "to drink some goggle-moggle. I managed to procure a bottle of rum, we found some eggs and powdered sugar, and set to work in front of a boiling samovar. Of course, we were not the only guests at this nocturnal feast, but the others remained, so to speak, in the wings; and it was one of them, Tyrkov, who involuntarily betrayed us, for the rum had a powerful effect upon him, and the proctor soon got wind of the disturbance, as there was noise and sounds of racing footsteps coming from our end of the wing. He notified the warden. After dinner, the latter observed the pupils closely and noted an unwonted degree of exhilaration in them. Interrogations and investigations began forthwith. All three of us came forward and declared we were the only ones involved and the only guilty parties."

This was a grave offense. On September 5, 1814, Frolov wrote the following report: "Malinovsky, Pushchin, and Pushkin had persuaded a servant to bring powdered sugar, hot water, raw eggs, and rum to their room. When this had all been delivered, they left the hall—with the permission of the proctors on duty—to go to their room, where, in a spirit of mischief and childish curiosity, they prepared a beverage called goggle-moggle and proceeded to drink it. Learning that I had been notified, they then returned to the hall, where I found them; I carried out an investigation on the spot and, after finding them guilty, ordered them, by way of punishment, to kneel throughout prayers for two days."†

But that was not the end of the matter. At that time, the headmaster was an Austrian named Hauenschild; he sent a report to the minister. And Count Razumovsky (the minister) came down from St. Petersburg, summoned the culprits to appear before him, admonished them severely and submitted the matter to the schoolmasters' senate.

"The senate," Pushchin wrote, "sentenced us (1) to remain on our knees for two weeks during morning and evening prayers; (2) in the dining room, where pupils were seated according to conduct, to go to the bottom of the table; (3) to have our names, with details of our offenses and punishment, recorded in the school's black book, which could affect our marks on the final examination.

"The first measure was applied *in toto*. The second was lightened: After a while, we gradually moved up the table again.

"As for the third, it was annulled three years later, thanks to the new headmaster, Engelhardt."

This event, like all the others, was immortalized in poetry: Every-

† About an hour each day was spent at prayers.

thing that happened at the school was a pretext for some poem, epigram or song.

Korsakov played the guitar, and set Pushkin's poem *To Delia* to music; the boys used to sing the ballad in chorus during recreations. Another pupil, Yakovlev, was a tolerable violinist and composed a tune for Pushkin's *To the Painter;* this melody was also a great hit with the boys. Comic couplets about the pupils or their teachers were sung as well—as, for instance, when the interim headmaster Hauenschild, sucking at his licorice and wrinkling up his eyes, was slowly approaching the recreation room one day and heard the following words yelped out by a chorus of vigorous young voices:

> In the hall when all's at peace,
> Oh wondrous, strange event!
> Here comes Satan gliding past
> With a licorice drop 'twixt his teeth.

Group storytelling parties, at which each person had to recite in turn, were another source of amusement. At these gatherings Pushkin improvised two tales which he recalled in later years and elaborated into short stories: *The Shot* and *The Snowstorm.*

Pushkin seldom emerged victorious, however, from these contests of eloquence and imagination. The boys preferred Delvig, who was a wonderful storyteller and notorious idler. Round, pale, nearsighted and languid, little Delvig never learned his lessons and never understood the questions he was asked in class, but he was passionately interested in mythology and romantic poetry, and he was by far the best liar in school.

"One day," Pushkin later wrote, "he described the campaign of 1807 to some friends as though he had been an eyewitness to the events. His tale was so vivid and plausible that it deeply stirred his young listeners' imaginations, and for days thereafter, curious fellow students would gather around him in a circle and ply him with questions about the details of the action. Our headmaster, Malinovsky, got wind of it and he too wanted to hear the tale of his adventures from Delvig's own lips. Delvig was ashamed to have to own up to his lie—as skillful as it was innocent, moreover—and decided to stick to his story in front of the headmaster; which he did, and so convincingly that any doubts the rest of us might have had about the veracity of his statements were quelled, until the day he confessed he had been lying all the time."

But little Delvig only deceived his companions in fun, and would never have lied to cover a misdeed.

"In children with rich imaginations," wrote Pushkin, "a propensity for lying is not incompatible with integrity or sincerity."

Delvig also wrote poetry and published in the school newspapers. He learned German from Küchelbecker and read Klopstock, Schiller and Goethe, while Pushkin continued to specialize in the French authors. In his poem *The Village*, written in 1814, he enumerated some of his favorites: "the rasping old man of Ferney," "the lazy sage Jeannot La Fontaine," "the giant Molière," Racine, Parny; and also Vergil, Homer and "sensitive Horace," Tasso, Juvenal; and the English poets Gray, Thomson and Milton. True to his childhood love, Voltaire was the author to whom he remained most firmly attached. He called him "poet of poets," "gray-haired old rogue," "rival of Euripides" and "matchless old man." Voltaire's airy irony, his audacity, his deflation of all idols were meat and drink to the boy. He longed to be like him one day—as soon as possible. As for the Russian authors: All the young scholars in the literary circle knew their works by heart, argued their merits, admired them and envied their renown: Zhukovsky, Batyushkov, Dmitryev, Derzhavin, Krylov . . . To keep abreast of the literary scene, Pushkin spent some of his own money on a subscription to the periodical *The Russian Museum*; its list of subscribers for 1815 mentions one "Alexander Sergeyevich Pushkin, at Tsarskoye Selo."

This at first glance unlikely passion for poetry in a group of preadolescents can best be explained by the novelty of literature in Russia. Russian poetry had been born at the beginning of the eighteenth century, with the sticky hexameters of Kantemir and Tredyakovsky; it quickly became organized, shook the clay from its feet and split into rival factions, and these schoolboys were the avid spectators of the first triumphs of national expression. Unlike their French contemporaries, they did not have the certainty that the new generation of authors was continuing a centuries-old tradition, they did not see themselves being carried along a mainstream whose source was in some far-distant headland.

No; *they were at* the source, they were witnessing the resurgence of a spring that had long flowed underground, quenching their thirst from a virgin cup. For them, literature was not history, it was the immediate present. They saw it being made before their eyes. It was discovering itself and they were discovering it, with amazement. Every new poem was essential. There was the intoxication of free words, unexpected rhymes, harsh, naïve melodies. They were eager to plunge into the fray, quickly, quickly; to begin to juggle with these rhymes, sonorous as glass beads. What were all other sciences compared to this supreme delight? The children of Tsarskoye Selo were drawn into the wake of the very first Russian poets. With his customary pomposity, Ilichevsky wrote to a friend: "So it is, dear friend, that we want to rejoice in the dawn of our literature, thrill to the flowering of the genius of Zhukovsky, Batyushkov,

Krylov, and Gnedich. But sometimes it is not a bad thing to lift the veil upon the past, to cast a glance upon the works of the ancestors of our national poetry, Lomonosov, Kheraskov, Derzhavin, Dmitryev. They hide treasures for all to find. It is also good to question the foreign authors (our fathers were their disciples), to converse with Racine, Voltaire, Delille, and borrow their inimitable beauties to enhance our own poems."

Pushkin's method of composition was recorded by Komovsky: "Ideas for poems came to him, not only during his free periods or when he was out walking, but in class, and even in church. Either he would screw his face all up, or his features would relax into a smile, according to the subject that had caught his attention. He would withdraw to a corner of the room to record his thoughts, biting his fingernails nervously, furrowing his brow, and puffing out his lips; then, in a low voice, with his eyes of fire, he would read over the lines he had just written."

The literary germ was so contagious that after the first group of students had left Tsarskoye Selo, a servant named Gabriel Zaytsev wrote a poem, too:

> You who will wield
> No saber or sword,
> But paper and well-trimmed quills . . .

The boys' inspiration fastened upon the most insignificant local incidents and trivial landscapes, and magnified them into poems. They sang of their pranks, their fellows' blunders, their teachers' failings and the beauties of the gardens surrounding the school. Deprived of outings and holidays, all they saw of the outside world was its ceremonial, official, historical aspect; the vast park with its lawns and avenues of trees, its grottoes, flower beds, marble bridges, its two palaces, its "prarie of roses"—which had been bereft of roses since the reign of Catherine II; and the blue lake in which a single white column was mirrored. Not far away, though, reveille sounded and banners flapped in the wind. In the evenings they could hear the military band playing noisily in the guards' camp. And sometimes, as they walked along the finely raked garden paths, the boys passed the tall silhouette of the emperor.

6. *War*

Being so close to the court and its concerns, the boys were wildly excited at the prospect of war with France. Ever since the meeting at Erfurt, the French alliance had been unpopular, to say the least, in Russia. Grievances against Napoleon were many and well-founded: There was the continental blockade—disastrous for Russian trade; the creation of the Grand Duchy of Warsaw; the fear of new Napoleonic campaigns in Europe; the double game of the French diplomats in Constantinople; the sudden breakdown of negotiations for a marriage between Napoleon and Grand Duchess Anna. All of these, strengthened by the treasury-minded urgings of England, forced Alexander I to break off relations again with the emperor of the French. Maneuvering diplomatically, he informed the Tuileries government that he would adhere to the terms of the treaty of Tilsit only if Napoleon's armies withdrew from Prussia and remained on the far side of the Oder. He knew perfectly well that there was no possibility of Napoleon agreeing to this, but he wanted to be seen as a pacifist, placing the responsibility for a new offensive squarely on Bonaparte's shoulders. As he predicted, Napoleon termed the Russian demands an insult to his honor, and in June 1812 the French army crossed the Niemen. Alexander then wrote the following letter to its chief: "If Your Majesty does not intend to shed the blood of Your Majesty's people for such a misunderstanding as this, and agrees to remove Your Majesty's forces from Russian territory, I shall disregard what has occurred, and some arrangement between us will still be possible. Otherwise, Your Majesty will compel me to consider Your Majesty solely as an enemy, whom I have done nothing to provoke." War had virtually been declared.

From the beginning of the year, the schoolboys at Tsarskoye Selo had been watching the troops go by on their way to the frontier. Cavalry regiments in battle dress paraded past along the mud- and snow-covered highroad. Their officers wore short fur-lined coats, the men peaked caps and greatcoats. There were Cossacks too, with beards and waxed mustaches, their bodies glued to their steaming mounts. They carried spears and sang. Later came new recruits in gray, their faces etched with dirt, fatigue and brutishness. The palace was empty and hollow. Meals were poor. Then the boys learned from their parents and teachers that the scattered Russian forces were not even offering a show of resistance to the invader. The French and their allies from Baden, Prussia, Saxony, Bavaria, Westphalia, Württemberg, Austria and Poland were pouring across Russia under Napoleon's command, and advancing at an alarming rate. They had reached Vilno. General Barclay de Tolly was relieved of command, and Kutuzov was placed in charge of the army. General Bagration gave battle beneath the old walls of Smolensk; then he abandoned the fortress and retreated toward Mozhaysk.

The pupils' imaginations were fired by every word of military news. Troops passing through Tsarskoye Selo could hear their cheers and applause from behind the grills. Every boy had his favorite hero. Volkhovsky revered the memory of Suvorov; Gorchakov wore his hair like the emperor and screwed up his eyes when he spoke. Little Malinovsky swore by Platov, the hetman of the Cossacks; but Küchelbecker stubbornly defended the disgraced Barclay de Tolly. On August 24, 1812, his mother wrote to him: "Barclay has shown that he loves his fatherland by accepting a secondary role after being commander in chief. I am writing this for you: Learn not to judge too hastily, and not to agree automatically with those who blacken the names of men who have once held high office. . . ."

In the school library, the boys fought over the newspapers, read every communiqué aloud, cut out the portraits of the leading generals. They traced the route of the Antichrist and his army on the map. Their teachers explained the campaign to them in class. "In the beginning," wrote Pushchin, "we saluted every regiment of guards that passed through Tsarskoye Selo. We were always there the moment they appeared, we even left class to go outdoors, we sent our fervent prayers to accompany them, we embraced our parents and friends, mustachioed grenadiers made the sign of the cross over us, without losing step as they marched. Oh, the tears we shed! . . . When the fighting began, some of our parents would bring us the latest news every Sunday. The library was always full during recreation period, we pored over every Russian and foreign paper, we argued and discussed ad infinitum. The smallest incident was magnified a thousandfold, our fears changed to hopes with the slightest improvement in the military situation. The teachers came in and taught us to follow the action, explaining details that we could not have understood without their help."

Myasoedov, another pupil, wrote: "One day, after saluting a passing company, the boys felt such a wave of patriotism sweep over them that when they were sitting down for their next French lesson, they threw the books on the floor."

The French colony, however, was suffering no hardship in Russia. M. de Boudry continued his classes at Tsarskoye Selo. Forced to comply with government orders, the French theater company in St. Petersburg performed patriotic Russian works translated into French, but it performed them nonetheless—with Mlle. George in the role of Princess Xenia, incarnation of Slavic heroism. Mme. de Staël, Napoleon's sworn enemy, wrote: "When I entered Russia, the French army was already deep in Russian territory, and yet the foreign traveler was never impeded for one moment by any form of persecution or difficulty: Neither I nor my companions knew a word of Russian, we spoke only French, the language of the enemies who were laying waste to their empire. . . ."

This meddlesome busybody, the "conspiring magpie" as she was called, thoroughly exasperated the Muscovites with "her speeches that were too long and her sleeves that were too short" and her obsessive conviction that the entire European drama was centered upon her own person, "as though Napoleon's sole object in invading Russia had been to pursue her." As the Baron de Montet put it, she would have liked to be seen "as one of the last remaining sovereign powers of Europe." Although her reception by Alexander I might have been more enthusiastic, at least she was not molested; and this indulgence toward her was a curious sign of the times, proving in itself, if no other proof were available, that in its opening phase the war of 1812 was a war of governments, not of peoples. Curious, too, to think that in November 1812 *Mérope* was performed in St. Petersburg with Mlle. Mars in the leading role; in 1814 Molière's *Les Fourberies de Scapin* was revived; in 1816 two French theater companies were formed in the capital.

At school, meanwhile, the outcome of the Battle of Borodino was anxiously awaited. Kutuzov, the old, the glorious Kutuzov, swollen with fat, his skin stitched together by scars, old, one-eyed Kutuzov was waging a decisive battle outside Moscow. "When I saw him," wrote Mme. de Staël, "I feared he would not be the equal of the fierce and powerful men who were swooping down upon Russia from the four corners of Europe." The first bulletin left some hope of victory: "The fighting was widespread and continued throughout the night, losses on both sides are heavy; those of the enemy, judging by their repeated attacks upon our fortified positions, must be greater than ours. . . ." In St. Petersburg, the bulletin was read aloud in St. Alexander's Cathedral and followed by a solemn Te Deum, cannon salutes and fireworks.

And then, overnight, Moscow was being evacuated and occupied by the French.

From the very first days of the war, Governor Rostopchin had tried to arouse a sense of patriotism and self-sacrifice in the Moscow citizenry. He was a fervent, disorganized and uncultivated man, who hung posters in all the streets, proclaiming: "Napoleon will freeze on the road . . ." or, "Forward, Christian army . . . May its numbers swell until they darken the light of day . . ."

He outlawed lynching, but ordered a man named Vereshagin to be lynched for predicting a French victory within six months. He advised against the evacuation of the city, but authorized the departure of "single women and men of female sex"(!). Then he organized the transfer of the chancellery, then he opened the prisons, then he distributed weapons to the populace, then he arranged processions of the sacred ikons through the city, then he sent for Platon, the metropolitan, who lay dying in a convent in the suburbs, and had him carried into Kremlin Square, to an altar hung with banners. Assisted by his deacons, the metropolitan climbed out of the coach. He was pale as a ghost beneath his white-hooded purple archbishop's mantle. He could not speak. He wept; and the crowd was shaken by a sob, deep-throated as the roar of an animal. The archdeacon spoke: "The metropolitan wishes to know whether he has succeeded in convincing you. Let all who promise to obey him kneel." The crowd fell to its knees. Whereupon the commander in chief brusquely announced: "The people of Moscow will not be delivered up to the enemy unarmed. Distribute the weapons in the arsenal. The defense of Moscow is in your hands."

After this, Rostopchin summoned "all brave men to assemble on the Three Mountains" to make one last stand. But there was no last stand; Borodino had been the last stand. A general, panic-stricken exodus began immediately. Lords great and small, tradesmen and merchants, civil servants and anyone else who owned a vehicle and horse had already fled. Some left inscriptions in French on the walls of their homes: *Le mot adieu, ce mot terrible,* or, *Je vous salue, ô lieux charmants, quittés avec tant de tristesse* ("The word farewell, that fateful word," or, "Hail, fair ground, so sorrowfully abandoned"). Long lines of carriages, carts and landaus stretched along the roads. Pushkin's parents and Uncle Basil had taken refuge in Nizhny Novgorod. The police force, fire brigade and all their equipment had been evacuated; but the French actors remained. They gave one last performance at the New Theater: *Nathalie, la fille du boyard,* by Daniel Kashin; the high point of the play was a fire. The performance was seen as an evil omen, and the theater burned down the same day. A strong wind fanned the flames, and soon the whole city was blazing like a torch.

Pushkin must have thought with horror of his family home lying in ruins, the smoldering gardens, the familiar streets buried under piles of smoking timbers, Uncle Basil's wonderful library reduced to a heap of ash among other ashes, and the Karamzin library, and so many other libraries and so many other of his childhood haunts.

Nizhny Novgorod, whither the Moscow nobility, wealthy businessmen and literary and artistic elite had fled, seemed strangled, wrenched apart and submerged by the influx of men, women, children and baggage. The refugees camped in a few cramped, underfurnished rooms: the Muravyevs and their three children shared three rooms with Batyushkov, Druzhnin, an Englishman, two governesses and six dogs. Uncle Basil was living in an isba, trying to find a fur coat for the winter, and existing on a capital of a few kopecks. The boys and girls met in the squares of Nizhny Novgorod and wandered among the carriages, telegas and broken-down coaches, wistfully recalling their elegant promenades along the Tverskoy Boulevard. A few Muscovites, however, had managed to salvage some money and were already giving plentiful dinners and organizing balls, at which young ladies in French gowns danced French quadrilles until they dropped, and cursed, in French, the foe of their fatherland. Initially prostrated by the thought of his lost library and wardrobe, Basil Pushkin began to pull himself together and gallantly strove to produce new witticisms. "Grief has deranged Pushkin's memory," the poet Batyushkov wrote. "Last night he was scarcely able to recite the tale of the nightingale, at the Arkharovs'. . . . All Moscow congregates at their place, or rather, all the dispossessed of Moscow; some have lost their home, others their land, others have nothing to eat but a crust of bread. . . . They complain and curse the French, speaking French all the while, and their patriotism can be summed up in these words: *point de paix* [no armistice]."

At the school, it was feared that Napoleon would march on St. Petersburg, and the administration was already making plans to transfer the boys to some northern city. Wardens and teachers made feverish preparations. Malgin, the emperor's tailor, came to fit the boys with short Chinese-style coats lined with sheepskin. This romantic exodus toward polar regions captivated the boys' imaginations; they began dreaming of a new life among eternal snows, ice and bears. In the end, however, they did not have to go. In October, Napoleon abandoned Moscow, burned, plundered and profaned, and the long retreat began. A contemporary poet celebrated the sacrifice of Moscow in these terms:

There were not enough tapers,
There was not enough wax,
We had but one taper to light
In the sanctuary of the Lord,

And the taper was Moscow.
It burns for the repose
Of all your souls, our friends,
And for the shame of our enemy . . .

The first Muscovites to re-enter the capital were aghast at the extent of the destruction. One of Mrs. Rimsky-Korsakov's daughters wrote to her brother, on November 9: "I have been back in our poor Moscow for five days. Ah, Grisha, my friend, you cannot imagine what has happened to Moscow. The city is unrecognizable, it is impossible to look upon the ruins without weeping. Only the walls of houses built of stone are still standing, and their stoves are being heated with the remains of the wooden houses. . . ."

Mrs. Rimsky-Korsakov herself wrote to her son, on November 12: "Moscow is nothing but rubble and corpses. Of 9000 houses, 720 are now standing, and one of them is mine. The gates have been torn off, and the windowpanes fell out when they blew up Ivan the Great Tower. . . . The house is so filthy that it would take a fortnight to clean it: 180 dogs have been living in it, and a captain of the first battalion of the guards, who slept in our beloved Varenka's bed. All the curtains have been torn; they poked holes in the leather and slashed the upholstery. . . . But they did not molest our people; they only took their fur coats. . . ."

She later wrote: "May God help you to capture this wild beast, this exterminator of Christian peoples."

While the Muscovites were returning to the ruins of their homes, the French army, starving, ragged, harried by bands of partisans, was abandoning the vast land of desolation and mystery. To their stupefaction, the Russian people and Alexander I discovered that they were victorious. Yesterday their enemy had terrified the whole world, today it was as though a weight had shifted in the heavenly scales, and fortune was slowly tipping toward Holy Russia. The collapse of the French army was somehow miraculous. The Russian troops were often repelled and sometimes beaten by their opponents, yet Napoleon's army continued to fray or melt away, company by company. The real cold had not come yet, but a thick, milky fog enshrouded the retreating columns. They crept forward, losing their way in a mirage of mists, enchanted paths, forests of snow. They surrendered to peasant women armed with scythes, to bearded muzhiks, to silent Cossacks who suddenly fell upon them out of the wasteland of pearl and unending cold.

Slaughtered at the Berezina, the French nevertheless managed to cross the river and keep moving, and they abandoned 100,000 corpses along the road between Smolensk and Vilno; the horses shied at them as they passed. They met lines of prisoners with blotchy faces being driven along by muzhiks armed with clubs and pitchforks. Leaning against the tree trunks, the frozen dead stood guard; dark waves of wolves engulfed the wounded where they lay on the plains.

On Christmas Day, Russia officially hailed the rebirth of her territory, which "twenty nations" had come to devastate. Kutuzov advised a cessation of hostilities, since the enemy had now crossed the frontier. But Alexander I fancied himself as a liberator, not only of his own people, but of all the peoples of Europe. His pride, his mysticism and his hatred of Napoleon drove him on; and the war resumed—in another country, but with the same men. There followed the Battles of Lützen, Bautzen, Dresden, Kulm and Leipzig. At last, exactly at noon on March 19, 1814,* Emperor Alexander I and the King of Prussia entered Paris.

The people of Russia went nearly mad with joy. After being universally despised, Alexander I was suddenly The Emperor par excellence, the liberator, the avenging angel. He was called "Agamemnon," "Blessed of God," "Russian deity" and "tsar of tsars."

On April 13 a courier from St. Petersburg arrived in Moscow to announce the capitulation of Paris, and the celebrations began. On April 23 a high mass was sung in the Kremlin, and the bells pealed continuously from dawn to dark for three days. The town was illuminated, there was dancing in the streets. One contemporary wrote: "The All-High has heard his creatures' prayers and the vandal has been stricken low. Here, though Moscow has been seared to the bone, the revelry is general, we are spending our last kopecks to celebrate the victory. The Circle gave a masquerade . . . so did the shopkeepers. . . . On the eighteenth there will be a great reception, in which your three sisters will have a part. . . . There is to be a melodrama. Vera Vyazemsky will act the part of Russia, little Lunin will be Europe, and Bakhmetev will play Glory. . . . Then a temple will appear, enshrining a bust of His Majesty the Emperor, surrounded by all the different nations. Sofya is Portugal, Natasha is England, the younger Shakovskoy girl is Turkey, and the other Shakovskoy is Germany; little Poltoratsky is Switzerland, one of the Visotskys is Italy and the other is Sweden. No one wanted to represent France or Poland. The young ladies will sing a chorus—the words are very fine—and crown the emperor's bust with flowers."

On July 27, 1814, the dowager empress gave a magnificent party at Pavlovsk to celebrate Alexander's return to Russia; the pupils from Tsarskoye Selo were invited. The high point of the evening was an open-air ballet, with a backdrop painted to represent "the outskirts of Paris and Montmartre with its windmills." From a box hung with rose garlands,

* March 31, 1814, by the Gregorian calendar.

the schoolboys watched the performance. "Our Agamemnon, pacifier of Europe, conqueror of Napoleon," wrote Baron Korf, "shone with all the majesty that can be attained by a mortal."

The way from the palace to the pavilion passed beneath a triumphal arch bearing the following inscription:

> O you who return from the war,
> This arch of triumph is too small for you.

Pushkin was immediately inspired to draw a caricature of Alexander I, swollen by too many copious dinners, advancing toward a great gate that was manifestly too narrow to admit him, while the panic-stricken generals of his retinue rushed up to enlarge the orifice with their sabers. This cartoon was much appreciated by the other pupils.

"After the performance," wrote Baron Korf, "we were taken back to school, on foot, without any tea, or so much as an apple or a glass of water."

Pushkin's feelings about Alexander I were complex: To his contemporaries, the emperor was the living manifestation of human inconsistency. Napoleon called him "a veritable Byzantine"; Chateaubriand claimed he was "crafty as a Greek." He was "the Talma of the North," "the Sphinx," "the foam on the waves."

In reality, Alexander I worshiped truth but was incapable of telling it. He loathed violence, and came to the throne through the murder of his father. He called himself a pacifist and waged war all over Europe for ten years. He deemed himself a liberal and was in fact a notorious tyrant. It seemed as though he was afraid of his inner self and, to forestall any display of a culpable softness, tolerance or understanding, imposed a discipline upon himself that was in conflict with his true nature.

While he was at school, Pushkin venerated him, like all his classmates. He wrote:

> And Europe, hanging its aging head,
> Stretched out to the knees of the liberating tsar
> Arms freed of the shackles of slavery. . . .[1]

Later, he was to say:

> In face and gesture both, he was a Harlequin.[2]

7. *The Young Lion*

Russia's triumphant reawakening coincided with Pushkin's first literary successes. He matured in an uneasy world, doubting himself when his country was facing defeat and blossoming with her victory. A few days before the tsar's reception at Pavlovsk, Pushkin published his first poem; he was fourteen years old. At his schoolmates' urging, he had submitted one of his poems to the *European Herald,* and on July 4, 1814, read his own lines in a universally known and respected periodical. From the handwritten sheets of *The Schoolboy Philosopher* he moved directly to the celebrated pages of the review; from the children's playpen he rocketed straight into the world of the adults. He was becoming an adult himself. Better still, he was becoming a poet. Like Zhukovsky, like Uncle Basil. His head swelled with vanity, he could hardly believe his eyes. It was to his credit that he did not boast to his companions.

The poem was called *To a Poet-Friend,* and Pushkin had signed it "N.k.ch.p." Other poems appearing in the same review in 1814 were signed with three numerals, 1-14-16. But Pushkin's official entry into the literary world took place on January 8, 1815, on the occasion of the qualifying examination for admission to the upper school. A large audience had been invited, and the Minister of the Interior in person was to preside over the board of examiners. Also, it was rumored among the boys that the aged and honored Derzhavin himself had promised to attend.

Prompted by Professor Galich, Pushkin wrote a poem entitled *Recollections of Tsarskoye Selo,* to be read at the end of the session. There was a rehearsal in the minister's presence, and on the appointed day, the guests duly filed into the great white, red and gold hall. There were the minister, the metropolitan, Count Uvarov, the interim headmaster, Leshakov, commander of the hussars, Field Marshal Saltykov, parents, friends, ladies with high-piled hair and quantities of uniforms, frock coats, lace jabots and decorations. Pushkin's father and Uncle Basil were also there, of course.

Pushkin has left a detailed description of the scene: "I only saw Derzhavin once in my life," he wrote, "but I shall never forget him. It was in 1815, at the school examination. When we heard that Derzhavin had promised to be with us, we were all terribly excited. Delvig went out on the steps to wait for him and kiss the hand that had written *The Waterfall*. At last, he arrived. He entered the vestibule and Delvig heard him ask the guard, "My man, where is the toilet?" This prosaic inquiry quite deflated poor Delvig, who changed his mind and came back to the assembly hall. Afterward, he told me what had happened with remarkable good humor and gaiety. Derzhavin was very, very old. He wore a uniform and high soft boots. Our examination tired him greatly. He sat with his head propped on one hand, expressionless, his eyes dull, his lip sagging, looking very much like the portrait of him in his dressing-gown and nightcap. He dozed until the beginning of the examination in Russian literature, when he suddenly came to life: His eyes shone, he was literally transfigured. Of course, it was his poetry that was being read, analyzed and praised. He listened so intently, it was extraordinary. At last my turn came. I recited my *Recollections of Tsarskoye Selo*, standing three feet away from Derzhavin. . . ."

At the first lines, the old man sat up and put his hand to his ear to hear better. He stared in astonishment at this strange youngster with the dark skin and woolly head, his eyes as hard and cutting as slivers of glass. The boy was dressed in his tight-fitting blue tunic with the red collar. White tights clung to his legs, and he wore little black patent-leather boots that were reflected in the floor of the hall. He stood very straight. He was tense and rather solemn; his sonorous, strained voice flung out the lines with a fine edge of violence. Derzhavin had never heard such a voice or such verse. It was a little like what he wrote himself. As a matter of fact, all the poetry written in Russia was like his, but there was a sort of easy assurance in these lines that was almost frightening. Was it even poetry? He felt like nodding in time with the lines. And how old could he be, this baby, fourteen, maybe fifteen? The young poet was speaking of the great gardens of Tsarskoye Selo stretched out in the moonlight, their long avenues, icy waters, cascades of pearl. He also alluded to the heroes of the century of Catherine the Great, of whose glory Derzhavin himself had sung.

But Catherine's century was gone, and other days had come, days of anxiety, quarrel and strife. Napoleon. The national war. The enemy crossing the sacred frontier of Russia:

Beyond lies the steppe with its heavy snows
    And the earth smokes with blood,
And the calm hamlets and cities blaze
And the glow spreads all across the sky.

. . . Tremble, Tyrant! For the hour of your fall is near,
Each of our soldiers will be a proud knight.
His only thought to win or die in battle,
For his faith, for his tsar!

The boy's voice grew deep and menacing as he described the enemy's advance across the forsaken land, the sacking of the towns, the deprivations of the peasants hiding in medieval forests and, at last, the burning of Moscow, whose flames, it seems, will roar through history forever.

Where are you, lovely Moscow of the hundred cupolas,
Wonder of our land?
There where the solemn city reigned,
Nothing but ruins remain.
Moscow! All Russians quake at the sight of your grieving face.
Gone, the palaces of noblemen and tsars!
The flames have consumed them all, the crowns of towers
And homes of great fortunes.
Along the boulevards of wealth,
In gardens and in fields,
Where the scent of myrtle hung and lindens shook,
Now there are embers, ash and dust.
Everything is dead, silence everywhere. . . .

The boy paused. All around him, people were sitting motionless. Derzhavin seemed frozen in mindless ecstasy. Then Pushkin threw back his head and proudly declaimed:

Take comfort, mother of Russian towns,
See how your invaders shrink,
They have felt upon their boastful company
The avenging right hand of the Lord.
See: they are running away, they do not turn to fight.
And their blood is flowing in long streams through our snow,
And in the night hunger and cold cut them down,
And at their backs the Russian sword pursues.

His voice grew taut, rose, stretched to the breaking point.

"Hearing those lines we already knew," wrote Pushchin, "we felt a cold shudder run through our bodies. . . ."

At the last words of the poem, old Derzhavin rose, all knotted and broken in his heavy red and gold senator's uniform. His wig had slipped to one side. Senile tears ran down his full-lipped, wrinkled clown's face. He shook hands on all sides. He wanted to clasp Pushkin to his bosom. He murmured, "I am not dead." But the boy had run away. They hunted high and low for him, but he was nowhere to be found.

Pushkin wrote: "I cannot describe my feelings: When I reached the passage where I speak of Derzhavin, my juvenile voice thrilled and my heart began beating with dizzying speed. I don't remember how I finished, I don't remember how I ran away. Derzhavin was enchanted. He called for me, he wanted to embrace me. . . . They looked everywhere for me, but I kept out of sight."

That same evening, after the examination, Count Razumovsky gave a dinner to which Pushkin's father was invited, and during which the minister spoke to him earnestly: "I should also like to teach your son the art of prose." At this, Derzhavin turned scarlet and exclaimed in prophetic tones, "Leave him as he is: a poet!" After reading other poems by Pushkin, he added, "This is the one who will take Derzhavin's place."[1]

Pushkin's father and Uncle Basil soon were bursting with pride. Their little Alexander's fame had soared beyond the walls of the school: He was being spoken of in drawing rooms with benign approval and curiosity, and Zhukovsky himself liked to recite the *Recollections of Tsarskoye Selo*. The poem was submitted to the *Russian Museum* and appeared in the April issue with the author's name in full at the end, accompanied by an elegantly flattering editorial comment which must have filled Pushkin's heart with joy: "For the communication of this contribution we sincerely thank the parents of the young poet whose talent gives such great promise."

Was the poem worth all this fuss? For a fifteen-year-old boy, its author handled language with exceptional confidence; he already knew how to choose and balance his words to fit an unfaltering rhythm; and his use of onomatopoeia was judicious and tasteful. He could duplicate the hammered, "bronze" technique of Zhukovsky, the conventional grandeur of Derzhavin. He was an apt pupil. He was far from being a master. His *Recollections of Tsarskoye Selo* is a speech, a pompous declaration, a well-built piece of rhetoric. Seen as a whole, it is cold, manipulated from without, although true emotion does break through in places in a sudden flash of lightning, before the poem relapses into academic and mythological reminiscences. Like the "archaics" he so detested, young Pushkin sought the noble word; he was intoxicated by "ires," "torches," "bards" and "skalds," "harps" and "lyres," "dawns" and "golden hours." Nevertheless, the poem can stand on its own by virtue of its rhythm and drive and its truly remarkable ease of composition; it was this apparent facility of versification that first amazed Pushkin's contemporaries.

After the publication of *Recollections of Tsarskoye Selo* in the *Russian Museum*, Delvig sent a poem entitled *Message to Pushkin* to the same review; and the appearance of this poem celebrating Pushkin's genius in one of the best periodicals of the time proves how quickly Alexander's reputation was made.

In 1815 Zhukovsky, then thirty-eight years old and basking in the full light of official fame, esteem and favor, made a present of his works to Pushkin, spoke to him of the "sacred destiny of poetry," and exhorted him to seek "pure renown" and shun compromise and facile execution.

Zhukovsky had just been appointed reader to Empress Marya Fyodorovna.* He was weak, affable, naïve and rather obsequious, but endowed with legendary kindheartedness. "It was impossible to know Zhukovsky and not to love him," wrote Viegel. "And for him, loving everyone, both near and far, had become a habit." From the very beginning, Zhukovsky felt a strong sympathy for the turbulent, incomprehensible Pushkin. He sensed his young friend's powers and foresaw the brilliant flowering of his genius. Sometimes Zhukovsky would read his latest composition aloud to Pushkin, and if the boy could not repeat it from memory, he concluded that his rhymes must be wrong and tried to alter them as his listener suggested.

In 1816 Karamzin, the historian, came to hear the young prodigy's poems. "N. M. Karamzin," Uncle Basil wrote to his nephew, "is coming to Tsarskoye Selo at the beginning of May. Love him, listen to him, respect him. The counsel of such a man can make your future, and perhaps that of our entire literature. We expect great things of you."[2]

Karamzin duly met Pushkin, questioned and soberly encouraged him, and said to him, according to his classmate Malinovsky, "Soar like an eagle, but do not falter in your flight." "And he," wrote Malinovsky, "his nostrils flaring as always in moments of strong emotion, returned to his seat, accompanied by the approving regard of all his fellow students."

Other famous authors came to admire the school's literary "phenomenon." Ilichevsky wrote to a friend of his: "How could you have missed the opportunity of meeting Karamzin, immortal historian of our nation?

* His background was strangely like that of Pushkin himself: Zhukovsky's father was a landowner in Tula. When war broke out between Russia and Turkey, he said to one of his peasants, who was about to go off and serve as canteen keeper in the army, "Bring me back a pretty Turkish girl, there's a good fellow; you can see how my wife is getting on."

The peasant did not realize that his master was joking, and returned with two Turkish girls, sisters, who were taken prisoner after the capture of Bender. One died; the other, Salkha, became the lord's mistress and produced a son: the poet. The landowner's wife suffered every form of betrayal and humiliation in silence. She had borne eleven children, six of whom died one after the other, and in the end, utterly drained by mourning and loneliness, she forgave her husband, took in his concubine and the bastard and reorganized her household, so that the master had two wives, the child two mothers, and everybody was happy. From his Turkish ancestors Zhukovsky had inherited a milky, matte complexion, a long, asymmetrical face and an admirable pair of almond-shaped eyes shaded by long, silky lashes. He grew up pampered, spoiled and protected, studied perfunctorily for a time, and, in 1802, published an adaptation of Gray's *Elegy* which immediately won him the praise of the literate public. His subsequent poetry fulfilled his early promise, and by 1812 he was regarded as the leading Russian poet of the new school.

It's shameful of you, my friend. We are hoping he will come to see us, and our hopes may be fulfilled, because he knows Pushkin and is very interested in him. . . . I must admit that before I came here I was not acquainted with a single one of our authors. But since I have been at school I have met Dmitryev, Derzhavin, Zhukovsky, Batyushkov, B. Pushkin, and Khvostov. . . ." The attention these great men lavished upon Pushkin increased his prestige among the schoolboys; he was surrounded by an aura of light and mystery. He had "the vocation." The other child-poets piously observed his progress, pouncing upon his most trivial scribblings. His success rubbed off on them, became their success; his fame merged with the fame of the school and the gardens of Tsarskoye Selo. Delvig, dear, blue-eyed Delvig, surreptitiously purloined his friend's poems and sent them to the distinguished periodicals of the day.

After the success of *Recollections of Tsarskoye Selo,* the Minister of Education in person commissioned Pushkin to write a poem celebrating *The Emperor's Return from Paris in 1815,* which he duly composed in the emphatic manner of his *Recollections:*

Fortune's child, forsaken by the gods,
No longer sees the Russian soil outstretched at his feet.
He flees . . . And vengeance thunders after him.
He topples from his throne . . . stiffens . . . and goes down!
Later, the grandsons of Russian warriors . . .
Will forgather, mute, around some tall old man
To listen. And he, with his stick,
Will slowly outline in the dust
The camp, the rows of soldiers, the forest and the hill,
And then, in a few short words, unstrained and true,
Will tell them the glory of olden days
And bless the tsar, his eyes filled with tears.

Upon completion of this opus, Pushkin wrote to the director of the ministry of education: "Your Excellency has kindly requested me to write a poem on the emperor's return; I have complied. If the sentiments expressed in it of love and gratitude to our great monarch do not seem totally unworthy of my noble subject, I should be happy if His Highness, Count A. K. Razumovsky, would deign to present to His Majesty this feeble effort of an inexperienced poet." Unfortunately, Pushkin's poem did not reach the emperor. However, a second commission followed: a poem to illustrate the wedding of William, Prince of Orange, and the Grand Duchess Anna Pavlovna, in 1816; this time, luck was with him. Empress Marya Fyodorovna, having decided to give a party for the newlyweds, asked the old poet Neledinsky-Meletsky to write an ode for the occasion. He could not deliver the goods on such short notice, and, on Karamzin's advice, made a special trip to Tsarskoye Selo to offer his commission to the youngest of the Russian poets. Pushkin accepted and met the deadline, and his lines were sung at the imperial reception:

Hush, the thunder is past,
The bloodstained iron lies lusterless,
The ominous wing of war
No longer darkens the village skies. . . .
Glory to the young hero!
With the others, heroes of Albion,
He went to the final battle
And avenged the Bourbon fleur-de-lis.

Empress Marya Fyodorovna was pleased with this composition, and made Pushkin a present of a gold watch and chain.

We must not be surprised at this sudden elevation of a fifteen-year-old boy, the serious consideration given to him, the respect, even, that was paid to him. In those days children matured early, both physically and intellectually; little girls were married off at fourteen, and youths of fifteen joined the army as commissioned officers and began commanding old soldiers with grizzled mustaches. In July 1812, when the two Raevsky boys fought at their father's side in the Battle of Saltanovka, they were aged sixteen and eleven, respectively.

In any event, Alexander Pushkin, intoxicated by all these marks of esteem and interest, wrote on in a state of feverish elation from 1815 to 1816. In 1814 he composed twenty-six poems; in 1815, twenty-seven; in 1816, fifty or more. He tackled the most lofty literary genres, paddled about in works of philosophy, strayed among morality plays, collided with heroic epics. We know nothing of his story *Fatam, or Man's Reason*, except that it was composed in the style of Voltaire's fables; we know no more of his comedy *The Philosopher*, to which Pushkin alludes in his diary (entry of December 10): "I have begun a comedy. I do not know if I shall complete it." His classmate Ilichevsky wrote, in a letter dated January 16, 1816: "Pushkin is now engaged in writing a five-act verse comedy entitled *The Philosopher*. The plot is good, and the beginning, that is, the first act, which is all he has written so far, looks most promising: The verse is flawless, and there are masses of funny lines. Please God he can finish his comedy—it is the first major *ouvrage*[3] he has undertaken, and he wants to begin his professional career with it when he leaves school. May heaven grant him success, and let the rays of his fame reflect upon his friends."

In a poem entitled *The Shade of Von Vizin*, written during the same period, Pushkin imagines the ghost of the writer Von Vizin, who died in 1792, being granted permission by Pluto to return among his colleagues on earth. The ensuing encounters between the living and the dead afforded Pushkin an opportunity to dole out epigrams and applause to the authors of his day. That same year, 1815, he planned a *Tableau of Tsarskoye Selo,* including: "1. A description of the park. 2. The palace, a day at Tsarskoye Selo. 3. The morning walk. 4. The afternoon walk. 5. The evening walk. 6. The inhabitants of Tsarskoye Selo."

He also tried his hand at theatrical criticism, in a stern analysis of comedy by Prince Shakovskoy called *The New Stern,* which was directed against the sacrosanct person of Karamzin. With the unimpeachable authority of his fifteen years, Pushkin asserted that Shakovskoy's play "contained not the slightest shadow of either plot or denouement," that the characters in a play should act, and not be "soporific preachers," and that Shakovskoy was "a man not totally devoid of wit, who notices the comic or super-subtle features of a society, goes home and notes down everything he has seen, and then pastes his observations into his comedies however they happen to fall."

Pushkin's literary activities, successes and ambitions formed a curious pendant to his racing about, wrestling and schoolboy pranks. Despite the visits from the great poets, despite Derzhavin's prophecies and Zhukovsky's encouragement and his imperial commissions, Pushkin remained a mischievous scamp, whose masters recognized his gifts but kept a close watch on his conduct. He noted in his diary, "Yesterday I finished the third chapter of *Fatam, or Man's Reason;* it is called 'Natural Law.' I read it to S.S. and in the evening amused myself by snuffing out all the lamps and candles in the hall. Excellent occupation for a philosopher. In the morning, read the life of Voltaire. . . ."

This same diary, comprising a few scant pages of disconnected notes, also introduces us to the young Pushkin's first experience of the torments of love.

8. *First Lessons in Love and Politics*

At a very early age, even before he went to school, Alexander Pushkin was attracted by women, intrigued, obsessed by the need to discover the significance of these weak, soft creatures who glided about him and whose praises the poets never wearied of singing. He speaks, as we have seen, of a first, unidentified object of love, who would seem to have crossed his path when he was about seven years old. And we know too that in 1811 he was eagerly half flirting with his uncle's mistress, the serf girl Annette Vorozheykin.

His reading of the French erotic writers aggravated his need for some of these secret caresses, stolen kisses and languorous fatigues. He was all agitated by this lore, gleaned haphazardly from books and conversations. He knew everything it was possible to know about women without ever having known a woman. To him, love was an occupation, a *raison d'être*, an art, a profession in itself, on the same level as poetry, and his entire life was to be divided between the two. Or rather, love and poetry were for him divergent manifestations of a single force. Even at school, more precocious and better informed than his fellow students, he amazed them by his display of "pure African" sensuality. As early as 1812, according to Gaevsky, he became enamored of the young Countess Kochubey, who was a frequent visitor to the school, and composed a poem called *Betrayals* in her honor. "N. V. Kochubey," wrote Baron Korf, "must have been Pushkin's first love." First love? A protracted stare, a few polite words, a smile from Miss Kochubey; and that was all. When the boys were finally allowed outside the school walls to visit the local nobility, Pushkin seized the opportunity to pay court to every female who appeared even remotely approachable. "Count V. V. Tolstoy, who lived in Tsarskoye Selo," Gaevsky later wrote, "had formed a private theater company of serf actors. The boys used to attend performances there and, like most of the other spectators, devoutly admired the 'inamorata' of the troupe." Her name was Natalya and she was not much of an actress; but in 1814 Pushkin dedicated two poems to her, *Natalya* and *To a Young Actress*. In the latter, he wrote:

> . . . Happy the man who stands onstage
> By the side of a charming actress,
> Presses her hand and dares to hope
> For his heart's desire in the wings.

It is unlikely that the schoolboy Pushkin, then aged fourteen, was ever granted "his heart's desire in the wings." But a swift kiss or two, a few furtive chambermaid caresses, were enough to set the youngster afire. The conscientious Komovsky tells us how Pushkin lost all self-control in the presence of the young ladies—his schoolmates' sisters and cousins—invited to school dances. "Pushkin," he wrote, "was so sensual that at the age of fifteen or sixteen, the mere touch of his partner's hand at a school ball would turn his eyes to flames, and his breath would quicken and whistle like the snorting of a fiery steed in a herd of fillies." Komovsky's remark provoked the indignation of another of Pushkin's companions, Yakovlev—who took exception only to the form, however, without denying the facts. "One may speak of an Arabian yearling in such terms," he wrote, "but not of Pushkin, simply because he has Arab blood in his veins." Wishing to amend his earlier remark, Komovsky drafted a second version: "The mere touch of his partner's hand set off an electric charge inside him so violent that everyone's attention would be focused upon him during the ball."

It was at one of these balls that Pushkin, by his own avowal, met his first "passion"—not Miss Kochubey, but Miss Bakunin, one of the empress' maids of honor and the sister of one of Pushkin's schoolmates. A very pretty girl she was, too, with whom the entire school professed to be in love. In his private diary, Pushkin described the impact of a chance encounter with her: "I was happy! No, I was not happy, yesterday: I spent the morning in torments of anticipation. With a feeling impossible to describe, I stood by the window and scanned the little snow-covered path: She was nowhere to be seen. At last I abandoned hope, then suddenly I met her on the stairs, delicious moment. How beautiful she was! How that black gown becomes the sweet Bakunin! But now I have not seen her for eighteen hours! Ah, what a state to be in, what torment! However, for five minutes I was happy." And, to define his anguish more explicitly, Pushkin quoted two lines of a famous elegy by Zhukovsky, applying them to his own plight:

> He sang love's praises but his voice was sad,
> For of love he knew only the torments.

This novice's passion for the young Miss Bakunin was shared by his friends Pushchin and Ilichevsky; all three inundated the young lady with their verse. Did Miss Bakunin respond to Pushkin's disguised or open declarations? Apparently not, for from the time of this encounter, unrequited love seems to become the poet's favorite theme. In *Desire*, composed in 1816, he wrote:

My days drag on lamentably,
Each passing second multiplies
The pangs of a hopeless love
And I writhe in the heavy grip of madness.

Elsewhere:

Love gives one instant of unspeakable joy
And the misery that follows lasts until death.[1]

The misery of being rejected by Miss Bakunin, however, did not last until the poet's death.

The truth was that Pushkin was in love with love; women were simply a pretext for his outpourings of passion and lyricism. The same year in which he was bemoaning Miss Bakunin's coldness and lack of compassion, he was also applying himself to the close pursuit of the chambermaids of the empress' maids of honor. One evening, as he was going along the dim corridors of the palace on his way to the guards' quarters, where the military band was playing, he passed the doors of their rooms. One of them, Princess Volkonsky, had a fresh-faced, bold young wench named Natasha as her maid, whom Pushkin, to relieve his boredom, often embraced and pinched in the shadows to the accompaniment of her frightened squeals. His pace slowed as he passed the princess' room. He paused to listen. He heard a sound of breathing, the rustle of a skirt close by. It must be Natasha, waiting for him. Groping forward in the darkness, he stretched his arms toward the body whose warmth was coming out to him in waves, caught it and clasped it to his breast, his lips seeking out a protesting mouth. At that moment a door opened, throwing a harsh beam of light into the vaulted corridor, and Pushkin saw to his horror that he was embracing a wrinkled, floury, beplumed old dress dummy—Princess Volkonsky herself. He thought he was going to faint, dropped his arms, cried out and bounded away, while the maid of honor stamped her feet and gasped imprecations in French and Russian. That same evening, Princess Volkonsky complained to her brother, who promptly informed the emperor of the indignities to which Her Imperial Majesty's maids of honor were being subjected, and the next morning Alexander I summoned Engelhardt, the headmaster.

"What is the meaning of this?" said the emperor. "Your children are no longer content with climbing over the wall to steal my apples and maltreating my gardener Lyamin's staff. . . . Now they are also lavishing their attentions upon my wife's maids of honor?"

The scandal could not be hushed up; Alexander I spoke of applying the lash to the overenterprising Pushkin. But Engelhardt successfully pleaded his pupil's cause and the emperor relented; if the truth be told, he was more amused than angered by the incident, for Princess Volkonsky was old, ugly and a harridan.

In the end the emperor said, "Very well. Let him write an apology, and I shall be his advocate; but tell him this sort of thing must not happen again." With a sly smile he added, in a low voice, "Between you and me, the old woman is probably delighted with the boy's mistake."

"Then he shook the headmaster's hand and went to join the empress in the garden."[2]

In his fury at the old princess for denouncing him to the emperor, Pushkin composed a scurrilous and graceless French quatrain which was an enduring source of delight to his schoolmates:

On peut très bien, Mademoiselle,
Vous prendre pour une maquerelle,
Ou pour une vieille guenon,
Mais pour une grâce—Oh, mon Dieu, non!

You may easily be taken, Miss,
For the patron of a bawdyhouse
Or for an aging tramp,
But for a Grace—good God, not that!

Engelhardt, who had rescued Pushkin from the lash, could not suspect that the young man would repay his kindness by creating a scandal in his own household. On this matter, Gaevsky wrote: "There lived with the Engelhardt family (his wife and five children) a young woman who had recently lost her husband; her name was Marie Smith, nee Charon la Rose. She was pretty, good-natured and witty, and she enlivened and united the little group that used to gather in their home. Pushkin became interested in her, and sent her a rather improper poem entitled *To a Young Widow*. But the young widow, who had not forgotten her husband and was expecting his child, was offended by her aspirant's poem and showed it to Engelhardt; this was the beginning of the animosity between headmaster and pupil that lasted until we left school."

Marie was justifiably ruffled by *To a Young Widow*, in which Pushkin simply commanded her to love him—on the ground that, as he put it,

You may rest assured, those in the other world
Sleep and do not wake.
No voice is dear to them,
And no care weighs them down.

Rejected by one woman, Pushkin turned to another. He was insatiable and engaging, and his sentimental research took no account of his subject's age, social position or reputation. The family of Karamzin, the historian, having moved to Tsarskoye Selo, he abruptly fell in love with Karamzin's wife, who was nineteen years older than he and, according to Viegel, "white, cold and handsome as a classical statue. . . ." Pushkin sent her a love letter "in prose," and, with pounding heart, awaited the reply from this thirty-five-year-old matron with the full-blown charms. "Naturally," wrote Bartenyev, the Pushkin scholar, "Katerina Andreyevna showed the letter to her husband. Together they had a good laugh over it, summoned Pushkin, and scolded him soundly. It was all very funny, and enabled Pushkin to become better acquainted with the Karamzins. From that day forward, he began to like them and see more of them."

In his *Letter to Lydia*, written in 1817, Pushkin alludes to other loves, more down-to-earth, less one-sided:

By his fleeting step,
By his voluptuous silence,
By his swift, trembling hands,
By the heat of his breath,
By his soft and burning mouth,
Do you know your lover?

No one knows the identity of this obliging Lydia, nor that of one Elvina to whom the young man addressed the following lines, entitled *To Her:*

What would I give, Elvina, one dark night,
To sweep you up in my arms,
Gaze upon you with languorous eyes . . .
. . . Listen in ecstasy and delight
To your fervent murmur, your weary pleas,
And in the shadow propitious to lovers' awakenings,
Drift off by my beauty's side.

It was in 1816 that the Venuses, Cupids and other ephemeral deities in the young man's poems began to give way to women who had bodies of warm flesh, a reassuring girth, thirsting lips, hands, breath, scents and experience. The initiator's name has remained a secret. But Pushkin's work reveals the approximate date of her appearance on the scene.

Did Pushkin's looks justify his conquests? His schoolmates called him "a mixture of monkey and tiger" and he himself wrote, in French:

Vrai démon pour l'espièglerie,
Vrai singe par la mine,
Beaucoup et trop d'espièglerie,
Ma foi–voilà Pouchkine.

A true demon for devilry,
A true ape by his face,
So much, too much devilry,
No doubt about it—that's Pushkin.

He was small, lean and nervous; his dusky skin, thick lips, strong, white cannibal teeth and, above all, his eyes—his eyes sparkling with glee—could not fail to impress the undemanding young women of Tsarskoye Selo.

During 1817, his last year at school, Pushkin went to the dogs with a will. A regiment of guards hussars was stationed at Tsarskoye Selo. Most of the officers were young aristocrats, cultivated, bold and bawdy, who had taken part in the foreign campaign of 1812–14 and were now resting from their labors, the chief activities of their convalescence being criticism of the government and pursuit of Count Tolstoy's actresses and the daughters of respectable families. Pushkin became attached to them, and forsook his studies even more than before for the pleasure of their company. The boys were now allowed to leave school after the last class of the day, and the young poet, interpreting this sanction rather broadly, took to staying out all night. "With the hussars," the prudish Komovsky wrote, "and unknown to the authorities, he would sacrifice to Bacchus and Venus. . . ." And the no less prudish Baron Korf noted in his memoirs: "Toward the end of our time at school everything changed, and in our free time we used to go not only to Teppers' and other respectable places, but also to Ambiel's sweetshop, and even to see the hussars. At first, we only went out on holidays and with written permission, but later it was every day of the week, without permission and unknown to the night watchmen, and sometimes we would come back very late at night. I even think some of us used to stay away *all night*, but I was never one of those. A small *Trinkgeld* to the porter would make everything all right, because the wardens and dormitory night watchmen would be asleep hours before. The circle in which Pushkin spent all his time was composed of officers from the regiment of guards hussars. In the evening after classes, when the others used to visit the headmaster or some local family, Pushkin, who could not bear any form of constraint, would be carousing freely with these gentlemen."

"These gentlemen" were named Molostvov, Salomirsky, Saburov, Chaadaev and Kaverin.

Kaverin seems to have been the model hero of this little world. He was five years older than Pushkin. After studying to an advanced level at the University of Göttingen, he fought in the war against Napoleon in 1813 and in 1816 was assigned to the regiment of hussars quartered at Tsarskoye Selo. He was a hard-drinking swashbuckler and notable womanizer. One day during the Russian occupation of Paris, he entered a fashionable restaurant and saw a group of young men order one bottle of champagne and four glasses, whereupon he ordered four bottles of champagne and one glass, proceeded to drink all four with his dinner, swallowed a few thimblefuls of liqueur with his dessert and walked out of the restaurant in a straight line, to the applause of the other customers. It was also told how he cured himself of an unmentionable disease by drinking iced champagne, how he drank rum instead of tea and how, at the end of a meal, he would ingurgitate a bottle of cognac in place of coffee. He took part in a few notorious duels, charmed and possessed a vast number of women, was ruined, grew old and eventually discovered the charms of religion. By the end of his life he was spending every cent he had on devotional articles, selling vigil lights and singing in the church choir. In 1817, however, Kaverin was a long way from imagining that he would end his days in active mysticism and penitence.

The schoolboy Pushkin, after composing some disparaging lines about the guards officers, was ordered to apologize and did so in a poem dedicated to Kaverin, in which he wrote, *inter alia,*

> . . . Feel only contempt for the jealous mutter of the herd:
> They do not know how Cythera and the Portico,
> Books and wine, can lovingly be joined. . . .

That same year, 1817, he also dedicated a quatrain to Kaverin, entitled *To the Portrait:*

> In him burn the fires of rum and war.
> He is a fearsome conqueror on the field of Mars,
> To men a sure friend, a danger to the damsels,
> And everywhere, a hussar.

In 1819 Kaverin wrote an entry in his diary concerning a gathering at which Pushkin had been present: "The champagne had been put on ice the previous evening. By chance, my lady of the moment (whom I employed to satisfy my sexual needs) passed by outside. We called her in. It was insufferably hot. We asked Pushkin to celebrate the occasion with a few lines of verse." His poem ended thus:

> When shall we four meet again together,
> With a few tarts, some drink, and a pipe?

By themselves, however, "a few tarts, some drink, and a pipe" would not have sufficed to bind Pushkin so strongly to his new friends. These guards hussars, led by Kaverin and Chaadaev, were not only gay dogs greedy for women, cards and wine. They were highly cultivated men who had served in the French campaign and had sampled the fruits of the Republic. In Paris, after the fall of Napoleon, their passion for military life had been transformed into a no less consuming passion for politics. Benjamin Constant's lectures—on the constitution, the rights of man and the citizen, and on equality, liberty and fraternity in the Republic—astonished and delighted these offspring of oriental despotism. They made comparisons between the benefits of French economic and political liberalism and the rigors of the tsarist state. They became friendly with Prussian officers of the Tugendbund, and even thought momentarily of founding a secret society to combat the abuses of imperial power. And after bathing in all this independence and civility, their return to Russia was a cold shower indeed. Slavery, trivial intrigues, bigotry, official espionage and beribboned inertia reigned on all sides. At the sight of their fellow countrymen they began telling each other, in the words of Yakushkin, that they were "a hundred years ahead of them." Even the triumphant figure of Alexander I became hateful to them after he concluded the Holy Alliance and restored all the thrones Napoleon had overturned.

Some of these men, including Kaverin, did join the secret society known as the "Union for Salvation," founded in 1816 by a group of young professional soldiers in St. Petersburg. And although the central figure in the group of hussars, the witty and elegant Peter Chaadaev, does not appear to have been a member of any political organization, he was always promulgating highly original and subversive theories to his comrades. Chaadaev was a handsome, slender man with a peaches-and-cream complexion, a broad forehead and a thoughtful expression. He took great pains with his dress and affected an exaggerated and cynical courtesy toward his companions. Pushkin was literally bewitched by this young dandy in uniform, and Chaadaev took a liking to the young poet too, and called him the "peripatetic philosopher."

Chaadaev was five years older than Pushkin; he spoke four languages fluently, was interested in English literature and philosophy and claimed to be a disciple of Locke. He convinced Pushkin of the weaknesses of French skepticism and the merits of an experimental approach to art and science. For a time, the schoolboy had let himself be subjugated by light, conventional, neoclassical poetry; Chaadaev revealed another poetry to him, another way of thinking: more serious, more human and real. Sometimes he would pick up a collection of verse, read a passage aloud to Pushkin and then criticize the author's language. Pushkin, dazzled by the music of the passage, would now discover, to his amazement, all the inaccuracies and contradictions it contained. Under his friend's tutelage he became more critical of himself and others. He began to see that poetry was more than a pastime: It was work. He learned that only precision, exactitude could produce a solid, finished, faultless poem. One day Chaadaev recited Derzhavin's *Traveler* to him, and Pushkin confessed that he found the following lines admirably melodious:

> The moon shines. Through the dense obscurity
> A traveler guides his skiff.

But, as his friend observed, if the moon were shining the obscurity could not be dense. Pushkin made good use of these lessons in common sense and artistic integrity.

Like the other officers, Chaadaev was shocked by the poverty of the Russian people, and dreamed of reorganizing his country along the lines of the Western nations. "Chaadaev was intelligent," a contemporary wrote, "and thought about things which had never occurred to Pushkin." This may be something of an overstatement, for Pushkin had read the French philosophers and knew the value of freedom of opinion, universal education and equality before the law. He had never been outside Russia, however, and it all seemed rather remote to him—very fine, but abstract. But here was a man just back from a place where these theories had actually been tried and had produced whole nations thriving in abundance and felicity. Here was a man who talked about Russia in terms of these ideals, and who wanted to find out how they could be made to work in Russia. Pushkin was blinded, as though some familiar ghost had suddenly taken on weight and substance at his side. In 1817 he wrote a quatrain entitled *For the Portrait of Chaadaev:*

> Heaven sent him into life, chained
> To the orders of the tsar. In Rome
> He had been Brutus, Pericles in Greece;
> Here: an officer of the hussars.

The following year he dedicated another poem to him, called *To Chaadaev:*

> . . . Listen, friend, it will come,
> The adorable dawn of bliss,
> Russia will have her awakening.
> On the ruins of despotism,
> It is our name they will inscribe.

Other boys at the school, Pushchin, Küchelbecker and Delvig, were also influenced by the philosopher-hussars. Pushkin and Pushchin's nocturnal conversations through the partition separating their cubicles became filled with new doubts, new interests and a social discontent far in advance of their years. Pushchin wrote, "Pushkin always agreed with me in respect of the common cause, the *res publica.*"

And Delvig maintained, according to Pushkin, that if fate had delivered both Nero and Titus into his hands,

> He would have struck Titus, not Nero,
> For Nero would have died without his help.

Pushchin, Delvig and Küchelbecker could not wait to join some group of conspirators and play the part of Brutus in the future overthrow of the empire. Burtsev—one of the officers in the Union for Salvation—said of Pushchin, "Judging by the ideas and convictions he has acquired at school, I consider him ready for action."

Pushkin, on the other hand, was not ready for action. He loved his comrades' cause, but too many other passions were also claiming him: poetry, women. Poetry first. He wrote of a vague revolution in the future, but he had no time for the tiresome job of preparing for it; and the officers, knowing how fickle he was, heartily applauded his verse and took good care to exclude him from their brotherhood. He was like a wild creature in their midst, intense, high-spirited, generous, brilliant and useless. In June 1816, when it was decided to give classes in military science to pupils wishing to take up a career in the army, Pushkin resolved to attend so that he might one day join the regiment of the guards hussars. A fervent admirer of the young officers of Tsarskoye Selo, he saw himself too

> Hiding his soul behind a helmet.

In 1815, in *Epistle to Galich,* he wrote:

> I shall don close-fitting breeches,
> I shall curl my arrogant mustache,
> My epaulets with gold will gleam,
> And you will see the boy of solemn muses
> Lost among the grim ranks of cornets.

But Pushkin's father would not hear of it: The paraphernalia for service in the guards cavalry cost a fortune, and the war had made considerable inroads in the family resources. By way of consolation, Sergey Lvovich proposed an infantry regiment, which was much less expensive. But this alternative was not acceptable to Pushkin, who preferred to renounce his martial vocation altogether. He did so without too much reluctance, it would seem, for although he did admire his hussar friends, he had some misgivings about the discipline that "chained them to the orders of the tsar." All his companions were preparing to be soldiers in flashing uniforms, civil servants in decoration-paved frock coats or closely watched, crafty ambassadors. He alone did not know what to be. He wrote:

> They are all one to me: uhlans and scribes.
> They are all one to me: helmets and laws.

I will not climb up to the captains,
I will not crawl up to the magistrates.[3]

Long before his final examination, however, he had made up his mind: In order to preserve his independence, he would have to refuse any official position and content himself with being a poet.

The examination, meanwhile, was a long time coming. To the students, that last year was endless and empty. On March 27, 1816, Pushkin wrote to Prince Vyazemsky, a poet and friend of Uncle Basil: "What can I say of our isolation? The school has never seemed so unendurable to me. . . . I assure you, in reality, solitude is absurd, no matter what those philosophers and poets say who pretend to have lived in the country and thirsted after silence and peace. True, the day of our release is approaching. One more year. But another whole year of 'plus' and 'minus,' rules, computation of interest rates, sublimity, admirableness. . . . Another whole year of sleeping beneath the lectern. . . . Ghastly! It is immoral to keep a young man under lock and key. . . . Being full of boredom myself, I am writing boring verse. . . ."

This lament would not seem wholly justified, in the light of the life Pushkin was actually leading at Tsarskoye Selo. His poems were anything but "boring" and the school's "locks and keys" yielded to the boys with disconcerting ease. Pushkin divided his time between the guards hussars and the hospitable drawing rooms of Tsarskoye Selo. He and his friends were regular guests of the Engelhardts, Mme. de Veglio, Count V. V. Tolstoy (owner of the private theater), and Baron Tepper von Fergusson, the school singing master. "Although he could not sing," wrote Baron Korf, "he was an excellent teacher," and he set the boys' poems to music. At his home they drank tea, chatted and sang and exchanged epigrams on set subjects. But the young poet's favorite haunt was the home of Karamzin, the historian. First conquered by the writer's wife, he was soon equally enamored of the rest of the family.

In the eyes of Russian society, Karamzin was the ideal man of integrity and moderation. His life was organized down to the minute, one could not help admiring him. He arose very early, took a walk before breakfast, swallowed two cups of tea, smoked one pipe and set to work. At lunch—frugal and carefully prepared—he drank one small glass of port and one mug of beer. In the evening before bed he invariably ate two baked apples. And no external event could compel him to deviate one hairbreadth from his routine. His work, like his life, was even and measured. After his initial success with a romantic novel called *Poor Liza,* he accepted, in 1803, the post of state historiographer, which carried an annual stipend of 2000 rubles, and began writing a *History of the Russian Empire;* by 1816 he had completed the first eight volumes. The emperor and empresses liked and respected Karamzin.

They called him "the angel"; Pushkin agreed that he had "an admirable soul," and Vyazemsky described him as follows: "In his relations with the emperor, Karamzin made a point of preserving his independence. . . . He never requested anything for himself, nor allowed anyone else to do so on his behalf, with the result that the emperor, although in a position to see how modestly he lived, had no idea that Karamzin often lacked the most basic amenities." His ability as stylist equaled his ability as historian, and he was regarded as the reformer of the Russian language. He was the first to perfect an easy, colloquial, "spoken" style at a time when his contemporaries, led by Admiral Shishkov, were all extolling the virtues of pomposity. "Karamzin," wrote Pushkin, "released the language from the yoke of its foreign oppressors, gave it back its freedom, returned it to its sources in ordinary speech." The whole younger generation of authors was "for" Karamzin and Zhukovsky, "against" Shishkov. The object of universal respect, affection and interest, the great man, aided by his wife and elder daughter, became host to all the masters of art and science in Russia.

Conversation in his drawing room at Tsarskoye Selo always turned on either literature or politics. Karamzin himself was a staunch supporter of Russian autocracy to whom serfdom was a patriarchal institution. He thought that if any difficulty arose in the administration of the empire, it must be the fault of the men in power, not of the system it was their duty to enforce.

After his indoctrination by the hussars in the worship of freedom and the abhorrence of physical and moral constraint, Pushkin must have found these reactionary views most distasteful. However, he liked the company of this man whose politics conflicted so strongly with his own, and the very ease with which he could adapt himself to different societies betrays the shallowness of the young Pushkin's convictions. He respected intelligence more than anything else, and both Karamzin and the hussars were intelligent. He enjoyed listening to first one and then the other as they defended their irreconcilable theories. And both sides were fond of him, because there was something slightly mad about him, irresponsible and droll, and because nothing he said was of any consequence. Karamzin even read him some chapters from his *History of the Russian Empire.* "The schoolboys come to see us," he wrote Vyazemsky, "the poet Pushkin, Lomonosov. . . . Their naïve earnestness amuses us. Pushkin is extremely witty."

Karamzin was constantly in touch with the progressive writers who had chosen him as their leader—a little circle of intellectuals composed of Zhukovsky, Bludov, Dashkov, A. I. Turgenev, Vyazemsky and Uncle Basil. Its opponents were the literary society founded by Shishkov and baptized "The Conversation Club of Friends of the Russian Language." Between the two schools it was a fight to the finish, of epigrams, messages and puns. Karamzin remained aloof from the struggle being waged in his name, but he encouraged its champions, applauded their victories and declared them to be the only "true Russian academy, all of whose members are intelligent and gifted young men."

In 1815 this "academy" took the name of Arzamas. Its meetings were gay, rowdy affairs, much talked about at school. Pushkin yearned to attend them, like his uncle. Most of the members already knew and thought highly of him; he already felt himself one of them. They had nicknamed him "the cricket."

At last, in May 1817, the final examinations began. The school was in a turmoil. After six years of communal living, the boys knew they were about to scatter to the four winds, to confront their various destinies and perhaps lose sight of each other forever. Mingled with the joy of release from supervision and lessons was the generous grief of separation. The boys embraced, vowed everlasting friendship, wept in secret and wrote farewell poems in each other's albums.

By the education they had received, by chance and the passing of time, this flock of miscellaneous children who had crossed the threshold of the school a few years earlier had now been welded into a coherent tribe; a single, shared feeling, a common mood had grown out of their imprisonment. In their case, "school spirit" was more than sentimental convention; the inmates of Tsarskoye Selo actually did think, speak and write in the school spirit. And all through their lives, the memory of the school was to act upon them as an irresistible and mysterious rallying call.

"We began," wrote Pushchin, "to make our preparations for departure. It was hard to leave our friends, though we were leaving them for a life long desired, with all the attraction and mystery of remoteness. . . . We spent our days in meditations and last farewells and oaths and vows, and our hearts were heavy. . . . Our albums filled with poetry and prose; I still have Pushkin's lines in mine."

On June 9, 1817, the course officially came to an end: "There was something quite unique about the ceremony," wrote Pushchin. "Our departure was as silent and unassuming as our arrival had been ostentatious. Emperor Alexander entered the same room as before, followed only by the Minister of Education, who was Prince Golitsyn at the time. The sovereign was not even accompanied by Prince Volkonsky, who had asked, or so everyone said, to attend.

"In the hall the pupils, teachers, warden and governor were assembled. Engelhardt read a brief account of the past six years of instruction; after him, Kunitsyn, secretary of the faculty council, read out the council's decision, which was approved by the emperor. Then we were presented to him in order of our places in the class, and our number was read out and the prizes we had won.

"The sovereign closed the ceremony with a fatherly little speech to the boys, and expressed his satisfaction to the headmaster and staff of the school."

After the imperial address, Pushkin read out a rather mediocre poem he had composed at Engelhardt's request, called *Atheism.* Then the school choir sang a farewell song with words by Delvig and music by Professor Tepper: "Six Years Passed, as in a Dream."

"The emperor," Pushchin continued, "was moved by the words and music, and he understood the tears in the eyes of both pupils and teachers. He took his leave of us with his usual benignity and, leaning on Prince Golitsyn's arm, began to move in the direction of the boys' rooms. Engelhardt warned him of the disorder they were in, owing to the preparations for departure. 'No matter,' said the emperor, 'I am visiting you at home today.' Indeed, everything was topsy-turvy in the dormitory, with clothes and boxes and suitcases lying about everywhere; it smelled of farewell. . . ."

When the emperor had gone, Engelhardt distributed the iron rings he had had made for them, as a keepsake and talisman. The boys said goodbye again, for the last time.

On the basis of Pushkin's performance in the examination, he was rated nineteenth in his class. In the Russian administrative hierarchy, this very undistinguished result conferred upon him the rank of undersecretary. For honors and prerogatives, an undersecretary in the civil service was equal to a lieutenant in the army or sublieutenant in the navy. Together with his schoolmates Küchelbecker, Lomonosov and Yudin, Pushkin was assigned to the foreign ministry. His school-leaving certificate read as follows:

"CERTIFICATE

"ALEXANDER PUSHKIN, pupil at the Imperial Lyceum of Tsarskoye Selo, has studied in that establishment for six years, and his achievement has been assessed as follows: in history of religion, logic, moral philosophy, natural, private, and public law, Russian or civil and criminal law—good; in Latin literature, political economy, and financial law—very good; in Russian and French literature and fencing—excellent. In addition, he has studied history, geography, statistics, mathematics, and German. In witness whereof, the faculty council of the Imperial Lyceum of Tsarskoye has presented this certificate to him, and affixed its seal thereunto.

"*Tsarskoye Selo, June* 9, 1817. The headmaster:

EGOR ENGELHARDT

The Secretary of the Faculty Council:

ALEXANDER KUNITSYN."

But to Pushkin this famous certificate, whose possession had been the sole object and motive for work or faith in so many of the boys, was a mere scrap of paper. The administrative career on which he was about to embark did not interest him. His diploma was a notebook, into which, with the help of his schoolmates, he had copied thirty-six of his best poems. On the cover, the title was inscribed in a firm hand: "Poems by Alexander Pushkin. Year 1817."

Pushkin was a severe judge in his choice of poems for this collection. He had actually written more than 120 in the course of his school career, but most of them were not exhumed or made public until after the author's death. Then, when one publisher included them among the author's complete works, there was an outcry from some of the critics, who called it a crime of lese majesty. These stuffy journalists claimed that Pushkin's memory was being defiled by the publication of work so puerile that the poet himself had disowned it, and said that by padding out the opening volume of the series with such trivia, the publishers were merely seeking to boost their sales, to the detriment of Pushkin's unsullied renown.

Belinsky, a Russian essayist, disagreed: "Pushkin's schoolboy verse," he wrote, "is important, not only because it shows us, by comparison with his later work, how swiftly his poetic genius grew and matured, but also, and most significantly, because it established the historical link between Pushkin and the poets who preceded him."

It is a fact that Pushkin's schoolboy poems mark an interesting transition between the style of the masters he venerated when he first began to write and his own style, which emerged so triumphantly a few years later.

At school, Pushkin learned his craft. His imitations of Zhukovsky, Batyushkov, even Derzhavin, helped to develop his skill. From these exercises he acquired an astonishing sureness of language. What he says is well said; but it is as though nothing had impelled him to say it. Only occasionally, when he speaks of Moscow in flames or some disappointment in love or his friendship for one or another schoolmate, do his words betray a touching sincerity; the rest is nothing but fine sounds and shaky allegory, a play of mirrors and reminiscences. With impatient ease, Pushkin essayed every poetic form. He experimented with the grandiose official style in the *Recollections of Tsarskoye Selo, Epistle to the Prince of Orange, The Conquered Paladin* and *Napoleon on the Island of Elba.* In these large-scale operations he employed the full, ponderous line of Zhukovsky, he struggled to find the high-sounding word, he transposed current events into a sort of epic past in which the heroes were all made of marble and the landscapes of painted cardboard. To an accompaniment of trumpet and drum, his larger-than-life men spoke a language more dignified than life and gesticulated for all eternity. Napoleon was the "son of Bellona"; Alexander I, the "worthy nephew of Catherine"; the English soldiers were "heroes of Albion." In the campaign of 1812, Russians and French alike fought with "glaives" and "shafts" and protected themselves with "shields and bucklers." It was all rich as plum pudding, and impersonal and artificial to a fault.

In his idyllic poems, Pushkin discarded Zhukovsky in favor of the suave and nonchalant Batyushkov, even going so far as to borrow the names of the other poet's muses—Chloë and Delia—and his mythological allusions and stereotyped comparisons. His first poems in this vein were haunted by Cupid, Mars, Apollo, Phoebus, Venus and Morpheus and their divers attributes. If he were writing of a feast, then goblets, roses, fresh crowns and myrtle would abound. If his subject were a poet, he was immediately surrounded by those muses, lyres, flutes, citharas and harps of gold. If it were a woman, the mood was all "sweet passions," "secret pleasures," "reveries," "cold, soft and splendid breasts" like "lilies" or "marble" or "snow." When he wrote of a landscape, his readers were plunged into a never-never world in which night "drapes her veils," the moon "sails like a white swan," paths open under "vaults of greenery," brooks "babble," breezes nod off to sleep and the scent of myrtle floats over all, agitating "the friendly dryads." Even when he was trying to describe a scene he knew, like Tsarskoye Selo or the farm at Zakharovo, his reading hid reality from him—he had read so much that he could no longer *see* anything with his own eyes. In his epigrams, again, he was trying to copy somebody, Voltaire or Parny. . . .

He transformed events at school until they became totally unrecognizable. Layers of sticky embellishment must be scraped away before reaching, embedded in some banquet of pupils "sacrificing to Bacchus," the goggle-moggle episode, or Count Tolstoy's shabby little actress beneath the mantle of a "priestess of Thalia." His philosophy was already fully formed: He loved sleep, idleness, wine, women, dreams, poetry, reading and friendship. But he also moaned—because it was the thing to do—that he was "fading," his youth was "flying away."

In reality, Pushkin had a veritable passion for life, but he wrote of it as one who had never lived, and let other people do all the feeling and seeing of the world for him, while all he knew of it came to him through the deformed reports of his contemporaries; and it was for the very excellence of his imitations that those contemporaries praised him. They saw themselves in him; in his poems they heard an amplified echo of their own voices, and what they liked in his ideas was the magnified reflection of their own. "I am not dead," Derzhavin had said. But now the pupil was ready and eager to cast off the mantle of his masters. And his work, at first glance indistinguishable from that of his Russian and

Western predecessors, already bore signs of the coming emancipation. They were few—a chance word here, an odd rhyme there, or, some would say, a "carelessness." But now and then the young man who had read too many books seemed to lift his head and forget the printed page, and then, for one brief moment, he spoke a new language. In a flash, one true adjective, one living verb, one sharp, authentic hue, leaps out of the decorous and melodious line. Why this commonplace word, glittering like a shard of glass in the doughy mass of the poem? Why this one trivial reference among so many high-flown notations? Pushkin wrote:

On the table of polished wood,
You will set a mug of beer,
And a jug full of punch.

Never before, as Belinsky pointed out, had any poet dared to write about a mug of beer or a jug of punch. In poems of that era, guests assuaged their thirst exclusively on "ambrosia" and "mead" served in "goblets." In his *Epistle to Galich*, Pushkin even went so far as to speak of pâté and trout; elsewhere, of "mustaches steeped in wine and rum,"[4] and in another poem,[5] of a "palisade devoured by nettles." His *Bova* openly declares:

I want everyone to understand me,
From the most humble to the highest.

In *The Village* he wrote of a kind old woman who served him "scented tea" and told him the local gossip:

In suchandso's garden
The cabbages are doing fine,
Thomas has beaten
His wife for no reason
And Anthony broke
His balalaika.
The old woman tells me all,
Knitting away at her skirt.

Any lesser poet would have sheered away in fright from this skirt, this balalaika, these cabbages and nettles and rum and trout and pâté and punch and beer. Today, when poets have the whole dictionary and then some at their disposal, these audacities seem childish; but then, they were the first stirrings of a literary revolution.

A copy of Benjamin Constant's novel *Adolphe* has been found with notes in Pushkin's hand. On page 61 of the 1824 edition, the poet furiously scored out several lines, where Constant had written: "I fling myself down on this earth, let it gape and devour me forever, I lay my head on the cold stone, let it soothe the raging fever that consumes me." In the margin Pushkin has written one word: "Lie!"

Between the boy who spoke as though by right of beer and nettles, cabbage and mustaches, and the man who, a few years later, was to call Benjamin Constant's romantic effusions a lie, the distance was infinitesimal. Pushkin was born at the frontier between two periods. He inherited the spirit of the French *encyclopédistes* and the decorum of the Russian poets in powdered wigs; he was a living link between Voltaire and Parny and the first European romantics. He could not be a latter-day classical poet, for he was too attached to visual truth and the simple expression of powerful emotion; nor yet a pure romantic, for he had too great a love of moderation, clarity and restraint. He must disdain both the facile allegories of Batyushkov and Zhukovsky's messianic mists. At seventeen, in a few furtive lines, he was already beginning to sound his own note. He saw clearly and observed accurately, despite the garlands of artificial jewels in which he draped himself, and he need wait no longer before rending the veils of convention. Then, he would cross that ideal line into a hard, sharply defined world of barren steppes, dung-spattered carriages racing down the roads, capacious homes in which girls of flesh and tears sat dreaming, ballrooms exploding with lights and music, gypsies camping under tattered rugs, and the great granite city whose river's swirling waters swelled and roared in a furious boil.

PART II

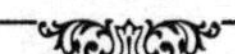

1. *From Drawing Room to Back Room*

On June 13, 1817, Alexander Pushkin was assigned to a post in the foreign ministry, with the rank of (roughly) tenth undersecretary and an annual salary of seven hundred rubles.*

He was eighteen. He was small, but remarkably lithe and agile; he was a first-class swimmer, an accomplished horseman, a redoubtable swordsman. The young sportsman-poet amazed his contemporaries. He was already a legend. How should he have been other than vain? Also, after six years of solitude and study, he was ravenous for romance and bright lights. He had more energy than he could use in six lifetimes. Busy, quick, heedless, insolent, audacious, superficial, he wanted to meet every famous man, hear every famous voice and become the most famous poet. To read the letters and memoirs of his contemporaries, one would think he had multiplied himself a thousandfold, every one elusive as a spring sprite. There were not one but ten or twenty Pushkins flashing through St. Petersburg, as though a pair of mirrors reflected his image and actions into the four corners of the capital. He was everywhere, he saw everything, he tried everything.

Appointed on June 13, he took oath on the fifteenth and promptly applied for three months' leave of absence to visit his parents, who were spending the summer on their farm at Mikhailovskoye. In his draft memoirs (1824) he noted: "After leaving school I went almost immediately to the Pskov estate belonging to my mother. I can still recall how enthralled I was with country life, the Russian bath, the strawberries, and the rest. But it did not last long. I loved and still love noise and crowds. . . ."

The Mikhailovskoye farm was set in a placid, pleasant landscape, with a stream, lakes and a horizon of blue hills on one side, a forest of moss-slippered pines on the other. All the furniture in the old wooden house

* Those of his schoolmates who had received better marks in the examination were given a higher rank and a starting salary of eight hundred rubles.

dated from the time of Grandfather Hannibal. There was a brother of the famous Januarius living nearby: Peter Abramovich Hannibal, another son of the Negro of Peter the Great, now a retired general. He was an old fellow of seventy, a lover of folk songs and dances and a despot by instinct and profession, whose favorite pastime was the distillation of alcoholic spirits, chiefly vodka.

Alexander Pushkin went to call on his Ethiopian ancestor. "Vodka was served," he wrote. "After pouring himself a glass, he ordered one to be poured out for me too. I drank it without flinching, which seemed to please the old Arab. A quarter of an hour later he called for more vodka, and repeated the performance five or six times before dinner. . . ."

Alexander soon lost interest in the quirks of his great-uncle. He cared less for Peter Abramovich's empty conversation and drinking bouts than for the company of his neighbors the Wulf-Osipovs, whose property, Trigorskoye ("Three Mountains"), lay not far away. The Wulf-Osipov household was composed of the lady of the manor, then thirty-six years old; her husband;† a son, Alexis, by a former husband; two daughters, Annette and Eufrasia; and a stepdaughter, Aline. An immediate friendship sprang up between Pushkin and the mother. She was a remarkable woman, energetic, cultivated and gay—an avid reader of German, French and English literature, who dreamed over the works of Klopstock and Richardson, drew allegorical designs in the margins of her books and managed both farm and family with a strong and steady hand. Throughout his life, Pushkin preserved a singular fondness for and loyalty to Mrs. Wulf-Osipov and her nestful of marriageable daughters. For him, Trigorskoye and its denizens were symbols of rustic bliss. In *The Village* he wrote:

> I love this meadowland with its fragrant haystacks,
> And bushes enlaced by singing rivulets. . . .
> Far off, two lakes spread out their blue expanses
> Where the fisher's sail blinks white from time to time;
> Chains of hills and patchwork fields,
> A few flocks grazing at the sodden banks;
> Farther off, smoking ovens and winged mills:
> It all breathes labor and felicity.

Although he savored the delights of the Russian countryside, Pushkin also found them very tedious[1] and began to long for the more substantial distractions of St. Petersburg. He returned to the capital at the end of August 1817, and there embarked upon a life of untrammeled feasting, fighting, fatigue and idleness.

He lived with his parents, who had rented an apartment on the Fon-

† He died in 1824.

tanka; but the singular atmosphere of that household was not conducive to the cultivation of a love of thrift and moderation or quiet evenings by the fireside in the bosom of the family.

Nadezhda Osipovna and Sergey Lvovich Pushkin had enrolled their younger son Leo as a boarder at the Pedagogical Institute. Their daughter Olga lived and languished at home. The apartment was poorly furnished and the service wretched. As in Moscow and everywhere else, the Pushkins lived for their public and sacrificed comfort to appearances. They ate badly, there were not enough plates, the footmen went about in rags; they haggled over kopecks and spent fortunes on evening clothes. "Pushkin's parents," their grandson Pavlishchev wrote, "were forever short of cash and as a result their children most often did not even have pocket money. The reception rooms were lighted with candelabra, but in my mother's room [Alexander Pushkin's sister]—she used to sell her brooches and earrings to buy a new dress—there was one tallow candle, purchased out of her own savings."

Pushkin's father was becoming increasingly stingy as he grew older. He lavished money on himself, but would do nothing to help his children in their financial straits. If Alexander wanted buckle pumps to wear to a ball, Sergey Lvovich would indignantly appeal to his ancestors to witness his tribulations and offer him a pair of shoes he no longer wore himself, dating from the reign of Paul I. If one of the children happened to break a liqueur glass, the father would grow angry and morose and sit with his nose in his plate and tears in his eyes.

"How can you be so miserable over one little glass that cost less than twenty kopecks?" the culprit would ask.

"I beg your pardon, sir," the father said with feeling. "Thirty-five kopecks it was, not twenty!"

If Alexander hired a cab in foul weather, he could be sure his extravagance would be thrown at his head the same evening. "When I was ill," he wrote his brother, "and would take a cab from the Anichkov Bridge, on muddy autumn days or during the coldest part of the winter, my father would always scold me for the eighty kopecks I had spent—which neither you nor I would have begrudged a servant."

"Upon leaving school," a contemporary wrote, "Pushkin found himself in the position of many young people returning to their families after a stay in some well-endowed and luxurious educational institution. In this case, the contrast was accentuated by the father's penny-pinching avarice, which could not fail to exasperate Pushkin. He did not scruple to provoke his father, moreover, with uncommon malice. One day he was taking a boat trip with several other people and his father. The weather was fine and the water so clear they could see the bottom. Pushkin took out a few gold coins and dropped them into the water one by one, admiring how they sank and winked in the limpid depths."[2]

This Byronic anecdote, whose authenticity some authors have contested, is true enough in essence, if not in fact. Far from stifling Pushkin's taste for frivolity and extravagance, the paternal avarice drove him to the opposite extreme. His duties at the ministry were exceedingly ill defined, and left him ample time to frequent both drawing room and brothel. His personal renown and his parents' connections gave him access to the best families: Count Buturlin, the Vorontsovs, Trubetskoys and Lavals. He went to every ball, he flirted with every woman. And his advances, it must be said, met with considerable success.

"He was not at all good-looking," his brother Leo noted, "but his features were lively and expressive. And although he was small, his lean, muscular body was admirably proportioned. Women liked Pushkin. . . . Whenever he was paying court to a woman, or even simply curious about her, his conversation became extremely charming. . . ."

Around 1829, Pushkin made two lists of his female conquests, which he called his "Don Juan lists." The first contained the Christian names of the women he had loved Platonically, and the second those of the women he had possessed, for the beauty of their bodies and the satisfaction of his own.

This collection has exercised the imaginations of Russian Pushkinists for nearly a century; for although some of the items may be readily deciphered, the remainder elude all attempts to attach a family name, social class, fate or face to some long-dead inamorata. Thus, many are the Helenas, Katerinas and Maryas whose identities have remained hidden behind the mask of that vague given name; but there can be no doubt about the fifth name on the Platonic list, the woman with whom Pushkin was "purely" in love in 1817: "Princess Eudoxia." This was Princess Eudoxia Golitsyn, then thirty-seven years old, nicknamed *la princesse nocturne*. On December 24, 1817, Karamzin wrote: "He [Pushkin] has fallen madly in love with Pythoness Golitsyn, and spends all his evenings there: He lies for love, he rages for love, but so far he does not write for love. I confess I should not have fallen for the Pythoness: Her tripod‡ sits on tongues of ice, not fire."

Vyazemsky paints this enigmatic creature in the following terms: "I know nothing of her first youth, but in her second and third youths she was supremely lovely in a cold, chaste way. She had expressive black eyes, heavy black hair falling in waves over her shoulders, a southern, olive skin, a kind and gracious smile. Add to this a wonderfully sweet and harmonious voice and manner of speaking, and you will have some notion of her charm. Her beauty was principally a beauty of line: She

‡ An allusion to the Delphic oracle. At the shrine of Apollo at Delphi, the priestess is said to have seated herself on a tripod to deliver oracles.

was reminiscent of a Greek statue. There was something unclouded in her, placid or indolent or congealed. By her birth and by the mutually agreed termination of her marriage, she was utterly her own mistress. Her town house was tastefully decorated by the brush and chisel of the best Russian artists of the period, and the lady and her surroundings set each other off to good advantage. . . . Everything breathed elegance and severity. In the evenings a select few would gather in her drawing room—I almost said her temple, for the hostess might well have been a sort of priestess of some pure and lofty cult. Her appearance and dress —picturesque, rather than slavishly following the mode—conferred upon her little circle an air, not of mystery, but of eccentricity. . . . One could have taken them for initiates, not friends. . . ."

A romanticized portrait of Princess Golitsyn shows her with a round, pale face, her eyes raised heavenward, her lips closed in a little grimace of illuminated solemnity. Her head is draped in the Roman manner, one shoulder is artfully bared. She was undeniably beautiful, and undoubtedly intelligent. "She does not want for distinction," A. I. Turgenev wrote, "and when it is a chair she sits on and not her tripod, she is a woman of some wit."

Princess Golitsyn was an anticonstitutionalist Slavophile monarchist—more so than Karamzin, perhaps more even than the emperor himself. After the defeat of Napoleon she appeared at a ball in national costume, her cornet on her head and laurel leaves entwined in her hair. She thought a flag with a cross in the center should be added to the Russian coat of arms, to commemorate the liberation of the native soil. Later, she led a campaign against Kiselev, a minister who wanted to introduce the culture of the potato, on the ground that that tuber was not indigenous and should therefore be refused entry at the frontier—like French constitutional notions. Her guests' liberal views pained the fair Pythoness, but she did not scruple to correspond with foreign aritsts and scholars. She later discovered the joys of mathematics, and even edited a work in two volumes entitled *On the Analysis of Force,* of which A. I. Turgenev wrote, "It is unmitigated nonsense."

"The princess sleeps all day," one of her servants testified in a police report, "and at night she writes papers and hides them. They say she is a believer, but I have been in her bedroom and her study and I could not see a single holy image."

When Balzac visited St. Petersburg in 1845, Princess Golitsyn, who knew him only by reputation, sent her carriage to him on the stroke of midnight with an invitation to attend her. Balzac rebelled at such treatment and dispatched a reply saying that in France the only person one sent for in the middle of the night was the doctor.

At the period of his life when Pushkin first knew Princess Golitsyn, it is not surprising that her affectation of mystery, her genuine beauty and her restless intelligence should have seduced him for a time. Accustomed to the little actresses and shopgirls of easy virtue of Tsarskoye Selo and St. Petersburg, he was struck dumb with admiration and respect for this almost incorporeal being who lived by night, fed on figures and books, had views on the Polish question and entertained the most famous figures of the day. He did not dare approach or touch her; he was too impressed by her funereal splendor: He loved her from afar, with diligence, with frenzy and with patience. He wrote:

I used to say: "Where in my country
Shall I find one solid mind, one true genius?
Do we have one man of noble soul,
Mightily exalted and fiercely free?
One woman whose beauty is not dead,
But living, radiant, compelling?"
. . . I had almost come to hate this land.
But yesterday I was privileged to see the fair Golitsyn
And my fatherland has now found favor in my eyes.

Young Pushkin's passion for the nocturnal princess lasted nearly ten years; but he remained faithful in mind alone. His worship of the "radiant, compelling" lady who had reconciled him with his homeland did not prevent him from seeking more immediate satisfaction in low dives, at stagedoors and among the professionals of love.

A. I. Turgenev's letters are most informative on the subject of the young man's dissipation: "Every day I scold Cricket-Pushkin for his laziness and refusal to learn anything. Add to that his predilection for vulgar flirtations and for the no less vulgar liberalism of the eighteenth century, and where can you find anything to feed a poet?"

Later: "Here, Pushkin's sole occupation is debauchery. . . ."

Or: "Idleness and laziness, like the dread exterminators of beauty and talent, hover over Pushkin's head. . . . Every morning he tells Zhukovsky how he has not been to bed the night before. He spends his days visiting the b—, me, or Princess Golitsyn, and in the evenings he plays cards. . . ."

The poet Batyushkov wrote to Turgenev: "It would be a good idea to lock up the Cricket at Göttingen and feed him on milk soup and logic for three years. Nothing good will come of him if he doesn't decide to settle down. Posterity will not distinguish him from his two namesakes. . . . But perhaps our prayers, and the muses, can save him."

In another letter Turgenev announced: "Pushkin is very ill. He caught cold standing outside the door of a w— who would not let him in, even though it was raining, because she was afraid to give him her disease. What a conflict, between principle, love, and debauchery!"

He also wrote: "I only see the light-footed Pushkin at the theater, where he puts in an appearance whenever he can spare a moment from his contemplation of the animals—he is spending all his time at the ticket office of the zoo, as he is in love with the attendant and has become her *cavalier servant.*[3] Thus, he can study animal behavior and simultaneously observe points of comparison between them and the ordinary sort of brute he doesn't have to pay to look at."

A. I. Turgenev was not alone in deploring the young man's conduct. Zhukovsky, Karamzin, Vyazemsky—all who loved and admired him—beseeched him to give up his rake's progress. They reminded him of his poetic mission. They warned him against disease. But Pushkin laughed at disease, and he was in too great a hurry to live to think about his poetic mission. He wrote to a friend: "Everything here is as usual; the champagne is in good form, the actresses too. One is to drink, the others to f—. Amen, amen, and so it must go. Yuryev's —— has been cured. I'm starting one, small, but that's enough. Vsevolozhsky is playing cards. The chalk rises in clouds, the money descends in torrents."

He also wrote, in a draft of a poem:

> Smote down by fate for my past crimes,
> I shall suffer a week, my stomach full of drugs,
> My blood thick with mercury and my soul with remorse. . . .

One or two quickly cured bouts of venereal disease were not enough to cool his ardor. In January 1818, however, a gangrene fever threatened to end his days. Parents and friends exchanged anxious letters. To cure him, Dr. Leyton plunged him into a bathtub filled with ice: Pushkin's robust constitution saved his life. He whiled away his convalescence working on a long poem, *Ruslan and Ludmila,* which he had begun at school. Friends who came to call found him stretched on his bed in a striped dressing gown with a skullcap on his head. Everything—tables, bedclothes, floor—was littered with papers and books. The lines were coming easily, the poem was good, he was pleased with himself.

But the moment he was on his feet again, he abandoned it and resumed his wild career, reappearing, with the face of one risen from the dead, in drawing room and theater, gambling house, dive and bordello. His looks shocked even his most charitable friends: His head had been shaved during his illness and he wore a little round skullcap. To complete his weird silhouette (he did so like to shock the prudes), he ordered a black frock coat with flapping tails *à l'américaine* and a straight-brimmed, Bolivar-style hat, and let his fingernails grow.

An actress, A. M. Kolosov-Karatygin, whom Pushkin often visited in those days, has left the following description of him:

"He could not sit still. He whirled about, hopped up and down, changed chairs, upset the sewing basket, tangled all the skeins of wool in my embroidery frame, moved the cards of a double solitaire my mother had begun to lay out. 'Will you calm down, grasshopper?' she cried. 'Will you ever stop rushing about?' Sasha would keep still for two minutes, and then he would start again. One day my mother threatened to 'cut the claws' of the insufferable Sasha—as she termed the enormously long fingernails he had grown.

"'Hold his hand,' she said to me, picking up her scissors, 'I'm going to cut them off!'

"I held Pushkin's hand, but he nearly brought the house down with his play acting, his sobs, moans and laments, and we laughed until we cried. . . ."

Pushkin soon replaced his skullcap with a chestnut-hued, lavishly curled wig, which immediately became a pretext for innumerable pranks. One day, he went to speak to the Kolosovs in their box at the Grand Theater. "We invited him to sit with us," A. M. Kolosov wrote, "for we imagined that there, at least, our scalawag would behave himself. Not for a moment! In the middle of the most tragic scene of the play, Pushkin began to complain of the heat, took off his wig, and started fanning his face with it. The people in the nearby boxes were spluttering with laughter and those in the orchestra kept turning to look at us. We tried to make him behave, but then he slid off his chair onto the floor and settled himself at our feet, hidden by the front of the box. Then he plunked his wig onto his head like a hat. You couldn't look at him without laughing. And there he sat, on the floor, throughout the entire performance, poking fun at the play and the actors."

A page[4] of Pushkin's gives an exact idea of the atmosphere of these gold- and velvet-filled theaters, where idle young people like himself paraded between the orchestra seats and yawned or applauded in all the wrong places, just to annoy the other spectators.

"Dramatic talent is formed by the public," Pushkin wrote. "What is our public? Before the curtain rises at an opear, tragedy or ballet, a young man strolls through ten rows of armchairs, treads on everyone's feet, talks to acquaintances or to people he has never seen before: 'Where have you come from?' 'Oh, I've been with Sem[enova], or Zozn[itsky], or Kol[osova], or Ist[omina].' 'Aren't you the lucky one!' 'She's singing—or dancing—today.' 'Oh, let's applaud, let's have an encore! She's so adorable!' 'She has such pretty eyes! And what legs! What talent!' The curtain rises. The young man and his friends move about from place to place, enthusing and applauding.

"In this, I am not condemning youth for being passionate and capricious," continued Pushkin (thinking of his own wild oats); "I know it deserves our indulgence. But can one trust the opinions of judges such as these?

"One more remark. Most of the people in the audience are too preoccupied with the fate of Europe and the fatherland, too weary from their day's work, too sober, too austere, too cautious in expressing their feelings, to take any part whatever in the appreciation of dramatic art, and Russian dramatic art in particular. If, at half past six, these same important persons leave barracks and council room and come to sit in their subscription seats in the first row of the orchestra, it is because it is a social obligation, far more than an entertaining occupation. . . . These high-ranking dignitaries, bearing upon their faces the uniform marks of boredom, arrogance, worry and stupidity inherent in their occupations; these regular front-row spectators, frowning through comedies, yawning through tragedies, sleeping through operas, attentive, if ever, only when looking at a ballet—these mighty persons, I say, must chill the most impassioned actor and fill his soul with inertia and lassitude—if, that is, nature has endowed him with a soul."

Pushchin often met Pushkin at the theater, and suffered to see him prancing through the orchestra in the company of a few fashionable gallants. He acted as though he were proud of his associates, he liked to make jokes for these ignorant dandies, who listened with an air of supercilious amusement. "Sometimes," Pushchin wrote, "when they waved to him from their seats, he would rush over to join them. I would say to him, 'What pleasure do you derive, my dear fellow, from hanging about with those people? There is not one in the lot in whom you could find anything sympathetic to our way of thinking.' He would hear me out in patience and then begin to tickle and hug me, which was his usual trick when he didn't have an answer. And the next thing, off he would go again with his lions of fashion. . . . Strange contradiction in this admirable person!"

Rigged out in his outlandish getup, with his wig on his head and his nails cut like claws (the longest protected by a little golden sheath), the insolent Pushkin was enjoying himself enormously and shocking the entire capital. He was equally notorious, as A. I. Turgenev put it, "for his small poems and his large profligacies." He had a huge circle of friends, frequenting princesses and prostitutes with equal assiduity and equal delight. He drove himself to exhaustion, drank himself silly, had fist fights in dives, sparkled in drawing rooms, talked of Byron with swooning ladies, wrote a poem in honor of Empress Elizabeth and some obscene verses on his venereal infections.

One day he wagered that he could drink a whole bottle of rum without losing consciousness, but for once he overestimated his capacity. When the bottle was empty he sat there, groggy, eyes closed, head motionless. Only the little finger of his left hand moved, curling and uncurling. His friends nursed him, brought him around, and when he was sober at last, he maintained that he had been moving his finger to prove he was still conscious. The jury accepted this explanation and ruled that he had fairly won his bet.

On another occasion he gathered together a few of his cronies and organized an expedition to the lowest dives in the city. "After dressing in filthy rags," a contemporary wrote, "they went off to get drunk in the cabarets, to observe the mores of those insalubrious places, and to sample their pleasures." At the Red Cabaret Pushkin, by his own admission, tried to start a fight, threw punches at a few Germans and worked off a little of his excess energy. He returned home covered with bruises.[5] To the reproaches of his father and mother, he replied, "Nobody would ever be noticed in the crowd unless he made a little noise."

His usual companions were Pushchin, Delvig and the eccentric Nashchokin, one year younger than he. Nashchokin had inherited a huge fortune from his father and was applying himself to its dilapidation with perseverance and imagination. He drank, lost at cards, ran after expensive actresses, ordered carriages from Vienna, bought up collections of marble vases, Chinese *objets d'art* and modeled bronzes and then, tiring of them, distributed them all to his followers. To encourage new talent, he commissioned every artist he knew to paint his portrait, thereby amassing some thirty effigies of himself, which he then gave to all his friends as souvenirs. He lived with his mother, but also rented an apartment on the Fontanka, whose address became famous. Pushkin was one of its most regular patrons. "Thither Nashchokin would repair," wrote a contemporary,[6] "after a night at cards or a spree; any of his friends were also welcome to spend the night, alone or in couples. The large staff of servants, under the orders of Charles the dwarf (who had a face like a tadpole), were instructed to lay out mattresses for anyone who came. . . . Couples were ushered into small individual cubicles, single men slept where they fell in the main rooms. The master of the house always came in last, asked how many were there that night, and mounted silently to his own little cell. In the morning, however, everyone had to meet for tea or coffee. . . . This led to some rather piquant introductions and incidents. . . . Sometimes, especially on Nashchokin's birthday, there would be a huge feast accompanied by quantities of bottles, after which the gallant officers of the guards and their fair damsels would call for Nashchokin's four-seater and install Charles inside it, surrounded by a bevy of young women in evening gowns, while they themselves, removing their uniforms and dressed only in breeches and shirt, would sit in the coachman's and *Vorreiter*'s places or clamber up behind and perch like footmen. Then the entire equipage would go tearing down the Nevsky Prospect at a gallop, along the Morskaya and into the busiest streets in town. Another time, on Pushkin's initiative, and again on Nashchokin's birthday, the latter's friends invited him to a party in his own house where, at the entrance, they presented him with a gift so outrageous that I cannot describe it."

"Always broke," wrote Baron Korf, speaking of Pushkin, "always in debt, sometimes without a decent coat to wear, embroiled in impossible intrigues, involved in numerous duels, on intimate terms with the owner of every dive, the madam of every brothel, and every prostitute in St. Petersburg, Pushkin was a perfect example of the most licentious debauchery."

Baron Korf, Pushkin's former classmate, had particular reason to dislike and vilify the poet: They lived in the same house and their manservants had quarreled over some trifling question of service. Korf took up his man's defense and soundly thrashed Pushkin's, whereupon Pushkin challenged Korf to a duel, but Korf haughtily replied, "I do not accept your cartel, for the matter is not worth it. You are Pushkin and I am not Küchelbecker."

This was a reminder of a lamentable duel that had taken place in 1818 between the poet and another ex-schoolmate, the goodhearted, earnest, innocent, tactless Küchelbecker. Upon leaving school he too had been assigned to a post in the foreign ministry, where he continued to write bad poetry and recite it to his associates, and Pushkin continued to make fun of him. One satirical quatrain of his stung Küchelbecker so deeply that he demanded reparation gun in hand. Friends interceded, but in vain. Only gunpowder and blood could obliterate the offense, and so the duel actually took place. Küchelbecker fired first and missed. Pushkin burst out laughing, flung away his pistol and ran to embrace his comrade, but Küchelbecker kept gesticulating and squeaking in a choked falsetto, "Shoot, go ahead and shoot!"

Pushkin explained that he could not shoot because the barrel of his gun was full of snow, the seconds decided to adjourn the encounter, and the two adversaries were reconciled around a samovar.

Pushkin was already an old hand at dueling. His quarrels and fights were becoming legendary. On March 23, 1820, Mrs. Karamzin wrote, "Pushkin fights a duel every day; thank God, they are not fatal, and the adversaries come back unscathed."

Thus, at the beginning of his life Pushkin felt a powerful need to tempt fate, to expose himself to every danger and calamity. He fashioned a destiny in his own image: highly spiced, contradictory, explosive. His only joys were in the extremes of pleasure and peril. On December 23, 1818, Police Commissioner Gorgoli sent the following report to P. I. Ubry, Pushkin's immediate superior in the foreign ministry: "On the twentieth of this month ministerial undersecretary and translator Pushkin, attached to the ministry of foreign affairs, attended the theater and sat in a box at the back of the orchestra; during the intermission he went into the orchestra and, passing between the rows, stopped in front of the seats occupied by Councilor Perevoshikov and his wife. Mr. Perevoshikov asked him to move, but Pushkin, interpreting the request as an insult, spoke indecently to him and insulted him in obscene terms."

Another of Pushkin's theater incidents had a ludicrous aftermath, related by the author Lazhechnikov in his memoirs. At the time, Lazhechnikov was sharing an apartment with Major Denisevich, a newcomer to St. Petersburg. The major was something of a brute, baldheaded, with blood-swollen cheeks. He was proud of his heavy epaulets that gleamed like portable suns; he was also an ardent pursuer of the ladies, adored the ballet, ate like ten men, slept like a log and could only be awakened by having a spoon thrust into his mouth.

"It happened one fine winter morning," Lazhechnikov wrote. "It was about a quarter to eight; I had just finished washing and gone into the next room, where the major was staying, to call for tea. Denisevich had gone out on a tour of inspection to the stables. I was hardly inside the room when three strangers entered from the antechamber. One was a very young man, short and thin, with curly hair and a Negroid profile. He wore a frock coat. Behind him stood two magnificent specimens, guards cavalry officers, with clanking spurs and sabers. The civilian came up to me and said, in a quiet, insinuating tone, 'May I inquire whether Major Denisevich lives here?' 'He does,' I answered, 'but he has just gone out; I shall send for him.' I was about to do so when Denisevich himself appeared. He was visibly taken aback at the sight of the two officers but quickly recovered and assumed an equally martial posture. 'What do you want?' he asked the civilian sharply. 'You know perfectly well,' replied the other. 'You told me to be here at eight (pulling out his watch); there are still fifteen minutes until the hour. That should suffice for the choice of weapons and meeting place. . . .' All this was spoken in a flat, calm tone of voice, as though he was talking about the arrangements for some friendly gathering. Denisevich turned red as a lobster and stammered, 'I did not ask you to come here for that. . . . I only wanted to tell you that it is not proper for a young man like you to shout in the theater in the middle of the performance and prevent your neighbors from hearing the play. . . . It isn't right.' 'You made your reproaches to me yesterday, in the presence of a large number of people,' said the civilian, raising his voice. 'I am not a schoolboy and I have come here to settle the matter in my own way. Which in this instance requires few words. Here are my seconds. This gentleman is an officer (pointing to me), he will certainly not refuse to act for you. Now, if you don't mind—' Denisevich did not let him finish his sentence. 'I can't fight you,' he said. 'You are a young man whom nobody knows and I am an officer.' At these words the other two officers burst out laughing; as for me, I turned pale and began to tremble with rage at the stupid and humiliating position my friend had got himself into. At the same time, I began to sense something odd about the whole affair. The civilian replied in a firm voice, 'I am a Russian nobleman. My name is Pushkin. My witnesses will confirm what I say. Consequently, there can be no *shame* for you in fighting me.'

"When I heard the name Pushkin it crossed my mind that this might be the gifted young poet to whom Zhukovsky himself paid homage, the coryphaeus of the intellectual youth of St. Petersburg, and I quickly spoke up: 'Is it not Alexander Sergeyevich whom I have the honor of addressing?'

" 'That is my name,' he answered with a smile."

Wishing at all costs to avoid such an absurd encounter, Lazhechnikov then asked the witnesses to set forth Pushkin's grievances. He was informed that on the previous day Pushkin had gone to the theater and been seated next to Major Denisevich. The play was poor, and Pushkin kept yawning insistently and muttering, "Intolerable! Intolerable!" Denisevich, who was enjoying the performance, remarked that Pushkin was preventing him from hearing the actors. Pushkin gave him a black look and continued as before, paying no heed to his remark. "I shall call the police and have you thrown out," said Denisevich. "That I'd like to see," Pushkin retorted, and went on yawning, whistling and groaning. When the play was over and the audience moving toward the exit, Denisevich caught up with Pushkin in the aisle and said, shaking a threatening finger at him, "Young man, you prevented me from hearing the play, and that is indecent and rude."

"I am not an old man, that is true," answered Pushkin, "but I shall tell you, my good officer, that it is still more rude to point at people and stop them in such a place. Where do you live?"

Denisevich gave him the address and arranged to meet Pushkin the next morning at eight. "I'll be there," said Pushkin.

After hearing the story, Lazhechnikov called Major Denisevich into the next room and persuaded him, in the end, to call off the duel. Denisevich went back and apologized. Pushkin listened with a haughty sneer on his face, coldly murmured, "I forgive you," and departed without shaking the major's hand.

Another contemporary, the author of an essay on the "school spirit," has left this portrait of the graduates of Tsarskoye Selo: "Their heads are hot, their mien arrogant, their voices insolent, their speech rapid. Their replies are edicts, their questions—commands. They all imagine that they were born too soon, that they are far in advance of their century, that the world sees them as geniuses, reformers, children of the future. . . ."

Arrogance, insolence, smug self-importance: These were indubitably Pushkin's gravest shortcomings. He believed he could get away with anything, he believed it was his duty, as a "liberal" and a poet, to get away with everything. His elders—Turgenev, Zhukovsky, Batyushkov, Karamzin and the rest—vainly tried to reason with him. They knew the true value of their boisterous troublemaker and watched over him like jealous mothers. If he shut himself up indoors for even two or three days, they immediately began to crow: "In spite of the debauched life he is leading, he is completing the fourth stanza of his poem," wrote Turgenev. "His first illness has been good for his work. . . ."

He also wrote: "What treasures there are in that head! What a pity he does not know how to husband them! . . ."

And Batyushkov exclaimed, clutching the manuscript of the *Epistle to Yuryev*, "Oh, how this rascal has begun to write!"

Zhukovsky: "What a wonderful gift! What lines! His genius haunts me like a ghost!"

Vyazemsky: "The devil-nephew's poem is marvelously written. But what an animal! We should lock him up in the yellow house; otherwise the little tiger will devour us all, us and our fathers too!"

Lastly, the carping Viegel wrote in his memoirs: "When young Pushkin left school, the members of the Arzamas hailed his arrival as a blessed event, a triumph. Zhukovsky in particular rejoiced, as though God had given him a son. But to me, the son was an ill-mannered rake, and it saddened me to see all the big boys trying, one after the other, to spoil their little brother."

2. *The Arzamas and the Green Lamp*

The Arzamas had adopted Pushkin before he left Tsarskoye Selo, but he could not be officially admitted to the brotherhood until he came to St. Petersburg. The Arzamas was a youthful, baroque organization, founded, as noted, to compete with Admiral Shishkov's reactionary group. It began after one of the "conservatives" had made fun of Zhukovsky in a comedy, *The Waters of Lipetsk*, and Bludov, an author who admired Zhukovsky, replied with a pamphlet entitled *The Vision in the Cabaret at Arzamas*.* Upon its publication, all the champions of the new Russian literature rallied around the author and Zhukovsky. The partisans even named their society the Arzamas in honor of the poet who had brought them together.

"It was," wrote one contemporary,[1] "a small group of young men united by a keen affection for the national language, literature and history. The tone of the society, or more exactly of its informal meetings, was essentially critical." This noncommittal assessment gives a false impression of the disorderly and hilarious proceedings of the Arzamas. True, its members did love the Russian language and Russian literature and history. True too, they studied and discussed the works of their contemporaries. But they were also gay and keen, and, in rebellion against the dusty severity of the old school, a spirit of high buffoonery presided at their meetings. The statutes of the society provided that every new member must pronounce a funeral oration at his initiation. ". . . However, the members of the Arzamas being immortal," the document went on, "it has been decided, in the absence of any deceased among their own numbers, to borrow those of the 'Conversation Club'† and tell them a few home truths now, without waiting for the judgment of future generations." Every member of the Arzamas had a nickname,

* A small town in Russia.

† "The Conversation Club of Friends of the Russian Language" was the reactionary group of which Shishkov was president.

which was scrupulously respected. Bludov was called "Cassandra," because a reactionary writer named Zakharov, a member of the Conversation Club, had died a few days after Bludov pronounced his funeral oration at a plenary meeting of the Arzamas. A. I. Turgenev was "the Aeolian Harp," because his stomach was always grumbling; Zhukovsky was "Svetlana," Vyazemsky was "Asmodeus," Basil Pushkin was "Well then, I'll tell you!" and Alexander was, of course, "the cricket," etc.

The president, drawn by lot at the opening of each session, wore a red bonnet to symbolize the coming literary revolution. New members also wore a red bonnet. When Uncle Basil joined, Zhukovsky organized a grotesque ceremony in the masonic style: First the unfortunate Basil was buried under a mountain of fur coats and compelled, sweating and panting, to listen to a reading of a complete French tragedy. Then he was dressed in a light tunic bedecked with shells, a handkerchief was tied over his eyes and he was paraded through the house. Next his masters brought him a bow and arrow, removed his blindfold, and commanded him to pierce the heart of a dress dummy representing bad taste. After completing this task, he was presented with a jellied goose, which he had to hold in both hands while Zhukovsky gave a very long and very solemn welcoming address. The jellied goose was the food fetish of the Arzamas: One was consumed at every meeting, and members addressed each other as "goose" or "honorable goose." The minutes of the meetings were drafted by Zhukovsky, as perpetual secretary of the society, and they were monuments of grandiloquent nonsense: "I gave a sermon and was seated, or rather inserted between the hospitable arms of an easy chair that part of the anatomy without which it is impossible to assume the seated position, and which serves as a head for the Chaldean members of the Conversation Club." He also wrote, "The criticism of the Arzamas must ride confusion astraddle."

Pushkin was delighted by this atmosphere of titanic tomfoolery, epic incoherence and warm friendliness. He loved the unspoken complicity that united the members of the brotherhood: All rejoiced in the success of each, and individual connections were put to the service of all. A. I. Turgenev, for example, spent half his time making official representations on his friends' behalf. When the emperor granted Zhukovsky a pension, Turgenev wrote to Vyazemsky: "If your Arzamas founding member's heart does not leap for joy out of your Arzamas founding member's chest and expend itself in magnificent Arzamas-style verse of thanksgiving to the Aeolian Harp, who has made all possible haste to transmit to you the first tidings of this item of Arzamas news, then you are no longer Asmodeus!"

The minutes of the meeting at which Pushkin was received into the society have not been preserved; we know only that he made a speech in verse glorifying the new Academy, "wearing a jester's cap, with bauble, laurel wreath and rods in his hand."

Around the middle of 1817, however, the brothers began to weary of their own joke. Admiral Shishkov's Conversation Club was defunct. The Arzamas were without a worthy adversary, their shafts of irony were falling on barren ground. A few voices were heard demanding the creation of a newspaper; and two new members, Orlov and N. I. Turgenev, became the self-appointed critics of the group's joyous frivolity. To hear them talk, the age of literary trivialities was over; the time had come to publish political journals, to concern themselves with the social education of the nation, to become serious, to grow up, to be important. The idea was debated, examined, accepted. A stern and gloomy program was drawn up. They all promised to act like grownups. Then, sadly, they parted; and the Arzamas died a natural death. Zhukovsky wrote its epitaph:

> The spirit forsook us. We lost our laughter,
> . . . We wrote statutes. And that was all. . . .

The demise of the Arzamas did not find Pushkin unprepared; another society had already welcomed him to its bosom. This was the "Green Lamp," founded in 1818 by the millionaire Vsevolozhsky and his friend I. N. Tolstoy. Once every fortnight Vsevolozhsky's home became the meeting place for a group of idle, brilliant "young roués," containing a high percentage of officers of the guards, hussars, uhlans and light cavalry. Lost among the braid and brandenburgs were a few select civilians: Pushkin, Delvig. At most there were a score of them, congregating in a large room lighted by a green lamp, symbol of hope. They all wore a special ring with a lamp engraved on the stone. The society's statutes invited its members to discuss the questions of the day in complete freedom and with a guarantee of absolute secrecy. Pushkin, Delvig and the dilettante officers read their latest poems to the company, Vsevolozhsky gave lectures on Russian history, while Barkov reviewed the theater season. There was some talk of play production, but much more of actresses, involving elaborate schemes to kidnap and possibly sequester them. And then, the members being young and loving freedom, progress and wit, they criticized the imperial government and its beribboned, stupidity-stuffed representatives:

> There we spoke and minced no words
> Of fools, of wicked dignitaries,
> Of professional kowtowers,
> Of the king who reigns on high;
> Sometimes, too, of the one below.[2]

After a thorough review of the failings of both celestial and terrestrial monarchs, the friends of the Green Lamp would sup in the company of maidens of easy virtue. Whenever one of the guests swore, Vsevolozhsky's Kalmuk footman was instructed to sing out, "I wish you good health" and present the offender with an expiatory cup; and as nobody watched his language, the expiatory cups followed in rapid succession. Heads grew hotter and speech more bold. To close the meeting, the gentlemen would go out on the town for a sensational tour of the brothels. Pushkin's first biographers,[3] who interviewed the poet's contemporaries, maintained that the Green Lamp was an exclusively and shamefully "orgiastic" association. Provocative *tableaux vivants* were arranged, representing Adam and Eve expelled from Eden and the holocaust of Sodom and Gomorrah. . . . Later biographers,[4] on the contrary, have tried to make out that the Green Lamp was another of the little revolutionary circles of that period; in their view it was a political club, serious and militant, a branch of the Union for Welfare. Both theories tell only part of the truth. The men in the Green Lamp were officers—rebellious intellectuals, no doubt, some of whom, like Tolstoy, Kaverin, Prince Trubetskoy and Tokarev, did belong to the Union for Welfare—but that does not mean the Green Lamp was a product of that hotbed of conspiracy. The Green Lamp was at subconspiratorial level: It was the playground of the soldiers of independence, where the big boys with the solemn faces came during their recreation period. Authority was attacked "with words"; but in that day, who did not attack authority "with words"? Revolutionary ideas were the fashion; you were an old fogy if you stubbornly persisted in praising the regime. In Chapter X of *Eugene Onegin*, Pushkin gave a true picture of the group:

> Veuve Cliquot, Château-Lafitte,
> Couplets, amical disputes,
> They were but games played in boredom,
> Laziness of our young heads,
> Playthings of overgrown boys.

There was too much Château-Lafitte and too much Veuve Cliquot, too many cards, too many bare-bosomed girls, too much laughter and too much wealth in all this for the Green Lamp ever to have been a center of conspiracy.

When the mild and temperate Küchelbecker was asked to join he declined, on the ground that "the society was ruled by debauchery and the excessive consumption of strong spirits."

Pushkin, however, had become the life and soul of this collection of worldly Jacobins, liberal rich men's sons, and officer Don Juans. He attended every meeting and, in addition to the regular sessions, never missed an opportunity to join "President" Vsevolozhsky in his gay dinners. They gambled their nights away together; once, in 1820, he suffered particularly heavy losses and had to repay his friend by selling him (for a thousand rubles) the printer's manuscript of his poems. Vsevolozhsky was in love with a young ballerina, a student at the Academy of Dramatic Art, and Pushkin used to escort his friend to the church there, "to pray to the Lord and contemplate Mlle. Ovoshnikov." Often, armed with lorgnettes, the two friends would post themselves at the window, waiting for the fleet-footed young lady to pass. "Every morning," Pushkin wrote, "the winged virgin flits past beneath Nikita's window on her way to rehearsal. As before, our telescopes are trained on her, and our —— as well. But alas, you scarcely catch a glimpse of her, and she doesn't see you at all!"[5] It was also at Nikita's window that Karatygin, the actor, first saw Pushkin, on his way home from a rehearsal. "At the window," he wrote, "were seated Vsevolozhsky and a stranger with a flattened nose, thick lips, and the dark skin of a mulatto. Dembrovsky [Karatygin's companion] leaned out of the carriage and bowed deeply to them. The mulatto raised his wig, began to wave it around his head, and called out something to Dembrovsky. We were much amused by these antics. I asked Dembrovsky, 'Who is that man?' and he told me it was Pushkin, the author, who was just beginning to be known, adding that his head had been shaved during a bout of gangrene fever and that he had written a poem on the subject."

One day Pushkin, Vsevolozhsky, Mansurov and a few others went to see a German fortuneteller named Kirchow. After laying out the cards, Madame Kirchow told Pushkin he would soon receive some money, a business proposition would be made to him in the near future, he would become famous, he would be twice deported and he would live a long time if, at the age of thirty-seven, he could successfully avoid a great danger in the from of a white head, a white horse or a white man (*weisser Kopf, weisses Ross, weisser Mensch*).[6]

When he reached home that evening, he found a letter from a school friend containing a sum of money in payment of an old gambling debt. A few days later, Orlov offered him a place in the horse guards. One by one, the other predictions came true. Pushkin always remembered his visit to the old German witch, and spoke of her with inhabitual respect and fear. In particular, he was obsessed by the idea of the white man. One day his friend Sobolevsky asked him why he had never joined a Masonic lodge or secret society, to which he replied, "It is because of the prediction about the white head. Don't you know that all philanthropic and humanitarian societies, even the Freemasons, have received directives from Adam Weishaupt‡ opposing the government's policies? How could I join them? Weisskopf, Weishaupt, it's the same thing."

‡ Adam Weishaupt, founder of the Illuminati (1748–1822). The Illuminati was a short-lived movement of republican free thought whose aim was to replace Christianity by a religion of reason. It was linked with various Masonic lodges and had its attraction for literary men like Goethe, fitting in with the idea of benevolent despotism as a vehicle for the Enlightenment.

3. Ode to Liberty

Alexander I's triumph was too much for him; he was incapable of administrating it. Facing the invader, he had seen himself as champion and knight-errant to Russia, Europe and the whole Christian world; the burning of Moscow, Napoleon's defeat and the prayers of the Russian people had turned him into an archangel. In response, the young skeptic discovered that he was indeed inspired by God; his faith, however, was not yet ritualistic, only vaguely Christian: "the Bible and I."

In 1815, on the advice of Baroness Krüdner, a fifty-year-old romantic mystic, he conceived the Holy Alliance, designed to subordinate the policies of major European powers to the principles of eternal Christianity. According to the act establishing the Holy Alliance, signatory monarchs undertook that their policies would henceforth be ruled by "the sublime truths embodied in the immortal Law of God the Savior."

Alexander's allies, however, and especially the Austrian diplomats, used the Alliance to further the interests of the monarchy. Without his ever realizing it, the tsar's Holy Alliance became a coalition poised to throttle any expression of the will of the people in Europe.

Liberalism was the first, the only foe of the Holy Alliance. Morality and religion were enrolled in the exclusive service of absolutism: Any uprising, even that of Christian Greeks against their Turkish oppressors, was regarded as an unpardonable revolt of subject against sovereign. Alexander, as leader of the Alliance, found himself also, and without wishing to be, the leader of the ultraconservatives. A strange fatality compelled him to oppose the liberal ideas of his own youth, as though it were impossible to be both a just man and a respectable master, a promoter of social progress and a potentate feared beyond the frontiers of his country; as though there were only two courses open to men in power: Either they could rule, with discipline, severity and rectilinear legitimism, or they could abdicate in the name of humanism. Several times Alexander I tried to return to the equalitarian principles he had learned from La Harpe; but it was dangerous to tamper with the amorphous mass of Russia; Russia was not ready for reform. So Alexander carried out his reforms elsewhere. It was easier. And safer. He insisted that Louis XVIII give France a constitution. He guaranteed the autonomy of Finland. He introduced a liberal regime in the new kingdom of Poland.

At the opening of the Diet of Warsaw in 1818, he announced in his speech from the throne that he intended to restrict absolute power throughout Russia. "The customs already existing in your country," he told the Poles, "have made it possible for me to introduce this constitution. . . . Thus you have furnished me with the means of giving to my own country that which I have long been preparing for it, and which it will possess as soon as the time is ripe for this matter of capital importance. . . ."

The intellectual youth of Russia received these statements with hope and amazement. The liberals immediately began to imagine that their daydreams would become realities overnight, by the emperor's will. "The Warsaw speeches," Karamzin wrote, "have deeply stirred the hearts of the young. They see the constitution in their dreams, they debate, they fancy themselves competent judges on every question. . . . It is at once sad and ridiculous."

Speransky: "The danger is that the great, obscure mass of the people have now become convinced not only that freedom has been promised to them, but that it is already theirs, and only the landowners are preventing it from being openly proclaimed, or are hiding the fact that it already has been. . . . It is terrifying and all too easy to imagine what the result of this could be."

After veering to the left, Alexander I, frightened by his own temerity, tried to steer his ship back on its course. The Russian people were not ready to take part in public affairs, they did not understand freedom, they would misuse it. Give them an inch, and they would demolish the whole imperial administration, plunder the nobles' castles, begin voting laws and taking justice into their hands. In Russia, curtailing the powers of the authorities was the same as fomenting revolution. Remarkable country, Russia!

Alexander I loved Russia sincerely, but he disliked Russians. To him, the inhabitants of his empire were ignorant, lazy, irrational, unruly and incomprehensible. He preferred the Germans: so obedient, virtuous and sentimental. German songs were sweet to his soul. German towns, symmetrical and scoured, flattered his love of order. Even German landscapes seemed more regular to him, more familiar, more human, than the endless plains and impenetrable forests of Russia. It was his dream to end his days in some smiling town on the banks of the Rhine, far from the intimidating, inscrutable, unpredictable little Russian muzhiks.

Meanwhile, Alexander I lived a life of order, cleanliness and exactitude. His face was round, soft, close-shaven. The little strips of his side whiskers were curled with precision. The cut of his uniforms was ideal. The top of his desk was carefully arranged. The papers submitted to him for signature were of uniform size. The furniture in his apartments was lined up as for a review. And the emperor suffered, because he could not organize Russia the way he organized his study. He would have liked to create a society in which every citizen occupied a preassigned niche, with a definite place of work, predetermined days of rest, recreation at fixed hours and ideas and attitudes supplied with his uniform. He dreamed of an immense civilian army—chiefs, underchiefs, reports, schedules, parades and discipline. In the army, the soldier is relieved of all care. He is a pawn in a row of pawns. He knows his rights and his duties, and he is happy.

In 1812, Alexander read a French book written by General Servan, proposing the establishment of military colonies on the outposts of the empire. The emperor leaped for joy. Militarize the muzhiks. Transform their isbas into barracks. Replace garrisons by colonies. Why hadn't he thought of it before? He had General Servan's book translated into Russian and submitted it to his most privy counselor, Arakcheev, for opinion.

This Arakcheev was the slave, the mirror image, the very shadow of his sovereign: "Of average height, stooped, with thick hair cut short and bushy; small, cloudy, cold eyes beneath a low, furrowed brow; a large, boot-shaped nose; thin, tight lips over which it seemed no smile had ever played."[1] Arakcheev worshiped the emperor as a deity. He trembled and crossed himself when he entered the ruler's study. And he did not steal from the state. What more could one ask of a counselor? Moreover, Arakcheev never gave an opinion on matters of general policy. He was there solely to assist Alexander in administrative affairs. Even then, for the most part, he confined himself to listening to the monarch's vaticinations and encouraging him in his wildest schemes. Arakcheev, like Alexander I, thought Russia was a land of hypocrites, sloths, braggarts and thieves. A thick, complicated people who must be brought to heel. And since they were all brutes, a heavy stick would be needed.

Arakcheev was fastidious and vicious. "Industrious as an ant," his colleagues said, "and venomous as a tarantula." He wore himself out over trifles, he was obsessed by detail. "If they see how I look to small matters," he liked to say, "they will be careful not to neglect great ones." This vulture also had a fierce temper; he became so furious at the

Gachina review that he tore off the soldiers' mustaches. It was also said he had bitten one of his servants on the ear. On his estate at Gruzino, offending peasants wore a collar of iron spikes, and the rods were pickled in brine. But the place was beautiful to the eye, well kept, well swept, with a profusion of Doric columns, white turrets and imperial emblems. Alexander I was fond of visiting this paradise of European symmetry.

"It is a charming place," he wrote after spending a few days there in 1810; "the order reigning everywhere, the cleanliness, the planning of paths and gardens, the kind of symmetry and elegance to be seen in the arrangement of the buildings . . . aroused my admiration."

At Gruzino, every blade of grass and every pebble had a justification. Russia would do well to metamorphose itself in the image of Gruzino—especially as there was no lack of distractions on this model estate; but they were cleverly concealed from prying eyes. In the garden, for instance, stood a little kiosk decorated with mirrors, where Arakcheev kept an interesting selection of obscene paintings and pornographic books: *Tendres étreintes conjugales et plaisirs pris avec les maîtresses*, and *Les amants et les époux, ou les hommes et les femmes, lisez, comprenez, et peut-être que vous voudrez en goûter* ("Tender conjugal embraces and pleasures enjoyed with mistresses"; "Lovers and wedded mates; or, men and women: Read, comprehend, and perhaps you will wish to sample").

Arakcheev had good taste; and so it was to this expert in alignment, leveling and supervised recreation that Alexander turned for the realization of his dream of military colonies. In 1816, one section of the province of Novgorod (where Arakcheev's estate was located) was converted into a camp. The governments of Mohilev, Kherson, Yekaterinoslav and Slobodsko-Ukrainsky were the next to be reorganized by imperial directive.

The process was as rigorous as it was logical. Regiments were installed in a district, and all the district's inhabitants automatically became soldiers. The militarized muzhiks were divided into companies, battalions and squadrons, forming the regiment's reserves. They were taught the art of soldiering and, in their "hours of freedom," worked in the fields to feed the army. What could be more simple?

Many picturesque and lice-infested villages were thus destroyed. The isbas were replaced by perfectly symmetrical, anonymous cottages. The muzhiks' beards were shaved. They were dressed in uniforms. Their new duties were literally beaten into them. Their children were also clothed at state expense and given preparatory military training. There was a time for everything: a time for plowing and a time for drill, a time for recreation and a time for procreation. The peasants marched to the fields in uniform, to the sound of the drums. They pushed their plows on command from the corporal. They began to sing on signal. The leaders kept exact inventories of livestock, farm implements and marriageable girls. Weddings were decided by military decree, and partners were often drawn by lot. Not one widow, not one old maid must there be. Compulsory copulation. Utilization of all available bodies. Resistance on sentimental grounds was not advisable. The reproduction of the species was promoted and controlled by administration. There had to be so many babies a year. Women who did not produce often enough were fined. On their tenth birthday, boys were enrolled in the children's troops. They learned to take steps of regulation length, hold their heads up, keep their chests out. Arakcheev and Alexander I, equally enamored of Prussian military methods, wanted their soldiers to be trained to hold their breath on parade, "so that their breathing should not be visible."

In the identical little pink or blue cottages, all with the same red steps outside, the same little white stone posts, the same little rows of frail, mass-produced birches, lived whole families in uniform. The cottages were divided by partitions. The first room, "gleaming with cleanliness," was reserved for important guests on tours of inspection. The soldier-muzhiks lived in the other room, damp and poorly ventilated. A framed list of the contents hung on the wall, and inspectors examined their condition at regular intervals. In the summer, from May 1 to September 15, all food was cooked outdoors. Head cooks would come to examine the indoor stoves and seal them with red wax. On September 15, not a day earlier or later, the soldier-muzhiks might break the seals and light fires indoors. The sweeping of courtyards, washing of rooms, care of livestock, nursing of infants, polishing of buttons and every other detail of daily life was provided for and described in articles of the regulations. The smallest violation was followed by corporal punishment, rods and racks being regarded as the mildest forms.

Alexander I and his minister were well pleased with their work; after all, they had acted in the interests of the country. The new measures improved the soldiers' lot, for in peacetime they would remain attached to their homes and families. With its magazines, schools and hospitals, the military colony would become a cultural beachhead. The muzhik, subjected to iron discipline, would be introduced to the beacon of European education. And the army would no longer cost the state a penny, because it fed and maintained itself! Economy and civilization in one: What could the militarized muzhiks have found to complain about?

And yet, the devils were complaining. They seemed reluctant to let themselves be enriched by their sovereign's bounty. Some were Old Believers and, in accordance with the laws of that sect, would not relinquish their beards, or asked to have them returned afterward, so they would be able to present them to God on Judgment Day.* Others were unhappy about changing all their clothes and habits overnight. They were used to their dirt and sloth, and failed to appreciate the benefits of military discipline. Others, again, moaned because they were married off against their will, or because their son was made a soldier, or because they had to do two jobs at once, bearing arms and tilling the soil. And still others claimed that privacy had become impossible in this prison of exactitude. And they were rebelling, the ungrateful wretches! The insubordination of these brutes would have to be quelled with blood! "The military colonies will continue to exist," said Alexander I, "if I have to pave the road from Petersburg to Chudov with corpses."

On September 5, 1819, Arakcheev submitted a report to his sovereign on the uprising at Chugunyev, which had assumed such proportions that the military tribunal had had to sentence seventy-five people to death. "Inspired by the feelings which are natural to a Christian," Arakcheev liked to think he had softened these harsh measures: He gave orders that the condemned men, instead of being executed, should be made to "run the gauntlet twelve times, through a battalion of one thousand men." Except that it was, in a word, more refined, this sentence was no different from the first—although a man with an elephant's hide and a strong heart might have some hope of survival, skinned alive and crazed with pain. For a start, Arakcheev sentenced only forty of the convicted men to be tortured by this method. Their comrades appealed for mercy, whereupon Arakcheev "thanked" the Almighty with his whole soul, and "promised the appellants to have recourse to imperial clemency." Alexander's reply must have surprised even Arakcheev: "I understand," the emperor wrote, "what your sensitive soul must have felt in the circumstances. I can also appreciate your foresight in the face of such grave events. I thank you sincerely and with all my heart for the trouble you have taken. . . ."

Of the condemned men's appeal or the possibility of suspending their sentences, not a word. On the contrary, the letter concluded: "The situation is painful, to be sure; but since it was unfortunately not possible to prevent these occurrences, there is no alternative now but to allow the violence and rigor of the law to pursue their course."

Alexander remaining adamant, the sentences were systematically executed. According to the report by De Malvirade, the French chargé d'affaires, 160 men met their death in this fashion, 26 women were also

* Barbers charged a fee for returning the bundles of venerable hair.

punished and sent to Orenburg and 56 officers incurred disciplinary penalties.

The Russian military and intellectual elite were thoroughly revolted by these repressive measures. Many new members came to swell the ranks of the secret societies during 1818–19, and there was open talk of "conspiratory circles"; but their importance has been grossly exaggerated, for these clandestine associations were united by no common plan or over-all program. Even the members of a single group held different political views: Some were revolutionaries, others liberals, or enlightened anarchists, or moderate constitutionalists. The only thing they had in common was their love of Russia and their hatred of Arakcheev.

At meetings of the Arzamas and Green Lamp, and in the homes of the monarchist Princess Golitsyn and the Turgenev brothers, Pushkin was involved in these political discussions. Everywhere, people were complaining, plotting and building the future in great phrases, and Pushkin followed the crowd: in his own way, however. He really was the *enfant terrible* of society. He rather fancied conspiracy, except that it demanded such precautions on the part of the conspirators. He wanted to laugh, he wanted to *do* things, and say whatever came into his head, whereas the professional revolutionaries were forever watching their actions and their words, keeping their voices down and looking the other way. He could never have kept his voice down or looked the other way. Plans and precautions and secrets bored him. Why couldn't one just love freedom and equality and flirt with girls and drink wine and play cards and say anything in front of anybody?

His school friend Pushchin, who had joined one of the secret societies, wrote in his *Recollections:* "My first thought was to confide in Pushkin. In his way, he was fighting for the same things as we—verbally, in writing, poetry or prose. Luckily, or unluckily, he did not happen to be in St. Petersburg just then. [He was at Mikhailovskoye.] If he had been, I am fairly certain I would have taken him with me from the start, because of my great friendship for him. Later, when I thought of putting my plan into action, I could no longer bring myself to tell a secret that was not mine alone, and one whose ill-judged disclosure could have jeopardized so much. The instability of his impulsive personality and his associations with untrustworthy people held me back. It was natural that Pushkin should notice a change in my behavior and begin to suspect that I was hiding something from him. He asked embarrassing questions, subjected me to interrogations which I eluded as best I could. I reassured him by telling him that he was doing good work for the cause, outside all the secret societies."

One day in January 1819, Pushkin was returning from a walk in the Summer Garden and decided to call on his friend N. I. Turgenev.

When he entered the drawing room he was surprised to find a gathering of sober individuals among whom he recognized Pushchin, Kunitsyn and Mazlov. The faces turned toward him expressed embarrassment and disappointment. His presence was clearly felt to be undesirable. These gentlemen, members of the Union for Welfare, were planning a new review, *The Archives of Political Science and Russian Literature*, which, according to its editor, was to be "the dove of salvation, the messenger from free shores."

Mazlov was reading aloud an article on statistics. The others, seated at a round table, were solemnly taking notes, smoking, drinking tea and spirits. Pushkin touched Pushchin on the shoulder and murmured in his ear, "What are you doing here? At last, I've caught you in the act!"

Then he went over and sat on a divan, feigning complete absorption in the design of the furniture and ceiling moldings. It hurt him to be excluded from this noble-minded fraternity. When the reading ended, he took Pushchin aside and resumed: "Why didn't you tell me you knew Turgenev? So this is your secret society, all present and accounted for? Do stop all this hiding about in corners, please; I assure you, old man, it's silly."

Pushchin gave an uneasy laugh, shrugged his shoulders and changed the subject.

"Looking at him," Pushchin wrote, "I again thought: Shouldn't I ask him to join us? It was up to him to accept or decline. But then another question came immediately into my mind: Here were his closest friends, who were also the most high-ranking members of our association; why had no one else thought of him? So the idea that frightened me had stopped them too: His inclinations were known to all, but he was not felt to be completely trustworthy."

Pushchin and his friends admired Pushkin, but they deplored his frivolity. He, a conspirator? Why, with two words blurted out in public or three brilliant lines scribbled on a tablecloth, he would have compromised the most carefully planned revolution in the world. Pushkin was not born to fight in the ranks. He must be allowed to act alone, away from the main body of troops, as a rooftop sniper. After all, he really was a noisy devil.

The conspirators did not want him? Never mind. Pushkin now set out to demolish the government with his own weapons; but whether he did so instinctively or in emulation of his friends one cannot say. These recent events infuriated him; Alexander I, Arakcheev, ministers, civil servants—anyone in any way connected with the government—deserved to be soundly thrashed. On October 27, 1819, he wrote to his friend Mansurov: "Tell me about the military colonies. I need to know everything about them. For I love you, and I hate despotism." How could

Karamzin go on singing the praises of autocracy? Pushkin had loved and admired Karamzin. Well, he had been wrong.

"One day," he wrote, "he [Karamzin] began to rehearse his pet paradoxes to me. I did my best to contradict him. I said, 'So you prefer slavery to freedom?' Then he grew angry and called me a calumniator. Respecting the wrath of a noble soul, I made no reply. We changed the subject. I got up to go. Karamzin was uncomfortable. As I was taking my leave, he rebuked me, but weakly, as though excusing himself. . . . Another time, when he was putting on his decorations to go to Pavlovsk, he scowled at me and then burst out laughing; I too began to laugh."

Another misunderstanding between the poet and the historian gave rise to an epigram, about which Pushkin used to say, "One of the best epigrams in Russian is attributed to me; but it was not the finest thing I ever did." It dates from 1818:

In his elegant, simply told history
He explains to us most objectively
How autocracy necessarily came about
And all the good effects of the knout.

The same year, Pushkin attacked the archimandrite Photius, Arakcheev's friend and colleague, and the darling of all the lady mystics of St. Petersburg:

Part fanatic, part pickpocket,
The only spiritual weapons he waves
Are opprobrium and cross, sword and knout.

Countess Orlov adored Photius and gave large sums of money to the monastery over which the holy man presided. For her, it was a unique mark of grace to be allowed to remove his boots and kiss his feet. She called herself Photius' "spiritual daughter," but there were many, and Pushkin foremost among them, who maintained that her relations with the archimandrite were of a more earthly nature. Pushkin wrote:

This so pious woman
Has sold her soul to God,
And her sinner's skin
To archimandrite Photius.

He also wrote, in his *Conversation Between Archimandrite Photius and Countess Orlov:*

"Now hear what I proclaim:
In body I am a eunuch, but in soul a man."
"Just what is it, then, you're doing to me?"
"Transforming your body into soul."

Golitsyn, the Minister of Education, was a notorious pederast; Pushkin is said to have written an epigram about him ending with the lines:

You must attack him from behind,
For that is his weaker side. . . .[2]

Finally, he boldly anathematized the abhorred Arakcheev, grand master of the military colonies, in a few lines which have since become famous:

Tyrant of all the Russias,
Headsman of all the governors,
He's master of the council,
Brother and friend of the tsar.
Full of wrath and lust for revenge,
Witless, heartless, ignoble;
At bottom, what is this underling
They call "faithful but not corrupt"?
At best, a common foot soldier.

These scathing compositions quickly made the rounds of the capital's youth. Before long, any lively and aggressive political epigram was being attributed to Pushkin. "Every offensive remark," he said, "every foul line that is written, is laid at my doorstep."[3] His witty sayings sped from drawing room to drawing room; he had already won countless friends and a few well-placed enemies. One contemporary wrote: "Not only did everyone know of all his unpublished poems—*The Village,* the verse on Arakcheev, the address to Chaadaev, and many more—but there was virtually not one half-literate cornet or ensign in the entire army who could not recite them from memory."[4]

Pushchin said the same: "In those days everybody was secretly passing his poems around, copying and reciting them; there were *The Village, Ode to Liberty, Hurrah! He's Back in Russia Again,* and other little pieces of the sort. There was no one who did not know them all by heart."

The three revolutionary poems cited by Pushchin deserve special mention: from *Ode to Liberty,* written in 1817, to *The Village* (1819), they are Pushkin's "liberal" bequest, covering this first phase of his career.

In his memoirs Viegel tells how the *Ode to Liberty* was written at the home of the Turgenev brothers, who lived across from the sinister Michael Palace, where Paul I was murdered. "Someone in the group," Viegel wrote, "was looking out the window at the deserted palace, doomed to oblivion, and asked Pushkin to write something on the theme. Pushkin had inherited Arab blood from his mother, and in his agility and the swiftness of his movements was very like the Negroes and other African peoples. With his customary ease, he leaped onto the big table that stood before the window, lay full length on the top, seized a pen and paper, and, laughing all the time, began to write. When his poem was finished, he showed it to those present and, God alone knows why, entitled it *Ode to Liberty*." In this improvisation Pushkin wrote:

I will sing of Liberty
And scourge the evil that sits on thrones. . . .
Shudder, pupils of blind fortune,
Tyrants of the world;
And you, courage, hear me. . . .
Rise up, dull slaves!
It was law, not nature, tyrants,
Put the crown upon your head;
You may be over the people,
But the law is over you.

Further on, Pushkin alluded to the tragic death of Louis XVI, overrun by his subjects. Then he turned to Paul I, assassinated in the Michael Palace with the foreknowledge and assistance of the reigning tsar, his son Alexander the Liberator:

Here come the furtive assassins,
Decked out in garter and star,
They are drunk with rage and wine,
Insolence and ambition.
The disloyal watchman is dumb,
Soundless, the drawbridge drops,
The hand of a mercenary traitor
Opens the doors of night.
Oh shame, oh terror of History!
Like wild beasts the janissaries
Charge, and their blows rain down;
The crowned monster sinks. . . .
And now know this, O kings:
Neither reward nor punishment
Nor altar nor prison bars
Can protect you any more;
If you will be first to bow your heads
To the certain force of the laws,
Then peace and liberty
Will defend your thrones.

In *Hurrah! He's Back in Russia Again,* Pushkin openly mocked Alexander's Warsaw speech, in which he promised a liberal constitution, not only to good little Poland, but to boorish Russia as well. The tsar is returning from his voyage and exclaims, upon entering an isba:

Know, O peoples of Russia,
What no one does not know:
I have ordered new uniforms
From Prussia and from Austria.
I am fat, well fed, in very good health. . . .

Standing over the cradle being rocked by Marya the peasant woman, the potentate declares that he is going to give his subjects liberty and equality:

At these words, the baby wriggles
Vigorously in his cradle:
"Can I believe? Is it possible?
Could it perhaps be true?"
His mother says, "Close your sweet eyes,
For our good tsar
Has finished his fairy tale. . . ."

In another poem, *The Village*, Pushkin adopted a fiercer tone to criticize the institution of serfdom and the cruelty of landowners:

Head down, docile under the pursuing lash,
The gaunt old serf struggles down the furrows
Of some implacable master.
Not daring to dream any more, or hope for them:
His little girls, growing up
To feed the lust of some vice-sodden old monster. . . .
Oh, if my voice could move humans!
Why this fire, burning vainly in my chest,
If I have not the dread gift of prophecy?
Shall I see, O my friends, the people freed,
Serfdom abolished by the hand of the tsar,
And on the soil of pure independence,
Will the sweeping dawn burst at last?

These "forbidden" poems give an exact idea of Pushkinian liberalism. Was he an intractable like the poet Rylyev, for whom there could be no compromise between tyrant and slave, tsar and subject? Rylyev and the other dyed-in-the-wool revolutionaries argued that the monarchy must be overthrown with violence and bloodshed, and that they must prepare for the coming of the people-king. Pushkin, on the other hand, held that the monarchy should be preserved, so long as it granted people freedom of thought and equality before the law. In his *Ode to Liberty* he predicted a future of peace and prosperity for the monarchs, if they could "bow their heads to the certain force of the laws." Let the kings respect legality, and their reign would be blessed. Let the kings be good kings, and they would not be asked to step down. In *The Village*, Pushkin wanted to see "serfdom abolished *by the hand of the tsar*"—the same idea as in *Ode to Liberty*. The poet is not calling for a bloody revolution, he only wants a little understanding on both sides. Freedom must be given to the people by the tsar, not wrested from the tsar by the people. Everything could be all right, he was saying, but people would have to co-operate.†

† This was so true that when Alexander I read *The Village* he asked General Vasilchikov to thank Pushkin for the sentiments expressed in the poem.

Government oppression was so intense at that time, however, and police surveillance so relentless, that every one of Pushkin's poems was hailed as a revolutionary declaration of dazzling boldness and novelty. Turgenev did not dare to send Pushkin's *Ode to Liberty* to his friend Vyazemsky, who was in Warsaw. "I'm afraid to send it," he wrote, "both for you and for him. The walls can have eyes, and even ears."

Vyazemsky wrote back: "Do send me Pushkin's poem; what a fraidy-cat you are! I have never been intimidated by anything or anyone. . . ."

A contemporary[5] related the following incident, which took place in a student residence hall around 1820: "One day a strange-looking fellow, lame and whey-faced, with his hair all disheveled, came to the door of No. 10. Today he would automatically be classed as a nihilist; in those days he was a perfect specimen of a liberal. 'Have you read Pushkin's *Ode to Liberty*?' he said. 'No? Well, in my opinion, it's a lot of custard. For me the revolution has got to be a real revolution, like the French one; bring on the guillotine!' Suddenly Katonov leaped off his bed, grabbed a chair and plunked it down bang! in the middle of the room. 'Listen, you scum!' he roared, 'who here dares to speak ill of Pushkin? Listen, I tell you!' And, rattling his chair, rolling his eyes, and gnashing his teeth, he shouted at the top of his lungs:

'I hate you, and I hate your throne. . . .'"

"Pushkin's writings," the author continued, "reached the people; any doorman with a smattering of learning knew them, and all the intellectual serfs—the architects, painters, and actors whom the gentry sent up to town to study, and who went back, still slaves, to their masters, in a state of exacerbated hatred. His poems were read in the garrisons too, by the common soldiers."

What was the official fame of a Karamzin or a Zhukovsky beside the wild enthusiasm which Pushkin aroused among students, freethinking officers and little shopkeepers and soldiers? He was the first poet to be elected by his readers. He was the first literary idol of the country. He was twenty years old.

4. Calumny

Pushkin's friends were worried by his notoriety; it was as though the poet were openly seeking scandal, as though he positively desired and were feverishly preparing for a catastrophe. With every fresh epigram and every new jest, he made himself more dangerously conspicuous to the authorities. His enemies were joining forces against him, and they were powerful, and their memories were long.

Pushchin relates that upon meeting the poet's father on the Nevsky Prospect one day, he went up and asked him the news of his son. Sergey Lvovich seemed tired and anxious. At length he said, "I'm spending the best part of my time these days wearing myself out trying to get my dear son out of trouble. No doubt you haven't heard his latest escapade?"

Pushkin was bounding from one escapade to another. After two and a half years of his futile existence in St. Petersburg, he was perishing with boredom and disgust. The social whirl, balls, intrigues, binges, affairs with overwilling girls—they all nauseated him. Something was lacking. His destiny was elsewhere. To shake off his inertia, he struck out left and right, ran every risk, challenged fate to single combat. His poems reflected this desperate satiety:

I am not the same, and golden hours,
Wild fire of youth, speed and mischief,
Love of poetry, love of independence,
All go by as in a misty dream.
So it is that sometimes, behind the festive glasses,
You will find me pensive and with lowered head,
And then you will understand the torment that gnaws at me. . . .[1]

In March 1820 he wrote to his friend Count Vyazemsky: "St. Petersburg is stifling, for a poet. I am hungry for new horizons. . . . My letter is boring because now that I have become a historical figure in St. Petersburg intrigue, I have grown dull myself, and am aging weekly, hourly."

Then began a pitched battle between the St. Petersburg elite and the disorderly little poet who had dared to revile it. There were whisperings, plottings and strange alliances going on all around him. It was suddenly rumored in the drawing rooms that Pushkin had been summoned to the secret department and whipped for his political poems. When a sympathetic soul[2] carried this tale back to Pushkin, he became literally insane with shame and rage. He was too vain to deal with such an insult by ignoring it. He wanted revenge. But against whom? Of whom should he demand justice? In his frenzy he exaggerated the accusation, imagining himself dishonored, lost, the laughingstock of the whole world. He, Pushkin! He, the loftiest, bravest, most pure of poets!

There was only one recourse: He would write to the emperor. A draft of a letter to Emperor Alexander I, written but never posted, has been found among the poet's papers. It was written in French, and it said: "I was twenty years old in 1820. . . . Thoughtless words, satirical poems (gave me much publicity . . . spread through the public). It was rumored that I had been summoned and w. in the s. ch.* I was the last to hear this tale, which was being told everywhere; I saw myself flouted (degraded) in public opinion, I lost heart; I fought back, I was twenty years old. I debated whether I should kill myself or murder Yo.† If the former, I would only confirm the rumor that dishonored me; if the latter, I would have no revenge because there had been no offense; I would be committing a crime, sacrificing to public opinion—which I despised —a man on whom everything depended and . . . for whom I felt an involuntary admiration. These thoughts decided me. Those were my thoughts. I confided them to a friend who agreed with me in every respect. He advised me to demand justice from the authorities. I saw the futility of that. I resolved to fill my speech and writing with so much indignation and vainglory that the authorities would finally be compelled to treat me as a criminal: I hoped to be sent to Siberia or the fortress for rehabilitation. . . ."

Siberia or the fortress. The only salvation he could conceive was in extremity. He wanted to see break that storm whose first rumblings he heard throbbing around him. He wanted to die and be born again. He was like a madman, calling the curse of the government down upon his head. He began telling everybody how he admired Karl Sand, who had assassinated the author-spy Kotzebue.

At the theater, in the middle of a performance, he announced, "This is the least dangerous time of year, for the ice is going down the Neva!" —meaning that people could act without fear of imprisonment, since the Sts. Peter and Paul Fortress, where political offenders were incarcerated, was on the far side of the river. Also, shortly after the assassination of the

* Whipped in the secret chancellery.
† Your Majesty.

Duc de Berry by Louvel, Pushkin, from his orchestra seat, handed round to his neighbors a portrait of the murderer bearing the inscription: "A lesson to kings." Again, when the tsar narrowly escaped being attacked by a young bear prowling in the Tsarskoye Selo gardens, Pushkin publicly exclaimed: "At last the man has been found,‡ but even then it was only a baby bear!"

Emperor Alexander I was informed of all the pranks and subversive verses perpetrated by Pushkin. He must have found the *Ode to Liberty* particularly offensive, with its allusion to his father's assassination in the gloomy Michael Palace. The monarch's irritation was intensified by Pushkin's attacks upon Arakcheev and other members of the government; and Arakcheev was said to have requested that some special punishment be devised for the poet.

Meanwhile, a man named Vogel, an agent of the secret police, went to Pushkin's home and offered his valet Nikita fifty rubles for his master's manuscripts. Nikita refused, and Pushkin, alerted, quickly burned his papers.

The next morning he was summoned to appear before Miloradovich, the military governor of St. Petersburg. On his way, he met the poet F. N. Glinka, then employed in General Miloradovich's offices. Pushkin was pale, nervous, preoccupied; in a few words he told Glinka of the attempted seizure of his papers and his order to go immediately to the military governor. What should he do?

"Go straight to Miloradovich," Glinka told him; "have no fears, don't worry about anything. He is no poet, but in his heart and in his chivalrous posing there is much of the poet's romanticism. People don't understand him. Go and open yourself fully to his noble heart, he will not betray your trust."

Pushkin followed Glinka's advice and went on to the governor's office.

"Three hours later," Glinka wrote in his *Recollections*, "I went to see Miloradovich myself on business. He was lying on his green divan, all wrapped in precious shawls; when he saw me he cried, 'Guess what, dear chap, Pushkin has just been to see me. I was ordered to arrest him and seize all his papers, but I thought it would be more elegant to invite him here and ask him in person to hand over his manuscripts. So he arrived, very calm, with a smile on his face, and when I mentioned the papers he replied, "Count, my poems have all been burned, so you will find nothing in my home. But if you like, I have them *here* (touching his finger to his forehead), and if you will send for some paper I shall write down everything I have composed (except what has been printed, of

‡ Meaning: who dares to attack the tsar.

course), and I will tell you which verses are mine and which are being circulated under my name." The paper was brought. Pushkin sat down and wrote and wrote . . . a whole notebook full. There it is (he pointed to the table by the window), behold. . . . Tomorrow I shall take it to the tsar. Do you know, Pushkin utterly charmed me by his nobility of speech and demeanor?'*

"The next day," Glinka continued, "I contrived to go to Miloradovich early, and was waiting for him when he returned from his audience with the emperor. His first words upon entering were, 'Well, that's that; the Pushkin affair is settled.' After taking off his dress uniform, he went on: 'I went into the emperor's room with my treasure, handed it to him, and said, "Here are all the poems that are being circulated, but it would be better, Sire, if you did not read them." The emperor smiled at my solicitude. Then I told him what had transpired. He listened attentively and then asked, "And what have you done with the author?" "I? Why, I announced Your Majesty's pardon to him." At these words, I thought the emperor seemed somewhat annoyed. After a moment of silence he spoke sharply: "Wasn't that a little premature of you?" Then he thought a while and added, "Well, since that's the way it is, we'll handle the matter differently. Let Pushkin be sent away, at our expense; let him go to the South, give him some suitable occupation and every mark of consideration." And that's how it was settled.'"

During the forty-eight hours pending the announcement of the imperial decision, Pushkin's friends were in a state of collective panic. There were rumors that he would be sent to Siberia. Pushkin's father sat and sobbed. Zhukovsky made the rounds of his official connections. Chaadaev besieged General Vasilchikov. Gnedich tackled Olenin, president of the Academy. Even Karamzin, against his better judgment, agreed to intercede on his behalf with the empress.

Karamzin valued Pushkin's talent but felt no pity or sympathy for him. He helped to rescue him, but disdainfully, as his letters show:

"Around the poet Pushkin," he wrote on April 19, 1820, "has gathered, if not a huge storm cloud, at least one small but rather threatening gray cloud. Under the flag of liberalism, he has written and circulated some poems on liberty, epigrams against members of the government, etc. . . . The police have been informed. . . . There is great apprehension about the outcome of the affair. Having long since tried every means I know of to subdue this daredevil, I had already abandoned the wretch to his fate and to Nemesis. Out of compassion for his talent, however, I agreed to intercede personally on his behalf, but only after

* It may be noted in passing that Pushkin omitted the epigram on Arakcheev.

extracting a promise from him that he would settle down at last. I do not know how it will end."

Later he added: "For several days Pushkin lived in a highly unpoetical state of terror on account of his poems on liberty and a few epigrams. . . . It would take too long to relate all the details, but if after this warning Pushkin does not mend his ways, he will be a devil before he ever goes to hell."

Lastly: "I made representations on his behalf, out of compassion for his talent and his youth. Who knows, he may reform. He promised me not to write anything against the government for two years."

Karamzin was fond of showing guests the place in his study that had been "watered by Pushkin's tears."

The supreme appeal was made by Engelhardt, the headmaster of the Tsarskoye Selo school, and by Capo d'Istria, who was Pushkin's superior at the ministry. Meeting Engelhardt in the gardens at Tsarskoye Selo, the emperor said:

"Engelhardt, Pushkin must be sent to Siberia; he is inundating all Russia with his subversive poems, all the young people know them by heart. I admire him for the courage he displayed with Miloradovich, but that doesn't really solve the problem."

"It will be done as you decide, Sire," the headmaster replied, "but permit me to say one word in favor of my former pupil: The extraordinary talent that is maturing within him merits consideration. Pushkin is already the pearl of our literature, and there is much to hope for in the future. Exile could have a very bad effect on the impassioned nature of this young man. I think he will be more readily swayed by Your Majesty's indulgence."[3]

Alexander I liked to imagine himself a man of enlightened generosity. "With Pushkin, he played the tsar," in the words of Turgenev.

By the emperor's order, therefore, undersecretary Pushkin was not expelled from St. Petersburg, but "transferred" to Yekaterinoslav in southern Russia, to the offices of General Insov, administrator of the southern colonies. Pushkin's friends were overjoyed: "The Pushkin affair has had a happy ending," Turgenev wrote. The poet's father composed a letter to Zhukovsky: "Dear Basil Andreyevich, I know how much I owe to you, Nicholas Mikhailovich [Karamzin], Turgenev, and the others. I shall never be able to repay you, but your memory will certainly be the last to visit my mind upon my deathbed. I am overwhelmed, dear friend, deeply overwhelmed; the tears prevent me from continuing. . . . As for Count Miloradovich, I don't know whether to throw myself at his feet or into his arms the next time I see him."

Pushkin appears to have seen his exile as deliverance. His fatigue and moral indigestion, his despair and shame would end with his residence in the capital. He was not being driven out, he was escaping. He was not going to die, he was about to begin to live. Anything would be better than this city of granite and fog, populated by uniforms, traversed by hostile faces, buzzing with flattery and deceit. Anything would be better than this organized idleness, these drawing-room conspiracies, these orgies and gamblers' quarrels, this agitation, and all these visits, and all these meetings, and all this falseness.

On May 6, 1820, Pushkin left St. Petersburg, with a sum of a thousand assignation rubles to cover his traveling expenses and a letter to General Insov from the foreign ministry. This document, which had been seen by Alexander I, was a sort of introduction, and its charitable and moderate tone were all to the credit of its author.[4] The "recommendation" was drafted in French:

"Mr. Alexander Pushkin, former pupil of the Tsarskoye Selo school and latterly attached to the ministry for foreign affairs, will have the honor of handing this note to Your Excellency. Its object is to place this young man under your tutelage and to ask you to accord him your benevolent protection.

"Permit me to give you some particulars of Mr. Pushkin:

"Beset with sorrows and troubles throughout his early childhood, young Pushkin left home without regret. His heart, devoid of filial affection, could know no passion but that of independence. As a pupil he soon showed proof of remarkable endowment. He made rapid progress at school, his mind was widely admired, but his character seems to have escaped the teachers' vigilance.

"When he made his entrance into society, his strength lay in his fiery imagination and his weakness in a total absence of those inner feelings which serve as principles until such time as experience has given us a true education.

"There are no depths to which this unfortunate young man has not sunk, just as there are no heights to which he cannot ascend by virtue of the transcendent superiority of his ability.

"He owes to his writings a certain notoriety, some very serious errors, and some very respectable friends, who will open the path to salvation for him, if it is not too late and if he will but resolve to follow it.

"A few short poems and, in particular, an ode to liberty, brought Mr. Pushkin to the attention of the government.

"Together with some great qualities of composition and style, the latter poem displays dangerous principles acquired in the school of the day, or, it were better called, in that system of anarchy which bad faith calls the system of human rights and the freedom and independence of peoples.

"However, MM. Karamzin and Zhukovsky, having learned of the

dangers to which the young poet had exposed himself, hastened to counsel him, brought him to recognize the error of his ways, and prevailed upon him to make a solemn undertaking that he would abjure them forever.

"Mr. Pushkin seems to have repented—if, that is, his tears and protestations are to be believed.

"His protectors, moreover, believe he is sincere, and that by removing him from St. Petersburg for a time, giving him some work to do, and putting good examples before him, he may yet become an excellent servant of the state, or, at least, a man of letters of the highest distinction.

"It is in accordance with their wishes that the emperor has authorized me to give young Pushkin a leave of absence and recommend him to you. He will be attached to you personally, and will work in your division as supernumerary. His fate depends upon the effects of your good counsel.

"Be good enough, therefore, to give him freely of it. Enlighten his inexperience by telling him that excellence of the mind is almost always but poor riches unless it be accompanied by qualities of heart, and there have been too many instances of men gifted with fine minds who have not sought protection in religion and morality against dangerous excesses, thereby bringing only unhappiness upon themselves and their fellow citizens.

"Mr. Pushkin seems to desire a career in the diplomatic service, and began in the foreign ministry here. I could wish for nothing better than to keep him, but he will not be allowed this favor except on your recommendation and at such time as you deem he has deserved it.

"You were not, I know, expecting such a commission, and if it is a troublesome one, you have only to blame the high and justified opinion in which you are held."

5. Ruslan and Ludmila

The garrulous and undisciplined young man being removed from the capital by the emperor's will was not only the author of a few epigrams and "underground" revolutionary poems: On March 26, 1820, six weeks before Pushkin left for southern Russia, Zhukovsky presented him with a dedicated portrait, which has been preserved in the national Archives. It is a lithograph, showing Zhukovsky with nose inclined and pensive eye, his chin burrowing into a wide turndown collar. Beneath the picture are four lines, written in a small, swift and exquisite hand: "To the conquering pupil from the conquered master, in memory of the notable day on which he completed his poem *Ruslan and Ludmila*, 1820, March 26, Holy Friday."

Pushkin had begun *Ruslan and Ludmila* in 1817, when he was still at school. He continued it through all the distractions and vexations of his life in Petersburg. He wrote between orgies, between exhaustions, or when he was ill. The poem came in pieces, corresponding to his moments of enforced leisure. And Pushkin's friends fretted and fumed at his negligence. On December 18, 1818, A. I. Turgenev wrote: "He hardly has time to write. But in spite of his dissipations, he is completing the fourth stanza of his poem. Two or three more . . . will see it finished. His first illness has been the first midwife to his poem."

February 12, 1819: "Pushkin is sick in bed. . . . Now he'll have to go back to his poem."

February 22, 1819: "Venus has harnessed Pushkin to bed and his poem."

August 17, 1819: "Pushkin is not here; he has retired to the country for the summer to rest from his Parnassian labors. His poem is almost entirely in his head. There may be a few passages on paper, but I doubt he could read us any excerpts from them."

August 19, 1819: "Pushkin has come back from the country, bringing a shaven head and the sixth stanza of his poem."

Pushkin would read sections of the poem at Zhukovsky's Saturday gatherings, at the Shakovskoys', or in the homes of other friends. A few passages were published in the *Neva Observer* and *Son of the Fatherland*. But the complete poem did not appear in print until July 1820.

Ruslan and Ludmila is a long, regular poem in six stanzas, with envoi, prologue and epilogue:

It is a tale of olden days,
A story from the depths of time.
Surrounded by his stalwart sons
And all his friends, in the banquet hall,
Vladimir-the-Sun is feasting.
He is marrying his youngest girl
To the intrepid Prince Ruslan. . . .

This legendary prince and princess have, of course, a legendary destiny. No sooner have the newlyweds withdrawn to their bedchamber and the bride let fall her veils, when

Thunder, lightning, all is fog;
The lamp grows dim, the smoke curls up.
Everything is dark, and trembles.

Chernomor the magician, "old abductor of beautiful women," has kidnapped Ludmila and hidden her in an inaccessible castle. Ruslan and three of his rivals saddle their steeds and set off in search of her, for Ludmila's father has promised to give his daughter's hand finally and irrevocably to the one who brings her back safe and sound. There follows a wild ride across the steppe. The heroes part at the crossroads. Ruslan meets an old sage who tells him where the unfortunate princess is imprisoned. Then he is attacked by Rogdai, a rival suitor. Adventures follow thick and fast. Meanwhile, deep within an oriental palace of gold, sapphire and brocade, the fair Ludmila weeps and calls for Ruslan day and night. When Chernomor, a horrible, glowering dwarf, bearded and humpbacked, enters her chamber and tries to caress her, she struggles, manages to seize hold of his magic hat and promptly becomes invisible. A rustle in the grass, the swing of a snagged branch, the plash of water caught and emptied by some aerial hand—by these alone can her presence be divined.

While Ludmila is thus eluding her abductor's clutches, and Chernomor is howling his lungs out and threatening his black-faced servants, Ruslan is still on the road. Having slain Rogdai, he comes to a broad valley strewn with yellowed bones:

He sees an ancient battlefield,
Open to the sky; here and there
Lie yellowed bones; on the hills
Breastplates sleep, and quivers,

Harnesses and shields all of rust;
A skeleton with sword in hand;
The grass nibbles a hairy helmet
Where rot the remains of a skull;
The hide of a paladin stretches out
Beside his stricken steed;
Arrows and lances bristle
Over the heavy, cloyed land,
Enlaced by the tranquil ivy. . . .
Nothing troubles the silence now
In this desert place; and the sun,
Stopped in an empty sky,
Illuminates a land of death.

Farther on, Ruslan comes to a halt in front of a hillock, which turns out to be the head of a giant, rooted for centuries in the earth.

An enormous living head
With sleeping eyelids
Snores beneath a high-plumed helm.
And the plumes, in the dark sky,
Weave like shadows.

To awaken the monster, Ruslan tickles his nostrils with his lance:

The head contracts and yawns,
Opens its eyes, and sneezes. . . .
A gust of wind, the steppe shudders,
Dust flies up, and owls flap off
From lashes, brows, mustache.

The reanimated head blows up a hurricane of wind and saliva to frighten the knight, but Ruslan pins his tongue to the ground with his lance. The vanquished head then admits that it is in the service of Chernomor. It is custodian of the miraculous sword which alone can cut off the magician's beard—and in that beard lies all the sorcerer's power. Clean-shaven, he will be nothing but a dwarf, helpless and dumb. Ruslan seizes the sword and continues on his way. One of his rivals is dead. The second has gone home. The third has been enchanted by a group of maidens who live in a dream castle, adepts of the art of love.

Days pass, the fields turn yellow,
Leaves fall in the woods,
The whistling winds of autumn
Hide the birds' lament.
A dense and heavy mist
Wreathes the barren hills.
Winter draws near . . . but Ruslan
Valiantly keeps his road
To the great north; and each day
New obstacles confront him.

He fights another knight,
A sorcerer, a giant.
He sees, as in a dream,
In a bath of milky fog,
The sea sprites swaying
On branches in the moonlight. . . .
A subtle smile upon their lips,
Silently they call him.

At last Ruslan reaches the gates of the palace in which his beloved is held captive. Spreading his awesome beard, the dwarf Chernomor rises into the air, falls upon the knight and stuns him with a blow of his club. Ruslan ripostes. The battle begins. His opponent stumbles, the prince grabs him by the beard, but with a desperate effort, the magician takes flight, carrying Ruslan along in his hairy wake.

The knight will not let go. The dwarf begins to tire, whines, begs for mercy, "amazed by the Russian strength." At last he alights. With one slice, Ruslan amputates his beard and rolls the trophy around his helmet. Then he enters the palace, the guards fleeing at his approach. He finds Ludmila. But she has fallen into a deep sleep and nothing seems able to arouse her from her enchantment. Ruslan takes her up in his arms and carries her away from the castle. His tribulations are not yet at an end, however. On his way home, he unwisely dozes off. One of his rivals, the traitor Pharlaf (the one who had gone home), surprises him lying by the side of his beloved, gives him three thrusts of his sword, sweeps up Ludmila and bears the sleeping beauty back to her father Vladimir-the-Sun. But even at Kiev, Ludmila refuses to wake, and Vladimir-the-Sun despairs. To make matters worse, the Pechenegs arrive and besiege the city. The Russians cannot hold out long against their foe's superior numbers. But Ruslan, left for dead by Pharlaf, has been found and nursed by the old sage he met at the beginning of his travels. His wounds heal and he rides to the rescue. At dawn, the citizens of Kiev hear anguished screams from the enemy tents:

They run to the ramparts and there they see
In the midst of the enemy troops
A splendid warrior on his horse.
Armed in tongues of flame,
He falls like a thunderclap, strikes, cuts,
And blows on his powerful horn.

In the twinkling of an eye Ruslan has decimated the infidel hordes, confounded the traitor Pharlaf, awakened Ludmila with a sacred ring and received the blessing of the aged Vladimir.

The moment it was published, this phantasmagoria unleashed the passions of the Russian public and critics. Never before had the printed word provoked such excitement and such wrath. It was as though some essential message had dropped from the sky. One had to take sides, be for or against. The author had gone into exile, but he had left a Roman candle behind him.

"It is impossible to find anything with which to compare the enthusiasm and indignation aroused by Pushkin's first poem," wrote the critic Belinsky. "Few works of great genius have caused as much furor as this poem, which could hardly be more juvenile or more lacking in that quality. The partisans of the avant-garde group treated it as a colossus, and glorified Pushkin for years with the curious title of 'bard of *Ruslan and Ludmila.*' Those in the other camp, the blind admirers of antiquity, flew into a tantrum when the poem came out, seeing in it everything that was not there, including atheism, and overlooking everything that was; that is: some fine lines, intelligence, an aesthetic sense, and occasional glimmers of true poetry."

And so it was: The entire army of conservative writers rose against Pushkin in a body. The critic of the *Neva Observer*[1] decried the poet's propensity for triviality: "The object of poetry," wrote this grave and well-informed man, "is beauty. It is only when talent sings of beauty that it deserves sincere homage and distinction. . . . The poetic beauties of *Ruslan and Ludmila* are marred by vulgar comparisons, obnoxious enchantments, voluptuous images, and expressions offensive to good taste." Further, "I do not care to argue the point whether it [*Ruslan and Ludmila*] may be called a poem; these days any tale, or nearly, that is written in a tone slightly higher than that of ordinary conversation is called a poem, whereas the name used to be given to works recounting heroic deeds of religion or virtue, or events upon which the fate of kingdoms hung."

These irritated mutterings were as an April shower in comparison with the vitriolic diatribe of the *European Herald* (or *Messenger*),[2] whose critic, a partisan of the conservative group, was horrified by the "vulgarity" of this new school which boldly disinterred and published old folk legends hardly fit to be told to children. The tone is typical of the views of "classical" authors of the day. The article says, *inter alia:*

"Now I would ask you to turn your attention to an object which, like Camoëns' Stormy Cape, has risen from the ocean depths and swum into the Russian literary sea. Here is the thing: As you know, our ancestors left us a meager literary heritage, a few tales and folk songs in all. What can be said of them? Since we preserve old coins, however ugly they may be, should we not also assiduously preserve these ruins of our ancestral literature? To be sure. You see that I am not opposed to research and the study of Russian tales and songs; but when I learn that our men of letters are becoming interested in these old songs for a very different purpose, are proclaiming their glory, their power, their beauty and their richness—no, thank you very much! . . .

"Cast an eye, I pray you, upon Nos. 15 and 16 of the *Son of the Fatherland,* in which an unknown poet has published passages of his poem *Ruslan and Ludmila.* I cannot judge the worth of the whole, but the excerpts I have read would try anyone's patience.

"For greater precision, or in order to demonstrate more effectively all the beauties of our ancient style, the poet adopts the expressions of the taleteller Yeruslan, as, for example:

"Do you laugh at me?
My beard will choke you!

"What do you think of that? Or:

"Circling the head, he halts
Before the nose, draws his lance
And tickles its nostrils.* . . .

"A tableau worthy of Kirsha Danilov, no?

"Further on, the head sneezes, and the echo also sneezes.† In another passage, the knight strikes its cheek with his heavy gauntlet.

"But spare me a recital of the whole, and allow me to ask you one question: If some bearded individual in peasant's coat and bast sandals should enter the Moscow Assembly of Nobility (I am imagining what is manifestly impossible) and begin to bellow, 'What's new, mates?' do you think such a jokester would be admired? For the love of God, let an old man tell the public through the pages of this review that it should close its eyes to such aberrations whenever they occur. Why allow these vulgar farces of old to be served up to you again? This is a low, common joke, unacceptable to the aesthetic sense of educated people, detestable, and neither funny nor entertaining. Dixi."

Mérimée, on the other hand, was delighted by the revival of the Slavic legends that so infuriated the Aristarchus of the *Herald.* He wrote: "To my mind, the outstanding feature of *Ruslan and Ludmila* is that it attempts to find in Russian folklore a less outworn and overwritten tradition than that of Greek mythology—outside which, in 1820, there was no salvation. His experiment was almost foolhardy, given the degree of intolerance of the 'classicals' of the day. He was trying to get off the beaten path. He lived in a world of aristocrats, and he wanted to penetrate the intimate, everyday world of the peasant."

* Many of the more circumspect readers seem to have found this detail objectionable. One French translator of *Ruslan and Ludmila* simply preferred to omit the passage.

† The same translator, presumably considering it unseemly to sneeze in a poem, left out this line as well.

Today we are left equally at a loss by the exaggeration on both sides. The critic of the *European Herald,* who damned Pushkin for resurrecting the old Russian legends, and Prosper Mérimée, who revered him for returning to the true source of poetry, were equally, totally and naïvely mistaken. Pushkin's poem did not create a new genre: Many of his contemporaries had already worked the same vein. The magician Chernomor, for example, was lifted bodily from Karamzin's *Elia of Murom,* Ludmila's abduction recalls the opening of various Russian tales previously refurbished by poets of the day,‡ Zhukovsky wrote of a castle inhabited by fair maidens, and the enchanted hat that confers invisibility upon Ludmila belongs in the repertory of legends edited in the eighteenth century.

As yet, Pushkin's knowledge of Russian folklore was restricted to the more or less faithful printed versifications current in his day. He consulted books, not oral tradition; he worked from secondary sources. The vocabulary of *Ruslan and Ludmila,* too, is very remote from the charming and archaic language of old Russian legend, and in general manner the work is reminiscent of Voltaire's *Pucelle,* Ariosto's *Orlando Furioso* or the fantasies of Hamilton.

As it stands, then, Pushkin's poem is a masquerade for high-brows, rather than a historical reconstruction: a fancy-dress ball, where boyars in false beards sip champagne as they chat with delicate young ladies in beribboned diadems. Beneath their old-fashioned costumes, Pushkin's characters have nineteenth-century souls, and the author himself speaks with a nineteenth-century voice. He does not put himself on the intellectual and emotional level of his prince and princess, he doesn't really believe their story; he merely tells it, raising a skeptical eyebrow and occasionally even poking fun at them. In a word, he is not sincere. For example, after describing the distress of the abducted Ludmila, he has the girl say:

I do not need your tents,
Your songs and feasts;
Fasting and deaf,
I shall perish in your gardens.
She spoke—and sat down to eat.*

Another bit of irony: Ludmila refuses to look into the mirror brought by Chernomor's servants. Here, Pushkin breaks off his narrative to observe, as a careful student of the French "galant" poets:

When an unhappy woman,
Flaunting custom and reason,

‡ Cf. also similar episodes in Wieland's *Oberon* and Ariosto's *Orlando Furioso.*

* The same French translator, decidedly anxious to restore Pushkin to respectability, has also omitted this line.

Fails to gratify the glass
With one swift, tear-dimmed glance,
Then she must be truly sad.

Elsewhere we read how Chernomor,

In fine fettle again, wishes to lay
At the feet of his captive virgin
His heart, his troth, and his mustache.†

Then, there is the opening of the fourth stanza:

Every morning when I wake,
I bless the Lord with all my heart
For having, in this modern day,
Created fewer sorcerers.

One would like to give more examples of these wry asides punctuating the pseudo folk tale background. Pushkin seems to be wavering between the naïveté of the Russian fairy tale and the bantering tone of Voltaire and Hamilton. Whenever he launches—with all due conviction—into some miraculous report, we may be sure he will contrive to shatter the illusion a few lines later with a snort of laughter. The "whole tale" does not, as Mérimée contends, have "an ironic twist"; but it is there, in the intermissions, the divertissements, the author's asides. "You were about to be taken in? Fools! You were about to be frightened? There's nothing but cardboard and smoke. You were about to take me seriously? But I'm only a drawing-room gossip!"

Throughout *Ruslan and Ludmila,* the terms Pushkin uses to qualify his work are significant: He calls it an after-dinner story, a "licentious song." He alludes to his "light and irreverent lyre," and says:

Alas! I am no Homer;
Only he can sing in noble lines
Of feasting Hellenic warriors
And the clash of foaming cups.
I am happier imitating Parny,
Celebrating with a gentle lyre
Naked bodies in the twilight
And the sweet embrace of love.

It should be observed, however, that this duality does not destroy the balance of the poem. Despite its mixture of epic recital, lyrical digression and mocking couplet, *Ruslan and Ludmila* is not a motley jumble. The whole work is structured, bound together, amalgamated by the author's talent. The music of the lines overrides the diversity of their content, unity of form replaces unity of substance. The melody is pure,

† Needless to say, the French translator did not consider it necessary to mention mustaches either.

articulated by a single voice from beginning to end. It is this miracle of the perfect orchestration of seemingly discordant themes that is the poet's unique secret, and one can only shudder to think of the literary monstrosity any lesser author would have produced using the same materials and methods.

For the modern reader, what remains of this youthful effort which provoked such excessive praise and censure when it was written? A well-made plot that never lags and has no unnecessary complications, a beguiling gaiety of manner, and an astonishing, a truly bewildering ease of composition. What would we not forgive the poet who created that desert battlefield, those twilights of times gone by, that dazzling assault beneath the walls of Kiev? Pushkin's lines flow, smooth and uncluttered. His rhymes are effortless, the difficulties of versification do not seem to exist for him—or else, rhyme is his natural and only means of expression. The heavy, stony, overaccented Russian line softens in his hands like virgin wax. He can do what he likes with it: He rolls it out, stretches, smooths it, throws it away and catches it again. And all around him, the experts with their cramped, smudged fingers look on in bewilderment and scowl: a juggler with words, a virtuoso of rhyme, a goblin of facility. Nothing more.

But if that is so, how is it that this twenty-year-old boy, endowed with such dangerous ease of expression, did not overload his poem? How did he refrain from drowning it in metaphor? How did he resist the temptation to open up flowery bowers on every side, and moonlit rotundas and balustrades for solitary dreamers?

This leads us to the true hallmark of Pushkin's work: moderation. He was a prodigious versifier who never ran away with himself, an extravagantly gifted man who was suspicious of eloquence. An idea he could illustrate in fifty lines he labored to encompass in four. If some effect were not essential to the over-all structure, he dropped it. Pushkin was so rich that he could easily afford not to display all his treasures; no sacrifice cost him anything. It is the reader who fills in, behind the poet's few brilliant strokes, the whole background of sentimental or visual implication, imagines the harvest where the poet has drawn one stalk of grain, populates the forest where he has planted one tree, invents features for the face where he has given only a narrow oval or a look. Thus, at the end of the poem the reader has in mind a description of a battlefield—a long bravura passage, a hallucinating fresco with apocalyptic lighting, funereal relief of detail, a horrible and tranquil expanse of horizon. He knows the topography of the scene, the color of the sky, the sun's reflection in the battered armor. Nothing could be added to this image, created—wasn't it?—in fifty firm lines? Look again: There are sixteen. But nothing is omitted. Every word is full of resonance, every gesture encompasses a thousand other gestures which are not described and yet we know we have *seen* them. The reason for this is that our minds, unconsciously, have been working in the wake of Pushkin's, and in the direction he indicated. Unknown to ourselves, we have filled in the details. Pushkin's wealth lies in what he suggests, not what he shows; in what he withholds, not what he gives. His simplicity, his classical moderation, are all to his credit, for these are great poetic resources.

"His restraint," wrote Mérimée, "and his tact, in selecting only the main features of every subject and discarding all trivial detail, would be considerable merits in any country. . . .

"Although he knows all the resources and all the astonishing wealth of his language, his thought is always formulated so simply that it does not seem possible to express it in any other way."

The truth, however, as we may see from his drafts, is that this man who "writes verse as easily as he breathes" revised every word of every poem: Pushkin was aware of his great facility, and this made him all the more exacting. He was suspicious of his own talent. He loved the collected, compact, pared line that drops onto the paper as naturally as an unpremeditated exclamation. He worked in spurts, evenings, mornings, between two rendezvous; but once his door was shut and his pen in his hand, he ceased to be the dandy of drawing room and brothel. He was Pushkin: a poet who knew what he wanted. He would not be satisfied with a brilliant approximation. He was not afraid to scratch out and write over, to search until he found the right word. He would not shun the craftsman's patient fury and felt no disdain for the craftsman's meticulous enthusiasm.

When he came to describe the night ride of Prince Ratmir, one of Ruslan's rivals, Pushkin wrote a first draft in his notes that had neither rhythm nor rhymes:

> He rode (among sinister boulders)
> Beside black rocks
> (Along sinister caverns) (centuries old)
> Through a gloomy wood, overpowered by the storm, on the
> Banks of the Dnieper. . . .

Two pages further on, we find:

> He rode between (among) boulders covered by forests
> Moss-laden boulders.
> And looked about
> In search of a resting place among (the bushes) among the trees.

From this emerges the final version:

> His horse at a walk beside the black rocks,
> The eyes of our prince sought
> A resting place for the night.

Elsewhere, Pushkin wrote this first draft to describe the meeting of Ruslan and Ludmila:

> Her breasts . . . her shoulders
> Her breasts and her legs are naked. . . .
> Her soft legs in their bonds
> Are naked
> And her half-naked charms
> In . . . nets entangled. . . .

The variations on this theme cover two full pages of manuscript. The official text, the conclusion of all these voluptuous stammerings, is contained in the following eight lines:

> Our prince falls at the feet
> Of his unforgettable beloved,
> Kisses her hands, breaks her bonds,
> Sheds tears of joy,
> Calls out her name; but the virgin sleeps,
> Lips and eyelids closed,
> And a dream of pleasure
> Lifts and swells her young breasts.

Every line in the poem is worked over, crossed out, starred, rewritten, surrounded by sketches of female profiles. Moreover, every correction is an improvement, and with each revision the author moves closer to that diamantine perfection which so amazed his public.

In 1824 Pushkin wrote: "Critics confuse inspiration and enthusiasm. Inspiration is a predilection of the soul to fix fleeting impressions and see through to the heart of ideas. . . . There must be inspiration in geometry as in poetry. Enthusiasm precludes serenity, which is essential to artistic creation. Enthusiasm does not imply an effort of reason, distributing each part to the advantage of the whole. Enthusiasm is ephemeral, discontinuous and therefore incapable of producing truly great and perfect works. Homer is incomparably greater than Pindar. The ode is on the lowest step of artistic creation. The ode does not require uninterrupted work, without which nothing great exists in the world."

In these lines Pushkin gives us the secret of his method: It is this miraculous *enthusiasm* that positively hurled him at his sheet of paper. Syllables poured through his pen. Rhymes rushed up, paired themselves off, piled up on top of each other. Images overran and destroyed each other. He was in such a hurry, so afraid to lose one drop of this shower of gold, that he noted down everything that went through his head. Sometimes he heard the music of a line, but the words that would fall into the cadence were still unformed: He left a blank. Or he would jot down end rhymes that had no lines, rhymes in the air, floating around some thought we shall never know. Often, he interrupted himself in the middle of a poem to attack some other subject: drafts of letters, personal reflections, testings of his pen. It would require ten or twenty agile hands to record all his intentions, and he was alone, struggling under the avalanche, under the weight of his fertile enthusiasm.

Once enthusiasm had left him, it was the turn of *inspiration:* Inspiration is calm and severe, she inspects the proceeds of the night, sorts, weighs up, rejects, accepts, orders. The skeletons of lines would detach themselves from the black mass of scribblings; and a beautiful, tranquil, gay work was born, out of the chaos of improvisation—for the works this hotheaded scatterbrain gave to the world are beautiful, and tranquil, and gay.

At the threshold of Russian literature—somber, prophetic, tormented—stands this young man surrounded by a halo of joy. The prelude to Gogol's caricaturish realism, Turgenev's artistic nihilism, Tolstoy's hatred of civilization, Dostoevsky's obsession with mystical torture; the prelude to all that spleen and blood, obscurity and suffering, was Pushkin and his astonishing gaiety.

Pushkin's message did not outlive its author. The secret of his vivacity died with the light of his eyes, and his spiritual sons are remote from him. They admired him, they envied him, but they did not imitate him. Perhaps he was inimitable.

He too exposed the heart's hypocrisies, the social cowardice, the injustice, misery and shame of his epoch. He suffered, and he wrote his suffering; but he was happy too, and then he wrote his joy: by turns merry and sad, skeptical and enthusiastic—he was all that. He loved life too much to be anything less. Specializing in one thing meant rejecting another, choosing one particular line to follow meant renouncing the excitement of knowing and trying them all. Therefore, he ran from bush to bush, swam in every stream and sang in every wind. He is prodigiously healthy and male; he is exceptionally complete. He makes one want to live. *Ruslan and Ludmila* is a minor work, but what zest and energy run through the poem from start to finish!

In 1825 he wrote:

Like the lamp that pales
In the dazzle of dawn,
False knowledge flutters and is consumed
By the sun of the mind.
Long live the sun! And down with night![3]

"Long live the sun! And down with night!" That had never been heard in Russia before Pushkin, and it was never heard again after he died. The sun set, and night descended upon the authors of the huge land. Then came the age of the sad men, who spoke of Pushkin as a lost god.

PART III

1. *The Caucasus and the Crimea: The Raevskys*

Pushkin's parents and friends greeted his departure with a sigh of relief. Disaster had been averted, imperial clemency had saved the poet from himself and his enemies. Pushkin, moreover, believed that it was he who had deliberately broken with the cold, petty St. Petersburg society, and saw his departure as a boon obtained after many threats and prayers, not as a punishment being imposed upon him. He had wanted to go and he was going, his head high. He even called himself a "voluntary exile" and said he had "rent the nets in which he had been languishing a captive. . . ."[1]

He set out on Ascension Day, May 6, 1820. Of his many friends, only Delvig and Yakovlev accompanied him as far as Tsarskoye Selo; then, after a brief leave-taking, the post coach rolled away in a cloud of sun-brightened dust. In a wide-brimmed hat and belted red blouse, Pushkin turned to confront his new destiny.

In those days it was a long journey from St. Petersburg to Yekaterinoslav, monotonous and fraught with danger. There were halting places in mid-steppe, arguments with post masters; one slept, jolted and lurching, in an odor of leather, horse dung and human sweat; there was darkness and sun, sun and darkness, for an eternity lasting ten days. And at the end of this Calvary, the drab, brand-new little town of Yekaterinoslav, with an unpaved main street, colonists' shanties and the dilapidated and empty palace of Potemkin.

Immediately upon his arrival, Pushkin went to see General Insov, administrator of the southern Russian colonies. Insov received him with paternal benevolence, examined him carefully out of the corner of his eye and left him alone. Pushkin found lodgings in a wretched little Jewish cottage in the Mandrikovka district. Having no definite duties in General Insov's offices, he saw no reason to go there more than three times in eighteen days; a government employee in name only, an abysmally idle supernumerary, he spent his time strolling through the forests, rowing and scandalizing the curious and prudish inhabitants of the little town. Some people[2] claimed they had seen him strutting about in transparent voile trousers in the governor's own drawing rooms. "You could see everything!" The ladies were horrified. Others told how, when a professor at the Yekaterinoslav theological seminary came to call on Pushkin, he was dismissed with the words, "Now you've seen me, yes? Then, good-bye!"

But these eccentricities did not last long. "Soon after my arrival in Yekaterinoslav," Pushkin wrote, "I became so bored that I went rowing on the Dnieper, bathed, and, as usual, caught a fever."[3]

While Pushkin lay on his bunk bed with chattering teeth, the town was welcoming another guest of note in the person of General Raevsky. The general, accompanied by his younger son Nicholas (nineteen), two of his daughters, Marya and Sofya (fifteen and fourteen) and his personal physician, was on his way to take the waters in the Caucasus. General Raevsky was famous for his exploits during the Napoleonic war. After the time when he had gone into battle accompanied by his two sons (the two aged eleven and sixteen), official lithography and poetry had nearly canonized him.

Pushkin was still at school when Nicholas, the younger boy, was assigned to the regiment of guards hussars quartered at Tsarskoye Selo; the beardless youth and the schoolboy poet met at Chaadaev's and immediately became fast friends. When Nicholas Raevsky heard that Pushkin was in Yekaterinoslav, he rushed off in search of the exile, and found him "delirious, in a Jewish thatched hut, with no doctor and no medicine except a jug of iced lemonade. . . ."[4] Pushkin, who thought the whole world had forsaken him, could not restrain his tears of joy at the sight of a familiar face. Nicholas hurried off to his father's physician, found him in bed and forced him to get up and accompany him posthaste.

"Doctor! I have found my friend here. He is ill. He must have help. Come quickly!"

"There was nothing to do but go," the doctor wrote in his memoirs, "so off we went. At length we came to a sordid little hut, in which I found a young man sitting on a wooden bunk. He was very thin, white and unshaven. 'Are you ill?' I asked the stranger. 'Yes, doctor, I wanted to have a little sport, so I went for a swim and I think I've caught cold.' After examining him thoroughly, I found that he was suffering from a high fever. Some sheets of paper were lying on the table in front of him. 'What are you doing to occupy yourself?' 'Writing poetry.' "[5]

Nicholas invited Pushkin to join his family, who were continuing their journey to the Caucasus. General Insov, Pushkin's superior and the official guardian of his good behavior, saw no reason to refuse this little excursion and sent the following letter to St. Petersburg, to justify himself: "Pushkin's health, which is so precarious despite his youth, coupled with the difficult situation in which he has been placed, have necessitated some assistance and a few harmless distractions; I have accordingly allowed him to leave in the company of General Raevsky, who was passing through Yekaterinoslav and willingly agreed to take him. I would refer you to Count Capo d'Istria in this matter, and I hope I shall not be chastised for taking this decision, or that it will be seen as an indulgence. He is a good boy, only it is a pity he has not gone further with his education: An intellectual veneer will never be more than a veneer."

The Raevsky family was traveling in an open barouche and two broughams. Feverish and weak, Pushkin was lifted into the barouche with Nicholas, leaving Marya, Sofya, an English tutor, a companion, the doctor and the general to squeeze into the other two overladen vehicles. Once on the road, however, the general saw that Pushkin was not fit to travel in the open air, so he ordered him to be moved into his own carriage, and on they went, like so many sardines.

Near Taganrog the travelers suddenly came upon the sea; the general's daughters jumped down and ran to the shore. Little Marya began to play with the waves, chasing them as they fell back swallowing their foam and running away as they returned. Pushkin watched in genuine delight: The dark-skinned, lively little girl was not pretty, but so graceful, so young and fleet as a cat! Charmed by the image of the fifteen-year-old child playing with the surf, he later wrote a sentimental verse about her:

> . . . I longed, like the waves,
> To lap your feet with my lips.

In Novocherkassk, the Raevskys stayed with the hetman Denisov, and at dinner Pushkin literally gorged himself on blancmange, whereupon his temperature shot up again:

" 'Help me, doctor!' 'Well then, do as I tell you!' 'I will, I will.' (More concoctions, more paroxysms and grimaces.) 'Don't go out without a coat.' 'Impossible, I'll suffocate.' 'Better to suffocate than have a fever.' 'No, I'd rather have a fever.' (More paroxysms, increasing in violence.) 'Doctor, I'm ill.' 'Because you're so mule-headed. Do as I tell you.' 'I will, I will.' "[6]

Nevertheless, as the journey continued, Pushkin gradually regained his fierce vitality, and was completely recovered by the time they reached the mineral springs of Goryachevodsk.

The Caucasus made a dramatic, indelible impression upon him. A city dweller, accustomed to the damp mists of St. Petersburg and the pastures and placid greenery of Mikhailovskoye, he was awed by the grandiose architecture of the mountains. Here he was only in the foothills, but in the distance he could see the soaring white towers. The air was keen. Torrents gurgled through the narrow gorges, fizzing like champagne. Eagles and mountain goats haunted the jagged peaks. All around, the Circassian tribes were waging their guerrilla war with the Cossack outposts. The wide, sun-filled spaces and elementary wildness of the land exalted the poet's love of freedom. In the sacred inscrutability of these heights, it became easier to hate the cities and their intrigues. He felt allied with the boulders, the snow, the gullies and waterfalls, against the little men of drawing room and antechamber. He was reaching out and touching true greatness. He wrote to his brother:

"I regret, my friend, that you were not with me to see this magnificent mountain range with its summits of ice, looking like strange, motionless, multicolored clouds far, far away in the glowing dawn; I am sorry you were not with me to climb the sharp five-ridged peak of Besh-Tau, or the Mashuk, or Iron Mountain, or the Rocky and the Serpent.

"The Caucasus, the southern boundary of Asia, is strange in every respect. The name and beneficent spirit of Yermolov dominate it. The Circassians are frightened, their hereditary insolence is on the wane. The roads are hourly becoming more secure, and large escorts are now almost unnecessary. It is to be hoped that this newly conquered country, from which Russia has so far gained no visible advantage, will bring us closer to the peaceable Persians."[7]

While admiring the majestic beauty of the Caucasus and avidly following the course of the guerrilla war between Cossacks and Circassians, Pushkin was also nursing his health, undermined by fever and assorted abuses. "I have spent two months in the Caucasus," he wrote in the same letter to his brother; "the mineral waters were absolutely essential to me and have done me no end of good, especially the hot sulphur springs. I also took sulphur baths, ferric water baths, and cold baths."

In 1820 the Caucasian mineral springs had a picturesque and primitive quality which they lost soon afterward. The water issued straight from the rocks. The bathhouses were mere log cabins. Rich summer visitors camped in tents on the banks of the wonder-working streams, in permanent fear of night raids by rebel mountain tribes. When Pushkin returned some years later, he recalled those improvised baths in the wilderness: "In my day," he wrote, "the baths were installed in improvised shacks. Most of the springs were in their natural state, gushing, steaming and pouring over the mountainside in all directions, leaving white or reddish trails where they ran. We drew boiling water in the bottom of a broken bottle. . . . I grant you that the Caucasian mineral springs are far more comfortable now, but I miss the charm of their former wildness, I miss the steep, stony paths, the bushes, the unguarded precipices whose ridges I used to scale."[8]

The Kalmuk tents, the caravans of grayish camels, the torrents, the distant rumble of avalanches, the unseen presence of the mountain tribes: Pushkin remembered them all in his later works:

> I heard your growling streams,
> Your thundering white avalanches,
> Your shrieking eagles and singing girls,
> And the wild Terek roaring,
> And the laugh of your far-off echo.

For the moment, he wrote nothing: He drank in the new light, colors, sounds, and made them his.

Even humans seemed better to him in this lofty, radiant land. Above all, there was the delightful Raevsky family. The general was a rustic, unassuming hero who laughed at all the legends the public had woven around his name. He denied having ever exposed his sons to enemy fire. "My boys were not with me in the battle," he said. "One of them was picking up shot in the forest, that was all. (He was only a child at the time and one ball went through his britches.) That was really all there was to it."

Napoleon had said that General Raevsky was the stuff field marshals were made of, and at the end of the war Alexander I offered to make him a count; but the general answered his emperor with the motto of the Rohans: *Roy ne puis, duc ne daigne, Rohan suis* ("King, I may not; duke, I deign not; Rohan I am").

Pushkin said of him: "This witness of the century of Catherine, this living monument of the year 1812, is a being free from all prejudice, a strong and sensitive nature. He involuntarily draws to him all who are capable of understanding and appreciating his great qualities."

An upright, unsophisticated, jovial man, the general had his hands full with his two sons and four daughters.

Nicholas, the second son, was a strapping lad with muscular neck and swelling chest, who could bend an iron poker in his hands. He was lazy, blunt, and affected a provocative "democratism." His father often complained of his uncouth ways. In 1824 he wrote, "Do take yourself in hand, my dear Nicholas. The tone of your jests in your father's presence and your habit of sprawling on the sofas in front of me and the young ladies and pulling your trousers up over your fat legs are most objectionable. You are intelligent, but so far you have done no more than any idiot, and I don't know if you will ever be capable of anything better."

Nicholas was no idiot, however. He was not afraid to criticize Pushkin's poems and suggest improvements, it was he who revealed Byron and André Chénier to the poet, and it was to him that Pushkin decided to dedicate *The Prisoner of the Caucasus.*

But the jolly and athletic Nicholas was as nothing compared to his older brother. Alexander Raevsky, who had been colonel of a guards light cavalry regiment, was taking the waters in the Caucasus, and it was in Pyatigorsk that Pushkin first met him and fell immediately under the spell of his arrogant, sneering, cruel personality. He was four years older than Pushkin, with a long, bony, emaciated body ending in a little bird's head. His mouth was a ragged gash, his brown eyes flickered, his cheeks and forehead were strewn with grimacing wrinkles. His whole being exuded condescending mockery, systematic negation. He was a cynic and skeptic in the Byronic mode, for whom there was not one individual or object in the world worthy of trust or admiration. God, nature, the good, love, friendship and freedom were so many empty words. How could you thrill to the look of a loved woman, once you had acquired a few notions of anatomy; and why should you honor your mother? Because she carried you "for nine months in a pocket full of water"? He rejected all ethical, social or aesthetic principles, and would not admit ownership of any human emotions. He had been put on earth to challenge all preconceived ideas and assumptions. In 1820 his father wrote: "He is so cold! I look for signs of tenderness or sensitivity in him, and find none. He does not reason, he argues; and the more he is in the wrong, the more irritating, even coarse, his language becomes. He and I have agreed never to discuss any subject whatever, and to avoid all conversation when we are alone. I think he does not believe in love, and as he is incapable of experiencing it himself, does not try to inspire it in others. I do all I can for him, whenever I can, but I conceal my reasons for doing so, as he is indifferent to my affection. His spirit is so contrary. He philosophizes on subjects he knows nothing about, and in such a complicated manner that logic becomes irrelevant."

Pushkin, however, was intimidated and overwhelmed by this somber-faced demon. Alexander Raevsky's eyes so fascinated him that he preferred to talk to him in the dark. With all candles extinguished, he would listen ecstatically while Raevsky destroyed his illusions. He believed that Raevsky's negation was the mark of innate wisdom, and that the lessons of this intellectual charlatan were the lessons of maturity. He wrote to his brother that Alexander Raevsky would be "more than famous," and subsequently made him the hero of his poem *The Demon:*

Our meetings were melancholy.
His smile, his wonderful eyes
And sarcastic speech
Filled me with icy poison. . . .

Rejecting love and liberty,
Sneering at life,
He refused to admire
Nature's greatest gifts.

Pushkin's romantic enthusiasm and adolescent naïveté transformed the selfish, bitter, envious, bilious, pretentious little officer into a sort of all-powerful Mephistopheles. The poet gaped and was silent before this lord of a very artificial darkness. He burned to be like him, to sell him his soul:

I was mournful, dull, unhappy,
But he conquered my soul
And bound my destiny
To his own dark fate. . . .
I saw only through his eyes,
My words were the echo
Of his disenchanted speech,
And I gave my ecstasy,
My faith, and my hope,
For an empty world.[9]

But however he strove to deny himself, Pushkin remained Pushkin. This association, which would have destroyed anyone else, was strangely beneficial to the poet. Alexander Raevsky added to his collection of character types, renewed his inspiration, and taught him, even better than Chaadaev had done, to eschew superfluity and vagueness in literature.

"Young writers," Pushkin wrote (the words might be Raevsky's), "usually do not know how to express the physical motions of passion. Their heroes are all tremblings, teeth-gnashings, etc. . . . It is grotesque, like a melodrama."

On August 5, 1820, Pushkin and the Raevskys left the Caucasus for Gurzuf, in the Crimea, where the general had an estate.

Southern Russia was still a newly conquered territory, only partly subdued. The Caucasian mineral springs were located on the frontier, and the very abstract line of demarcation shifted daily in the course of the fierce border warfare. At the beginning of 1820, the Circassians had crossed the frozen Kuban and attacked the Cossack outposts and villages. The rebel mountain tribesmen were greedy for fair female captives, whom they resold to the Turks or traded for arms and ammunition—a lady of quality was worth her weight in gold—so General Raevsky had his group accompanied by an armed escort. About their perilous journey, Pushkin wrote: "I saw the banks of the Kuban and the frontier villages. I admired our Cossacks, always in the saddle, always ready to fight, always alert. I passed the territories of the free, rebel mountain tribes. We were escorted by sixty Cossacks and dragged a loaded cannon behind us, with lighted fuse. Although the Circassians are fairly quiet just now, they cannot be trusted, and might easily attack an eminent Russian general in the hope of a big ransom. Where an impecunious officer can pass safely in a post carriage, an Excellency runs a heavy risk of being lassoed by some *Chechenetz*. You can imagine how this specter of danger appealed to my inventive mind. . . ."[10]

In another letter, to his friend Delvig, Pushkin described the second part of the trip:

"From Asia we crossed into Europe [i.e. from Taman to Kerch] by boat. I went immediately to the so-called tomb of Mithridates, the ruins of some tower or other; I picked a flower to keep as a souvenir, and lost it the next day without a qualm. The vestiges of Panticapaeum left me equally unimpressed: I saw the ruins of streets, a half-filled ditch, some old bricks, and that was all. From Theodosia to Gurzuf we traveled by sea. At night I could not sleep; there was no moon, the stars were brilliant. Ahead, in the mist, stretched the southern mountains. 'There is Chatir-Dag,' the captain told me. I could not make out Chatir-Dag, nor did I care. I fell asleep before dawn. Meanwhile the ship had anchored, within sight of Gurzuf. I awoke to a fantastic sight: The multicolored mountains were dazzling, the flat thatched roofs of the Tartar huts looked, from afar, like beehives glued onto the mountainside; poplars stood up straight between them like green pillars. On the right, the towering Ayu-Dag, and all around the blue, pure sky, the still sea, and the radiance of the southern air. . . .

"At Gurzuf I lived like a recluse, bathed in the sea, and gorged myself on grapes; I felt immediately at home in the southern climate and luxuriated in it with all the laziness and insouciance of a Neapolitan lazzarone. I loved to wake at night and listen to the sound of the sea for hours. There was a young cypress close to the house; every morning I went to visit it and in the end I felt something akin to friendship for it. That is all I remember of my stay at Gurzuf."[11]

All? Not quite. For although the Crimean landscape had a good deal to do with Pushkin's euphoria, the presence of the Raevsky girls was by no means irrelevant to it.

"All his daughters are adorable," Pushkin wrote to his brother; "the eldest is an exceptional woman. Judge for yourself whether I was happy, living carefree and idle days in the midst of a charming family—the kind of life I love so much and have never known; a beautiful southern sky, an exquisite site, splendors of nature that fill the imagination, mountains, gardens, sea. . . . My friend, it is my dearest hope to see the southern shores and the Raevsky family again."[12]

At Gurzuf, Pushkin stayed with the Raevskys in a mansion known as the "Duc de Richelieu's house," a sort of two-story château overlooking the sea, all balconies, windows and galleries, with its own huge garden. There was an old library, in which Pushkin discovered Chénier and re-read Voltaire with fervor. Aided by Nicholas Raevsky, he also tried to decipher the poems of Byron in the original; when a new word puzzled the young translators, they went to Nicholas' elder sister Katerina, who spoke English fluently and gladly answered their questions. In this spacious residence, its doors and windows ever open to the breeze, Pushkin was welcomed by the members of the Raevsky family whom he had not previously met: the general's wife and two elder daughters, Katerina, twenty-three, and Helen, seventeen. With little Sofya and Marya, that made four girls to flirt with; what more could he desire? Katerina was a beautiful creature with a thin face, a small mouth and huge, candid, soulful eyes. She was extremely willful, and was nicknamed "Marfa Podestà" in memory of a heroine of a medieval chronicle who was mayoress of Novgorod and fought for the city's independence. Pushkin based the character of Marina Mnishek in *Boris Godunov* on this "lofty virgin." In 1825 he wrote: "My Marina is a splendid wench, a real Katerina Orlov [Katerina Raevsky married General M. F. Orlov in 1821]; but don't tell anyone."

Pushkin fell in love with Katerina, of course. But the young lady received his attentions with an amicable smile, nothing more; she tolerated him. Pushkin put her name on his Don Juan list.

His feelings for her sister Helen were more ethereal. Helen was a ravishing girl, tall and slender, with eyes as blue as the Tauric sky. She was timid, chaste and so delicate that her parents feared for her life. Unknown to anyone, she translated Byron and Walter Scott into French and tore up the pages as soon as she had written them. Finding some scraps of paper beneath her window, Pushkin pieced them together and congratulated the girl on her translation.

As for Marya Raevsky, a small, lively, mischievous, graceful brunette: Some say she was the secret passion of his life. Marya, however, who married the Decembrist leader Prince Volkonsky in 1825, firmly denied that Pushkin had ever felt anything but friendship for her.

"As a poet," she said, "Pushkin felt obliged to fall in love with every pretty woman and every girl he met. In reality, he was in love with his muse, and transposed everything he saw into poetry!"

Pushkin himself wrote: "I have been more or less in love with every pretty woman I have ever met.[13] All of them have laughed at me. All, except one, played the flirt with me."

All except one: Perhaps he was thinking of Marya?

Leaving aside the question of an exclusive passion, Pushkin must certainly have been attracted by this child who was unfolding and becoming a woman before his eyes. But the more genuine his affection, the more reticent his approach. He might pose as a Don Juan in front of less virtuous creatures, but he became tongue-tied in the presence of someone he sincerely respected. He said nothing to Marya; or if he did, she did not understand him. Too young, perhaps; in those days she was still in the care of her English governess and her nanny, and her ideas did not extend beyond climbing the steep mountain path or dabbling her feet in the waves. But later? No letter or document has survived to reveal the destiny of this unshared love; Pushkin's works alone attest to its strength and persistence. From this period date his first poems on the theme of the unknown, adorable and irreplaceable woman who has not responded to his love and whom he is trying to forget.* He immortalized Marya's childish play in *Eugene Onegin*, gave her name to the heroine of *The Fountain of Bakhchisarai* and her features to that of *The Prisoner of the Caucasus*; to all appearances, his *Poltava* is dedicated to her as well:

> Will a poet's dedication
> As in the past his love
> Go unnoticed by you
> And receive no answer? . . .
> The empty desert where you dwell
> And the last sound of your voice
> Remain my sacred treasure
> And the only love of my soul.†

He sang of her eyes, "Clearer than day, Blacker than night. . . ."

The climate and scenery of Tauris intensified Pushkin's emotions; he exulted, he suffered and he rejoiced in his suffering and exultation under this blue sky. Marya, Helen, Katerina, the murmuring sea, the jagged rocks, the poplars, cypresses, grapevines, myrtle, olive groves, Tartar huts—all blended wonderfully together. The truth of the matter is that Pushkin was probably in love with the country and all three girls at once. They formed a single three-headed being, an entity endowed with every female charm and every danger. But the entity was not favorable to the poet; his love was unrequited. Neither Marya, Helen, nor Katerina listened to his pleas. Never mind; he did not need the sun's consent or that of the trees and flowers to love them. Besides, time was passing. He had to be thinking of the return trip; life must go on.

At the beginning of September, Pushkin and Nicholas Raevsky left Gurzuf together. "We traveled along the Tauric coast," Pushkin wrote to Baron Delvig, "and M——[Muravyev]'s *Journey* awakened many old

* Actually, Pushkin had expressed similar sentiments in some of his Tsarskoye Selo poems, but then he was only following a literary fashion.

† The reference to "the empty desert": Marya, having married Prince Volkonsky, followed him into exile in Siberia after the Decembrist uprising. A first, excised version of these lines has been found among Pushkin's drafts, in which he had written: "The cold wastes of Siberia . . ."

memories, but the terrifying crossing of the ravine gave me no new ones. We went up on foot, on steps carved into the cliff, holding our Tartar horses by the tails. That amused me greatly. On the other side of the mountain the first thing I saw was a birch, a northern birch! My heart sank; already I was beginning to miss the South, even though we were still in Tauris and I could still see poplars and grapevines. I was very impressed by the St. George Monastery, with its steep steps going down to the sea. I saw the ruins of the Temple of Diana. Mythological legends seem to be more congenial to me than historical ruins. . . . I was ill when we reached Bakhchisarai. I had already heard of the strange monument of the lovelorn khan. K——‡ had described it to me very poetically, calling it the 'fountain of tears.' When I went inside the palace, I saw a dilapidated fountain with water coming out of a rusty pipe a drop at a time. I went all around the palace, angered by its ruinous condition and the semi-European arrangement of some of the rooms. N.N. [Raevsky] dragged me almost by force to see the ruins of the harem and the khan's cemetery. . . .

"Now tell me why this south coast and Bakhchisarai have such inexplicable attraction for me? Why do I have this great desire to return to places I left without a backward glance? Memory is a magician that exalts everything it touches."

Pushkin's leave of absence was coming to an end. He had to go back to General Insov's offices. While he had been away, however, the general had transferred his headquarters from Yekaterinoslav to Kishinev, in Bessarabia.

‡ An allusion to Katerina Raevsky?

2. *Kamenka.* The Prisoner of the Caucasus

On September 21, 1820, Pushkin entered Kishinev, a little town of low houses and twisting, mud-inlaid streets, and around mid-November he left it again, with General Insov's permission, for the Davydov estate* in Kamenka. General Insov granted his poet-clerk two weeks' leave, but Pushkin did not return until the second half of March. The indulgent general, however, made no protest at this inexcusable delay. On December 15, 1820, a month after Pushkin's arrival, the eldest Davydov son wrote to him: "With Your Excellency's permission, Alexander Sergeyevich Pushkin is still our guest here; he was planning to return to Kishinev with General Orlov, but, having caught cold, he is not yet in a condition to travel. I think it my duty to inform Your Excellency of this fact and to assure you that as soon as Alexander Sergeyevich's health will permit him to do so, he will return to Kishinev with all due speed."

Insov's reply, dated December 29, 1820, was that of a kindly father, not an executive jealous of his authority: "I had been anxious about Mr. Pushkin, fearing that he might have disregarded the sharp frost, wind, and blizzards, started on the return journey, and come to grief on the way, owing to the dreadful state of the roads across the steppes. Your letter of the fifteenth inst. has reassured me, and I hope that Your Excellency will not allow him to undertake the voyage until he has sufficiently recovered his strength."

Pushkin was happy on the Davydov estate: There was an enormous house, an artificial grotto, a pavilion with a billiard room, a library, a serf orchestra and singers, good food, good wine, a few pretty women, some jolly friends. On December 4, 1820, the poet wrote to Gnedich: "I am now in the territory of the government of Kiev, at the home of the Davydovs, two likable and learned hermits who are half brothers (through their mother) of General Raevsky. My time is spent in aristo-

* Old Mrs. Davydov was General Raevsky's mother; Leo Denisovich Davydov was her second husband.

cratic dining and democratic conversation. A short while ago our company—now dispersed—represented, for a newcomer, a curious mixture of original minds, people famous throughout Russia. Few women, much champagne, much wit, many books, a few poems. . . ."

The company at Kamenka was genuinely interesting. Old Katerina Nikolayevna Davydov was a niece of Potemkin's, and so rich that the initials of all her estates could be put together to form the sentence "Leo loves Katerina." The house was full of children, nephews, nieces, strange friends who had been installed there for months, distinguished parasites. On feast days the noble dame fired a salute on her private cannon.

Then there were the two Davydov brothers—Basil (twenty-eight), known for his revolutionary opinions, and Alexander (forty-seven), known for his gluttony and marital misfortunes. Alexander was tall, stout, muddleheaded, but refined; he came to life only when seated before a well-garnished table. During the occupation of France, he asked to be quartered in some town of high gastronomic repute. Pushkin wrote about him: "Alexander Lvovich was a second Falstaff: gourmand, cowardly, a braggart but no fool, totally devoid of principles, full of self-pity and obese. He had one distinctive feature, however, which gave him added charm: He was married. Shakespeare never had time to marry off his bachelor, and Falstaff died without knowing the joys of cuckoldom or fatherhood."

In *Eugene Onegin* Pushkin wrote of

A magnificent cuckold,
Ever content with his person,
His dinner, and his wife.

Alexander Davydov belonged to no clandestine organizations and snored through his guests' political discussions. His brother Basil, on the other hand—a war hero and retired colonel—was an influential member of the Union of the South. All the local revolutionaries met in his home: On November 24, his mother's birthday, every liberal for miles around assembled at Kamenka, ostensibly to wish the chatelaine many happy returns of the day. On that occasion, Pushkin met the future Decembrists Yakushkin and Okhotnikov, and the very remarkable General Orlov, a rabid conspirator, author of a petition to the emperor demanding the abolition of serfdom, instigator of a "humane discipline" in the units under his command and former member of the Arzamas—whose downfall he had precipitated, moreover, by attempting to introduce serious political discussions into the meetings. He was about to marry the lovely Katerina Raevsky, and her family had also come to Kamenka, to Pushkin's great joy. There was a swarm of military men too, both active and retired, but all of them inspired by the same hatred of the government and the same dream of social reform. These uniformed plotters were actually meeting to prepare a vast secret assembly, which was to take place in Moscow in January 1821. The peasant uprisings and the brutality of the government's repression fostered their illusions. Their idea was not to start a people's revolution, but to overthrow the tsarist regime by a military coup, and then, once the country was liberated, to establish the constitutional system of their choice. The Spanish revolution, the Neapolitan revolution of July 1820, the Portuguese revolution of August 1820 had all been preceded by military *coups d'état;* they would follow the example of these pioneers of independence.

"Have a whiff of Spanish tobacco," Pushkin wrote, "and sneeze, and sneeze again."[1] And in his *Epistle to Basil Davydov* (1821), he spoke of his friends who were filling

> . . . The cup of liberty
> With chilled, flat wine,
> And tossing it down their gullets
> With toasts to Victory, Theirs and Hers;
> But They are playing games in Naples,
> And She will not survive.

"They," of course, were the Italian Carbonari, and "She" was freedom.

The revolutionary Yakushkin recounted one memorable evening at Kamenka: "We spent our evenings in Basil Lvovich's rooms, and these nocturnal conversations were of the highest interest to us all. Raevsky [the general], who suspected the existence of the secret society but was not himself a member of it, was terribly intrigued to know what was going on. He did not believe my visit to Kamenka was accidental, and he dearly wanted to learn the reasons for my presence there. On the last evening, Orlov, Basil Davydov, Okhotnikov and I determined to behave in such a manner that he would be completely confused and unable to guess whether we did or did not belong to a secret society. To keep the discussion more orderly, we elected Raevsky chairman of the meeting. With a half-amused, half-solemn air, he began to conduct the proceedings. When we became too unruly he would ring a bell, nobody was allowed to speak without permission, etc. At one point, having requested and been given the floor, I attempted to prove that it was impossible to set up a secret society in Russia that could really accomplish anything. Raevsky began to contradict me, enumerating all the instances in which a secret society could act successfully and with good effect. To refute his statements, I said, 'It is easy for me to prove that you cannot mean what you say. Let me put one question to you: If there were such a secret society now in existence, I am sure you would not have joined it?'

'I most certainly should have done,' he answered. 'In that case, give me your hand,' I said. And he held out his hand; whereupon I burst out laughing and said, 'Of course, this is all a joke.' Everyone else began laughing too, except Alexander Lvovich Davydov, that magnificent cuckold, and Pushkin, who was terrifically excited and had been thinking all along that a secret society either existed or was about to be founded then and there, and that he would become a member of it; but when he saw the whole thing turned into a joke he stood up, all red in the face, and said, with tears in his eyes, 'I have never been so unhappy as I am now. There I was, seeing my life ennobled and an ideal goal rising up before me, and the whole thing was nothing but a nasty farce.' At that moment he was truly beautiful."

As in St. Petersburg, Pushkin was again sitting in the very thick of a conspiracy and being rejected by the conspirators. No matter how many revolutionary poems he wrote, no matter how often he was sent into exile for his love of freedom and hatred of Arakcheev and his clique, still they wouldn't trust him. With him, they drank to independence, they declaimed subversive poems, they gave him comradely pats on the back, and that was all. He was denied entry to the crucial negotiations, he was kept waiting in the antechamber of revolution. A civilian. A baby. A poet. That was what he was to them. It drove him wild to stand thus scratching at the door of history.

Repelled by serious manhood, Pushkin fell back on frivolous femininity. "Much champagne, few women. . . ." True, there were not many women at Kamenka. But Mrs. Davydov, the "magnificent cuckold's" wife, was as good as a harem. The fair Aglaia was born de Gramont; she was French, and thirty years old. She had a plump face, a pert nose, a soft and velvety mouth, a downy bosom. Her grace, her wantonness, her eternal coquetry turned the head of every general and cornet who came to the Kamenka estate. Aglaia was happy only when she was in the center of a ring of admirers, and there was always someone around to admire her. Pushkin himself fell in with the custom of the house and paid court to the pretty Frenchwoman, out of habit and because he had nothing better to do. But she wanted to play the romantic heroine in the grand manner, and the poet, frightened by her intensity, beat a hasty retreat before obtaining anything more from her than smiles and a brush of the lips. These flutterings with fat Alexander's wife irritated Pushkin, and he relieved himself by composing epigrams:

Some have had my Aglaia
For their mustache and braided coat,
Some for money—that I understand;
Or because they were French.

Leo was no doubt impressive,
Daphnis sang so well;
But tell me, my Aglaia, what
Your husband had you for?

Pushkin sent this epigram to his brother with the comment: "For the love of Christ, don't let it get around. Every word of it is truth."

In another epigram, he preached restraint to the eager Aglaia:

Let us leave impassioned fevers . . .
(Our day is drawing to a close)
You, my dear, to your oldest girl,
And I to my young brother. . . .

Pushkin's allusion to Adèle, Aglaia's eldest daughter, was not fortuitous. She was a very pretty lass of twelve, and he was not above bestowing some of his attention upon her. "Pushkin imagined," Yakushkin wrote, "that he was in love with her; he kept ogling her, coming up to her, clumsily teasing her. One day at dinner he was sitting beside me all flushed with emotion, and stared at the pretty little girl so insistently that the poor thing didn't know what to do and was on the verge of tears. I took pity on her and, lowering my voice, said to Pushkin, 'See what you're doing; your indecent leering has completely upset the poor child.' 'I want to punish the flirt,' he replied; 'at first she was very sweet to me and now she's playing cruel and pretending not to see me.' I had great difficulty in turning the incident into a joke and bringing a smile back to his lips."

Between political discussions with his hosts, amorous disputes with Aglaia and gazing at little Adèle, Pushkin also found time to write. In fact, he wrote a great deal. There is a group of lyric poems dating from his stay at Kamenka (*The Clouds . . .*, *The Water-Nymph, I Have Lived to Bury My Desires*), which seem to be the dying echoes of his passion for Marya Raevsky. In them, Pushkin speaks of the Tauric coast, the "tender myrtle" and "somber cypress," and his forsakenness, making him like the last leaf on a tree twisted by the winter wind:

I live on, gloomy and alone,
And wait: When will the end come?

Also at Kamenka, Pushkin completed his first long poem in the Byronic mode: *The Prisoner of the Caucasus*, the manuscript of which bears the date "Kamenka, February 20, 1821."

According to Davydov, Pushkin transformed the billiard room into his study. He wrote *The Prisoner of the Caucasus* lying on his stomach on the billiard table, in such a state of creative intensity that he could not tear himself away from his work even for meals: "One day," a contemporary[2] noted, "Pushkin was called for dinner; he told the valet to bring him a clean shirt, as he wanted to change before going in, then returned to his writing. The man brought the shirt, Pushkin wrote on; the man stood there with the shirt over his arm, Pushkin didn't even look at him, and went on writing, writing. . . ."

The Prisoner of the Caucasus, begun in August 1820, was finished on February 20, 1821, but not published until September 1822. Its subject is disarmingly simple: A Russian is taken prisoner by a Caucasian mountain tribe, and escapes with the help of a Circassian girl who has fallen in love with him and drowns herself after giving him his freedom. But this trite idyll was the pretext for a display of pyrotechnics of great artistic refinement; the poem is a piece of "fictionalized journalism," but of what quality!

All nineteenth-century society knew of the Caucasus was what they read in the bulletins of their victorious armies. Derzhavin and Zhukovsky had, it is true, devoted a few resounding lines to the noble wildness of the landscape and the warlike ways of its inhabitants; but neither of them had bothered to verify their information at first hand, whereas Pushkin had actually seen the mountains whose motionless splendor he sang of, and the rebel warriors who captured his hero. His concern for veracity appears in a letter he wrote to Gnedich on March 24, 1821: "From the bare summit of Mt. Besh-Tau I could only glimpse the snow-covered peaks of Kazbek and Elbrus in the distance. By rights the action of my poem should have taken place on the banks of the roaring Terek, on the Georgian frontier, in the wild gorges of the Caucasus. But I put my hero in the monotonous plains where I spent two months myself, and where only four mountains can be seen, very far apart, the last folds of the Caucasus."

Pushkin's memories of his travels with the Raevskys gave body to his new poem, which was, thus, both Caucasian and Raevskian, i.e. visual, "scenic," and imitative of Byron, for the Raevskys were "mad" about Byron and Pushkin was still under their influence.

Like Byron, he used the theme of the European transported to an exotic civilization, who seduces a native woman. Like Byron, he employed a narrative style broken by questions, songs, abrupt digressions. His prisoner, too, might well have appealed to Byron's stormy genius—but he also, and strongly, puts one in mind of Chateaubriand's René. Both the Russian and the French heroes are melancholic, *enfants du siècle*. They both fall in love with a "savage" woman who comes to them by night. Both are freed. And behind each lies the corpse of his beloved. Chateaubriand had looked for his local color in little-known America, and Pushkin for his in the Caucasus, as yet totally unsung. But the similarities between Pushkin's work and those of Chateaubriand and Byron end there. Pushkin is lighter, more discreet, more classical than his predecessors. He avoids Chateaubriand's declamatory passages. He is not carried away by the sound of his own voice. He controls himself. He also differs from Byron, in that he loses his hero in the landscape. Byron's heroes have a streak of full-blown satanism, they overpower everything with their bleak grandeur, they monopolize the interest of the poem. In Pushkin, on the other hand, the characters are rapidly and lightly drawn; they scarcely touch the ground, they blend into the light of the sky and the shivering of the foliage; it is when they try to be Byronic that they cease to be real. In July–August 1825, his "Shakespeare phase," Pushkin wrote to N. Raevsky, "How petty the 'tragic' Byron seems by comparison. Byron never imagined more than one character in his life (Women have no personalities: They have passions, when they are young, and that is why it is so easy to portray them), he merely distributed parts of his own personality among his different characters: His pride went to one, his hatred to another, his melancholy to a third, etc. . . . and that is how, out of one full, somber, and vigorous personality he created a number of insignificant ones. That is not tragedy."[3]

This comment could be turned against the author of *The Prisoner of the Caucasus*, for in his hero Pushkin meant to protray himself. "The character of the prisoner doesn't come off," he wrote. "Proof that I am no good as the hero of a romantic poem."

In fact, Pushkin put only a tiny fraction of himself into his creation. He did not give him his young, gay, virile mind; he gave him only his attitude of the moment, which was inspired by his reading of Byron. He made him a man with a troubled and romantic past, betrayed by his friends, persecuted by calumny, consumed by ennui. Trying to enrich him, he succeded only in diminishing him. The Circassian woman, although hardly indicated, is more believable than her lover. True, she is only a passion, in the manner of Byronic women; but an elemental, strong, proud passion.

Pushkin was a severe critic of this youthful work. In the draft of a letter to Gnedich, he wrote:

"The faults of this tale, poem, call it what you will, are so blatant that for a long time I could not make up my mind to publish it. The simplicity of its plan verges on imaginative bankruptcy; the descriptions of Caucasian customs (the best parts of the poem), not being related to the action, are no better than geography lessons or tourists' journals. The main character (and there are only two) would be better in a novel than in a poem. And what kind of character is he? Who could be interested in a young man who has lost all his sensitivity as the result of a few vague misfortunes about which the reader is told nothing? His inertia, his indifference to the savage cruelty of the mountain tribes and the beauties of the Circassian girl might be natural enough, but what is there in them that could move anyone? It would have been easy to enliven the tale with episodes arising out of the plot. The Circassian who captured my Russian could have been the lover of the woman who freed him; her mother, father, brother might each have had a role and a personality. But I omitted all that: out of laziness, in the first instance; and secondly, because all these sensible reflections came to me after both sections of the poem had already been written and I no longer had the energy to start over again. . . . You see that I am not blinded by paternal affection where *The Prisoner of the Caucasus* is concerned. Still, I confess to being fond of it, without quite knowing why. It contains some lines which are dear to my heart."[4]

In 1829, when he made a second trip to the Caucasus, Pushkin found a "smudged and blotted copy" of his poem at Kars. "I read it eagerly," he wrote in his *Journey to Arzerum.* "The whole thing is weak, young, unpolished, but contains much that is accurately sensed and expressed."

In *The Prisoner of the Caucasus,* as in *Ruslan and Ludmila,* poverty of plot is masked by wonderful richness of orchestration, fluent, unfaltering language, and uncompromising perfection in the choice of detail. Before Pushkin, Russian poetry had been a sort of garden for innocent gallantries. There were odes, epistles and epigrams. Poets sang of their hearts' delights, the cooing of doves, the bleating of lambs, the prostrations of shepherds at the feet of their shepherdesses and floods of tears in the gloaming. The first romantics repudiated this curled and perfumed Arcadia *à la française,* but only to fall into a universe as artificial as the one they had cast off. In the place of pastorals, green pastures and babbling brooks, they offered moonlit cemeteries, cardboard boulders, plunging torrents, phantoms with fluorescent trains, death's-heads and melancholic dreamers in capes as black as their consciences. Carried away by their hatred of classicism, they overshot the mark. Between these two literary camps, their premises equally false and naïve, Pushkin miraculously kept his balance and his wits about him. In opposition to the lovers of ribbons and powder puffs, and the amateurs of gloomy night rides and precipices, Pushkin tried to see straight and speak true. How did this twenty-year-old manage to remain uncontaminated by fads? Where did he find the confidence that enabled him to innovate? Who gave him the audacity to stand alone? In the days of noble words and plebeian words, poetic animals and prosaic animals, epistolary lighting effects and lyrical lighting effects, this boy sat his hero down to dine on real food, put the correct weapons in his Circassians' hands and did not disdain to tip his hat to the fermented mare's milk of the Caucasus. And with all its shortcomings, his poem was better than the airiest of legends. Writing of a storm in the mountains, he said:

> At his feet clouds steamed,
> Dust from the steppe whirled in the wind,
> Frightened elk sought refuge
> Between piles of boulders,
> Eagles flew out from the cliffs
> And mounted shrieking to the sky,
> And the storm drowned the voices
> Of horses and bawling oxen.
> Suddenly, rain and hail
> Hurtled from the sky with the flashes.
> Torrents harrowed the earth,
> Tearing away ancient rocks,
> Pouring over the steep slopes.

The picture has the sober black-and-white precision of a photograph. Elsewhere, Pushkin writes of Circassian games; in another place, of the men coming back to the village from the fields, with the sun glancing off their scythes. Further on, the Aoul sleeps:

> The steppe sinks into darkness,
> The rocky peaks grow dim.
> The white huts of the Aoul
> Pale in the moonlight.
> The pines fall asleep above the water.
> The eagles' cries have ceased.
> And the mountains relay
> The far-off roll of galloping herds.

Last comes the escape by night, the Circassian's suicide and the prisoner's arrival at the Russian lines:

> Already before him in the mist
> The Russian bayonets gleamed,
> And Cossack sentinels called
> From the top of the rise.

Mist, bayonets, the call of the Cossack sentinels. There strokes, no more; but three exact strokes. Pushkin, this contemporary of the romantics, had a passion for precision and verisimilitude. The critic of the *European Herald* (1823) upbraided him for describing a traveler asleep "in his wet burka"† at the back of a Circassian hut.

"It would have been simpler," he observed, "for the man to remove his burka and dry off."

This remark exasperated Pushkin: " 'In his wet burka,' " he wrote to Vyazemsky. "Burkas are rainproof and only get wet on the outside.

† A Circassian overcoat.

Therefore it is possible to sleep in one if you have nothing else to wear, and absolutely pointless to dry it out."[5]

In the poem he had written:

Fate gave to him
Few exquisite *nights.*

The censor, offended by the allusion to nocturnal pleasures, replaced "nights":

Fate gave to him
Few exquisite *days.*

Pushkin's wrath: "The censor has butchered me. I will not, must not, cannot say 'days' in that line. *Nights, nights,* for the love of Christ, *few exquisite nights.* It has to be nights, because she couldn't come to him in the day. Look at the poem. And why is night more improper than day? Which is the hour of the twenty-four that so offends the sensibility of our censor?"[6]

In another letter to Vyazemsky, Pushkin defended the "verisimilitude" of his work: "One more word on the subject of *The Prisoner of the Caucasus.* You tell me, sweetheart, that he is a dog because he doesn't weep over the Circassian maiden, but what more could he say? 'He understood all' expresses his feelings completely. You must not explain everything, that's the secret of the charm. Other people wish the prisoner had leaped into the water to save the Circassian. You just try it! I have swum in the rivers of the Caucasus. You could drown in them yourself, and the devil take me if you could pull anyone else out of them; my prisoner is an intelligent, logical man. He is not in love with the Circassian. Therefore he was right not to drown himself."[7]

The poem's epilogue[8] angered Vyazemsky, because in it Pushkin wrote of the military glory of Generals Kotlyarevsky and Yermolov:

"I wish Pushkin had not put all that blood in the last lines of his poem," he wrote to Turgenev. "What kind of heroes are Kotlyarevsky and Yermolov? What is so noble about the fact that they annihilated the primitive tribes like a black plague? The idea of being celebrated for such actions turns my blood to ice and makes my hair stand on end. I am sorry about Pushkin: His enthusiasm is anachronistic!"

In fact, Pushkin was torn between his desire to celebrate the Russian victories and his compassion for the natives who were being hunted down and hacked to bits in their mountains. His drafts show his hesitations and conflicts of conscience during the gestation of the poem. In the end, trying to remain neutral, he gave credit to both the exploits of the Circassian rebels—"proud sons of freedom"—and the courage of the Russian leaders and their men.

The Prisoner of the Caucasus aroused at least as much excitement as *Ruslan and Ludmila,* if not more. The censor forbade the inclusion of the author's portrait in the printed version of the poem,‡ but his image, voice and message were in the hearts of all educated young Russians.

Even the critics had to soften their assaults upon the new prophet. The *Son of the Fatherland* was forced to concede, "The local color in this work is rendered with freshness and accuracy. There is an oriental accent in the scenes, sentiments, and style."

In 1823 the Imperial Theater in St. Petersburg presented a ballet based on *The Prisoner of the Caucasus,* with the celebrated Istomina in the role of the Circassian woman.

But all Pushkin knew of his triumphs at the other end of Russia was what he could glean from his friends' letters and the accounts of passing travelers.

‡ Page 49 of the copy submitted to the censor contained the following "Observation," furiously scratched out by the bureaucrat's pen: "Thinking that our readers will want to preserve an image of the early years of the poet whose first works display such exceptional promise, the publishers append a portrait of the author drawn in his youth."

3. Kishinev

In March 1821 Pushkin left his friends in Kamenka to return to the "accursed town" of Kishinev, where General Insov had moved his offices.

Kishinev was an Asiatic town, full of vermin, tortuous streets and dreariness. "The town is large," a contemporary of Pushkin's wrote, "but badly planned. The streets are narrow, with innumerable passageways. There are few houses in stone or wood—cabins, rather. . . . In the evening I took a walk in the garden, there were a few officers, some Moldavians in tall, round hats (the richest, the most prominent), others in hats not so high; all wore a kind of kaftan similar to a priest's cassock, but multicolored. Under the kaftan they wore a second, narrower kaftan, then a skirt, then trousers. The women dress in European fashion. There are many Greeks, Serbs and Albanians, who wear beautiful costumes. Few Turks. . . ."[1]

This heterogeneous population thronged the streets and cafes. The tall wizards' bonnets jostled scarlet fezzes, turbans, the top hats of civilian bureaucrats and the plumes of preening soldiers. Every dialect was spoken, from Moldavian to Russian, Greek to Jewish and Turkish to Armenian. Violins squeaked in the low-ceilinged taverns, where noble-headed ancients sat cross-legged smoking their pipes and staring into space. Teams of oxen barred the road to spanking Viennese barouches. And in one hall of the casino, with a blare of brass, the military band rehearsed their quadrilles and mazurkas for the next ball.

Upon his arrival the poet reported to General Insov, who welcomed him like a son. As Pushkin had no money, the general invited him to live in his own home, a pretty, clean, spacious building brightened by a garden, grapevines and an aviary: Insov was such a botany enthusiast that he had had the outside walls of the house covered with frescoes of rare plants. Pushkin occupied two rooms on the ground floor, one for himself and the other, a sort of antechamber, for the faithful Nikita Kozlov. The windows, protected by iron bars, gave onto the garden, and at the bottom ran the river Byk. "A table by the window," wrote Bartenyev, the Pushkin scholar, "a divan, a few chairs, a scattering of papers and books, blue walls bearing the traces of pellets of soft wax deposited during target practices—such was Pushkin's room." He ate at Insov's, slept at Insov's and was theoretically employed by Insov. But it was not so much he who submitted to the general's orders as the general who submitted to his caprices. This kindly man with the bulldog head regarded Pushkin as an individual of a rare species, to be handled with care. He admired, he even loved the brilliant scamp, and secretly smiled at his follies.

On April 13, 1821, Count Capo d'Istria wrote to Insov: "A short time ago I sent young Pushkin to Your Excellency. It would be useful to me, especially in the present situation, to know your opinion of this young man: Is he now obeying the dictates of his own heart, which is fundamentally good, or those of his subversive and unwholesome imagination?"

On April 28 Insov replied: "Pushkin is living in my house, and behaving himself; despite the troubled times we are now traversing, he is not actively involved.* I have set him to make a Russian translation of the Moldavian laws which were originally written in French, and with this work and other administrative tasks, his time is fully occupied. Inspired by the feelings common to all dwellers on Parnassus who try to imitate certain fashionable authors,† the ideas he expresses in our conversations are occasionally rather fanciful. But I am sure that with time and age this will pass. . . . In the capital, he was paid an official salary of seven hundred rubles; now, without this, and receiving no material assistance from his parents, he sometimes has no decent clothes to wear, despite my solicitude. I accordingly feel called upon to ask you to see that he is paid the same salary here as in St. Petersburg."

Insov's prayer was answered. Pushkin's parents had indeed forgotten their son, but the old general stepped in to replace the defective family, and thanks to him Pushkin again had his seven hundred rubles—little though they were for the place he aspired to occupy in society.

And a strange society it was. There were two clans, Russian and Moldavian. The Russians were all, or nearly all, revolutionary officers. There were Orlov and Okhotnikov, whom Pushkin had met at Kamenka; and Pestel—grand master of the Union of the South, and a member of the Union for Welfare: the most rabid, the most uncompromising, the "reddest" conspirator in all Russia. There was Veltman, who wrote bad poetry; Gorchakov, who was a nice lad but nothing more; and Alexeyev,

* Insov is alluding to the Greek uprising.
† Probably a reference to Byron.

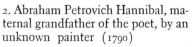

2. Abraham Petrovich Hannibal, maternal grandfather of the poet, by an unknown painter (1790)

3. Alexander Pushkin in his youth, engraving by E. Heitmann (1822)

4. Young Pushkin writing verse

5. Delvig, water color by Yakovlev

6. Sergey Lvovich Pushkin, the poet's father. Drawing by Hampeln (1820)

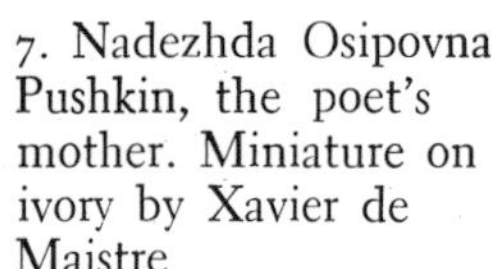

7. Nadezhda Osipovna Pushkin, the poet's mother. Miniature on ivory by Xavier de Maistre

8. Pushkin reads his verses to Derzhavin during the examinations in the Lycée. Painting by Ilya Repin

9–11. Pushkin's caricatures, self-portraits:

9. Young Pushkin (1821)

10. Two profiles

11. Alexander Pushkin wearing a Circassian costume (1829)

12. A. The bridge on boats in St. Petersburg in 1820, engraving from that time

12. B. "The Bronze Horseman"—the statue of Peter the Great on Senate Square in St. Petersburg (1810)

13. Pushkin in exile in the Bakhchisarai Palace, from a painting by Chernetsov

14. Engraving of the Lycée of Tsarskoye Selo, housed in a wing of the Great Palace, where Pushkin went to school

15. Leo Sergeyevich Pushkin, the poet's brother

16. General Insov, the fatherly protector of Pushkin when the poet was first exiled

17. Calypso Polichroni, to whom Pushkin dedicated his poem *To the Greek Girl*

18. Prince and Princess Vyazemsky

16–18. More of Pushkin's caricatures:

Bologovsky and, lastly, Liprandi, who had asked permission in 1820 to enlist in the Italian people's army and was demoted to the ranks as a result. He was surrounded by an aura of mystery. He had no regular income, yet he lived expensively and entertained lavishly. He loved parties, yet he always looked excessively mournful in company. He was impassioned in his own speech, yet he always tried to pacify others in an argument. "It was impossible that Pushkin should not have been attracted to his original personality," wrote Gorchakov. "Apart from his caustic wit and his erudition, there was something poetic in his manner, action, speech, his whole way of life."‡ Pushkin himself said, "He is a good friend to me and (proof positive of his nobility and intelligence) there is no love lost between him and our government."[2]

From St. Petersburg to Kamenka and Kamenka to Kishinev, Pushkin found the same atmosphere of demagogical debate and conspiracy. On April 9 he wrote in his diary: "Spent the morning with Pestel; a man of wit in every sense. My heart is materialist, he said, but my reason rebels against it. We had a metaphysical, political, moral, etc. conversation. He is one of the most original minds I know. . . ."

Pushkin arrived in Kishinev at the beginning of the Greek insurrection. In March 1821 Alexander Ypsilanti crossed the Prut and, from Iaşi, launched an appeal to his countrymen to rise against the Turkish oppressors: "Greeks, the hour has come. It is time to avenge our religion and our fatherland. . . ." In response, armed bands poured down from the mountains to fight the Ottoman army with flintlock and saber. It was all exceedingly brave, unorganized and puerile. In Kishinev, the news of the revolution excited both Russians and Moldavians. The conflict was so close at hand, the cause so great; and overtones of Antiquity gave such glamour to these heroes with the thick mustaches and powder-blackened hands!

"Everywhere you went," Veltman wrote, "people were talking about the events in Greece; it was remarkable, the interest people took in this affair. The news ran like wildfire through the Greek population of Kishinev. Turbaned princes and bonneted boyars went from house to house in their Viennese carriages, exhibiting letters they had received from abroad."

Serbs, Romanians, Albanians, Bulgarians and Greeks flooded the town with their strongboxes, their harlots and their portable patriotism. Pushkin was in transports of enthusiasm and impatience. That struggle for freedom he had talked about so often with the officer conspirators of St. Petersburg and Kamenka was suddenly becoming a reality, here on the outposts of the empire. So it was true that a people could con-

‡ This same Liprandi, it may be observed, who thought so little of the government, ended his career as an agent of the secret police.

quer its independence by armed force? It was true that plots, proclamations and meetings could foment a genuine uprising? But what was Russia going to do about it? Was it possible that the very Christian tsar would let his Orthodox brothers in Greece be cut to pieces for the greater glory of the Mohammedan Turks? Pushkin wrote to Alexander Raevsky: "Here is news of an event which will have very serious consequences for the future, not only of this country, but of the whole of Europe. (And Russia in particular.) Greece has rebelled and proclaimed her independence. . . . On February 21 Prince Alexander Ypsilanti, with his two brothers and Prince George Cantacuzino, arrived in Iaşi from Kishinev, where he had left his mother, wife, and two brothers. . . . There he published proclamations which spread rapidly through the countryside, declaring that the Greek phoenix was about to rise from its ashes, that Turkey's final hour had come, and that one of the great powers was supporting this noble movement. The Greeks have flocked to serve behind his three standards. . . . Everyone is terribly excited. All the Greeks' thoughts are bent toward the same end: the independence of the fatherland. In shops, on the streets, in bars, everywhere, crowds of Greeks are congregating. They are selling their possessions for ridiculous sums, buying sabers, guns, and pistols, talking about Leonidas and Themistocles, preparing to join the regiments of the blessed Ypsilanti. . . . Strange sights. Two nations [Italy and Greece], both long sunk in a condition of negligible mediocrity, are rising from the dust at the same moment and re-entering the world political arena revitalized. Ypsilanti's first step was sublime and courageous. He is starting out at twenty-eight, having lost one arm in a good cause. Now, dead or alive, he belongs to History. An enviable fate. . . . One important question. What will Russia do? Will we occupy Moldavia and Wallachia as 'pacifist' mediators, or will we cross the Danube as allies of the Greeks and enemies of their enemies?"

On April 2 Pushkin noted in his Kishinev diary: "Spent the evening with N.S. Charming Greek woman. We talked about Ypsilanti; of the five Greeks in the room, I was the only one who spoke like a Greek: They were all despairing of the success of the Etaireia, but I am absolutely certain Greece will prevail."

On May 7 a young Frenchman left Kishinev to enlist in the Greek army, carrying a letter from Pushkin to Ypsilanti: Pushkin's excitement was so intense that he was proposing to leave Russia and fight in the ranks with the Greeks. He wrote to Gnedich: "I will not be seeing you again for a while. Events give me a presentiment that our separation will be very, very long." He even wrote a poem entitled "War," glorifying his own lust for battle:

> Why delay the horrors of these battles,
> What are they waiting for to begin?

In August 1821, still hoping Russia would come into the war on the side of Greece, he wrote to Turgenev: "If there is any hope of war, for the love of Christ leave me in Bessarabia."

His need to serve a cause was so imperative that he actually did join the Masonic lodge "Ovid No. 25" that year, and participated joyfully in its political discussions and plans to change the face of Europe. He felt that here, at last, he was acting; in fact, he was only killing time.

"I was a Freemason," he wrote in 1826, "a member of the Kishinev lodge, whose activities led to the suppression of all the other lodges in Russia."

One day General Insov received a letter from St. Petersburg, dated November 19, 1821: "His Imperial Majesty has learned that Masonic lodges have been established or are about to be established in Bessarabia under the direction, for Kishinev, of a certain Prince Zutzo. . . . With him must be Pushkin, who is attached to Your Excellency and over whose conduct you have been asked to keep a close watch. . . . As for Pushkin, His Majesty should be told how he has been behaving and why you have not seen fit to remark upon his activities in the Masonic order. . . ."

Insov replied on December 1: "Mr. Pushkin, who is employed in my offices, is conducting himself perfectly well. . . . The information regarding his affiliation with a Masonic lodge is incorrect, for he could not have joined such a lodge even had he wished to do so, there being no Masonic lodge here."

The police were watching Pushkin. It was already known in St. Petersburg that he was "publicly, and even in cafes, maligning not only the military administration, but the government as well."

It was true, Pushkin was maligning everybody. He was dissatisfied with everybody. He was angry with Russia for not supporting the Greeks and with the Greeks for not deserving support. Yes, even the Greeks disappointed him. Their ideal had been beyond the reach of nineteenth-century men. Too soon had come the sordid compromises, jealousy, treachery, wanton cruelty. Differences had arisen between the leaders of the insurrection, Vladimiresco and Ypsilanti. Vladimiresco represented a Romanian democratic movement, while Ypsilanti only aspired to defeat the Turks so that he could set up a bourgeois Greek regime in Greece. The great goal of independence faded into the background; the war became a pretext for plunder, the capture of towns and torture of prisoners. The Turks mutilated the men, sold the girls, spitted and roasted the children, tied the women up in sacks with starving rats, cats and poisonous snakes. The Greeks cut the throats of the Ottomans, sparing only the rich, who might be able to pay ransom. Pushkin was increasingly shocked and disgusted by these barbarians who were dishonoring the cause they had championed. In 1824 he wrote, in a letter to N. A. Raevsky: "We have seen the new Leonidases in the streets of Odessa and Kishinev; several of them are known to us personally, and we can certify their utter worthlessness. No notion of military science, no grain of honor, no enthusiasm; they have somehow contrived to be insipid even now when their conversation should be of moment to any European; the French and Russians here treat them with a contempt which they merit only too fully; they accept anything, even beatings, with an imperturbability worthy of Themistocles. I am neither a barbarian nor an apostle of the Koran, I am intensely interested in the Greek cause, and it is for that very reason that I am so infuriated by the sight of these wretches posing in the sacred role of the defenders of freedom."[3]

He expressed himself even more strongly in a letter to Prince Vyazemsky: "Greece disgusts me. The Greek issue may be viewed like that of our Negro brothers: It is to be hoped that both will be delivered from a condition of intolerable servitude, but it is unforgivable childishness for the civilized peoples of Europe to begin raving at the mere mention of Greece. The Jesuits taught us about Themistocles and Pericles, and we imagined that a dirty tribe of brigands and shopkeepers could be their legitimate successors and the heirs to their academic celebrity."[4]

The failure of this revolution prompted Pushkin to write the following lines:

> Give no freedom to the flocks:
> Flocks are for slaughter and shearing,
> Their heritage, down through the ages,
> Is the club and the yoke with a rattle.

What a gulf there was between liberal theory and liberal practice. And what a caricature of the struggle for independence, these bandits' brawls beneath the blue sky of Greece. What was one to believe? Whom was one to trust?

Disillusioned with politics, Pushkin worked off his excess energy in pursuit of women, provoking scandals and rushing into duels all over town. As in St. Petersburg, his moral confusion expressed itself in a fresh wave of devilry and provocation.

Life in Kishinev was deadly. Work for General Insov was nonexistent. St. Petersburg was at the other end of the earth. And mail was slow. The poet chafed; several times he implored his friends to have him recalled to the capital. From letter to letter, his hopes gradually sank: "If I am given permission to come back, don't tell a soul, I want to fall upon your heads like a roof full of snow." Again: "My friend, I so want to see you again. I have business in St. Petersburg. I don't know if I shall be able to come, but I am trying."[5] "I'm hanging on, I may get to you yet. But not before next year. I wrote to Zhukovsky, he doesn't answer; I wrote to the minister, not a word; O my friends, carry my prayer to Augustus."*[6] "I am sloshing about in the Moldavian mud and the devil knows when I'll get out of it."[7]

He compared himself to Ovid, exiled from Rome, or to a captive looking out of his prison window at the free, powerful flight of the eagles.

He thought even his friends had forsaken him.

"Not one friendly voice reaches me in my desert."[8] "You are one of the few of all the fleeting friends of all my fleeting youth who remember me."[9] "Nobody writes to me. Moscow, St. Petersburg and the Arzamas have completely forgotten me."[10] "Delvig has not written one word to me for a year."[11]

The isolation was bad enough; but on top of that, he had no money.

Pushkin's parents sent him nothing, or as good as. "My father has had an inspiration," he wrote to his brother Leo, "he is going to send me my clothes; remind him for me."[12]

His annual salary of seven hundred rubles was not even a drop in the bucket. *The Prisoner of the Caucasus* brought in a paltry five hundred more. He "was dying of poverty."[13] To disguise his indigence, he resorted to artificial eccentricity: The memoirs of the day describe the poet's singular silhouette, dressed in Moldavian, Jewish, Turkish and gypsy costume, with an eighteen-pound cudgel in his fist and a pair of pistols stuck through his belt. One of his contemporaries[14] wrote: "He often used to walk in the municipal gardens, each time in a different disguise. One saw him attired as a Serb or Moldavian, his women friends lent him their clothes—in those days the Moldavians wore cassocks. Or as a Turk or Jew, speaking with a Jewish accent. Even when he was not wearing some costume, he would contrive to have one of his coattails fastened to his shoulder and the other one trailing on the ground—that, he said, was being dressed *en général*. He often went to the metropolitan church with Insov, who would sit up in front near the choir, while Pushkin kept to the back where the general could not see him. All the time he was kneeling and prostrating himself on the floor, he would be making faces at women he knew, smiling or shaking his finger in front of his nose as if to scold or warn them of something."

Every morning Pushkin spent hours lying on the bed in his room in General Insov's house, firing pellets of bread or wax. The ceiling still shows traces of his marksmanship. Or if a friend came to call, Pushkin would thrust a foil into his hand and force him to parry his attack. In the summer he wandered about the room naked, writing or declaiming

* Alexander I.

poetry until he was hoarse—and woe to anyone who disturbed him. At night he would play cards, drink and argue with a few officer acquaintances. There is the story of how, one evening, having caught sight of a pretty girl inside a shop in Kishinev, he rode his horse through the door. And of how he amused himself teaching Moldavian curses to General Insov's parrot, who promptly repeated them to a visiting priest. And of how, in a quarrel with a native of Kishinev, Pushkin whipped off his boot and struck the poor man full in the face with it. And of how, another time, when he had been drinking, he had a run-in with a fellow named Lanov, a local administrator.

"You are a babe in arms," said Lanov; "you can still see the milk on your mouth."

"There's wine on yours," Pushkin retorted.

A duel was narrowly avoided.

Dueling and cards: two ways to stake one's life on a gesture, and Pushkin never missed an opportunity to try his luck. It is hard to know exactly how many meetings he had "on the field of honor" in Kishinev. A dozen, no doubt, perhaps more.

In October 1820 he quarreled with Colonel F. F. Orlov, one of General M. F. Orlov's brothers, a redoubtable colossus of a man who had lost a leg as the result of a war injury. Alexeyev, Orlov, Pushkin and Liprandi were playing billiards in a local tavern and drinking numerous glasses of djonka. The liquor had excited Pushkin; he couldn't keep still, he laughed at nothing, pushed the other players, prevented them from taking aim, moved the balls around the table. Orlov grew annoyed and called Pushkin a "schoolboy," and Alexeyev added that "schoolboys deserved to be punished." At these words Pushkin turned white, poured out a stream of violent abuse, smashed the balls all over the table top and challenged Orlov and Alexeyev to a duel. The meeting was set for the following morning at ten. "I'll show them I'm not a schoolboy," muttered Pushkin. Liprandi had great difficulty in reconciling the adversaries, but the duel was finally canceled and replaced by a friendly supper.

A few months later, in June 1821, Pushkin had a fresh altercation, this time with a certain Deguilly, a "*ci-devant* French officer." Deguilly declined to fight it out on the field, so Pushkin wrote him the following letter in French:

"Notice to Mr. Deguilly, French ex-officer. It is not enough to be half a fraud, you've got to go all the way. On the night before a f—ing sword fight one does not go writing lamentations and last wills and testaments under the nose of one's wife, one does not invent cock-and-bull stories for the local authorities just to make certain one will not get scratched; one does not compromise a second on two occasions, or a general who deigns to allow a bootlicker inside his door. I knew exactly what would happen, I'm sorry I didn't take a bet on it. Now it's over, but watch out!

"I am, Yours as you deserve, Pushkin. June 6, 21.

"Further, take note that in future I shall know, if the need arises, how to assert my rights as a Russian gentleman, since you wish to know nothing about the rights of dueling."

Even this letter, however, was not enough to calm Pushkin's wrath. He was boiling. To relieve himself, he grabbed his notebook and, among the drafts for some admirable poems, drew a picture of a man, barelegged and in shirt sleeves, with a caption in French: *Ma femme! . . . ma culotte! . . . et mon duel donc! . . . Ah! ma foi, qu'elle s'en tire comme elle voudra, puisque c'est elle qui porte culotte . . .* ("My wife! . . . My britches! . . . and what about my duel! . . . Well, she'll have to manage the best she can, since she's the one who wears the britches!").

Later that year, another incident actually brought Pushkin onto the field. He was playing baccarat with an officer named Zubov, and losing as usual. He suspected the other man of cheating, and, standing up, announced that he considered it unfair to have to pay a debt contracted in such circumstances. Zubov challenged Pushkin, and the two met at the Malina dueling ground. Pushkin arrived with a bag of cherries in his hand. Facing his adversary, who was already taking aim, Pushkin calmly continued to eat his cherries and spit the stones in the direction of the officer. Zubov fired and missed. Pushkin had not blinked. Instead of taking his turn, he asked: "Are you satisfied now?"

At his words, Zubov came running up to embrace the poet, but Pushkin stopped him with a gesture.

"That would be too much," said he.

And strolled dignifiedly away, carrying his bag of cherries.

Pushkin used this encounter in 1830, when he was writing his short story *The Shot*. His hero also ate cherries while a pistol was being aimed at his head, and refused to shoot once his adversary had received satisfaction.

In January 1822 he had another quarrel and duel with another officer, Colonel Starov. This incident began at the Kishinev casino, where the entire local cosmopolitan upper crust used to gather. The ladies wore expensive gowns from Vienna, the men wore turbans or high Moldavian bonnets. There was dancing, and Pushkin loved to dance. One night, having worked himself into his usual frenzy, he asked the orchestra to play a mazurka. Then a young officer, newly arrived at the garrison, called for a waltz. The orchestra, obeying the first command, swung into a wild mazurka—giving a civilian precedence over an officer! Indignant, Colonel Starov called the young officer over and ordered him to demand an apology from Pushkin.

"But how can I speak to him, sir?" the young man stammered; "I have never even met him."

"You don't know him?" said Starov. "Very well, never mind; I'll go myself." At the end of the dance he marched over to Pushkin.

"You have been guilty of an impertinence to one of my officers," he said. "Apologize to him, if you please, or you will have me to answer to."

"Apologize for what?" retorted Pushkin. "I don't know what you're talking about. But as far as you are concerned, I am your servant."

"Very well, until tomorrow, Alexander Sergeyevich."

"Excellent, Colonel."

The duel was set for nine the next morning. Starov was renowned for his bluster, his marksmanship and his acute sense of his own dignity. Pushkin was proud to have such an opponent and eager to match forces with him. He awaited the hour of the meeting in a state of nervous gaiety, as though it were a party being given in his honor. He urged his second, Alexeyev, to hurry with the preparations, for he wanted to be first on the field. By the time the two men reached their destination, however, a snowstorm of fearful violence was sweeping over the countryside. The barrier was set at sixteen paces. Pushkin fired first, and missed. Starov fired with no better result. The colonel then asked the seconds to reduce the distance to twelve paces.

"That's better," Pushkin agreed. "It's cold out."

The seconds, their fingers stiff with cold and their eyes blurred with tears by the wind, struggled to reload the guns. Finally, Starov and Pushkin took aim once more. Two shots rang out. Neither man was hit. Starov and Pushkin asked the seconds to shorten the distance again, but they refused point-blank, and the duel was postponed.

"See you soon, Alexander Sergeyevich," said the colonel.

"Until the next time, Colonel," said Pushkin.

On his way back, Pushkin stopped at a friend's home and left the following note on his table:

> I'm alive,
> Starov
> Safe and sound,
> The duel goes on.

That day Liprandi, Alexeyev and other friends made a series of visits in an attempt to negotiate a reconciliation, ending in an interview between the colonel and the poet at Nicoletti's restaurant.

"I have always respected you, Colonel," said Pushkin, "which is why I accepted your cartel."

"And it was a good thing you did, Alexander Sergeyevich," Starov replied. "For you have thereby risen in my esteem; I must own, by the way, that you conduct yourself as well under fire as behind your desk."

And that was the end of it. But the town of Kishinev was ringing with the story. Young Pushkin's *sang-froid* in the face of an opponent as tough-skinned as old Starov was much admired. "I have known Alexander Sergeyevich to lose control of himself," Liprandi wrote, "sometimes to the point of insanity; but in moments of danger, when he was facing death and, like the rest of us, showed his true self, he became utterly calm and collected. . . . When matters had reached the dueling stage, he would walk onto the field as cold as a block of ice. . . ."

Two days later Pushkin was in the billiard room at Nicoletti's and heard some young Moldavians talking in low voices about his duel with Starov. He listened. They were unanimous in applauding his courage and belittling the conduct of the colonel. Pushkin threw his cue into a corner, went over to the group and said in a loud voice: "Gentlemen, the way in which Starov and I settled our differences concerns no one but the two of us. I warn you that if you have the audacity to criticize Starov, a man for whom I have the highest regard, I shall take your words as a personal affront for which each and every one of you will have to answer to me!"

The startled young men apologized to the poet, who swept triumphantly from the room.

A short while later, the wife of a Moldavian boyar named Todoraki Balsh, vexed by Pushkin's indifference to her, tried to provoke him by alluding to the duel. The scene took place in a Kishinev drawing room.

"How tedious!" said Pushkin. "If only I could fight to defend someone else's interests!"

"Fight to defend your own, instead," the young woman said.

"Against whom?"

"Well, there's always Starov. I seem to think you didn't end your quarrel with him as well as you might have done. . . ."

Pushkin flew into a temper, told her she could be thankful she was only a woman, announced that he was going to demand an explanation from her husband then and there, turned and strode to the gaming table presided over by Todoraki Balsh, a full-bearded boyar of consequence and a member of the Bessarabian supreme council. He demanded an apology from this august personage, who spluttered, grew angry and ran to ask his wife what it was all about. The young woman insisted that Pushkin had been impertinent to her. Balsh returned to the gaming room and solemnly articulated: "How can you demand an apology from me when you yourself have had the audacity to insult my wife?"

Pushkin went berserk, snatched a candlestick and began brandishing it like a club. Fortunately, it was taken away from him. The next day, after the intervention of a few officers, Balsh agreed to make amends to the poet. The Moldavian arrived at the rendezvous clothed in a long, flowing tunic, his paunch well to the fore, his expression lofty.

"I have been asked to make you an apology," he said. "What kind of apology do you wish?"

Pushkin said not a word, raised his hand, slapped the boyar with all his force and pulled a pistol from his pocket. There was no duel: General Insov ended the argument by placing Pushkin under house arrest for two weeks.

Pushkin's clashes with the Moldavians were frequent, and in order to placate the plaintiffs and keep his lodger in check, poor Insov was often forced to lock him in his room and confiscate his boots. "Careful, Pushkin," some Moldavian would say, more temerarious than the rest; "if you go on like that they'll be taking your boots away again."[15]

"Old Insov put me under arrest every time I thrashed a Moldavian boyar," Pushkin wrote in 1824. "It's true that the good old mystic would come to see me in my prison and talk to me about the Spanish revolution."

From Moscow, Vyazemsky wrote to Turgenev: "Our Pushkin in Kishinev has walloped a boyar and had a pistol fight with a colonel. No blood spilled. They say he behaved splendidly on the latter occasion. . . . He has no money. He has even gone into a decline, it appears, from melancholy, boredom and poverty."

Melancholy, boredom and poverty were effectively what drove him to provoke everyone he met, to disguise himself, fight, get drunk, play cards—and chase the ladies. Wherever Pushkin went, women appeared and romance ensued. At no time in his life was he free of the chains of love. Always, there would be a swarm of Maryas, Eudoxias and Natalyas with interchangeable faces fluttering around him.

The wives of the great Moldavian lords dressed in the European fashion, they had French teachers and governesses, and they had their "at home" days, but their servants were no better than a tribe of ragged gypsies, and their homes were a potpourri of external opulence and colorful squalor.

"Go through the doors of any one of these stately residences, which would not disgrace the main square of a large European city," Veltman wrote. "You cross a vestibule full of Armenians; a piece of cloth will be pulled aside to let you pass; then you traverse a hall large enough for a detachment to maneuver in; another red curtain, in the left or right wall, will be drawn aside and you will find yourself in the divan room, where you will be met by the lady of the house, in a European gown under a sleeveless jacket covered with gold; or it may be the master himself who will receive you, and involuntarily, you will think to youself:

"He's important, very important, very, very important.
His mustaches are at least three inches long,
His fine gray beard must measure two full ells,
The amber stem an archine, the pipe five sagenes.
He's important, very important, very, very important.

"You are invited to sit on the divan; some nondescript Armenian enters, wearing a purple velvet tunic and a silver-gilt breastplate, a Turkish cashmere turban on his head, a scarf—also Turkish—tied around his waist, and a yataghan at his side; over his arm he carries a square of gold-embroidered muslin, which he will use to wipe the precious pipestems. . . . He offers you a pipe and places a copper saucer on the floor beneath the hearth. At the same time a tattered, barefoot little Bohemian girl, her hair in a bush of snarls, presents the 'dulchez' and a glass of water on a tray."

Pushkin has left a portrait in verse of those massive Moldavian females burgeoning in the semiobscurity of the "divan rooms":

Their legs folded beneath their arse,
Staring at bowls of fresh preserves,
The ladies, like Egyptian gods,
Sit and sweat in silence.

One or two of these plump, mute women caught the poet's eye, however, and few resisted his advances.

"Pushkin was fond of going to parties and evening receptions," Gorchakov wrote in his memoirs, "and everyone was always glad to invite him. He took part in all the balls and auxiliary entertainments, he loved cards and dancing. At every reception he found someone new to admire, becoming the latest idolater of yet another idol. I often heard him say, 'What a gorgeous creature! I can't live without her!' And the next day this gorgeous creature would be replaced by another."

In 1821 Pushkin himself wrote, to Nashchokin: "All the pretty women here have husbands, and in addition to the husband, a gallant, and in addition to the gallant, someone else to keep them from growing bored."

Pushkin was enamored, among others, of the Schreiber girl, who was seventeen, pretty and shy; Mrs. Vakar, a bit low-slung, but witty and not overtimid; little Sandulaki, dark, keen and spritely; Commander Solovkin's wife; the senior official Eyfeldt's wife; the graceful Moldavian girl Rossetti, whose tiny, light feet often visited his dreams; a Jewess;

somebody named Prunkul; a local gypsy; and a host of others. But although every woman drew him, none detained him. Only two names on the Don Juan list date from his Bessarabian period: Pulcheria and Calypso.

Pulcheria Bartholomey was the daughter of a rich Moldavian, a man who was inflated, mustachioed and of a pensive turn of mind. He had an enormous ballroom built onto his house, and his favorite pastime was to sit there cross-legged on a divan and watch the revolving dancers as he sucked on his pipestem. From her father, Pulcheria had inherited a sort of vegetable indifference. Her beauty was immobile and cold. Her conversation was nonexistent. And she was incapable of experiencing any emotion whatever. Veltman, who knew her well, described her in these terms: "Pulcheria was a fresh young girl with a full, round figure; she preferred to express herself in smiles, but her smiles were not those of a coquette: They came straight from an untroubled and wholesome heart. No one, of all who knew her during those years, can recall that her eyes ever singled anyone out; for her a man, whoever he might be, was an individual with a head, arms, and legs. . . . Observing Pulcheria, who looked to be about eighteen, I often wondered if she were not a masterpiece of art, rather than nature. Her movements might all have been performed mechanically, by an automaton. I watched her walk, and it seemed to me that there was something strange, inexpressible about the way she moved. I studied her eyes; her wonderfully serene expression followed every turn of her head. Her complexion and hands were so fine that they seemed to be covered with suede skin."

Pushkin admired this doll; there was something grandiose, something divine in her imbecility. He danced with her, he courted her. When he paid her a compliment she would answer in French, with a dreadful Moldavian accent: "Ah, what a one you are, Mr. Pushkin! How you do go on!"

These two sentences, according to contemporaries, represented Pulcheria's entire romantic vocabulary. But Pushkin was such an amateur of lovely forms and colors that he forgave the poor girl for being both dumb and unable to conceal it. He loved her for the freshness of her skin, the color of her eyes, the shape of her lips. He is believed to have written the poem *A Virgin* for her:

> I have warned you: fear that amiable virgin
> For her strange power compels every heart.

That was doing her a considerable honor; but in spite of her adorer's declarations, both in prose and in poetry, the girl remained as unmoved, as mineral, as congealed as ever. Pushkin grew weary of the "Ah, what a one you are"s and the "How you do go on"s, and moved on to new horizons.

Calypso Polichroni had two enormous advantages over Pulcheria: She was more intelligent and she was more approachable. Her mother was a Greek refugee who had fled Constantinople in 1821 and set herself up as a fortuneteller in Kishinev. The old witch received her clients in a black velvet bonnet covered with cabalistic signs. When she went into her trance, her hair stood on end and lifted the enchanted object off her head, a curious spectacle that was much appreciated by the youth of Kishinev. Pushkin, however, was more interested in the girl than in her magician mother. Calypso Polichroni was small, thin and flat-chested. Her long face, painted pink in the Turkish style, was not without grace. Her features were fine, her hair thick, black and fragrant, her elongated eyes bespoke a world of experience and sensuality. This otherwise perfect ensemble was unfortunately marred by an aquiline nose that cleaved her face from top to bottom. Calypso spoke Greek, Turkish, Arabic, Moldavian, French and Italian. She had a melodious voice; Pushkin liked to hear her sing the oriental laments—now languid and despairing, now harsh and panting like the gusty breath of love. But Calypso had more than her voice to make the poet forget her long nose and hollow chest: She was rumored to have been Byron's mistress, and Pushkin was much intrigued by the thought of possessing a woman whom Byron had known only a few years before. Caressing her was like communing with the English poet. On April 5, 1823, he wrote to Vyazemsky: "I shall introduce you to the heroes of Skulyani and Seku, Yordaki's comrades in arms, and a Greek girl who has been kissed by Byron."

To this voluptuous girl with the trenchant nose and the eyes like bright black olives, Pushkin dedicated a mass of drawings and notes and one poem, *To the Greek Girl:*

> You were born to illumine
> The imaginations of poets. . . .

Pushkin had one other serious affair, with the wife of a rich Kishinev landowner named Inglesi. The man was fiercely jealous of his wife, who was beautiful and of a roving disposition. The legend tells how he nearly surprised the faithless one in Pushkin's company, how the lovers only just had time to run for cover in a nearby cottage and how the husband challenged Pushkin to a duel. But General Insov put Pushkin under house arrest again and advised Inglesi to leave town, with Mrs. Inglesi. They say she was inconsolable, and died of heartbreak in a foreign country.

Pushkin's notebooks attest to the existence of yet another passion, as intense as it is unidentifiable. The draft of a letter has been found, written in French and addressed to an unknown woman: "I do not write to affront you, but because I have the stupidity and weakness to confess my absurd passion to you, and I want to speak openly. Do not put on airs, it would be unworthy of you; coquetry would be a frivolous and above all pointless cruelty; nor would I be convinced by your anger; in what can I offend you? I love you with so much force and tenderness, so little pretension, that even your pride cannot be injured. . . . Attribute this confession to my exaltation, to a state of distraction I could no longer control, bordering on physical faintness. I ask for nothing, I do not know myself what I want, and yet I . . ."

The draft of another letter has been found among the poet's notes, addressed "to a few unknown ladies" of Kishinev. The text is in French: "Yes, indeed I have guessed the identity of the two charming women who deigned to remember the hermit of Odessa, erstwhile hermit of Kishinev. A thousand times I have kissed these lines that remind me of so much madness, torment, wit, grace, so many evenings, mazurkas, etc. . . . Good God, you are cruel, Madame, to suppose I could enjoy myself in a place where I can neither meet nor forget you. Alas! sweet Maygyn, far from you [I am] distraught, ill-tempered, my wits go all astray. . . ."

The Pushkin scholars have identified the sweet Maygyn as a certain Marie Ralli, a friend of Pulcheria Bartholomey's.

"She was," wrote Liprandi, "a girl of eighteen, a friend of Pulcheria's, but far prettier in figure and form; also, she was three years younger than Pushkin. He was particularly fond of dancing with her."

Several love letters. But what happened to the rest? A few women's names. But how many more, of whom we know nothing? Pushkin loved, sang and forgot so many in his life! Young and middle-aged, short and tall, blonde and brunette, quick-witted and silly, bold and bashful. Today these creatures, once flesh and blood, live on only in two or three words scribbled in the margin of a notebook.

4. *Ovid*

Even with all his gambling, damsels, duels and dancing, the monotony of life in Kishinev was turning his blood to molasses. A trip to Kamenka, another to Odessa, a tour of Bessarabia with Liprandi gave him only the briefest illusion of freedom. But all the time he was being unconsciously enriched by these places, their history and legends.

In his memoirs Liprandi has given an account of his Bessarabian tour with Pushkin. Of their stay in Akkerman (Belgorod-Dnestrovsky), he wrote: "One minute Pushkin would be flirting with our host's five husky, ripe daughters, and the next he would be over at the whist tables taking bets. . . . His bursts of laughter rang out in every corner. . . . We reached Tatar-Bunar at dawn and stopped there to rest and have something to eat. While the chicken was being roasted, Pushkin wrote, as usual, on scraps of paper which he then stuffed carelessly into his pocket, took out again, studied. . . . [At Izmail] when I came in around midnight, I found Pushkin sitting Turkish-fashion on a divan surrounded by a swarm of bits of paper. He swept them all together and thrust them under his pillow. . . . After emptying a carafe of wine, we went to sleep. . . . When I opened my eyes, I saw him sitting in the same place as on the previous night, in the same position, in his nightclothes, and again surrounded by his scraps. . . . He had a pen in his hand and was beating time with it as he read out something in a low voice. His head was nodding with the rhythm. Seeing me awake, he put all his papers away and busied himself getting dressed."

Their trip lasted nine days, from December 14 to 23, 1821. But those nine days away from the "accursed town" were enough to revive his need to write. They were traveling through unsubdued territory, where whole battalions of "bandits of honor" were hiding out: deserters from the Greek armies, revolutionaries, escaped political prisoners and professional criminals. Their chiefs were formidable men such as Urzul, who claimed the right for bandits "to seize by armed force the goods of certain lords who, fearlessly and with utter impunity, despoil the serfs attached to them."[1] The exploits of these robber chiefs and their companions reminded Pushkin of an event which had taken place in Yekaterinoslav while he was there, and the moment he returned to Kishinev he began to write a poem, *The Robber Brothers.*

"This piece," he wrote, "was based on an actual event: In 1820, when I was in Yekaterinoslav, two bandits, chained together, swam across the Dnieper; their pause to rest on the island and the drowning of one of the guards are not invented. A few lines are reminiscent of *The Prisoner of Chillon,* but so much the worse for me. My meeting with Zhukovsky had nothing to do with it, since my poem was written at the end of 1821."[2]

Also: "I have burned the *Brothers* and it's a good thing I did. One fragment is still in existence, Nicholas Raevsky has it. If the low-class expressions 'tavern,' 'knout' and 'prison' do not shock the sensitive ears of the readers of the *Polar Star,* have it published."[3]

Notwithstanding Pushkin's affirmations, *The Robber Brothers* was apparently never completed.*

"For style, I have never done anything better," he said of it. The new poem was principally an experiment in folk literature. The general tone is set in the opening lines:

> Not crows collecting round
> A pile of rotting bones
> Down on the banks of the Volga at night.
> But bandits gathering by firelight.

The lines recall the first verse of a Russian folk song:

> Not white swans settling,
> Not falcons soaring,
> Not turtledoves cooing
> But the chatter of thieves.

The whole poem is cast in the same rough, cruel tone.

"I would have liked," Pushkin wrote in November 1823, "the Russian language to retain a sort of biblical rusticity. I do not like to see it being infiltrated by European graces and French delicacies. Roughness and simplicity suit it better."

N. N. Raevsky thought the poem contained "admirable examples of that simple, true language which our public has not yet learned to understand."[4]

Belinsky wrote that "elements of real life had found their way into this poem" and praised Pushkin for not hesitating "to introduce real

* "Pushkin," Mrs. Orlov wrote, "has sent Nicholas a part of a poem which he does not dare to have printed, or even finish. The idea is a weird one, showing in my opinion the influence of his reading of Byron."

Russian robbers into his work instead of the traditional Italian or Spanish ones, and arm them with broad knives and clubs instead of daggers and pistols."

Other unfinished works date from the same year, 1822: the story of *Vadim*, who lived in Novgorod in the ninth century and was an apostle of civic independence; and *Tauris*, inspired by the Crimean scenery, the opening lines of which announce a lyric novel on a vast scale.

The only major poem Pushkin actually completed during that period, however, was the scandalous and satanical *Gabriliad*. In fact, it was so scandalous and so satanical that some scholars have tried to deny his authorship. Pushkin could not have stooped, they say, to ridicule the Virgin Mary, the Archangel Gabriel and the whole of Christianity in this manner. This must be a fake—apocryphal, perhaps. And throughout his life the poet himself refused to admit he had ever written it.†

In the Pushkin archives, however, on page 28 of notebook 2365, surrounded by a tangle of drawings of women's profiles, silhouettes and a portrait of Goethe, appear these few revealing words: "The Holy Spirit convenes the Archangel Gabriel, confesses its love, and makes him its go-between. (Gabriel is in love.) Satan and Mary."

The outline of *The Gabriliad*. There can be no doubt. Pushkin is uncontestably the author of the poem. And to top it off, he seems to have written it during Easter week (April 3–9, 1821)!

Like all government employees, Pushkin was required to fast throughout the week and to attend religious services virtually nonstop. General Insov set the tone. What with his sacred but very physical hunger, the liturgical chants, the news of the Greek revolution and his general hatred of exile, Pushkin must have been very nearly possessed, in the medieval sense of the word. He could not tolerate any form of coercion, and he wanted to ridicule the Church because he was *forced* to go to church, he wanted to be a devil because he was *forced* to behave like an angel.

On Easter Sunday, he amused himself by writing:

Christ is risen, dear Rebecca.
And here I stand ready, my Jewess,
To place into your hands what tells
Jew from Orthodox Christian.

The *Epistle to Davydov* was written the same day and in the same vein:

I have become good and grave.
I fast, I pray, and I believe
God will pardon my faults
As the emperor my poems. . . .

† *The Gabriliad* was not included among Pushkin's complete works until after the 1917 Revolution.

Besides, my haughty mind
Rebels against myself,
And my atheistical stomach
Will not digest the Eucharist. . . .
One might manage, if the blood of Christ
Were a good Château-Lafitte
Or a Clos-Vougeot, perhaps,
But what they give us, if you can conceive,
Is diluted Moldavian wine.

The Gabriliad, the outline of which is written in the same notebook as the lines to Rebecca and the *Epistle to Davydov*, closes this cycle of revolt against the Church.

It is a parody of the Annunciation, in the style of the *Galanteries de la Bible*, Parny's *La Guerre des Dieux* and Voltaire's *La Pucelle d'Orléans*. In the course of a single day, the Virgin Mary is possessed by Satan, the Archangel Gabriel and God in the form of a white pigeon. This threefold initiation is related by Pushkin in some five hundred graceful and mischievous lines. The fable contains neither metaphysics nor pornography: It is not his intention to refute Christian dogma as a philosopher, and he is too much of a poet to be merely depraved. Therefore, he jokes. But on such a theme, jest is surely a more serious offense than outright aggression? If an author makes a virulent attack upon religion, then the problem exists for him and he is tormented by it. But Pushkin simply laughs at the Church, the Virgin, God and the Son of God with terrifying unconcern. He does not even honor God with his rage. He does not deny God, he ignores him. He treats him as he treated Chernomor the magician in *Ruslan and Ludmila*.

"Pushkin has just sent me one of his finest pieces of mischief," Vyazemsky wrote on December 22, 1822. And Yakushkin: "I have just read his *Gabriliad*. I think it is the best of all his long poems."[5]

It is true: The lines of *The Gabriliad* are wonderfully pure. Pushkin polished them lovingly, although he knew the poem would never be published, and even handwritten copies would have to be circulated without a signature. *The Gabriliad* was written for the pure pleasure it gave to its author and a few friends.

Its epilogue, in which the poet speaks of his own future, is ghoulishly ironic, in view of the fact that Pushkin died young, killed because of a woman who did not love him, did not understand him and may have been unfaithful to him. Here it is:

Days pass. Time, no doubt, unknown to me,
Will whiten my hair with silvery powder.
A sumptuous marriage at the altar rail
Will unite me forever to some gentle girl.

Oh sacred comforter, the ancient Joseph,
Bending my knee, I pray to thee—
Defender, protector of cuckolds—
I pray, and await thy blessing:
Have mercy, grant me peace and tranquility,
Have mercy, and grant me too—hear me out—
An easy sleep, trust in my wife,
Calm in my home, and my neighbor's affection.

While he was working on *The Gabriliad,* Pushkin was also preparing another poem, lyrical, colorful and clear as spring water. *The Fountain of Bakhchisarai* was begun in 1821, abandoned, resumed the following year and completed in 1823. In Pushkin's own words, the work was closely modeled on a story he had heard from "the lips of a young woman," presumably Katerina Raevsky.

The sky, rocks and lush vegetation of Tauris. The ruins of the harem which Pushkin had visited on his trip with Nicholas Raevsky. The memory of long, infatuated evenings with Katerina or Marya. Byron too. These are the components of this impassioned, naïve poem. Pushkin wrote about it, "*The Fountain of Bakhchisarai* is weaker than *The Prisoner.* The poem is dominated by references to Byron, who was my idol in those days."

The subject did not want for grandeur, however: Girey, the old khan, vain and cruel, has fallen in love with the beautiful Maria, whom he has brought back from Poland and installed in his harem at Bakhchisarai. His former favorite, Zarema, a Georgian woman, suffers from his sudden indifference. She steals into Maria's room and threatens to kill her if she does not restore Girey's love. A few weeks later, Maria mysteriously dies. The guards immediately seize Zarema and drown her. The inconsolable khan builds a marble fountain in his palace, in memory of the "doleful Maria."

It would have been interesting to study the birth and growth of a sense of chivalry in this primitive and brutal Tartar. All Girey knew of womanhood was the female livestock of his harem, washed, polished and perfumed according to ritual. His notions of love were simple and animal. It never occurred to him that one could sigh at a woman's feet, or respect and feel compassion for her. Suddenly, this tearful alien destroys all his preconceptions. He feels surges of aching tenderness for her. He grows up, transformed by her sole presence. But Pushkin neglected the potential here; he failed to see what could be made of this emotional transfiguration. He was concerned only with Zarema's jealousy of Maria, and as a result the poem lost in originality. A flaw in composition, thus; and weaknesses too in character portrayal. As in *The Prisoner of the Caucasus,* Pushkin does not really place his heroes, and he dresses them in Byronic colors. Girey is a Childe Harold, brave, moody and arrogant. The women are perfect examples of the same race. Byron created two kinds of women: violent, jealous and vindictive, like Gulnare in *The Corsair* (Zarema the Georgian is one of these), or tender, loving, docile and melancholic, like Zuleika in *The Bride of Abydos* (such is Maria the Pole).

But once again, Pushkin saves his poem by an admirable exterior. Our attention is not held by the khan or Zarema or Maria, but by the harem, with its undercurrent of murmur, the games of the women and their smooth, heavy bare skin, the slow stride of the eunuch, the starry nights of Tauris, the bloom of all that flesh, those perfumes of voluptuousness, those fountains of tears; they all spread and flower in another world. It is the music of the language, the choice of rhythms, rhymes and words that enchants us, not the substance of the poem. Here the words are infused with oriental resonances, the syllables adhere as though coated with honey. The nightingale is a different nightingale, more intoxicated and solitary than ours. The rose is a different rose, too full-bodied and heavily scented for our climates; the water of the fountains is too pure and fine for our hands and faces. Pushkin seems to have a different vocabulary for each country, climate and theme he illustrates; and yet, in poem after poem, he uses the same words, with the same meanings.

While he was working on *The Fountain of Bakhchisarai, The Gabriliad* and *The Robber Brothers,* Pushkin was also writing a host of short lyric or satirical poems, incidental verse, odes, epistles to friends and verse descriptions of historical events or scenes. His notebooks contain entangled stanzas from contradictory poems. He was simultaneously writing the scurrilous *Gabriliad* and the noble address to Chaadaev. Toward the end of June 1821 he wrote *The Dagger,* a political poem "dedicated to Brutus, Charlotte Corday and Karl Sand, the murderer of Kotzebue": When the law sleeps and God is occupied elsewhere, then may be seen the avenger's dagger glinting in the shadows . . . the necessity of the dagger in world history; the posthumous glory of political murderers. But in this revolutionary poem, Pushkin criticizes the French revolution. His liberalism was too moderate to condone massacre and mass hysteria. When spilled in such quantities, blood disfigures and perverts the pure concept of independence.

> Contemptible, dark and bloody,
> The hideous executioner towers
> Over the body of guillotined freedom.

In 1825 Pushkin wrote to Zhukovsky on the subject of this poem: "I promised Karamzin not to write anything against the government for two years—and I have kept my promise. *The Dagger* is not directed against the government, and although from the viewpoint of style its lines are not the most elegant imaginable, in intention it is guiltless."

On July 18, 1821, the news of Napoleon's death reached Kishinev. In his notebook Pushkin wrote, in French, "July 18, 1821. News of the death of Napoleon. Ball at the Armenian archbishop's."

Elsewhere: "In 1820 O—— said: revolution in Spain, Italy, revolution in Portugal, constitutions here, constitutions there. . . . Milord monarchs, you did a foolish thing the day you dethroned Napoleon."[6]

Napoleon's death inspired Pushkin to write a new poem on the former emperor of the French. At school, like everyone else, he had called him "bloodthirsty tyrant" and "Antichrist." But time had passed, and brought the restoration of the Bourbons, the legitimist exactions of the Holy Alliance, the Spanish, Italian, Portuguese and Greek revolutions, all weakening the prestige of Napoleon's conquerors. With every passing month it become more obvious that the European sovereigns had acted solely in their own interest. By opposing Napoleon, they had been defending autocracy and their own skins, nothing more. Napoleon, after all, was the heir of the Revolution, whereas they were only the heirs of their fathers. Their halo had already begun to dim, and the balance was gradually restored, Napoleon's popularity reaping the fruits of their blunders. Defeated, he was admirable. Dead, he became a legend. People began to miss him. By 1821 Pushkin had stopped insulting him—he called him "a great man," endowed him with "divine intelligence" and "noble thoughts":

Scathing shame upon the wretch
Who dares on this fateful day
Offer one inept reproach
To his uncrowned shade.
Glory! He gave the Russian people
A destiny worthy of their size,
And from the oblivion of exile,
Bequeathed freedom to the world.

In addition to the works mentioned above, the list for the "Kishinev years" should also include a large number of poems such as the excellent *Ovid,* the amusing poem *To My Inkwell* and *The Song of Oleg*—a fine piece of work in a sonorous, emphatic style; *The Black Shawl,* a Moldavian song; and various addresses to women and the muses. And lastly, it was in Kishinev, "on the night of May 28, 1823," that Pushkin began to write *Eugene Onegin,* the novel in verse that was to take him more than seven years to complete.

Kishinev was a long way from the capital, true; but the repressive campaign of Alexander I reached out to the farthest confines of the empire. Myriads of bureaucrats and spies were skulking in the shadows. There was surveillance, there was writing of reports, there was a race to see who could denounce the most people fastest. General Orlov had prohibited the flogging of the troops under his command. He had instructed a young officer, V. F. Raevsky, to devise literacy courses for the men. He had exhorted his subordinates to treat the soldiers with kindness. These generous measures aroused the deepest suspicions of the government secret agents. On January 1, 1822, Orlov gave a party in the riding academy, with a table set for the men as well as the officers. Officers and men seated under the same roof: That was not liberalism, it was indiscipline! It was the beginning of revolution! On February 5, at 1 P.M., Pushkin went to see V. F. Raevsky.

"Hullo, old man," said Pushkin, speaking very rapidly and in a strange voice.

"Hullo, what's up?"

"Sabaneev has just left Insov. They talked about you. I don't like to listen at keyholes, but I kept hearing your name, so I began to pay attention. Good old Insov, you know how he loves you, was staunchly defending you. They talked a long time. There was a lot I couldn't catch. . . ."[7]

V. F. Raevsky burned his papers, but he was arrested the next day and incarcerated in a fortress on grounds of conspiracy. Shortly thereafter, the revolutionary Union of the South was dissolved and a ukase of August 1, 1822, ordered the closure of the Masonic lodges.

The reactionary trend made itself felt in literary circles as acutely as in the army. Censorship was intensified to the point of absurdity, the most inoffensive works were torn to shreds. Birukov, the censor, had become the terror of all men of letters. He slashed his way through their texts, disfiguring them and fulminating in the name of an antiquated morality. Against him and his clique, Pushkin wrote his *Epistle to the Censor*, which could only be circulated in manuscript form but very quickly found a large audience:

Like a soured eunuch you prowl about the muses;
Neither fine feelings, wit, nor grace . . .
Nothing could move your frozen mind.
The glance you cast on every side is false, oblique;
Mistrusting everything, you find poison everywhere. . . .
What is it you fear? The man who seeks distraction
In mocking power, law, and custom
Will not, you may be sure, come your way;
He remains unknown to you, all of us know why,
And his message, far from Lethe's banks,
Roams the world without your seal. . . .

Pushkin spoke with the voice of authority: Most of his poems were thus roaming the world, unsigned by their author and unblessed by the censor's seal.

His work was the very image of his life—brilliant, mischievous, satirical, grave or rebellious by turns, and sometimes sad as death. He wrote according to his mood and he wrote to express his mood. He did his best to occupy the dull days of his exile; but they were beginning to grow terribly long. Ten, twenty times he had hoped an act of imperial clemency would permit him to return to St. Petersburg. He had a genuine need to see life in the capital again. A professional need, in the first place: How could he argue with a censor who was operating two thousand versts from Kishinev? How could he supervise the publication of his poems? Friends had to do it all for him—well intentioned, no doubt, but often clumsy.

"You like *The Black Shawl?*" he wrote to his brother. "You're right; but it was so badly printed. Who on earth was responsible for it? I smell Glinka!"[8]

And again, to Bestuzhev: "I enclose my Bessarabian dreams and hope you will find them to your taste. Give my respects to my old friend the censor. I foresee difficulties with the publication of my poem *To Ovid*. . . . But the little old woman [the censor] can be got round, for she is remarkably dim-witted."[9]

To "get round" the little old woman on this occasion, *To Ovid* had to be printed without a signature—there were two asterisks at the end of the poem. It was not until January 1823 that Pushkin received the copy of the *Polar Star* in which it had been published, through the agency of Bestuzhev. Periodicals took forever to cross the Russian steppe—not to mention payments! The civilized world was so incredibly far away from this ghastly Bessarabian desert! So far away, and yet it was for it that one had to go on living, suffering and writing.

There was another question tormenting the poet: He had learned the name of his calumniator in St. Petersburg—it was Count Tolstoy "the American," a gambling swashbuckler of low repute. Lieutenant Longinov, Pushkin's companion in Kishinev, wrote in his diary on June 15, 1822: "People were saying he had been whipped in the secret chancellery. . . . He wants to go to Moscow this winter, to fight a duel with a certain Count Tolstoy, the American, who was the chief author of this calumny."

Friends, enemies and business, all were calling Pushkin northward. From letter to letter, his itch to escape became a delirium. He couldn't wait, he was too bored. At the beginning of October 1822 he wrote a letter in French to his brother Leo which reveals the full measure of his pessimism, pride and gloom:

"You will be dealing with men you do not know. Always begin by thinking the worst of them; then you will not have to alter your opinion much. Do not judge them by your heart, which I believe to be noble and good and which, moreover, is still young; scorn them with infinite courtesy. That is the way to guard against the petty prejudices and passions which will affront you when you first go into society. Be cold with everyone: Familiarity is always bad. . . . No little kindnesses, divest yourself of whatever altruism you may possess, people will not understand it and will readily interpret it as servility—always delighted to judge others by themselves. Accept no favors. A favor, nine times out of ten, is a piece of perfidy. No protection, either, for it is degrading and creates obligations.

"I should have liked to warn you against the attractions of friendship, but I haven't the heart to harden your soul in the years of its fondest illusions. Whatever I could say to you of women would be utterly wasted. I would only point out that the less one loves a woman the more certain one is of having her, although that kind of possession is good for no one but an old eighteenth-century chimpanzee. As for the woman you truly love, I can only hope with all my heart that you may have her. Never pardon a deliberate offense; use few words or none, and do not repay insult with insult.

"If your fortune or circumstances will not permit you to shine, do not try to cover up for what you lack; instead, go to the opposite extreme: The bitterness of cynicism is convincing to superficial minds, whereas the petty maneuvers of vanity render you ridiculous and contemptible.

"Never borrow money, live in destitution instead. . . .

"These principles I offer you are the fruits of painful experience."

A few months after composing this sentimental testament, Pushkin made one last attempt to escape from Kishinev. Weary of indirect appeals that led to nothing, he decided, on January 13, 1823, to write to Nesselrode (the Foreign Minister) himself, asking for leave to spend two or three months in St. Petersburg. He wrote in French: "Your Excellency: Being attached by His Majesty's order to the governor general of Bessarabia, I cannot come to St. Petersburg, where I am called by the affairs of a family I have not seen for three years, without special permission. I therefore take the liberty of writing to Your Excellency to implore you to grant me a leave of two or three months."

Nesselrode transmitted the appeal to Alexander I, and the reply, dated March 27, 1823, was finally sent to General Insov: "His Majesty has deigned to instruct me to inform Mr. Pushkin through Your Excellency that it is impossible to grant him the leave he requests at this time."

Pushkin's last illusions collapsed; and now that he had lost all hope of returning home, life in Kishinev seemed more unendurable than ever.

He had to do something; he begged Insov to give him even the tiniest "change of air," if only a trip to Odessa. At least Odessa was in Europe! Touched by his protégé's lamentations, Insov gave him permission to go to Odessa in late May or early June 1823.

It was in Odessa that Count M. S. Vorontsov, governor general of southern Russia, was about to establish his headquarters, and Pushkin's friends in St. Petersburg and Moscow now applied themselves to obtaining his transfer there. Vyazemsky wrote to Turgenev: "Have you spoken to Vorontsov about Pushkin? He absolutely must take him on. Let the good souls do whatever is necessary, especially now that Pushkin really does want to settle down, and boredom and melancholy are poor counselors."[10]

This letter crossed in the mail with one from Turgenev: "I have spoken to Nesselrode and Count Vorontsov about Pushkin. He will take over from Insov and try to save his morals while allowing his talent to develop and strengthen."[11]

On June 15 Turgenev wrote again: "I have spoken personally with Vorontsov on two occasions, explaining Pushkin's problems to him and what he should do to save him, and I think it will be all right. A patron, a good climate, the sea, history—he will have everything; as far as talent goes, I trust him; unless he loses his head completely."

Pushkin was literally enchanted by his second trip to Odessa: "I have left my Moldavia and come to Europe. The restaurants and the Italian Opera remind me of the good old days and have made a new man of me. Meanwhile, Vorontsov has arrived and given me a very cordial welcome; he tells me I am to come under his orders now, and remain in Odessa."[12]

Pushkin was jubilant at the thought of leaving the "accursed town" of Kishinev and the society of the ignorant Moldavians, but the prospect of abandoning Insov pained him, and he had some apprehensions about the new experience that lay ahead and the new man he would have to contend with. He went back to Kishinev to take his leave of the people he had known there.

"Everything looked as though it would be fine," he wrote to his brother, "and yet my heart was seized by some new dread."

Having embraced his friends, paid his debts and packed his bags, Pushkin returned to Odessa at the beginning of July, leaving behind him in the little Moldavian town a few pretty and disconsolate women, two or three companions who missed him sincerely, a considerable number of enemies who were heartily glad to be rid of him and the good old General Insov, gruff and anxious, who kept repeating to everyone he met: "It won't be so easy with Vorontsov! Ah, why did he leave me? I loved him like my own son!"

PART IV

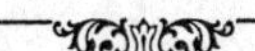

1. *Odessa*

In summer, all the windows had to be kept shut; otherwise, one was buried alive by the fine black dust that whirled down the streets. Pedestrians masked their faces with their capes. The friable soil crunched between the teeth, clogged the nostrils, burned the eyes. Nevertheless, the inhabitants of Odessa preferred it to the tenacious autumn mud. With the first rains, the city sank into a deep mire. Crossing the street became a perilous undertaking, for one might easily lose a shoe. Carriages ground to a halt, stuck fast in the center of town. Ladies in evening dress stepped out onto wooden pontoons, and teams of oxen were brought up to replace a pair of straining thoroughbreds at the head of a barouche. Post Street was chained off because of the danger of carriages becoming bogged down. Ribas Street was not much better. And to top it all off, there was a shortage of drinking water. A cask of water from the Dnieper cost a ruble. During periods of drought, the owners of hotels and boardinghouses distributed one bucketful of water per family per day. And yet, with all these minor inconveniences, the city was growing and expanding by leaps and bounds.

In 1793 the Duc de Richelieu had laid the foundations for a town which was destined, by virtue of its commercial port, to become a meeting place for the goods, men and ideas of all nations. A French *émigré*, the Comte de Langeron, continued Richelieu's work, and it was thanks to these two Frenchmen that the city of Odessa was born, stone by stone, in the opening years of the nineteenth century. When Pushkin came to live there, in July 1823, it looked like an agglomeration that had sprung up overnight. Two-storied "European" houses stood side by side with shanties built of wood and dried mud, Jewish hovels and Moldavian lean-tos, and behind the long gray palisades stretched empty lots where the local dogs hunted and howled. None of the streets were paved; but the old Turkish fortress was already being demolished and the game-filled undergrowth was being cut down to make a boulevard.

Here a church sprang up, over there a chancellery, hospital, garden, barracks, customs office, "quarantine." Saws were screeching, pulleys creaking, hammers pounding rhythmically on all sides. Wooden scaffoldings outlined the future against the light from the blue sky.

In recent years colonists had been pouring into Odessa. Serfdom had been abolished in the district; land was being distributed, and with land came liberty, and with liberty, wealth—for in a commercial port there is always money to be made. Wheat, rye, barley, tallow, linseed came into it and went out of it again, and all one had to do to snatch a few rubles on the wing was be there. Foreigners came, as well as Russians: Greeks, French, English and Jews were amassing fortunes in trade and commissions. There were already over thirty thousand inhabitants.

Whoever makes money wants to spend it, and for that there was the Italian Opera. In the intermissions, the audience went outside and sat on the stone blocks encircling the building to eat ices brought over from the nearby cafe. There were also restaurants, secret gambling dens, brothels, "European" hotels: in a word, all the attractions of the big city, for a public of wide-eyed country hicks. For a moment, after being deprived of all distractions during his stay in Kishinev, Pushkin imagined he was in Europe. He thanked his friends for pulling him out of the Moldavian mud. "One has to have spent three years in a stifling Asiatic jail as I have done," he wrote to Turgenev, "to appreciate the right to breathe the air of Europe, even if it isn't free." Chapter VIII of *Eugene Onegin* contains a tribute to the charms of Odessa:

> The sky there is calm for days on end.
> Trade, active and profitable,
> Hoists sail above the waves. . . .
> The golden Italian tongue
> Resounds gaily down the street,
> Where pass the arrogant Slav,
> The Frenchman, Spaniard and Greek,
> Armenian and fat Moldavian. . . .

To be sure, there was that dust, and the mud, and the desolation of the surrounding steppe, and the shortage of drinking water.

> But never mind: The evil is but middling bad,
> Especially when there is wine to drink
> That has entered duty-free.

Elsewhere, Pushkin describes his day:

> Sometimes, when the dawn cannon
> Thundered out on board ship,
> I would race down the steep slope
> That led to the edge of the sea. . . .

After a morning walk along the waterfront, spattered with sea foam and giddy from the wind, he would go into an inn to swallow a cup of thick, black Turkish coffee, and look out on the theater square, alive with short-tempered, shouting merchants. Despite the volume of its sea traffic, Odessa was still without an exchange, so the businessmen assembled outside the theater, chewing on their cigars—the distinctive mark of their trade:

The merchant goes to look at the flags,
To see if the heavens are bringing back
The fine sails he has been waiting for.
What new shipments have come into port,
What goods are still in quarantine?
Are the wine casks there?
And the plague? And fire?
Is there war or famine
Abroad? What's new?

While the merchants took inventory of their cargoes, the young people who had nothing else to do would invade some restaurant that had received a fresh consignment of oysters. That evening, the same young people would meet at the theater. In his early days in Odessa, Pushkin was a passionate fan of the Opera and the music of Rossini, the "European Orpheus." He loved:

The play of questing lorgnettes,
Rendezvous in the wings,
The prima donna, the ballet,
And the box where some young
Merchant's wife, lovely and vain,
Sits dreamily enthroned amidst
A court of willing slaves.

And the spectacle of the southern night:

It is late, the town is sleeping,
Night weighs, tranquil and hot.
Not a breath. The moon climbs.
A light and limpid veil
Drapes the sky. And all is still.
Only, the Black Sea murmurs.

However, all the polyglot agitation of the port, the calm beauty of the nights, the culinary accomplishments of the Greek and French restaurants, and even the Opera could not long distract him from his melancholy. Once the town lost the appeal of novelty, it quickly became unbearable. He was bored, there as in Kishinev, there as everywhere.

He arrived at the beginning of July, and on August 19 he wrote to Vyazemsky: "I am bored, my good Asmodeus. I am ill, I wish I could write, but I can't get a grip on myself." And to his brother, on the twenty-fifth of the same month: "I am in a foul mood . . . and this letter has not dispelled it."

His laments follow with monotonous regularity:

"Here everything is boredom and cold. I am freezing beneath the southern skies. . . ."[1]

"I am bored, and that is the refrain of my entire existence."[2]

"I have become boring . . . and sedate."[3]

Pushkin was happy only when he felt surrounded, supported, loved—not for his writing, but for himself. The presence of one true friend transfigured him; but nature's greatest glories could not hold him long, if there were no companion capable of understanding him with whom he could share his joy. In Odessa as in Kishinev, he sought in vain that atmosphere of warm exchange, virile communion, youthful high spirits. He lived at the Hotel Renaud, in a corner room with a balcony overlooking the Black Sea. Viegel, with whom Pushkin liked to talk, lived in the next room, and Liprandi, having also been transferred to Vorontsov's service, joined them there. But were these friends? No, only comrades, and their superiors were not much better. In Kishinev, at least, there had been good old "Papa Insov," who had provided him with a family. But in Odessa he was under the orders of Count Vorontsov, and there was decidedly nothing of the father, nor even of the enlightened patron of the arts, about him.

A fine-looking man, though, this Vorontsov: tall, lean, elegant, with chiseled features, thin lips, a hard expression. He had been brought up in England and affected a clipped, sibilant British accent. His personal physician was English: Mr. Lee; his secretary was English: Mr. Jackson; and he had an English groom for his English horses. His phlegm, his liberalism, his imperturbable correctness of manner were also copied from the purest British models. He was known as "the lord." He took himself for a viceroy and Odessa for his capital, where he maintained a court of servile flatterers, young *arrivistes* and frustrated intellectuals. He interested himself in social welfare: He reigned, in other words. He reigned voluptuously. He divided his princely activities among three residences: The first, by the seashore, was reserved for small, intimate dinners; the second, in town, immense and brand-new, housed his family life and official receptions; while in the third, in the municipal gardens, he received his suppliants. They were legion, too, the suppliants. They shuffled humbly in the dust before the little king's door, and Vorontsov treated them all with frigid equanimity and an English smile. The more there were of them, the happier he was. But the more amiable he became, the more he was to be feared, for he dissembled his feelings, out of cunning or politeness. As a gentleman. And he always, always got what he wanted. Whoever resisted him was defeated from the start.

Pushkin tried to resist. Vorontsov met him with the master's indulgent kindliness toward a gifted subaltern whom he is determined to protect and charm. But Pushkin was not asking for protection or charm. He was not an undersecretary, he was a writer and a member of the Russian aristocracy; in short, he was Vorontsov's equal. That was what the other man refused to understand. "Vorontsov is a vandal, an ignoble courtier and a niggling egoist," he wrote on July 14, 1824.[4] "He wanted to see me as an undersecretary, while I, to be quite truthful, imagined I was something rather different."

Again, in a letter to Bestuzhev written in June 1825: "In this country, writers belong to the upper nobility and have both the pride of the aristocrat and the artist's sensitivity; we do not wish to be protected by our equals. That is what this dog of a Vorontsov won't understand. When he sees a Russian poet coming into his antechamber with an epistle or an ode, he forgets that he also comes demanding deference, as a gentleman whose lineage goes back six hundred years. That makes a devil of a difference in approach."

The "difference in approach" widened daily. It drove Pushkin wild to be treated with condescension by a man he did not like and could not respect. Vorontsov's august posing exasperated him. He missed the jollity and simplicity of old Insov. "Insov was very fond of me," he wrote. "Whenever I had a fight with the Moldavians he would put me under house arrest and bring me French magazines to relieve my boredom. His Excellency Count Vorontsov did not put me under arrest and brought me no magazines, but, knowing approximately as much about Russian literature as the Duke of Wellington, he was excessively —— to me."[5] In the same piece he also wrote, "General Insov is a good and venerable old man. His soul is Russian: He does not give preference over all his compatriots, celebrated or obscure, to the first English tramp to come along; he no longer flirts with women, being past the age for it; he does not fear mockery, because he is above it; he is not empty-headed; he does not listen to calumny. . . ."

Pushkin already thought all that, but he was not yet saying it. Vorontsov sensed the poet's hostility, however. He had intended to attach him to his person, make him into a satellite who would be flattering to his prestige, a sort of court poet. But the court poet would not take the bit; this little civil servant, without status or position, this starveling, this upstart, had the audacity to put on airs with him—some present! Insov might better have kept his godson in his lice-ridden, stinking hole of a Kishinev. However, Vorontsov was too much a man of the world to show his annoyance. He continued to invite Pushkin to official functions, and Pushkin, also trying to hide his resentment, continued to attend his dinners and balls.

Vorontsov's receptions were starched and sumptuous. "Pushkin," Liprandi wrote, "was always very reserved and glum. [One day] as we were getting up from dinner I collided with him, and seeing that he was searching for his hat among the pile, I asked him, 'Where are you going?' 'Home to bed,' he answered, and added, 'These aren't dinners like Bologovsky's or Orlov's or even . . .' He left his sentence unfinished and walked out of the room."

Pushkin's gloom and irritation were intensified by his penury. At Kishinev he had been fed and boarded by Insov. In Odessa he could count on nothing but his own resources, that is, seven hundred rubles a year; and even they arrived inexcusably late. The salary for his last four months of service, which he should have received in September 1823, was not paid until February 1824: "225 assignation rubles and 1 silver ruble."

But hotels, restaurants, cards and theaters were expensive. There were his parents, of course, but Pushkin was a stranger to them. At least where money was concerned. On August 25, 1823, barely a month after his arrival in Odessa, he wrote to his brother Leo: "Explain to my father that I cannot survive without money. Thanks to the state of the censor today, I cannot live by my pen; I was not taught to be a carpenter; I cannot become a professor, even though I do know sacred history and the four rules of arithmetic. It's not my fault if I am a government employee and unable to resign. Everything and everybody fails me. On whom am I to rely, if not on my relatives and parents? I won't be kept by Vorontsov and that's flat. Necessity can drive me to desperation. It hurts me to see my father's indifference to my predicament, although his letters are all very amiable."

He was riddled with debts, and any money he laid hold of immediately went to pay off his innumerable creditors. A local cab driver told how Pushkin had hired him to make several trips into the country around Odessa, and had never paid him. Finally, the driver went to his lodgings: "I go into the room. He is shaving. I come up to him and say, 'Your Nobility, I would like my money, please.' He starts insulting me and rushes at me with his razor. I take to my heels. Good God, he nearly cut my throat. . . . One morning I'm out in the square, there where the exchange is, and I see Pushkin has opened his window and is calling all his creditors. I go up to him: 'Here are six rubles for each trip,' says he, 'and never show your face to me again.' "[6]

At the beginning of December 1823 Pushkin wrote the following letter[7] to General Insov: "General, I enclose the 360 rubles I have owed you for so long; please accept them with sincere thanks. As for excuses, I haven't the heart to make any. I am ashamed and humiliated to have been unable to pay you before, and the simple reason is that I have been absolutely penniless."

It was no more than the truth; and here he could not parade about, as he had done in Kishinev, costumed as a Jew, Greek or Moldavian. Living in the big town necessitated a certain decorum, and decorum was expensive. To the population of Odessa, Pushkin was a lean, nervous little man with a skin of bronze and thick African lips, in a black fitted coat, considerably worn but buttoned to the throat, a black hat with an olive sheen and a heavy ironclad cudgel. (He said he carried it to strengthen his wrist for duels.) His hair was ill-kempt, his expression fever-bright. He was poor. He was arrogant. He was alone.

In March 1824, however, his finances took a turn for the better, and hope revived. In the past, Pushkin's literary efforts had brought him little more than a reputation and a good deal of trouble. He received nothing for poems published in periodicals, and it was thanks to the efforts of Gnedich that he had been given a five-hundred-ruble pittance for his *Prisoner of the Caucasus*. The same was true, moreover, of every other Russian writer of the day, for whom literature was supposed to be a pleasant pastime, not a means of gainful employment. They would have felt dishonored to exchange their spiritual melodies for filthy lucre. Not being remunerated, their work was also unprotected. It could be reprinted and disfigured, and authors had absolutely no recourse against enterprising publishers. In 1824, for example, an employee in the third division published a German version of *The Prisoner of the Caucasus*, with the Russian text on the facing page. Pushkin, whose opinion he had not asked and to whom he had not paid a kopeck, had no choice but to accept this violation. "It was," he wrote, "the first case of literary fraud."

Pushkin was the first Russian author who dared to defend his rights, and also the first who pretended to live by his pen. He invented the profession of literature. With a nerve that left his correspondents speechless, he wrote, "Would you like to buy the whole poem? [*Prisoner of the Caucasus*] Length: 800 lines. Length of line: 8 feet. The whole divided into two cantos. I am selling cheap, because I don't want the goods to grow stale."[8]

"I consider my poem finished, as a cobbler might a pair of boots, and I intend to sell at a profit."[9]

"I am happy to hear that the *Fountain* is popular. I wrote it for myself, and am only publishing it because I need the money."[10]

After sending Vyazemsky *The Fountain of Bakhchisarai*, Pushkin wrote to his brother: "You know that I have twice asked Ivan Ivanovich,* through his ministers, for a leave, and that my application has twice, very politely, been refused, so there is nothing to do now but write to him directly: So-and-So, Winter Palace, opposite the Petropavlovsk

* Pushkin's name for Alexander I (the equivalent of John Johnson or Jones).

Fortress. Or else I should pick up my hat and stick and softly steal away to see what's happening in Constantinople. . . . If only I had some money; but where can I find it? As far as fame is concerned, it is difficult, in Russia, to content oneself with that. Fame in Russia may do for a Kozlov, surrounded by the flattery of all his St. Petersburg cronies, but no man with any self-respect can feel anything but contempt for it. *But why did you sing?* To Lamartine's question I would answer, I sang as the baker bakes bread, as the tailor cuts cloth, as the doctor treats patients: for money, for money, for money. That is what I am, in all the nakedness of my cynicism."

Further on, Pushkin berates some of his friends for circulating manuscript copies of his poems before they were printed, in the belief that they were doing him a service. But then, he reasoned, no one who had read them would dream of buying the volume, and there would be that many fewer sales.

"Pletnev writes that *The Fountain of Bakhchisarai* is in everybody's hands. I thank you, my friends, for the infinite pains you take with my fame; but it remains to be seen whether those who already possess a manuscript of the poem will be tempted to buy a copy of the printed version; however, we must not fret over trifles. The poet is not to think of his living; like Kornilovich, he must write in the hope of wresting one small smile from the lips of the fair damsels. Upon my soul, I am disgusted unto nausea with it. Wherever I look, I see nothing but dirt, ignominy, stupidity. Will it last much longer?"

But the commercial success of *The Fountain of Bakhchisarai*, from which Pushkin had hardly expected to make a fortune, astounded the poet and every other Russian author of the day. Vyazemsky, who negotiated with the printer, secured a princely fee for the author: three thousand rubles for six hundred lines, or five rubles a line. The printer also had to pay five hundred rubles to an agent, and publishing costs could not be less than five hundred rubles. That made four thousand rubles disbursed before the book ever appeared on the shelves; but sales covered them in a matter of days, and the printer even made a tidy profit. Thanks to Pushkin, the concept of authors' royalties entered the Russian literary world.

Pushkin received his miraculous three thousand rubles on March 8, 1824, in Odessa, and wrote to Vyazemsky the same day: "I thank you with all my heart, dear European, for your unexpected letter and for the package. I begin to have some esteem for our publishers, and to believe our profession is really no worse than another. . . . Luckily for me, I do not belong to the eighteenth-century school: I write for myself and I publish for money, not for the smiles of the fair sex."

The commercial success of the volume was such an unprecedented event in publishing annals that Vyazemsky wrote an article about it in the *Literary News:* "The manuscript of Pushkin's little poem was purchased for three thousand rubles; it contains a bare six hundred lines; hence, the line (and what a line, too, we would point out to the exchange experts, a little eight-foot line!)—the line, as I was saying, comes to five-odd rubles. . . . The name of Ponomaryev, who bought the manuscript, deserves to become famous among printers for giving this example. His ability to estimate the worth of a work of art without reference to its dimensions and weight has secured him the respect and gratitude of all who care about culture. To our great satisfaction, we may add that he made an error in his calculations, and the audacity with which he overturned the laws of commerce has already been recompensed by a justly merited profit."

Three thousand rubles! "I shall pay off all my old debts. And I shall start a new poem," wrote Pushkin.

Indeed, the old debts made short work of the money; but even when it was gone and the pleasures it had purchased forgotten, Pushkin was left with one gratifying certainty: Henceforth, he could survive on the income from his work, and his profession was a true one.

2. *Amalia and Eliza*

Pushkin's official duties were nonexistent. He had no definite job. And he did not consider it necessary to put in an appearance at the office. He correctly regarded the seven hundred rubles allotted to him by the government as compensation for the rigors of exile, not as payment for the services of a scribe. No one, moreover, reproached him for his lack of zeal.

As in Kishinev, he spent his days writing, walking, drinking and playing cards with casual companions.

"We eat well," he wrote to Viegel in November 1823; "I drink like Lot of Sodom and my only regret is that there is not one girl in sight. A few days ago we had a little bachelor party. I presided over the drinking part of the evening, and everybody duly got sozzled, after which we made a tour of the brothels."

The romantic Pushkin could not long survive, however, without romantic attachments. In Odessa he became the inseparable companion of a "retired pirate," Ali the Moor. This Moor Ali, or Morali by contraction, was a handsome athlete with mighty muscles and a copper-hued face. His features were strong and sharp, his wrists slender, his black eyes as though outlined in coal. He wore a red silk shirt, a short red woolen jacket decorated with gold braid, full trousers tied with a Turkish sash, a pair of damascened pistols and embroidered slippers on his feet. His head was covered down to the ears by a turban of thin white material. He spoke Italian and French. He was gay, playful, a hearty drinker. And it did not discomfit him to be reminded of his pirate days. Byron would no doubt have loved him for his dark past; Pushkin loved him for his cheerful present.

"When I came in at eight one evening," Liprandi wrote, "I decided to stop by Pushkin's room. I found him in excellent spirits, sitting in his shirt sleeves on the knees of Ali the Moor. This Moor, who came from Tunis, had been captain of a merchant ship, or of his own vessel. He was an extremely jolly fellow, thirty-five years old, of average height, robust, with a tanned, slightly pock-marked face, but pleasant to look at withal. Ali was very fond of Pushkin, who always called him the pirate. . . . Pushkin did not bother to move when I appeared. He commended the Moor to me and added, 'I feel a bond with him; who knows, perhaps my grandfather was a cousin of some ancestor of his?' At this, he began to tickle him, which annoyed the Moor and delighted Pushkin."

All that was Byronic about Morali was his title, his costume and the color of his skin; to Pushkin, the Byronic soul was personified by the "sarcastic and frigid" Alexander Raevsky. In Odessa, the poet renewed his acquaintance with the sickly demon of the yellow, wrinkled, smooth-shaven face, the evil black eyes, the harsh laugh and disillusioning mind. As in the Caucasus, he was fascinated by this provincial Mephistopheles; he still blew out the candles in order to converse with him in the dark. He made himself humble, he played at being afraid; maybe he really was afraid. However, as time wore on, he seems to have understood his companion's morbid vanity more clearly. His artificial infernos became wearisome in the end, his eternal negations monotonous. He even disparaged friendship. Love, marriage, patriotism, duty, liberty—that was all very well. But friendship! Perhaps it was for relief from the sneering Raevsky that Pushkin turned to the enthusiastic young poet Tumansky, who worked in Vorontsov's offices. In Pushkin's words, Tumansky was "a good lad, but something of a liar." In Tumansky's, Pushkin was "a nightingale," the "Jesus Christ of our poetry." With Tumansky, Schwartz, Varlaam and many more, Pushkin rolled from restaurant to theater and theater to casino. The food was not bad at Dimitraki the Greek's, and it was excellent at César Automne the Frenchman's. His wine cellar was considered to be the best in Odessa. After Pushkin's death, César graciously shared his impressions with the poet's worshipers: "He preferred Saint-Peray to every other kind of champagne, and I always kept some bottles of the best in my cellar."

But it was not only César Automne's wine cellar that drew the "carefree boys" of Odessa. Downstairs, there was a secret gaming room, where a throng of civil servants, merchants and idle youths crowded around the tables. Sometimes the bank took several scores of thousands of rubles a night. Among the punters, there were always a few professionals who roamed throughout Russia, living on their nocturnal earnings.

At the Opera the same civil servants, merchants and idle youths applauded Desiro the basso, Morinelli the tenor, Amati the prima donna and the little Marconi. But the show was as much in the audience as onstage. Everybody knew everybody else, and intermissions were an uninterrupted stream of visits from box to box, chatter from orchestra seat to orchestra seat, hand-waving and rotation of lorgnettes. When the

French soprano D'Angeville-Banderberg tried to introduce Parisian vaudeville to Odessa, there was an uproar. People took sides for and against her, Gallomanes and Italophiles went about calling each other "pig," and box-office receipts soared. Pushkin adored these quarrels. He loved the opera, the singers, the lights, the pretty women leaning forward in the velvety caverns of their boxes, the thunder of the orchestra, and then going outdoors under the calm, starry sky. He would have given twenty official dinners for one evening at the Opera. However, attendance at official dinners was compulsory. Vorontsov did not trifle with etiquette.

At the court of Vorontsov, Pushkin met the meek and timid Kaznacheev, secretary-general of the chancellery, and his overbearing wife, who wrote verse and kept a literary salon for provincial scribblers; and Naryshkin, the sleepy husband of a woman adulated by every young man in Odessa. "Ah, my friend," Tumansky wrote, "if you only knew how lovely and graceful Olga is! . . . When she waltzes, in her blue gown light as mist, one could fall on one's knees before her without shame." Pushkin shared Tumansky's views on the subject of Mrs. Naryshkin, and Count Vorontsov himself was not insensitive to the lady's provocative charm.

Another member of Vorontsov's "suite" was Guryev, the governor of the town—a greedy fool, a digestive tube, "a walking stomach," as Viegel put it. Then there was Blaramberg, whose daughters Zenaida and Helen, both lively and attractive, appealed to Pushkin and inspired him to write some incidental verse. There were also the kindly Leks, and Sinyavin, and the Polish woman Sobanskaya, a proud statue with whom Pushkin was fleetingly in love; and Sturdza the monarchist, and the Frenchman Sicard, and the Comte de Langeron, who had been Vorontsov's predecessor as governor of the southern colonies and was consoling himself for his fall from grace by writing tragedies on the Neapolitan revolution; and the odious, servile Brunov, whose entire face sloped away behind a monumental jaw. Brunov came to one costume ball dressed as the knave of hearts, and said to Vorontsov, "The knave of hearts renders homage to the king of all hearts." At the same ball Von Tom, the Austrian consul, arrived disguised as a large book, the spine inscribed in gilt: Tome the First. A man named Sabaneev came with his frock coat covered with all the foreign decorations he had won in his European campaigns; this disguise was not appreciated by the consular corps, and soon afterward an order arrived from St. Petersburg prohibiting the use of foreign medals, crosses and stars as fancy-dress ornaments.

Pushkin went to the ball masked and wrapped from head to foot in a long black domino. He admired the costumes, danced, flirted apathetically with some of the young faces animated by the heat and light of the ballroom—and went home, weary and saddened by so many futile words and gestures. His whole life was a masquerade. Everyone around him wore a mask, their souls were as disguised as their bodies. He was not at ease in this rich, noisy, revolving crowd. "At one in the afternoon," Liprandi noted, "we found Pushkin sitting cross-legged in bed, writing as usual. He was in a temper about the costume ball of the previous night. He told us some of the things that had taken place, and seemed particularly incensed by Brunov's toadying salute and Vorontsov's smug little smile. . . . Pushkin was unhappy in Odessa, chiefly because of the society he was apparently more or less obliged to frequent. I noticed a kind of *abandon* in Pushkin's attitude. . . . He had grown unaccustomed to, and had lost the taste for, life in aristocratic and family circles ruled by etiquette. . . ."

Unable either to live in seclusion or to put up with the society of the first families of Odessa, Pushkin was equally furious with himself and the people who persisted in inviting him.

In a letter dated June 16, 1824, the poet Tumansky described the women of the Odessa of Pushkin's day in the following terms: "The lack of social training is far more evident in the Odessa women. Married women (including the lovely and sweet-tempered Mme. Riznich) avoid men, hiding their simple-mindedness or their ignorance behind a mask of modesty. Unmarried girls cannot seem to find the right tone: Either they are too reserved, or they are coarse; some are too gay, they know too much and make no effort to hide the fact. . . . It is certain that a girl who is a little free in her ways is more interesting than a mute provincial maiden or an affectedly modest married lady."

As always, Pushkin was in love with a vast number of young women and girls in Odessa. His companions said of him, "The object of his passion might change, but the passion was always the same." He cared more about his success as a woman-killer than about his success as a poet. For him, flirting was an amusing, essential and hygienic exercise. He called it "making *coquetteries*." And the ladies were grateful to him for taking such pains to amuse them. "That is why," wrote the Pushkin scholar Annenkov, "despite his celebrated negligence of attire and the irregularity of his bold features, Pushkin aroused such tenderness in their hearts, and left behind him memories which nothing could efface."

For the "Odessa period," his Don Juan list contains two names: Amalia and Eliza.

Amalia Riznich was married to a rich Odessa merchant. She was said to be of German and Italian extraction. She was young, tall, slender, with an intense pallor of face, a long, silky throat and vast, light-infused eyes. Unbound, her hair fell in a jet curtain to her knees. As she had big feet, she always wore full-skirted gowns cut like riding habits, with a mannish hat and a veil trailing on the ground. This raiment only added to her charm. All the young men in Odessa were more or less in love with her. Her eccentric dress and doubtful reputation had closed the drawing rooms of Vorontsov and his associates to her, so she entertained in her own home. Bachelors rushed to her *soirées dansantes*, dinners and whist parties. Her husband looked on in bewilderment at the flood of aspirants undulating about her; he was eclipsed by her, happy in her success and certain of her fidelity.

Pushkin was an assiduous guest in the Riznich home. Like the others, but more than the others, he was bewitched by the lovely Amalia. His love for her made him giddy, literally swept him off his feet. He wanted to kidnap her and feast in solitude on the light from her eyes, the luminous elasticity of her skin, the broad caress of her lips. But she was surrounded by a swarm of adorers, many of them rich and clever. And she liked to be courted. "One day," Pushkin's brother wrote, "in a fit of jealousy, he ran five versts bareheaded under a blazing sun, in a temperature of 90°." Pushkin's chief rivals were the landowner Sobansky and, most important of all, Prince Yablonovsky. In 1823 he wrote:

Why do you try to be nice to them all?
Why do your lovely eyes, tender and mournful,
Hold out insane hopes to them all?
Don't you see, in the thick of the heated crowd,
Deaf to every voice, alone and mute,
How I struggle with my solitary anguish. . . .
What if I ran away? Your eyes would not follow,
Full of terror and beseeching.

Amalia Riznich was not, however, indifferent to Pushkin's passion. She gladly allowed herself to be kissed and caressed by him; but she did not refuse herself the same pleasure in other arms:

But answer me, how did my chief rival,
Finding me alone with you the other day,
Dare to salute you in so perfidious a way?
What is he to you? Will you answer? By what right
Does he turn pale and play the jealous lover?
But you love me! . . . When I am alone with you,
You seem so sweet, your lightest kisses
Are so burning! The words of love you whisper
Come straight from your heart and do not lie. . . .

In his poem *Night*, Pushkin may be relating his amorous experiences with Amalia:

In the shadow, your great eyes sparkle before me,
You smile, I hear a voice that murmurs:
My friend, my sweet friend, I love you . . . I am yours.

Toward the end of 1823 Pushkin's love for Amalia Riznich was "a malady comparable to the plague," a "black rage," a "fever," a "madness." Pushkin himself was frightened by it. His beloved, however, was pregnant—presumably the work of Riznich the merchant. At the beginning of 1824 she gave birth to a son, fell ill, began coughing blood and had to go to Italy. Yablonovsky, Pushkin's chief rival, followed her, and she died of tuberculosis in 1825. Her husband, his suspicions finally aroused, abandoned her, and so did her lover; she died very much alone and in great misery. Pushkin did not hear of her death until July 29, 1826, when he wrote this elegy for her:

An insensitive mouth announced this death.
  I listened, indifferent.
Where is love, where its torments? In my heart,
  For the poor shadow, so light,
For the sweet memory of days that are gone,
  There are no more songs, no more tears.

This tenuous phantom, which Pushkin believed doomed to oblivion, haunted him for years, however. In 1830, on the eve of his marriage, he wrote:

You said to me: "One day soon,
Beneath the blue of an unchanging sky,
Among the olive trees, my friend,
Our lips will meet again."
Your beauty, your many sufferings,
Are inside a funerary urn.
But the kisses you promised me?
I am waiting. You owe me them.

She was dead, and he was still waiting for her kisses, and cried out:

Come back, O adorable phantom,
As I knew you of old,
Fair and chill as the dawn,
Or contorted in pain,
Or like a distant star,
Or like a sound, a breeze,
Or a terrifying specter,
I don't care! Come back! Come back!
I do not call you here
To punish those whose spite
Has struck you down, my friend,
Or to learn about the other world,
Or to relieve the jealousy
That clutches at me. . . . But I want
To tell you it hurts, I love you still,
I am yours. . . . Come back! Come back!

Amalia Riznich's departure in May 1824 affected Pushkin less than the news of her death in 1826. At the end of 1823 his amazon was pregnant, and he was presumably unable to see very much of her. He began to lose interest; by the time she left, he was used to being without her. He loved her, assuredly, but already in memory, in his mind. Another woman hastened his recovery. And that other woman was no other than the wife of milord the viceroy, the Anglophile potentate himself, Vorontsov.

Eliza Vorontsov did not come to live in Odessa until September 6, 1823. At that time she too was pregnant, and Pushkin did not meet her until after her confinement, which took place in October. It was, thus, in November or December of 1823 that he made the acquaintance of the undisputed queen of Odessa. The rise of his passion for her coincided with the decline of his passion for Amalia Riznich. One took the other's place; it was only fair.

At that time Countess Vorontsov was a little over thirty. She was the daughter of a Polish count and had been brought up so strictly that the moment she was married, she fell into a positive frenzy of parties, flirtations and extravagance. Her long-repressed youth blossomed at a time when others had already given up the race. This delayed adolescence delighted everyone, beginning with Vorontsov and ending with Pushkin, and including Alexander Raevsky.

All of Eliza's contemporaries agreed that her beauty and grace were exceptional: "With the lightness and coquetry characteristic of Polish women," Viegel wrote, "she desired to please, and no one could do it better. She was young in body and soul. She did not possess what is commonly called beauty; but her eyes, although small, looked at you with a tenderness that pierced you through and through; her smile was incomparable, it was an invitation to kisses."

Vsevolozhsky: "I can find no words to describe the loveliness of Countess Vorontsov, her wit, her exquisite manners."

A portrait painted in the 1820s shows Eliza Vorontsov with her head inclined over her shoulder. Curls spill casually around the sides of her sensitive face. She has a pale, high, finely shaped forehead, and the skin of her neck is somehow luminous. Her eyes express a studied mournfulness and tenderness. Her lips form the ghost of a smile, calling through the canvas to another breath and other lips.

Pushkin must have loved the countess from their first meeting. She was attractive, intelligent, sensual and well-bred. She was also the wife of the execrable Vorontsov, a detail that only added spice to the adventure. As for Eliza Vorontsov: At first she was merely intrigued by this slightly seedy poet whom everybody said was the lover of Amalia Riznich. She saw him at the Opera, at dinner parties, at her husband's receptions. At the latter, the company was always divided into two groups. One besieged the count in the billiard room; the other, smaller and more select, courted the countess in the drawing room. Pushkin, of course, was in the second group. The countess liked to talk to him. She laughed at his puns. She tried, out of sheer curiosity, to learn the details of his latest passion. But that was all. And for a long time Pushkin resigned himself to the hateful role of *cavalier servant*. His main rival was that evil spirit Alexander Raevsky, who, while denigrating love in general, had fallen in love with Eliza Vorontsov in particular. They were cousins; he, therefore, could see her elsewhere than at official receptions. And the good gossips of Odessa affirmed that he did not scruple to court and console his appetizing relative in every sense of the word. They even whispered that Raevsky was using Pushkin as a screen, to divert the count's suspicions. He called Pushkin his friend, but did not hesitate to compromise him in order to save his own skin. He denounced him. He accused him. Sometimes he even made fun of him. And the trusting Pushkin came to him for advice!

However, the months went by, and despite Alexander Raevsky's exertions, Eliza Vorontsov began to listen to the poet with a more compassionate ear.

In May 1824 Vera Vyazemsky, the wife of one of Pushkin's best friends, came to Odessa with her two children; her doctor had prescribed a season at the seashore. She was the confidante of Eliza Vorontsov, and through her Pushkin could come closer to the object of his affections. Vera Vyazemsky's letters prove how irresistible Pushkin could be when he set out to please. At first annoyed and distant, Vera Vyazemsky finally gave the poet all her sympathy, and may even have been a little in love with him herself. Pushkin's name crops up in almost every letter she wrote to her husband:

"I can give you no good account of Basil Lvovich's nephew. His mind is utterly perverted, no one will ever control him. . . . I do what I can to calm his poor head."[1]

"I begin to think Pushkin is not so bad as he seems."[2]

"What a chaos there is inside his poor head! I often feel sorry for him, but more often, he makes me laugh."[3]

"Pushkin absolutely refuses to write on the death of Byron; I think he is too busy, and most of all, too much in love. . . ."[4]

"I am trying to adopt him like a son, but he is as unruly as a page boy; if he were not so homely, I should have said a cherub; really, everything he does is pure childishness, but even so he will come to grief by it one day."[5]

"I am beginning to feel a real <u>friendship</u>[6] for him. Don't worry. I believe he has a good heart, but his misfortunes have embittered him. . . . He talks to me quite openly about his troubles and his passions, and at least it passes the time."[7]

"I am very fond of him and he lets me scold him like a mother."[8]

A dangerous intimacy developed between Pushkin and Vera Vyazemsky. He often stayed in her home, amused her with his chatter and grimaces and played with her children. And in this blessed abode Pushkin also met Countess Vorontsov. The poet and the two women friends would go for walks along the beach. They would hire a boat, row out to sea and land on some wave-beaten rock to listen to the hurl of the huge, roaring breakers, streaked with foam and sparkling in the sun. Sometimes a giant wave would come and soak them to the skin, and then they would have to hurry back ashore to repair their coiffures and change their clothes. Was it in Vera Vyazemsky's house, or at the edge of the sea, or on some surf-ringed reef that Eliza Vorontsov and Pushkin exchanged their first kiss? No details of this amorous adventure have survived, but his poems, and the testimony of a few contemporaries, give proof that his love was at last requited.

"Princess Vyazemsky told me something of Pushkin's stay in Odessa and his relations with Count Vorontsov's wife; I had suspected as much, before knowing it," wrote Pletnev.

"M. S. Vorontsov's wife was not conspicuous for her domestic virtues, and, like her husband, had secret liaisons," wrote a contemporary named Eshliman.

"Today, Hebert (the son of Lady Pembrock-Vorontsov) sang *The Talisman;* little did he know that he was singing the story of his adorable aunt [Countess Vorontsov]," wrote Vyazemsky.

More than any epistolary allusions, however, the incident of the "talisman" proves the reality of the poet's affair with the wife of the "lord."

Toward the end of Pushkin's stay in Odessa, Countess Vorontsov gave him a gold ring engraved with Hebraic characters. Pushkin never parted with it. Long afterward, he continued to receive letters sealed with signs like those on his ring. The poet's sister said that on the days when such letters came, he would lock himself in his room, speak to no one and refuse to come out. Countess Vorontsov would not have given the ring —the talisman—to a mere acquaintance, however much of a poet he might be. She gave it to her lover, as confirmed by Pushkin in *The Talisman:*

> There where the waves spray
> The feet of solitary reefs . . .
> A loving enchantress
> Gave me her talisman.
> She told me with tenderness:
> You must not lose it,
> Its power is infallible,
> Love gave it to you.

Among the drafts dating from the spring of 1824 appear these crossed-out lines: "A wild grotto. . . . This haven of love is always filled with a dark, moist coolness. . . . There the growl of the frustrated waves is never still."

Also: "At the edge of the waves, a solitary grotto beneath a boulder—haven of love—throughout the summer's heat it is full of cool darkness."

In the same notebook:

> In the cavern where, exiled,
> I would read the soothing Koran,
> The angel of consolation appeared
> And gave to me a talisman. . . ."

All these transparent allusions re-create the setting: the rocks, cool shadows and marine murmurs where Pushkin and Eliza Vorontsov first embraced. Other poems attest to the authenticity of their passion, such as *The Burned Letter:*

> Suddenly the flame shot up, flared, and
> The thin smoke uncurled with my prayers.
> Already the magic seal yields its signs
> To the bubbling wax, oh, mirage!

After composing his lyric *Conversation Between the Bookseller and a Poet,* Pushkin began to fear that he had revealed his mistress's identity in his poems, and ingenuously suggested to his brother: "Would it not be possible to change the date of *Conversation* to 1823?" He presumably hoped to mislead his readers in this way. *The Angel, Proserpine* and parts of *Eugene Onegin* were dedicated to the same woman—in the latter, the gentle features of the heroine Tatyana were still another confirmation of the power of Eliza Vorontsov's eyes and smile.

After Pushkin left Odessa, Alexander Raevsky, who was then in Alexandria with the Vorontsovs, wrote the following letter[9] to the poet: "I shall put off for another letter the pleasure of describing the sayings and doings of our fair compatriots; now, I shall speak to you of Tatyana.* She took your misfortunes very much to heart, and instructs me to tell you so; it is with her permission that I am writing to you. Her sweet and kind soul saw only the injustice of which you were victim; and she has expressed it with all the grace and sensitivity that are so natural to Tatyana."

* That is, Eliza Vorontsov.

3. *David, Goliath and the Grasshoppers*

Even before he learned that Pushkin was courting his wife, Count Vorontsov had classed him as an enemy. The complacency and independence of this undersecretary who took himself for a genius had exasperated the "lord" from the outset, and when he heard, through Alexander Raevsky, that Countess Eliza was not indifferent to Pushkin's attentions, his dislike turned to genuine hatred. He felt himself flaunted by the little man with the monkey face and the illustrious name. He considered him devoid of talent but possessed of every conceivable vice. However, he allowed none of his fury to show and continued to receive Pushkin at his dinner parties with the same icy politeness. A silent war began between the administrative Goliath and his literary David. Vorontsov's entourage sided unanimously with him against Pushkin. Every day Pushkin felt himself more unwanted in this society of obtuse officers and high officials who were all devoted to the government. On January 17, 1824, one General Skobelev sent the following statement to the central authorities: "Would it not be better to forbid the person named Pushkin, who employs his exceptional talents to detestable ends, to publish his subversive poems altogether? . . . If, in exchange, the author of these shameful verses could have a few strips of flesh removed from his back, it would be so much the better. What is the point of showing indulgence toward a man who is wholeheartedly condemned by the voices of all respectable citizens?"

Goaded by his collaborators, prodded by Raevsky, inflamed by his wife's provocative attitude toward the poet, the phlegmatic Vorontsov finally determined to be rid of Pushkin at any cost. On March 27, 1824, he sent a hypocritical missive to Nesselrode, the Foreign Minister, explaining why it would be better to remove Pushkin from Odessa. Pushkin met too many flatterers there, he said, who praised his works and fostered his illusions of literary omnipotence, "whereas he is still no more than a feeble copy of an extremely dubious original: Lord Byron."[1]

This young man needed moderation, and to that end he should be sent somewhere else. "It would be no use," Vorontsov wrote in so many words, "simply to return him to General Insov, for apart from the fact that he would be hardly any distance from Odessa, he would nevertheless escape my surveillance. Kishinev is so near that those same people could seek him out there; and in Kishinev, too, he would fall in with extremely bad company among the young boyars and Greeks."[2]

Tormented by vindictive jealousy, Vorontsov wrote a second letter, more insistent than the first, on May 2, 1824, without waiting for Nesselrode's reply: "With regard to that, I repeat my plea: Deliver me from Pushkin; he may be a fine young man and a good poet, but I do not want him around me any longer, either in Odessa or in Kishinev."[3]

At last, on May 16, Nesselrode replied. The emperor shared the opinion of the governor of southern Russia with regard to Pushkin, "but as to the final decision to be taken, he will give me his orders in the near future."[4]

Pushkin, who was undoubtedly aware of Vorontsov's machinations, took his revenge in a spate of epigrams:

David was a little man,
But he did vanquish Goliath,
Who was a very big general
And a little more than a count.

Or:

Half milord, half tramp,
Half sage, and half hick,
Half bastard now, but one presumes
He will make a whole one yet.

The two men met and chatted politely in drawing rooms and at the huge, heavily laden dinner tables, but the same hatred envenomed both their hearts. One vented his spleen in epigrams which made the rounds of the town before the ink was dry, the other in weighty official letters and office conspiracies. Events came to Vorontsov's aid: Just then, the south of Russia was being devastated by a plague of locusts. On May 22, 1824, Vorontsov sent the following order to Pushkin: "You are to visit the districts of Kherson, Elizavetgrad, and Alexandria, and obtain the following information in each town: Where have the insects landed, in what numbers, what action has been advised to exterminate them and how has it been followed up. You are also to inspect the places which have been most badly affected by the invasion, evaluate the effectiveness of the methods of clearance being employed, and consider whether the measures adopted by provincial committees are adequate. Your observations are to be submitted to me personally."

Pushkin was not the only government employee in Odessa to be sent on a similar mission, but it was more insulting for him than for any of his colleagues. He fancied himself a famous poet, a personality in the Russian literary world, and here was Vorontsov, taking advantage of his higher rank, sending him to study the habits of grasshoppers and the progress being made with their extermination! This was better than a whole volume of epigrams. It reminded Pushkin that in the eyes of authority he was just another undersecretary. It drove him deeper into his misery. It would make him the laughingstock of his enemies. Behind his ornately gilded desk, icy and calm, full of hatred, distinguished and urbane, Vorontsov gloated. With one stroke of his pen, he had avenged his honor both as flaunted chief and ridiculed husband. Pushkin wanted to bite him, slap him, disembowel him, that milord, that tramp, that smooth-faced bastard with the elegant manners.

"A few days after I arrived in Odessa," wrote Viegel, "Pushkin burst into my room in a frightful state of agitation, to tell me that serious trouble was in store for him. Several underlings from the governor general's office and other provincial administrations had just been chosen to take charge of the action to arrest the invasion of locusts that was working its way across the steppe. Pushkin was among them. Nothing could have been more humiliating for him. . . . To spare him, the goodhearted Kaznacheev [secretary-general of the chancellery] delayed the order and even tried to have it annulled. So did I, but it was wasted effort. At my first words Vorontsov turned white, his lips began to tremble, and he said to me, 'My friend, if you wish to preserve the amicable relations that have obtained between us in the past, do not speak to me again of that scum.' After a pause, he added, 'Or of his worthy friend Raevsky.' His last words surprised me and awoke certain suspicions."*

Enraged by Vorontsov's intransigence, Pushkin wrote a letter to Kaznacheev the same day, but did not send it until three days later, May 25, 1824:

"Being unfamiliar with administrative procedure, I do not know whether I am entitled to protest against His Excellency's instructions. I take the liberty of explaining my position frankly. For seven years I have never concerned myself with the service, I have not written a single report, I have had no official dealings with any superior. Those seven years are therefore wasted as far as any promotion is concerned, and as you are well aware. Any complaints on my part would be out of place. Writing verse is my profession, and it gives me a living and independence. I think Count Vorontsov would not wish to deprive me of either.

* Concerning Raevsky's relations with the countess.

I may be told that I am receiving a salary of seven hundred rubles and must continue to serve. . . . I have accepted those seven hundred rubles, not as the salary of a civil servant but as compensation paid to an exiled slave. I am ready to give them up the moment I cease to be master of my time and activities. If I had wanted to serve, I should have asked for no better chief than His Excellency; but, feeling my total incapacity, I have already renounced all the advantages of a diplomatic career. I know this letter will ruin me, as they say. If the count orders me to resign, I am prepared to do so, but I feel that by changing one dependency for another I shall lose a great deal and have no hope of gaining anything. . . .

"One more word: Perhaps you do not know that I suffer from an aneurysm. I have been carrying my death inside me for eight years. Any doctor will give me a certificate. Is it really not possible to leave me in peace for the short time I have still to live?"

The aneurysm was imaginary. Pushkin had a varicose vein in one leg and was not seriously incommoded by it. But he did not want to overlook any argument that might convince the count. It required much urging from Raevsky and other friends before Pushkin would consent to obey Vorontsov's orders; but in the end he left, with leaden heart, to exterminate the cursed locusts. And after listening to their metallic hiss across the steppe and observing the efforts of the rescue teams, standing thigh-deep in the living, yellow mass, Pushkin returned to Odessa and submitted his report to Count Vorontsov. Some contemporaries said it was in verse:

> The locusts were flying, flying,
> Then they came to earth,
> They crawled, they ate up everything,
> And then flew off again.

Pushkin's official report on the locusts has not been found. Perhaps he refused to write one? He had definitely made up his mind, in any event: Resignation was the only possible response to the affront he had received. Kaznacheev, the secretary-general, considered his resignation (dated June 8) a mistake, and wrote to Pushkin explaining his fears. Pushkin replied: "I am very sorry indeed that my resignation has caused you so much distress, and I am sincerely touched by your concern. As to your fears regarding the possible consequences of this plan, I do not see that they are justified. . . . I aspire only to independence (forgive me the word, in favor of the thing); and if I have courage and perseverance enough, in the end I shall obtain it. I have already overcome my repugnance to sell what I write in order to make a living, and that was the biggest hurdle; I write only under the influence of inspiration, but once the lines are written I see them as merchandise to be sold at so much apiece. I cannot conceive the consternation of my friends (and I am not very sure who are my friends), and I am weary of having my fate dependent upon the digestion of some superior; I am vexed at being treated in my own country with less regard than the first English errand boy to come along, parading his platitudes and his gibberish. There is no doubt but that Count W—— [Vorontsov], who is a man of wit, will be able to discredit me in the opinion of the public. That is a flattering triumph for him, and one I shall allow him to enjoy to his heart's content, in view of the fact that I care as much for the opinion of that public as I do for the adulation of our journalists."[5]

A few days later Pushkin wrote to Vyazemsky: "I have quarreled with Vorontsov, and engaged him in a polemical battle ending, on my side, with my resignation. But what will the authorities do? I don't know. . . . Don't say anything about this. The whole thing has made my head whirl."

Meanwhile, Pushkin's resignation had been forwarded to St. Petersburg with an "explanatory" letter from Vorontsov. For Pushkin, June and July were months of exacerbated love and intense anxiety. Would he be understood by the authorities? Would they recall him, end his exile, give him the freedom he had earned by so much suffering?

In St. Petersburg the "Pushkin affair" was pursuing its course with ponderous deliberation. But then, Alexander I's police intercepted a letter from the poet to Vyazemsky, containing the following passage on religious belief: "I am taking lessons in pure atheism. There is an Englishman here, a deaf philosopher, the only intelligent atheist I have ever met. He has disgorged a thousand pages to prove that the existence of an intelligent being, a creator and regulator, is impossible—and seized the opportunity, in passing, to demolish all puny proofs of the immortality of the soul. A less consoling theory than the other, whatever else may be said of it, but unfortunately a highly probable one."

Thus we have: Pushkin's tender of resignation, plus Vorontsov's cover letter of "recommendation," plus this unfortunate observation on atheism. Everything was against Pushkin, the game was lost before it began.

On June 27 Count Nesselrode wrote to Vorontsov: "The emperor has also taken a decision in the Pushkin affair. He is not to remain with you, but His Imperial Majesty has asked to see the instruction I shall be giving you in the matter, and this cannot be done until next week."[6]

Pushkin's friends were furious with their poet, their eternal nuisance; they outvied each other in accusing him: "Pushkin alone is at fault," Turgenev wrote Vyazemsky on July 1. "He is simply asking for trouble. Now where can we put him?"

"He has been up to more of his tricks, this time ending with his resignation," Vera Vyazemsky wrote to her husband; "all the blame is on his side. He tried to make a fool of a person who was important for him, and he succeeded; it became known and he is no longer, and quite rightly, viewed with favor."[7]

"Ah, the little devil!" Vyazemsky replied. "I am really very unhappy about him. . . . However, people who do not know how to respect talent, even the talent of a madman, are wrong."

A "little devil," a "scatterbrain," a "madman." Nobody understood him. Pushkin was stupefied to find himself alone in his wretchedness.

"Why do you scold me in your letters to your wife?" he wrote to Vyazemsky on July 15. "Because of my resignation? You mean, because of my independence?"

While Turgenev was trying to "arrange matters" through his connections in high places, while Countess Eliza Vorontsov was trying, vainly, to wrest some knowledge of Pushkin's fate from her husband, while Pushkin was trying to persuade Vera Vyazemsky to lend him some money and reserve him a place on a ship bound for foreign parts, Count Nesselrode wrote his final report and submitted it to the emperor for approval. His letter left St. Petersburg on July 11, 1824, and reached Odessa on the twenty-fourth of that month.

"Unfortunately, everything indicates," he wrote, "that Pushkin is now thoroughly penetrated with the negative principles which manifested themselves so ominously at the outset of his career. You will be able to see this for yourself in the enclosed letter [the one on atheism]. The emperor has instructed me to send it to you. It has been appropriated by the police for, passing from hand to hand, it was known to everyone. In consequence whereof, His Majesty has ordered me, as a legal punishment, to strike Pushkin from the list of employees of the foreign ministry, for misconduct. However, His Majesty does not wish to leave him completely unsupervised; for, taking advantage of his independent position, he would undoubtedly propagate among ever wider circles the perverse ideas he clings to, and would compel the authorities to take radical steps against him. To avoid this, insofar as it may be possible, the emperor thinks that in the present circumstances it will not be enough to dismiss him. He must be confined to his parents' property in the government of Pskov, under the surveillance of the authorities there. Your Excellency will hasten to inform Pushkin of this decision, which he is to observe in every particular, and will send him without delay to Pskov, providing him with the money for post horses."[8]

By the time the letter reached the office in Odessa, Vorontsov had already left with his wife, their small daughter and the more intimate members of his court for a holiday in the Crimea, and so it was the governor, Guryev, who summoned Pushkin on July 29 to announce the news. Pushkin was shattered. He had hoped that his resignation would release him from administrative slavery and exile; but instead of liberating him, the emperor was simply transferring him to another jail. In Odessa, at least, there was a theater, restaurants, shops, women, a semblance of intellectual and social life. And they were taking even that little joy away from him. He was being driven into an ignorant, deserted province, a country where there was nothing but trees and wind, where an echo would be the only answer to his voice. He was being buried alive, killed off in the heart of nature. It was all very well for old folk to retire to the country. But he was young, wasn't he? And talented, and his friends cherished him, and women were not insensitive to him. By what right were they depriving him of everything that was life to him?

White-faced and shaking, he heard fat old Guryev proffering confused condolences. A paper was held out to him. Mechanically, he read: "The undersigned hereby undertakes to leave Odessa without delay and to travel, following the itinerary which has been given to him by the governor of Odessa, to the city of Pskov. He will not stop on the way in any place of his own choosing, and immediately upon his arrival in Pskov he will report, in person, to the civil governor of that town."

Pushkin turned the paper over and read: "The distance from Odessa to Pskov has been estimated at 1621 versts. For this journey undersecretary Pushkin has received, for the hiring of three horses, the sum of 389 rubles 4 kopecks."

Guryev said, "Sign." He signed. And walked out of the office, dazed by his misfortune, forgetting his gloves and hat on the table. Bareheaded, he ran to Princess Vyazemsky. Once again, he implored her to arrange his escape. There were so many ships riding at anchor in the harbor. The horizon was so vast, the earth so big. Why did he have to stay in this accursed Russia?

When Prince Vyazemsky learned of the government's punitive measures against Pushkin, his impatience with the poet gave way to honest indignation against the authorities. Now it was no longer Pushkin who was "mad," but those who were relentlessly conspiring to destroy his career.

"How can they," he wrote,[9] "employ such brutal measures to drive a man to distraction and despair? Who is the author of this inhuman assassination? For it is assassination, to bury a keen, intense young man in the solitude of a Russian village. The government must have been misinformed by mendacious gossip. A man is not sacrificed for one hasty remark, one unfortunate poem. . . . Do the people who decided such a measure even begin to realize what it means to be exiled in a Russian village? A man would have to be a saint to survive such torture. I fear for Pushkin! At his age, with his soul that is an abyss of boiling flames (to borrow Kozlov's expression for Byron), there can be no hope that his work, his literary activities alone can satisfy him. . . . I must confess that in my view Pushkin's exile will be his *coup de grâce.* I see no way out of his predicament. And why is he not allowed to go abroad? The publication of his works would guarantee him a living for a few years. Tell me, for the love of God, how the cudgel of Peter the Great, who has not patterned himself after his master in the tomb, could fear the prose or poetry of a mere child? The fine old tree of orthodoxy is full of sap and blossoming abundantly. If Orpheus himself were to appear and intone a seditious chant, nobody would budge an inch. How can the government fail to understand? How can it fail to realize its strength? All the poets in the world could howl their lungs out, nobody would hear a sound. . . . The Titans did not sing hymns to the gods when they wanted to drive them out of heaven."[10]

Uncle Basil's funeral oration for his nephew was more succinct: "*Les sauterelles l'ont fait sauter,*"† he kept repeating, with a satisfied smile on his lips and a small, senile tear in the corner of his eye.

Pushkin had one day in which to pack and make his farewells. He was summoned to see Guryev on July 29; on the thirtieth, heavyhearted, he left a town in which, as in so many others, he had thought he would be happy. He was leaving his dear friend Vera Vyazemsky. He was leaving his mistress Eliza Vorontsov. In his suitcases, stuffed among the shirts, socks and cravats, he carried the manuscripts of a few poems: *The Demon, To the Sea, To the Foreign Lady;* an unfinished poem, *The Gypsies;* and the first two chapters of his verse novel *Eugene Onegin.* His valet Nikita Kozlov, silent companion of all his misfortunes, followed his master.

The coach sped across a sandy, salt landscape, enclosed in a nimbus of dust. Ruts in the road occasionally upset the scaffolding of suitcases and bundles. Clumps of yellow grass began to appear. At last, the steppe opened out before them, answering in all its green, opaque immensity the transparent blue immensity of the sky. It was hot. The birds flew heavily. Horseflies clung to the gaunt, foam-covered team. The driver cursed and swore. At Nikolayev, the travelers stopped at a sort of lice-ridden inn whose bedbugs proved so aggressive and voracious that Pushkin preferred to spend the night in the carriage. They started again at dawn. On the way, Pushkin determined to stop and see a friend of his, Rodzyanko. The carriage passed through his village and drew up in front of the house. Pushkin leaped down and strode briskly into the hall.

† At least a triple pun. Literally: The grasshoppers have made him hop/got rid of him/blown him up.

An eyewitness[11] wrote: "Pushkin was wearing a red Moldavian cape and full trousers of the same color. He had yellow slippers on his feet and a Turkish fez with a long tassel on his head. His hair came down to his shoulders. In his hand he carried a big staff with an iron crook on the end, like those used by shepherds on the steppe. . . ."

They changed horses at Chernigov and stopped again for the night. The next morning, in the hotel lobby, a seventeen-year-old boy named Podolinsky, fresh from the University of St. Petersburg, was observing the arrivals and departures with an amused eye, when his attention was caught by an odd-looking figure whom he judged at first glance to be the buffet attendant. "His getup," Podolinsky wrote, "was quite outlandish: full yellow nankeen trousers that bagged at the top, a rumpled Russian shirt tied at the waist with an old, worn black sash, long, thick, curly, uncombed hair. Suddenly this individual walked up to me and asked, 'Are you from the Tsarskoye Selo school?' I was still wearing the jacket of my uniform, which is similar to theirs. Considering his curiosity misplaced and not wishing to engage in conversation, I answered rather curtly.

" 'Well!' the speaker exclaimed, 'so you were with my brother!'

"This left me completely at a loss, and at last I inquired more civilly what the name of his family was.

" 'I am Pushkin; my brother Leo was a boarder at the same school as you.' "

Stage by stage and landscape by landscape, Pushkin drew nearer to Pskov. On August 6 he was at Mogilev. The sky was blue, the military band was playing loudly outside the riding academy. The streets were thronged with a colorful, sauntering crowd. A carriage inched wearily down the center of the road, and before it walked a small, thin man, tanned and grimy. He wore a "Russian-style" red silk shirt and high boots, and a fez with a black tassel perched on top of his thick curly hair. A coat of military cut hung from his shoulders. He carried a walking stick, and people stood aside to let him pass. Intrigued by this apparition, a young officer named Raspopov, who was a nephew of Engelhardt's and had known Pushkin at Tsarskoye Selo, ran to the post hotel and asked to see the list of travelers. To his amazement, he discovered that the man in the red shirt was undersecretary Pushkin. Paying no heed to the postmaster's warnings, he rushed into the waiting room where Pushkin was sitting, seized his hands, and cried out:

"You are Alexander Sergeyevich. You don't remember me, I'm sure. I am the nephew of Engelhardt, the headmaster; on holidays I used to come over to Tsarskoye Selo from the cadet corps and you and Delvig made me recite poetry."

Pushkin embraced Raspopov and said, "I remember, I remember. . . . Sasha, you were some cadet!"

"I was so overjoyed at this unexpected meeting," Raspopov wrote in his recollections, "that I rushed off like a madman to find my fellow officers, who had been with me a moment before. I told them Pushkin was in town. We all hurried back to the hotel. Our enthusiasm was indescribable. Pushkin called for champagne. We drank to the health of everything we could think of. But that wasn't enough: We picked Pushkin up in our arms and carried him to my rooms, which were close by. . . . He seemed delighted by our joy. He was gay, and in a charming mood. Suddenly he sprang onto the table and began reciting poetry. . . . After that, we lifted him down and swung him in our arms. Then Prince Obolensky cried out, 'Gentlemen, this triumph exceeds the usual limits of our felicity, and must be marked by some exceptional event. Gentlemen, let us prepare a champagne bath for our guest!' Everybody agreed. But Pushkin smiled and said, 'My friends, I thank you from the bottom of my heart; it is true, that would have been an excellent idea. I can think of nothing I would like better than to splash about in a champagne bath. But I am in a hurry, and must get back on the road.' It was four o'clock in the morning. All of us accompanied him back to the hotel in a body, where we drank more champagne and bade him farewell."

With the first light of day, the coach jolted off again, along the bumpy roads of White Russia. Pushkin's head was heavy from the champagne and faces and shouts of joy. How "the young" loved him! Just as much as "the old" detested him, no doubt! On his side, he had the adolescents, the unknown officers, the cultivated businessmen, the lonely women of town and country, all who knew no other law but the law of the heart. But against him rose the army of government employees as starched as their uniforms, the governors, ministers, courtiers and the emperor himself. He was the center of the field of forces. Upon him converged passionate hatred and adoration. Upon him. Upon this wretched black speck. Upon this poor head of a man who believed he had been born for dreams, not combat. Would he be able to withstand all their assaults? Or would he fall, torn apart by so many conflicting emotions?

Nikita Kozlov snored, sprawling across the seat. Trees passed, indifferent and black. The road came alive, stone by stone, in the dawn light. In two more days, Pushkin reckoned, he would reach the end of his journey. Then, in the humble house at Mikhailovskoye, covered by weeds and dust, he would begin his new exile, an exile that might end only with his life.

PART V

1. *The Family Circle*

At last, after ten days on the road, Pushkin's carriage wheels rolled onto the poor, parched soil of the province of Pskov. The road, irrigated by wide, caked ruts, cut through a vast expanse of fields of rye, wheat, buckwheat, flax and hemp. Oases of birches ringed by mossy bogs announced a village in the distance, and finally the village itself hove into view: the humpbacked isbas, the beehives hollowed out of felled tree trunks, the little church with its green cupola, the heaps of rounded stones deposited by Ice Age glaciers and the flocks of geese guarded by ragged infants.

Disregarding his instructions, Pushkin decided not to present himself to Von Aderkas, the governor of Pskov, but to proceed directly to Mikhailovskoye, where his family awaited him. He was already re-creating the little Pushkin estate in his mind: He saw the "terrace" stretching alongside the ravine above the Sorot, a winding stream that linked two placid lakes; he remembered the old house: low and long, the worm-eaten wooden walls above greenish masonry foundations, the twenty windows full of sky, the two entrances, the tottering front steps, the outbuildings, the shallow garden separated from the serfs' hamlet by a palisade. So many fond scenes, secret monuments, childhood hiding places. His parents were there. How would they greet him? As pariah or prodigal? No doubt, the pathetic Sergey Lvovich would not be able to resist a small speech in the style of the Roman paterfamilias. His mother would have a fit of nerves. The old nanny would shed a few tears. He hoped so; he tried to believe so. Here: The road was already leaving the dense pine forest, the carriage was turning into the straight, level lane to Mikhailovskoye. In the distance, he could see the wall around the house and the garden overgrown with bushes and weeds. He had arrived. He was home. There was his old residence. His new prison.

All the Pushkins were there—Sergey Lvovich, Nadezhda Osipovna, Leo and Olga—and to the poet's surprise they welcomed him with open arms. He had misjudged his parents, he now saw: Sergey Lvovich was selfish, stingy, self-pitying and grandiloquent, but he cherished his son and was sincerely glad to see him again. As a mother, Nadezhda Osipovna was somewhat erratic, perhaps, a shade excitable, but charming, intelligent, sensitive. Both had aged in the four years since he had last seen them, but that only made them more human. And his nanny, Arina Rodionovna! The years had shriveled and creased her gentle face; she was continually sniffling. And Olga, sweet, loyal Olga! Already a tall young lady dreaming of marriage with her forehead pressed against the windowpane. And Leo! A husky lad of nineteen, who gambled, drank and chased women—just as he should be, in short. A fervent admirer of his brother. An ally. And the old furniture, the old trees, the secure old images of bygone times. Pushkin nestled into this bed of memories and ancient habits. He discovered with astonishment the voluptuous warmth of family affection. He was happy—so happy that he put off the moment when he would have to tell them why he had come back to Mikhailovskoye. As yet, nobody knew what had happened. Sergey Lvovich was ignorant of his son's imbroglio with Vorontsov and his expulsion from Odessa. With sublime innocence, he assumed that Alexander had been granted an imperial pardon and was released from exile, carefree and cleansed of shame. The patriarchal honeymoon was soon over, however, once the unfortunate Sergey Lvovich had been disabused by his neighbors and official notifications from the governor of Pskov. His son had not changed. A renegade, atheist, good-for-nothing, revolutionary, that's all he was! The old scenes resumed, at an accelerated pace: Sergey Lvovich played them for tragedy, with heavenward eye-rollings, tears, clasping of hands and exhortations and maledictions uttered with heavy tremolo. And, from dawn to dusk, "Think of your sister," "Think of your mother," and "Think of your father!"

Von Aderkas, the governor of Pskov, was furious with Pushkin for not bothering to report to him before going to Mikhailovskoye. He summoned him a few days after his arrival, admonished him severely and made him sign a statement in which the exiled poet promised to remain at Mikhailovskoye, to show proof of "good and moral conduct," to associate only with the right people, to write nothing improper and to make no subversive statements. The poet was placed under the surveillance of a close neighbor, Rokotov, the son of the marshal of nobility of the province of Pskov. But the cowardly Rokotov, wanting no part of the responsibility thus thrust upon him, hastened to wriggle out of his obligation with a plea of ill-health. A more accommodating stool pigeon would have to be found. They decided to try Pushkin's own father: "If State Councillor S. L. Pushkin would undertake to supervise his son's behavior, the said son might remain under his tutelage and be exempted from surveillance by some outside gentleman, especially in view of the fact that Pushkin senior is such an eminently respectable and honorable person."

To avoid having an outside nose poked into his family affairs, Sergey Lvovich agreed to the proposal and proceeded to transform himself into a living statue of Morality and Law. Fear of the authorities, respect for his pledge and a natural propensity to dramatize the most trivial events of his existence inspired him to release a flood of recommendations, prohibitions and reproaches upon his son's head. Throwing himself into his new role, he began spying on Alexander's every move, subjected him to humiliating interrogations and decreed that he had the right to open his mail and be informed of all his thoughts. He was terrified that Alexander might lead his brother and sister astray, and their neighbors and the whole Russian nation. He trembled to think that he might be accused of showing indulgence toward a being who bore his name. He began to pose as a noble father, but all he became was ridiculous and odious.

As a result of his father's vaticinations and his mother's tight-lipped reprobation, Pushkin went berserk with rage, humiliation and weariness: "What I foresaw has come to pass," he wrote[1] to Princess Vyazemsky. "My presence in my family has merely added to my already very real sorrows. (The government has had the effontery to ask my father to act as its agent of persecution.) To hear them talk, I am wholly and solely to blame for my exile; I am dragging them with me in my disgrace; I am preaching atheism to my sister, who is a heavenly creature, and to my brother, who is very funny and very young, who used to admire my verses and now most assuredly finds me a bore. My father had the weakness to accept this bargain, which puts him in a false position in regard to me. The result of all this is that I spend every moment I am not in bed either on horseback or out in the fields. Anything that reminds me of the sea grieves me, the sound of a fountain causes me physical pain; I think if I were to see a blue sky I would weep with rage, but thank God the sky is gray here, and the moon looks like a turnip."[2]

Memories of the southern sky, the sea and the passionate Eliza Vorontsov had followed Pushkin all the way to the flat and dreary fields of his home province, and the quarrels resulting from Sergey Lvovich's niggling disciplinary campaign merely aggravated his son's ill-humor; silence led to sulking silence, remonstrance to remonstrance and argument to argument, until a full-scale explosion shook the entire household. Pushkin related the details in his letter to Zhukovsky of October 31, 1824:

"My good friend, I place myself in your hands: You be my judge. When I first arrived, everybody welcomed me with open arms, but that did not last long: My father, frightened by my exile, kept saying that it would be his turn next; Pechurov (the marshal of nobility at Opochez), who was appointed to take charge of me, had the audacity to suggest to my father that he might open my letters, or in other words become my spy; and my father's crazy temper and touchiness made it impossible for me to have it out with him. I decided to say nothing. My father began to scold my brother for listening to my lectures on religious belief. Still I said nothing. Then a letter came, concerning me. Wishing to put an end to this painful business, I went to my father and asked leave to speak frankly. . . . He flew into a rage. I bowed, got on my horse and left. My father called in my brother and ordered him to have nothing more to do with the monster, the *fils dénaturé.** . . . (Zhukovsky, think what my life has been, and judge.) I too began to boil. I went back to my father, found him with my mother, and told him everything that had been on my mind for the past three months. I ended by saying that this discussion would be our last. Then, taking advantage of the absence of witnesses, my father ran out shouting all over the house that I struck him, that I tried to hit him, I raised my hand against him, I nearly committed violence upon his person. . . . I am not trying to justify myself to you. But what is he hoping to achieve with this accusation of physical assault? Hard labor in Siberia and civil disqualification? Save me, if only by having me put in a fortress or the Solovetsk monastery. I need not tell you what my brother and sister are going through because of me. I repeat: Save me.

"A.P. 31 Oct.

"Hurry: Everyone in the house knows of my father's accusation. Nobody believes it, but they talk about it. The neighbors know too. I don't want to have to prove my innocence to them. And imagine what will happen if the government hears about it. It would sicken me to have to convince a court that my father's words were calumny, and besides, there is no court for me. I am *hors la loi.*"†

At first, panic-stricken by his father's threats, Pushkin determined to blow his brains out. Then he changed his mind and wrote to Von Aderkas: "His Majesty the emperor has deigned to send me to live on my parents' estate, thinking thereby to alleviate their grief and the harshness of my sentence. But the government's grave accusations have seriously disturbed my father and aroused suspicions in him which can be forgiven only out of consideration for his age and tender affection for his other children. For his comfort and my own, I have accordingly resolved to ask His Imperial Majesty to deign to transfer me to some for-

* Unnatural son.
† Outside the law, an outlaw.

tress, and I solicit Your Excellency's intervention, as a final favor, to this end. . . ."

Fortunately, the messenger who was to deliver this letter did not find Von Aderkas in Pskov and brought it back again. Fortunately, too, Zhukovsky, who had been asked to arrange for the poet's incarceration in a fortress or monastery, did not have time to act—for any such step would have given publicity to the incident and irrevocably ruined Pushkin's chances with the authorities.

Pushkin's brother went to St. Petersburg and reassured the anxious Zhukovsky, explaining that this was purely a family quarrel, that nothing would come of it and that the fault lay equally with father and son. Toward the middle of November, Zhukovsky wrote to Pushkin:

"I do not want to write anything in reply to the letter in which you told me of your quarrel with your father, for I do not know which of you is guilty and which innocent. Both your letter and what Leo has told me prove, as far as I am concerned, that you are as much to blame as he.

"The only response I can make, to everything that has happened to you and every misfortune you have brought upon your own head, is—poetry. You are more than talented, you have genius. . . . You were born to be a great poet. Be worthy of it. That sentence sums up all the preaching I have to do. I stand on a desert shore watching a mighty athlete struggle in the waves; if he can exert his full strength, he will not drown. . . . Athlete, swim!"

Pushkin, his fury abated, wrote back to his "guardian angel": "I am so sorry, my good, my honorable friend, to have brought you all this fuss and worry: But what else could I do? I was exiled for one line of one silly letter; what would I be if the government heard of my father's accusations? It smells strongly of the hangman and the salt mine. Afterward, my father said, 'What a fool! Now what is he trying to explain away? If he had even made one move to strike me, I would have had him bound on the spot!' Then why did he need to accuse his own son of an imaginary crime? 'Why? He dared to make rude gestures when speaking to his father!' Yes, but a gesture means nothing. 'He killed his father verbally.' A figure of speech. . . . Think what you will, in this business poetry is no help to me at all. . . ."

During these weeks of domestic tension, Pushkin avoided the house and spent his days in the country, or at Trigorskoye, the home of his old friend Mrs. Osipov, flirting with her daughters and actively plotting his escape from Russia.

Pushkin's brother left Mikhailovskoye‡ at the beginning of November; his sister Olga followed a few days later. At last, Sergey Lvovich

‡ To go to St. Petersburg.

solemnly foreswore all further supervisory duties and left for St. Petersburg with his wife, on November 19, 1824.

Relations between the poet and his parents had been broken off. Pushkin was left alone, with winter coming on, in the ramshackle house at Mikhailovskoye, lost in the desert with no true friends, no literary life, no books, no amusements. He set up his headquarters in a room overlooking the courtyard. It was a sinister hole; the wall covering had rotted into tatters, the floorboards were rough and uneven, the ceiling was black with soot. One table. Two chairs. A divan. A wooden bed, with a roll of canvas shoved under the corner where a foot had broken off. A bookcase. On the floor, scraps and shreds of manuscripts, chewed goose quills, dust balls, periodicals, books. . . . Across the hall was his nanny's room, where the seamstresses worked. The rest of the house was closed off, and, to save money, Arina Rodionovna did not heat the rooms.

What now? Autumn and solitude beckoned the poet to work. He peopled his loneliness with the figures of his imagination. Deprived of friends, both male and female, he summoned to his den the heroes and heroines of his poetry. He lived with them. He feasted upon their docile company. He listened to their voices, answered their questions, relieved himself in their passions, their tears and their laughter. On September 5 he completed stanza 38 of Chapter III of *Eugene Onegin;* on the twenty-eighth he wrote his *Conversation Between the Bookseller and a Poet;* on October 10 he finished *The Gypsies.* Around mid-November he wrote to his brother: "Do you know how I spend my time? Before lunch, I write. I eat late. Afterward, I ride. In the evening I listen to my nanny's tales and fill the gaps in my wretched education! What wonders they are, her old tales! Every one is a poem. . . ."

Arina Rodionovna told the poet the legends of his land. Night barred the doors and windows; the rain drummed softly against the panes. Vast expanses of earth, leaves and murmuring water enclosed the house. The shuttles clicked in a nearby room. A rat scuttled across the dusty parquet. The vigil light cast a dim glow on the old woman's puckered face. Her mouth moved, swift, retractile. And out of it issued a voice from another age. Many times, Pushkin wrote of the solitary evenings he spent in the company of this fair companion:

Our decrepit hovel
Is all dark, all sad.
Why do you sit there, old woman,
Mute by the corner of the window?
Is it the long sobs of the wind
That weary you, my friend,
Or have you drowsed off
To the murmur of your wheel?

Let us drink, steadfast companion
Of my poor young years!
No more sorrows! Where's the jug?
Let our hearts be gay!

Later, there was:

Companion of my evil days,
My sweet, old-fashioned friend,
At the window of your room
You watch like a lookout,
And the needles move more slowly
In your wrinkled hands.
You see the empty door,
The black, unending road,
And sorrow, and forebodings,
And worries press your heart.

After her death, Pushkin wrote:

The old woman is no longer there; behind the wall
I do not hear her slow and heavy tread,
Or the orders she would cry out all day long.
I shall not go again on stormy nights to hear
Her tales remembered from the depths of my infancy,
Yet always beautiful, like the songs of my land,
Like the pages of some old book in which you know
The exact place and worth of every word. . . . Sometimes,
From her simple talk, her counsels, her fond reproaches,
There would ebb into my tired heart
A quiet gaiety. I was, in those days,
Still very young and full of crazy surge and thrust. . . .

Now, it was not the tales of gallant chivalry like *Ruslan and Ludmila* that charmed Pushkin's long evenings: These were real folk tales, passed from age to age by anonymous creatures with sun-tanned faces and hard-working hands, faithfully reiterated by the old woman on a night like any other night of the last ten centuries. Now, Pushkin had ceased to sneer at the remote adventures of sorcerer and paladin, princess and golden fish and Tsar Saltan. He forgot he had ever read Parny and Voltaire, and that he was living in an age of irony and sophistication. He accorded to these figures the religious awe they deserved. He believed in them. He feared and loved them with the candor of a child. And when he came to speak of them in his turn, he did so devotedly, brusquely, using his old nanny's words and sighs and phrases. His education had taken him away from the people. Now, he was coming back—without, however, completely neglecting his more formal instruction, for his letters to Leo were filled with clamoring for books:

"Poetry, poetry, poetry! Byron's *Conversations*. Walter Scott. Now, there is food for the soul. Here is something you can get me: *Historical Notes on Stenka Razin,* the only poetic figure in Russian history."

"Send me the works of Lebrun, odes, elegies, etc. . . . *The Life of Emelka Pugachev;* Muravyev's *Travels in Tauris.*"

"The Bible, the Bible! But it absolutely has to be in French!"

"Dear fellow, if it's in any way possible, find, buy, borrow or steal Fouché's *Mémoires!* I think he is more interesting than Byron."

"Dear heart, send me some mustard, rum, something marinated, and some books: Byron's *Conversations,* Fouché's *Mémoires,* Sismondi (literature), Schlegel (plays). . . . I would also like the new edition of the *Anthology of Russian Poetry;* but it's expensive: seventy-five rubles. I wouldn't pay that for the whole of Russia."

"If possible, send me the latest Genlis, *Childe Harold,* Lamartine (who must be nonsense, I think)."

"Fouché, Schiller's plays, Schlegel, *Don Juan* (beginning with the sixth canto), the new Walter Scott, *The Siberian Courier,* complete . . . wine, wine, rum (twelve bottles), mustard, orange-flower water, a suitcase, some Limburger cheese, a book on horsemanship, I want to start training colts like Alfieri and Byron."[3]

In his Mikhailovskoye hermitage, Pushkin set feverishly to work, reading Shakespeare, Schiller, Goethe, Alfieri, Byron, Moore, Saadi, Cervantes, Dante, Petrarch, Milton, Tacitus. But all the prestige of these towering figures could not overshadow his old nanny. Their era lived comfortably side by side with Arina Rodionovna's folk tales, as though united by some mysterious kinship.

At the beginning of November Pushkin was called to Pskov by the governor. Pskov was a historic citadel, girded by great walls with venerable towers and bristling with palaces, churches and miracle-working monasteries; it seemed benumbed by memory. It had lived too much to hope to live again; all that spoke in it was its great past. The stones of its buildings, its soil, its tombs and even the sky above it evoked the gloom and glory of ages long gone by. "You are near Pskov," Rylyev wrote to the poet, "where the last sparks of Russian freedom were smothered. . . . It is an inspiring region. Would it be possible for Pushkin to leave it without celebrating it in a poem?"

Pushkin did celebrate it, but in a play, not a poem. The ghosts of Boris Godunov and Dmitry the Impostor were already edging into his life, and passed, very quickly, into his work: By the end of 1824 Pushkin was drafting the opening scenes of *Boris Godunov.* But while he worked on his tragedy, he was also writing the *Imitation of the Koran, Eugene Onegin* and short poems and other minor pieces. This multiple, intense, fruitful labor did something to lessen the rigors of exile.

However, the moment he laid down his pen and raised his eyes to the window, framing an immobile landscape of brush and black trunks, boredom gripped him in its jaws. When the cold set in and the first wet, whirling snow fell, the solitude of Mikhailovskoye became lugubrious. The house shrank into itself, a tiny, creaking spot in the midst of a frozen wasteland, a rudderless ark in the tempest. It lived an inward, latent, vegetable life, lulled by the whine of spinning wheels, traversed by the steps of familiar serf girls, embalmed by kitchen odors, subsisting on its own reserves, far from human commerce.

Pushkin longed to flee this hostile place. His brother Leo and his neighbor Mrs. Osipov knew of his schemes. On November 22, 1824, Mrs. Osipov wrote to Zhukovsky: "If you think the air and sun of France or some other country beyond the Alps are salutary to Russian eagles and would do no harm to ours, then let this remain an eternal secret. But if you think otherwise, try to prevent it from taking wing."

And in December Pushkin wrote to his brother: "Wulf is here. I have said nothing to him yet, I am waiting for you. Come out from St. Petersburg, with Delvig, perhaps. We absolutely must settle all this."

And, hoping to avert the suspicions of the police, he added, with piquant ingenuousness, "The Petersburg gossip about my running away annoys me intensely. Why should I run away? It is so nice here. When you come, we will talk about the bank, correspondence and Chaadaev's residence [he was living abroad at the time]; those are points you can already investigate."

But Leo could not come to Mikhailovskoye soon enough, so Pushkin laid his plans with Mrs. Osipov's son Wulf, a student. Wulf was planning to go abroad early in the summer of 1825, and offered to take the poet along, disguised as his valet. Pushkin had little faith in this fanciful scheme and rather than chance it he decided to trot out his aneurysm again—that is, his varicose vein. Professor Moyer, a surgeon in Dorpat, was to obtain the government's permission for the "patient" to come to him for treatment. From there, Pushkin hoped to make his way out of the country. And once across the frontier, he would be free. The conspirators devised a special code to use in their letters. Hearing that Pushkin was ill, Zhukovsky began to worry and offered to apply for permission for him to leave Mikhailovskoye. By covert allusion, Pushkin tried to make him understand that the aneurysm was only a pretext. "I have been living with my aneurysm for ten years now," he wrote, "and with God's help I shall put up with it another two or three. There is no great urgency, therefore; only, I am stifling in Mikhailovskoye. If the tsar were to send me abroad for treatment, that would be a favor for which I would be eternally grateful, to him as well as to my friends. . . . Trusting entirely to you, I enclose a draft of a letter to the emperor; I do not think there is anything shameful either in making the request or in the way it is formulated."

The letter to the emperor was written in French: "I should resolutely have borne my disgrace in respectful silence had necessity not compelled me to break it. My health was seriously impaired in early childhood, and until now I have had no means of treating it. In addition, an aneurysm I have been afflicted with for the past ten years urgently requires operation. The truth of what I allege may easily be confirmed. In the past I have been accused, Sire, of presuming overmuch upon your generosity, and I confess that today, it is to that quality alone that I appeal. I implore Your Majesty to allow me to retire somewhere in Europe, where I shall not be without support."

Zhukovsky and Karamzin did not dare send this plea to the emperor, and replaced it by a needlessly pathetic missive from Pushkin's mother, in which Nadezhda Osipovna begged the sovereign to allow her son to undergo treatment "at Riga or in any other city it may please His Majesty to name."

The response to this staggered everyone: The emperor authorized Pushkin to go, not to France, Italy, Germany or even Riga, but to Pskov—that is, the town nearest to Mikhailovskoye, in which there was no doctor.

Pushkin's reaction to this mark of grace was a sarcastic letter to Zhukovsky which deserves to be quoted in full:

"I was profoundly touched by His Majesty's unexpected indulgence, particularly as our governor has already said that I might live in Pskov; but I was adhering strictly to the orders of the higher authorities. I have now investigated Pskov's medical resources, and have been recommended to one Vsevolozhsky, a highly skilled veterinary surgeon who is well-known in scientific circles for his tome on the care of horses. Even so, I have elected to stay on at Mikhailovskoye, although I remain filled with humble gratitude for the paternal solicitude of His Majesty.

"I fear that my tardiness in acting upon the imperial favor may be interpreted as negligence or a hateful obstinacy on my part; but who could credit ingratitude so diabolical in any human heart?

"The truth is that I have given little thought to my aneurysm for the past ten years, and I see no imperative need to concern myself with it now. I shall continue to wait, until the emperor's humanity impels him to allow me to choose my own place of residence and a doctor to whom I may accord my trust at leisure, not one imposed upon me by decision of the higher authorities."

Pushkin's fit of pique exasperated his friends in both capitals. What more did he want? He talked about aneurysms; they offered him a specialist. He was given permission to live in Pskov; he refused, and must needs go on posing as a martyr, so unreasonably! Really, he was never satisfied, he was nothing but an embittered maniac.

"Thus far," wrote Zhukovsky on August 9, 1825, "you have wasted your life with an extravagance unworthy of you and painful to us; you have exhausted yourself physically and morally. Now it is time to settle down. Your life until now has been a clever epigram, but it was intended to be a sublime poem."

Vyazemsky too sent the poet an interminable letter, on August 28, 1825, in which he said, *inter alia:* "By refusing [the trip to Pskov], you have directed the authorities' suspicions to your mother, who now looks as though she were trying to presume upon the emperor's good will. . . . You are ruining your chances for the future; by this refusal you have aroused fresh misgivings concerning your intentions, plans, hopes. . . . Are you the only man on earth who suffers? Does no one else have to put up with misfortunes resulting from conditions that exist not only here, but all over Europe? If you are hit a little harder than the others, you have only your pedestal to blame, for being higher than the others. Let us be fair: Are you not partly responsible for what has happened to you? You sowed your seeds with no thought for the climate, the frost has done its work, and there's an end of it. I do not say your fate is to be envied, but I do say it could be worse, and will be if you make no effort to improve it and if you persist in undoing all your friends' efforts on your behalf. If you continue to destroy everything they achieve, in the end you will paralyze them completely. . . . You boast of your exile; but in this country exile, like literature, is not a distinction or profession, it isn't even a recognized condition. . . . Disgrace is not the key to popularity here. . . ."

Pushkin must have been stunned by this letter. So: Even his closest friends thought his rebellion was outrageous. They simply accepted the existence in Russia of a crushing authority against which one could not fight, with which one had to come to terms or perish. They were exhorting him to compromise ignominiously, for the sake of popularity. They were ordering him to be obedient and patient for his own peace of mind. They were calmly condemning him to slavery: "Too long you have gone against the current, now swim with it."

On September 13 Pushkin replied to Vyazemsky: "It is easy for you to accuse me of ingratitude from the height of your carefree leisure, but if you were in my boots (which God forbid), you would no doubt be even more rabid than I. My friends make representations, and meanwhile I go from bad to worse. In the heat of the moment I lose my temper and curse them; then I think again and thank them for their good intentions, like a Jesuit; but I am no better off than before. I have stuck to my aneurysm for five years, it was my supreme argument for release, *ultima ratio libertatis*, and suddenly this last hope is swept away by that confounded authorization to go and get myself treated in the very place of my exile. My friend, I assure you that my head reels in spite of myself. You are concerned about my health. Many thanks. But this is a hell of a life, and I would rather die at Mikhailovskoye without treatment. No; at this point, friendship becomes the ally of tyranny, taking pains to excuse it, to shield it from my hatred. You offer to send Moyer to me, who could, of course, perform the operation in the Siberian salt mines; you tell me not to complain any more (this time, not even in prose, much less in poetry, which is a horse of a very different color!), you order me never to become angry again. . . ."

Having had a good bellow, Pushkin returned to his monotonous existence of an exiled poet in a remote rural mudhole.

"Here the rain murmurs, the wind murmurs, the forest murmurs, everything murmurs, and what a bore!"[4]

For months he had been writing, reading, yawning, sleeping, eating, bathing, riding, hitting balls around his old billiard table and whiling away the evenings with the old nanny who radiated fairy tales. Anyone else would have committed suicide or turned to drink; but his astonishing vitality protected him from going soft, in either mind or body. He was forever young, quick, curious, combative, intense. Sometimes he was even gay, for no reason: because it was a fine day, or because he saw a fresh-faced peasant girl washing her rags in the stream, or because he received a letter from Odessa, or because he was eating some sweet preserves. His misery did not make him selfish, far from it: In December 1824, after hearing about the flooding of St. Petersburg, he wrote to his brother: "This million [to be distributed to the poor] is all well and good; but what about salt, and bread, and oats, and wine? It would be well to think of all this, for the winter, individually or in a body. I am obsessed by this flood. . . . If you want to help a few poor wretches, do so, please, without any publicity, oral or written."

The year 1825 began with a great joy. Zhukovsky and Vyazemsky were too cautious to risk a visit to the poet, Turgenev had even advised Vyazemsky to cease writing to such a compromising correspondent, and all his friends were treating him like the carrier of a deadly disease; but good old Pushchin, the merry comrade of Tsarskoye Selo and St. Petersburg days, decided to set out and give his season's greetings to the "hermit of Mikhailovskoye."

Turgenev vainly tried to dissuade him: "What? You want to go out there? Don't you know he is under double surveillance by police and clergy?"

"I know all that," Pushchin answered. "But I also know that one cannot refuse to see a friend after five years of separation, and when he is in such an abominable situation. Besides, he is hardly a hundred versts away. If I am stopped, I shall simply turn back."

"I wouldn't advise you to try. But, after all, suit yourself."

And Pushchin left for Mikhailovskoye, where he arrived on January 11. He stayed only twenty-four hours, but those twenty-four hours were the most beautiful, the fullest, the most rewarding hours the friends had ever shared. Pushchin describes them in his *Memoirs*, and his account is still so full of life and warmth that it deserves to be quoted in full:

"In Ostrov, which I reached at nightfall, I bought three bottles of Veuve Cliquot, and the next morning, we were already nearing the devoutly desired end of our journey. The sledge turned off the road and glided through the woods along a hilly track. Going down a hill, just before reaching the farm, which lay out of sight behind a dense curtain of pine, the sledge tipped so far into a rut that the driver fell off his seat. . . . We picked up the reins again, and the horses galloped on between the drifts. There was no danger, they couldn't shy because they were in the woods and the snow came up to their chests on both sides. . . . There was a sudden sharp turn, and we plunged through the half-open gates and under the porch, the sleigh bells jingling furiously! Impossible to stop at the door; the horses slithered past and finally came to a halt in the deep snow of the courtyard. I turned around, and saw Pushkin on the steps, barefoot in his shirt, with his arms raised. I need hardly say what I felt at that moment. I leaped out of the sledge, threw my arms around him and dragged him indoors. It was fiercely cold, but there are times when one is in no danger of catching cold. We stared at each other, we hugged each other, without a word. He forgot that he should put on some clothes, I forgot my coat and hat all covered with frost. It was getting on for eight o'clock. I was in a daze. An old woman came running up (Pushkin's nanny) and found us still in each other's arms, just as we were when we entered the house: him half naked and me covered with snow. A tear finally blurred my sight (that same tear fogs my glasses now, thirty-three years later, and prevents me from writing), and we returned to our senses. . . . Alexander's room was near the door, looking out onto the courtyard; he had seen me through the window, after hearing the sleigh bells. In this little room were his curtained bed, a writing table, a divan, a bookcase. . . . Poetic disorder reigned: Everywhere lay sheets of paper covered with scribblings, bits of chewed, burned quill (always, from his schooldays, he had written with such tiny bits of quill that it was almost impossible to hold them). The door opened directly from the hall. Opposite was another door, leading to the nanny's room, where there were a large number of embroidery frames. I looked around for someplace to wash and clean up after the journey. The door to the rest of the house was closed, and the rooms were unheated. We managed the best we could bustling about amid a hail of questions: 'Where? How? When?' Etc. Most of them went unanswered. Then coffee was served. We sat down and lit our pipes. Our conversation became more coherent. . . . I found Pushkin as high-spirited as ever, but more serious than before; that impression, however, may have been caused by the situation. My visit made him happy as a child; he kept saying he couldn't believe we were really together. His old vivacity showed in everything he said, in every memory he recalled. . . . In appearance he was much the same, except that he had let his side whiskers grow. . . . He told me that during the past four months he had begun to resign himself to his new life, but that at the beginning it had been very difficult; he told me, too, that he was on excellent terms with the muses and was working industriously and fruitfully. The only thing he regretted was his sister's absence, but he would not have allowed her to spend a whole boring winter in the country out of affection for him. He sang high praises of his Trigorskoye neighbors and wanted to take me to meet them, but I refused, saying there was so little time to talk alone. We told heaps of jokes and anecdotes and laughed heartily at them all.

". . . Then we went into the nanny's room, where the seamstresses had already assembled. I immediately noticed one small form that stood out sharply from the rest, but I did not pass on my deductions to Pushkin. . . . He guessed my mischievous thought right away, however, and answered with a meaningful smile. That was all I needed; I winked back, and everything had been said without recourse to words. The nanny circled solemnly about in the midst of her young regiment, knitting a stocking. We admired the girls' work, teased them a little, and went back to his room. It was time for dinner. Alexis [Pushchin's servant, whom he had brought with him] drew the cork on the first bottle, and we began a series of toasts to Russia, to the school, to absent friends, to freedom. A second cork suddenly flew off all by itself and hit the ceiling; we poured out some champagne for the nanny, and offered homemade liqueur to the other servants. The whole household was overjoyed; they became quite boisterous, drinking enthusiastically to our reunion.

"I had brought a copy of *Wit Works Woe*;* Pushkin was very pleased to have it, for the comedy was then available only in manuscript, and he had not read most of it. After dinner, sipping his coffee, he began to read it aloud.

"As he read, we heard someone approaching outside. Pushkin glanced out the window, showed signs of embarrassment, and hurriedly opened a breviary that was lying on the table. Noticing his embarrassment but

* Comedy by Griboedov.

not guessing the cause, I asked, 'What's the matter?' He had no time to reply: A little ginger-haired monk was already in the room, introducing himself as the superior of a nearby monastery. I went up to be blessed. Pushkin followed, and then asked him to be seated. The superior had obviously been informed of my arrival and had come to try his wits with me. . . . Tea was served. Pushkin called for rum, for which the monk apparently had a liking. He drank two glasses of tea, not forgetting his rum, and then left, apologizing once again for disturbing our conversation.

"I was delighted to be rid of the intruder, but I was sorry for Pushkin's sake; he had become quiet as a schoolboy while the superior was in the room. I told him how sorry I was to have been the cause of this visitation. 'Don't think of it, my friend. He would have come anyway. I am under his surveillance. Why talk about such nonsense?'

"And, as though nothing had happened, Pushkin took up his reading where he had left off. . . .

"Then he recited a few of his own poems, mostly fragments which were later included in his greatest works. He also read the opening of his *Gypsies*, which he was planning to send to the *Polar Star*. . . .

"It was after midnight. A little supper was brought. The third cork popped, to accompany our farewells. We embraced, telling each other we would soon meet again in Moscow—a feeble hope, but it did something to lessen the pain of separation after a day that had passed so agreeably and so swiftly. The driver had already harnessed the horses, the bells were jingling outside the door, the clock struck three. Our glasses touched once more, but we were sad; we had a presentiment that we were drinking together for the last time, that we were drinking on the eve of an eternal separation. Without a word, I threw my coat around me and ran to the sledge. Pushkin said something more, but I wasn't listening, I was looking at him: He had stopped on the steps, with a candle in his hand. The horses pulled away toward the hill. I heard, 'Farewell, my friend.' The gate creaked shut behind us."

Pushkin must have stood on the steps for a long time. The wavering candle flame flicked light onto the blue snowdrifts in the courtyard. Beyond, the scene dropped off into cold, hollow night. Sleigh bells tinkled in the depths of a dream forest sprinkled with stars. Silence flowed back to the house in slow waves. It was over. Pushkin went to his room. He looked at the empty bottles, sniffed the odors of coffee and tobacco. All that was left of this happy reunion. Arina Rodionovna was doing something in the hall. Birch logs crackled in the stove. Pushkin was alone again. And for how long?

In April Delvig came. Pushkin had been expecting him since February: "I am impatiently awaiting Delvig." "I can't bear it any longer, I want to see Delvig." "Delvig, what has become of you?" "Delvig still hasn't come!" "My arms are opened to Delvig." "Baron Delvig has not yet arrived." The sentences come back insistently in letter after letter.[5] At last, on April 22, Pushkin wrote to his brother: "I was so happy at the baron's arrival! He is delightful. Our young ladies are all in love with him, but he is as insensitive as a log."

Delvig spent ten days at Mikhailovskoye, during which the two friends read each other their works, exchanged advice and compliments, compared views on literature, the imperial government, women and wines, played billiards and basked in the adulation of Mrs. Osipov's daughters, and even wrote a joint poem. Then Delvig too went away. Once again, Pushkin stood at the top of the steps and listened to the sad, fading jingle of the bells and the voice of a friend calling "Farewell!"

He hoped someone else would come; but no one did. His whole life long, he was to remember this waiting, and the sound of bells in the empty countryside: "Is someone coming? Is it for me?"

In *Count Nulin* he wrote:

Beneath the window, gravely,
Squawking turkey cocks strut
Behind a sodden rooster. Three ducks
Splash joyously in the pool.
In the muddy courtyard a girl
Hangs her washing over the fence.
The weather's changing. It even
Looks like snow. Suddenly,
The far-off jingle of bells.
He who has lived long months
In dreary solitude knows
How the sound of far-off bells
Can overpower a heart. . . .
Closer . . . closer . . . the heart leaps . . .
But the sound flies on past us
And drops, and dies on the horizon.

When Pushchin, implicated in the Decembrist uprising, was sent to Siberia, the poet wrote him a message of loyal friendship:

My first and my best friend,
I used to bless my lot
When, in my lonely courtyard
Carpeted with pallid snow,
Your bells rang out so merrily.
Now, therefore, I pray
That Providence may let my voice
Bring solace to your soul.

Pushkin never saw his childhood friend again.

2. *Trigorskoye*

In the winter Pushkin often rose early, ran down to the stream, broke a hole in the ice with his fist and plunged into the chilly water. Then he saddled his horse and galloped across the fields to get warm again, or practiced shooting his pistol over by the bathhouse, while the servants crossed themselves at every detonation. Or he would go for a walk, juggling with his heavy stick. He would throw it up in the air, catch it as it fell and toss it up again, laughing at his skill. Some days, though, he would spend the whole morning in bed, refusing even to dress in order not to interrupt the flow of inspiration. He would putter about the billiard table playing "two-ball" billiards until lunch, and then go back to work.

His diversions were curious: He amazed the priest of a local church by ordering a requiem mass for Lord Byron. "Today is the anniversary of Byron's death," he wrote to Vyazemsky on April 7, 1825; "yesterday I ordered a mass for the repose of his soul. The pope was quite nonplused by my religious fervor, and gave me a communion host dedicated to the memory of one servant of the Lord, Boyar George. Enclosed herewith."

To his brother: "I have ordered a mass for Byron (this is the anniversary of his death . . . it reminds me a little of the mass ordered by Frederick II for the repose of Mr. Voltaire's soul)."

All who witnessed his life at Mikhailovskoye agreed that Pushkin paid no attention to the farm itself. The management of the land was entrusted to the village starets, and that of the house to his old nanny. The peasants were fond of their master, whom they regarded as a harmless and jolly nitwit. They laughed at him because he went walking in the fields in a red Russian-style shirt and full trousers, with a straw hat and his ironclad cudgel. "He was good and easygoing," one reported, "but a little touched in the head, as it seems; one time when I was on my way to Mikhailovskoye, I saw him coming toward me, and all of a sudden he stopped as though a tree trunk had hit him on the head. I was scared and hid in the rye field. I peeked out, and there he was talking out loud to himself, changing his voice and waving his arms around, exactly like a crazy man. . . . We often used to see him in the villages when the festivals were on. He would come dressed in a red shirt and oiled boots, and would stand over by the little girls' choir and listen and listen to their songs. . . ."

Thanks to his garrulous and sententious old nanny and to these slow and rudimentary peasants, their eyes aglint with malice, Pushkin was learning to know the people. He never missed a village feast, and was especially fond of the fairs held outside the gates of Holy Mountain monastery: He would turn up in his red blouse and boots, his straw hat raked over one ear, his side whiskers blowing in the breeze, his heavy stick in his fist, and prowl along the booths where sugar, wine, fruit, poultry and bolts of cloth and sewing cotton were sold. He would heckle the vendors, and shock the local gentry with his dress. Then he would mingle with the buyers, listen to the beggars' songs and pick up their refrains, beating time with his big staff. Or he would squat beside some blind storyteller and close his eyes, the better to hear the old tales. The people around him had not changed since the days of Boris Godunov: the same innocents with their prophetic speech, the same blind *conteurs*, the same meek, ragged beggars, the same bawling vendors, the same powerful, docile serfs. Merely looking at them, he felt the anonymous horde of his tragedy rise within him, dense, surging, muttering. He noted their phrases, their proverbs. He took lessons in simplicity from them—while around him the fancy folk in their fancy clothes shrugged and turned away: "Crazy as ever, that Pushkin!"

I. Lyapin, an Opochez merchant, wrote in his diary: "1825—May 29. At the Holy Mountain. Friday. Here I had the chance to see Alexander Sergeyevich Pushkin, who, so to speak, amazed me by the eccentricity of his attire. For instance, on his head there was a straw hat; then, he wore a red linen blouse belted with a blue sash; in his hand he held an iron stick; his black side whiskers were extremely long, more like a beard; and with his very long nails, he was peeling oranges, which he then ate with great relish (I think he ate half a dozen of them)."

Pushkin was enchanted by the Russian folklore and the speech of the common people. "The study of old songs, tales, and so forth . . . is indispensable to the acquisition of a full knowledge of the resources of the Russian language," he said.

Also: "Young writers: Listen to the speech of the people, you will learn far more from them than from the articles in our reviews. . . ."

And: "The spoken language of the people deserves to be studied exhaustively. Alfieri studied the Italian language at the fair in Florence; it would not be a bad idea for us to listen, now and then, to the words of some old Moscow bigot who manufactures communion hosts. These people speak a remarkably pure and regular language."[1]

Pushkin felt equally at home at the fair and in the drawing room—he was the man of every milieu, every country, every age; and so, after a joke with the peasants at the fair, he would go off to call on the mistress of Trigorskoye, where he charmed the girls and drank tea, telling faintly scandalous anecdotes. He was positively ravenous for female conquests, and his desire to please made him almost handsome.

Trigorskoye was a paradise of flowing locks, flying skirts, soprano squeals, virginal pouting, caresses and sweet protestations. From the trees to the very stones, from flowers to faces, everything in this pretty kingdom was feminine.

The road to Trigorskoye led through a dense stand of pine with violent, twisted roots; then it dropped down to the mist-shrouded lake, climbed again to the edge of the wood and rolled out onto the plain, which was dominated by three steep hills in the distance. Two were crowned with sparkling churches; on the third lay the village of Trigorskoye and the home of its masters. The house was all in wood, rather like a vast hangar or some huge abandoned riding school. Large, badly planned rooms. Simple, solid furniture. Wheezing clocks. A dim painting of the temptation of St. Anthony. An untuned clavichord. Around this antiquated but comfortable hulk stretched the grounds of Trigorskoye, with avenues of blue shadow, caverns of greenery, a linden-framed esplanade that was used as a "ballroom," a pond sheathed with pale silver, benches conducive to reverie, a terrace sloping over the Sorot and a bathhouse in which guests of note, such as Pushkin and Yazykov, sometimes stayed. Pure air, bird songs, the chink of china dishes, the perfume of tea and preserves, and the laughter of smooth-cheeked young ladies: They were what Pushkin loved most in his friend's ramshackle, hospitable domain.

"My only social resource," he wrote, "is a dear and old neighbor whom I often visit; I sit listening to her patriarchal conversation, while her daughters, who are quite dreadful in every respect, play Rossini (which I sent for) to me."[2]

To his sister: "Apart from the mother, your friends at Trigorskoye are insufferable idiots."[3]

Trigorskoye was full of girls; and of course there is nothing more unstable, irritating, stupid, incomprehensible, exciting, exceptional and useless than girls. One day they tease you, and that day they are "insufferable idiots." The next they are full of remorse, and it is impossible not to be touched by their grace and mystery.

The females of Trigorskoye were many and different. Mrs. P. A. Wulf-

Osipov, the owner of the estate, had three children by her first husband Nicholas Wulf:* Alexis, aged twenty, a student in Dorpat and old friend of Pushkin; Annette, aged twenty-six; and Eufrasia, called Zizi, aged sixteen. By her second husband, Ivan Osipov,† the mistress of Trigorskoye had two more girls, Marya and Katrina, both hardly more than babies.

Mrs. Osipov was a plump, forceful, energetic lady, at once sentimental and practical, idealistic and authoritarian: She would sigh her way through some German Romantic poet and write marginal notes in French in the works of Young ("There is a consoling thought! . . . Ah! happy hearts!"), but came out of her euphoria with a jerk to cuff a clumsy servant or scold her little girls for straying too far into the garden. A dreamer, in deference to the fashion, but by instinct shrewd, prudent and thrifty, Mrs. Osipov ruled both farm and family with a firm hand. She viewed Pushkin's presence in her aviary with misgivings. The little girls were very impressionable and totally inexperienced. Their innocent coquetry might lead to more serious experiments. She herself was not insensitive to the poet's charm. She admired his poems and liked his unruly boyish laughter, his jests and compliments. But she was forty-four years old, and a widow, she knew what life was. Whereas Annette and Zizi were obvious targets for this swarthy seducer with the devil's eyes and long fingernails. Annette was a tall girl, dreamy and soft, with a round face and soulful eyes, who lived on tragic phrases and lofty sentiments. She loved Pushkin fervently and insistently. She was prepared to sacrifice everything for him; but Pushkin only laughed at her romantic effusions.

"I have quarreled with Annette. She bothers me,"[4] he wrote to his brother. And Annette, jealous, humiliated, woebegone, played the love-lorn maiden down the garden paths and behind the backs of the tapestry-covered armchairs.

Zizi, on the other hand—delicate and small, blond and sparkling, flighty and full of merriment—Pushkin liked very much. He liked her for not being imaginative, or even intelligent, and for having as her rarest qualities the ability to run like a deer, burst into peals of mirth, dart mocking glances and make djonka in a little silver jug. Zizi, however, repelled the poet's advances, and he was caught at his own game. He insisted, became agitated and began a hot and earnest pursuit of the little girl of sixteen whose head had been turned by her first conquest. He compared her to a crystal champagne glass, he pretended to be "intoxicated by her presence." "Eufrasia is sulking. She is adorable," he wrote to his brother. And added her name to his Don Juan list.

* Who died in 1813.
† Died in February 1824.

Pushkin also paid court to Mrs. Osipov's stepdaughter Aline, and to Netty Wulf, a cousin of the Wulf-Osipov girls. In March 1825 he wrote to his brother: "I have fallen in love. . . . Do you know Annette's cousin—Anna Ivanovna Wulf [Netty]? *Ecce femina.*"

Annette was jealous of Netty and Aline; Netty was jealous of Zizi; Mrs. Osipov was jealous of Annette, Zizi, Netty and Aline. Novels wove and unwove in every corner. Intrigues sprang up overnight, for a look or the touch of a foot. The very air they breathed was a dangerous aphrodisiac. Sparks flew from the ladies' hair, and their palms were moist. And in the middle of all this agitation strutted Pushkin and young Alexis Wulf, his twenty-year-old companion. Two men for all those women.

Alexis was a student, and a great expert in erotic science. He claimed to have learned from Pushkin all the secrets of irresistible seductiveness. He called himself the poet's pupil, the Faust to his omnipotent Mephistopheles, but the truth of the matter was that he had far outstripped his master. While Pushkin was still allowing himself to become entangled in the snares of love, Alexis Wulf had reduced all problems of passion to a cold and vulgar algebra. Cynical, sensual and calculating, he approached every woman as an enemy to be defeated. No sentiment. Method. He wrote in his diary: "Yesterday I began to teach [my ladylove] the technical terms of love. Afterward, following the precepts of Mephistopheles, I filled her imagination with voluptuous images; women, having once tasted of this delicious fruit, will fall into the power of any man who can offer them new varieties, and lose interest in all other forms of amusement; everything seems base and dreary to them in comparison with the language of love. As an experiment, I want to see if I can enlighten her, if I am capable. I must begin by telling her of my amorous exploits." He tested his powers on his cousins, with excellent results. "I led her through every conceivable stage of sensual delight, but did not tamper with her virginity," he wrote of one. Aline, his sister by marriage, also acted as a willing guinea pig.

The two confederates now launched their campaign against the dames and damsels of Trigorskoye. They went into battle, each for his own account, while poor Mrs. Osipov looked on helplessly at the confused flutterings of her girls, quick to wound and quick to heal, preoccupied, soft and cooing with love.

The moment Pushkin entered the house, a general tumult began. He would arrive around three in the afternoon, leaping into the drawing room through the open window.

"The moment he came," Marya Ivanovna Osipov wrote, "everything turned into confusion; laughter, teasing, shrieks resounded from room to room. . . . How quick he was! Impossible to make him hold still! Forever on the go, running about. . . ."

At the beginning of 1825, however, Pushkin's thoughts began to stray from the Trigorskoye girls. There was someone else on his mind: a niece of Mrs. Osipov's, named Anna Petrovna Kern. She had promised to come to Trigorskoye, and she was such a beauty!

Pushkin first saw Anna Petrovna Kern in a St. Petersburg drawing room in 1819. He tried to court her then, but in vain: She rebuffed him sharply and left him nothing to remember but a chilling glare and a pair of white shoulders. This admirable creature was the wife of a senile old general who, being unable to satisfy her himself, plainly advised her to apply elsewhere. One time, he even dragged her by force into the room of a young nephew who was living in their house and who, having been forewarned, lay waiting, half naked on his bed. In exasperation, Mrs. Kern left her husband and returned to her family in the government of Poltava, where she began a serious affair with a local landowner, the pornographic poet Rodzyanko. Rodzyanko was in correspondence with Pushkin, and Anna Petrovna Kern with her cousin Annette.

"While I was living in the government of Poltava," wrote Mrs. Kern, "I was writing to my cousin Anna Wulf [Annette]. Pushkin often came to see them. She talked to him about me and contrived to repeat everything he said. In one letter she wrote, 'You made a great impression on Pushkin when you met at the Olenins';‡ he keeps saying, she was too dazzling.' "[5]

In the margin of another of the obliging Annette's letters to her cousin, Pushkin wrote: "An image passed before our eyes, we saw it and shall see it no more."[6]

With every letter Pushkin edged a little closer to this ill-married and ill-consoled young woman, while she too began to look more favorably upon the poet whose work she admired. Across the miles, they sought each other, driven by the same hunger. Knowing that Mrs. Kern was "on intimate terms" with Rodzyanko, Pushkin wrote to his friend on December 8, 1824: "Tell me what sort of person is this A.P.K. who puts such nice compliments to me in her letters to her cousin. She is said to be a charming little thing, but it is easy to talk at such a distance. By the way, knowing your proclivity for love and your exceptional talents in every field, I think your own business must already be settled, or half settled, anyway. Congratulations, my dear."

Further on, Pushkin asked Rodzyanko to show his letter to Mrs. Kern. Mrs. Kern was not offended. Mrs. Kern found him very witty. Mrs. Kern even agreed to begin a purely frivolous correspondence with the poet.

‡ President of the Academy of Arts; it was at his home that Pushkin met Anna Petrovna Kern in 1819.

She was sensual and passionate. She prized Pushkin's work. She wanted to meet him in earnest.

In June 1825, at last, she came to spend three or four weeks at Trigorskoye. Their first encounter was singular.

"We were all at table," Mrs. Kern wrote, "when Pushkin burst into the room with a big cudgel in his hand. I was sitting next to my aunt, who introduced him, and he bowed deeply without uttering a word; his shyness showed in every gesture he made. I could find nothing to say to him either. . . ."

How beautiful she was, and distinguished, and knowing! He compared her to an angel of purity and delicacy; yet he was not ignorant of her dubious past. The tone of their letters thus far had seemed to betoken a few weeks of agreeable dalliance with no involvement on either side, a sort of exercise in gallantry *à la française*. And here he found himself all timid and stammering, trembling with terror and desire—in love. Simply, idiotically, wonderfully in love. He didn't know how to behave in front of her. By turns he was gay, mocking, in despair, humbly sweet and stupidly jealous. He went to Trigorskoye every day. He listened to Mrs. Kern sing Venetian barcaroles. He read *The Gypsies*, which he had just completed, to his lady friends. His eyes glared daggers at the incorrigible Alexis Wulf, who was also trying to ensnare his cousin.

Mrs. Kern received the poet's more or less open declarations without demur. She too felt intrigued, infatuated. With a shiver of delight, she ventured out into deep waters. She was ready to lose herself in his arms. The two young people undoubtedly had at least one opportunity to come together; but Mrs. Osipov, fearing a scandal, hastily arranged for her niece's departure for Riga, where a husband without rancor and without desire was awaiting her.

On the day before she left, the ladies from Trigorskoye, both single and wedded, were taken to see Mikhailovskoye by Pushkin.

"The weather was superb," wrote Mrs. Kern; "the June night, lit by a fine moon, was filled with coolness and the fragrance of the fields. We divided ourselves into two parties: my aunt and her son in one carriage; Annette, Pushkin, and I in the other. Never, before or since, have I known him to be so simply happy, so likable. He joked without malice or sarcasm, he admired the moon and even forbore to call it 'stupid,' and said, 'I love the moon when it lights a pretty face.'[7] When we reached Mikhailovskoye, we did not see the house but went directly into the old abandoned garden, where there were long avenues lined with ancient trees over whose tangled roots I stumbled more than once, to my companion's alarm. My aunt, who was behind us, said, 'My dear Pushkin, do the honors of your garden for Madame.' Quickly, he gave me his hand and began to run, as hard as a schoolboy who has been given permission to go outdoors and play. I cannot recall the details of our conversation. He mentioned our first meeting at the Olenins', speaking of it with passion, rapturously; he said, 'There was such an air of purity about you; weren't you wearing something like a cross?'[8]

"The next day I was to leave for Riga. . . . He came in the morning, bringing as a parting gift the second chapter of *Eugene Onegin,* in uncut manuscript. Between the pages I found a folded sheet of stationery bearing the lines:

"I remember the wonderful moment . . .

"Just as I was about to slip this poetic gift into a little box, he looked at me for a long time and then snatched the sheet from my hand and would not give it back; I had great difficulty in getting it again; what thought had come into his mind at that instant, I have no idea."

When he came to give this woman a token of affection as eloquent as his poem, Pushkin was suddenly afraid he had made a mistake. Was she worthy of his adoration? Would she not laugh at him, later, with some passing lover? She seemed so animal! But all she had to do was speak or lower her gaze, and she became an angel again. Angel or beast? Angel and beast. He loved her both ways, for her soulless body and her bodiless soul. It was for her that he wrote:

I remember the wonderful moment
When you leaped into my eyes
Like a fleeting mirage,
Like a spirit of pure beauty. . . .

But to Rodzyanko, he wrote a poem in which the "spirit of pure beauty" is celebrated in a very different voice:

I applaud, my friend, her desire
To bring children into the world.
Happy the man whom she invites
To share in this pleasant toil.

The moment Mrs. Kern left Trigorskoye, however, whatever reservations Pushkin might have been entertaining fell to dust. He wandered like a starving man down the avenues where she had walked, sniffed the air where her head had paused, picked up the pebbles and twigs her hand had touched. At night his whole body burned to think of that fair, succulent flesh he had allowed to escape him and now craved like food. He wrote to Annette Wulf, who had gone to Riga with Mrs. Kern:[9] "I am writing after having made myself thoroughly and miserably drunk. . . . All Trigorskoye is singing . . . and it crushes my heart; yesterday Alexis and I talked for four hours. We have never had such a long conversation. Can you guess what has suddenly united us? Boredom? Shared sentiments? I have no idea. Every night I walk in my garden and say, 'She was there'; the stone she tripped over is on my table next to a wilted heliotrope, and I am writing a lot of poetry—all this, if you like, looks very much like love, but I swear to you that it is nothing of the kind. If I were in love, I should have been in convulsions of rage and jealousy on Sunday, whereas I was merely annoyed. . . . However, the thought that I am nothing to her, that after awakening and occupying her imagination I have been only a plaything for her curiosity, that the memory of me will not distract her one instant in the midst of her triumphs or add one shade of darkness to her sorrows, that her lovely eyes will fasten upon some conceited fool in Riga with the same rending and voluptuous expression: No, I cannot bear to think of it, tell her I shall die, no, don't tell her! She would laugh at me, the delicious creature. . . . Cursed arrival, cursed departure!"

Annette Wulf must have wept scalding tears over this declaration of love intended for her cousin. If only she were in her place! If only she could give Pushkin what he was searching for in someone else, give until he cried "Enough!"

Pushkin, moreover, soon dispensed with her services as go-between and began writing directly to Mrs. Kern: "I had the weakness to ask your permission to write, and you had the irresponsibility or coquetry to accord it. A correspondence can lead nowhere, I know, but I haven't the strength to resist the desire for one word from your pretty hand. . . . I take up my pen again, for I am dying of boredom and can think of nothing but you. I hope you will read this letter alone. Will you hide it close to your heart? Will you write me a long reply? Write everything that comes into your head, I implore you. If you are afraid of my fatuity and do not want to compromise yourself, camouflage your writing, use an invented name, my heart will know you. . . ."[10]

With every letter, Pushkin's passion grew less ethereal: "I reread your letter from top to bottom and keep saying to myself, my darling, my wonder, my divine! . . . and then, oh, the dreadful woman! . . . You tell me I do not know your character? What do I care about your character? I don't give a damn about that! Since when are pretty women supposed to have characters? What matters is eyes, teeth, hands, feet (I would add heart, except that your cousin* has cheapened the word). You say it is easy to know you. You mean, to love you? I am inclined to agree, and am myself proof that it is true; with you I have behaved like a boy of fourteen. . . . How is the gout of your esteemed spouse? I hope he had a rousing attack of it two days after you arrived, serves him right. If you knew what a mixture of aversion and respect I feel for that

* Annette Wulf.

man! My divine, in the name of heaven, let him gamble and have gout, it's my only hope."[11]

Meanwhile, Faust-alias-Alexis Wulf had also left Trigorskoye, en route for Dorpat, but stopped off in Riga to answer the call of Mrs. Kern, and soon replaced Pushkin in the affections of that incandescent young woman.

Pushkin's jealousy reared its head: "What are you doing with your cousin [Alexis]?" he wrote. "Report to me, truthfully. Hurry him off to his university. . . ."[12]

Again: "Listen: I'm telling you the plain truth. You have contrived to make me jealous at a distance of four hundred versts; what would it be like at four hundred yards? I should very much like to know why your cousin did not leave Riga until the fifteenth of this month and why his name fell off the tip of your pen three times in your letter to me?"[13]

Later: "You swear by all that's holy that you are flirting with no one and yet you *tutoyez* your cousin. . . . Jealousy apart, I advise you, as a sincerely devoted friend and without fancy phrases or affectations, to break off this correspondence. I cannot conceive what you hope to accomplish by playing the flirt with a young student (who is no poet) at such a respectable distance."

The more uncertain his hold on the young woman's heart, the more he fumed to be so far away and to have no other means of defending himself but letters and sighs. His love was becoming an obsession.

"It is night," he wrote to Mrs. Kern, "and a vision of you appears before me, mournful and voluptuous; I seem to see your eyes, your half-open mouth. Farewell! I seem to be at your feet, I embrace them, I can feel your knees: I would give all the blood in my body for one minute of reality. Farewell, and believe in my delirium; it is ridiculous, but true."

He even laid plans for her flight, their meeting, their life together: "If your worthy husband becomes too much of a bore, then leave him; but do you know how you should do it? You leave the whole family there, take the post for Ostrov, and get off at . . . where? Trigorskoye? Not at all: Mikhailovskoye. That is the fine scheme that has been running through my mind for the last fifteen minutes. But can you imagine how happy I would be? You will say, 'And the scandal, and the noise?' Hang the scandal! The scandal is done when the husband is left; the rest is nothing, or almost. It's a splendid, romantic scheme, you must admit. . . . But tell me seriously—coldly, that is: Shall I see you again? The thought that I may not gives me goose flesh. You will tell me to console myself. Fine! But how? Fall in love? Impossible, until I have forgotten your transports. Leave the country? Hang myself? Get married? They all present considerable difficulties. I couldn't face them. . . .

If you come, I promise to be terribly good; I shall be gay on Monday, rapturous on Tuesday, tender on Wednesday, dancing for joy on Thursday; Friday, Saturday and Sunday I shall be whatever you choose, and at your feet the whole week long."[14]

Mrs. Kern did return to Trigorskoye, in October, and when Pushkin was at last face to face with the object of his passion, he thought no more of writing hymns to her, only of using her. Once assuaged, his love lost its sting, and when the angel departed again it, in turn, had lost its wings.

3. *Work*

While busily rebuffing Annette, plaguing Zizi and sighing at the feet of Mrs. Kern, Pushkin also found time to write, effortlessly and steadily. His intellectual life had never been as intense as it was during his village exile. The women of Trigorskoye were mere shadows flitting in the margins of his work. He would join them for a moment, then return to his studious solitude. There were two of him; but then, there were always two of him—an overgrown scamp with a sweet tooth for pretty women, drinking bouts, fencing, gaming and love letters; and a scrupulous and fertile poet. First one, then the other would catch the light; first one, then the other was the truth. Some of his friends never knew both sides. He passed through their orbits showing one phase only, and they judged him on that phase and were mistaken.

At Mikhailovskoye Pushkin finished *The Gypsies,* which he had begun in December 1823. He had visited gypsy camps in Bessarabia; during his trip to Akkerman and Izmail, in particular, he had been able to take a closer look at these proud creatures, verminous, independent, hospitable, incomprehensible. He talked to the bear trainers and the handsome, brown and supple girls who read your palm and stole your watch with an engaging smile. He had loved them. And he re-created them accurately in his poem.

In its Byronic subject and form, this poem belongs to the cycle of Pushkin's southern works. Once again, in *The Gypsies,* we find that somber hero of nebulous origins who has fled his urban fetters and is relentlessly pursuing himself. This rebel—Aleko—eventually joins a band of Bohemians, a people who have no commerce with law and live according to divine will. To him, they are the sole possessors of truth. Aleko chooses one of their women, Zemfira, the daughter of the chief, and adopts the savage and noble life of the camp.

But Aleko is torn by a tragic conflict. His concept of human dignity is so absolute that he cannot live according to the narrow conventions of society: He aspires to total freedom, for himself and for others—at least, he thinks he does. But as soon as anyone interferes with his interests, the civilized man, the old burgher, the stick-in-the-mud jurist, come surging to the fore. He has married Zemfira, and Zemfira is unfaithful to him. Now, if he practiced what he preached, he should not mind; but he is jealous. He refuses to another the freedom he demands for himself, he calls for help upon the laws he has spurned. The man who rejected the very idea of property suddenly finds himself fiercely proprietary; the man who rejected punishment can think of nothing now but revenge. His passions have turned him inside out, he is no longer a principle personified, a walking virtue à la Jean-Jacques Rousseau. He is a man. An egotist.

An attack has been made upon his property, his peace of mind, his honor and his wife, so he kills. He kills Zemfira and he kills Zemfira's lover. And stands, drunk with rage, awaiting the verdict of the tribe; but his cruel and stupid act is utterly beyond their comprehension. It never occurs to them to punish the murderer, only to flee him. Zemfira's father buries the corpses, then turns to the assassin:

"You are wicked, bold man. Go,
And peace be with you."
He spoke, and the noisy host
Broke camp and went
Far from that sad place. Soon,
Everything had vanished
Over the horizon of the steppe.
One lone wagon
Covered with a threadbare rug
Remained on the scene of the crime.
As, when winter comes,
In a pale and misted dawn
When the last flock of cranes
Rises from the fields
And speeds, calling, to the south,
One stays behind,
Stricken by a fatal shot,
Her wing limp and bleeding.
Night was falling. In the wagon,
No one made a fire,
And no one, all night long
Slept beneath the canvas hood.

The poem, thus, illustrates a moral and social defeat. Modern man is not made for freedom. Should he obtain it, he would no longer know how to use it. Passions are everywhere. In towns, villages and nomad tents.

Even in ragged tents
Live tormenting dreams. . . .

The poem's design is spare, precise. And the rare touches of color are placed by a master's hand. In *The Gypsies,* Pushkin made extensive use of dialogue, and began to acquire a taste for the play of speech between his characters. This was his preparatory exercise for *Boris Godunov.*

The dialogue in *The Gypsies,* however, is not always smooth. It is often strained, affected, needlessly bombastic; and the murder scene is handled rather melodramatically. But the rest is admirably sound. The descriptive passages, in particular, have great purity. For instance, here is the camp, at the beginning of the poem:

> Between the wheels of wagons
> Half covered with tattered rugs
> Fires burn. Each family
> Cooks its stew. Horses graze
> Nearby; behind one tent
> A tame bear sprawls.
> The steppe hums with the work
> Of the band, getting ready
> To leave the next morning.
> Women sing, children shout,
> Iron clangs on the anvil.
> But the silence of sleep
> Soon spreads through the camp.
> And the only sound on the plains
> Is the neigh of a horse, a dog
> Howling afar; the fires go out.
> Sleep. Far up the serene sky,
> The luminous moon lights
> The silent camp. . . .

Mérimée was particularly impressed by the passage describing the band on the move:

> The whole camp moves off at once,
> Flows over the empty plains.
> Asses carry children at play
> In deep woven baskets.
> Husbands and brothers, women, girls,
> Young and old follow the train.
> Shouts and curses, gypsy refrains,
> Growl of the bear, clanking
> Its restless chains.
> Gaudy hues of ragged clothes,
> Half-naked infants and elders,
> Howling dogs, barking dogs,
> Wheeze of the bagpipe,
> Creak of heavy wagons,
> It is all poor, broken, wild;
> But so full of motion, so alive. . . .

"Speaking of *The Gypsies,*" Pushkin wrote in his notes, "one woman remarked that there was only one honest character in the whole poem: the bear [the tame bear which Aleko exhibits to villagers to earn his living]. The late Rylyev was indignant because Aleko was a bear trainer who passed the hat to a crowd of idlers. Vyazemsky ventured a similar comment. Rylyev asked me to make Aleko a blacksmith, as that would have been more noble. Better still, of course, I might have made him a government employee or a landowner, instead of a gypsy. Although it is true that there would then have been no reason to write the thing—*ma tanto meglio.*"*

In May 1825 Zhukovsky wrote to Pushkin: "I know of nothing more perfect in style than your *Gypsies*. . . . But, my dear friend, what is your purpose? Tell me, what are you trying to prove with your hero? How do you want to be remembered by the fatherland that has such need of great figures? What a pity that we cannot agree!"

What disturbed Pushkin's friends in his latest work was the antiheroic nature of his hero—in other words, his humanity. The Rylyevs, Vyazemskys and Zhukovskys were not ready to accept a personality as contradictory as that of Aleko. They had been fed on a diet of monolithic statues. If a protagonist were inspired by some lofty ideal, then he must either lead it to victory or die for it. Pushkin, fifty years ahead of his contemporaries, gave them a man torn between his mind and the promptings of his instincts. A vulnerable man, a real one, like themselves. Like himself. Could this still be called art? Could one make art out of ignoble sentiments, ambiguities, criminal regressions? Could one make art out of material gleaned from the close observation of everyday life?

The journalists, however, praised *The Gypsies*, although they recovered their habitual spleen at the sight of Pushkin's next poem, *Count Nulin.*

"In 1825," Pushkin wrote, "I was in the country, and, rereading *Lucrece*, a rather weak poem by Shakespeare, I said to myself, now what would have happened if it had occurred to Lucrece to give Tarquinius a slap in the face? That might have cooled his ardor and forced him to beat a shamefaced retreat. Lucrece would not have killed herself, Publicola would not have flown into a rage, and the world and the course of history would have been different. I thought of writing a parody on Shakespeare's theme. I was unable to resist the double temptation, and wrote my poem in two days."

Two mornings' work: December 12 and 13, 1825, and there is the poem, complete and humming with life. Count Nulin is returning from a long voyage in Europe; his carriage overturns and he is forced to take refuge in a château inhabited by a young, comely and melancholic

* But so much the better (It.).

woman. The husband, a rabid hunter who abandons his wife for days on end, is not at home, and the forsaken lady joyfully welcomes this new companion, prepossessing, eloquent and clever, whom heaven has sent to relieve her monotony. But Count Nulin attempts to push the entertainment a little further than the laws of hospitality permit. He creeps into his hostess' bedroom at night, and is rewarded for his presumption by a princely smack on the face. Crestfallen, he retires to his quarters and goes off to town the next morning. After his flight, the young woman tells all to her hunter-husband, and the anecdote flies from château to château. "And who had the biggest laugh?" asks the poet:

The husband? Far from it!
He was in a frightful pet. . . .
Only neighbor Lidin laughed,
A gentleman of twenty-three.

Such is the tale. Thin, banal, nonexistent; but on this cheap canvas Pushkin embroidered a picture full of bright and beguiling color. He never wrote more fluently. Enjambments, unlikely cadences, dashes of common speech, whimsical rhymes; Lord, but he could prattle masterfully! And Lord, how close to us he was in language and in thought, this man of 1825. In three words, he sets his characters and scenes. And off to the hunt, with the thrashing pack of hounds barking and straining at their leads. And on to the Russian autumn, full of mud and rain. But soon the snow will come. And on to the chatelaine's evening with Count Nulin, who sings songs from Paris to her while the night watchman strikes his gong in the dark courtyard. The opening of the poem is so peremptory, so "direct" that it might have been written yesterday:

Let's go! Let's go! The horns resound.
The whippers-in, in full array,
Are a-horse since break of day.
The hounds writhe in a solid pack.
The master comes out onto the steps,
Stands watching, fists on hips,
His handsome countenance alight
With joy of life and majesty.
He is belted into his tunic, wears
A Turkish sword at his side,
A horn on a light bronze chain
And a flask well filled with rum.
His wife, in frilly nightcap,
Hugging a fluffy shawl,
Stares out through the window
With sleepy, peevish eye,
At the pack of springing hounds.
Here comes the husband's horse.

One firm hand on the withers,
One foot thrust into the stirrup,
He bounds into the saddle, cries,
"Don't wait for me!" And rides
Out of the yard to the highroad.

Here is the count's arrival: the jingle of carriage bells, then silence. The vehicle has tipped over in the ditch. The mistress of the house sends her servants to bring in the unknown traveler, the unhoped-for guest:

Quick! Quick! the footmen run.
Natalya Pavlovna fusses and frets,
Twists a curl, grabs a shawl,
Draws the curtains and pushes up
A chair, and waits! Heavens!
Here they come! At last, they're coming!
Muddy, caked with grime from the road,
Mortally wounded and sad to behold,
The team can scarcely drag.
Behind it, limping pitifully,
A young man and his French valet,
Who keeps saying, "Allons, courage!"†

And here is the evening. Nulin is answering his hostess' questions:

"And the theater?" "Pitiful, pitiful.
C'est bien mauvais, ça fait pitié.
Talma's lost his voice, he's done!
Mademoiselle Mars is aging fast!
As for Potier! Le grand Potier,
He alone can hold his own
Before the country's cheering crowds."
"And who is everyone reading now?"
"Still D'Arlincourt, Lamartine. . . ."
"And where are they wearing the waistline?"
"Very low . . . it comes to here. . . .
Permit me to cast an eye
Upon your toilette . . . ribbons,
Fluting, an embroidered design,
All quite in the latest fashion."

The simple tone, the studied absence of poetic effects, the alert irony were all new to Russian literature, and Pushkin was well aware of it; he regarded *Count Nulin* as one of his best-written works. But neither censor nor critics agreed. The censor would not pass two lines, one concerning a serf girl who "played the flirt with her master," and the other referring to Count Nulin, who, after slipping into the lady's room at night and edging up to her bed, "reached out to stroke the coverlet."

† All the phrases in French are in that language in the original.

The journalists were shocked by the "almost pornographic" frankness of Pushkin's theme. They reverted to their ancient quarrel of the noble word and the plebeian word, things poetic and things prosaic. How dared Pushkin talk about mud puddles, turkeys, cigars, silver candlesticks and hairbrushes? Was that an arsenal worthy of an emulator of Apollo? No; with *Count Nulin*, Pushkin was wasting his talent and degrading the nation's literature. The critic of the *European Herald* went so far as to intone with solemnity that the poem was "a cold sore on the widowed countenance of Russian literature." In his notes, Pushkin wrote: "*Count Nulin* has given me a lot of trouble. It was deemed (forgive me the expression) pornographic. That, of course, was the opinion of the press (for the public liked my poem). No journalist would defend it. A young man has the audacity to enter a young woman's room at night, and the young woman slaps his face! Dreadful! How dare anyone write such filth? The author asks what the ladies of St. Petersburg would have done in Natalya Pavlovna's place? What impertinence!

"Still on the subject of my poor tale (which, incidentally, was written with the most salubrious and proper of intentions): The whole of classical antiquity and the whole of European literature were mobilized against me. I concede the virtuousness of my critics. I concede that they were genuinely shocked by *Count Nulin*. But how on earth, in a matter of decency, could they hold up the ancients as their ideal?

"Those gentlemen have hit upon a curious method for judging the moral level of a poem. One has a niece of fifteen, another a young lady friend of fifteen, and whatever the parents of these girls forbid them to read is automatically classed as indecent, immoral and pornographic!"

Pushkin also wrote a great many lyric poems in 1825, the most important being *October 19* and *André Chénier*.

Pushkin turned to André Chénier, poet and martyr of the French Revolution, to glorify the hero of pure independence, i.e. himself. Like Chénier, he was a lover of freedom and a foe of monarchist constraint. But, also like Chénier, he hated blood, civil war and everything that deformed a generous impulse. The hope was so great, its achievement so base. It was but a step from ideal to caricature, from the poets' revolution to the revolution of Robespierre and Collot d'Herbois:

Having brought down the kings, we hoist into their seats
An assassin and a pack of executioners! Horror and shame!
But thou, O Sacred Liberty,
Pure divinity, hast no blame in this.

"Have you read my *André Chénier in Prison?*" Pushkin wrote to Vyazemsky. "Judge it as a Jesuit; that is, according to its intention."

The censor deleted every reference to the French Revolution—forty-four lines. But handwritten copies of the condemned passage circulated in every drawing room and barracks in Russia.

While writing these more modest works, Pushkin was also continuing the long, essential work he began in Kishinev in 1823 and finished "seven years, four months and seventeen days later."

On November 4, 1823, Pushkin wrote to Vyazemsky: "As far as my activities are concerned: I am now writing, not a novel, but a verse novel—a very different thing, something in the style of *Don Juan.* I don't even dream of printing it; I'm writing it just as it comes. Our censor is so crotchety that there's no way of suiting our field of action to his vision. Better not to worry about him; just take it or leave it."

On November 16, to Delvig: "I am writing a new poem in which I prattle and prate unforgivably."

On December 1, to Turgenev: "I am writing a new poem, savoring my own spleen. Two cantos are already finished."

In January 1824, to his brother: "It is my finest work. . . ."

From Kishinev to Odessa to Mikhailovskoye, the poem advanced steadily. The first chapter was completed on October 22, 1823; the second, begun immediately afterward, was finished during the night of December 8, 1823. Pushkin started on the third, and finished it at Mikhailovskoye on October 2, 1824. The fourth, fifth and sixth chapters were written at Mikhailovskoye and occupied him until August 10, 1826.

That day, when he put down his pen and pushed back his pile of papers, smudged and littered with nervous doodles, Pushkin had completed the major part of his novel. It was a whole in itself, it already existed independently of him; it was already his masterpiece. Six cantos out of nine, two parts out of three, were ready for the press. The first canto was published separately on February 15, 1825, and prefaced by the following remark: "This is the beginning of a long poem which will probably never be finished. A few cantos or chapters of *Eugene Onegin* are ready. Composed under favorable circumstances, they show signs of the lightheartedness that typified the early works of the author of *Ruslan and Ludmila.* The first chapter is complete in itself. It describes a young socialite's life in St. Petersburg around 1819, and is reminiscent of *Beppo,* the humorous poem of the somber Byron. Perceptive critics will not fail to note the total absence of structure; but we take the liberty of calling the reader's attention to certain qualities which are seldom found in a satirist: an absence of wounding personal allusion, and scrupulous honesty in the humorous portrayal of fashion and custom."

This moderate and good-humored preface gives a clear enough idea of the author's intentions when he began his great work. When he first took up his subject, he saw it, as usual, only as a "pretext for poetry." He never thought of structure or character or plot. He did not try to arrange the contents of his imagination or memory into a novel. He did not want to write a novel, but a "verse novel . . . in the style of *Don Juan.*"

A real novel requires a solid substructure and the subordination of all poetic material to that structure. The novel Pushkin was envisaging had no structure at all; the poetic material would simply accumulate as inspiration brought it, in personal reminiscences, fond asides to friends, sentimental verse, morbid meditation, stanzas dedicated to the tiny feet of a woman or the blue grace of Tauris. . . . The thread of the story painfully gropes its way along between these admirable obstacles. It stops, vanishes underground, surfaces further on, spreads until it fills the horizon and shrinks again to a gurgling rivulet.

The division of the poem into regular stanzas facilitated digression. Like Byron in *Don Juan,* Pushkin adopted the method of the numbered stanza for *Eugene Onegin.* Each unit forms a musical and logical whole, a poem in itself; and the work was built simply by adding these units together. The stanza of *Eugene Onegin* was devised by the poet in 1822, when he was toying with the idea of writing his *Tauris.* There are fourteen lines to a stanza, in the following pattern: a quatrain of alternating rhymes, a quatrain of paired masculine and feminine rhymes, a quatrain of introverted rhymes and a rhyming couplet (or: abab, ccdd, effe, gg).

The rhyme pattern is the same throughout: The metrical scheme of *Eugene Onegin* is as strictly respected and unvarying as its content is arbitrary, proving once again that Pushkin attached less importance to his theme than to its orchestration.

When he started, he wanted his treatment to be very free and satirical, and the first two cantos were composed in that spirit. But beginning with the third, satire gives way to pure lyricism: Pushkin began to care about his characters, to believe in them. Thereafter, his inspiration was informed by a virile tenderness and lucidity. Byron was buried, Byron was left behind: Pushkin had come into his own. In 1823, when he wrote, "I am savoring my own spleen," he was also talking about "cynicism" and "mockery," and announcing a work "in the style of *Don Juan.*" By 1825 his tone had changed: "Really, you are wrong," he wrote to Bestuzhev; "you persist in being suspicious of *Onegin,* yet it is my finest work. You compare the first chapter to *Don Juan.* Nobody admires *Don Juan* (the first five cantos, that is, for I have not read the rest) more than I do, but that poem has nothing in common with *Onegin.* You talk to me about Byron's British satire, you confront it with mine, and you insist that mine must be like his. No, my friend, there you ask too much of me. Where do you see the satire in me? There's not a trace of it in *Eugene Onegin*. . . . The very word 'satirical' should not have appeared in the preface. Wait until you see the next chapter."

Thus the poem, begun in Pushkin's brilliant and humoristic early manner, was continued in his later style, more calm and human. The work developed and aged with its author, it followed him through adolescence and into maturity, it followed his life and lived with his life. More perfect, more uniform, it would have been less moving. To read *Eugene Onegin* is to spend seven years with the man who dreamed and transcribed this tale, sharing his mistakes, his rages, his pride, his victories and defeats, his sorrows, his landscapes, his faces, his solitude and his duration.

Eugene Onegin is a rich young man, handsome, idle, blasé, who lives a vain, sophisticated life in St. Petersburg and, like all the other young "dandies" of his generation, is bored. He is well-read, well-bred, well-dressed. He speaks French. He makes the ladies laugh. In his dressing room:

> Combs there were, and steel nail files,
> Scissors straight and scissors curved,
> And brushes, too, of every kind
> For fingernails and teeth.

His days are an exhausting succession of parties, performances, dinners, suppers and intimate triumphs. Reading of this hero, a composite of all the idle young men of the age, one is reminded of Chaadaev, Kaverin, Vyazemsky, Raevsky and Pushkin himself.

Here is Onegin at the theater. He has arrived late. He edges between the seats:

> . . . Treads in passing on some feet,
> Turns and aims his opera-glass
> At a box of women he doesn't know,
> And examines all the balconies:
> Yes, that's clear: All the faces
> And all the gowns are absolutely awful.
> Then he bows, left and right,
> To a few acquaintances, and casts
> A fishy eye upon the stage,
> Turns and says, with gaping yawn,
> "They're all about fit to retire."

After exhausting the pleasures of the capital, reading all the books in his library and loving all the women he meets, Onegin has lost his taste for life and laughter. Just then, a landowner uncle of his conveniently dies. He inherits the estate and goes off to the provinces, hoping that a change of scenery will cure him of his melancholy. He settles into the château in which his uncle:

> Nagged the housekeeper forty years,
> Peered out his window down to the yard,
> And solemnly swatted flies.

But there too Onegin is bored. To amuse himself, he tries to manage his estate on European lines and improve the lives of the peasants—to the righteous indignation of his neighbors. One, however, becomes his friend. This is young Lensky, poet and philosopher. His candor, frankness and childish enthusiasm amuse Onegin, only too ready to make fun of him. Lensky believes in God, fears the torments of love and writes of eternal affinities. He sees the world through the blue mists of poetry and finds it dreadfully sad that Onegin has acquired such a black view of men and things. The two friends, Pushkin said, were as opposite as "fire and ice, stone and wave, verse and prose." But their endless arguments bring them closer together.

Lensky is in love with a young lady of the district, Olga Larin, and insists that Onegin must meet his fiancée's family in order that he may understand more fully the reasons for his joy.

Now, there happen to be two young ladies in the Larin family—Olga, who is pretty, sweet-tempered, spritely, neat, plump and vapid; and Tatyana:

> Untamed, mournful, mute,
> Fearful as a doe,
> She seemed a little child,
> A stranger in her family.

Tatyana loves Richardson's novels and chill dawns above the half-awakened trees, and long reveries by dancing candlelight. She is ardent and naïve, intelligent and gullible, dreamy and decided, arrogant and bashful. She is all secrecy, all contradiction. Elusive and withdrawn, like a real girl. Never had Pushkin created a character with so much life, so much flesh and blood, as this little provincial. We have come a long way from the stereotyped Circassian of *The Prisoner of the Caucasus*, the Polish woman of the harem, or Zemfira in *The Gypsies*. Those were ink-and-paper heroines who fade into nothingless before this new creature who lives and breathes for our greater joy. Who was Tatyana? Pushkin himself has told us: Tatyana combines the features of all the many women he had loved, from the little Bakunin to Marya Raevsky to Eliza Vorontsov. She is the repository of all the enigmas, the sacrifices, the incomprehensible reserves he had encountered. She is the distillate of his passions, the best of his memories, the best of himself.

Onegin, however, is unmoved by this wild little girl. He has inhabited an artificial world for so long that he is unable to perceive reality in the form of Tatyana's heart. He finds her more interesting than Olga, that is all, and says so to Lensky in so many words.

Tatyana, however, falls desperately in love with the handsome stranger, so nonchalant, elegant, glacial and sneering. He is so different from her neighbors, so like the heroes of her English novels! There is so little about him that is "true" or "believable"! Tatyana dreams, dreams, dreams herself sick. Her old nanny, a living portrait of Arina Rodionovna, surveys her decline with tender concern. Finally, the proud and stubborn little girl determines to make a supreme gesture: She writes a letter to Onegin.

Pushkin made this letter a masterpiece: Its naturalness, purity and unassuming delicacy are the work of a psychologist of the first order, its music that of a master composer. For generations it has rung in the memory of every Russian man and woman:

> I am writing, need I do more?
> What else could I say to you?
> I know it will be easy for you
> To punish me with your scorn.
> But if you feel any pity at all
> For the sorry state I am in,
> You will not abandon me.
> At first, I wanted to keep still:
> Believe me, I never would
> Have confessed this great shame,
> If I had preserved any hope
> Of seeing you in these parts again,
> Even if only now and then,
> If only once a week,
> Of hearing your dear voice,
> Saying one word to you, and then
> Dreaming, dreaming, day and night,
> Until the next time you came.
> But they say you are unsociable.
> You find the village dull.
> And there is nothing brilliant about us. . . .
> But we like to have you come.

It was Tatyana's letter that settled the fate of the rest of the poem. Under the spell of his own creation, Pushkin abandoned his bantering tone and became serious, profound. Onegin too is touched by the missive from the little provincial—Tatyana expresses herself simply, she appears to be very fresh, unspoiled, sincere: The master seducer does not feel it would be right to dishonor her. At their first meeting, he suavely explains how, if he had the least intention of settling down and founding a family, it was she he would choose. But marriage repels him, so she must not cherish vain hopes. She will love again. She will forget him. And it will all be for the best. Pleased with his paternal sermon, Onegin goes off convinced that he has behaved like a gentleman, whereas in fact he has only wounded a being of rare quality. Tatyana suffers in silence.

Onegin continues to be bored in his château. Autumn comes, bringing its sour wind, dead leaves and mud. And Pushkin, in passing, gives us this striking picture of the countryside at the approach of the cold season:

Dawn rises, misty and chill;
Nobody goes to the fields any more;
The wolf prowls the highroad
With his mate, howling with hunger;
The horse hears, snorts and shies
And the quick-witted rider
Plies his crop and gallops off.
The cows are no longer seen
Plodding early out of the barn.
At noon the shepherd's horn
Does not call the flock to pasture.
Inside the isbas, young girls
Hum as they spin, while
The flame of the vigil light
Whips and wavers before them.

Then:

It is winter. . . . The happy muzhik
Retraces the road in his sledge,
His old nag, smelling the snow,
Breaks somehow into a trot.
A master's sleigh glides past,
Tearing off gasps of white plumes.
The driver is wearing his sheepskin
And around it a scarlet belt.
Here comes a stripling running along,
Harnessed to his own sled,
Where a mangy pup sits in state.
The devil's hands are frozen stiff,
They hurt and he wants to laugh,
And from behind the window
His mother looks sternly out at him.

The Larins give a party for Tatyana's birthday, and Onegin is invited. Diversions are rare in the country, and the slightest hint of a banquet will bring all the neighbors for miles around. Onegin accepts. But Tatyana, shy and embarrassed, avoids him and will not meet his eyes. Then, for fun, Onegin pretends to pay court to his friend Lensky's fiancée, the playful, laughing Olga. Lensky is outraged, he thinks he has been betrayed. On the advice of a swashbuckling braggart, who is extremely touchy where other people's honor is concerned, he challenges Onegin to a duel.‡ The two men meet in a setting of frozen white. They remove their coats, take up their positions, raise their pistols and walk slowly toward each other. A shot. Lensky falls, dead.

Dead! Where now the upheavals,
The valorous young thrust
Of emotions and ideas,
High, tender, vain?
Where the yearning for love,
The thirst for work, for knowledge,
The fear of sin and shame;
And you, more hidden thoughts,
Signs of another life,
Dreams of sacred poetry?

Onegin, appalled at his deed, runs off the field, deserts his house and sets out on a long trip across Russia.

The sixth canto of *Eugene Onegin* closes with Lensky's death.

Pushkin was pleased with his work. He did not finish it until four years later; but what he had written there was solid. In this poem, more than any other, he rang true. Leaving the shepherdesses, the copses and groves and fountains to the old school, and the moonlit cemeteries and perambulating sorcerers to Zhukovsky, he created an aesthetics of reality, with the colors, actions and thoughts of everyday life. He proved there was poetry, too, in a gleaming samovar, a mangy dog and the face of a plain little girl with tear-swollen eyes and dry lips. He proved that poetry was not in the objects described but in the heart of the person describing them. He proved all that, and he was hardly twenty-six years old. In addition, he had to transform the taste of his public, teach it new concepts, prepare it for himself. Both readers and critics were conditioned by English and German romanticism, and here Pushkin had suddenly turned his back on them and produced *Count Nulin* and the opening cantos of *Eugene Onegin:* He must be stopped!

On February 12, 1825, Rylyev wrote to Pushkin: "*Onegin* is inferior to *The Fountain of Bakhchisarai* and *The Prisoner of the Caucasus.*"

N. M. Yazykov: "I should not like to have written what I have read of *Onegin*. . . . I dislike *Onegin*, dislike it enormously; I think it is the worst thing Pushkin has done."

Bestuzhev, in his letter of March 9, 1825, criticized Pushkin's subject as being too ordinary: "Talent is a gun, its subject a bird. Why do you want to go firing off a cannon at a butterfly? . . . The higher the subject, the more force you need to embrace, comprehend and animate it.

‡ This character was based on Pushkin's old enemy, Tolstoy the American.

Otherwise you look like a gnat on a pyramid, an ant trying to carry an eagle's egg. . . . I see [in the character of Onegin] a dandy dedicated body and soul to the mode; I see a man of the type I meet by thousands every day. . . ."

Bulgarin himself claimed to know "dozens of Onegins."

They all reproached the poet for concerning himself with people and settings that were too commonplace. Brought up in the cult of the exceptional being, they could not understand Pushkin's insistence upon introducing into the world of poesy a man like other men, a young woman whom they had the impression they had met many times, a country house like the ones they owned themselves, an adventure of which they might themselves be the heroes. They resented his choosing his characters from their own ranks. They resented his making them into heroes. Before, they had felt safe: The heroes were always robbers and gypsies and solemn, vaguely English young men. But an ordinary father, a proper young lady, a well-brought-up society lad could certainly never be the stuff of literature. Well, Pushkin was changing all that. It was flattering, one supposed. But it was also a nuisance. And for art, it was incontestably a loss.

Nevertheless, the book sold well. The public was easier to please than the connoisseurs. In Slenin's shop alone, seven hundred copies went in two weeks. The author was sure of his success, and proud of his achievement.

While his readers were familiarizing themselves with this study of contemporary mores, Pushkin had already moved on, or rather back, into Russia's past. From the nineteenth century, he shifted to the final years of the sixteenth, from Onegin he turned to Boris Godunov, from a playboy to a tsar. But his approach to the work of art never altered: Whatever his subject, he treated it with the same precision and avoidance of excess.

Before sitting down to write the opening scenes of *Boris Godunov*, Pushkin did a great deal of research and documentation. He meant his creation to be unassailable. He meant to regenerate the Russian theater. He felt called upon to be a pioneer in dramatic art, as he had been in poetry. Old chapbooks, sixteenth- and seventeenth-century chronicles, and Karamzin's history provided the factual background for the period he wanted to re-create; and Shakespeare's tragedies gave fresh impetus to his imagination.

In the spring of 1825 he wrote Nicholas Raevsky that he was beginning work on a tragedy. On May 10 Raevsky replied: "Thank you for the outline of your tragedy. What can I say about it? You will never want for brilliant ideas, but you lack the patience to carry them through.

So now you are to found a national theater too. On the question of patience: I would have liked to see you consult Karamzin's sources instead of relying on his interpretation of them. Don't forget that Schiller took a course in astrology before writing *Wallenstein*. . . . Whether your tragedy is good or bad, I can safely predict that it will have a great effect on our literature. You will give life to our hexameter, now so heavy and inert; you will add movement to dialogue, so that it begins to resemble conversation instead of the grammar-book phrases of which it has been constructed until now. And you will finally bring us to accept the simple, natural language which our public still does not understand—despite the excellent models it has been given in *The Gypsies* and *The Robber Brothers*. You will knock poetry off its stilts."

To knock poetry off those stilts, to write dialogue that had the flexibility of actual conversation, to establish a "verisimilitude" that was more than skin-deep—those were indeed Pushkin's aims. His reply to Raevsky shows very clearly the thoughts that were going through his mind, on the subject of the past shortcomings and future possibilities of the theater.

"I see literally no one," he wrote at the beginning of August 1825, "except my old nurse and my tragedy, which is coming along and I am pleased with it. Writing it, I began to think about tragedy in general. Both classical and Romantic authors have always tried to follow the principle of verisimilitude, but that is exactly what is impossible in the theater.

"1. Leaving aside questions of time, etc., what on earth can have 'verisimilitude' in a hall divided into two parts, in one of which two thousand bodies are sitting who are supposed not to be seen by those on the stage?

"2. Language. As an example: After listening to a tirade by Pyrrhus, La Harpe's Philoctetus says, in the finest French, 'Alas! I hear the sweet sounds of the Grecian tongue, etc.' Look at the ancients: their tragic masks, their double characters; wasn't all that a perfect, conventional 'untruth'?

"3. Time, place, etc., etc. The true geniuses of tragedy never bothered with verisimilitude. Look how Corneille brought out his Cid. Oh, you want your rule of twenty-four hours? Well, here it is! And thereupon you cram enough events into them to fill four months. In my opinion, nothing could be a bigger waste of time than to try to fiddle with the old rules: Alfieri thought the aside was a ridiculous convention so he abolished it; then he lengthened his monologues and imagined he had revolutionized the scheme of tragedy; what childishness!

"Verisimilitude must be in situations, and truth in dialogue—there is the real rule of tragedy. I have not read Calderón or Lope de Vega, but what a man that Shakespeare was! I can't get over it! How puny the 'tragic' Byron looks beside him! . . .

"There is another mania: Once you have invented your character, you are supposed to make every line he speaks, however farfetched, conform to the particular nature of that character (like the pedants and sailors in Fielding's old novels). A conspirator has to say 'Give me a drink' with a conspiratorial air; how absurd. Look at Byron's Harold (*ha pagato**); that monotony, that affected laconicism and perpetual fury; are they natural? Whence the uneasiness and uncertainty of the dialogue. Read Shakespeare; he is never afraid to compromise his characters, he lets them speak with all the range and spread of life, for he knows he will be able to give them their own special language when the time comes.

"You ask me: Is your tragedy a tragedy of character or costume? I have chosen the easier form, but tried to combine the two. I write and I think. For most of the scenes, a little brainwork is enough; when I come to one that needs inspiration, I wait, or omit it; this is a completely new way of working for me. I feel that my soul is fully developed, I can create."

My soul is fully developed, I can create. Those were not empty words: In the literary forcing shed of Mikhailovskoye, Pushkin had matured fantastically. He was sure of his talent. He knew what he wanted. New paths opened up before him wherever he looked. In composition, Pushkin's southern poems had been weak; in *Boris Godunov*, inspiration and reason came together. He followed a definite plan, he considered the balance between scenes, he went back over his dialogue, ventilating and interweaving speeches with more patience than he had ever shown before. He built a monument in which there was not one loose stone. Later, he wrote: "Like Montaigne, I can say of my drama, 'It is an honest piece of work. . . .' My study of Shakespeare, Karamzin and our old chronicles gave me the idea of reviving in dramatic form one of the most tragic periods in modern history. I wrote in utter solitude, with no outside distractions. From Shakespeare, I took the free, broad design of his characters, his bewildering multiplicity of types of scene, and his simplicity; for the sequence of events, I followed Karamzin; and through reading the old texts, I tried to reach the mentality of the people of that time and their language. My sources were rich."

In his notebooks, he also recorded some principles of dramaturgy which deserve to be quoted:

"What is the meaning of tragedy? What is its aim? Man and the people. The destiny of man, the destiny of the people. That is why Racine

* He paid for it (It.).

is great, even with all the formal restrictions he placed upon his tragedies. That is why Shakespeare is great, even with all his irregularities and his carelessness and awkwardness of execution.

"What does a playwright need? Philosophy, impartiality, the political mind of a historian, perspicacity, a lively imagination, an absence of prejudice, even toward his most cherished ideas. Freedom.

"We are always saying that art must imitate the graces of nature, and that its highest merit is to be useful. Then why are painted statues (which, being colored, are closer to their models) less pleasing to us than sculptures in bronze or marble? And what is the utility of Titian's Venus or the Apollo Belvedere?

"Verisimilitude is alleged to be the first rule, the very foundation of dramatic art. And what if it were proved that by its very essence dramatic art precludes verisimilitude?

"Drama was born in the market place and began as a diversion for the people.

"The spirit of our age demands enormous changes on the stage.

"I am absolutely certain that the democratic principles of Shakespearean drama are better suited to our theater than the aristocratic formulae of Racine's tragedy."

The pages of his notebook are filled with such reflections. Today we take them for granted, but at the time they were extremely daring. The Russian theater as Pushkin conceived it did not exist; there was only an endless series of adaptations from French classics and pseudoclassics —overrefined, empty and pretentious, and horribly lifeless.

Following Shakespeare's example, Pushkin ignored the unities of time, place and action. *Boris Godunov* is divided into twenty-four short, violent scenes, taking place over a period of several years and in many different settings, and involving the common people, boyars, monks, tsar and his Polish enemies. Thus it is the whole of society that is brought to life again through the poet's voice. The fate of the heroes is bound up with that of the people. Pushkin does not make an artificial distinction between the individual and the group; he simply throws more light on one or the other as the action requires: Sometimes, the chorus of common people is alone onstage. Similarly, the tone varies from one episode to another: Noble periods alternate with common speech, iambs with prose, the buoyant light of palaces with the golden semidarkness of a monastic cell. And yet, there is an underlying unity in this many-hued, apparently disjointed work. There is nothing extra, nothing superfluous; every wall, every face and every word is important; remove one and the entire edifice will sway and collapse onto its foundations.

As Pushkin said himself, his tragedy is both "of character and of costume," both Romantic and classical, Shakespearean and Racinian—or Shakespearean, as dreamed by Racine. The structure, the crowd movements are the work of a disciple of Shakespeare, but it was an admirer of Racine who imagined the heroes' personalities, regulated their passions, confronted and adapted them in the light of the ultimate disaster. Racinian in substance, Shakespearean in form, Pushkin's tragedy is a summit of world literature and deserves to be better known.

The year is 1598. Tsar Fyodor has just died. Throughout his reign, he was sheltered, dominated and blinded by his brother-in-law Boris Godunov, who has contrived, by exile and assassination, to remove any boyars who might stand in the way of his ambition. He is even believed to have caused the murder of Fyodor's brother Dmitry, so that the tsar dies without an heir. The throne of Russia is empty, the Russian people are without a sovereign; they offer the crown to Boris Godunov, as the man closest to their late ruler. But Boris refuses: He wants to frighten everyone, to be felt to be indispensable; and it is only after the boyars and clergy have pleaded with him that he finally consents to mount the throne.

His speech in the Kremlin is lofty and noble:

> Thou, patriarch father, and you, the boyars:
> Before you this day I have laid bare my soul,
> You have seen with what deep fear and humility
> I have accepted the charge of supreme power,
> So heavy did the duties of my office seem to me. . . .
> Man of saintliness, my august predecessor,
> May you, from heaven, behold your servants weep,
> And may you give to him you love,
> Whom miraculously you have raised,
> Your holy blessing upon his reign.
> I only wish to rule for the glory of the people,
> To be just and merciful, as you were.
> And you, boyars, I am counting on your help.
> Serve me now as you served him before,
> When I still shared your labor and your pains,
> When the people had not yet chosen me.

The boyars are dumfounded by this speech: Godunov is only being crafty, of course, and they know it, yet they feel that he is genuinely uplifted by his new dignity. He is sincere when he asks for Fyodor's blessing.

Godunov the tsar has forgotten Dmitry's murder, but Godunov the man remembers, and the tragedy proceeds from the struggle between tsar and man, between the master of Russia and the murderer of an innocent boy, between the deciding mind and the flinching heart.

Five years after the coronation of Boris Godunov, the scene is transported to a dim Moscow cloister in which an old monk sits writing the chronicle of his age by the trembling glimmer of a vigil lamp. Near him sleeps Gregory, a young novice. The monk speaks as he writes:

> Perhaps in days to come some studious monk
> Discovering this sere, anonymous account,
> Will light his lamp as I do here,
> Brush away the dust of centuries,
> And recopy these true reports,
> So that the descendants of Orthodox Russians
> Will know the history of their motherland,
> Revere the august memory of their tsars,
> Glorify their works, their greatness and their virtue,
> And quietly implore the Saviour's mercy
> Upon their many sins and black intrigues.
> I am old, and yet I seem to live again,
> And all my past comes back before my eyes.
> Was it so long ago that it ran, surging
> And twisted like the waves upon the sea?
> It is calm now, and never stirs:
> Not many faces have remained in my memory,
> And few words come where I am now.
> But dawn is near, my light will soon go out;
> Just one more word, one final word. . . .

At this, Gregory wakens. He has had a strange, disturbing nightmare: Standing at the top of a high tower, he was being cursed by a great crowd below. What can it mean? The old man comforts his companion. He speaks of the past, of Ivan the Terrible, and Fyodor, and the assassination of young Dmitry, who was seven years old when the traitors struck him down, and would now be nineteen. Nineteen, just Gregory's age.

Gregory is struck by the coincidence; a mad scheme hatches in his brain. He escapes from the monastery, eludes his pursuers, crosses the frontier and presents himself at the court of Poland, where he has himself acclaimed as the Tsarevich Dmitry, heir to the throne of Russia. He tells the incredulous onlookers that he was able to escape his executioners and that another child was killed in his place.

The news reaches the Kremlin, where Boris Godunov is suffering from visions and insomnia. Remorse has been gnawing at him for years; his sister, Fyodor's widow, is dead; dead, too, his daughter's betrothed. He has lavished gifts upon the people, and the people do not love him.

> I feel sick, my head is whirling,
> And bloody children dance before my eyes.

He can find no peace except in the company of his son and daughter. Gently, tenderly, intelligently, he prepares his son for the arduous profession of ruler, and when he speaks to his children he is no longer the criminal potentate or the assassin of Dmitry; he is a kind, though somewhat sorrowful, father.

When he hears of the arrival in Poland of the man who calls himself Dmitry, pretender to the Russian throne, Boris Godunov feels both alarm and relief. This Dmitry is an impostor, he must be arrested and hanged! But what if, by some miracle, he were the real Dmitry, and had somehow escaped death? Then he, Boris Godunov, would be cleansed of guilt. Which should he hope, which fight for? The throne, or peace of mind; bloody renown, or honest oblivion? The throne. He is tsar before all else; the tsar in him stifles the man. Better to rule, even with remorse, doubt, fear and prayer, than to abdicate and lose his own power and that of his children. He orders the closing of the frontiers and takes steps to prevent the rumor of resurrection from spreading. He acts as a ruler; but he is dogged by horrible fears. Vengeance is born from crime: He deceived the people to gain the throne, and this impostor must be the answer to his deceit. Two lies, one destroying the other—Godunov's lie, and the lie of the false Dmitry. What a strange combat: God seems to have willed this contest between frauds; and how ghastly, this skirmishing over the corpse of a child! Godunov struggles against his fate:

> Ah, I can't breathe. . . . Leave me. . . . I must collect my wits.
> I felt all my blood rush up into my face
> And drain heavily back to the depths of my body.
> This must be why, every night for thirteen years,
> I have dreamed of a child whose throat was being cut.
> Yes . . . yes . . . that must be why. At last I see.
> But what is he, in God's name, this dread foe
> Marching against me? A hollow name, a shadow?
> Could a shadow tear my mantle off, a shapeless sound
> Deprive my children of their rights?
> I must be mad! And what am I so frightened of?
> Blow upon the phantom, it will vanish.
> That's settled. I will refuse to fear it.
> But neither should it be ignored. . . .
> How heavy your crown is, O Prince Monomachus!

But Boris Godunov is not alone in doubting his strength on the eve of combat; his adversary, Dmitry the Pretender, also falters. He has fallen in love with the beautiful and proud Marina, daughter of the Palatine Mnishek. Marina is contemptuous of Dmitry, but she covets the Russian throne and would follow the tsarevich in order to become tsarina. She would make a marriage of intrigue, of ambition; but that is what Dmitry refuses to understand. He wants to be loved for himself, for his paltry defrocked monk's carcass, for his low birth, for his tangible flesh. He could lie to populations, armies, kings and courts, but not to this woman. He suddenly feels compelled to confess.

The Impostor—Do not torture me, Marina, my beautiful,
Do not say it is my name and not myself
That has found favor in your eyes. You don't know
That by those simple words you break my heart.
What? If, by some accident . . . O hateful fear! . . .
Tell me: If blind destiny had not accorded
To this body an illustrious birth,
If I were not the son of Tsar Ivan,
The child the world has now so long forgotten,
Then . . . then, tell me, would you love me still?
Marina—You are Dmitry. You can be no other.
And I wish to love only him.
The Impostor—No! It's too much!
I will not quarrel with a corpse for a woman
Who has given her whole heart to him:
I dissemble no more, I shall tell the truth.
Know that Dmitry is dead, buried,
And will not return. But do you want to hear
Who I really am? Please yourself!
Listen, then. I am a ragged monk,
Wearied by the life of oblivion in his cell. . . .

Marina is extremely angry; having learned the true value of her aspirant, she rejects him fiercely, and says she feels soiled by his presence. Vainly, the false Dmitry pleads for mercy:

I never could have lied to you, Marina,
To me you were a blessed image
At whose feet any lie was sacrilege.
And it was jealous love, and it was blind love
Made me confess!
Marina—What is there to be so proud of?
And who asked for your confession?

Faced with Marina's adamant refusal, Gregory realizes his mistake and switches back to his former role.

The Impostor—I am the tsarevich. I am ashamed to crawl
Thus at the feet of an upstart Pole.
Farewell, then, for the acts of bloody war
And the grave concerns of my new destiny
Will soon displace the grief of thwarted love. . . .
Marina—And what if I revealed, before it is too late,
Your presumptuous lie to those who listen to you now?
The Impostor—What do you think? Do you hope I'll be afraid
Of you? Who will they believe? A Polish vixen
Or the tsarevich of Russia? You should know,
Too, that no one—king, pope or noble—
Is truly fooled by my claim.

They little care if I be Dmitry or not:
I am a pretext for their quarrel, for their war.
And that is all they need: Know it. As for you,
Poor rebel, your lips will soon be sealed.
Farewell.

MARINA—Don't go, tsarevich; at last you
Begin to speak like a man and not a youth. . . .
It is high time! Wake up! Delay no more!
March straight to Moscow at the head of the troops!
Occupy the Kremlin, mount the throne,
Then send me your nuptial courier.

Heartened by Marina's change of mind, the impostor takes command of the Polish army and dissident Russian troops, and crosses the frontier. In the first battle, the army of Boris Godunov routs the invading forces, but his victory has decided nothing: The soldiers of the false Dmitry may be beaten, but the false Dmitry himself has won. The Russian people are swept away by the image of this young prince who was believed murdered and is now miraculously returning to chasten the assassins and assume the hereditary throne. His shining sword is the sign of resurrection. Hordes rush as though bewitched to serve behind his banner, cities throw open their gates to him, roads level as if by magic, leading him to the Kremlin—where Boris Godunov, hagridden and at the end of his strength, suddenly collapses during an audience, blood spouting from his ears and mouth. When he regains consciousness, he calls for his son. The end is near. He must confess to the one who is to take his place on the throne of Russia. In a toneless voice, he begins his long story:

I was born a subject; and should have
Died a subject, too, in anonymous shadow,
But I was able to rise to power. How?
Do not ask. You have no guilt to bear.
You will reign after me, it is your right.
And I shall answer, alone, to God, for everything.
O my beloved son, do not be proud,
Or delude yourself as to your own worth.
You come to the throne in a troubled time,
For he is dangerous, this strange impostor.
The name he hides behind strikes terror. . . .

After giving his son the supreme counsel of his experience, exhorting him to be merciful, to respect the teachings of the Church, to be cautious and never to fail in filial devotion, virtue or dignity, Boris Godunov slowly dies in the arms of the patriarch, surrounded by black-robed priests. After his death and the defection of the best generals in his army, the false Dmitry enters Moscow in triumph, to be acclaimed by the people as the new tsar, the only true tsar of Russia. The final scene takes place outside Godunov's residence. Guards have been stationed before the door. The dead tsar's son and daughter are seen at a window. A seething crowd looks up at them, some expressing pity, others demanding their instant execution. Boyars arrive and enter, followed by archers. There are sounds of battle, cries, then silence. Boyar Mosalsky comes out on the steps:

> MOSALSKY—People! Marya Godunov and her son have taken poison. We have seen their corpses. (The people, horrified, fall silent.) Why are you silent? Cry, long live Tsar Dmitry Ivanovich! (The people remain silent.)

This swift, abrupt scene in prose ends the tragedy of *Boris Godunov*. The author, primarily a lyric poet, was never as impersonal as in this play. The speeches of each character—Boris, the false Dmitry, Marina Mnishek, the historian-monk, the visionaries, peasants and boyars—have a distinctive ring. Pushkin disappears behind his characters, behind his settings. After seeing or reading the play, the spectator or reader feels that "everything has happened as it should." Whatever minor errors of fact the work may contain, it must, one feels, express the essential historical truth. The Russia of the sixteenth and seventeenth centuries, with its density, its particular flavor, its hidden soul, its weight of flesh and blood, its voice and language, is more convincingly presented in *Boris Godunov* than in any academic tome.

Pushkin liked his play. In October 1825 he wrote to Vyazemsky: "May I introduce you, my friend, to a romantic tragedy, the chief character of which is Boris Godunov. My tragedy is finished; I have read it over aloud, to myself, and I clapped my hands and cried, 'Bravo, Pushkin! Bravo, you clever dog!' My innocent is a highly amusing chap; and as for my Marina, you would have —— her because she is Polish and not a bad-looking wench at all (something on the lines of Mrs. Orlov, did I tell you?). The others are also very nice people, except for Captain Margeret, who swears abominably. The censor will never pass him. Zhukovsky thinks the tsar will pardon me for this tragedy: I, personally, have my doubts, m'love. Although it was written in a spirit of staunch loyalty, I have not succeeded in hiding my ears entirely under my grandmother's bonnet; the tips keep sticking out!"

Pushkin was right to fear for the future of his play. It came too early upon a world that was not ready for it. He never succeeded in getting it produced, and it was not even printed until December 1830. The critics, as he had predicted, were devastating. Polevoy criticized him for adhering too closely to the facts of official-history-according-to-Karamzin: "Already, from the dedication, we knew we would be shown a Godunov à la Karamzin, and those words are enough to seal the fate of Pushkin's drama. His great talent, and all the power of his writing, could not save him. He has cast himself into chains of his own forging."[1]

Plaksin wrote: "There is neither unity nor scope in the action of *Boris Godunov:* For in the beginning, all the force is concentrated within the character of Godunov, and after the fourth scene everything changes and the dramatic focus is transferred to the Impostor. Boris can hardly be said to exist for the rest of the play, and yet the play goes on."[2]

For the critic of *Galatea,* Pushkin's work was "a mass of scenes bound together by neither time, place, nor a methodical sequence of events; in a word, it is pure disorganization."[3]

Others held that "there was not a single profound character"[4] in the play, that "Boris' farewell scene with his son is too long,"[5] that it was unforgivable to speak of feeling "sick"[6] in a tragedy, that "out of three scenes it is hardly possible to extract thirty lines of real poetry," that it was "admirable prose"[7] and nothing more.

Lastly, Nadezhdin wrote, in 1831, "A great fall for Pushkin. Boris Godunov has cut his throat like he cut that of Tsarevich Dmitry."

Later generations reversed this opinion; by the middle of the century the critic Belinsky was saying, "Pushkin's *Boris Godunov* still stands out from the host of pseudo-Russian tragedies in solitary splendor, sober, with a magnificent purity of style, a dignified and classical simplicity—a giant among pygmies."

For Russian critics of today, *Boris Godunov* remains a peak of the dramatic and poetic art of every country and every age.

4. *The Decembrists*

On November 7, 1825, Pushkin finished the last scene of *Boris Godunov*.

On November 19 Emperor Alexander I died suddenly in Taganrog. The news reached Mikhailovskoye at the end of the month, and Pushkin's response to it was a thrill of impious exhilaration: Alexander's death meant the disappearance of his intimate enemy, his liberal tyrant, the man responsible for his exile and ruined youth. At last, the pseudo great man was no more. At last, he could hope again.

Alexander I had no son and his two daughters had died in infancy, so the succession passed to the eldest of his surviving brothers, Constantine. Pushkin rejoiced at the prospect: "As a loyal subject," he wrote to Katenin on December 4, 1825, "I should be grieved by the emperor's death; but as a poet, I look forward in joyful anticipation to the accession of Constantine I. There is much that is romantic about him: his stormy youth, his campaigns with Suvorov, his hatred of the German Barclay are reminiscent of Henri IV. Also, he is intelligent, and one is always more at ease with intelligent men. In a word, I have confidence in him."

Pushkin was justifiably hoping for a full pardon. But without waiting for it, he began planning a trip to St. Petersburg incognito; he counterfeited a "travel permit" to the capital, bearing the names of two Trigorskoye muzhiks, one of whom was called "Alexis Kokhlov, height two archines four vershoks, hair brown, clean-shaven. Age twenty-nine" —a rough description of Pushkin. On second thought, however, and in view of the trouble this was likely to create for his neighbor Mrs. Osipov, Pushkin voluntarily gave up this scheme. But oh, how he wanted to know what was going on back there. Why were they so long about proclaiming the accession of Constantine I? Why had he not been called back to his friends? News took such eternities to reach this Godforsaken hole. And his friends in St. Petersburg were so negligent about writing. If somebody didn't do something, they might even forget to appeal to the new emperor! "Take it or leave it," Pushkin wrote to Pletnev at the beginning of December; "it isn't worth cudgeling your conscience over, and for the love of God don't ask the tsar for permission for me to live in Opochka or Riga; what the devil would I do there? What you must do is ask him to let me return to St. Petersburg, or else go abroad. I would like to come to the capital because of you, my friends, so that I can share one more joke with you before I die; but it would, of course, be more sensible for me to leave the country. What is there for me to do in Russia?"

Finally, on December 11, unable to bear the uncertainty and full of forebodings, Pushkin decided to make a dash for St. Petersburg. Without permission, without preparation, on impulse. But obstacles and strange omens began to appear on all sides, as though the trees and houses, animals and even the rural sky were determined to restrain him. On his way to Trigorskoye to take leave of the Wulf-Osipov family, a hare crossed the road. On the way back another hare bounded past him, with flattened ears and outflung paws. When he reached Mikhailovskoye, the poet learned that the servant who was supposed to accompany him was sick in bed. He chose another to replace him. But all these evil omens troubled him; he was no longer certain, he felt only too strongly that he was going against some higher will. Still: The carriage was ready, it was time to leave, he left. But then, he crossed a priest in black going down the snowy road. That was too much. Pushkin was superstitious; he told the driver to turn around, and went home again, shaking with fury and worry. He opened a book and tried to read, but his mind kept wandering —to St. Petersburg and his friends. What were they doing? Were they doing as he had told them, preparing his appeal to Constantine I? Were they even thinking of him at all?

On December 12 and 13, 1825, Pushkin wrote *Count Nulin* to occupy his mind and relieve his rattled nerves. While he worked away in his smoke-filled cubbyhole at Mikhailovskoye, his friends in the capital of mist and granite were gathering for the great revolt.

The moment was propitious, since Russia was effectively without a tsar. Upon the announcement of the death of Alexander I, Grand Duke Nicholas had sworn allegiance to his brother Constantine, the viceroy of Poland, who, as first-born, should have succeeded to the deceased emperor. But in 1823, when he married his Polish second wife, Constantine had written to the tsar renouncing his claim to the throne. Alexander I had accepted his abdication and made it official in a decree of August 16, 1823, naming his younger brother Nicholas as heir to the Russian throne. But he determined to keep his decision secret; he gave the original of the text to the Archbishop of Moscow and deposited copies in the Council of Empire, Senate and Synod, in envelopes marked "Keep until I call for; if I have not done so before my death, open immediately thereafter, before doing anything else."

On the death of Alexander I, Constantine, acting on these arrangements, had his brother Nicholas proclaimed emperor. But in Moscow and St. Petersburg, the high officials of the empire, who knew nothing about Alexander I's secret decree, swore allegiance to Constantine. Nicholas, having also taken oath to Constantine, did not consider himself entitled to mount the throne; while Constantine, having taken oath to Nicholas, refused to regard himself as emperor of Russia. Nicholas wanted to meet his brother to straighten it all out; the brother saw no need for a meeting. The road between St. Petersburg and Warsaw was overrun with galloping dispatch riders. The divided and uneasy populace felt lost without a leader and did not know what to think. Then, on the evening of December 12, it was officially announced that Grand Duke Constantine maintained his refusal and would not come to St. Petersburg, forcing Nicholas to ask the army and population to revert to their original oath—a delicate operation, as he was dealing with a nation of fundamentally religious and disciplined people; also, Nicholas was not loved by the rank and file, who knew him to be crude, cruel and authoritarian. And: The conspirators were ready for action.

The oath-taking was set for December 14, 1825. On December 12 Nicholas wrote: "The day after tomorrow I shall be emperor of all the Russias or I shall be a corpse." At 8 A.M. on December 14 he told palace dignitaries, "Even if I am emperor only for one hour, I shall prove I am worthy of it." He felt isolated, threatened. Count Miloradovich, the governor of St. Petersburg, was affecting a perfunctory optimism; the generals were fighting shy; the emperor had no empire, no subjects, no ministers and no army—in fact, he had inherited nothing, and had everything to conquer.

Meanwhile, the members of the Union of the North and Union of the South were preparing an armed uprising for December 14. On the evening of the thirteenth there was a plenary meeting in the home of Rylyev, the man in whose home Pushkin had planned to stay. Many of his friends were present: the Bestuzhevs, Prince Obolensky, Pushchin, Yakubovich, Küchelbecker, Prince Volkonsky, Odoevsky. . . . Civilians, officers, poets, idle aristocrats, all smoking, eating, shouting, arguing and embracing each other at the wrong moment. Each man had his personal plan of attack and his own version of a constitution all drawn up, and had no time for those of his neighbors. There was only one point upon which all the revolutionaries were in agreement: They had to overthrow Nicholas I or perish in the attempt. But which battalions could they rely upon? But how to compel the emperor to capitulate? But who to name in his place? Rylyev said, "There is little hope of success, but we have to try; this attempt will serve as an example and bear fruit later." He also said, "It is better to be taken prisoner on the public square than to die at home in bed. . . ."

The conspirators separated at 2 A.M., filled with apprehensive enthusiasm.

The next morning, December 14, 1825, the members of the Senate and Synod assembled to swear allegiance to Nicholas; but alarming reports soon began to arrive from the Winter Palace. The officers of the Moscow regiment had told their men that Constantine had been thrown into a dungeon and had forbidden them to take oath to Nicholas. Directed by its officers, the regiment had formed a quadrangle in Senate Square, and other rebel regiments were joining it. The men were shouting, "Long live Constantine and Constitution!" having somehow got the impression that "Constitution" was Constantine's wife. A huge crowd had gathered on the square, from which only the tall equestrian statue of Peter the Great emerged. Count Miloradovich came forward to pacify the mutineers, but Kakhovsky, one of the conspirators, aimed a pistol at him and fired, and Miloradovich fell, mortally wounded, from his horse. Meanwhile, Grand Duke Michael had managed to rally a few loyal units against the Decembrists; the rebel troops stood their ground, not knowing what else to do. Prince Trubetskoy, who was supposed to lead the insurrection, had not turned up. The soldiers were hungry. Bread and vodka were sent for, but there was not enough to go around. The men were freezing on their feet, stamping, grumbling, taking pot shots at the opposing forces.

At three in the afternoon Nicholas sent General Orlov's cavalry against them; the horses slipped and slithered on the ice, the rebels drove them off with sticks and stones—the charge failed, and many men were wounded. Then Nicholas ordered his men to open fire with case shot. The first volley hit the cornice of the Senate, the second fell square in the midst of the rebel troops. The scene became a bloody tumult. Ignoring their officers, the men fled, pelting along the English Quay and swarming down onto the frozen Neva in an attempt to reach the far side, but the ice gave way under their weight and most of them drowned. Night was coming on. The fires that had been lighted around the Winter Palace illuminated heaps of corpses. The emperor had won a decisive victory.

Inside the palace, Nicholas I wrote to his brother: "Dear, dear Constantine, your will is done, I am emperor, but at what cost, good God! At the cost of the blood of my subjects! Miloradovich mortally wounded, Shenshin, Friedrichs, Sturler all seriously injured. I hope that after this dreadful event it will be possible to unmask the most diabolical of conspiracies. . . ."

During the night of December 14–15 Nicholas interrogated the rebel leaders, one by one. He used cunning, violence, cajolery and dignity in turn, like an actor playing his favorite scene. He extorted a confession from Rylyev by promising two thousand rubles to his family, he wept with Kakhovsky over the woes of Russia, he seduced Obolensky by offering to pass a letter to his father, he promised to pardon Bestuzhev if he would swear to become a loyal subject again—but Bestuzhev answered, "There, Sire! That is exactly what we are complaining about, that is why we conspired. It is a colossal abuse that the emperor should always be able to do exactly what he pleases. . . . Let justice take its course."

The interrogations and investigations ended in a monster trial with 121 people in the dock, nearly all of noble birth, and 13 colonels among them. Five were sentenced to death: Pestel, Rylyev, Michael Bestuzhev-Ryumin, Kakhovsky and Muravyev-Apostol. The people were shocked by the executions of Colonel Pestel and Rylyev, the poet: When the hangman pulled away the support, their nooses snapped and they dropped to the ground, breaking most of their limbs. Another noose was thrown over their heads and, bleeding and mutilated, they were hanged again, for good.

All the others were deported to Siberia.

One evening, a few days after the uprising, Pushkin was at Trigorskoye. Mrs. Osipov and her daughters were drinking tea and chatting merrily away with their guest. Suddenly the maid announced that Arseny the cook, who had been sent to St. Petersburg to sell apples and buy sugar, had come back and was asking to speak to her urgently. Arseny, red-faced and breathless, erupted into the drawing room and told how there had been revolts in St. Petersburg, and shootings, and people killed and arrested. Pushkin turned pale, clenched his teeth and turned away. He answered the girls' questions with vague talk of conspiracies and implicated friends, quickly took his leave and went home to Mikhailovskoye. They must all have been caught and convicted: Pushchin, Küchelbecker, Rylyev and the rest. And if he hadn't seen those two hares and that providential pope, he would have reached St. Petersburg on December 13 and been arrested himself the next day on Senate Square. But there; he had stayed behind. And his comrades were paying for him, paying for all Russia. What could he do? He burned his biographical notes, containing names and details that might have been useful to the government. Then he thought of going to St. Petersburg; and again gave up the idea. What for? He would only be arrested, and what good would that do him, or anyone? The *coup d'état* had failed;

nothing could save the martyrs to the cause of freedom now. He might as well accept the disaster, bow his head, wait, go on living. Go on living in spite of everything. Perhaps it really was impossible to fight the authorities? Perhaps one really had to come to terms with them? But then, what about freedom? An empty word? A pretext for bloody, futile battles?

The doors were blocked by snow, frost lay its lace against the sealed windowpanes, the stove wheezed and the days were endless, in this silent, shapeless solitude. Pushkin felt buried alive. Finally, shaking off his torpor, his scruples and his shame, he decided to appeal for permission to return to the capital. In January 1826 he wrote to Zhukovsky: "I have not written to you earlier, firstly because I was less concerned for my own fate than for those of others, and secondly because I was waiting for a safe means of getting my letter to you. Here is the thing: The government must be convinced that I had no part in the conspiracy and no political connections with the rebels of December 14. Through the newspapers, it has promised to disfranchise anyone possessing information relating to the conspiracy who has not immediately reported to the police. But who, apart from the government and the police, did not know about it? People were talking conspiracy on every street corner, and that is one of the arguments for my innocence. And yet I am still under surveillance by the local police; it would be easy to prove I had political conversations with any of the accused; and a good many of them were my friends. Now, supposing the government wished to end my exile, I would be prepared to come to some understanding with it (if necessary), but I warn you absolutely that you must not answer for me. My future conduct will depend on circumstance, on the government's attitude toward me, etc. I think one might say to the tsar, 'Your Majesty, since Pushkin is in no way implicated in this affair, would it not be possible to allow him to return at last?'"

Around the same time, Pushkin also wrote to Pletnev: "Could not Zhukovsky find out whether I can hope for a return to favor? I have been in exile six years now, and no matter what they say, I am only twenty-six. The deceased emperor exiled me to the country for two lines against religion; I don't see that anything else I have written can be held against me. Can our new emperor forbid me to go and live in some warmer climate? And if that is impossible, then is there no way for me to come back to St. Petersburg, tell me? Forgive me, my friend. I am bored. I can't stand it any longer."

While trying to arouse the government's compassion for his own fate, Pushkin was also worrying about those of his Decembrist friends; he was even a little ashamed to be making such a fuss about his freedom and comfort when Pushchin, Küchelbecker and Raevsky were probably in chains.

"My dear baron," he wrote to Delvig in January 1826, "you are anxious about me—quite needlessly. I am a peaceful man. But pray God my anxieties about others are equally unfounded! I have been told A. Raevsky is under arrest. I have no doubt as to his political innocence; but his legs are bad, and the damp of the camp barracks would kill him. Try to find out where he is and set my mind at rest."

Elsewhere: "What is happening to you all in St. Petersburg? I know nothing, nobody writes to me any more. You must think I am in Nerchinsk. You are mistaken, I have no intention of going there, and I am tormented by my ignorance of the fate of people with whom I was on friendly terms. I pray they will be pardoned by the emperor."[1]

"I impatiently await the decision that will determine the fate of those poor men, and the publication of the details of the conspiracy. I have great faith in the magnanimity of our young tsar."[2]

"What has happened to Ivan Pushchin? I was told the sentence would be announced on the twentieth, that is, today. My heart is heavy, but I am firmly convinced of the goodness of the tsar."[3]

At last, on February 27, 1826, Pletnev replied to Pushkin's anxious entreaties: "Zhukovsky asks you to write him a serious letter, in which you say that while you intend to keep your private opinions, with which no one has any right to interfere, you have no more thought of playing with words for purposes hostile to a regime which has now been universally accepted. After such a letter, he hopes to see you soon on his doorstep."

This provoked a fresh outburst from Pushkin: Begging for mercy meant deserting his friends. But refusing an opportunity meant condemning himself to more years of exile. And he could live alone no longer; he would go mad if he stayed on in this deadly wilderness.

On March 7, 1826, he wrote a letter to Zhukovsky which, as he said, "wears a courtier's tricorne and patent-leather pumps": "I commend myself to your friendship, and here set forth the history of my disgrace. Vorontsov forced me to resign. My health, which had been poor for some time, and a sort of aneurysm requiring immediate treatment, provided adequate reason for my return to the capital. His Majesty did not deign to take these details into consideration. Ordering my expulsion from the service, His Majesty exiled me to the country on account of a letter written three years ago, in which I expressed certain views on the subject of religious belief which were superficial and, no doubt, blameworthy. The accession of Emperor Nicholas Pavlovich gives me joyful hope. Perhaps His Majesty will deign to alter my condition? Whatever my political and religious beliefs may be, I shall keep them to myself, and make no pretense of entering into an insane conflict with the established and necessary order."

This letter cost Pushkin a violent effort over his pride and his loyalty to his friends. He was almost sorry he had written it, and he was even sorrier when he received Zhukovsky's incomprehensible reply, dated April 12, 1826: "Don't be angry with me for delaying so long in answering your two letters; I have not been well and haven't the energy to write. . . . What can I say about your wish to leave the provinces? In the present situation, nothing can be done to help you. Your wisest course is to stay peacefully in the country, reminding no one of your existence, and to write, to write for posterity. Let these troubled times go by. I cannot conceive your reasons for writing your last letter: If it is intended only for me, it is very odd. If you want me to show it about, it is insane. Of course you are not implicated; but your poems have been found among the papers of every one of the accused—not the best way to reconcile yourself with the government. You know how I love your muse and how I cherish your reputation; I value poetry, and am not unaware of the fact that you were born to become a great poet and the pride and joy of Russia. But as far as order and principles are concerned, I hate every disgusting thing you have ever written. . . . Talent is nothing; principles are all that counts. . . . I shall end where I began: Do not try to return to St. Petersburg now. It is too soon. Write *Godunov* and other things like that; they will open the doors to freedom."

On April 7 Delvig also wrote to remonstrate with the poet: "My friend, try to live on remote and glorious hopes, and work for the edification of your nephews. . . . Wait until the coronation, then we will be able to approach the tsar, then you can begin looking forward to a new life."

In a letter of April 14 Pletnev said, in turn, "My advice and the advice of all who love you is to spend this summer in the country."

And Vyazemsky added his voice to the chorus of solicitude: "Stay where you are like a good boy, and write, write poems and send them to be printed."

Vyazemsky's letter, dated May 10, arrived too late: On May 11 Pushkin sent an official appeal to the tsar, through Von Aderkas, the provincial governor: "Your Majesty: Having had, in 1824, the misfortune to arouse the late emperor's wrath by expressing certain superficial views on the subject of atheism in a letter, I was expelled from the service and exiled to the country under the governor's supervision. Today, trusting in Your Majesty's magnanimity, filled with sincere remorse, and absolutely determined not to interfere with the established order by expressing my personal opinions (I am prepared to substantiate this promise with a written undertaking, and my word of honor), I have resolved to submit the following appeal to Your Majesty: My health, which was undermined in my early childhood, together with a sort of aneurysm, requires continual care, as medical certificates will confirm. I therefore take the liberty of requesting permission to go for treatment either to Moscow or abroad."

A pseudo-official document was appended to his plea:

"The undersigned solemnly undertakes never to become a member of any secret society whatever, and further certifies that he has never been and is not now a member of any such society, and has never even been aware of its existence.

"10th Undersecretary
Alexander Pushkin."

A few days later Pushkin wrote to Vyazemsky: "You who are not in chains, how can you remain in Russia? If the tsar gave me my freedom I would not stay one month. We live in a sad country, and when I think of London, the railways, steamboats, English newspapers, and Parisian theaters . . . the sight of my sinister Mikhailovskoye plunges me into boredom and frustration. In the fourth canto of *Onegin* I describe my own life. One day you will read it and inquire, with an approving smile, 'Where has my poet gone? He does have talent.' And you will hear, 'Away to Paris, never to return to accursed Russia!' Now, isn't he a clever devil! Farewell."

On July 13 the 5 Decembrists who had been sentenced to death were hanged, and the 120 others deported. The previous night Pushkin dreamed that five teeth fell out of his mouth. When he learned the terrible fate of his friends, he was sick with fury and shame. He wrote the victims' initials in his notebook, drew gibbets from which five long, thin bodies dangled, scribbled, "And I, too, might have" and "I saw in a dream . . ." And finally, he composed his admirable poem *The Prophet*, ending with the lines:

Arise, prophet of Russia,
Don your shroud of shame,
Go, the noose around your neck,
To face the execrable assassin.

His friends' ghosts haunted him, assailed him day and night. He grappled with them, trying to reach beyond the injustice, cruelty and stupidity of the world. He fought them with all his naïve optimism, all his need to laugh and love and sing and drink and sleep.

A letter he wrote to Vyazemsky on August 14, 1826, expresses his feelings: "You find my letter [to the emperor] too cold and dry. It could not be otherwise. It is a good thing it was already written. Now I could not lift my pen to do it."

And: "I keep hoping, about the coronation. The hanged are hanged. But penal servitude for 120 friends, brothers, comrades; it's atrocious!"

In the meantime Pushkin's mother had also sent a plea to the emperor for a pardon for her son, "suffering from an aneurysm, with no one to help him, but conscious now of his past errors." A police report has been found, too, dated July 19–24, 1826, and written by secret agent Boshnyak, who had been sent to investigate Pushkin's behavior in the country:

"I learned that Pushkin went to the fair at Holy Mountain monastery in a Russian shirt with a pink sash, a straw hat, and an ironclad staff in his hand. He is said to live very quietly and to be very circumspect; he never speaks of the government and there are no tales about him circulating among the people. . . .

"Pushkin lives quietly; he often says, 'I write all the nonsense that comes into my head, but you will never see me in the galleys. . . .'

"Sometimes he goes for a ride and, after reaching his destination, orders his man to turn his horse loose, on the principle that every animal has a right to some freedom.

"Pushkin knows no one and sees no one, except Mrs. Osipov.

"To my question, 'Does Pushkin try to incite the peasants to revolt?' Father Johan answered, 'He takes no interest in such matters and lives like a young virgin.'"

The good cleric was perhaps overstating his case when he compared Pushkin to a young virgin. Pushkin was never dominated by a single idea, occupation or person. It would be a mistake to imagine him exclusively absorbed by any preoccupation, political, poetic or amorous. Everything in him called out and responded to everything else. He wept over his friends and caressed his girls, cursed the tsar and slept with the peasants, wrote poems and manicured his nails. He was multiple, diverse, blown by every breeze, a butterfly: Every pleasure and every danger beckoned to him simultaneously. He could only possess the whole of himself when he was alone in his room with his papers and books.

The winter and spring of 1826 were a difficult time for the poet. Torn between his desire to return to St. Petersburg and his fear of finding it empty of his old friends who had been arrested after the December uprising, Pushkin sought distraction in multiplying his depradations upon the Trigorskoye aviary. Mother, daughters, cousins—all were grist for his mill.

The year of his grand passion for Mrs. Kern had been 1825; 1826 was that of his demoniacal experiments with the mind and body of the gentle

Annette. He vented his boredom upon this soft and easy prey. Adored and idolized by the girl, he amused himself by teaching her tantalizing caresses, upsetting, alarming, rejecting and recapturing her, as the whim took him. In one poem, *A Scene from Faust,* which he wrote in 1826, there are the lines:

> But why is my heart heavy
> With sorrow and gray tedium?
> Glutted with love, I contemplate
> The victim of my desire
> With exquisite disgust.

Mrs. Osipov anxiously observed the moves in Pushkin's game with Annette in her role of lamb-led-to-slaughter; she feared the worst, but did not know that "the worst" was no longer to be feared.

In February 1826 Mrs. Osipov, Annette and Pushkin spent a few days in Pskov. In town, he found Annette more appealing than at Trigorskoye, and proved it to her, to the poor girl's joy. "We were completely reconciled in Pskov," wrote Pushkin, but the "reconciliation" was not at all to Mrs. Osipov's liking. Her daughter insisted that she was jealous, and perhaps she was; but perhaps she also saw that it was necessary to remove Annette, if a catastrophe were to be averted. She hurriedly set out, with Annette in tow, for Malinniki in the government of Tver. Pushkin, weary and surfeited, went back to Mikhailovskoye to receive a stream of endless and half-demented letters in French from the love-ridden young woman. She claimed that her mother envied her, she rehearsed Pushkin's past conquests, Mrs. Kern, Netty Wulf and so many more. . . . She said she no longer believed in Pushkin's love, but hoped she was mistaken about him. She made a transparent attempt to arouse his jealousy. Her letters, probably unread, piled up on the poet's desk:

"Do you know, I am crying as I write to you? It compromises me, I feel it; but it's stronger than I am, I cannot help myself. It is almost certain that I am to stay here [at Malinniki]; my dear mother has arranged it all without consulting me; she says it is dreadfully inconsistent of me not to want to stay now, when last winter I wanted to go away, even by myself! You see how you are to blame for everything; should I curse or bless Providence for having sent you to cross my path at Trigorskoye? And if, after this, you are angry with me for staying, you will be a monster, do you hear, sir? I have found a delightful cousin here who loves me passionately and asks for nothing better than to prove it in your own manner, if I wanted. . . . He cannot bear the thought that I have spent so much time in the company of such a terrible libertine as you. But alas, I feel nothing when he comes near me, his presence does not arouse the slightest emotion in me. . . ."[4]

"Lord, it is decided that I am to stay here! Yesterday I had a dreadful scene with my mother about my departure. She said in front of all the relatives that she was definitely going to leave me here. . . . If you knew how sad I am. I really do believe, like A.K. [Mrs. Kern], that she wants you for herself and is leaving me behind out of jealousy. . . . A.K. is to come here too; there will be no rivalry between us, though, each seems content with her position—which does you honor and proves our vanity and credulity. . . . Heavens, how pleased I should be to have a letter from you; do not deceive me, for heaven's sake, tell me you don't love me at all, that might make it easier for me. I am furious with my mother; really, what a woman! Besides, some of this is your fault!"[5]

"If you received my letter, in heaven's name destroy it! I am ashamed of my madness, I shall never dare to look at you if I do see you again. . . . Today she [Maman] joked about our parting in Pskov, she thought we showed too much affection: 'He supposes,' she said, 'that I didn't notice.' (What do you think of that?) Anyway, all you have to do is be yourself, to deceive her and prove to her that you haven't even been aware of my absence. What an aura of enchantment I was seduced by! How well you know how to feign emotion. I agree with my cousins that you are a very dangerous man, but I shall try to be more sensible in future."[6]

"Lord! What I felt, reading your letter. . . . I would have been happy with it if I had not remembered you writing others like it, and even more passionate, in my presence, to A.K. [Mrs. Kern] and Netty. I am not jealous, believe me; if I really were, my pride would soon get the better of my feelings, yet I cannot prevent myself from telling you that your conduct hurts me. Farewell for now. If you feel as I do, I shall be happy. Lord, could I ever have believed I should be writing such a sentence to a man? No, I shall cross it out. Farewell again, I am making a face at you, since you like them. When shall we meet again? Until that moment I shall not live."[7]

Poor Annette was not to see Pushkin at Trigorskoye again; and it was no doubt for the best. What would she have said and done, had she known her lover's latest exploits? While she was writing those impassioned letters from Malinniki, Pushkin was consoling himself in her absence by sleeping regularly with a farm girl, a fresh, full-bodied lass named Olga Kalashnikov. Olga was one of the regiment of seamstresses employed by Arina Rodionovna, the nanny. Pushkin first noticed her in 1825. After an untroubled and comfortable liaison lasting nearly a year, he perceived that his mistress was pregnant. "Leo Sergeyevich Pushkin," Liprandi wrote (in April 1826), "told me that his brother was having an affair in the country, and was now addressing himself to the object of his affections in more practical prose, rather than poetry."

Pushkin was ashamed and angered by his blunder. Olga's father had recently been appointed steward of Boldino, another Pushkin farm, and Olga was to join her parents there in May 1826. Her thickening profile, however, hinted strongly at her condition. The other sewing girls were already whispering and pointing at the unwed mother-to-be, and Arina Rodionovna was scowling and muttering imprecations under her breath at her scoundrel of a master. What would the old man and woman say when they greeted their daughter, dishonored by the young lord of Mikhailovskoye? What could be done to protect the girl? How could a scandal be avoided? And what to do with the baby?

Early in May, Pushkin wrote to Vyazemsky: "This letter will be handed to you by a good and charming girl whom one of your friends has had the imprudence to get with child. I appeal to your humanity and friendship. Take her in, give her what money she needs, and send her to Boldino (our family estate, where there are hens, roosters, and bears). As you see, there is material in this letter for a whole chapter in the style of Zhukovsky, on the subject of the *pope*; only, posterity must remain ignorant of our philanthropy. I also implore you, with paternal affection, to take care of the child to come, if it is a boy. I should not like it to be sent to the Foundlings' Home. Could it not go to some village for the time being, Ostafyevo, for example? My dear fellow, I am ashamed, in truth, but this is no time for sentiment."

A few days later: "Did she give you my message? Isn't it true that she is a sweet girl?"

Vyazemsky replied: "I have just received your letter, but have not seen the messenger in person, for it was given to me by one of your servants. The messenger herself leaves tomorrow with her father and family for Boldino, where the old man is to be steward. . . . How could I keep the girl here, and what purpose would that serve? . . . Here is my advice: You must write your prodigal father-in-law a semiaffectionate, semirepentant, semisignorial letter in which you confess all and beg him to take charge of his daughter and the child she carries. Appeal to his sense of responsibility, remind him that with God's help you will be his master one day, and will then see whether or not he has heeded your instructions."

Pushkin followed Vyazemsky's advice, and Olga's father readily grasped the potential advantages for himself in his "shame." Whatever he did, Pushkin would not dare to demote him: He was steward for life. Olga gave birth to a son, and the existence of this illegitimate child did not prevent her, a few years later, from marrying a little provincial bureaucrat with a scrap of land and thirty serfs. Olga became a "lady." But her husband drank so voraciously that the scrap of land and thirty serfs were soon mortgaged to the hilt. Olga wrote to Pushkin: "Forgive me for having bothered you about that money we needed to repurchase my husband's serfs: They are not worth owning. I only asked you in order to please my husband . . . but he never understands my thoughtfulness, because he himself is the most thoughtless man in the world, and I have lost all hope in him, and he will not earn another crust of bread, and he is behind all the nasty work that goes on, and most of all, he is a drunkard and a profligate."

No one knows what became of the accommodating Olga Kalashnikov. And Pushkin's son? A little muzhik, probably, with dark skin and thick lips; some people claim he was still alive at the turn of the century.

While Pushkin's appeal for pardon wafted from office to office with decorous leisureliness, a pile of reports which boded no good for the poet's future was mounting up on the desk of Nicholas I. Every one of the rebels of December 14 knew Pushkin's "liberal" poems, they all referred to him in their interrogations, his name was continually assailing the emperor's ears.

Peter Bestuzhev, for example, told the investigating authorities: "My liberal ideas were implanted in my mind by unprinted poems like the *Ode to Liberty*, *The Village*, *My Apollo*, and certain epistles which created difficulties for our celebrated poet Pushkin."

In his official statement Divov said, "My liberal ideas were inspired by the reading of certain manuscripts, particularly the subversive poems of Pushkin and Rylyev. . . ."

Bestuzhev-Ryumin's testimony: "Everywhere, I heard Pushkin's poetry being recited enthusiastically. That anchored my love of liberal ideas more and more firmly within me."

From his fortress, Baron Steingel wrote: "What educated young man has not read and loved Pushkin's poems on freedom?"

Pushkin! Pushkin! Always Pushkin! Those Decembrists seemed to have gorged themselves on his infamous writings! This dangerous chatterbox must be investigated more closely. Police agent Locatelli noted, in his report for June: "Everyone is surprised to see that the famous Pushkin, long known for his subversive ideas, has not been questioned about the conspiracy."

In July Boshnyak, another agent of the police, was sent to spy on the poet; then, at the end of the month, police in Moscow seized a poem entitled *December 14*, which was a stream of abuse directed at the tsar and his new chief of police, Benkendorf. The lines were by Pushkin, beyond any doubt—that same Pushkin who was appealing for pardon had dared to write:

> Having brought down the kings, we hoist into their seats
> An assassin and a pack of executioners! Horror and shame!

What Nicholas I and his staff did not know was that the offending lines were from the censored passage in Pushkin's *André Chénier*, or that they referred to the French Revolution and not to the recent Russian incident. An ingenious copyist had simply retitled the passage *December 14*, and that was enough for the emperor and Benkendorf, who immediately saw themselves as the targets of the attack upon Robespierre and his bloodstained mob. Benkendorf ordered a search made for any person possessing a copy of the poem; two poor devils were brought in, questioned, mildly maltreated and admitted that the lines were by Pushkin. Benkendorf told his friends, "Those lines are so foul that you would have denounced your own son if you found out that he had dared to write them!"

Nicholas I's notions of literature were those of a provincial old maid; he had no conception of Pushkin's talent, but the fact that every enemy of autocracy sang his praises so unreservedly rendered his celebrity all the more suspect. He wanted to see this man, question him himself, hear his political views from his own mouth and save or damn him according to his replies. The appeal for a pardon and the affair of the subversive poem were both in his hands. Why wait?

On August 28 General Dibich recorded the imperial decision: "Order to Pushkin to come immediately [i.e. to Moscow, where the coronation ceremonies were to take place]. A *Feldjäger* to be assigned to escort him. Pushkin will be allowed to travel under ordinary conditions, in his own carriage, without any of the restrictions placed upon persons under arrest, but accompanied by the *Feldjäger*. Pushkin must be brought to me as soon as he arrives. Notify the governor of Pskov."

On the night of September 3 a constable from Pskov arrived at Mikhailovskoye. Pushkin was warming himself by the stove, tossing log after log onto the fire. When he heard who was there he leaped up, snatched a pile of papers from his desk and stuffed them into the flames —he always kept any compromising documents within arm's reach. He was surely about to be arrested because of some "liberal" poem or absurd denunciation. He would be sentenced. Deported to Siberia. Arina Rodionovna was already raising her arms to heaven and bursting into loud sobs at the sight of the threatening epaulets of the officer in the corridor.

"Don't cry," Pushkin told her. "They will give me plenty to eat. Wherever the tsar sends me, he will give me bread."

The officer had come into the room and was jingling his spurs, anxious to be off again. Pushkin sent for his pistols, which he had left at Trigorskoye.

"Mr. Pushkin, I don't like the look of those pistols," said the constable.

"I can't help it," answered Pushkin. "I can't go anywhere without them. They are my sole distraction."

Pushkin buttoned up his long overcoat, kissed Arina Rodionovna, bade farewell to a few sleepy servants and left the house in the company of the imposing officer. He was sure he was doomed, but felt curiously purified by this latest blow. He was going to suffer like the others, and for the same cause. That was good. At Pskov, however, the governor and *Feldjäger* disabused him: He was not charged, the emperor merely wanted to see him and speak to him personally. His pressing invitation was a sign of benevolence, not suspicion. From Pskov, Pushkin wrote a letter, dated September 4, to Mrs. Osipov: "I imagine, Madame, that my sudden departure with a *Feldjäger* will have taken you as much by surprise as it did me. The fact is that nothing can be done without a *Feldjäger*; I have been given one for added safety; according to a most amiable letter from Baron Dibich, I have every reason to be proud of the fact. I go straight to Moscow, where I should be on the eighth of this month, and as soon as I am free again I shall hurry back to Trigorskoye, the home of my heart forevermore."[8]

On the evening of September 4 Pushkin and Feldjäger Valsh left Pskov for Moscow. Pushkin's courage had returned; he joked with his companion and recited poetry. The driver pushed his team; at every posting station new horses appeared as if by magic. As they raced through the villages, the pigs and hens scattered before them, and children standing by the wayside waved their grubby little hands at the travelers. Pushkin was galloping to meet the emperor of all the Russias. They covered the seven hundred versts between Pskov and Moscow in four days.

PART VI

1. Nicholas I and Pushkin

"The emperor," wrote the Marquis de Custine, "is taller than the average by half a head; his aspect is impressive, albeit somewhat stiff: In his youth he acquired a habit of fastening his belt above the kidneys, so tightly as to push his abdomen up under his ribs. His profile is Grecian, with a high forehead, depressed toward the rear, a straight, perfectly formed nose, a beautiful mouth, a noble face, oval but a shade long, and an expression that could be called Teutonic rather than Slavic. His movements and gestures are deliberately imposing. He is always on display, he never forgets for one moment that people are looking at him. . . . The emperor of Russia is a military chief, for whom every day is a day of battle."

Lacroix, in his *Mystères de la Russie,* remarked: "He has the most autocratic physiognomy imaginable, he is despotism personified, a flawless illustration of absolute power. . . . There is something starched, strained and unnatural about this sovereign; or rather, something pedantically official. . . . His movements have grown stiff as the result of his constant wearing of a uniform, and his gestures have acquired a peculiar artificiality. One might say he is always keyed up for battle, never without his gorget."

Nicholas I loved two things: dress parades and mathematics. He would speak of "we military men" and "we engineers." He always wore a uniform, and would have liked to see every Russian equipped with a special form of dress suited to his functions and rank. His passion for exactitude, symmetry and hierarchy was reminiscent of Alexander I. Like Alexander, he considered it indispensable for administration, justice, education and human relations to be regulated by military discipline. Like Alexander, he dreamed of transforming the nation's entire moral and material life into a neat game of chess. Like Alexander, he was a wholehearted advocate of militarized society and unqualified autocracy. But whereas Alexander's love of order had been a manifestation of some strange and dolorous mystical complex, in Nicholas it was simply a mania. Nicholas had a horror of mysticism, he did not understand it and was afraid of it. In his view, mysticism was quicksand beneath a monarch's feet, and calling upon divine will to justify the acts of a terrestrial sovereign was the shortest route to self-contradiction. God had no part in the waging of wars, the drafting of laws or the building of roads, and the role of a tsar was to build roads, make laws, win wars and keep a firm grasp on his throne. Now, the security of the monarchy had been momentarily shaken by the uprising of December 14 and a few sporadic outbursts in provincial districts and regiments; Nicholas I accordingly began his reign by reinforcing army regulations and expanding the civilian police. Russia was transformed into a vast concentration camp guarded by agents of the secret police. Benkendorf, newly appointed chief of the third section (major crimes, religion, aliens, correspondence), blandly wrote: "One resource of the secret police, and a capital one, is the interception of correspondence, for it is effective always and everywhere. All that is needed is a series of postmasters in selected towns who are known for their trustworthiness and devotion. . . . That is a beginning, but it is not enough; informers are also necessary. Now, upon whom can we rely?"

By such measures, Nicholas I hoped to make Russia powerful and glorious. Discipline, orthodoxy, respect for tradition and love of the tsar, "chosen of God"—such was the program he submitted to his people. No more dissonant voices in the nation's choir, no more liberal initiatives, no more exalted personal destinies. Every subject was a stone in a pyramid, with the monarch at the top.

Despite his authoritarian ambitions, Nicholas I was a sane, limited, honest and conscientious man. He set an example of strict morality: work at regular hours, constitutional walks and quiet evenings at home. He was determined to present the image of a model husband and father; he venerated his wife, and if he chanced, now and then, to be unfaithful to her, it was with all the consideration and precautions befitting her imperial rank. Meticulous and practical by nature, he liked books that did not require him to think about social or metaphysical problems. Paul de Kock was his favorite author. With him, there was no danger: Evil was punished and virtue rewarded, and there were amusing episodes to entertain the reader between two passages of solid mawk. Nicholas I had never read Pushkin's lyrics, or if he had, he had forgotten them. Pushkin, for him, was two pieces of paper: an appeal for grace and a subversive poem about December 14, signed by the same name.

This was the man Pushkin was about to meet, and on this man his fate depended—an opaque, glacial, distant colossus. A drum major with a literary blank between the ears and exaggerated political pretensions. What could these two have in common? How could they communicate?

When Pushkin and Feldjäger Valsh reached Moscow on September 8, the poet was immediately conducted to the Chudov monastery, where Nicholas I had established temporary residence. Pushkin would have liked to wash and brush up a bit before going to face his judge and master, but the instructions were formal: "Straight to the palace. For an audience." He was to have an imperial audience, he, the exile, the friend of the Decembrists—really, there was something prodigious about this adventure!

Muddy and begrimed, his side whiskers flying, his nose a bright pink and his forehead covered with fever spots, Pushkin hurried along behind the perfumed and curled aide-de-camp who was leading him to the imperial apartments. Lackeys in scarlet livery. Petrified sentinels. A door opening. Pushkin was in the study of Nicholas I.

It was a vast, calm, imposing room. Gray light filtered through the window. Sheets of glazed paper gleamed on a bronze-incrusted table. A marble chimney piece framed a log fire, blazing, radiant, magnificent. And in front of the fireplace stood a very tall man, squeezed to the bursting point in his uniform, with fat hips, a stomach stretched like a drum and an expansive chest. Luminous, oddly motionless eyes gazed out of a matte white face. Pushkin was looking at the tsar of all the Russias. He shivered. His old doubts and fears welled up within him. Why this interview? What did they want with him? Which was it to be, salvation or perdition? He was carrying his latest poem, *The Prophet*, in his pocket:

> Arise, prophet of Russia,
> Don your shroud of shame,
> Go, the noose around your neck,
> To face the execrable assassin.

If Nicholas I threatened to send him to Siberia, he would simply hand him the poem; he would go out in glory, at least.

Nicholas I studied the poet with curiosity; it rather pleased him that Pushkin should be so bedraggled after his journey. At last, he spoke.

"Good morning, Pushkin, are you glad to be back?"

Surprised by the pure, metallic voice, Pushkin inclined his head a shade lower than he had intended.

"My brother, the late emperor," Nicholas continued, "sent you to the country in exile; I have decided to pardon you, as long as you never write anything against the government again."

"Your Majesty," replied Pushkin, "I have not written anything against the government for a long time now, and in fact I have hardly written anything at all, since *The Dagger*."

"You were friendly with quite a few of the men I sent to Siberia."

Pushkin squared himself.

"Yes, Majesty, I respected and liked many of those men and my feelings toward them have not altered."

"How could anyone be a friend of that swine Küchelbecker?" said the emperor with a frown.

"We always took him for a fool, and what surprises us is that he was sent to Siberia along with so many men of sense and intelligence."

The emperor permitted himself a smile; he quite liked the nerve and frankness of this Pushkin. He went on.

"What are you writing these days?"

"Hardly anything, Your Majesty. The censor is very strict."

"But why must you write things the censor cannot pass?"

"Perfectly innocuous writings are forbidden," Pushkin said. "The censor acts quite indiscriminately."

His tone was growing heated. The emperor moved to the table, leafed through some papers and held out a copy of the poem now entitled *December 14*. Pushkin heaved a sigh of relief. At last he knew why they were after him! He blurted out the whole story of the unfortunate poem: The lines were an unpublished fragment of *André Chénier*, they referred to the terrorists of the French Revolution. Nicholas I was apparently satisfied by this explanation. His mask unfroze slightly. A smile widened his long lips. As he had moved away from the fire, Pushkin, who was shivering and chilled to the bone, went over to warm his legs in front of it. He had quite forgotten protocol; he felt safe, he thought he had probably won. Was it possible that this same man, with the affable face and measured gestures, had sentenced so many young men animated by such lofty ideals to death and deportation? Was it possible that this man who was about to pardon all his crimes had been heartless enough to send Pushchin and Küchelbecker to prison and execute Rylyev? Pushkin gave a mighty sniff, for he had caught cold on the road. The emperor's voice recalled him to reality.

"If you had been in St. Petersburg, would you have taken part in the uprising on December 14?"

Pushkin's eyes sparkled.

"Beyond any doubt, Majesty. All my friends were in the conspiracy, it would have been impossible for me to let them down. My absence alone saved me, for which I thank God."

His reply flattered Nicholas' sense of chivalry: The poet must think him very grand indeed, to utter such a truth to his face. A nature as exceptional as this deserved special treatment. Why not enlist him in the service of the monarchy? He had talent, a reputation and a rather winning naïveté which might easily be exploited for the benefit of the regime—not to mention the fact that in St. Petersburg it would be easier to keep an eye on the young man's behavior.

"Have you made up your mind to change your ideas?" asked Nicholas. "Do I have your word of honor that you will mend your ways, if I give you back your freedom?"

Pushkin looked apprehensively at the emperor standing before him—the impenetrable face, all of a piece, the eyes of steel in which two immobile lamps gleamed. He felt that his whole life hung on his reply. Would he deny his faith and recover his freedom, or stand by his convictions and go back to rot in the country? Nicholas fascinated him: If he had spoken to the tribunal as he had just done in this room, he would certainly have been thrown into a fortress. But the tsar understood the nobility of his principles. How could he resist such generosity? How could he refuse such amazing magnanimity?

The emperor's large white hand was outstretched, open, toward Pushkin. In it Pushkin placed his small, dirty hand with the long fingernails. He felt as though he were falling off a cliff. He closed his eyes in exhaustion, shame and rapture.

"You have been foolish long enough," said the emperor. "I hope you will be more sensible after this, and there will be no more quarrels between us. You will send everything you write to me. From now on, I shall be your censor."

Pushkin's heart flooded with an infinity of gratitude. Free! Free! He was free! And he had not sold his soul, he had not humbled himself before this smiling potentate. Giddy and weak, he allowed himself to be led into the next room, filled with uniformed courtiers. Facing all those masks frozen in expressions of honeyed respect, Nicholas I loudly declared, "Gentlemen, here is the new Pushkin. Forget the other."[1]

Pushkin left the imperial apartments with buckling knees and tear-blurred vision. Mechanically, he reached into his pocket. His poem, *The Prophet*, was gone. Had he dropped it in the emperor's study? Nicholas would find it, be very justifiably enraged, and that would be the end of his promise. Pushkin's forehead was beaded with cold sweat. His heart thudded in his chest. His mouth went dry. He had stopped, paralyzed, halfway down the grand staircase. Suddenly he spied a scrap of paper on a step below, stirring in the draft, and immediately recognized it: *The Prophet*. Saved.

A few days later Pushkin carefully rewrote the last verse. The revised poem reads as follows:

Parched with the thirst of the spirit,
I was wandering in an unlit desert,
When a winged seraphim
Appeared to me beside the path.

With his fingers light as daydreams,
He bent and brushed my eyes.
My pupils widened, like those
Of an affrighted eagle.
He also touched my ears,
They filled with the pealing of bells;
I understood the shudder of the skies,
The flight of angels over the world,
The surge of submarine beasts,
And the fever of bursting seeds.
Then, leaning toward my lips,
He tore out my vile tongue
That talks too much and lies too much,
And with his bloody fist
Implanted in my dead throat
A viper's caustic sting.
With his sword he opened my breast
And plucked out my quivering heart,
And then between my cleft ribs
He thrust one glowing ember.
I was lying, alone, like a corpse,
When the voice of God called out to me:
Arise, prophet! Listen, behold!
Grow tall and full with my will,
And go, over land and sea,
To burn men's hearts with my word.

As soon as he left the emperor, Pushkin had himself driven straight to Uncle Basil's, where he stayed to lunch and heard the latest gossip of both capitals; then he went to find Vyazemsky in the Turkish bath. The friends embraced in the rich steam of the sweating room. They had so much to tell each other. Vyazemsky was an immovable monarchist, but he could not stomach the repression of the rebellion of December 14. "At the first opportunity, I shall leave Russia for a long time. . . . At present, Russia seems completely rotten to me, drenched in blood; I cannot and will not go on quietly living on the square where men have been executed. . . ."

Vyazemsky also tried, no doubt, to moderate Pushkin's naïve elation.

That evening, at a ball given by the Maréchal de Marmont—Duc de Raguse and ambassador of France—Emperor Nicholas I gaily announced, "Today I had a long conversation with the most intelligent man in Russia: Pushkin."

The news of Pushkin's return to grace flew from drawing room to drawing room. He arrived on September 8; on the tenth there was a reading of *Boris Godunov* at Sobolevsky's, and on the twelfth he went to a performance of a comedy by Shakovskoy entitled *Aristophanes* at the Moscow Grand Theater. His appearance in the orchestra was hailed by a long, welcoming murmur; every eye and smile was directed upon the lean, agile little man with the dark skin and bushy hair. "It's he! The author of *Ruslan and Ludmila, The Prisoner, The Fountain of Bakhchisarai, Eugene Onegin,* the exiled poet, the friend of lonely hearts!" A contemporary wrote, "The theater was filled with courtiers and officers, government officials and foreign diplomats. The highest and most brilliant society of St. Petersburg and Moscow. When Pushkin entered the audience . . . a murmur went up all over the theater. His name resounded on every side. Everyone looked at him, he was the center of attention. At the exit, a crowd surrounded him, he was pointed out from afar, being so easily recognizable by his light-colored hat."[2]

Another contemporary told how, in the street, "a compact crowd followed the singer of Elbrus and Bakhchisarai," and "people cried out ecstatically, 'Show him to us, show him to us!' " A lady poet of the day wrote these lines on Pushkin's progress through the town:

The crowd pushes forward;
I hear, "Look, he's coming,
Our poet, our glory,
Everybody's darling."
Distinguished though small,
Bold, quick and knowing,
He walked past in front of me.
And long afterward
My dreams were ruled
By his Arabian profile
And lighted by his fierce eye.[3]

Delvig informed the poet that his servants had danced for joy when they heard Pushkin was back in town. The old author Izmailov wrote, in a letter dated September 29: "I envy Moscow. It has crowned an emperor, now it crowns a poet. . . . Forgive me, I was forgetting myself: Pushkin deserves the celebrity of a Petrarch or a Tasso, but the Muscovites are not Romans and the Kremlin is not the Capitoline."

The *Ladies' Journal* contributed the following: "All or nearly all the ladies of Moscow have now made the acquaintance of the author of *Onegin,* which will only render the perusal of the future gifts of his noble muse the more pleasurable to them."

Thus, from society ladies to courtiers to students to companions to soldiers and servants of every description, it really seemed as though the whole of Russia were welcoming Pushkin and hailing him as its greatest man and most cherished son. Pushkin was amazed, intoxicated and deeply moved by his own renown. For long years he had lived remote from the public he sustained with his poems. He had talked and sung into the blue, with only an occasional letter to bring him an echo of favorable regard, or a neighbor or two to compliment him on his work. But the bulk of his readers, the anonymous mass who were listening for his voice, where were they? What did they think of him? And suddenly, after his sooty little room at Mikhailovskoye and the motionless landscape outside its window, after the familiar face of his nanny and the empty road and the long shadows of the forest, after all that solitude and all that silence, here in the center of the city, under the full blaze of the lights and in the thick of the noise, he was meeting the living bodies of his worshipers. For a poet, that human contact, that flat reality of skin, voice and warmth, were strange: He could not believe that these unknown people who were staring at him, following and applauding him, touching his clothes and asking for his autograph, had really become his friends by the sole virtue of his talent. He could not hear enough of their praise, and did not dare to hope that such rich rewards would continue for the rest of his days. He was honestly glad he had accepted the offer of Nicholas I. As Princess Volkonsky wrote to him: "A great Russian poet should write either out in the steppe or in the shadow of the Kremlin, and the author of *Boris Godunov* belongs in the city of the tsars."[4]

Among so many wonderful days, October 12 was particularly golden. At the request of a few friends, he had agreed to read *Boris Godunov* before a considerable gathering in the home of Venevitinov. The journalist Pogodin wrote: "It is impossible to render the impression the reading made upon us. Even now—forty years later—I thrill at the mere memory of it. We were expecting a majestic high priest of art, and we saw a man of very average height, even rather small, with long hair curling at the ends and lively, dancing eyes. He was full of movement. His gestures were rapid, his voice pleasant. He wore a fitted black coat, a vest of some dark color, buttoned to the chin, and a carelessly knotted cravat. . . . The audience listened to the first scenes in silence and calm; or, more accurately, in a sort of astonishment. As he progressed, the impression grew stronger. Everyone was overwhelmed by the scene of the historian-monk and Gregory. Some felt feverish, others had goose flesh. Their hair stood on end, they could not contain themselves. Some leaped out of their chairs or exclaimed aloud. Some had tears in their eyes, others were smiling beatifically. There was a silence. Then applause. At last, the end came. We looked at each other for a long time, then hurled ourselves upon Pushkin. There were embraces, shouting and laughter, tears and compliments. . . . Champagne was served; Pushkin seemed utterly dazed by the affection of the educated young people of his century. . . . I cannot recall how we parted, nor how we found our way home. But few of us slept that night, so shaken were we by that reading."

Most of the members of Pushkin's audience on that occasion were young university students, infatuated with Romantic literature and German philosophy. They asked Pushkin to help found a new review, the *Moscow Herald.* It was to be completely different from both *Son of the Fatherland,* which catered to the vulgar tastes of the mass, and the *Moscow Telegraph,* "which covered every conceivable subject from the study of infinitesimals to recipes for cockscombs in wine and the proper way to wear one's ribbons on the shoes that were in fashion that season." Pogodin was to be editor in chief of the *Moscow Herald;* Pushkin, the Polish poet Adam Mickiewicz, Baratynsky, the two Venevitinov brothers, the two Kireyevsky brothers, Obolensky, Sobolevsky and others were contributors. Pushkin hoped to receive an annual retainer of ten thousand rubles. On October 24 the founders of the new review met for a triumphal dinner. The meal was copious, noisy and hilarious. Everyone drank and talked and shouted himself hoarse, full of plans for articles, the coming literary renaissance, criticism of other reviews, personal anecdotes, toasts and compliments.

Pushkin was greatly impressed by Mickiewicz, an elegant, handsome figure with the face of a statue, black hair, sad eyes, a smooth smile: He found him irresistibly attractive. Mickiewicz was a profoundly and thoroughly cultivated man, whereas Pushkin had picked up his knowledge as he went along, from odd books and acquaintances. Mickiewicz was distinguished, grave and honorable, and alongside him Pushkin looked like an ill-mannered scamp, always about to pull a face, always off to drink, gamble or reach for a woman. Mickiewicz lived for art, Pushkin for the pleasure of living. However, a cordial friendship grew up between them, and each sincerely admired the other's work. "Together, they offered the most curious spectacle imaginable," one contemporary wrote. "The great Russian poet, who ordinarily reigned at any literary gathering, became quite retiring when Mickiewicz was present; rather than do all the talking himself, he tried to draw the other man out, and seemed always to be seeking his approval." Whenever Mickiewicz would improvise a poem for his friends, Pushkin listened in stupefaction, for Mickiewicz improvised brilliantly in both French and Polish. He would be given a subject, any subject; he would close his eyes and think for a moment, then suddenly open them, throw back his head and begin to speak, in verse, with an assurance that dumfounded his listeners. He never had to seek his words, he never hesitated over a rhyme, he never changed a line or corrected himself. . . . His face was almost disfigured by ecstasy. His eyes gleamed. His listeners felt a sacred shudder run through them, like fear. After one of these improvisations Pushkin stood up, electrified, with tears in his eyes, and began to shout, "What genius! What sacred fire! What am I beside him?"

Pushkin and Mickiewicz were invited to all the best homes in Moscow. They were the two prize exhibits of the season. "Moscow is full of noise and festivities," wrote Pushkin, "so much so that I am already tired of it and beginning to yearn for my Mikhailovskoye, that is, my Trigorskoye."[5]

In Moscow Pushkin lived with his friend Sobolevsky, a stalwart, tall young fellow with a face like a happy satyr and beautifully tailored clothes. He was a connoisseur of the fair sex, precious books, good food, rare wines and practical jokes. He was rich, depraved, cynical, intelligent and willful, and he amused Pushkin, who called him "the stomach" and "Falstaff." In February 1827 Pushkin wrote: "Sobolevsky swears and storms around as much as ever; spies, dragoons, prostitutes and drunkards are littered about the place from morning to night." In addition to the drunkards, prostitutes, dragoons and spies to which Pushkin alludes, Sobolevsky also entertained all the young intellectuals of Moscow. His dinners and dances were celebrated for their inventive lavishness. Even the staid Mickiewicz came and visibly enjoyed himself. From dinners *chez* Sobolevsky, Pushkin moved on to costume balls *chez* Mrs. Rimsky-Korsakov and private theatricals *chez* Princess Volkonsky. Wherever he went, he was surrounded and adulated, extravagantly. Everywhere, he was implored to recite some unpublished passage from *Eugene Onegin* or compose a little incidental verse for the albums of the young ladies of the house.

At Mrs. Rimsky-Korsakov's, Pushkin paid court to her daughter Alexandra, who walked but "scarcely touched the ground," whose breast "lifted indolently," whose velvety gaze was "incomparable."

At Princess Volkonsky's, he listened to music and played charades. One day, having to represent the rock of Moses, he wrapped himself in a shawl and, when the guest personifying the prophet touched him with a rod, raised one edge of his cloak, drew forth a jug of water, and poured it on the floor; this jest earned him a playful smile from the princess and a sentence in her singsong French: "Bad boy that you are, Alexander, to have showed the rock like that!"

The police, meanwhile, were keeping a close watch on Pushkin's depradations in the Muscovite salons. In a report to Benkendorf, Colonel Bibikov wrote: "I am keeping the author Pushkin under the closest possible observation. The houses he chiefly frequents are those of Princess Zenaida Volkonsky, the poet Prince Vyazemsky, ex-minister Dmitryev, and Zhikarev the attorney. The main subject of conversation is literature. He has just written a tragedy called *Boris Godunov*, which is to be read to me; supposedly, there is nothing liberal in it. It is true that women cover him with flattery and spoil him; once, for example, when he expressed a desire to take up some form of service, several persons cried out at once: 'Why serve? Enrich our literature with your sublime creations; are you not already serving the nine sisters? Has there ever been a finer service than that?' Another said, '*Vous servez déjà dans le génie*,'* and so forth."

In June 1826 secret agent Locatelli wrote, still more disapprovingly: "Everyone is surprised to see that the famous Pushkin, long known for his subversive ideas, has not been questioned about the conspiracy."[6]

Von Fok, another of Benkendorf's associates, wrote a dispatch containing the following: "This individual [Pushkin] is generally known to be a philosophist† in every sense of the word, that is, he professes systematic egotism, scorns all other men, holds both sentiments and virtues in contempt, and has a ruthless determination to procure for himself the pleasures of life at the expense of all that is most sacred. He is an ambitious man, consumed by hunger for desire [sic], who, it is remarked, is so wild and unruly that it will be necessary to give him a good talking-to at the earliest opportunity. It is said that the sovereign received him favorably and that he will not live up to His Majesty's confidence."[7]

These reports alone are proof that despite the promise given by Nicholas I, the authorities were still deeply suspicious of Pushkin. He, however, could not have cared less just then: He was reveling in his triumph and his amusements. At the end of one month in Moscow, he was already in love with four or five young ladies: "S.P. is my good angel," he wrote to Vyazemsky, "but the other is my demon; this interferes most annoyingly with my poetical and romantic meditations." The other, "the demon," was probably Alexandra Rimsky-Korsakov. The "good angel," S.P., was known on earth as Sofya Pushkin; she was a distant relative of the poet, just twenty years old, tall, slender, undulating and famous throughout Moscow for her Greek profile, her transparent, blue-shadowed skin, her eyes black as coals and her regal shoulders. Pushkin saw her once in a box at the theater, and a second time at a ball. Two meetings were enough. She was beautiful, she was good, she was irreplaceable. Why not marry her? At Mikhailovskoye, marriage had seemed a monumental idiocy to him, and he had written to Vyazemsky: "A lawful wedded wife is like a sort of bonnet you put on to keep your ears warm; but before you know it, it has smothered your whole head. You may be an exception, but I think, even so, you would have been wiser to remain a bachelor for another ten years. Marriage saps the soul."[8] In Moscow, however, it attracted him. He felt eroded, surfeited by too many ephemeral affairs. He began to long for

* "*Le génie*"—genius; also—the engineer corps.

† The French *encyclopédistes* were called *philosophistes*, and so, by extension, were all rationalists; but Von Fok has probably misapplied a term then in vogue.

a secure home, a devoted wife. Around Sofya Pushkin he wove an image of evenings by the fireside and a multitudinous progeny. There was only one difficulty: A man named Panin had been courting Sofya for two years, and she did not seem indifferent to the homages of this regular suitor. Pushkin tried to explain his torments to the girl, but he was bashful, as he always was with the women he thought he loved for real and forever. He made out a very weak case for himself: He switched from cheerfulness to mournfulness to absent-mindedness to dreaminess to exaggerated chivalrousness, with the result that Sofya Pushkin mistrusted him. In despair, he went off to Mikhailovskoye, instructing a mutual friend named Zubkov to make representations to the cruel one on his behalf. Would he be able to sway her? Would he obtain her consent? At Mikhailovskoye, Pushkin convalesced from his urban dissipations and awaited the verdict. On November 9, 1826, he wrote to Vyazemsky: "In one sense I am glad to be back in the country. One feels a certain poetic exhilaration in returning a free man to one's former prison. Do you know, I'm not being sentimental, but the greetings of my servants, my serfs and my nanny, I swear to you they gave my heart a bigger surge of joy than all the praise and recognition, the pandering to my conceit, the dissipation, etc. I shall be with you on the first, she has ordained it."

He was late for the rendezvous: A road accident delayed him, and December 1 found him not at Sofya's feet but languishing in a country inn, playing cards, gambling away the fourth chapter of *Onegin* and bemoaning his fate. He wrote to Zubkov: "Dear Zubkov, you have had no letter from me and here is why: I wanted to fall upon you like a bomb on December 1, that is, today, and so I set out by the post from my accursed village five or six days ago, on account of the miserable state of the roads. The Pskov drivers could think of no better way to make haste than to overturn me in the ditch; I've cracked a rib, my chest is bad, I can't breathe, I am gambling out of pure fury and losing. Enough of that; as soon as I feel at all better I shall come on by post. . . . I am twenty-seven years old, dear friend, it is time I began to live, I mean, to be happy. You will say that happiness is not everlasting: Do tell! Anyway, it is not my own happiness that worries me; could I be otherwise than the happiest of men, with her? But I tremble to think of the fate that may be in store for her, I tremble to think that I shall not be able to make her as happy as I wish. My past life—so unstable and tempestuous, my erratic nature, at once jealous, oversensitive, violent and weak: That is what gives me moments of painful hesitation. Should I bind the future of a being so gentle and fine to that of a nature so gloomy and ill-starred? God, she's so pretty! and I have acted so absurdly. My friend, try to efface the bad impression I have made upon her, tell her I am more steady than I look, and the proof is . . . for the proof, tell her anything that comes into your head. That horrible Panin has been in love for two years and is planning to propose after Easter; I saw her once in a box at the theater and another time at a ball and the third time I asked for her hand! If she thinks Panin is right, she must believe me mad, mustn't she? Then explain to her that it is I who am right, that once one has seen her there can be no hesitation, I cannot be trying to seduce her, and have therefore done the right thing by coming straight to the point; that once one loves her it is impossible to love her more, just as it is impossible to find her more beautiful with time, for it is impossible to be more beautiful. Angel, persuade her, implore her, frighten her of the hideous Panin, and marry me."[9]

But Sofya was less frightened of the "hideous Panin" than of the nice little Pushkin. When he finally reached Moscow on December 20, it was to learn that Sofya was betrothed to his rival. The news left the poet unmoved, utterly unconcerned by the loss of the woman he had thought he loved to madness. He was actually surprised by his sudden coolness. Was he incapable, then, of a great and enduring passion? Was he past the age of sighing and waiting?

Or were his fresh annoyances to blame for the short duration of his broken heart? For, from the very beginning of his sojourn in Moscow, Pushkin was again beset with complaints and official persecutions. It had been too good to be true. Everything had been going too well. The freedom which the emperor had granted him was nothing short of miraculous; in a letter dated September 30, 1826, Benkendorf had written in so many words: "Not only does His Imperial Majesty not forbid you to live in the capital, but he gives you complete freedom in this respect, provided only that you request written permission in advance. . . . Your works will henceforth be subject to scrutiny by no one; there will be no censorship of them; the emperor in person will be the first judge of your creations and your sole censor."

How could you fail to credit the autograph signature of Benkendorf? How could you doubt that you had been set free when the chief of police himself was pleased to inform you so? Thanks to Nicholas I, Pushkin might believe himself the only truly free man in Russia. He was living in a fairy tale, no? "The tsar has exempted me from censorship," he wrote to Yazykov on November 9, 1826. "He himself is to be my censor. An incalculable advantage. So we shall hurry *Godunov* along."

Now, both the emperor and Count Benkendorf had a highly personal idea of freedom. Upon learning that Pushkin had given readings of *Boris Godunov* in some Muscovite drawing rooms, Benkendorf wrote to him on November 22 in the following terms: "Today I have received information relating to a reading of your new tragedy which you are alleged to have given at a certain gathering. I must ask you to inform me instantly whether this report is true or not. I am certain, moreover, that you are too reasonable to fail to appreciate the true value of His Majesty's exceptional mark of favor, and will strive to be worthy of it in every respect."

Pushkin landed with a thud. Was he forbidden to read his writings to friends before presenting them to Nicholas I? Was he forbidden to seek the opinion of a few connoisseurs before submitting his poems for imperial approval? Why, every writer needed an exchange of ideas about his latest work. From reading to reading and controversy to controversy, he corrected, rounded off, polished his text. If he could no longer "try out" his poems on a select group of listeners, he would soon forget the very existence of his public, and find himself writing for the four walls of his room. Of course, Benkendorf didn't care a fig about the exigencies of the literary profession. He had never read anything in his life and never would, he was suspicious of all writers on principle and a priori. The imperial instructions were explicit; Pushkin had only to conform to them. A week later, sweetly, humbly, Pushkin replied to the chief of police: "I did read a tragedy to a few people in Moscow (not from any desire to be disobedient, of course, but because I had misinterpreted the royal will of His Majesty). I accordingly believe it my duty to send the tragedy to you in the exact form in which I read it, so that Your Excellency may judge the spirit in which it was written; I have not dared to submit it to the emperor before, wishing to amend a few improper lines. As I have no other copy, I make bold to request that Your Excellency return it to me after reading it. I would add that I am loath to importune an official burdened down with responsibility with my petty literary affairs. At the request of their editors, I have also given some poems to various reviews and almanacs, and apologize to Your Excellency for this unwitting error. . . ."

The same day he wrote to Pogodin, editor in chief of the *Moscow Herald:* "For the love of heaven, hold everything signed by me at the Moscow censor's office. Such is the will of the higher authorities. . . ."

After sending his manuscript of *Boris Godunov* to Benkendorf, Pushkin impatiently sat down to await results. He was beginning to suspect that he had been hoodwinked, but secretly hoped that the poetic, historical and moral qualities of his tragedy would surprise and convince the emperor.

On December 9, 1826, Benkendorf informed Pushkin that the manuscript of *Boris Godunov* had been returned and that he counted in future upon receiving "the smallest efforts of his brilliant pen." Nicholas I, having no time to waste in frivolous reading, had ordered Benkendorf

19. Emperor Nicholas I in Cossack uniform, by Sverchkov

20. Engraving of Red Square and the Kremlin in Moscow, 1820

21. The family estate, Mikhailovskoye, where Pushkin lived in exile (1824)

22. Painting of Alexis Wulf by N. Chade

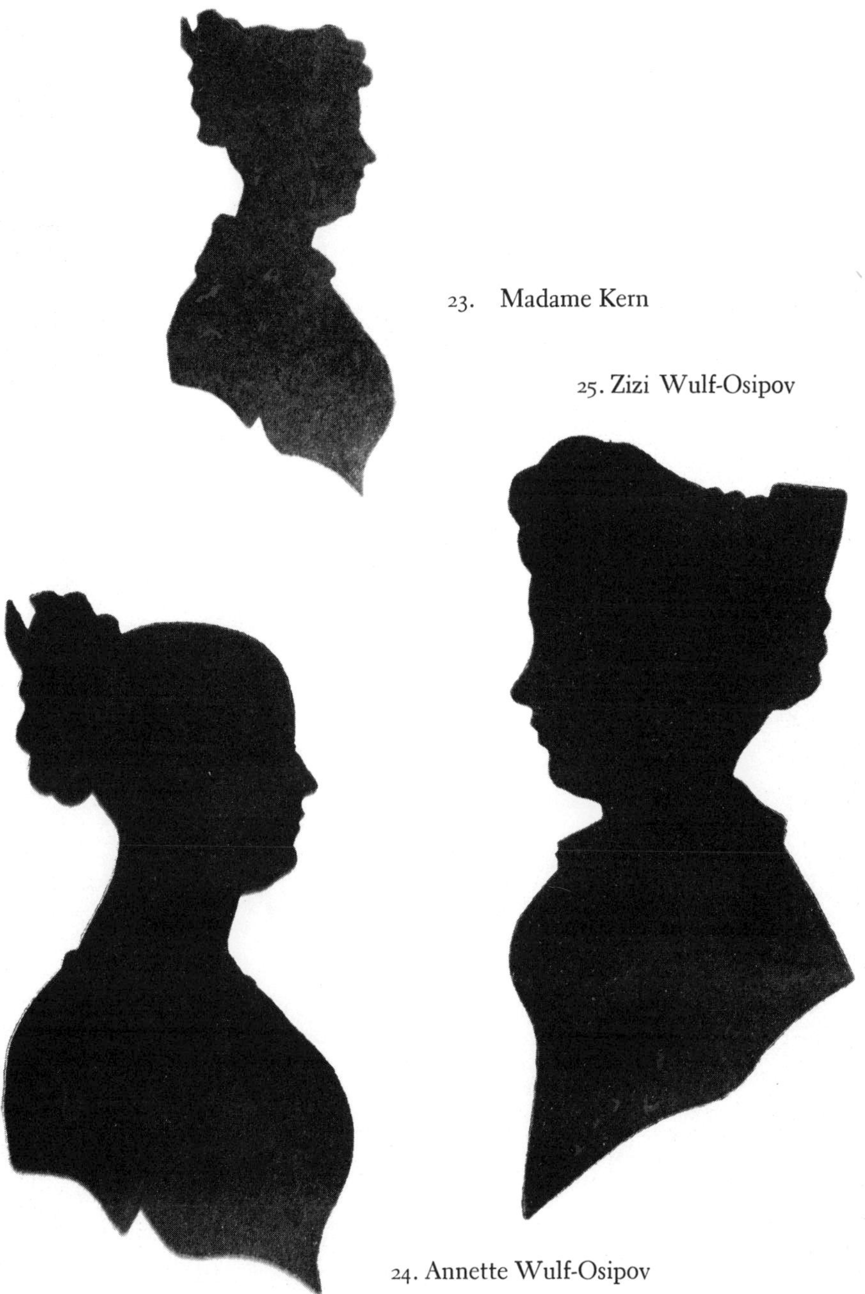

23. Madame Kern

25. Zizi Wulf-Osipov

24. Annette Wulf-Osipov

23–25. Silhouettes of several ladies who first knew Pushkin while he was in exile at Mikhailovskoye

26. Pushkin's study at Mikhailovskoye, where he wrote *Boris Godunov,* several chapters of *Eugene Onegin*, numerous lyrical poems

27. Marya Raevsky, believed by some to be one of the great loves of Pushkin's life

28. Sofya Pushkin

29. *La Princesse Nocturne,* Princess Eudoxia Golitsyn

30. Alexander Pushkin

31. Zhukovsky, by Esterreich (1820), lithograph offered to Pushkin by Zhukovsky with a dedication

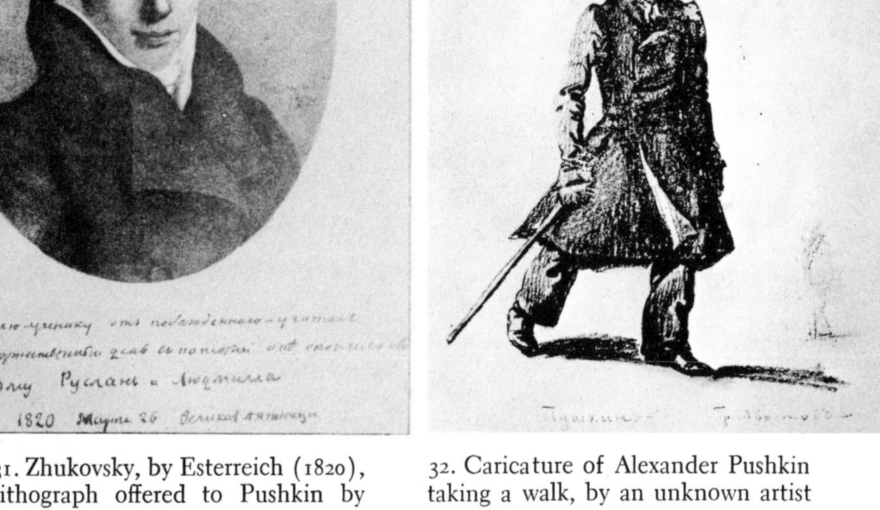

32. Caricature of Alexander Pushkin taking a walk, by an unknown artist

33. Princess Volkonsky

34. Natalya Pushkin, wife of the poet

to have the play analyzed "by someone trustworthy, to keep the matter from being noised about." In this instance the "someone trustworthy" was the critic and informer Bulgarin, who flipped through the pages of the tragedy and pronounced it execrable: "There is nothing solid in the play; it is all separate scenes, or more accurately, extracts from Volumes X and XI of Karamzin's *History of the Russian Empire*. . . . The literary merits of the play are far less than we imagined. . . . It is like a series of conversations drawn from Walter Scott. Few fine orations, few ringing lines. . . . The play certainly cannot be performed, as patriarchs and monks have never been represented on the stage."

Nicholas I contented himself with this one-sided judgment and did not have the curiosity to open the manuscript himself. On December 14 (five days after receiving the play), he replied to the poet, through Benkendorf: "His Majesty has deigned to read your work with the greatest pleasure, and in the margin of the report on it which I submitted to him, has kindly written in his own hand, 'I consider that Mr. Pushkin would achieve his purpose more nearly if, after detailed expurgation, he were to transform his comedy into a story or historical tale in the style of Walter Scott.' I am flattered to be the echo of the very benevolent attention accorded by His Majesty to your distinguished talent."

Pushkin had expected anything but that. The emperor and Benkendorf, neither of whom had the slightest taste, culture or literary authority, were commanding him to turn his play into a historical novel à la Walter Scott! The authorities were within their rights when they prohibited antigovernment pamphlets, certainly; but to refuse a work on the ground that its form did not take the emperor's fancy was carrying the limits of autocracy a little too far! So the public no longer had anything to say in Russia! So the emperor had decided to replace the public as arbiter of the qualities and weaknesses of a piece of poetry! He was extending his sovereign infallibility to the realm of inspiration! He now claimed to be sole possessor of truth in matters of style and prosody as well as politics and administration! Whatever displeased him did not have the right to exist! Well, in that case, why didn't the emperor become a writer himself? First soldier, first architect, first engineer, first father and first author of all the Russias. Rewrite *Boris Godunov?* Not likely. Fuming, Pushkin shelved his useless play and, on January 3, 1827, wrote his reply to Benkendorf: "It is with a sense of profound gratitude that I read Your Excellency's letter informing me of the benevolent opinion which His Majesty has deigned to express with regard to my dramatic poem. I agree that it has more features in common with the historical novel than with traditional tragedy, as His Imperial Majesty was good enough to point out. I regret, however, that I have not sufficient courage to begin again what I have already written. . . ."

In the meantime, another of Pushkin's works had been submitted to the tsar for approval. This time, it was a report on state education which Nicholas I had commissioned the poet to write. It never entered Pushkin's head that the emperor's invitation to expound his views on the question of education was a trap. He did not understand that the sovereign was giving him a test in civic obedience, an examination to see if he could graduate from the class of "liberals" to the class of loyal subjects, and so he took great pains to present his views on the subject of the instruction of young people truthfully, trying at the same time to avoid a clash with the imperial susceptibilities. He told Alexis Wulf: "I was acutely embarrassed when Nicholas I asked my opinion on the subject. It would have been so easy to write what was expected of me, but how could I let slip such a wonderful opportunity to do something good?"

Two complete drafts were necessary before the author considered these pages of "vile prose" presentable. Ostensibly, the report was based on an imperial manifesto of July 13, 1826; with such an unimpeachable primary source, Pushkin hoped to cover himself. The only parts of the manifesto he actually used, of course, were those that agreed with his own opinions. "It is not to any method of education," said the manifesto, "but to idleness of mind—more pernicious even than idleness of body—and to the absence of a solid foundation of knowledge, that are to be imputed this confusion of ideas which gives rise to violence in emotions, this delight in half learning, and this fascination with extremist fantasies that lead first to moral corruption, and finally to catastrophe."

Pushkin quoted the paragraph, but hastened to add: "Better yet, let us say that education alone is capable of preventing more folly and public calamities."

The manifesto proclaimed that the nobility should "strive to improve national educational methods and eschew foreign instruction."

In his report, Pushkin did not hesitate to comment: "As far as foreign education is concerned, it is pointless to prohibit it. In view of the fact that, firstly, few would take advantage of the concession, and secondly, the instruction imparted by foreign universities, for all its inconveniences, is far less noxious than that administered by our own fathers, it need only be subjected to the same restrictions as private tutoring. We see how, political fanaticism notwithstanding, N. Turgenev, who studied at the University of Göttingen, showed remarkable moral probity and moderation—the results of true culture and profound knowledge—in comparison with the disorganized mentalities of his accomplices."

And he followed this up with: "The abolition of corporal punishment is indispensable. From the outset, a sense of honor and humanity should be inculcated in pupils. . . . During the first years of study, history should be a simple chronological recital of events, without moral or political dissertations. Why seek to impose a unilateral orientation, which cannot be consistent, upon youthful minds? In the final history course, however (especially where modern history is concerned), the method should be completely altered. The differences between mentalities of different peoples may be impartially illustrated, along with the derivation of the exigencies of and necessity for the state; no trickery, no distortion of the republican spirit or denigration of the assassination of Caesar, as has been the current practice for two thousand years: Brutus should be shown as the defender and avenger of the traditions of his fatherland, and Caesar as an arrogant interloper. As a general rule, it is pointless for young people to wait to be introduced to republican ideas until they enter society, for they then offer all the appeal of novelty."

Benkendorf transmitted these pages to Nicholas with the laconic comment, "This young man is already returning to the paths of reason."[10] But Nicholas I disagreed. He read the report with mounting displeasure: twenty-eight question marks in the margins of the manuscript attest to the monarch's anger. He furiously underlined such assertions as "the abolition of corporal punishment is indispensable" and "Brutus should be shown as the defender and avenger of the traditions of his fatherland." There are three question marks opposite "the differences between mentalities of different peoples may be impartially illustrated." Nicholas I did not want to know anything about the mentalities of the peoples. Peoples did not have mentalities. They had a tsar, who acted as their mentality. And Pushkin was wrong not to understand that.

The letter forbidding Pushkin to publish and produce his tragedy was dated December 14, 1826. On December 23, nine days later, the poet was informed of the observations which his "well-intentioned" report had suggested to the emperor.

"His Imperial Majesty," Benkendorf wrote, "has deigned to observe that your principle, that education and genius [Pushkin had not mentioned genius] provide the only basis for moral perfection, is a doctrine which is dangerous to public security; it has led you yourself to the brink of the abyss and precipitated a large number of young people into it. Morality, exemplary dedication and zeal should be preferred to inexperienced, immoral and purposeless instruction. A properly ordered education should be built upon these foundations."

This time, Pushkin got the message. He was being reminded of his wayward youth, indirectly reproached for his ingratitude, told that genius was dangerous and zeal alone worthy of consideration and favor. In the eyes of the emperor, thus, talent was a stigma. The emperor mistrusted great men. All he wanted was courtiers. Could it be possible? Pushkin remembered how Nicholas I had greeted him, his noble stature, his white face, his proud, calm gaze, the heavy white hand outstretched. Perhaps the emperor had been misinformed? Perhaps he was misled by his entourage? Perhaps he should still be loved, and only Benkendorf and his gang of secret agents detested?

On December 26 Pushkin saw little Marya Raevsky again, the "daughter of the Ganges" whom he had so passionately praised during his travels with General Raevsky through the Caucasus and Crimea. She was no longer the dark, sharp-tongued little girl who used to play in the waves and elude the clutches of her governess. At nineteen, she had married Prince Sergey Volkonsky—a man almost twice her age, for whom she felt no affection—in obedience to her parents' will. When her husband was arrested with the Decembrists, however, she decided to join him in Siberia of her own volition. Deaf to her father's imprecations, her brother's sermons and the threats of everyone around her, she abandoned her child and family and went, stopping briefly in Moscow en route, to spend a few days with her sister-in-law Zenaida Volkonsky. At a party on December 26 everyone saw her as an angel of abnegation, courage and sorrow. Pushkin contemplated her in wonderment. Tears came to his eyes when he heard her whisper to a singer, "Again, again! Think that I shall never hear any more music!"

Pushkin crushed her feverish little hand in his and told her how he admired her devotion and how he would come to visit her beyond the Urals. As he spoke, he thought what he might have become if he had married this child whose last hours of freedom he was sharing. How much better she was than all these pretty debutantes. How much better than he himself. A few days later, when the wife of Muravyev, another Decembrist, also left Moscow to join her husband in Siberia, Pushkin gave her a message in verse for the brave little Marya Volkonsky:

> In the depths of the Siberian mines,
> Keep that haughty patience. . . .
> The heavy chains will fall,
> The prison doors will gape. Outside,
> Freedom will await you,
> Your brothers will hand back your sword.

He also gave her a poem for his poor friend Pushchin. What would Benkendorf have said if he had known of these messages to the "wretched criminals" of December 14?

The police bureau was busily spying, reading Pushkin's correspondence with his friends, and their subterranean reports were steadily accumulating. On January 13, 1827, a new "Pushkin affair" came before the military tribunal, still concerning that ill-starred poem *December 14*—the passage from *André Chénier*. At his interview with Nicholas I, Pushkin had given a full explanation of the matter, and supposed he had nothing more to fear from the inquisitors; but the military authorities were unwilling to be convinced. After questioning the two men, Molchanov and Alexeyev, who had been found guilty of possessing the poem, the commission instructed the chief of Moscow police to summon Pushkin with a view to determining "whether the incriminated lines were actually written by him, when and why they were composed, and how they came into the hands of these other persons."

On January 27 Pushkin signed the following statement: "I am the author of these lines. They were written long before the late events and formed part of my elegy *André Chénier*, which was published, with some deletions, in the volume of my collected poems. They refer explicitly to the French Revolution, of which André Chénier was a victim. . . . Except by preposterous misattribution, these lines cannot be associated with December 14. I do not know who gave them this incorrect title."

In good faith, Pushkin considered that this second explanation of the *December 14* must finally have satisfied everybody, and so, during the first few months of 1827, he abandoned himself to his noisy and dissipated life in Moscow with no further thought for the warnings he had received. He went out often, ran from ball to ball, gambled for high stakes, danced, fluttered around the ladies, waltzed from den of thieves to drawing room and from drawing room to dressing room. He went to bed late and got up late, and every morning his antechamber was filled with friends, admirers and supplicants. "Judging by all I have seen and heard here," wrote P. L. Yakovlev on March 21, 1827, "Pushkin is lounging on a bed of roses. The whole town knows him. Everybody is interested in him. A group of distinguished young people has gathered about him, just as, in olden days, anyone with any sense was to be found in the proximity of the great Arouet. . . . Pushkin looks very different: He has grown fantastic black side whiskers that give him a positively diabolical air. But apart from that, he is the same as ever, agile, quicksilver, changing in a minute from merriment and laughter to gravity and meditation."

The poet's misfortunes with Sofya Pushkin had not soured him on girls or the idea of marriage. On the contrary: His desire for a bride was becoming obsessive. He was drawn to every great house that harbored an unclaimed virgin. He prowled about their families with hollow belly and greedy eye. He loved right and left, indiscriminately. He was almost simultaneously in love with Sofya Pushkin, the Urusov sisters, the Ushakov sisters and Alexandra Rimsky-Korsakov. In 1826 the first and the last of these heartless maidens brought him to grief; by 1827 he had moved on to the Ushakov girls. The younger, at sixteen, was infatuated with a certain Colonel Kiselev; the elder, seventeen, was free and accessible to Pushkin's charm. Her name was Katerina. She had ash-blond hair twisted into long tresses, lively blue eyes, a full-lipped smile, a slender waist and unobtrusive "charms." She was gay, mocking and mischievous. Pushkin delightedly commented that she was "neither woman nor boy."

"It appears," one young lady of Moscow wrote in her diary, "that our famous Pushkin intends to entrust his future to her and has already deposed his arms at her feet; in other words, he is in love. That is all the rumor. I have heard it said more than once that all the time he was in Moscow he had eyes for no one but Miss Ushakov; at balls and out walking, he spoke only to her, and when she did not happen to be at some gathering, Pushkin would sit the whole evening brooding in a corner, and nothing could arouse him. . . . My encounter with them confirmed the truth of these rumors. In their house, everything speaks of Pushkin—on the table you will find his works, *The Black Shawl* and the *Bohemian Song* will be in the music albums, and his *Talisman* sits on the piano. The family album is full of his drawings, verses and caricatures, and in every conversation the name of Pushkin is heard continually."[11]

Pushkin was seriously contemplating marriage with the pretty Katerina; yet he did not speak out. He felt so comfortable in this friendly house, full of dimpled laughter and tender looks; they say he went there as much as four times a day, just to chat with Mrs. Ushakov, or listen and write down the old Russian songs she knew by heart, or tease little Elizabeth Ushakov and her fiancé Kiselev, or pay court to Katerina, or write incidental verse and scribble caricatures, at the whim of his inspiration. The Ushakov album has been preserved; it contains some rapid sketches, economical and sure, showing a true gift for draftsmanship; light poems, witty sayings—and that famous Don Juan list.

On May 26, 1827, Katerina Ushakov's sister wrote to their brother: "I find Katerina greatly changed; all she can speak of these days is Pushkin and his great works. She knows them all by heart. She is completely insane, I can't imagine what has come over her. At this very moment, she is reading *The Prisoner of the Caucasus* aloud."

Katerina added a few lines to her sister's letter: "He has gone to St. Petersburg, maybe he will forget me, but no, I want to believe, I want to hope he will return. . . . The town is empty, what ghastly tedium (a favorite expression of Pushkin's). Farewell, brother dear, I am, as ever, your Katerina . . . and the 'angel' of someone else."

Despite his esteem for the Ushakov establishment and his affection for Katerina, Pushkin was still buzzing around other lights.

The Ushakovs had two daughters, but the Urusovs had three—whose beauty was equaled only by their brainlessness. Pushkin seldom chose a woman for her intellect, however. Sofya Urusov, to whom he was particularly drawn, was celebrated for her—unsophisticated is perhaps the word—repartee. To a suitor who inquired what she was reading at the moment, she replied, "I am reading a little pink book and my sister is reading a little blue book."

Pushkin must have been entranced by this absence of literary interests: He did not want to be loved for his talent, but for his comely countenance, his caustic wit and his honorable birth. "He went to the home of Princess Urusov almost every evening," Semevsky wrote, "and was always in fine fettle, very witty and talkative. He had an inexhaustible store of improvisations and jokes. He often amused his listeners by telling old Russian folk tales. Sometimes everyone would gather around a huge round table, and Pushkin would carry the whole room away to a fantasy world peopled by sorcerers, elves and werewolves. His inspiration magnified the old tales he had picked up during his long residence in the provinces; he told them skillfully, in the authentic style."

His pursuit of the Urusov debutantes nearly cost him his life at one point. A man named Solomirsky, a moody admirer of the youngest sister, took advantage of one of the poet's ill-timed witticisms to challenge him to a duel. On April 15, 1827, the poet replied with a succinct note: "Now, if you wish; bring a second. A.P."[12]

The seconds had great difficulty in averting the encounter and effecting a reconciliation.

By the spring of 1827 Pushkin had already had enough of Moscow and its eligible young maids. The trouble over *Godunov*, the *Report on State Education* and *André Chénier* had told on his nerves; he was increasingly gloomy, irritable and preoccupied. He yawned at balls. He didn't know what to do with himself. The young intellectuals of the *Moscow Herald*, whose admiration had formerly been such a great consolation to him, now vexed him with their childish pretentiousness. They had all gorged themselves on Schelling. They would say, "the first sign of poetry must be mystery," or "the poet lives in exile outside the real world, in the universe of his fantasy." But Pushkin was a dedicated realist, the first and most pure of Russian realists. Also, the boys on the *Moscow Herald* were enamored of nebulous terminology, battles of metaphysical concepts, religious dialectics and "the abysses of thought and feeling"; whereas Pushkin, the pupil of Voltaire, scorned their stammering attempts to explain the unexplainable, trap the absolute in nets of syllogism and mount to God on ladders of words. On March 4, 1827, Pogodin, the editor in chief of the *Moscow Herald,* wrote in his diary: "To Pushkin. Disquisition against philosophy; unable to make any specific rebuttal, I remained silent. But convinced that his position was absurd."

Two days earlier, Pushkin had written to Delvig: "You complain to me about the *Moscow Herald* and German metaphysics. God knows how I loathe and detest it! But what can I do? A bunch of hot-blooded stubborn chaps have put their heads together, and they pull one way and I the other. I say to them, 'Gentlemen, what pleasure can it procure you to decant thin air? That's all very well for Germans, who are already saturated with positive knowledge. But for us? . . .' The *Moscow Herald* is in the ditch, and asks: 'What is the essential nature of a towrope?' The essential nature of time, in any event, is such that I wish to waste no more of it on any *Herald.* So much the worse for them if they won't listen to me."

Conceived in an atmosphere of misty metaphysics, the *Moscow Herald* was a dismal failure—a bare six hundred subscribers the first year, with a marked decline thereafter. Pushkin's name alone could not guarantee sales; he was swamped by the philosophers, and rival reviews were doing their utmost to demolish his reputation.

Pushkin's glory reached its apogee during the winter of 1826–27, and plummeted as spring wore on. The public had made too much of him in the beginning for him to have any chance of continuing on the crest of such a wave. His success sowed seeds of bitter envy on all sides; anonymous enemies were busy about his perdition. So-called liberals accused him of foreswearing his republican loyalties for the sake of vain pleasure and the right to peacock about in Moscow. It was whispered that he had forgotten his old friends, betrayed his work, sold himself to the emperor, gone to work for Benkendorf as a spy. Pushkin had published a poem called *Stanzas,* in which some claimed to see a glorification of Nicholas I. In it, the poet advised the ruler to follow the example of Peter the Great:

> Be like him tireless,
> Firm in power and merciful.

The final word ought to have reassured the friends of the Decembrists, but the smear campaign was already launched. Protest as he might, nobody would listen to him. Epigrams circulated about him. Suddenly, he felt set apart, suspect to liberals and police alike. Rejected by both. Caught in a crossfire. And it had happened so quickly, like a blue sky suddenly laden with thunderclouds. Weary and disgusted, Pushkin decided to flee the town that had borne him in triumph and was now grinding him underfoot. He wrote to Benkendorf asking for permission to go to St. Petersburg, where his parents were. On May 3 Benkendorf replied: "His Majesty, in authorizing your departure for St. Petersburg, has deigned to say he had no doubt that a gentleman's word to his sovereign to conduct himself nobly and correctly would be punctiliously honored."

"A gentleman's word . . . to conduct himself nobly and correctly . . ." What was the matter with them all, forever doubting him?

On May 19, 1827, Pushkin was to leave Moscow for St. Petersburg; that evening his Moscow friends and a few contributors from the *Herald* met in Sobolevsky's country house. Pushkin came late. "The candles had already been brought," wrote Polevoy, "when he arrived, preoccupied, morose, speaking without a smile (always a sign of ill-humor in him). He left immediately after supper. His carriage drew up and he went off without a kind word to anyone. His attitude, I recall, left a very unpleasant impression on us all."

Three or four months earlier, the artist Tropinin had painted a portrait of Pushkin; all his friends agreed that it was a hallucinating likeness. More than the finished canvas—smooth, polished and rather cloying—it is the first sketch that represents him so truthfully: a ravaged, violent face, harshly lined, with thick, sensual lips and protruding eyes; an unhappy, defensively proud expression, heavy-lidded. Bushy side whiskers and long, crisp-curling hair. An open collar, poorly anchored by a loose cravat. Pushkin had been marked by his struggles, by worry, by every form of excess. But a last youth shone undefeated in his face: the youth of his mind, which would withstand the wear of men and years.

2. *St. Petersburg*

"I leave tomorrow for St. Petersburg," Pushkin wrote to his brother, "to see my 'beloved parents,' as they say, and sort out my finances. . . ."

He had not forgotten the ridiculous scenes at Mikhailovskoye, the spying and shouting and paternal lecturing; all he felt for his parents now was a sort of helplessly affectionate disgust.

Of late, Sergey Lvovich had been telling the world how he adored his son, and how his son did not understand him. Pushkin was not deceived by this sentimental about-face, which coincided too nearly with his return to grace. He knew his father to be vain and false, a pathetic and pusillanimous socialite, and his mother was not much better. Both hoped to profit by the privileged position which imperial favor had conferred, or so they imagined, upon their son. Since Nicholas I had pardoned his wild oats, he was their son once more; since he had won the emperor's trust, he was again worthy of their love. The poet himself, however, was in no hurry to meet his parents; at most, he would be glad to see his big sister Olga. His brother Leo was off in the army in the Caucasus, and military service had done nothing to improve his boastful, superficial, idle nature. Pushkin's closest friends were all in prison or deported; only Delvig was left. And Delvig had been foolish enough to get married. St. Petersburg, thus, was just as empty, stupid, tedious and insalubrious as Moscow.

"What can I tell you, Madame, of my stay in Moscow and my arrival in Petersburg?" he wrote to Mrs. Osipov in a letter dated early June 1827.[1] "Our two capitals are equally insipid and senseless, albeit in different ways, and as I aspire to impartiality I would say, if asked to choose between them, that my choice would be Trigorskoye, rather like Harlequin, who, when asked whether he preferred to be broken on the rack or hanged, replied, I prefer milk soup. I shall soon be leaving and am absolutely determined to spend a few days at Mikhailovskoye; meanwhile, I salute with all my heart yourself and everything near to you."

Thus, Pushkin left St. Petersburg almost as soon as he got there, this time to escape to the country, the little wooden house at Mikhailovskoye and the Trigorskoye girls. By July he had resumed the pattern of his life in exile: Sometimes he worked twelve hours a day, lying on his bed in a litter of paper, pens and chewed pencils. Now and then he would go out, to play billiards, ride his horse, tease old Arina Rodionovna, have a little flirt with the Trigorskoye demoiselles, bruise some delicate heart, lift some light skirt and come home famished and feverish. During the autumn of 1827 he wrote several lyric poems and began the first Russian historical novel, *The Blackamoor of Peter the Great,* about his famous ancestor Hannibal, who was captured by the Turks, conscripted into the sultan's seraglio, and sent to Peter the Great by the Russian ambassador in Constantinople. "The main action of the story," Pushkin said, "will be his wife's infidelity; she gives birth to a white baby, for which her husband shuts her up in a convent." He began the work eagerly, but never finished it. The first six chapters, however, are wonderfully vigorous and self-assured. In his prose novel as in his verse tragedy *Boris Godunov,* he succeeded in giving life to the figures history had petrified. There is Peter the Great, with his own personal gestures, his particular warmth, odor, gait and voice. The figures around him are all three-dimensional. The opulence of the French court during the regency of the Duc d'Orléans, the imperial assemblies, the boyars' arguments—everything is seen, observed, described as though by the most painstaking eyewitness.

In his recollections, Alexis Wulf recorded a visit to Pushkin while he was working on *The Blackamoor of Peter the Great:* "September 16, 1827. Dined yesterday with Pushkin at his mother's place, until recently his place of exile; he has just come from St. Petersburg to rest from his dissipations in the capitals and write in freedom. (Others contend that it is because he has lost too much money gambling.) I went up the rickety steps and into the worm-eaten hovel of the foremost Russian poet. I found him in a little red Moldavian hat and a dressing gown, seated at his writing table, which was littered with the numerous articles of toiletry that mark the follower of the mode; also on the table, Montesquieu snuggled cozily beside the *Bibliothèque de campagne* and the *Journals of Peter I.* In addition, buried beneath a pile of Russian almanacs, were an Alfieri, Karamzin's monthly periodicals and *The Interpreter of Dreams.*"

Nail files and Montesquieu, the *Interpreter of Dreams* and *The Blackamoor of Peter the Great:* This jumble of trivial objects and great ideas is a fair summary of the poet's whole life. Admirably organized on paper, singularly disorganized in deed; man of maturity in thought, infant in emotion.

If he had lived as he wrote, Pushkin would have been a calm and happy man; if he had written as he lived, he would have been a wild-eyed, puerile, verbose romantic. But he managed to separate the two, and every failure in his earthly endeavors was offset by an enduring success in the world of poetry.

Pushkin came to Mikhailovskoye in late July and left at the beginning of October; on the way back, he stopped at a posthouse at Borovichi, where he joined in a game of cards and lost sixteen hundred rubles in a few hands. At the following station, he decided to seek consolation in Schiller.

"But I had hardly read three pages," he wrote in his notes, "when four troikas escorted by a *Feldjäger* came into the station. I went out to look at them. One of the prisoners stood leaning against a column. A tall young man, pale, thin, with a black beard. . . . Suddenly he looked at me so piercingly that I turned toward him involuntarily. We stared and stared. . . . And I recognized Küchelbecker. We threw ourselves into each other's arms. The guards pulled us apart. The *Feldjäger* grabbed my arm, shouting threats and insults. I didn't hear a word he said. Küchelbecker fainted. The guards gave him some water, dragged him over to the troika, and the convoy set off again."

The guards were transferring the unfortunate Küchelbecker, sentenced to perpetual solitary confinement, from the Schlüsselburg (Petrokrepost) fortress to Dünaburg (Daugavpils); and in transit from one prison to another, chance had brought about this meeting between Pushkin and his old schoolmate. In all that space and all that time, their paths had chosen to cross before the door of a Russian inn—Pushkin the free man, Küchelbecker the convict. Two friends, childhood playmates.

Sobered and grieved by this vision of the wretched, lovable fool, so pallid, worn and weakened, Pushkin turned back to his drawing rooms and triumphs, his fashionable women, theaters and restaurants; while Küchelbecker, victim of his convictions, went off to languish in silence, buried in some damp prison block. "And I too might have . . ." At the mere thought of it, Pushkin was sick with shame for having accepted the imperial pardon, and more determined than ever to enjoy every instant of his incalculably precious and perilous good fortune.

In St. Petersburg Pushkin took two modest rooms in the Hotel Demuth. He saw little of his parents. When father and son met on the street, they exchanged ceremonious greetings but did not converse. As usual, Pushkin stayed up until all hours, and read and wrote in bed. "When someone came to see him," Polevoy wrote, "he would get up, sit at his dressing table, and, as he talked, clean, shape and buff his nails, which were so long they could properly be termed claws. Sometimes I would find him at another table—a card table—with a stranger, and then he would hardly speak at all. . . . He played for very high stakes, and lost heavily, as always! It was sad to see this remarkable man in the grip of such a crude, foolish passion."

Pushkin had always loved games of chance, but in 1827 his love turned to a veritable malady; he grew faint at the mere sight of a green cloth and a deck of cards. No reflex could restrain his urge to stake everything, to challenge fate, to provoke fortune or ruination. That fatal fall of red or black, best or worst, suited his adventurous spirit; he would have liked his whole life to be played in casts of the die or cuts of the cards, up in some corner of heaven. And who knows, perhaps it was.

Sobolevsky, having joined Pushkin in St. Petersburg, encouraged him in these vain, demeaning pursuits. One of Von Fok's police reports, dated October 1827, announced: "The poet Pushkin is here. He seldom stays at home. Sobolevsky drags him to theaters and cabarets, and feeds him and pays for his drink. He is known as 'Pushkin's stomach.' Politically, Pushkin is behaving himself."

In May 1827 Volkov, a general of the civilian police, had already informed Benkendorf that, "With regard to the poet Pushkin, as far as I have had time to ascertain, he is extremely well received everywhere and is apparently less concerned with poetry than with cards, for the moment; he has traded his muse for the 'Mouche,' which is the most fashionable game just now."

And so, in the absence of understanding parents, true friends or absorbing love affairs, Pushkin drifted from tavern to tavern and wasted his time playing cards and toying with the season's beauties of birth both high and low, while Benkendorf's secret agents watched his every move, recorded his every word and sent reports to their chief which sound more like hospital bulletins. "Pushkin is better. Pushkin is losing at cards. Pushkin speaks well of the emperor. Pushkin has read his tragedy. . . ."

"He [Pushkin] is still a worthless playboy, but if we can guide his pen and his speech, that will be something, at least."[2]

"Pushkin's conduct has shown some improvement, as far as politics are concerned. He is sincerely devoted to the sovereign and even says he owes his life to him, for exile and incessant restrictions had made him so disgusted with life that he was about to commit suicide."[3]

"The well-known author Pushkin, heedless of the emperor's benevolence, continues to circulate compositions injurious to the government and even to the emperor, in both verse and prose."[4]

In June 1827 *The Gypsies* appeared in the bookshops, and Benkendorf froze in his tracks at the sight of the cover design: an overturned goblet, a sword, a serpent, the severed links of a chain, a piece of parchment and branches of laurel in the background. What was the hidden meaning of this weird assortment of objects? Surely, that broken chain must be an allusion to the uprising; that sword, an incitement to assassination; and the serpent, parchment and laurel, a homage to "liberal" poets. Adorning a volume by any other author, Benkendorf would never even have noticed the baroque composition. But with Pushkin, one had to be so careful; not one word or deed of his was innocent! Oblivious to ridicule, with gravity and ponderation, as though this were an affair of State, Benkendorf wrote a letter, dated June 30, 1827, to General Volkov in Moscow:[5] "Be so good as to scrutinize this [the design], dear general, and you will readily be persuaded that it would be important to ascertain who chose it, whether the author or printer, as it is extremely unlikely to have been selected at random."

General Volkov replied, on July 6: "It is known to have been the author's choice; he selected it from a book of samples of type faces submitted to him by Mr. Semen. . . . It would not be an easy matter to analyze the design. . . . To my mind, the overturned goblet of pleasure, the poison-bearing serpent, the sword signifying vengeance and the document signifying treason, are all related to his subject. Moreover, the design was not made in Moscow. Mr. Semen got it from Mr. Firmin-Didot of Paris."

This affair, for a wonder, went no further; but other "Pushkin affairs" were waiting, wound up and ready to spring, in the shadows of the administrative offices.

There was the old business of *André Chénier/December 14,* to begin with. Pushkin supposed the declaration he had signed in Moscow had put a stop to police proceedings: far from it. From committee to commission and *rapporteur* to *rapporteur,* the Pushkin file grew great with fresh menaces. On March 25, 1828, the tribunal's findings were submitted to the Senate. After scrutinizing the poem backward and forward, the senators confirmed its subversive content (despite the fact that it referred explicitly to the French Revolution), but agreed that the author was exempted from punishment by the imperial amnesty of August 22, 1826. Pushkin was not "acquitted," he was "pardoned"—of the crime of insulting the Russian monarchy by writing a poem against the French Revolution. . . . The senators, sublimely untroubled by this glaring absurdity, demanded that Pushkin sign a promise to publish nothing that had not first been approved by the censor, "under pain of severe penalty."

On July 28, 1828, the Senate's conclusions were approved by the Council of State, with the following further provision: "Considering Pushkin's misguided attitude toward the events of December 14, 1825, and further considering the spirit of his poem published in October 1825 [*André Chénier*], he should be kept under secret surveillance."

The members of the Council of State had been the stern judges of the Decembrists, and to them Pushkin was a dangerous satellite of the conspiracy; so they were now delivering him, bound hand and foot, to the mercy of the pack of secret agents, constables, paid spies and voluntary informers.

Pushkin knew nothing of the diabolical net which had just been thrown over his head. He still believed, in flashes, in the imperial promise. He could not have imagined that the emperor was under the thumb of his own police, or that a corps of bureaucrats grown green in the shadow of their dossiers could be the most powerful force on earth. Humiliated and exasperated by this damnable administrative procedure, Pushkin was simply relieved to be told, early in August, that the *André Chénier* affair had been settled for good.

He breathed too soon. On May 28 the servants of a retired captain named Mitkov had testified to the ecclesiastical authorities that their master had corrupted them by reading "an indecent work entitled *The Gabriliad*." Mitkov was arrested on July 4. On the twenty-fifth a special commission ordered the governor of St. Petersburg to summon Pushkin and interrogate him with a view to determining whether he was the author of the poem.

After *André Chénier, The Gabriliad*. After insults to the regime, insults to the faith; a bad subject, a bad Christian; an enemy of the tsar and an enemy of God. At the beginning of August, when the governor of St. Petersburg informed him of this new charge, Pushkin felt himself doomed. Admitting to *The Gabriliad* meant condemning himself to a prison camp, and this juvenile opus was not worth a hairbreadth of his freedom. Exile was sacred only when the cause was sacred: Pushchin had been sent to Siberia for defending his revolutionary ideals, whereas Pushkin would have to go on account of a joke at the expense of the Virgin Mary and the Archangel Gabriel. Nonsense; a travesty.

From the first interview, Pushkin stoutly denied having written the poem: "He stated," reads the governor's report, "that the poem was not by him, that he first came to know of it at school, in 1815 or 1816, and copied it then." The emperor was suspicious of this version, and ordered Pushkin recalled for further questioning; the second interview took place on August 19, 1828, and at its conclusion Pushkin signed the following declaration: "The manuscript [of *The Gabriliad*] was circulating among the officers of the regiment of hussars, but I am absolutely unable to recall who passed it to me. I burned my own copy, probably in 1820. I would add that none of my words, even those I most deeply regret having written, show any trace of atheism or blasphemy against the Church, and that makes the opinion which attributes this shabby work to me all the more distasteful."

Having denied his poem, and suspecting that his letters were being opened by the police, Pushkin wrote to Vyazemsky, on September 1, 1828: "You ask me to come to Penza, but I am likely to be going much farther than that—in a beeline straight to the east. I now have a truly idiotic affair on my hands: *The Gabriliad* has at last come to the attention of the authorities, it has been attributed to me, I have been denounced and shall probably have to answer for someone else's mischief, unless Prince Gorchakov comes back from the hereafter to claim his royalties. Let this remain between us."

The reference to Prince Gorchakov, who, being dead, could not defend himself, was too obvious to throw the police off the scent, and only added to the evidence against the poem's true author.

After reading Pushkin's statement, Nicholas decided to vary his tactics: "Count Tolstoy will summon Pushkin and tell him that I, being personally acquainted with him, take his word, but that I wish him to assist the government in its search for the person capable of perpetrating such a piece of infamy and insulting Pushkin by circulating it in his name." On October 2 Count Tolstoy, a member of the investigating commission, summoned Pushkin and informed him of His Majesty's exceptional mark of favor.

Nicholas, who knew that the surest way to manipulate Pushkin was to appeal to his honor, had decided to play upon his sense of nobility again: Only treat him with indulgence, the tsar calculated, and he would feel impelled to confess his sins. With Count Tolstoy, however, Pushkin could not bring himself to speak out. His fear of reprisals fought with his impulse to dazzle the emperor by his honesty. In the end, he asked if he might write directly to the emperor, without passing through the intermediary of the investigating commission. Permission was granted, and he wrote a letter to Nicholas I forthwith, which he sealed himself and handed to Count Tolstoy. In it, he admitted that he was the author of *The Gabriliad.* Nicholas had scored again; for the second time, he had got the better of Pushkin by acting the part of magnanimous sovereign.

The Moscow interview and Pushkin's confession placed in the tsar's hands a creature totally disarmed and filled with gratitude and admiration: The emperor indulged himself by forgiving him.

On December 31, 1828, Nicholas announced his decision: "I am aware of all the details of this affair. The matter is closed."

Once more Pushkin was saved; but he felt humiliated by this continual game of pardon and accusation. The emperor was playing cat-and-mouse with him. He would give him a caress, send him spinning with a flick of his paw, pluck him up, blow some life into him and pin him down to squeeze it out again. Pushkin was ashamed of *The Gabriliad,* he wanted to disown the tasteless joke of his early youth. But was he going to have to keep paying for the rest of his life for every little folly he had ever committed? *André Chénier, The Gabriliad*—the list was open; what else might they not unearth, with a little cunning and perseverance, to use against him? Once the police take an interest in you, they never let you go; once the emperor has noticed you, you forfeit all right to your own private life.

Nicholas I was a great tsar and Pushkin respected him as an individual, but he hated him as an autocrat; he admired the man and detested the office. His response to the sovereign's clemency was his famous *The Anchar,* a condemnation of the very principle of monarchy.

The anchar is a tree whose leaves secrete poison. One man sends another to gather the poisoned foliage and die. The first man is a prince, the second is nothing. The image of autocracy.

Out in a thirsty, lifeless desert
On sun-scorched earth
The anchar stands, grim sentinel,
The only anchar in the world.
A poison seeps beneath its bark
In the blaze of midday sun,
And when evening comes, congeals
Into thick, transparent gum. . . .
Birds will not go near the tree,
The tiger avoids it, the wind
Flowing over the tree of death
Carries afar its fetid stench. . . .
But a man of haughty mien
Sends another to the anchar tree.
And the other, docile, goes. At dawn
He sets out home with the poison.
He carries the sluggish liquor:
One branch of wilted leaves,
And drops of icy sweat
Run down his livid brow.
He arrives, staggers and falls
On the rug inside the tent,
And the poor slave expires
At the feet of his invincible prince.
And with that poison, the prince
Anointed the tips of his willing darts
That sped then, sowing death
To neighbors in other lands.

Two protagonists, the "invincible prince" and the "poor slave." The poet says,

> But a man of haughty mien
> Sends another to the anchar tree.

The "invincible prince" is "a man," the "poor slave" is "another" man; but the first has power of life and death over the second. Why? Because he is prince, king, emperor. Nicholas I was made like Pushkin, with the same flesh and blood and bones, yet Pushkin had to crawl before the image personified by this other self, his kindred, his brother. He had to obey him as slave obeys master. He had to run to the poison tree at a word from the potentate "of haughty mien." After expressing his hatred of absolute power, Pushkin turned to its mindless worshipers, the blind cohort of courtiers, and dedicated to them his poem *The Populace.*

> We are weak and perfidious,
> Debauched, malicious and ungrateful,
> Eunuchs frozen in our hearts,
> Defamers, slaves and fools. . . .

Continuing, the poet refused to moralize for this perverse clan; he claimed for art the right to be useless. Later, he wrote: "Poetry is above morality. Or at least, completely different from it. Good Lord, what business of the poet's are questions of good and evil? At most, he may concern himself with their poetical aspects."

Thus, Pushkin defended personal freedom against the emperor in *The Anchar,* and artistic freedom against his court in *The Populace.* He so wanted to be free, free to write and live as he pleased, and his thirst for independence only increased with the rising barriers of police constraint. Another man would have been defeated by the ordeal of Pushkin's existence in St. Petersburg; but he worked on, suspected, harassed and exhausted. On October 2 he was interrogated by Count Tolstoy about *The Gabriliad;* on the third, instead of collapsing, he began his great poem *Poltava.* He did not know what fate Nicholas I had in store for him. It was possible that tomorrow or the next day his career and his life would be shattered. It was possible that this newborn work would become a stillborn work. So what? He worked. In fact, he worked with more determination than ever before, as though he had all eternity to express his thoughts, as though he were not facing imminent arrest, as though there were no tsar or Benkendorf or police or courtiers in Russia.

The little room in the Hotel Demuth was dark and miserable. Rain splattered against the panes, wind whistled beneath the door. The cold, the damp and the glowering ugliness of the sky, however, kept Pushkin at his desk. "He wrote all day long," Yusefovich said in his recollections. "He even saw lines of poetry in his dreams, and would leap out of bed at night to write them down in the dark. When he was hungry, he ran to the nearest tavern, but the lines of poetry never left his head. He bolted down whatever was put before him and went back to his room, still at a run, to write down the thoughts that had come to him in the street or while he was eating. He wrote hundreds of lines a day. When he could not organize his thoughts in poetry, he wrote in prose. Then he corrected what he had written, sometimes throwing out three quarters of his first version. I have seen drafts so covered with revisions that it was impossible to make out a word of them; there would be a bottom row of words, all crossed out, surmounted by several more tiers of words, also crossed out, so that there was not a speck of white left on the page."

The poet began *Poltava* on October 3, 1828. On the thirteenth of the month A. N. Wulf noted in his diary, "Went to see Pushkin, who read me his nearly completed poem." Pushkin himself said, "I wrote *Poltava* in a few days; I could not have spent any more time on it and would have given it up unfinished."[6]

Poltava shows signs of his haste: not in the writing, which is as admirably true and sober as ever, but in the lack of balance between the different episodes, due to the pull of conflicting plot lines. He had two subjects: the culpable loves of young Marya and old Mazeppa; and Mazeppa's treachery, the war between Sweden and Russia and the victory of Peter the Great. In this poem case history and history, instead of converging, negate each other. The lyric is drowned by the epic, Marya's face is buried in the dust of battle, and Peter the Great, who should have remained in the background, towers over all the other figures in the drama. Composed at breakneck speed, *Poltava* resembles a rosary of poems linked by a common context: It has no over-all cohesion, although every bead, taken separately, is a miniature masterpiece.

In his notes Pushkin wrote: "What a horrible subject. Not one good or noble sentiment. Not one consoling feature. Seduction, malevolence, treachery, ruse, cowardice, cruelty. . . . But what interested me was the forcefulness of the characters and the long, tragic shadows overlying all that horror."

Marya, daughter of the rich Kochubey, is in love with Mazeppa, hetman of the Ukranian Cossacks; she rejects all other suitors and will look at no one but the violent, solemn old man with the white mustache and the legendary past. Kochubey, who was a companion in arms of Mazeppa years before, is scandalized by his daughter's unnatural passion. He refuses the hetman's proposal of marriage, whereupon Marya elopes with her venerable lover. Flouted, humiliated and despoiled, Kochubey determines upon revenge. He knows Mazeppa's politics: While affirming unwavering loyalty to Peter the Great, the hetman is secretly negotiating with Charles XII of Sweden and preparing to mobilize his

Cossacks against his master, the tsar. Kochubey reveals Mazeppa's treachery to Peter the Great, but the tsar refuses to believe him and delivers Mazeppa's accusers into the hands of their would-be victim. So, after abducting Kochubey's daughter, Mazeppa now sees her father being led into his own dungeons. Mazeppa is a primitive being, uncomplicated and hard. He has no acquaintance with pity, remorse, moral obligations or fear of damnation, and obeys only his own will. Nevertheless, he hesitates to tell Marya that he has had her father arrested and is preparing to execute him like a common criminal. For although he himself has betrayed Peter the Great, he cannot bear the thought that anyone else should betray him—not he, Mazeppa. He says to Marya:

MAZEPPA—Do you love me?
MARYA—Do I love you?
MAZEPPA—Whom do you cherish most, your father
Or your husband?
MARYA—My sweet,
Why ask such a strange question,
Why cause me needless pain?
I want to forget my family. . . .
MAZEPPA—Listen: If one of us two
Had to die, and you alone
Were judge between us,
To whom would you give death,
Whom would you allow to live?
MARYA—Stop! You tear my heart,
You torture me. . . .
MAZEPPA—Answer!
MARYA—You are white, your voice is harsh.
Don't be angry, I am ready
To sacrifice anything for you!
Only, your words frighten me.
Be quiet.
MAZEPPA—Remember, Marya,
What you have said. . . .

The scene has great dramatic tension, and is dry, cutting, cruel, in keeping with the hero's character. After leaving Marya, Mazeppa goes down into the garden:

The Ukranian night is mild. Above,
Stars shine in the limpid sky.
The air is frozen in sleep.
The silver poplars shiver.
But dark forebodings
Sting Mazeppa, the stars
Stare down on him from the sky
Like sober, mocking eyes.

The poplars, shoulder to shoulder,
Confer with each other like judges
And the hot shadow of the night
Is stifling as a prison to him.

If he wants to reign, he will have to sacrifice Marya's father—the old fool, the imbecile traitor who tried to discredit him with Peter the Great. Well, what of it? When the time was ripe, Mazeppa would call out the Ukranian Cossacks, join the troops of Charles XII and repay the tsar's good faith by pulling him down from his throne. And Marya? She would suffer, no doubt, and curse the hetman when she learned he had killed Kochubey. But in politics there was no place for sentiment. If you listened to the women, you would never leave your fireside. The future of the Ukraine was worth a few female sobs. Mazeppa saw that it had been a mistake on his part to yield to the temptation of love. A great man must stand alone.

You cannot harness gazelle and hound
To a chariot of war.

While he is fretting and accusing and justifying himself (for the first time in his life, perhaps), Marya's mother slips into the palace, makes her way to her daughter's room and falls weeping at her feet.

THE MOTHER—The scaffold is up, only you
Can calm their frenzied wrath.
Save your father!
THE DAUGHTER—What, my father?
What scaffold?
THE MOTHER—Don't you know?
You're not in a desert, you live
In a palace, you must know
How fierce a foe the hetman is,
How he strikes down his enemies
And how the tsar humors him. . . .
Shake yourself, my child, Marya,
Run to him and fall at his feet,
Save your father, be our angel. . . .
Your eyes will stay his arm.

Mother and daughter rush out to implore mercy for Kochubey. Meanwhile, on the field where prisoners are executed, the headsman is standing before the crowd, chaffing the onlookers as he strokes his ax. The scene is compellingly precise:

The drum rolls. Hearts leap.
The road, like a long snake,
Writhes and unrolls.
In the middle of the field, the scaffold.

Laughing, the executioner strolls,
Fierce, awaiting his prey.
With his white hand he heaves
His heavy ax aloft in play,
And jokes with the populace. . . .

Mazeppa arrives, and the prisoners are led in. The ax rises, gleams and strikes off Kochubey's head, then that of his accomplice:

The executioner wrapped a hand around their hair,
Lifted them with one powerful arm,
And shook them at the crowd. . . .
It was over; the slow-moving crowd
Drifted away toward the town,
People talking to each other
About errands to run and things to buy.
Slowly, the field emptied.
Then, crossing the path,
Two poor women appear,
Weary and gray with dust.
They come trembling forward
To the place of the last ordeal:
"You're too late," someone says,
Pointing to the fields.
Over there, the platform was being
Dismantled, a pope in his black gown prayed,
And two Cossacks were loading
The coffins onto a cart.

Anxious, tormented and gloomy, Mazeppa returns to the palace to find Marya missing. He sends people to look for her; they come back empty-handed. Marya has fled with her mother. Mazeppa bows to fate. Having sacrificed love for power, he begins to assemble his men to fight the tsar. The third canto of the poem describes the famous Battle of Poltava, in which the forces of Peter the Great met and routed the armies of Mazeppa and Charles XII.

Poltava! The battle begins,
Shots crackle, salvos
Gut the living walls. . . .

Defeated, Charles XII and Mazeppa flee into the country on horseback. After a long ride, Mazeppa begins to recognize the landscape. He lies down by the bank of the Dnieper, trying to sleep. But Marya appears, and by her speech and strange laughter, Mazeppa understands that she is mad.

Pushkin called *Poltava* "my most solid piece of work, the one in which almost everything was original. . . ." In fact, *Poltava* has the same weaknesses of composition and strengths of style as some of his southern poems.

"He's flat, your poet," Flaubert said to Turgenev when the latter was singing Pushkin's praises. What Flaubert, the lover of metaphor, called flatness was the absence of metaphor. For the author of *Salammbô* there could be no poetry without a wealth of simile. He was addicted to heavily underscored contrasts, exaggerated details, blows to the solar plexus and bellows and crashings of gongs, romantic thunderclaps soothed into tender zephyrs. But the scaffolding of a poem such as *Poltava* was far too lightweight for such facile effects. Pushkin's work is informed by geometrical clarity; it is pure and fine, unadorned, limpid as water. It is all a play of nuances in which the smallest touch of color takes on far greater value than in the image-swollen texts of Hugo, Flaubert or Keats. Four lines describe the scaffold being taken apart on the edge of the steppe, the praying priest and the Cossacks loading coffins onto a wagon. The scene is reminiscent of a dry point by Rembrandt: the barest minimum, but perfect and complete in itself. Three lines sketch the executioner joking with his audience while he waits for his victims, yet we see him more clearly than if Pushkin had devoted a page to him: "his white hands." All we know about him is that he has white hands, but those white hands gripping the ax express a whole personality. *Poltava* is the final state of a poem a hundred times larger and a thousand times more colorful; the precious precipitate of a maelstrom of lines and rhymes. It is the supreme analysis, the ultimate residue, hard, brilliant and indestructible, of a poetic raw material whose wealth would have led any lesser writer astray. Pushkin offers us an essential poem, divested of everything approximative, shorn of every transition and every experiment. In his head he decanted, discarded, wore out all the accessory images and left upon the paper only the "solution" to the intermediary problems. It is for the reader to reverse the process, enriching the work with all that has preceded it.

Despite its indubitable qualities, *Poltava* was severely censured by the critics, if not by the public. The columnist of *Son of the Fatherland* wrote that Pushkin's Mazeppa was "not an opportunist, not a villain, not even a wretch; at most, a malicious imbecile."[7] Marya's love for Mazeppa was beyond comprehension: "Why did she fall in love with this ancient, why did she reject all the young men, why did she run away from her father's home and grant her favors to a dyspeptic, sick old hetman as though he were Adonis? . . . The reader cannot credit it."

Pushkin replied: "Love is the strangest of passions. I do not refer to the many instances in which ugliness and stupidity have been preferred to youth, intelligence and beauty. But think back to the lessons of mythology, Ovid's *Metamorphoses*, Leda, Phyllis, Pasiphaë, Pygmalion, and you will agree that they are all fit subject matter for poetry. And

Othello, that old Negro who seduced Desdemona with the tales of his travels and battles! In my poem, Mazeppa acts exactly in accordance with historical fact, and his speech illustrates a historical personage. It is not enough for critics to decree that a character is an imbecile; they must also prove it."

The *Northern Bee* wrote: "The poem is divided into three cantos; the cantos are composed of fragments or distinct episodes, like the slides of a magic lantern."[8]

The critic Nadezhdin had the temerity to say: "In my opinion *Poltava* is a veritable Poltava for Pushkin. Thanks to his poem, he has suffered the same fate as Charles XII."

Other critics tut-tutted over his use of "mustaches" and "creakings," and such trivial expressions as "Get up!" and "It is time!"

To the latter, Pushkin replied, "I shall never sacrifice the truthfulness, the rightness of an expression to the demands of provincial snobbery or the fear of being called 'populistic' or 'Slavophile.' . . ."

On October 19, 1828, still smoking from the creative fires of *Poltava*, Pushkin went to the annual reunion of the alumni of the imperial school. "There were present," the minutes record, Delvig, Ilichevsky, Yakovlev, Korf, Stephen, Tyrkov, Komovsky and "Pushkin-the-Frenchman, hybrid of monkey and tiger."

The friends drank and laughed and lamented the absence of Pushchin and Küchelbecker, grew moist-eyed at the memory of their bygone youth and parted company in the small hours of the morning after wishing a bon voyage to Pushkin, who was leaving directly for Malinniki, the Wulfs' estate in the government of Tver.

Pushkin had been planning this trip for more than a month. On September 11, 1828, Alexis Wulf wrote in his diary: "I saw Pushkin; he wants to go to Malinniki with my mother, which displeases me very much, because it would be bad for her reputation and that of my sister; and for my sister, it would be bad for other reasons." One is tempted to smile at this high-minded concern being expressed by Alexis Wulf, Pushkin's erstwhile pupil in the amatory arts—the Faust, the Lovelace of Trigorskoye, who was almost simultaneously the lover of Mrs. Kern (Pushkin's old flame), one of the Osipov girls and Delvig's wife. He kept a journal in which he recorded his conquests, tactics and rebuffs. He specialized in virgins, bringing them to the point of "ecstasy" but leaving their precious maidenheads intact. Nevertheless, where his sisters were concerned, this expert in gallantry feared the potency of a science which had procured so many conquests for himself, and his fears were justified.

Pushkin was compellingly attractive to the sentimental Annette and the mischievous Zizi, and to their mother, the practical, plump, respectable and dreamy Mrs. Wulf-Osipov; not to mention the friends and cousins of the household. He had literally maddened and dishonored Annette, whose love letters we have seen. And Zizi, now twenty, was aching to follow in her sister's footsteps. "Judging from various indications," wrote Wulf, "her youthful imagination has also succumbed to the irresistible Mephistopheles."

The whole female clan of Trigorskoye, now transported to Malinniki, was working itself into a stew, fluttering about in preparation for its rapturous capitulation. In the huge house built of ship timbers with a colonnaded entrance, dark, low-ceilinged rooms and mahogany furniture upholstered in coarse material, the poet's arrival was preceded by feverish altercation and negotiation. Dresses were exchanged, confidences whispered, perfidious advice proffered, faint sighs uttered and perverse private prayers offered up by vigil light or along the garden paths. Pushkin was coming! The monster! The angel! We're so afraid of him! And it's so lovely to be afraid! At last he came, and was greeted by a bouquet of tender faces. Their laughter, their bittersweet provocation and the prospect of a little enjoyment rapidly effaced the bleak memory of the capital. Among all these girls, these devoted, demanding females, Pushkin forgot *André Chénier, The Gabriliad,* Benkendorf and Nicholas I. He felt ten years younger; he was gay, keen, seductive, mocking, affectionate and vigorous as never before. He flitted from one maiden to another, teased, caressed and provoked microscopic jealousies, court revolutions and corridor intrigues. He was reprimanded. He was detested. He was admired. He was loved. He was happy. On October 27, 1828, he wrote to Alexis Wulf: "I was received with all the deference and indulgence befitting my rank. I am told you are not nearly as good as I am (morally, that is), which does not mean I may hope for success as great as yours. I supplied, truthfully and innocently, the particulars requested of me regarding your conduct in St. Petersburg, which gave rise to a few tears and some unspeakably unkind expressions such as 'Oh, the worthless man! Oh, the vile, base person!' But I pretended not to hear. I take this opportunity to inform you that Marya Vasilyevna Borisov is a flower in a desert, a nightingale in a virgin forest, a pearl in the sea, and that I intend to fall in love with her in a day or two."

And to Delvig, in November: "I am enjoying myself here. I love Praskovya Alexandrovna [Osipov] with all my heart; what a pity she is always indisposed and anxious. The neighbors come to inspect me as though I were the hound of Munito. . . . A few days ago there was a gathering at the home of one of our neighbors and I had promised to go. The children of a relative—spoiled brats—absolutely insisted on coming too; their mother gave them some raisins and prunes, hoping to slip away while they were occupied with them. But Peter Markovich [Mrs. Kern's father] came running up to excite them, crying, 'Children, children, your mother is deceiving you! Don't eat those prunes, go with her; Pushkin will be there, he is all made of sugar with a behind of apples; they're going to cut him up and everybody will have a piece.' The children began to scream, 'We don't want prunes, we want Pushkin!' Willy-nilly, they had to be taken, and came running toward me licking their chops, but stopped in bewilderment when they saw I was made of flesh and blood instead of sugar. There are lots of pretty little girls (or just plain girls, as Boris Mikhailovich says I must call them); my dealings with them are all platonic, however, and as a result I am putting on weight and recovering my shaky health. Farewell! Place a kiss from me on your navel, if you can reach it."

In another letter to Delvig, Pushkin continued: "I am having a very good time here, loving country life as I do. They are laboring under the illusion that I have come to work on *Onegin*, and they use me as a werewolf to frighten the children. I, meanwhile, take trips on the ferry and play whist for eighty kopecks a game, savoring the delights of virtue and shunning the snares of vice. Tell that to our ladies. I shall come back to them. . . . Enough, I begin to wander."[9]

At Malinniki, while caressing little Zizi, simpering at pretty Marya Borisov and running after other transient petticoats, Pushkin also finished the seventh canto of *Onegin*, wrote the dedication to *Poltava* (to Marya Raevsky), and composed a few lyric poems, including the strong and sinister *Drowned Man*. Then, having worked, laughed and loved his fill, he left Malinniki in December and went to Moscow to try out his latest creations on a few trustworthy friends.

"Pushkin is here for three weeks," Vyazemsky wrote to Turgenev. "So far he has fallen in love with no one, and his former passions have more or less forsaken him. Yesterday he was to go to the Korsakovs'; so far I have heard no news of the occasion. I have asked him to come to Penza with me; he says he would like to, but I don't count on it because in the meantime he will surely have fallen in love."[10]

From Moscow, Pushkin went back to the Wulfs in their harem at Malinniki, where Alexis Wulf, lately come from St. Petersburg, had relieved him as chief slayer of fair maidens, and the sentimental skirmishes resumed at an even hotter pace than before—for now the combat was no longer being waged by Pushkin alone, but by Pushkin in partnership with Alexis. The two were joined in "an offensive and defensive alliance" against the weaker sex. Alexis Wulf noted in his diary—a precious source of information, incidentally, on the sentimental mores of the age: "For Epiphany [January 6, 1829], we received Pushkin, 'the glory of our days, heaven's favorite poet,' as our Kostroma poetess

Gotovtsev calls him. He has brought a little distraction into our group. His brilliant wit of the man of the world is very welcome in company, particularly female company. He and I have concluded an offensive and defensive alliance against the fair ones, and my sisters are now calling him Mephistopheles and me Faust. But Marguerite [Katerina Velyashev, a sixteen-year-old cousin of Alexis Wulf's], notwithstanding the counsel of Mephistopheles and the pressing attentions of Faust, has remained unmoved, our efforts are all in vain. . . . Little Marya Borisov and Natalya Koznakov have also slipped through my fingers. . . . At dinner we made Frederika (a pretty girl from Hamburg whom my uncle brought back from one of his military campaigns and later married) drink Lunel, as well as a German woman from Riga, half governess and half maid, and the steward's fiancée, and a lively little sprite who is the daughter of the former local pope. . . . I mention her because I had quite a comical adventure with her. . . ."

The comical adventure was singularly like that of Count Nulin, related by Pushkin in the poem of that name. Having pursued the pope's daughter all day long, Wulf determined to visit her bedroom that night. The "victim" gives the following account of Alexis Wulf's nocturnal visit: "I woke and saw a young man on his knees by my bed, leaning his head toward mine. 'Ayee! Who are you?' I cried. 'Hush, hush, I'm going right away,' he stammered. And he went. When Pushkin heard the story, he seemed delighted by it and was very nice to me afterward: 'Splendid! Well done!' he would say; 'Old Alexis thought every door was open to him and he didn't even need to warn people he was coming, but events have proved him wrong.' "

In the home of Alexis Wulf's uncle Pavel Ivanovich, Pushkin divided his time between Zizi and the pope's daughter, to Mrs. Osipov's acute annoyance: "Pavel Ivanovich," she would say, "opens his door to every comer and treats the daughter of a pope as the equal of my own girls."

"When we went into the dining room," wrote the daughter of the pope, "Alexander Sergeyevich Pushkin gave one arm to me and the other to Mrs. Osipov's daughter Eufrasia [Zizi], who was just my age. He sat between us at table and served us with equal attentiveness. When the dancing began in the evening, he danced with us in turn, first with her, then me, and so on, and Mrs. Osipov grew angry and left. Eufrasia Nikolayevna [Zizi]'s eyes were full of tears, I don't know why. Maybe because, after the meal, Pushkin showed us the portrait of an unknown woman and insisted that she was a great beauty; everyone else looked at the portrait and echoed his admiration. That must be what upset her. But she was devouring him with her eyes."

The pope's daughter, little Mayra Borisov, little Velyashev, little Zizi; Pushkin harried each blossoming quarry in turn, and ultimately ensnared and led Zizi to her decisive defeat, whereupon she became wan and distraught, and began to weep at the drop of a hat. Alexis Wulf observed in his younger sister "a sort of languor which admirers would find charming but which reminds me strongly of Liza Poltoratsky and the agonies of unrequited love; I believe I am not mistaken."

On all sides handkerchiefs were sodden, eyes downcast, lips sighing and being sweetly offered, and Pushkin was drunk with youth and love. Then, gorged with honey, his head heavy and his feet weary from too much dancing, he began to think of going back to St. Petersburg. He left, with Wulf, on January 19.

On the way, he composed a poem for the blue-eyed Velyashev girl, promising to forget her grace and mocking laughter in the glittering tumult of the capital:

For if I do not, I shall set out again
And come straight back next year
To see this peaceful place once more
And love you till November. . . .

"At the posting stations," Wulf wrote, "we played chess, while the horses were being changed; and on the road we talked of current events, literature, women and love. Pushkin talks well; his keen and penetrating mind instantly grasps the point of a conversation, but it is that very faculty which explains his sometimes superficial and one-sided judgments. . . . He knows women better than anyone. Thus it is that, possessing none of those outward attributes to which the fair sex is always attracted, he gains their indulgence by the sheer radiance of his intelligence."

Women, women, always women—Pushkin's entire existence was infested by and cluttered with women. Their babbling cohort thrust figures more worthy of esteem into the background; carried away by the whirlwind of his sentimental pleasures and pangs, Pushkin failed to mention his deeper afflictions. Thus, we know nothing of the great bereavement that marked the year 1828 for him: Arina Rodionovna, his nanny, his most loyal confidante and oldest friend, died in St. Petersburg. The soul went out of the tumble-down house at Mikhailovskoye. His childhood slipped its moorings and floated away. Suddenly, he was a generation older.

3. *Love in Town*

Returning to St. Petersburg on January 19, 1829, Pushkin promptly forgot his rural idylls in a fresh round of cards and conquests.

"His conduct," Nikitenko wrote in his diary, "is unworthy of a man who speaks the language of the gods and aspires to transform living images into ideal beauty. It is too bad that such moral contradiction should be joined to such supreme natural talent."

Among Pushkin's notes for *The Queen of Spades* (1832–33) is the following autobiographical comment: "Four years ago I was living a very disorganized life in St. Petersburg. There was a group of us, all young men of means only recently brought together by circumstance. We dined *chez* Andrié, but without appetite; we drank, but without joy; we went to S.A. (Sofya Astapova), who kept a house of ill repute, but without necessity—simply to infuriate the poor woman with our feigned indifference; we killed the daylight hours as best we could, and in the evening we met in the rooms of one or another of our group to spend the night, cards in hand."

During one of these vigils Pushkin chalked on his coat sleeve the lines which were to become the epigraph for the first chapter of *The Queen of Spades:*

Days of rain, days of wind,
They often met together,
And staked, God forgive their souls,
Fifty to a hundred.

Everything the poet earned went at the card table. He was registered on the Moscow police list of inveterate gamblers: "No. 1 Count Fyodor Tolstoy—skillful gambler; No. 22 Nashchokin—gambler and lover of scandals, noted for the number of reports he has occasioned; No. 36 Pushkin—well-known gambler in Moscow."

Pushkin, the well-known gambler. The police forgot that he was a poet, too. Vyazemsky wrote to him: "All I hear is complaints from the

Karamzins—that you have disappeared from their lives without a trace—and an anonymous rumor that you are gambling madly. Is it true?"

To this letter Pushkin replied: "While Kiselev and Poltoratsky were here, I led the life I sang, in

"Days of rain, days of wind,
They often met together . . .

"Now we have all scattered. Being without a fixed residence, I have plunged into society. Without your copper Venus, I should already have died of boredom. She is superbly consoling and good, and has promoted me to the rank of pander to her ladyship."

This "copper Venus" who had managed to lure Pushkin away from the card table was the Countess Agrippina Zakrevsky, a splendid creature with dark skin, ardent eyes, fever-flushed cheeks and insatiable appetites. Consumed by her thirst for love, she left a trail of passions, catastrophes, poems and burgeoning jealousies behind her. She exhausted her lovers, physically and emotionally, and exhausted herself in the process. By turns mocking and forlorn, cynical, provocative and languid, she seemed to be forever seeking her place in the world. When Pushkin knew her, this hysteric in the grand manner had already annihilated a large number of aspirants, one of whom was the poet Baratynsky, who wrote:

She is a drunken bacchante!
Her fire is of fever,
Not the fire of love.

And:

You moan like a Magdalen,
You sneer like an Undine.

Fatal beauty, copper Venus, Undine, Magdalen, Cleopatra—Countess Zakrevsky had no very clear idea herself who she was, or what she wanted, from men, the world or God. Nevertheless, she fascinated Pushkin. An eyewitness said, "Not long ago Pushkin, on a visit, scolded her for paying more attention to some stranger than to him. Then he grew angry and planted his long claws in her hand so deeply that he drew blood."[1]

Pushkin himself wrote:

Your confessions, your languid laments,
Your smallest whimpers, I hoard
Like a miser. The language
Of love has made me giddy!
But no more of such talk.
Tell me nothing of your thoughts,
I fear the fire that consumes you,
I do not want to learn what you know.

For a few months Pushkin wore himself out loving and trying to satisfy this maenad, enduring her fits of laughter and tears, her orgiastic demands, her metaphysical doubts, her vapors, her indispositions and her jealousies. (He dedicated a few short poems to her, included her in *Eugene Onegin* and placed her on the section of his Don Juan list devoted to consummated victories.) Then, when he had had enough, he turned away in search of calmer comforts. Toward the end of this absorbing liaison, he wrote to Mrs. Khitrovo: "Proper women and lofty sentiments are what I fear most in the world. Long live tarts! . . . Shall I tell you frankly? I may be elegant and proper in what I write, but my heart is completely base and vulgar and my inclinations all third-estate. I am drunk on intrigue, romance, correspondence, etc. . . . It is my present misfortune to be involved with a person who drives me to distraction, although I love her with my whole heart."[2]

Mrs. Eliza Khitrovo, to whom Pushkin made this avowal, was a woman of forty-six, the daughter of Field Marshal Kutuzov and mother-in-law of Count Ficquelmont, the Austrian ambassador to St. Petersburg. Her drawing room was a sort of intellectual stock exchange for the latest political and literary news of St. Petersburg, and she presided over it with ponderous, patient, placid, middle-aged grace. Massive and inclined to stoutness, she claimed to have the handsomest shoulders in Russia and kept them on permanent display in scandalously low-cut gowns. This curious need to exhibit her nearly deflated charms earned her the nickname of "Liza the naked." "It is time to throw a veil over the past," Perovsky said, contemplating her proffered attributes. The author Sollogub wrote that she rose late and received her first callers in her bedroom; she would say to them urbanely, "Do sit down. . . . No, not in that armchair, that's Pushkin's chair. . . . Not on that settee, that's Zhukovsky's place. . . . Oh well, sit here on my bed, that's everybody's place. . . ."

In reality, Mrs. Khitrovo's adventures were far fewer and less spectacular than those of Countess Zakrevsky. Eliza Khitrovo was kind, charitable, sensitive and loyal. The moment she first caught sight of Pushkin, she became wildly infatuated with him, obsessed by him body and soul. For him, she delightedly descended from *grande dame* to maidservant; she surrounded her god with a myriad maternal anxieties, hygienic recommendations, coy demonstrations. Pushkin probably responded to this opulent passion once or twice, and then lost interest in the handsome matron with the aggressive décolleté. However, even when deprived of more immediate consolations, Eliza Khitrovo continued her public and private cult of her idol. Everybody knew about this late-blooming and unrequited passion, for Liza the naked could no more hide her feelings than her shoulders. Friends of the ill-assorted couple called Mrs. Khitrovo "Erminia" in allusion to Tasso's heroine, the faithful and unrewarded lover of Tancred. Pushkin's mother wrote to her daughter: "Alexander . . . goes for walks in the Summer Garden with his Erminia. . . . Your brother really is extremely droll." Pushkin was well aware of the oddity of this liaison, and, having a morbid dread of ridicule, he laughed at his self-appointed high priestess and tried every way he could think of to get rid of her; but there was no getting rid of Eliza. She would put up with anything, as long as she could go on seeing her poet. "If you can make Eliza fall in love with you," Pushkin wrote to Vyazemsky in 1830, "you will be doing me a precious favor. I saved my sanity by leaving not my cape, but my shirt in the clutches of that woman, and she is still flooding me with letters and packages." "She embarrassed him beyond words," a contemporary wrote, "but he could not bring himself to offend her openly, even though he threw her daily letters into the fire unread."[3]

A few of her letters survived, however, all of them in French; they give an exact picture of the nature of Mrs. Khitrovo's affection for the poet:

"Just when I begin to be reassured about your trip to Moscow, I have to start worrying about your health; I am told you are ill at Trigorskoye. Your pallor was one of the last things I noticed about you before you left. . . . I don't know whom to ask in order to learn the truth, this is the fourth time I have written you. Tomorrow it will be a fortnight since you left, it is inconceivable that you have not written one word to me. . . . Forbid me, if you wish, to speak to you of myself, but do not deprive me of the happiness of being your messenger. I can tell you the news of society, foreign literature, the probability of a new ministry in France; alas, I hear everything before anyone else, the only thing I lack is happiness.

"How I love it that you are loved! Even though I am meek and inoffensive and resigned with you (and despite your antipathy on that account), do, at least once in a while, tell me that you have received my letters. I should be radiant at the mere sight of your writing!"

Later: "Henceforth, my heart and private thoughts will be an impenetrable secret to you, and my letters as they should be. . . . Make any use of me you like, and do not hesitate. I am in a position to do a great deal for others, and am precious to my friends; I have nothing to lose, I can speak to the people in authority, I never balk, weather, season, nothing discourages me, my body does not know my weary heart, I am afraid of nothing. . . . Even after I have drowned my love for you in my tears, I shall remain the devoted, gentle and harmless being who would plunge into a frozen river to save you, for that is how I love—even those I love little."[4]

By turns gratified, ashamed, moved to pity, embarrassed and annoyed, Pushkin played the cherub to this maternal and voluble mistress for some time. It was she who kept him in touch with the rest of the world, through her daughter, who was married to the Austrian ambassador. Thanks to her, he received foreign newspapers and books and could keep abreast of political and artistic events in Europe. That alone was enough to keep him on the good side of the ardent Eliza.

But neither "bacchante" Zakrevsky nor "Erminia" Khitrovo could satisfy the poet's longing for fresh fields to conquer. As the years passed, his fascination with the mystery of maidenhood grew stronger. At Trigorskoye, it was the newly nubile Zizi and her friends who drew him; in Moscow, it was Alexandra Rimsky-Korsakov, the Urusov sisters, Sofya Pushkin (who had rejected him) and Katerina Ushakov (whose future he still did not despair of sharing); in St. Petersburg, the Chosen One was a girl named Anna Olenin, twenty years old, the daughter of the president of the Academy of Fine Arts.

For three years, Anna Olenin had been maid of honor to the empress. With a wasp waist, rounded bust, shining blond hair and small, sugary lips, she had the mincing grace of a Greuze. In her father's drawing room assembled the elite of the Russian aristocracy and artistic world. Every May the Olenins emigrated to their country home at Pryutino, near St. Petersburg, and the guests came flocking after them in such numbers that the farm's seventeen milch cows could not provide enough fresh cream for the house. At Pryutino, there was little talk of politics and much of literature, few games of cards and many of charades. Mickiewicz, Vyazemsky, Zhukovsky, Brüllow and Glinka were regular guests. Pushkin began assiduously paying court to Miss Olenin. He did not really care very much about her, but she was a *virgo intacta*, gay and bright, and he felt obliged to reward her for it. He wrote poems in honor of the "pensive genius," "childlike simplicity" and "expressive languor" of her look, he compared her to "a Raphael." One day, by mistake, she used the familiar form when speaking to him, and Pushkin wrote for her the poem *Thou and You*, ending with the lines:

> I stand, thoughtful, before her,
> Not daring to look away,
> And say, "How lovely you are!"
> Thinking, "How I love thee!"

Wordplays on Anna Olenin's names are scattered through the pages of Pushkin's notebooks; there are "Aninelo . . . Etenna . . . Olenina. . . ." And even, "Annette Pushkin."

Anna Olenin, of course, kept a diary in French. In it, Pushkin was the hero of a childish novel written in the third person. One passage reads:

"One of the poet's singularities was a passion for tiny feet, which he confessed to preferring over beauty itself in one of his poems. In addition to a presentable exterior, Annette possessed two things: eyes which were sometimes pretty and sometimes stupid; but her foot was really very small indeed, and hardly any of her friends could wear her shoes.

"Pushkin had remarked upon this advantage and his eager eyes followed the young Olenin's footsteps across the slippery parquet.

"He had recently returned from six years in exile. Everyone—men and women—eagerly showered upon him the attentions always given to genius. Some did so because he was in fashion, others in the hope of receiving some pretty verse and making their reputation that way, and others out of true respect for genius; but the majority did so because of the favor he enjoyed with the emperor, who was his censor.

"Annette had met him when only a child, and ever since, she had enthusiastically admired his enticing poems.

"She too wanted to show some mark of her esteem for the famous poet, and chose him for a partner at a dance; her fear of being ridiculed by him made her lower her gaze and blush as she went up to him. She was stung by the nonchalance with which he asked where her place was. The idea that Pushkin might think her a silly goose was hurtful, but she answered unaffectedly and did not venture to ask him to dance again that evening.

"Then it was he, in turn, who came to invite her, and she saw him approaching. She gave him her hand, turning her head aside with a smile, for it was a happiness envied by everyone there.

"I wanted to write a novel, but it bores me, I would rather not do it at all, and simply write my diary.

"I saw Pushkin's portrait again, I am pleased to have sketched it so well. You could recognize him in a thousand!"

On May 21, 1828, Vyazemsky reported to his wife: "At Pryutino we found Pushkin and his amorous grimaces. The countryside is quite pleasant, especially in view of its proximity to St. Petersburg. . . . But the mosquitoes make it a veritable hell. I have never seen such swarms of them. . . . I could not have stayed even one day, the next morning I should have gone mad and beaten my head against a wall. Mickiewicz called it "a day of blood." As for Pushkin, he was covered with bites, but mildly exclaimed as he fended off a cloud of them, 'How exquisite!' "

In a previous letter, dated May 7, 1828, he wrote: "Pushkin believes and is trying to make everyone else believe he is in love. . . ."

Indeed, Pushkin wanted so desperately to make others believe he was in love with Anna Olenin, and to believe it himself, that in the end he proposed to her. But the marriage did not take place; some said her father, having learned of Pushkin's trouble with the police over *The Gabriliad,* refused his consent, while others maintained that it was Pushkin himself who was afraid to go any further, failed to turn up for the betrothal dinner and begged her parents to consider his proposal null and void.

Whatever the truth of the matter, Pushkin's quest for a fiancée was not over.

His sister Olga had better luck: She was married in 1828—but at thirty, and in what circumstances! In January 1826 a drab, hard-working, respectable young man named Pavlishchev had asked for Olga's hand, but Pushkin's parents would have none of such an unprepossessing suitor. Sergey Lvovich waved his arms, stamped his foot and wept, and Nadezhda Osipovna ordered Pavlishchev never to darken the doorway again. Some time later, the lovers met at a ball and, under cover of the cotillion, danced "two turns" together. Nadezhda Osipovna, glimpsing them in the tightly packed crowd of couples, rushed up to her thirty-year-old daughter and shook her vigorously in front of the whole assembly. Olga swooned. The next night she left, was secretly married to Pavlishchev and went home again with no one the wiser.

"That morning," wrote Zhukovsky in a letter dated February 4, 1828, "she went to see her brother Alexander (at the Hotel Demuth) and said to him: 'Sweet brother, go tell our parents I was married yesterday. . . .' The astonished brother briefly flew into a rage, but being a sensible man at heart, he saw that a bad peace was better than a good quarrel and went off to the parents to break the news. Sergey Lvovich fainted. A surgeon was called in to bleed him. Pushkin noticed that his father, supposedly unconscious, was arguing with the surgeon and trying to teach him how to apply the leeches. . . ."

The parents forgave Olga and instructed their son and Mrs. Kern to welcome and bless the couple. The ceremony was to take place at Delvig's apartment. It was chilly. In the ancient paternal carriage, Pushkin and Mrs. Kern found themselves alone together for the first time since their impassioned hours at Trigorskoye. Pushkin had long since lost interest in her, and she no longer felt anything more than a calm and sincere affection for the poet. They made a curious couple—old lovers and new friends. They were sad. Perhaps they were thinking of all they had lost? Perhaps they envied the fate of this man and woman they were about to bless for life, while their union had lasted a few days at most? Perhaps, too, they simply had nothing to say to each other.

The adventures of Olga and Pavlishchev and the efforts of the loyal Delvig, deceived husband but faithful friend, brought Pushkin and his family together again. Delvig even arranged a formal reconciliation.

But in spite of his praiseworthy attempts, Pushkin could not love his parents: For him, Sergey Lvovich, with his parrot's beak, his taut little paunch, his saliva, tears and pitiful chatter, and Nadezhda Osipovna, with her haggard face, her unfriendly eyes, her tantrums and her mincing ways, were nothing but puppets. His real family, his true parents, were not Sergey Lvovich and Nadezhda Osipovna, but Delvig (they kissed each other's hands when they met in the street), Vyazemsky, Nashchokin, Sobolevsky, Glinka, Mickiewicz, Mrs. Kern, Mrs. Osipov and Mrs. Karamzin (the historian's widow). They were his family, they were the ones who helped him to endure his boredom.

"I have been back in St. Petersburg a week," wrote Pushkin, around January 25, 1829. "I found the whole of high society in a turmoil. Everybody is madly gay. 'Raouts'* are all the rage; how did we never think of them before? We were born for 'raouts,' for to have a successful one you need neither intelligence nor humor nor conversation nor politics nor literature. You simply tread on people's feet as on a carpet, then say you're sorry, and that takes the place of conversation."

Pushkin had long been weary of St. Petersburg, its "raouts" and police, its eligible debutantes and willing wives. He needed new horizons, he needed to be revived—so badly that in the spring of 1828, when he heard that hostilities had broken out between Russia and the Ottoman Porte, he had asked Benkendorf for permission to serve in the regular army. Benkendorf had given him an appointment for April 18, but failed to keep it. Pushkin returned to the charge in a letter dated the same day. Benkendorf replied that "all the places were taken." Then he suggested that the poet might participate in the campaign by joining the third section! Pushkin in the third section, Pushkin a police agent! The joke was a little flat. The poet fell sick with rage, and begged to be allowed to go to Paris. Refused again. But one of Benkendorf's agents advised him to enlist in Paskevich's army on the Caucasian front.

"Excellent idea," exclaimed Pushkin. "I'll think about it."[5]

And promptly forgot about it for almost a year.

Then, in March 1829, the desire for a change of scene seized him again. Fearing another refusal, he neglected to apply to Benkendorf and told no one of his plans. First, he would go to Moscow; from there, he would set out for Tiflis. And from Tiflis, perhaps across the frontier. . . . For him, the ideal was always just over the horizon. He wore himself out pursuing it, from house to house, smile to smile, year to year, while his own heart began to falter and fresh lines etched their way into his face.

* *Raout* (French) = a party.

In Moscow, Pushkin stayed with his friend Nashchokin: Nashchokin the openhanded madman, the model profligate, the poorest rich man in all Russia. He spent his money with truly inspired extravagance, buying up marbles, Chinese *objets* and bronzes for which he had absolutely no desire, paying a fortune for a minute fragment of the candle which had lit the face of the actress Aksenov in her finest role and having it mounted in a silver case; throwing away forty thousand rubles on a two-story doll's house made of glass and filled with tiny furniture and curios, all of which, from settees to teacups and chandeliers to tablecloths, were made by the leading artisans of Vienna, Paris and London.

Gambling, losing, winning, inheriting, borrowing, Nashchokin scaled summits and plunged into abysses that would have given anyone else vertigo; but he throve on his strange destiny. Pushkin loved him for his good humor and intelligence—for at heart the spendthrift, lazy great lord was sad. Pushkin listened to his tales in fascination and tried to get him to write his memoirs. It was Nashchokin who told Pushkin the story of Dubrovsky; it was Nashchokin's life he thought of writing in a novel to be called *The Russian Pelham.*

But Pushkin had not come to Moscow just to see Nashchokin; still obsessed by the idea of marriage, he was hoping the second capital might produce that model fiancée he had sought elsewhere in vain, before he set out for Tiflis. In fact, he was quite prepared to give up the Caucasus and his deeds of heroism altogether, if only somebody would offer him a desirable, steady woman in exchange. Of all the girls he had met, Katerina Ushakov was decidedly the one most deserving of his confidence. Back he went, therefore, to this friendly house; but only to be met by disappointment again. Having heard of Pushkin's betrothal to Anna Olenin in St. Petersburg, Katerina Ushakov had become engaged herself, to Prince Dolgoruky. Pushkin despaired. He tried to justify himself, he explained how he had broken off his engagement to Anna Olenin, he listed all the temptations of life in St. Petersburg; but to no avail. Then, he told Katerina's parents that Prince Dolgoruky was unworthy of such a match, giving conclusive evidence in support of his arguments and ultimately convincing them: Katerina refused to marry the prince; but, having acquired a clearer view of Pushkin's constancy, she also advised him not to seek her hand in marriage. Pushkin accepted his fate with a smile: Katerina would remain single, which was almost as good as marrying him. He continued to frequent the Ushakovs, as fond friend and unthreatening lover. He drew more sketches in her album and dedicated new poems to her. Katerina replied with other poems and sketches. The couple disparaged each other's flirtations, teased, sulked and perhaps regretted that their relationship was henceforth condemned to mere friendship.

The drawings in the album illustrate the preoccupations and subjects of mirth of Katerina and Pushkin. One of the caricatures shows Miss Olenin fishing for fiancés with rod and line. Another shows Pushkin with enormous side whiskers and eyes glittering with covetousness. "Go! Get thee gone! Leave me! Your hands are unworthy," the caption reads.

On another page there is a sketch of the head of a young and beautiful woman, accompanied by the caption "O, woe is me! Kars! Kars! Farewell, light of day! I die for thee!"

Kars, a Turkish fortress reputed to be impregnable, was Pushkin's nickname for another young Muscovite. Her name was Natalya Goncharov. And while Pushkin was joking with Katerina, his deepest thoughts had already turned to her.

Pushkin had met Natalya Goncharov during his previous stay in Moscow, in the winter of 1828–29. In his memory, she was a girl of sixteen, dazzled by the bright lights and music of the ball. That evening she had been wearing an ethereal white gown and a simple circlet of gold in her hair. She was timid, pure and beautiful. After a few months away, Pushkin found her even more timid, pure and beautiful. No hesitation: Natalya was the ideal fiancée, the perfect partner, God's messenger on earth. With determination, Pushkin began to frequent the same homes as the Goncharovs. Then, having been reconciled with his old enemy Tolstoy-the-American, he chose this man, into whose head he had previously sworn to fire a bullet, to act as his ambassador extraordinary to the Goncharov family. Pushkin's suit was received with reservations. He was poor, he had a dreadful reputation; true, he wrote poetry, but a good poet could never make anything but a bad husband. In short, Mrs. Goncharov considered that her little Natalya, so pretty and fresh, deserved something better than a vague Pushkin with no fixed income and no official future. As for Natalya, all she felt about the poet was a sort of flattered bewilderment. He interested her because he published, or so they said, very pretty poems. But he had such a funny face. And such long nails! And he danced peculiarly, like somebody with a fever. Still, he was nice. He paid court to her. One must be polite to people who pay court to you. The mamans take care of the rest.

Natalya's maman saw Count Tolstoy. Tolstoy pleaded the poet's cause, Mrs. Goncharov that of her daughter. "He has such talent." "She is so beautiful." "He loves her so." "We must beware of these sudden infatuations." "Then what do you advise?" "Patience."

Tolstoy returned with sighs and evasive promises, but Pushkin had been too frightened of an outright refusal to feel anything but joy at Mrs. Goncharov's response. He was not being dismissed, he was being told to wait. Of course, it was true: Natalya was a mere child. Her mother's concern was comprehensible. But how was he, Pushkin, to wait such a long time? He was in a terrible hurry. His guts were on fire. If it went on much longer he would kidnap Natalya, he would do something insane! . . . First of all, he must get out of Moscow. He could not bear to trail around after this little maiden, counting the months and weeks and days that separated him from his marriage, watching her maturing figure, her awakening gaze, the new assurance of her smile. He was totally in the grip of his nuptial obsession. He needed the Caucasus, the outdoors, mountains, armies, dangers and adventures, in order to forget the Moscow debutante. He already loved her so much that he preferred not to see her at all if he could not hold her in his arms. All or nothing: He was like that.

"Byron went to Greece," they told him, "and died there! Don't go to Persia, don't make yourself more like him than you already are."[6]

And: "Don't tell me you are going to Georgia. That place is hostile to literature. It has already taken Griboedov away from us!"[7] Griboedov, the author of *Wit Works Woe,* had been assassinated in Teheran that year by rebel Moslems.

But no threat or caution could stop the poet; on May 1, 1829, he sent a letter in French to Mrs. Goncharov: "I should be writing on my knees, shedding tears of gratitude, now that Count Tolstoy has brought me your reply—your reply that is not a refusal, you allow me to hope. However, if I still murmur, if sorrow and bitterness mingle with my joy, do not accuse me of ingratitude; I can understand a mother's prudence and tender concern! But forgive the impatience of a heart that is sick and intoxicated with happiness. I am leaving now, carrying away in the depths of my soul the image of the celestial being who owes her existence to you. If you have any orders to give me, please transmit them to Count Tolstoy, who will be in touch."

Later, in April 1830, he wrote to Mrs. Goncharov again, also in French, enlarging upon his love and sudden departure: "When I saw her for the first time, people were just beginning to be aware of her beauty; I loved her, my head whirled, I asked for her, your reply, vague as it was, gave me a moment of rapture; I left the same night for the army; if you ask me what I intended to do there, I will swear to you that I hadn't the faintest idea, but some involuntary anguish drove me out of Moscow; I could not have borne your presence or hers. I wrote, I hoped, I waited for an answer; none came. The errors of my youth passed before my eyes; they were all too great, and calumny has made them even worse; and they have, unfortunately, become widely known. You might have credited the rumors; I did not dare complain, but I was in despair."

Pushkin left Moscow on May 1, 1829; unknown to Benkendorf, he had obtained a return travel permit for Tiflis.

4. *The Journey to Arzerum**

From Moscow Pushkin went first to Kaluga, then to Belev, Orel, Novocherkassk and Stavropol. The trip was slow and uneventful, the coach was perpetually bogged down in mud, the inns were full, the only distractions were drink, food and the conversation of the postmaster or a sore and sleepy fellow passenger. However, "the transition from Europe to Asia," Pushkin wrote, "became hourly more perceptible. The forest disappeared, the hills dropped away, the grass grew thick and coarse. . . . Kalmuks have settled near the station buildings. Hideous, hairy goats graze just outside their tents. A few days ago I went to see one on the inside. The whole family had assembled for lunch. The pot was bubbling on a fire in the center, and the smoke escaped through a hole in the roof. A very handsome young Kalmuk girl was there, sewing and smoking a pipe. I sat down beside her. 'What do they call you?' '——' 'How old are you?' 'Eighteen.' 'What are you making?' 'Trousers.' 'For whom?' 'For myself.' 'Kiss me.' 'No. It's shameful.' She had a very pleasant voice. She offered me her pipe and began eating. The pot contained a mixture of tea, tallow and salt. She held out a cup to me. I didn't want to refuse and swallowed a mouthful of the liquid, trying not to breathe. I think no other folk cookery has produced anything more unspeakable. I asked for a bite to eat. I was given a piece of dried mare's meat. And contented myself with that. After this exploit, I thought I deserved a reward, but my haughty beauty gave me a whack on the head with her balalaika. Intimidated by the Kalmuk courtship customs, I hastened out of the tent and away from the Circe of the steppe."

At Stavropol Pushkin again saw those clouds on the horizon whose stationary majesty had surprised him nine years before. "They were still the same, and in the same place. They were the snowy peaks of the Caucasus."

* The modern spelling is Erzerum.

From Georgyevsk Pushkin went to the mineral springs of Pyatigorsk. Houses had sprung up and avenues unrolled in the once barren landscape, but his memories of the Raevsky family were untainted by these municipal embellishments. Pushkin thought of the demon, Alexander Raevsky, of his brother Nicholas and of the proud little Marya, who was sharing the exile of a husband she did not love. How many faces had passed before his eyes, never to appear again. Was there one in the world that would accompany him to his death? Natalya, perhaps? On May 15, at Georgyevsk, thinking of her, he wrote:

All is calm. Night is coming down over the Caucasus.
The stars are shining above.
I feel sad and weightless. My pain is so pure.
My pain lives on you.

Sanctified by memory, Natalya followed the poet on his travels. She haunted the valleys, trees, streams and sky. She was present everywhere in nature, she was nature itself.

At Yekaterinograd Pushkin bought a Circassian costume, a saber, a dagger and a brace of pistols, and hired horses to take him to Vladikavkaz. The roads were uncertain; those going deeper into the country had to wait until a post came through and travel in convoy, escorted by Cossacks, infantry and cannons. It was known as "taking advantage." On May 18, 1829, at dawn, the drum roll brought everyone out onto the square. There were at least five hundred persons in the caravan: civilians decked out with brand-new weaponry, sitting uneasily on their mounts, officers curveting around the ladies, oxcarts, green tarpaulins, uniforms, shouts, laughter, pale dust.

"To the roll of the drums," wrote Pushkin, "we started off. First came the cannon, surrounded by infantry. Behind it stretched a line of open coaches, carriages, soldiers' chariots in transit from one fortress to another, and the two-wheeled arabas brought up the rear. Along the sides of the column ran herds of horses and buffalo, with Nogai herdsmen in burkas carrying lassos. I enjoyed it all very much, but soon tired of it. The cannon crept along, its wick smoldering, and now and then a soldier went up to light his pipe from it. The pace at which we were traveling (the first day we scarcely made fifteen versts), the unbearable heat, the shortage of provisions, the restless nights, and the perpetual creaking of the native arabas jarred on my nerves. . . . At the edge of the sky, the peaks of the Caucasus rose higher every day. . . ."

At last, on May 21, the column entered Vladikavkaz, unmolested by the mountain tribes. "The Circassians detest us," Pushkin noted. "We have driven them out of their free land; their villages are in ruins; whole tribes have been annihilated. With every hour, the survivors are retreating deeper into the mountains, sending out their raiding parties from bases there."

On May 23 Pushkin left Vladikavkaz and plunged into the heart of the range. No more cannon; only a small escort of Cossacks armed to the teeth. The road wound up the left bank of the Terek. On either side rose sheer walls of basalt and porphyry, topped by dizzying crags on which the clouds snagged and tore. "The deeper we went into the mountains," he wrote, "the narrower grew the gorge. The strangled Terek roared and hurled its agitated waters over the boulders blocking its way. The rocky base of the mountain was gnawed away by the stream. I went on foot and kept stopping all the time to wonder at the somber beauty of the scene. The sky was overcast, the clouds dragged heavily along the peaks. Not far from Lars, I halted at the rear of the convoy, unable to take my eyes off the enormous boulders buffeted by the Terek. Suddenly a soldier came running toward me shouting, 'Don't stay there, sir, you'll be shot. . . .' The Ossete brigands, being safe in the gorges, fire on travelers across the Terek."

The following day they met a gang of Turkish prisoners clearing the roadway—first sign of the distant war. Now the convoy entered a doomsday landscape: The granite walls drew closer together, bristling with sharks' teeth, piercing spires and towers, sugar pinnacles; and the Terek, increasingly constricted, choked in fury, spitting out curls of spray and numbing the ears with its roar.

"A strip of sky like a ribbon stretched blue over your head. The rivulets falling in pulverized jets from the rocky heights reminded me of that strange painting by Rembrandt, *The Rape of Ganymede*. The lighting in the gorge would have been exactly to his taste. . . . Not far from the post, a narrow bridge leaps boldly over the stream. Crossing it, you feel as though you were inside a mill. The bridge is continually vibrating and the noise of the Terek is like the sound of wheels turning millstones. . . . But one's sensitivity is soon sated. Hardly twenty-four hours later, the roar of the Terek and its distorted cascades, the rocks and the precipices no longer held my attention. My mind was completely preoccupied by my impatience to reach Tiflis."

After Kobi, the last outpost on the northern slope, the climb became carpeted with wet snow. Avalanches split off the peaks and slid into the void with a deafening roar. In some places, galleries with inclined roofs protected the path leading to the Pass of the Cross, so called because a granite cross had been erected there in 1824 to commemorate General Yermolov's victory. On the other side, gentler slopes and a new warmth in the air announced the approach of Georgia. "The sudden transition from the Caucasus to Georgia," Pushkin wrote, "is exquisite. A southern breeze begins to blow upon the traveler. From the summit of Mount Gut, the view opens out onto the valley of Kashgar, with its rock-dwellings and gardens and the clear Aragvi snaking down in a ribbon of silver, the whole drawn in miniature against a background of a precipice three versts high, scaled by a perilous path. We went down into the valley. A new moon was rising in a serene sky. The evening air was soft and warm. I spent the night in the house of T. on the banks of the Aragvi. The next day I bade farewell to my congenial host and continued on my way."

At last, at 11 P.M. on May 27, Pushkin entered Tiflis, where he hoped to find his brother Leo and his friend Nicholas Raevsky. Their regiment had already moved on, however, so Pushkin wrote to Count Paskevich, the general in command of the army, for permission to go to the front. While waiting for the reply, he spent his days strolling around the town and, as usual, shocking the natives and local bureaucrats. Tiflis was really a most curious place. The mannerly buildings of the European town squared away to the north, but Pushkin carefully avoided that district. He far preferred the dusty, smelly streets of old Tiflis, with their shops full of oddments, open-air kitchens, armorers forging daggers under the eyes of the onlookers, tailors squatting needle in hand, saddlers exhaling a rainbow of powerful odors, jewelers besieged by white women with black eyes and rug merchants seated among their sails of multicolored wool like figureheads on some royal caravel. The crowd was made up of Georgians, Armenians, Persians, Tartars, Circassians, Ossetians, Germans, Russians and French, all gaily haranguing and jostling, all buying or selling. Urchins herded loiterers out of the way of a file of shaggy camels or an araba carrying oxskins filled with Kahetian wine.

Pushkin reveled in this cosmopolitan throng. One day he was seen strolling arm in arm with a Tartar. He played knucklebones with the street urchins. He went to the bazaar in evening dress with an officer's coat over his shoulders.

These innocent occupations did not prevent him from becoming acquainted with the notables of the place. He questioned them about the life, customs and folklore of the Caucasian peoples. He listened to and wrote down Georgian songs. He read. And what joy and pride he felt, too, when he discovered the extent of his fame! Even in this remote outpost of the empire, even in this little world of civil servants and soldiers, everybody recited and admired his works. The Tiflis intellectuals invited him to dinners and suppers and glorious banquets, one of which took place in a vineyard on the banks of the Kura. It was an unforgettable occasion for the poet.

"I had assembled everything of the best," wrote the organizer. "Different kinds of orchestras; singers, dancers, nautch girls, troubadours of all the Asiatic peoples living in Georgia. The garden was lit by colored lanterns and candles were set among the branches of the trees. In the center stood a shield bearing the initials of our guest of honor. . . ."

The guests shouted "hurrah!" The champagne fizzed over the rims of the goblets. A feverish orchestra played the overture to *La Dame Blanche*. In the midst of this merry din, Pushkin giddily shook moist hands, returned anonymous kisses, thanked total strangers, gasped for breath and drank like a fish. At the end, his admirers seated him by force on a mound decorated with flowers and boughs.

"Each of us in turn," the organizer went on, "came up, glass in hand, and explained to the poet in his own way how happy he was to see Pushkin among us. To all these compliments he made no reply, but the tears in his eyes showed the gratitude he felt at that moment."

At last, on June 8, Pushkin received permission to join the army. On the tenth he rode out of Tiflis with one guide, changing mounts at the Cossack posts along the road. On June 11, somewhere near Fort Gergera, a weird incident befell him. "After a short rest," he wrote, "I was continuing my journey when suddenly, above the sheer bank of the torrent, I saw the fortress of Gergera. Three waterfalls tumbled down the tall boulders, growling and boiling with foam. I crossed the stream. Two oxen were coming down the steep path toward me, pulling an araba. The drivers were Georgians. 'Where are you from?' I asked. 'Teheran.' 'What are you transporting?' 'Griboedov.' It was Griboedov's body, en route for Tiflis."

First, the encounter with Küchelbecker the convict, and now this meeting with Griboedov the corpse: Fate was amusing itself by setting these hair-raising reminders in his path. Some phantom always happened along just as he passed, to chill him with terror or remorse. "I did not think I would be seeing our Griboedov again," he later wrote. "When we parted last year in St. Petersburg, just before he left for Persia, he said to me, 'You don't know those people; you'll see, we'll have to use knives with them.' "[1]

Pushkin reached the little Cossack post of Gumri in a driving rain. It was night. Inside the tent, twelve Cossacks lay sleeping in a row. Pushkin stretched out beside them, soaking and feverish, and dropped off immediately. He awoke at dawn: "The sun was rising. A white mountain with twin peaks stood out against the clear sky. 'What mountain is that?' I asked with a yawn, and heard the answer: 'Ararat.' Great is the power of words! I stared hungrily at the biblical mountain, I saw the ark coming to land on its summit, full of hope for resurrection and life; I saw the crow and the dove, symbols of punishment and reconciliation, flying away."

The poet saddled his horse and left, with another Cossack, for the Russian frontier on the Arpachai River: "Ahead gleamed a river which we had to ford. 'There's the Arpachai,' said the Cossack. The Arpachai, our frontier. That was as good as Mount Ararat. I galloped up to the bank in a state of indescribable emotion. I had never seen foreign soil. For me there was something magic about a frontier. Since my earliest childhood, travel had always been the favorite subject of my daydreams. For many years I had lived like a nomad, roaming over the country, but never before had I escaped the confines of endless Russia. With a thrill, I urged my horse into the river, and the good animal carried me to the Turkish bank. But the river had already been taken: I was still in Russia."

On June 12 Pushkin finally reached the newly captured stronghold of Kars, but the army was no longer there; so he set out once more, with a young Armenian guide, to join the Russian camp twenty-five versts from town on the banks of the Karshchai. On June 13 he found his brother Leo, sun-tanned, full of vigor and vainglory, and his friend Nicholas Raevsky, who had recently been made a general.

That same day Pushkin went into the field with the regiment of Nizhny Novgorod dragoons under Raevsky's command. The proximity of danger made his blood boil. Did they really exist, those Turks whom everyone in camp kept talking about and only he had never seen? Would he be allowed to risk his life at last, to sneeze in the virile reek of gunpowder, slash out with his saber and be carried away in a glorious gallop to the East? Pushkin's childish eagerness amused the officers.

" 'Where are the Turks? Am I finally going to see them?' he kept asking. 'I mean those Turks who charge at you, howling and waving their swords. Please give me a chance to meet these people I have come such a long way to see, and at such great expense!' "[2]

Pushkin's prayer was answered sooner than even he may have wished. "We were still eating, with Pushkin, at Raevsky's, in the company of his brother Leo and Semichev," wrote one of the officers in the regiment, "when they announced that the enemy had been sighted at the forward posts. We rushed out to our horses, which had been saddled since morning. Before I could even get clear of camp I found myself in the midst of a group of battling Cossack and Turkish cavalry. Semichev was there and asked if I had seen where Pushkin had gone. We both galloped off in search of him and found him cut off from the dragoons and charging, naked sword in hand, at the Turks who were riding to meet him. When they caught sight of us and Yusefovich's lancers coming to the rescue, the Turks turned tail and Pushkin, to his annoyance, did not have a chance to try his saber on an Ottoman pate; but he kept close to us after that. The Turkish attack was repelled at every point, and after chasing them back to their stronghold we returned to our base position before nightfall."

Numerous witnesses confirmed this incident. One saw Pushkin "seize the lance of a slain Cossack and rush at the enemy cavalry. The Don Cossacks were quite nonplused at the sight of this unknown hero in their midst, wearing a Circassian round hat and coat."[3]

Another wrote in his recollections: "When the main body of Turks had been turned back, we saw a rider coming toward us at full tilt: It was Pushkin, in civilian coat and top hat. Pulling up his horse two or three paces from Paskevich, he doffed his hat, spoke a few words to the general from Raevsky, and returned with the reply."[4]

This civilian in Circassian burka and top hat intrigued the soldiers, who took him for a "German pope." The German pope joined wholeheartedly in the life of the camp, became immersed in the concerns of the men and told everyone he saw that he had never slept so well as in his tent or eaten so well as out of a mess tin.

"I enjoyed camp life tremendously," he wrote. "The bugle awakened us at dawn. Sleeping in a tent is extraordinarily healthy. At dinner we washed down our shashlik with English beer or champagne iced in the Tauride snowdrifts."[5]

But he was still frustrated, he could not work off his excess energy, he wanted a real fight. And the Turks were prudently refusing to commit themselves. At last, one day, a Cossack patrol collided with the main body of the Turkish army of Zeraskir, coming from Hassan-Kaley. "When Pushkin heard the news," a contemporary noted, "his African blood blazed and he began to leap up and down and clap his hands, saying that this time he was surely going to come to blows with the Turks."[6]

But General Paskevich was watching, and he did not like the looks of this tourist-soldier, this bellicose poet. To protect Pushkin from his own temerity, he contrived to keep him at his side. Hemmed in by official solicitude, Pushkin fumed at being cheated of his fight, but he did not dare try to give Paskevich the slip. So he stayed at the rear, following from afar the maneuvers of the troops in blue and the multicolored horde of the Turks. He was living the war on a map. He was surrounded by old men. Paskevich was spoiling his war.

In reality, the war had become a strategic procession through an abandoned country. The enemy had ceased all resistance, and were retreating in disorder toward Arzerum.

Arzerum capitulated on June 27, and Pushkin and the Russian troops made a triumphant entry into the Asiatic town. The frightened Turks stood on the flat roofs of their dwellings, watching the soldiers march through their streets. The Armenians crowded after the liberators, shouting and gesticulating and pushing each other under the very boots of the infantry. Street urchins scampered in front of the horses, making the sign of the cross and yelping, "Christians! Christians!" In the Russian camp, Pushkin found the general in conversation with a toothless and voluble old pasha. The pasha wanted to know the identity of the man in civilian dress and round hat.

"He is a poet," he was told.

The pasha crossed his hands over his heart, bowed gravely to Pushkin and said, "Blessed is the hour in which we meet a poet."

"We have had a letter from Pushkin, written in Arzerum," wrote Delvig. "He is having a grand time and is fully occupied, with drinking, eating and swaggering about, nagaika in hand, on a Cossack horse."[7]

Pushkin conscientiously toured the town, inspected the mosques and cemeteries and saw the harem of Zeraskir. He kept hoping the Russian troops would continue their offensive and he would finally be able to kill a few of those infidels who stubbornly refused to fight. But Paskevich, apprized of his intentions, summoned him and said, "Mr. Pushkin, I am sorry for you: Your life is precious to Russia, and you have no place here; I therefore advise you to leave the army immediately."

Pushkin bowed stiffly and fled, crimson with anger and humiliation. They were rejecting him. Like a craven civilian. Like an incompetent. So: Nobody would take him seriously, neither the revolutionaries, who would not let him into their plots, nor the military, who shooed him away from their battles. Was he good for nothing but writing verse?

Meanwhile, a plague had broken out in Arzerum, and Pushkin soon began to think that Paskevich had not been entirely wrong to send him home again.

"The idea of the plague is extremely unpleasant," he wrote, "especially when one is unaccustomed to it. To overcome my repugnance, I determined to take a walk through the bazaar, and I had stopped in front of an armorer's shop to examine some dagger or other when I felt a touch on my shoulder. I turned: Behind me stood a horrible beggar. He was pale as death, with tears dribbling out of his red, purulent eyes. The thought of the plague came into my mind again. I pushed him away in disgust and went home, very dissatisfied with my walk. But curiosity got the better of me: Next day I went to the plague camp with a doctor. I dismounted and took the precaution of placing myself upwind of it. A patient was brought out of the main tent: He was chalk-white and he staggered like a drunk. Another lay unconscious. I saw two Turks holding one man by the arms, undressing him, feeling him over, as though the plague were no different from a common cold. Contemplating their indifference to danger, I was, I confess, filled with shame at my European squeamishness, and quickly went back to town."[8]

On July 21 Pushkin abandoned Arzerum, without having killed any Turks, captured any cannons or laid hands on any plague victims.

On August 1 he was in Tiflis again, where he made a pilgrimage to

Griboedov's grave; and on the sixth, after a fresh round of receptions, praises, suppers and banquets, he set out to revisit the Caucasian mineral springs. Three days after his departure the *Tiflis News* published the following item: "On August 6 Alexander Pushkin, back from Arzerum, left Tiflis en route for the Caucasian mineral springs. All friends of art will now await the admirable gifts with which Pushkin's genius, stirred by his memories of the Caucasus, cannot fail to enrich our literature."

The journalist's desire was soon satisfied. The poet's second visit to the Caucasus inspired an autobiographical essay, *The Journey to Arzerum*, and many poems: *The Ravine, The Hills of Georgia, Delibach, The Don, The Caucasus, The Monastery on Mount Kazbek*.

"In the morning, passing by Mount Kazbek," Pushkin wrote, "I saw a miraculous vision: Shreds of white clouds were streaming through the peaks; the isolated monastery, lighted by the sun's rays, seemed to be sailing through space on a sea of mist."

On reaching Vladikavkaz, Pushkin found some Russian newspapers in the home of a friend and pounced upon them feverishly. His name was mentioned—but only as a pretext for petty, nastily critical remarks. He sadly recalled the banquets in Tiflis, the crown of flowers, the toasts, the music, the exhilarating war, the old pasha's compliment: "Blessed is the hour in which we meet a poet!" This poet was clearly less blessed to the money-grubbing pen-pushers of St. Petersburg than to the brave and unsophisticated folk who dwelled in the outposts of the empire. "An article of insult," Pushkin wrote, "was my first greeting from my gracious fatherland."

Disgruntled and unhappy, Pushkin returned to gambling with a vengeance. At Pyatigorsk and Kizlovodsk, he alternated his mineral baths with protracted sessions at the card table. Having lost what little money he possessed, he set out from Kizlovodsk for Moscow on September 8, after borrowing a large sum to cover his traveling expenses—most of which passed from his pocket to that of his fellow passenger, a rabid gambler and insatiable toper named Durov.

But Pushkin had already ceased to be seriously concerned by money, critics, Turks, banquets, battles or the snow-capped peaks of the Caucasus. From posting station to posting station, the image of Natalya Goncharov began to haunt him with increasing persistence. He was going to see her again, after so long. He was going to marry her, perhaps. With such great prospects in store, there could be no room for regrets.

PART VII

1. *The Goncharov Family*

Natalya Goncharov lived with her three brothers, two sisters, mother and father in a long, low wooden house with enclosed courtyard and outbuildings on Great Nikitskaya Street. In 1807 the father, an official in the foreign ministry, had married a young woman of such fascinating beauty that the lover of Empress Elizabeth Alexeyevna had become enamored of her, and had rashly neglected his mistress-sovereign for her sake. As a result, the young Mrs. Goncharov was compelled to leave the court, and her husband resigned his post at the ministry to devote himself to the management of his family estate. The Goncharovs lived comfortably; they were prospering, producing children and contemplating the future with confidence, when fate struck the thriving household a terrible blow. In 1814 Mr. Goncharov fell from his horse, fractured his skull and emerged from his illness "melancholic." In time, his melancholy turned to madness. His wife tried and failed to have him committed; he lived in a dreamworld, a stranger to everyone and everything, rising out of his lethargy only to scream incoherences and pursue his wife with a knife. His fits of rage terrorized the children; the girls especially dreaded this father who had reverted to an animal state.

Mrs. Goncharov was forced to take over the actual running of the estate; but Mrs. Goncharov was no businesswoman. Unsupervised and ill-managed, the property rapidly deteriorated. Land, crops and the labor of the two thousand serfs attached to the estate brought in next to nothing. There was no money. The furniture grew shabby, wardrobes threadbare and meals singularly ascetic.

The memory of her former opulence only added to Mrs. Goncharov's discontentment. Accustomed to living on a grand scale, she suffered from her straitened condition and was terrified that "people" would criticize her. She worried so much about what "people" would say, she was so desperate for respectability and so addicted to moral commonplaces, comfortable marriages, stable positions and official distinctions that she seemed an obsessive old woman before her time. And yet, she was no fool; but she was soured, authoritarian, tactless in speech and awkward in gesture and excessively devout into the bargain. She had converted one room of the house into a private chapel, its walls covered with ikons and banked with burning candles and vigil lights, where a priest came to say mass every Saturday and on the eve of feast days. The remainder of the time, Mrs. Goncharov vegetated in the center of a galaxy of nuns and verbose visionaries who flattered her, promised her eternal grace, scrabbled in her purse, sold relics and maligned their benefactress' servants and friends. With their aid, Mrs. Goncharov became more superstitious, mistrustful, narrow-minded and tyrannical with every passing year. Her daughters were brought up more strictly than novitiates in a convent. They rose at dawn and were in bed by ten. If their mother called them at an unusual hour, they immediately assumed they had committed some grave sin and entered the room crossing themselves and whispering King David's psalms. The children were forbidden to raise their voices or to engage in serious conversation with a guest. They were forbidden to read any book that was even "tinged with romanticism." They were forbidden to argue at table. The slightest infraction of the regulations was punished by a prompt and rousing slap. For the rest, the young ladies' education was limited to dancing and French: For girls are made to marry rich husbands, and you cannot marry a rich husband unless you know how to speak French and dance a quadrille.

Mrs. Goncharov's two older girls were not particularly prepossessing: Katerina was tall, heavily built and vague, and Alexandra had an unpleasant squint. Mrs. Goncharov had invested all her matrimonial hopes in her youngest daughter, Natalya. Natalya's beauty was worth all the estates and serfs in the empire. Thanks to her, they could expect a liberal return of fortune.

But there was no time to lose. In 1828, when Natalya was only sixteen, Mrs. Goncharov gave her a spectacular launching into an unsuspecting world, and the world was properly dazzled. Every amateur of pretty women was enchanted by the cold, timid nymph. The private diaries and letters of the day bear witness to this chorus of acclaim:

"In my lifetime I have seen beautiful women who may have been more alluring," wrote Count Sollogub, "but never have I encountered one as wholly and classically perfect of face and figure. She was tall, with a deliciously slender waist and splendid bust, above which her delicate head swayed like a lily; I have never had occasion to contemplate a profile as fine and regular as hers, and what skin, what teeth, what eyes, what ears! Yes, she was a real beauty, and it was natural that her presence should make even the most charming women turn pale with envy.

She always seemed reserved to the point of coldness, and spoke little."

"A creature perfect in face and form," wrote Countess Ficquelmont.

"The figure of a goddess and a delicious face," wrote Bulgakov.

"She is very young, pretty and white-skinned, with regular features and knowing eyes," wrote the poet Tumansky.

But although her contemporaries were unanimous in their praise of Natalya's physical attributes, few insisted upon her character or intelligence. For the fact was that Natalya possessed neither.

Still giddy from the lights and noise that greeted her when she left her parents' home, she made her curtsies, danced, displayed herself, spoke as though she were reciting and strove to follow her maman's instructions in every particular. Little by little, however, she acquired a taste for masculine flattery and low-cut gowns. To her stupefaction, she saw that she was queen of the ball, and began to revel in her role with the simplicity of a child. But she was not there to revel; that gown had not been bought for her to revel in, or that camisole, those ribbons and that fan. This vast outlay of capital was going to have to show a profit, and at short-term.

But the season of 1828 came to an end without producing a single suitor. Unless you could count that Pushkin, that poet, who was said to earn a great deal of money and to spend even more, and had the police at his heels wherever he went. Slim pickings. Nevertheless, he must not be discouraged altogether: They could always fall back on him if Natalya did not land someone better next year. Probably it was no longer enough to be beautiful and know how to dance, speak French and embroider to attract the serious attention of these gentlemen! The modern suitor wanted a dowry too!

Pushkin departed for the Caucasus, however, and the season of 1829 opened triumphantly. Natalya was even more admired than before, people whispered that Prince Meshchersky was thinking of asking for her hand. Mrs. Goncharov was in seventh heaven. Her only fear was that Pushkin would come back, with his amorous outpourings, his protracted visits, his four-page letters, his feverish eyes and trembling hands. He might well turn Natalya's head; he could ruin everything. Ah, if only he could have stayed at Tiflis and died, like Griboedov, or fled to a foreign country, or taken a native wife. All that money spent on frills and furbelows, perfumes and laces, just to land one little man with a Negroid lip and uncombed side whiskers. What an affront to a mother! What a humiliation for a well-bred girl!

But the months went by, Pushkin did not come back and Mrs. Goncharov took heart. By her reckoning, she could last one more season. And God, to whom she was fervently praying, would not leave her with Natalya on her hands after so much effort and extra expenditure.

But there came a rainy September morning, when Natalya's brothers were drinking tea in the dining room and Mrs. Goncharov was still in bed, and a great blow was heard at the door. Someone came into the antechamber and flung off a coat. One rubber galosh sailed through the half-open door and landed at the foot of the laden table. The children stood up openmouthed. Pushkin made his entrance. His face was tense with emotion, his clothes rumpled from the voyage. He had come back from the Caucasus that very day, and his first visit was to the Goncharovs. Scarcely able to breathe, he asked if Natalya were at home. The children ran to warn their mother and sister. Mrs. Goncharov had a truly rude awakening; with her pillows plumped up behind her, she rapidly determined upon a new course: This famished aspirant must be sent away, and Natalya forbidden to see him except in her presence.

With this plan firmly in mind, Mrs. Goncharov received Pushkin—in bed, her face still congealed with sleep and her expression bleak. She answered his questions evasively, talked about the weather and Natalya's youth and social triumphs. And Natalya, duly sermonized by her mother, seemed more cold and distant than ever. Pushkin understood that he had lost. The hopes that had borne him up throughout his long journey collapsed before his eyes. Natalya would belong to someone else. Like all the others he had wanted. What a void in his heart, suddenly. What pointlessness in his existence. He found himself back in the street, woebegone and useless.

"What torments awaited me at my return," he wrote to Mrs. Goncharov afterward. "Your silence, your coolness, Miss Natalya's greeting, so vague and absent-minded. . . . I did not have the heart to speak out. . . ."[1]

His despair was short-lived, however, for mournful resignation and mental and emotional inactivity were foreign to his nature. He loved life too much to be disheartened. In his existence, every low was a prelude to a new high—no straight lines, only zigzags. Ushered out by one young lady, he ran to console himself with another; it was both a conscious method and a natural impulse. From the Goncharovs, thus, Pushkin fled to the Ushakovs, where sweet Katerina welcomed him with unfeigned joy. He let himself be teased about his matrimonial misfortunes, and the games resumed, the satiric jingles and the album of sketches, whose pages were now adorned with such items as Pushkin on horseback, lance in hand, wearing a round hat and his Circassian burka; or a panoramic view of an Asiatic town crowded with flat-roofed houses and minarets ("Arzerum conquered by me with the help of God and Katerina's prayers"); or a stern-faced woman in nightcap, who was "the maman of Kars"; and others.

Well, if nobody would have him as a husband, he would become a lover again, a Don Juan whose list of victims was not yet full. After spending three weeks at the feet of Katerina Ushakov, Pushkin went to that veritable breeding ground for girls, Malinniki, where he hoped to collect on "certain debts" from the beauties of the government of Tver. On October 16, 1829, he wrote to Alexis Wulf:

"On my way from Arzerum to St. Petersburg I made a little detour to the right . . . to collect on certain debts long overdue. . . . I have the honor to submit to you herewith an account of our affairs and those of others:

"1. At Malinniki I found only Annette, with a swollen cheek. . . . She greeted me with her customary amiability and informed me as follows: (a) Eufrasia [Zizi] and Alexandra had gone to Staritsa to admire the new uhlans; (b) Alexandra's imagination was occupied partly by the fine figure and rump of Kusovnikov and partly by the wonderful whiskers and lisp of Yurgenyev; (c) La Marguerite is growing more beautiful and innocent with every passing hour. (Annette this instant tells me she does not agree.) I have been in love with Netty for three days now. . . . We have recently learned that before going to sleep Netty makes the sign of the cross over all the objects around her bed. I must endeavor to procure (as token of my all-pure love) a chamber pot blessed by her. . . ."

Upon receipt of this letter Alexis Wulf wrote to his sister Annette: "Alexander Sergeyevich sends me news of the lovelies of Tver. I think time has no effect upon him, he has not changed in the least, he is everywhere and always the same. The return of our young ladies has undoubtedly detached him from Netty, upon whom he was lavishing his affections—whether as a substitute for someone else or simply to pass the time. . . . According to my letter from Anna Petrovna Kern, he has already gone to St. Petersburg; she shares your opinion, and says he is more cynical than before."

Pushkin's cynicism was the reaction of a healthy organism to Mrs. Goncharov's refusal. He always treated his afflictions with a dose of mischief and impertinence. And also, a dose of work: At Malinniki, Pushkin wrote a few stanzas of the eighth canto of *Eugene Onegin*, and composed his best lyric poems on the Russian winter. In November he went to St. Petersburg, where he had not been for months. And after one week he was already exclaiming, "Oh, the tedium! The tedium!"

The gray sky, the slushy snow, the sour-faced houses and the population of tight-lipped civil servants soiled his memories of Caucasian radiance. And then, St. Petersburg was also Nicholas I, and Benkendorf—who was furious with Pushkin for running off to the Caucasus without his permission. The moment he left for Tiflis, the chief of police had ordered the poet to be kept under secret surveillance all the time he was in Georgia; and on October 14, when he was back in Moscow, Benkendorf wrote: "His Majesty the Emperor, having heard through public rumor that you were traveling in the Caucasus and have visited Arzerum, has instructed me to inquire whether anyone authorized you to undertake this voyage. As for me: I demand to know why you found it expedient to break your word to me and go to the Caucasian provinces without first informing me of your intention."

Pushkin had expected a scolding, but this was a little stiff; he was being treated like a schoolboy caught in the act, he was being reminded of his "word." Humiliated and annoyed, Pushkin replied with a letter dated November 10, 1829:

"It is with the deepest sorrow that I have learned of His Majesty's displeasure with regard to my journey to Arzerum. Trusting in Your Excellency's indulgent and generous kindness and the interest you have always deigned to take in me, I make bold to appeal to them once more and give you a frank explanation.

"Having reached the Caucasus, I could not resist the desire to see my brother again, who is with the Nizhny Novgorod dragoons and whom I had not seen for five years. I thought there would be no objection to my going on to Tiflis, and once there, I discovered that the army had already left. I wrote to N. Raevsky, a childhood friend, for permission to come to the camp, where I arrived on the day of the crossing of the Sagan-Lu.

"Being in the camp, I found it difficult to avoid taking part in the operations, and so it was that I followed the campaign, half soldier and half tourist.

"I realize how false my position appears, and how rash my behavior; but at least it was not only rash, and the thought that any other motive could be imputed to it would be intolerable to me. I would suffer total disgrace rather than pass for ungrateful in the eyes of the person to whom I owe everything, and for whom I am ready to lay down my life; those are not empty words."[2]

St. Petersburg society had lost all appeal for Pushkin. His friends found him silent, tormented, embittered. He often set out in the early morning to walk to Tsarskoye Selo, and as he walked he laid fresh plans for flight or marriage—for him, they were the same thing, a means of escaping from himself, a door into an unknown universe. He had thought he would be able to forget Natalya Goncharov, to bury her beneath new faces. But the girl haunted his dreams; her refusal had hurt him more deeply than those of Katerina Ushakov, Sofya Pushkin and Anna Olenin. Was he truly in love? For the first time in his life? Was there no antidote to this sweet poison that was thinning his blood and bringing an occasional rueful smile to his face? On October 23 he wrote:

All right, let's go! I'm ready, friends, to follow you
Anywhere, anywhere you will guide my steps,
Anywhere, anywhere to flee that haughty maid!
I will go to the end of the Chinese Wall,
I will go to feverish Paris, over there. . . .
I am ready, friends, let's go; but say,
Will my pain die away on the road?
Will I forget that regal virgin who is destroying me,
Or shall I come back to her one day, to offer up
The homage of my heart to her young wrath?

The poem expressed the poet's state of mind so accurately that two weeks after writing it, he rephrased it in prose in a letter to Benkendorf: "Since I am neither married nor attached to any service, I should have liked to travel, either in France or Italy. If that is not possible, however, then I beg as a favor to be allowed to go to China with the mission which is about to leave."[3]

In the same letter Pushkin also requested permission to publish *Boris Godunov:* "It would be onerous, in view of my small fortune, to be deprived of the fifteen thousand rubles my tragedy might bring in, and it would also be a pity not to publish a work on which I have spent so much time and with which I am very satisfied."

It must have placed a strain on Pushkin's credulity to imagine that Nicholas I would ever let him leave Russia, just as the false solicitude of Benkendorf's reply must have made him smile: "His Majesty, believing that travel in foreign countries could do no good for your financial situation and would only distract you from your other occupations, has not deigned to accede to your request. Similarly, your wish to accompany our mission to China cannot be granted, for all the places in the delegation have already been assigned and could not be altered without notifying the court of Peking."[4]

A few days later Pushkin went to a ball at the French embassy in civilian dress, whereas all the other representatives of the nobility were wearing the uniforms of their provinces. Nicholas I chose to misinterpret this vestimentary eccentricity, and wrote the following note to Benkendorf, on January 28: "You might tell Pushkin that I found it extremely rude of him to appear in evening dress when we were all in uniform, and that he might at least order a gentleman's uniform."

Benkendorf transmitted the text of the imperial remonstrance to Pushkin with admirable promptitude.

Really, that was too much. Not only were they forbidding him to go abroad, not only were they opening his letters and following him from town to town like a malefactor, but now he couldn't even wear the clothes he liked. Imperial protectiveness was being extended to the cut of one's coat, the style of one's coiffure and the shape of one's buttons. An autocratic tailor was Nicholas I, for whom personal freedom began with one's underclothes. How was it possible to live in such a prison of regulations? Quickly, to Moscow and marriage, and the haven of a warm, close family! Pushkin's dreams returned to Natalya Goncharov and Katerina Ushakov. In February 1830 he wrote to Vyazemsky: "Is it true that my Goncharov is about to wed Prince Meshchersky of the Archives? And what is little Ushakov, also mine, doing these days? I intend to come to Moscow very soon."

In Moscow, meanwhile, the trading in Natalya Goncharov's beauty was brisk. The imperial court had recently arrived in the old city of the tsars, and festivities were proceeding at breakneck pace. Prince Golitsyn, the military governor, organized a series of *tableaux vivants* in his salons, enacted by the young ladies of high society. As Dido's sister, Natalya Goncharov charmed every eye, and was particularly remarked by Nicholas I. During the ball after the performance, one of Pushkin's friends danced with Natalya at length, spoke flatteringly of the poet and succeeded in gaining the ear of Mrs. Goncharov herself.

The truth was that Mrs. Goncharov was beginning to regret having sent Pushkin away. This third season was costing even more than the previous ones, and serious suitors were no more plentiful than before. Prince Meshchersky looked as though he was not going to deliver the goods: compliments, piercing glances, flowers—and nothing to back them up. But Mrs. Goncharov's resources would not survive another season. She now considered, therefore, that it would have been wiser not to drop Pushkin; he should have been kept on the line, as a last resort. She spoke to the poet's friend with unprecedented civility and asked him to give her regards to Pushkin, which commission the friend assiduously performed. Pushkin was stunned by this kind word, this greeting from "the maman of Kars." Did that mean all was not lost? The "haughty maid" was still within reach? There was no time to lose. He must go to Moscow, with or without permission. He went.

Alerted by his agents, Benkendorf immediately sent him the following message: "To my great surprise, I hear that you have decided to leave for Moscow without first informing me, as had been agreed between us. This decision on your part compels me to ask what has led you thus to break your word. I should be only too pleased if the motives for your action were sufficiently respectable to justify it. But I believe it my duty to warn you that whatever difficulties you may incur can only be attributed to your own behavior."

From Moscow, Pushkin fired off a pert reply to this reprimand: "In 1826 His Majesty the Emperor gave me permission to live in Moscow, and the following year you yourself, Excellency, allowed me to go to St. Petersburg. Since that time, I have spent every winter in Moscow and every autumn in the country, without ever requesting prior permission and without ever receiving the slightest remonstrance. . . . From the beginning of the winter, it has been my intention to go to Moscow. When we met out walking not long ago, Your Excellency asked me what my plans were, and I was pleased to inform you accordingly, whereupon you even deigned to remark, 'You are always out on the road!' "

Pushkin reached Moscow on March 12, 1830, and attended a concert the same evening. The first person he saw in the audience was Natalya Goncharov, cold, smiling and lovely, against a background of red velours, lights and fluttering mother-of-pearl inlaid fans. He was not sorry he had come.

2. *Literary and Sentimental Skirmishes*

"The thaw, my laziness, and Miss Goncharov are keeping me in Moscow," Pushkin wrote a few days after his arrival.

He went out seldom and spent whole days in the home of his friend Nashchokin, smoking his pipe and reading until he was numb. Sometimes, his host dragged him to see the gypsies, when he would listen to the songs of Tanya the Bohemian and order blinis and champagne for the whole chorus. He also went to see the Ushakovs, less for Katerina's sake, however, than because his itinerary took him past the windows of Natalya Goncharov's house. If the edge of a curtain were lifted and a silhouette glided past behind the steamy window, he was happy for hours.

While his friends were negotiating with "the maman of Kars" on his behalf, Pushkin dreamed of tender scenes of domestic bliss. He was increasingly tempted by quietude, comfort, domestic occupations and fidelity rewarded. Slowly, the paterfamilias that lurks in every male and usually rears its head around his thirtieth birthday was ripening within him. This new development in his personality charmed and faintly alarmed him, and also distracted him from his work.

"I am horrified to see how little he is writing," Sobolevsky noted on March 28, 1830.

Pushkin's fascination with Natalya Goncharov was not the only reason for his literary inactivity, however: In recent weeks the press of both capitals had launched a merciless offensive against him, led by three critics, Nadezhdin, Polevoy and Bulgarin.

Back in 1829 Nadezhdin had written that Pushkin was "cluttering up Parnassus with the bric-a-brac of his glittering small change."

And: "Poor, poor poetry! How long must she languish in the prisons of Nerchinsk, the gypsy tents and robbers' dens? Is it possible that she can speak of nothing but vice, fury and wickedness? What is this curious antipathy for all things good, pure, melodious, pleasing and high-minded? . . ."

What infuriated the poet most in these accusations was that their sole object was to portray him as a man of doubtful morals and revolutionary artistic ambitions. According to Nadezhdin, Pushkin was "a Robespierre of literature." On April 23, 1830, Pogodin invited Nadezhdin and Pushkin to dine with him together, in a vain attempt to effect a reconciliation between them.

Polevoy, Pushkin's second adversary, had been offended by a poem dedicated to Prince Yusupov, which was, according to the critic, a congeries of craven flattery. In a supplement to the *Moscow Telegraph* Polevoy announced that the prince had invited Pushkin to dine with him every Thursday as a reward, for the poet's kind sentiments and pretty rhymes.

But Pushkin's fiercest enemy was unquestionably Bulgarin, of the *Northern Bee.* He came originally from Poland, grew up in the St. Petersburg cadet corps, joined the French army and fought the Russians, and then settled in Russia at the end of the war. Swollen, bloated, with pendulous lip, purulent eyes and a harsh voice, his appearance was as unalluring as his personality. He was no ordinary journalist: He was the director of the *Northern Bee,* and had purely and simply sold himself to the third section. He published articles dictated by Benkendorf, set the authorities onto his literary foes, wrote secret reports and took commissions for recommending shops, restaurants and other commercial enterprises to his readers. This official blackmailer and paid police informer turned into a raging tiger if anyone dared to interfere with his pecuniary or artistic interests. Now, in 1830 Delvig, Pushkin and Vyazemsky decided to found a new review, the *Literary Gazette,* so Bulgarin immediately opened fire on them as competitors—especially after an article in the *Gazette* had been rash enough to disparage his latest novel, *Dmitry the Impostor.*

In writing the book, Bulgarin had lifted whole scenes from Pushkin's *Boris Godunov,* a task made all the easier by the fact that it was Bulgarin whom Benkendorf had asked some years before to analyze the play for the emperor, and he had simply taken advantage of the opportunity to make some useful notes.

Upon learning of Pushkin's charge against him Bulgarin wrote, on February 18, 1830: "To my utter amazement, I have just heard from Olin that you claim I plagiarized your tragedy of *Boris Godunov,* transposing the poetry into prose and turning scenes from your play into scenes for my novel! Alexander Sergeyevich, be worthy of your own celebrity! Can I be accused of such an idiotic thing? I have not even read your tragedy. . . . I hear you intend to publish a statement that I stole your work in the *Literary Gazette!* How will the public react? You will have to furnish proofs. . . . Does the fact that two people treat the same subject mean one must have stolen from the other? . . ."

Pushkin was not convinced by Bulgarin's exhortations, and so, in the absence of a sound defense, the journalist-spy resorted to the time-honored trick of counterattack. First, he condemned Pushkin's latest work, Canto VII of *Eugene Onegin,* on the ground that the poet had failed to produce a hymn to the glory of the Russian army after his trip to the Caucasus. This perfidious slur cast doubts on Pushkin's patriotism. "We had thought," he wrote, "that the great events on the eastern frontier which have astounded the world and earned Russia the unanimous respect of civilized nations might have stirred the genius of our poets. But we were mistaken. The famed lips have remained sealed, and into the desert of our poetry wanders *Onegin* again, pale and puny. . . . The heart cringes when the eye beholds this bleak tableau. . . . There is not one idea worthy of note in the whole of this watered-down Chapter VII, not one feeling, not one image. A total abdication. A failure. Our hopes have been deceived."

Bulgarin was pleased enough with his article; but to make his vengeance complete, he wanted to insult the man as well as his work. Pushkin suspected him of plagiarism? Why not accuse him of the same thing? Delighted with his idea, Bulgarin also wrote, in his *Northern Bee:* "For Canto VII of *Eugene Onegin,* the poet has liberally helped himself to the play *Wit Works Woe,* and also, do not be angry with me, to a certain well-known novel" (meaning his own novel *Ivan Vyzhigin*).

The *Literary Gazette*'s ironic retort: "There is a still more serious charge of plagiarism [i.e. than that of *Vyzhigin*] to be leveled at Pushkin: that he borrowed from *Dmitry the Impostor,* and with the help of his plunder was able, with his habitual cunning, to produce the historical tragedy of *Boris Godunov*—even though, by some strange concourse of circumstance, it was written five years before the inception of Mr. Bulgarin's historical novel."

The echoes of this quarrel speedily spread beyond the literary circle and rose into the government stratosphere. Nicholas I even got wind of the affair, and condescended, rather unexpectedly, to write to Benkendorf as follows: "I was forgetting to tell you, dear friend, there is another article against Pushkin, most unimaginative and unjust, in today's *Bee;* it demands some form of action. I would therefore ask you to summon Bulgarin and forbid him in future to publish any literary criticism whatever and, if possible, forbid his review."[1]

But Benkendorf was backing his spy, and replied to the emperor: "Your Majesty's orders have been executed; Bulgarin will not make any further criticism of *Onegin.* I have read the article, Sire, and must confess that I find nothing personal in it against Pushkin; moreover, the two authors have been on quite good terms for a couple of years. [Wherever had he got that idea?] Bulgarin's pen, ever loyal to the authorities, merely deplores the fact that a journey through the Caucasian mountains and the great events which have immortalized these past few years have not done more to inspire Pushkin's genius. . . . I enclose an article against *Dmitry the Impostor*,[2] so that Your Majesty may see how Bulgarin is attacked. If Your Majesty has read the book, you will have found its contents very interesting, monarchistic in particular: the triumph of legitimacy. I could wish the authors who attack the book to write in the same spirit; for an author's writings are his conscience."[3]

Nicholas was only half persuaded by Benkendorf's blandishments, and added a note to the report on *Onegin:* "I am by no means defending the author, who would have done better not to abandon himself to this form, which is highly entertaining but far less heroic than his *Poltava*."[4]

While Nicholas I and Benkendorf were thus attempting to arbitrate the conflict, Pushkin and Bulgarin were filling the columns of their respective reviews with abuse. At the climax of the battle Bulgarin published an article entitled *Anecdote,* which was about Pushkin although it did not mention him by name. In it, he wrote that the poet was "by nature a Frenchman, serving Bacchus and Pluto more faithfully than the Muses, who has expressed no useful truth, no lofty ideas, or elevated sentiments in his work, whose heart is cold and lifeless as an oyster, and whose head is like a child's rattle, filled with resounding rhymes but empty of ideas. . . . He hurls his rhymes at everything holy, boasts of his liberal views to the people and slyly grovels at the feet of the mighty. . . ."[5]

Pushkin was literally floored by this new affront. What would Natalya and her mother say when they read it? And how was he to get back at this plagiarist, this informer, this counterfeiter, who was protected by Benkendorf himself? "They have set the dogs on Pushkin," wrote Shevyrev. And Pogodin: "It saddens me to see how deeply these scurrilous insults wound him. . . . *O irritabile genus!*"

In his anxiety over the possible repercussions of Bulgarin's *Anecdote* upon his sentimental affairs, and in the absence of support from any other quarter, Pushkin lost his head and turned to the one man on earth who would not and could not understand him: Benkendorf. On March 24, 1830, he wrote to the chief of police:

"Despite four years of unwavering good conduct, I have not managed to secure the trust of the authorities. It pains me to see how every move I make arouses suspicion and ill will. . . . If, thus far, I have escaped official disgrace, I owe it not to any knowledge of my rights and duties, but to your personal benevolence. But if tomorrow you cease to be minister, the following day I will be 'inside.' Mr. Bulgarin, who claims to have some influence over you, has become one of my most ruthless enemies because of a critical review which he attributes to me. After the infamous article he has written about me, I believe him capable of anything. I cannot refrain from informing you of my relationship with this man, for he could do me infinite harm.

"From Moscow, I was intending to go to the country, in Pskov; if Nicholas Raevsky comes to Poltava, however, I crave Your Excellency's permission to join him there."[6]

On April 3 Benkendorf replied:

"I cannot see quite why it pleases you to imagine your position as precarious; I do not find it so, and it seems to me that it depends solely upon you to make it still more firm. You are wrong, also, to believe me influenced against you by any force whatever, for I know you too well. As for Mr. Bulgarin, I have never spoken to him about you for the simple reason that I do not see him more than two or three times a year, and of late, only to reprimand him. But I admit that your recent precipitous departure for Moscow must have aroused suspicion.

"With regard to your request to go to Poltava to see Nicholas Raevsky, I am to inform you that His Majesty, to whom I submitted the question, has deigned to reply that he most particularly forbids you to make this trip because he has reason to be dissatisfied by the recent conduct of Mr. Raevsky. You will consequently be persuaded that by following my good advice, you will avoid a recurrence of the *faux pas* you have so often committed in the past, without consulting me."[7]

Since no help was to be forthcoming from Benkendorf, Pushkin decided to fight alone. On April 6 the *Literary Gazette* published an article by him on a police official named Vidocq, whose personality was strangely reminiscent of that of Bulgarin: "Imagine to yourselves a man without name or country, subsisting on a daily fare of gleanings from informers, married to one of those poor creatures whose functions necessitate her constant surveillance [Bulgarin had married a prostitute], a sort of low cad, shameless, contemptible; and then try to imagine what the works of such an individual could be. . . . Who would have believed it? Vidocq is sensitive! He flies into a rage on reading a journalist's criticism of his style. He writes reports against his enemies, accuses them of debauchery and liberalisn, and carries on about honorable feelings and independence of convictions."

This article created a furor. One St. Petersburg bookseller informed the public that he could sell authentic portraits of Vidocq to his clientele: pictures of Bulgarin, subtitled "Vidocq." At this, Bulgarin lodged an official complaint, after which the "portraits" were confiscated by the police and the censor's office prohibited the publication of any further articles on "the French police agent Vidocq." Pushkin countered with an epigram:

That you are Polish is no great evil . . .

Then Bulgarin, losing all restraint, attacked again, in the *Northern Bee:* not Pushkin's work, not even his person, but the respectability of his ancestors: "It is said that Byron's high birth and aristocratic eccentricities, coupled with a deplorable mentality, have turned the heads of poets and versifiers in many countries, all of whom have begun talking about their six hundred-year-old lineage. Pray heaven that this instills in them a desire to be worthy of their ancestors (if they have any); but even so, it cannot give more fluency or spirit to their verse and prose. . . . It is public knowledge that a Spanish-American poet and fervent emulator of Byron, who is the offspring of a mulatto or mulatress, I forget which, began to claim that one of his ancestors was a Negro prince. City Hall archives subsequently established that there had indeed been a lawsuit between a captain and his lieutenant over the disputed possession of a Negro. The captain proved that he had bought the man for a bottle of rum. Little did he think that day, that a certain maker of verse would later boast of his descent from this Negro. *Vanitas Vanitatum* . . ."

To this outrage, Pushkin replied with a broadside:

Figlarin* in his study says
My black forefather Hannibal
Was purchased by a captain
For a bottle of rum.
That was the captain
Who awakened our land
And piloted our ship
On its course to sovereignty.
He saw my ancestor's true worth
And the Negro he had bought
Grew up, loyal, by his side,
More friend than slave.
Figlarin, new-inspired, now calls me
A bourgeois with pretensions
To nobility. But he:
Who heads his family tree?
A nobleman from Bourgeois Street.

"Bourgeois Street" was the prostitutes' district of St. Petersburg, and it was in one of its brothels that Bulgarin had found his wife.

* Surname for Bulgarin.

This exchange of articles, epigrams and personal insult was not to Pushkin's liking. He defended himself because he had to, but he would gladly have dispensed with a controversy whose echoes were attracting the attention of both the authorities and his potential mother-in-law. Despite drawing-room gossip and the advice of the nuns' conclave, however, the poet's matrimonial prospects were looking brighter every day. He was being received regularly and cordially in the Goncharov home, where he chatted with Natalya, who smiled and blushed at nothing and Mrs. Goncharov, who did her best to appear amiable. But her eyes never ceased their scrutiny of her candidate son-in-law, weighing him up, taking him apart, piercing his soul in an attempt to read his innermost thoughts. Sometimes, if Pushkin spoke disparagingly of certain religious beliefs or allowed himself a reservation about the sacred person of the late Emperor Alexander I, she would fly into a temper and complain of his atheism, his revolutionary ideas and even his past misdemeanors, whereupon Pushkin would grow bearish, Natalya would sulk moist-eyed and Mrs. Goncharov would go off to pay a visit to her private chapel at the back of the house, after which order would be restored and Pushkin would leave Natalya's home with the impression that he had gained another inch or two of ground. Around the fourth or fifth of April, he was emboldened to broach the subject of marriage. Mrs. Goncharov heard him out with a welcoming smirk and put three fateful questions to the poet, exhorting him to answer truthfully and only after careful thought:

1. Did he believe, despite a youth of dissipation whose every detail was common knowledge in Moscow, that he was capable of giving happiness to a child as pure as Natalya?

2. Would his financial position enable him to satisfy Natalya's needs, for she was accustomed to want for nothing and deserved to occupy the highest place in the highest Russian society?

3. Was he not on ambiguous terms with the authorities, and under police surveillance?

Pushkin asked if he might reply in writing. Back in his rooms, he sat down to ask himself what he really felt, and was surprised by the anguish that poured into his heart. Until that day, he had been struggling blindly and desperately to conquer an unattainable virgin. Now that victory was within his grasp, a thousand furtive apprehensions came to torture him. Would he be happy with Natalya? She was so beautiful, so indifferent, so young! . . . Perhaps it would be madness to unite his destiny to that of such a frivolous nature? In a noble burst of honesty, he wrote Mrs. Goncharov a lengthy letter explaining his qualms and seeking her counsel:

"Now, Madame, that you have given me permission to write to you,

I find myself taking up my pen with as much trepidation as if I were in your presence. I have so much to say; and the more I think, the more gloomy and depressing my thoughts become. . . . But I shall try to explain myself.

"Only habit and long intimacy could secure me your daughter's affection; I may hope she would come to care for me in the end, but I have nothing alluring to offer her; if she consents to marry me, I shall see it only as proof of the tranquil indifference of her heart. But, surrounded by admiration, homages, temptations, will her tranquillity endure? She will be told that it was a cruel stroke of fortune that prevented her from making some more equal, more brilliant match, one more worthy of her—such comments may indeed be sincerely meant, and it is certain she will take them so. Will she not have regrets? Will she not see me as an obstacle, a fraudulent abductor? Will she not come to detest me? God is my witness that I am ready to die for her, but the thought of having to die and leave her a widow, dazzlingly beautiful and free to choose a husband the next day, is pure hell.

"Let us talk money: I pay little heed to it. My fortune has been enough for me in the past. Will it suffice once I am married? Nothing on earth could induce me to allow my wife to go without, or be unable to occupy her rightful position, to shine and enjoy herself. She has the right to demand it. To satisfy her I am ready to forgo all my own tastes and pleasures, those of a completely free and adventurous existence. But will she not murmur that my place in society is not as brilliant as she deserves, or as I should wish it to be?

"These are some of my anxieties; I tremble lest you find them all too reasonable. There is another, which I cannot bring myself to consign to paper. . . ."[8]

The anxiety which could not be consigned to paper related to his surveillance by the police; in all the other points, Pushkin was devastatingly clear-sighted. He saw the future in the cold light of day. He knew he was heading for ruin. . . . It was as though he had been blinded by a premonitory vision.

But when the vision faded and his letter was in the post, his courage returned. There were the same old chairs, objects, familiar faces. . . . What a fool he had been to let himself become so dejected. This marriage was not such an ominous undertaking as he imagined. Natalya would eventually grow to love him and his work. They would have children. . . . If only Mrs. Goncharov would not use that insane letter as a pretext to refuse her daughter's hand!

The next day, April 6, was Easter; while the bells were pealing riotously all over town, Pushkin sat awaiting the answer to his strange confession. He described those hours in an autobiographical fragment which he marked "translated from the French" to divert suspicion: "She whom I have loved for two years, whom my eyes proclaimed everywhere the first, with whom a meeting was to me a blessing, God! she is almost mine! The pause before the last card, the torments of remorse, the dreams of the night before a duel are as nothing by comparison. The fact is that it is not only her refusal I fear. A friend of mine used to say, 'I don't understand how anyone can make a proposal of marriage unless he knows beforehand and beyond any shadow of a doubt that he will be shown the door.'. . . To marry! The words are easy to say. I am getting married. That is, I am sacrificing my independence, my luxuries, my roving life, my solitude and my inconstancy. I am doubling an already incomplete existence, and I shall begin to think in the plural: 'we.' Happiness is the goal of life, but I have never looked for it: I could get along without it. Now I need enough for two, and where am I to find it?"

While Pushkin was thus expatiating upon the pros and cons of the step he had taken, a servant brought him the reply. The poet opened the envelope with shaking hands. It was: Yes. He wanted to run straight to his betrothed. He had brought no evening dress. He borrowed Nashchokin's. Throw on a coat, knot a cravat, smooth down his hair—so much bother! In the same fragment, supposedly "translated from the French" (in which Natalya is called Nadenka), he wrote: "I have been accepted. Nadenka! Angel! She is mine. Every gloomy doubt is vanquished by that radiant thought. I leap into a carriage, race through the streets, here is their house. I go into the antechamber; already, from the servants' fluster, I understand that I am the fiancé. A disturbing thought: All these people knew the secret of my heart, they have all been talking about my love in their ancillary language. The mother's eyes are red. Nadenka is called. She comes, pale and embarrassed. We are blessed. Nadenka holds out her cold, limp hand. The mother begins talking about trousseaux. Thus, our hearts have no more secrets. Today it is family news, tomorrow it will be public news."

Leaving his fiancée's home, Pushkin blissfully contemplated the sunlit town, the new grass starting between the paving stones, the painted eggshells heaped at the entrances of the houses. Through the baker's grille wafted smells of fresh pastry, sweet cream cheese, and paschal confectionery. The sky was blue, bells were ringing, birds were flying high and swift. Pushkin joined in the great springtime carol; he felt full of pride and vitality, he was triumphant. A little worried too: He was going to have to think about trousseaux, income, land, milliners. He was going to have to write his parents, and Benkendorf.

To the former he wrote, in French: "I am going to marry a young woman whom I have loved for a year, Miss Natalya Goncharov. I have her consent and that of her mother. I ask your blessing, not as an empty formality, but because I am profoundly convinced that it is necessary to my well-being."

The occasion being a solemn one, the father's reply was also in French: "A hundred thousand blessings upon the day of yesterday, my dear Alexander, for bringing us the letter from you. It filled me with joy and gratitude. Yes, dear friend, that is the word. I had long forgotten the sweetness of the tears I shed in reading it. May heaven shower its blessings upon you and the sweet companion who is to make your happiness. . . . I have some land which came to me in entail from my late father: two hundred peasants, without let or hindrance; I give you full and complete use of them already. They can produce four thousand rubles a year now and perhaps in time will give more. . . ."

Pushkin also wrote to Benkendorf, asking him to allay Mrs. Goncharov's fears on the subject of his relations with the police. It was an extremely difficult letter for him to compose. How ridiculous, that his precious secret had to be endorsed by mustachioed confidential agents with epaulets and Brandenburgs.

"General," he wrote on April 16, 1830: "It is most distasteful to me to have to write to the authorities about a purely personal matter, but my position and the interest you have been good enough to take in me compel me to do so. I am to marry Miss Goncharov, whom you must have met in Moscow; I have her consent and that of her mother. Two objections were raised: my fortune, and my relations with the government. To the former, I was able to reply that my resources were sufficient, thanks to His Majesty, who has enabled me to earn a respectable living from my work. But as to my position: I was unable to deny that it was unclear and dubious. Expelled from the service in 1824, I am still under the cloud of this stigma. I left the school in 1817 with the rank of tenth undersecretary, and never received the two additional grades to which I was entitled, my superiors having failed to include me in the lists and I not having bothered to remind them. With the best will in the world, it would now be very trying for me to return to the service. A completely subsidiary post such as my rank would qualify me to hold would not be suitable. It would distract me from my literary occupations, which are the source of my livelihood, and would only cause pointless and needless distress and worry. I must, therefore, think no more about it. Mrs. Goncharov is afraid to give her daughter to a man who has the misfortune to be in disfavor with the emperor. My happiness depends upon a kind word from him for whom my devotion and gratitude are disinterested and boundless. . . ."[9]

Benkendorf's reply was a masterpiece of subterfuge, in which compliments, rebukes, advice and protestations of sympathy were artfully interwoven:

"His Imperial Majesty, having learned of the marriage you are about to contract and expressed his benevolent approval, has deigned to observe that he trusts you have carefully examined your conscience before taking this step and have found yourself to possess the necessary qualities of heart and character to make a woman's happiness, particularly a woman as delightful and interesting as Miss Goncharov.

"As to your position in relation to the government, I can only repeat what I have so often said to you before: Your position is perfectly in accordance with your interests and there can be nothing unclear or dubious about it unless you choose to make it so. Prompted by his wholly paternal concern for you, His Majesty the Emperor has deigned to instruct me, General Benkendorf—not the chief of police but the man in whom he is pleased to place his confidence—to observe and guide you with his counsel. No police have ever been given orders to place you under surveillance. The advice which, as a friend, I have given you from time to time cannot but have been useful to you, and I hope you will come to find this increasingly true. What shadow can be cast upon your position in this respect? You have my permission to show this letter to anyone to whom you think it should be shown."[10]

The same letter informed Pushkin that the emperor authorized the publication of *Boris Godunov*.

"Victory, dear heart," Pushkin wrote to Pletnev at the beginning of May. "The emperor has authorized me to publish *Godunov* in all its virgin splendor. . . . If you only knew what a little wife I have found myself!"

And to Benkendorf he sent a letter of heartfelt thanks, which Von Fok transmitted with the following comment: "I append to my letter a scribble from your famous Pushkin. These lines are typical of him in all his heedless irresponsibility. Unfortunately, he is a man who thinks about nothing but is ready for anything, all his actions are dictated by the impulse of the moment."[11]

The official betrothal of Alexander Sergeyevich Pushkin and Natalya Nikolayevna Goncharov took place on May 6, 1830. Opinion as to the desirability and prospects of the union was divided:

"You, as our foremost romantic poet, owed it to yourself to wed the foremost romantic beauty of our generation," wrote Vyazemsky.

"Our greatest Muscovite beauty, Miss Goncharov, is to be pitied. She is marrying Pushkin," wrote Mukhanov.

"My sister tells me of the forthcoming marriage of Pushkin and Miss Goncharov, the most perfect beauty in Moscow. I wish every happiness to the couple, but what real hope can anyone have who knows Pushkin's vices and mentality. . . . How many pairs of horns will crown his brow; for his first act will be to pervert his wife!" was the opinion Wulf recorded in his diary.

Bulgakov attributes the following assessment of his marriage to Pushkin himself: "Do not imagine it will be the last foolish thing I shall ever do."

And Mrs. Khitrovo, the eternal Erminia, wrote to him: "It is the prosaic side of marriage that I fear for you. I have always believed genius could thrive only in perfect independence, maturing through a series of ordeals, and that a perfect, positive, uninterrupted, and, in the end, rather tedious and monotonous happiness emasculated men and led to obesity and humdrummery rather than great poetry! And after a moment of personal pain, that is the thought that struck me most forcibly."[12]

Pushkin replied, on May 19, 1830: "Your thoughts on my marriage would be perfectly correct if you had seen me in a less poetic light. The fact is that I am humdrum and wish for nothing better than to become obese and happy, although one is easier to achieve than the other."[13]

In reality, Pushkin was no longer very sure whether in asking for Natalya's hand he had brought off a master coup or made a disastrous error. She was, of course, adorable, desirable, unique—but what a pity she was not also an orphan. With every day that passed, the altercations between Pushkin and Mrs. Goncharov grew fiercer and more frequent. Pushkin wanted the wedding to take place as soon as possible, but Mrs. Goncharov was being difficult. She was still of the opinion that she had made a bad bargain when she gave her daughter to Pushkin, and she held the poet to blame for this misalliance. She never missed an opportunity to pass on to him all the gossip that was circulating on his account, to pity Natalya, or to bewail the meagerness of these literary marriages. Pushkin gritted his teeth, avoided open clashes and rushed about collecting from his debtors, paying off his own gambling debts and making preparations for the couple's future. Mrs. Goncharov surveyed all this petty money-grubbing activity with disdain, and finally announced that she would not marry her daughter without a trousseau. It was a matter of principle. Pushkin must understand that "poor Natalya" would be the laughingstock of her friends if the betrothal basket were not overflowing with expensive gifts. But where was the money to be found to order gowns in sufficient quantity and of sufficient splendor? Mrs. Goncharov had no resources at all, and Pushkin was hardly better off. Secretly hoping that a more desirable match for Natalya might still be found, Mrs. Goncharov accordingly announced that she wished to postpone the wedding. But Pushkin would not hear of it. What a madman he was, that man. A veritable Negro! He even boasted that he could pay for a trousseau! He badgered Natalya's grandfather, who lived at Polotnyany Zavody, until the old man promised to provide a dowry for his granddaughter—on one condition: Old Goncharov had a huge and hideous bronze statue of Catherine II in his cellar. If Pushkin could obtain the government's permission to melt it down, the sale of the metal should easily cover the cost of a trousseau, because it must be worth something like forty thousand rubles. Pushkin wrote to Benkendorf. Permission was granted. But then the experts appraised the value of the metal at a maximum of seven thousand rubles, whereupon the grandfather said it was really not worth the trouble of bringing it out of retirement, and instead of providing a dowry, begged the poet to obtain a little government pension for him in his old age.

This setback nearly discouraged Pushkin. But he went to St. Petersburg to collect a few more debts and see to the publication of *Boris Godunov*.

"No police have ever been given orders to place you under surveillance," Benkendorf had written on April 28. But on July 18 Miller, the chief of Moscow police, signed the following report: "Alexander Sergeyevich Pushkin, who is subject to secret police surveillance, left Moscow on the sixteenth of this month for St. Petersburg. During his stay here, we observed nothing reprehensible in his conduct."

The poet's friends in the capital were amazed by the new man who confronted them, proud and austere. Pushkin thought continually about his fiancée, he spoke of her ecstatically, impatiently, to all who had not met her. His happiness, so to speak, clothed him in his Sunday best. He wrote respectful and flowery letters to Natalya:

"I kiss the hands of Natalya Ivanovna, whom I do not yet dare to call maman, and yours too, my angel, since you will not yet allow me to kiss your lips."[14]

"I seldom go out. Your arrival here is impatiently awaited. All the lovely ladies ask to see your portrait and will not forgive me for having none to show them. I console myself in its absence by spending hours on end in contemplation of a blond madonna who is your absolute twin; I would have bought her except that she costs forty thousand rubles."[15]

The blond madonna was probably one by Perugino which Pushkin saw in the home of his friend Smirnov. He told everyone he was getting married so that he could have his own madonna at home, and dedicated a sonnet to Natalya entitled *Madonna:*

My wish is granted, since the Lord has offered
You to me on earth, O my madonna,
Pure symbol of the most pure beauty.

The date for his wedding to the madonna was set for May, then postponed until September. On August 10 Pushkin left St. Petersburg, his affairs in order and his old loves interred, to return to Moscow, his chilly fiancée, and his scalding mother-in-law-to-be. On the fourteenth he arrived. On the twentieth Uncle Basil died, his ill-timed demise forcing Pushkin to delay the wedding for another six weeks.

There were other, more serious obstacles: While Pushkin was away, Mrs. Goncharov had allowed herself to be set against him, and was now demanding more time, further explanations and additional expenditure. Scene followed scene, with "the maman of Kars" dropping words like "debauchery," "indigence," "police," and "atheism" into the discussion, along with the name of every woman and girl Pushkin had ever loved. She shouted. Pushkin shouted back. Natalya was too frightened to disagree with her mother or offend her fiancé. Passive and tearful, she sat, a spectator to the conflict between the rage-empurpled matron and the wrath-green little man with the demented eyes and great claws. In his heart, Pushkin reproached Natalya for her apathy. He felt she was a sort of object-prey, not an ally: a piece of merchandise, a thing. On August 31 he was to leave for Boldino, to take possession of the farm and serfs his father had given him. On the eve of his departure, he quarreled with Mrs. Goncharov so violently that when he rushed out of the house, he felt sure that all was over between him and the entire family. Before leaving Moscow he wrote three letters, all of which are significant.

To his fiancée, first, he sent a laconic note: "I leave for Nizhny uncertain of my fate. If your mother is determined to break off our marriage, and you to obey her, I shall subscribe to whatever reasons she may choose to give, be they even as rational as the scene she made yesterday and the insults she is pleased to proffer so liberally to me. Perhaps she was right, and I wrong to believe for a moment that happiness could be for me? In any event, you are perfectly free, and I give you my word of honor never to belong to anyone else or to marry at all. A.P."[16]

To Princess Vyazemsky, he wrote the same day: "I am leaving, after quarreling with Mrs. Goncharov. The day after the ball she made the most ludicrous scene you could imagine. She said things to me which in all conscience I could not accept. I do not know whether my marriage has been broken off, but the opportunity is there, I have left the door wide open. . . ."

Lastly, to Pletnev:

"Dear chap, I must unburden myself to you. What a deplorable business! Oh, the tedium, the tedium! The life of a thirty-year-old fiancé is more abominable than thirty years of the life of a professional gambler. The affairs of my future mother-in-law are in a dreadful way. Every day my marriage is postponed a little longer. In the meantime, my enthusiasm begins to wane, I think of the cares of married men and the delights of bachelorhood. Also, all the Moscow gossip reaches the ears of my fiancée and her mother, and leads to more misunderstandings, pointed innuendoes, precarious reconciliations; in a word, I am neither unhappy nor happy. Autumn is approaching, my favorite time of year: Usually, my health improves then, and my literary work calls me. But instead, I am supposed to be spending my time on a trousseau and a marriage that will take place God knows when! It is not very cheering, all this. I am going to the country. God knows whether I shall be able to work there, or recover the stability without which it is impossible to create anything more than Kachenovsky's epigrams!

"There, dear fellow, one must never go looking for trouble. What devil drove me to dream of happiness? As if I were made for happiness! Freedom should have been enough for me. . . . It is all very sad, my friend."

Pushkin left Moscow in a state of uncertainty. He would have preferred a clean break to this slow poison of doubt. Sometimes, he felt what a relief it would be not to have to think any more about trousseaux or Mrs. Goncharov or a home for the future couple or his husbandly carpet slippers. But the next moment he was sick with anguish at the thought that Natalya might one day belong to some pomaded gentleman "of the Archives" or a general bloated with unhealthy fat and covered with decorations.

The road was monotonous. It was hot. At the second station out of Moscow, Pushkin learned that a cholera epidemic had broken out in the government of Nizhny Novgorod and that travelers and nonresidents were evacuating the infected area. Postmasters and peasants advised him to turn back; but the very thought of seeing Moscow again chilled him with aversion, and he determined to push on. He was almost glad to risk his life for such a paltry reason; death itself would be preferable to the worries that had been dogging him for weeks: "If I had not been in such an evil temper when I left for the country," he wrote to his fiancée afterward, "I should have returned to Moscow from the second station, when I heard that Nizhny was being decimated by cholera. But as it was, I would not have dreamed of turning back and desired nothing more than the plague."[17]

On September 3 Pushkin reached Boldino without mishap.

3. *Boldino*

The village of Boldino was a wretched huddle of hunched, thatched isbas. On a rise overlooking the hamlet stood the master's house, built of wooden uprights with plank roofing, and surrounded by a crooked palisade. No garden. No flowers. The courtyard was a sea of mud, inhabited by scrawny, cackling fowls. On all sides stretched the steppe, rolling, bare, yellow. A strong odor of ammonia and rotting vegetation rose from the black earth. Slow-moving, lazy, dirty peasants prowled the fields like phantoms. Pushkin was enchanted with the ugliness, the poverty, the sinister monotony of the scene. This cloud-torn sky, this empty space and solitude were exactly what he needed to forget Natalya. But five days after his arrival he received a letter from her, recalling him to Moscow and promising to marry him "with or without a trousseau." It was hopeless; that child and her rags and her dowry and her mother would pursue him to the ends of the earth. Couldn't they let him catch his breath for one moment? Did they think he had nothing better to occupy his mind than dresses and columns of figures? Pushkin replied in tones of restrained civility: "My very dear, my very sweet Natalya Nikolayevna, I thank you on my knees and implore your forgiveness for the worry I have caused you. Your letter is charming and has completely reassured me. My stay here may be protracted by an unforeseen development: I thought the land my father gave me was a separate piece of property, but it turns out to be part of a village of five hundred peasants and there will have to be a division. . . ."[1]

We must look elsewhere for Pushkin's real response to her letter. On September 9 he scribbled in the margin of a manuscript: "Letter from Natalya. You'll see: What will happen is that nothing will happen."

The same day, he opened his heart to Pletnev: "My melancholy thoughts have fled and I am resting. Cholera morbus reigns on all sides. Are you acquainted with that animal? At any moment it may come to Boldino and devour us all to a man. . . . You cannot imagine how cheering it is to run away from one's fiancée and begin writing. . . . I had a very sweet letter from her today, promising to marry me even without a trousseau. We can always find a trousseau somewhere. She calls me back to Moscow. . . . Ah, my good fellow, what an exquisite place this village is! Only think! The steppe and nothing but the steppe: of neighbors, not a trace. Ride as far as you like, write as long as you please, nobody to disturb you. I shall prepare some of each for you, prose and verse."

In this bleak setting, Pushkin savored a calm he was never to know again. He busied himself minimally about his estate, heard the peasants' grievances, read out his instructions to them—in the church, if you please!—regarding the perils of cholera, signed official documents to hasten the division of the land and muzhiks, rode his horse over the grassy plains, flushed birds in the skimpy undergrowth and returned to the old wooden house, covered in mud and soaked to the skin, in joyful anticipation of the work awaiting him on his desk. There, between four cracked walls, with the rain slashing at the landscape of mud, puddles and sky behind the windowpanes, he exiled himself from time and space. Eternity began on the sheet of white paper beneath his hand. Never had so many thoughts and melodies assailed him before; his body was the center of an extraordinary magnetic field, he was vibrating in unison with the world. And the lines that flowed from his pen had a perfection that charmed even him. In *Autumn,* he wrote:

In my head hums a swarm of thoughts,
And light rhyme runs out at their call,
Fingers reach for pen and pen for paper.
A flash, and the lines pour freely out,
As on a dozing, motionless ship,
When suddenly all hands leap to the rigging,
Below, aloft, the sails fill in the breeze,
The mastodon shivers and cleaves the seas.

From time to time he received a letter from his betrothed, recalling him to the life he had left behind and would have to return to one day.

On September 16 the court of estates legalized Sergey Lvovich's donation to his son. Pushkin began to think of going back, but without enthusiasm. Quarantine barriers had been set up around several areas. The roads were full of ruts and water. And then too, the silence of Boldino was a poor preparation for the inevitable offensives of Mrs. Goncharov. He even wondered if it would not be more sensible to give up the whole idea of marriage. No woman was worth the sacrifice of this wonderful freedom. On September 29 he wrote to Pletnev: "It was my mother-in-law, not I, who put off the marriage because of the trousseau. I was furious. My mother-in-law began to treat me more and more coldly and to seek stupid quarrels with me, to my intense exasperation. I became utterly depressed and sank into despair. I did not want a break and was not looking for a break; but then I realized that the break had come, and have consoled myself as best I could. All you say of society is true, and therefore I am right to fear that the aunts, grandmothers and sisters will turn my young wife's head with their inanities. . . . Baratynsky says the only happily married men are imbeciles. . . . I have completed my business here and am setting out for Moscow across a series of quarantine barriers. . . ."

On September 30 Pushkin left Boldino, but without much hope of getting through: "I have just been told there are five quarantine barriers between here and Moscow," he wrote to Natalya, "and that I shall have to remain a fortnight inside each one; add it up and imagine what a foul mood I must be in. . . . Cursed be the hour in which I decided to leave you for this fine country of mud, plague and fire, for that is all we see. . . . Do not laugh at me, for I am really very angry. Our marriage keeps retreating as I advance, and isn't this plague and its quarantines the worst joke fate has yet invented?"[2]

Thus, on September 29 Pushkin was writing to Pletnev that "the only happily married men are imbeciles" and on September 30 he was telling his fiancée how he cursed to see their wedding day delayed. He was as sincere on the twenty-ninth as on the thirtieth; he was telling each of them the truth. He was afraid of marriage, yet he could not marry fast enough. He adored his freedom, yet he was determined to lose it. He exulted in solitude, yet he longed for the day when he would share his entire life with another.

He set out on September 30, stopping first to call on a neighbor, Princess Golitsyn, who advised him against attempting to cross the quarantine barriers. According to her, the epidemic had spread to Moscow, the city had been evacuated, and all access to it was prohibited until further notice. Pushkin went back to Boldino, alarmed at the thought that his fiancée might be ill or have fled to some remote province.

"It is forbidden to enter Moscow, and here I am confined to Boldino," he wrote to Natalya on October 11. "In the name of heaven, dear Natalya Nikolayevna, write to me, even if you are not in a mood for writing, and tell me where you are. Have you left Moscow? Is there any road that will lead me to your feet? I am completely at a loss, I really do not know what to do. It is plain that our wedding will not take place this year (confounded year). But you have left Moscow, haven't you? It would be unpardonable to court danger deliberately at the height of an epidemic."[3]

On November 4 he wrote again: "On the ninth you were still in

Moscow. My father wrote and told me so; he also wrote that our marriage is off: Isn't that enough to make me hang myself?"[4]

Break off his engagement? What an absurd idea! Pushkin would have been only too happy to remain at Boldino had he not been forced to do so; but any obstacle placed in the way of his fancy was enough to make him want, automatically and desperately, to oppose it. The quarantine barriers were separating him from Natalya, so it became absolutely imperative for him to go to her. It was impossible to get to Moscow, so Moscow became the city of paradise. Early in November the anxious Pushkin set out again, but at the first barrier the inspector refused to let him pass, so back he went to Boldino once more, to write to the governor of the province for a new travel permit certifying that the population of Boldino had not been contaminated by cholera.

"Still at Boldino, at Boldino forever," he wrote to Natalya on November 18. "My father keeps writing that our marriage is off. One of these days, he will probably tell me you are married to somebody else! It's enough to drive a man mad."[5]

At last, a few letters from his fiancée reached him; but after how long! No, Natalya had not left Moscow, and she had no intention of breaking off their engagement, as she informed her betrothed in a series of colorless little schoolgirl missives censored by her mother. On Mrs. Goncharov's initiative, she exhorted the poet to observe all fast days, attend church services and return to God through prayer and contrition. Was he not being kept at Boldino by some nasty liaison with his neighbor, Princess Golitsyn? "How could you imagine I was staying in Nizhny for the sake of that Princess Golitsyn?" he replied. "Have you ever seen Princess Golitsyn? She alone weighs as much as your whole family put together, including me. . . ."[6]

Pushkin's agitation subsided, his patience returned. Cholera, the uncertainty of his marriage, the numerous suitors who were undoubtedly besieging Natalya in his absence, the money for the trousseau, the slowness of the mail, the problems of the estate: He continued to worry about all that, of course. But he also found relief from all that in his work.

As a child, Pushkin had been enchanted by the formal gardens of Tsarskoye Selo, with their miniature grottoes, historic monuments, temples of Eros and velvety greensward. That was his neoclassical period. Then came the snow-capped summits of the Caucasus, the gorges of the Terek, the Black Sea fringed with boulders and cypresses and the deserts of Bessarabia, and to their magnificence corresponded his southern, Romantic poems. Finally, with the forests of Trigorskoye, the lake, the river Sorot and the old house lost in its overgrown garden, had begun his period of Russian realism.

Pushkin perfected his new style at Boldino, where everything was conducive to sobriety of thought and expression. The drab, unrelieved, unhappy landscape intensified his love of spare, true poetry. Contemplating this scene, all in dull hues and inelegant lines, he saw that he had not been wrong to repudiate the artificial temptations of Romanticism. He felt himself called upon to celebrate those humbler beauties which poets of the past had deemed unworthy of record. A scrawny, twisted tree trunk and a puddle of water were just as much objects of pure beauty as a blue lake and the Italianate silhouette of a cypress. How could the critics fail to see that anything could be the subject of a work of art, provided that the artist himself were good enough? Oh, how he would love to have one of those partisans of florid, rumbling bombast beside him now at Boldino, to show him the naked, forsaken charm of that slope with its sparse grass, those two frail sloe trees, that broken-down fence, and that sky rent by ribbons of mist. Oh, but solitude was sweet! Oh, but it was sweet to work, when autumn had shorn the land. He wrote:

My rubicund critic, my full-bellied mocker,
Ever ready to rail at my desolate muse,
I am calling you. Come here, sit beside me.
Together we shall try to divert ourselves a bit. . . .
Look before you: a few shabby isbas,
Beyond, the black earth, a sloping plain,
And over all the thick line of cloud.
Where are you, sunny fields, dark forests, brooks?
In our courtyard near the low fence
Two puny saplings stand to charm our gaze.
Just two saplings; and one of them
Was stripped by the recent downpour,
And the yellow, sodden foliage of the other
Will pile up in the puddle with the first gust.
That's all. Not even a dog prowling the road.
Oh, here comes a muzhik, with two women behind him:
Bareheaded, a child's coffin under his arm;
From afar he shouts to the pope's lazy boy
To call his father and open up the church.
"Run. We're late. Have to have a quick funeral."

What could be sharper, more cruel and tender, than this short poem? Not one word too many, not one indulgence, not one concession to the reader's sensitivities. A single spot of color in all that gray and black: the yellow leaves. Yet the sadness that emanates from this sketch will never leave us. We know everything about this village sunk in the mud, this rough, stingy, hurried peasant who will have no truck with grief, and those two women who follow him without uttering a word of their pain. We can almost imagine what happens next. And what happens next has a poignancy far more potent than that of the gypsy Aleko, the robber brothers or the inmates of the harem of Bakhchisarai. Pushkin understood his own evolution so well that he wrote, also at Boldino:

Sleep, O torments of my youth.
Of old, I could sing only
Of deserts, the wash of waves,
The sigh of surf, and rocky cliffs,
The lofty ideal of the virgin,
And her ineffable sufferings.
But for a new age, new dreams . . .
I have watched the calming
Of the yearnings of my spring
And into the poet's goblet poured
A goodly measure of pure water.
Other images waylay me now:
I love the sandy slope,
The two sloes before the isba,
The postern gate, the lowly fence,
A few gray clouds in the sky,
The grange and its heap of straw,
The pond beneath the willows
Where ducks paddle and splash.

At Boldino, Pushkin came into the full possession of his art, and all his creative powers were unleashed. In a letter to Pletnev, dated December 9, 1830, he said: "Just between us, I will tell you that at Boldino I have written as I have not written for a long time. Here is what I am bringing back: the last two chapters of *Eugene Onegin*, VIII and IX, ready for the printer; a short story in octaves (a matter of four hundred lines), which we will publish anonymously. Several dramatic scenes or little tragedies: *The Covetous Knight, Mozart and Salieri, The Feast in Time of Plague,* and *Don Juan* [known as *The Stone Guest*]. And I have also written some thirty poems. Not bad, eh? And that's not all. Keep it to yourself, but I have composed five prose tales that will make Baratynsky rear and whinny, which we shall also publish without an author's name."

All that in less than three months. It makes one's head spin.

The two final chapters of *Eugene Onegin* to which Pushkin refers were actually composed before he came to Boldino, where he only revised and polished them. He also completed another chapter, intended to be Chapter X, which he had in mind when he went to Arzerum. It was to tell of Eugene Onegin's encounter with the Decembrists, and opened with a highly caricaturish portrait of Alexander I:

Weak but cunning despot,
Lazy dandy with balding brow . . .

and continued with a reference to the war with Napoleon and the origins of the secret societies in Western Europe and Russia. By the time he reached stanza 17, however, Pushkin realized that it could never be published in his lifetime. People had been sent to Siberia for less. Fearing a perquisition, the poet burned his manuscript of Chapter X and transcribed the text on loose leaves, using a code. The device was simple: He wrote the first lines of each stanza in order on one sheet, the second lines on the next, and so forth . . . so that in order to reconstruct the first stanza one had only to read the first line on each page, and for the second stanza the second lines, etc. Most of these loose pages were lost, and scholars have only been able to put together the first four lines of each stanza, and two and a half stanzas found intact among his rough drafts.

On September 25, 1830, Pushkin wrote the table of contents of *Eugene Onegin*, a verse novel in three parts and nine cantos. The third part contained:

Canto VII–Moscow
Canto VIII–Onegin's Travels
Canto IX–The Great World

The following year, he deleted "Onegin's Travels" (ex-Chapter VIII) and appended Onegin's letter to Tatyana. After revision and pruning, thus, the third section included only Canto VII, "Moscow," and the new Canto VIII (formerly IX), "The Great World." It was at Boldino, however, that the poem was actually completed. Apart from minor alterations, it stood then as we know it today.

"Kishinev–May 9, 1823.
Boldino–September 25, 1830.
7 years, 4 months, 17 days,"

Pushkin noted after finishing this huge canvas, of which he once said that he would never reach the end.

At the close of Chapter VI, Onegin had repelled Tatyana's ingenuous advances and killed the poet Lensky, fiancé of the coquettish Olga, in a duel. Then he went far away from the calm countryside to which he had come in search of peace only to abandon it covered with blood, leaving behind him a fresh grave and a young girl wild with love and horror.

Canto VII tells of Tatyana's shame and remorse in her now empty world. Olga's grief is soon forgotten, and, after burying Lensky, she gaily weds an uhlan, as "unpoetical" as possible. But Tatyana is unable to forget either the murder or the murderer. The malevolent inscrutability of Onegin, whom she should hate, frightens and fascinates her. She has been bewitched by this spirit of evil that whirled through her life with a sneer, and Olga is no longer there to take her mind off her morbid thoughts. She lives in a dream, sleepwalking. One day she visits Onegin's estate, and a servant allows her to go through the house. She piously contemplates the couch covered with its rug, the armchair, the little objects on the table, the lamp, the books. She picks up a volume, turns the pages, stops. Onegin had marked with a cross or made a groove with his fingernail alongside the passages which had held his attention. Reading this text of signs and symbols, Tatyana discovers the true face of the man she loves and does not love: "a Muscovite draped in Childe Harold's cape," a soulless playboy, a professional Don Juan—that is what he was. And yet, she cannot accept it. She rebels against these words, these printed phrases coming between her and her ideal image of Onegin.

Meanwhile, prompted by her neighbors, Tatyana's mother decides that her daughter is really far too pale and nervous and it is high time she was married. Now, all good marriages are made in Moscow, Moscow is the auction block for fiancées, and so the great voyage must be made. Informed of her mother's plans, Tatyana is deeply grieved by the thought of leaving the scenes of her childhood and her love. She goes for long walks, bidding farewell to every tree and flower, and the trees and flowers become the confidants of her sorrow. At last, winter comes and it is time to leave:

A wagon and three sledges
Hold the household goods;
Pots and pans, chairs and trunks,
Jam pots, bundles of clothes,
Plump eiderdowns, caged roosters,
Vases, basins, and more and more . . .
The whole motley treasure!
Here are the servants, already
Choking back their heavy sobs.
Eighteen horses are led up
And harnessed. Hastily
The cooks throw meals together.
Men load the sledges; drivers,
Women shout themselves hoarse.
The bearded outrider shinnies up
A shaggy, gaunt old nag.
The whole household runs to the door
To say good-bye to their masters. . . .

Then comes the journey along the snow-covered roads, the arrival in Moscow, and Tatyana's introduction to her countless cousins, who find her charming but excessively naïve and set immediately to work to change the way she does her hair and tell her all the secrets of their hearts. Numbly, Tatyana submits. Nothing moves her any more, nothing interests her. Onegin has killed all her desire to live or love, and the young gallants sense this so clearly that they leave her standing, a wallflower, at the ball.

Heat, milling crowds,
Music, candle flames,
Sparkling lights, flying couples,
The beauties' fine toilettes . . .
Noise, laughter, bustle, bows,
Gallops, mazurkas, a waltz.
Standing beside a pillar,
Surrounded by her aunts, Tatyana
Looks at it all and sees nothing.
She hates the din of society,
She is stifling . . . oh, how she longs
To see her gentle countryside again,
The village and the shabby serfs,
And her lonely retreat, enlivened
By a clear, running brook,
And her flowers, and the old books,
And the cool shade of the lindens,
Where *he* met her before. . . .

While Tatyana stands there, lost in her nostalgia, the aunts have spied a general, paunchy, inflated and carpeted with medals, who never takes his eyes from the girl's face. They exchange looks, jog Tatyana with an elbow:

"Quick, look over on your left. . . ."
"On my left? What? What is it?"
"Never mind! Look, I say . . .
In that group, you see, in front of you . . .
Between those two; in uniform . . .
Oh, he's going away. . . . Ah, he's turning back. . . ."
"Who? You mean that fat general?"

Chapter VII closes with the look exchanged by Tatyana and the fat, glory-swollen general. Chapter VIII opens with another ball: Eugene Onegin has come back to Moscow after several years. All the lands he has visited and the people he has met have done nothing to fill the void in his heart. He is sadder and more disenchanted than ever. He wanders like a phantom through a world he despises and from which he expects nothing. And Pushkin shares his hero's envy of those

Who were fops at twenty,
Married at thirty,
And at fifty, had paid
All their debts. . . .

They were imbeciles, but they were happy. They ran the universe, and they suffered no brain-gnawing torments.

> But it is sad to think
> That our whole youth was vain.
> Once or twice we played her false;
> She plays us false again and again. . . .

In the crowd of bemedaled and costumed puppets, Onegin singles out a young woman whose regal loveliness, unaffected gestures and open countenance appeal to him.

> Women clustered around her,
> Matriarchs beamed upon her,
> And men bowed very low to her
> Their eyes fixed upon her face.

Struck by this apparition of grace, Onegin thinks he recognizes her as the girl he knew long ago in the country. He turns to one of his friends, a general, and, raising his lorgnette, asks the name of that person by whom everyone seems so captivated.

> "What? Well, you have been out of touch!
> Let me introduce you."
> "But who is she?" "She is my wife."

Tatyana had married the old general, out of apathy and disgust. In a flash, Onegin realizes what he has lost by spurning the little provincial maid. Upon meeting Onegin again, however, Tatyana does not move an eyebrow. She makes vague small talk, to which Onegin replies, trying to fathom the secret of her serenity. Suddenly he feels that this woman alone can cure his all-consuming boredom. It is she he has been seeking all over Russia, it is of her he has been dreaming under all the heavens of his voluntary exile. And now that he has found her at last, she is married to somebody else. No matter; he must see her again. He will live to conquer her. That adipose general is no serious rival. In love for the first time in his life, Onegin writes a desperate letter to Tatyana, confessing his error, his wasted life and the impossibility for him to survive without her:

> To see you every hour of the day,
> Follow every step you take,
> Lovingly surprise
> Your smile, your look;
> To listen, the better to understand
> What makes your perfection,
> To tremble with remorse before you,
> Grow pale and die . . . what ecstasy! . . .

There is no reply. Now it is Onegin's turn to suffer the pangs of disprized love. He drags from drawing room to drawing room in the hope of meeting her. He sees her in his dreams, talks to her in his loneliness, imagines exquisite encounters that set his blood on fire. At last, at his wit's end, he breaks all the rules of propriety and enters the young woman's rooms unannounced, to find her in floods of tears, his letter in her hand. Onegin falls at her feet, kisses her icy fingers. She raises him, and speaks. She reminds him of the sermon he gave her long ago because she had dared to write to him:

Then, no doubt, in that desert,
Far from Moscow and its opulence,
I did not take your fancy. Why
Have you caught up with me now? . . .
I wish I could exchange
All this tinseled masquerade,
This luxury and noise and smoke,
For my books and my old garden,
Our modest country house,
Those places where I used to see
You, Onegin, long ago;
And for the quiet cemetery
Where my old nanny sleeps
Beneath her cross and boughs. . . .
Happiness was so close then,
So simple. . . . But my destiny
Is all laid out. It may well be
That I was wrong to yield! . . .
Well: I know how you worship
Pride and honor.
I love you (why deny it?),
But I am the wife of another man,
And shall belong to no one but him.

Having spoken, Tatyana leaves the room. Onegin is left alone, shattered by her words. In the corridor, a jangle of spurs is already drawing near. The general enters. The scene ends. And the poem.

Perhaps Pushkin was thinking of Natalya when he wrote that final chapter, still not knowing if she was to be his wife; perhaps he was imagining some future meeting with the girl he should have married, who would then be bearing another man's name; or perhaps this was a foretaste, on his hero's account, of his own frustrations once the simple girl he knew had been transformed into an unapproachable *dame*. Whatever the cause for it, this section of the poem is written in a new style. No more Byronism, no more psychological stereotypes: The Tatyana and Onegin of Chapter VIII are flagrantly "human." The development of each is logical. Onegin's late-awakening love rings true: When Tatyana abandons herself to him, he rebuffs her and gives her the casual advice of a worldly older brother; but as soon as she holds back from him, he cannot live without her. He is subjugated by both what she was and what she has become, child and woman, past and present. A man who has asked too much, refused to be content with ordinary joys and ruined his life by trying to make it unique: That is Onegin.

Yet he was not wrong to repudiate, one after another, all the scenes and faces that passed before his eyes, since there did in fact exist one setting and one face that could have given him happiness: a calm rural landscape and the pensive face of a girl. All the rest was fake. He had been looking for a diamond in a mountain of anonymous bits of glass, had held it in his hands an instant and thrown it away without recognizing it; that was his mistake. Hence, behind his mask of irony and boredom, Onegin was hiding a world of untapped affection. His heart was capable of true love, and it was only absence of opportunity that had led him to think he must be insensitive. In the instant chosen by fate, the urbane, posturing playboy suddenly finds himself more vulnerable than a schoolboy with his first crush. This last touch saves Onegin from the charge of romanticism: He ceases to be a social concept, endowed with voice and features for the convenience of the story, and becomes a man, an imperfect creature like the rest of us.

Eugene Onegin stands out as the first hero of the "realistic" novel. Pushkin had long since introduced realism into his scenery; with Onegin he introduced it into his characters as well. The prisoner of the Caucasus, Aleko and Mazeppa were artificial beings in a real setting; Onegin is a real being in a real setting.

Tatyana is portrayed with the same authenticity as Onegin. She is the purest figure in the whole of Russian literature, and Pushkin's achievement was to make her mature with the years without losing any of her initial purity. The *grande dame* must be very different from the little girl, and yet faithful to her past. Corresponding to the purity, tenderness and soulfulness of the provincial maiden, the married woman had to possess a moral texture that was equally fine, but distinct. The second Tatyana had to be the "result" of the first, not a copy or a caricature. Pushkin solved the problem by subtracting from the second Tatyana the naïveté he had given to the first. The Tatyana Onegin had known believed in fairy tales, took care of beggars, worried about animals and lived by the season. She was a child of field, flower and storm, candid, unspoiled, ignorant of men; all she knew of love came from the accounts of Richardson, Rousseau, Mme. de Staël and Mme. Cottin. And the first handsome, witty, mocking man to appear before her, as though escaped from the pages of a fashionable novel, she loved so innocently that she could think of nothing else to do but tell him so.

Rejected by him, married to the general she did not love, a social queen, adulated, praised and covered with gifts, she secretly remains a little girl yearning for solitude, fresh air and romantic declarations. But she has learned to be careful, to hide her emotions. People see her as a beauty, content with her lot and sure of her powers. And to those who do not know her, the second Tatyana can have nothing in common with the first. Even Onegin does not see; to realize his mistake, he has to surprise her weeping over his letters. Unmasked Tatyana confesses her subterfuge:

> I wish I could exchange
> All this tinseled masquerade,
> This luxury and noise and smoke,
> For my books and my old garden . . .

She even admits that she still loves Onegin, but only to add that her life has been decided and she will not fail in honor. Before, it was hard for her to confess her emotion to the handsome stranger who had fallen like an angel into her isolation; how much harder now to send him away. But she has given her word and knows her duty; and she loathes the petty, clandestine arrangements and guilty, furtive pleasures in which most women delight. She does not react like a sophisticated socialite accustomed to amorous fraud, but like the proud, upright and clearhearted little girl who grew up in the country. Despite appearances, she has not changed, she lives up to her past. Her action reminds one of Marya Raevsky, who, after her loveless marriage to the Decembrist Prince Volkonsky, seventeen years her senior, abandoned family, fortune and child to follow him to Siberia when he was condemned to penal servitude.

Like Onegin, but more than Onegin, Tatyana is flesh and blood; and however hostile to this pair the critics may have been, the readers were not misled. With each new chapter, Onegin and Tatyana gained a wider audience; they lived all over Russia, in town and country, palace and barracks, in the hearts of the men, women and girls who shared an unspoken kinship. They were even more "alive" than their author, they were everybody's friends. And when he ended their story, so simple and beautiful, Pushkin must have saddened many who had chosen them for companions in their loneliness.

As a recreation from this enormous poem which had accompanied him through so many years and triumphs and defeats, Pushkin wrote a series of short plays and prose stories at Boldino, each of which is perfect in its way.

Pushkin's brief tragedies are "crisis" tragedies, containing only the critical scenes. They have been stripped to a hard, irreducible core of passion; there are no secondary characters, no exposition and no conclusion. He had material for a five-act play, and indulged himself by treating it in a few pages. These dramatic sketches, however, are so packed with substance that they assume in the reader's mind the proportions of a work whose every ramification has been explored.

For each of his four dramatic essays, Pushkin chose a different period or setting. Trapped at Boldino, he amused himself by traveling in his mind. *The Covetous Knight,* thus, is medieval; *Mozart and Salieri,* "modern"; *The Feast in Time of Plague* is set in England, *The Stone Guest* in Spain. A single inspiration lies behind all this diversity, however; one dominant idea seems, perhaps unconsciously, to have guided the poet through all four "Boldino plays." He was thirty. He was probably about to marry. It was a crucial moment. Looking into his past, he tried to extract from his own experience the principle of an ideal approach to life. Was it right to live as he had done, letting himself be tempted by everything chance happened to place in his path, frittering away his time, strength and intelligence; or should one struggle against the current, combat fate? Submit or oppose? Accept or propose? Unwittingly, Pushkin was posing the whole problem of Providence.

The Covetous Knight shows the conflict of two concepts of human destiny. There is a son, spendthrift, superficial, reckless, brutal, caring only for the pleasure of the moment—a Dionysiac. And a father: a miser who plans and calculates, and who aspires, by virtue of his gold, to rule the world and conquer chance, perhaps even God. His son says about him:

> He lives like an aged dog. Shut up in his frozen
> Vault, he subsists on water and dry bread,
> And never sleeps at night, but runs and barks,
> And the gold lies dormant in locked chests.

In his dungeon, the old miser indulges a strange passion; his monologue, as he peers into his coffers overflowing with coin and precious stones, is a profession of faith:

> Everything is subject to my will. Like a demon
> I can, but if I will, rule the universe;
> If I will, I can build palaces,
> Watch a laughing, dancing troupe of nymphs
> Come scampering into my sumptuous gardens;
> The muses will come bearing offerings,
> Unbridled genius will heed my laws,
> Hidden virtue and long nights' toil
> Will humbly wait upon my nod. . . .
> I am master of everything. No one is master of me.
> I command all desires. My mind is at peace,
> For I know my strength. And that is enough for me. . . .

Unlike Molière's miser, that of Pushkin does not inspire laughter; he is sinister, because the heart of his passion is a philosophical concept. The higher his heap of gold, the nearer its master to God. He is already all-powerful, he already knows the pride of having foreseen everything, being able to command everything. Just a few rungs more, and he will be immortal. But those last few rungs are insurmountable. He will die, and he knows it; and after his death, all this painfully amassed wealth will be squandered by his son—his son, who has spared no effort to merit his good fortune, for he lives only to drink and laugh and fight and sing. This conflict between the man who wants to dominate fate and the man who lets himself be led by circumstance ends with the prodigal's victory over the miser: After a fierce quarrel, the knight expires and all his treasure is frittered away into a thousand anonymous hands.

In *Mozart and Salieri* the "miser" and the "prodigal" are seen from a different angle. The miser is Salieri, an inoffensive, careful, hardworking, reasoning composer, who has slowly made his way to fame, who loves his art and serves it through the noble sufferings of creation. He has talent, he knows; but he also knows that he does not have genius.

Opposite him stands Mozart, the "prodigal," whose works pour out with miraculous ease, who seems to have no knowledge of toil or doubt or failure or envy, who is so limpid, gay and unthinking that he is an offense to artistic integrity, as conceived by Salieri. He is a personal affront to Salieri, who both hates and admires him, and regards his genius as a sign of divine injustice.

> Where is justice, then, O heaven! when talent,
> When immortal genius, instead of crowning
> Devotion to art, abnegation, hard work
> And struggle, and unremitting prayer,
> Shines down to light a madman's brow,
> An idle wastrel. . . . O Mozart, Mozart!

Salieri is incensed when Mozart asks him to listen to one of his works played by a blind fiddler on an untuned instrument. And when, after sending the fiddler away, Mozart sits down at the harpsichord to play his latest composition, Salieri cries:

> . . . You were coming to me with that music,
> And yet on the way you could stop at the tavern,
> And listen to that old, blind fiddler. . . .
> Good God, Mozart! You are not worthy of yourself! . . .

Salieri's remonstrances sound curiously like those addressed to Pushkin by his friends. Like Pushkin, Mozart did not kneel down and worship his own creations. Like Pushkin, Mozart did not organize his entire existence around his work. Both sang when they felt like singing and lived the way they wanted to live. They scattered the riches of their hearts and minds to the four winds. People said about Pushkin:

"His conduct is unworthy of a man who speaks the language of the gods."[7]

"How can one throw away such a beautiful life?"[8]

Just so, Salieri says of Mozart: "Good God, Mozart! You are not worthy of yourself!"

After Mozart leaves, Salieri feels positively invigorated by his hatred. Mozart is too pure a genius not to be dangerous. He was not made for this low world. In fact, his artistic "usefulness" can even be contested, because there will be no one great enough to replace him when he dies:

> . . . If Mozart lives a long time
> And attains still higher summits,
> Will our art be elevated thereby?
> No; it will sink back to darkness at his death,
> For he leaves no one to come after him.
> Therefore, he is useless! Like some cherub,
> He has honored us with a few celestial songs
> To awaken within us children of the dust
> A will to fly, then flies away himself.
> Well then, fly! And the sooner the better!

Then, acting in the name of all obscure, hard-working men of talent, all those who know their limits and cannot equal Mozart, Salieri decides to kill him. They meet in a restaurant; Mozart has been troubled, uneasy, ever since a stranger dressed in black came to his home to commission a requiem from him. He is haunted by the fear of death, and asks Salieri whether it is true that Beaumarchais poisoned someone. "Genius and evil are incompatible!" he says.

Thereupon, Salieri pours poison into Mozart's glass. The other man sees nothing, drinks and sits down at the harpsichord to play his latest work, his *Requiem*, for Salieri.

As he plays, Salieri weeps:

> At last, I can cry. My sickness is deep, yet sweet.
> I feel as though I have performed my duty.

With Mozart dead, diligent and well-meaning men can live at peace in their pettiness, never suspecting it is Salieri they owe it to.

Like Mozart and the son of the miserly knight, Don Juan in *The Stone Guest* also throws his life away. His struggle is that of the completely free prodigal against a society whose coffers are filled, this time, with rules. Exiled from Madrid for killing the Commander in a duel, Don Juan flouts the king's decree and returns to the city in search of fresh conquests. He meets Doña Anna, the Commander's widow, on her way to the cemetery to pray at her husband's grave. This is his first glimpse of the wife of the man he struck down in fair combat. She is beautiful. He decides to seduce her, and to that end disguises himself as a monk and posts himself in the cemetery near his victim's statue. In front of the funerary monument, ignoring the silent reproach of the tomb, he engages Doña Anna in conversation. At first, he speaks to her as a holy man, then as a plain man, then as a lover. But he cannot admit to her that he is also Don Juan, her husband's murderer, and calls himself Don Diego, a Spanish gentleman.

The unhappy widow, at first taken aback by the stranger's boldness, is soon confused, weakening, yielding to the charm of his language; she tells him he may visit her at home. Don Juan exults; she is not like other women, he had thought to seduce her and finds himself seduced instead. Ah, how right he had been to despise convention and superstition, to let himself be borne by the tide of his instinct—to act as a "prodigal." He must be beloved of God; everything he undertakes succeeds at the first try. His head turned by this latest exploit, he begins to imagine himself omnipotent. He builds his luck into a "system," and imperceptibly slips from the ranks of those guided by events, like Mozart and the knight's son, into the category of those who, like Salieri and the miser, believe they can force destiny to conform to their calculations. He wants to try his strength, to defy fate: Sacrilege, punishment, death itself hold no more fears for him. Out of bravado, Don Juan invites the Commander's statue to Doña Anna's house, where he may surprise his young widow in the arms of her new lover. The statue nods acceptance, and Don Juan is terrified by this sign from the other world. But he is too sure of himself to refuse the challenge; and besides, he loves Doña Anna better than he has ever loved anyone else. Ignoring the warning, he goes to see the inconstant woman, whose confusion is a positive incitement to attack. He dizzies her with high-flown speech, entices, unseats, persuades her, until her defenses are reduced to an adorable flutter. He confesses his true identity and admits to slaying the Commander. Even so, the young woman, under his spell, allows him to kiss her. Don Juan is triumphant, stronger than laws, religions, God himself; he feels so elevated that the very notion of evil melts within him. Like Pushkin to Natalya, Don Juan confesses his sins to his angel, his "madonna," Doña Anna, and promises to mend his ways through love of her:

> I bear a heavy burden in my weary heart.
> Many years, I was a scholar of debauchery.
> But I saw you at last. Since that meeting,
> I believe I am reborn to something new.
> Loving you thus, it is virtue that I love;
> Before her, humbly, and for the first time ever,
> I bend my shaking knees and do homage.

After obtaining her promise for another rendezvous the following day,

Don Juan is about to leave, when the Commander's statue appears, takes Don Juan's hand in his grasp of stone and bears him off to the fires of eternal damnation. Don Juan dies, crying out the name of his last and only true love, Doña Anna.

The Feast in Time of Plague is, in a sense, a logical extension of *The Stone Guest*. Don Juan flaunts death in the person of the Commander, while the jolly band of *The Feast* gather to muffle with their song and laughter the moans of the plague victims who are expiring by hundreds in the city. It was Pushkin's own experience, more than his reading of John Wilson's tragedy *The City of the Plague*, that prompted him to write on this bizarre theme. Cholera was decimating the countryside around Boldino, every day the poet expected the epidemic to reach the village and begin killing off his peasants and servants; his mind was on his own perhaps imminent death, he was haunted by the thought of the last breath, the final abyss. When he first came to Boldino, he wrote to his fiancée: "I desired nothing more than the plague."

He also wrote in his notebooks: "I continued my journey as you, it may be, have made your way to a duel."

Pushkin transmitted this sense of stolid courage and Asiatic unconcern to his characters, one of whom exclaims:

> Some strange charm compels us
> To rush into battle, lean over the abyss,
> Sail through the tumults of the sea
> Amid heavy fog and towering waves,
> And into hurricanes of sand;
> And to breathe the air of plagues. . . .
> Everything that speaks of death
> Arouses in the heart of mortal man
> An inexplicable thrill of pleasure.

The miser-knight dreads death, Mozart is obsessed by the black-garbed stranger who has commissioned his *Requiem*, Don Juan flaunts the silence of the cemetery to invite the dead man's statue to a fatal rendezvous, the merrymakers of *The Feast in Time of Plague* sing of the sensual allure of danger on the brink of eternal night. The principal actor in all four of these dramas, then, is death.

The short stories Pushkin wrote at Boldino are transpositions of the plays into prose, with the same acerbity of style and the same economy of character. His dramatic essays are compact five-act tragedies, and his short stories are compact novels, propelled by the same inspirational force.

In *The Shot*, for example, we meet Mozart and Salieri again, but dressed in Russian uniform. Silvio is an officer in the hussars, swashbuckling, hard-drinking, quarrelsome, jealous, authoritarian. He is very proud of his reputation, and knows he has earned it. But along comes a new recruit to the regiment, a rich young man of great family: "In all my life I had never met such a brilliant pet of Fortune," says Silvio. "Imagine youth, brains, the most reckless bravery, an illustrious name and so much money he could never want for anything, never even count it. . . . My supremacy was shaken."

Silvio-Salieri conceives a hatred for this new version of Mozart and challenges him to a duel. But the young man arrives (as Pushkin did for one of his Kishinev duels) with a capful of cherries in his hand. The young man fires first and misses, and philosophically resumes his meal of cherries, spitting the stones in the direction of his adversary. In the face of such contempt for death, Silvio feels his lust for revenge escaping him. He refuses to kill the man who seems, just then, to set so little store by life.

"Just as you wish," the other says; "you are still entitled to your shot, and I am always at your service."

Silvio retires from the army and composes himself to wait, before claiming his right, until his insouciant foe has discovered something to live for. Several years later he learns that his rival is happily married and settled in the country. Silvio goes to see him.

"I have come to fire my shot," he says.

The reaction of the married man is no longer that of the young officer. He loves his family, his home, the whole way of life he has built; he is afraid to die, and Silvio takes cruel pleasure in his discomfiture.

At last he says, "I will not shoot. I have seen your confusion and your fear; we are even. You will remember me. I leave you to your conscience."

And, after firing his pistol into a painting on the wall, he leaves.

Like *The Shot, The Snowstorm* is a panegyric to impulse. Its moral is that faith in blind chance is often rewarded, and submission to the vagaries of fate may lead to a happy ending. Marya Gavrilovna wants to marry a corporal, appealing and respectable but poor, against her parents' wishes. They decide to elope, and find witnesses and a country pope to bless their union. On the appointed night the young man sends his sleigh to his beloved and sets out for the church. But on the way he is blinded by a snowstorm, goes hopelessly astray and does not reach the church until daybreak. The door is locked, there is no one in sight, he has missed his marriage. That morning Marya Gavrilovna, whose parents never noticed her absence, suddenly falls ill. In her delirium she cries out the name of her beloved, and her parents, fearing for her reason, resign themselves to the marriage and write to the corporal giving their consent. Shame and consternation! The young man replies that he will never wed Marya Gavrilovna; and she, on her side, rejects all other suitors. The War of 1812 breaks out, the young man is killed. Marya

Gavrilovna, at first inconsolable, eventually allows herself to be won over by a young colonel of the hussars named Burmin. She loves him, he loves her, but neither dares speak out until Burmin is finally driven to confess to Marya Gavrilovna that he would very much like to marry her, but he is already married—to a woman he does not know and will never see again. He tells how, early in 1812, he was going to join his regiment when he was caught in a snowstorm, driven off his route, and finally came to a halt, exhausted and furious, by a little church. The door was open. Some people standing in the doorway came rushing out, shouting, "This way! This way!" The priest pointed to a sobbing girl and asked, "Do you wish me to begin?" Burmin the prodigal, the thoughtless lady-killer, found the situation so comical that he exhorted the priest to perform his duty.

"'We were married. "Now embrace each other," someone said. My wife turned her pale face to me. I was about to kiss her.

"'"Ah! it's not he! It's not he!" she cried, and fell in a swoon.'"

Burmin fled, delighted with his criminal joke. But now he repents of it, because it is an obstacle to his marriage with Marya Gavrilovna. But while he is speaking, Marya Gavrilovna gradually revives and finally exclaims, "My God! My God! So it was you!" Thus chance, which had brought about the wedding of Burmin and Marya Gavrilovna, was merely anticipating the desires of these two people who were destined to love each other and did not know it. And if Burmin finds happiness with his resurrected wife, it is because he was willing to let chance have its way with him.

It is chance again, and a hoax, that comes to the aid of the protagonists of *Mistress into Maid*. Like *The Snowstorm*, *Mistress into Maid* turns on a confusion of identities. The heroine, Liza Muromsky, is a prose version of the Tatyana of *Eugene Onegin*—how could one fail to recognize her in this description: "Those who have never lived in the country cannot imagine the charm of the provincial miss. Brought up in the pure, fresh air, in the shade of her apple trees, her only knowledge of life and the world comes from books. Solitude, unconstraint and her reading soon awaken emotions and passions in her which are unknown to our frivolous town beauties. The sound of carriage bells is an adventure for her; a trip to the nearest town marks an epoch in her life, and the visit of a guest leaves a lasting and sometimes indelible memory. . . ."

The young hero of *Mistress into Maid* has something of Onegin about him, too—but without his fatal flaw. "In spite of that ominous ring he wore, his mysterious correspondence, and his melancholy, disenchanted air, Alexis was a good, keen boy with a pure heart, capable of appreciating innocent simplicity."

The young people's parents are not on speaking terms, and the children must abide by the quarrels of their elders. But Liza, her curiosity piqued by gossip about the new arrival, dresses up as a peasant girl, meets Alexis in the forest, and charms him with her grace, gaiety and intelligence. Alexis is a full-fledged romantic, and begins to dream of actually marrying the girl he believes to be the blacksmith's daughter. In the meantime, the parents have become reconciled and now plan to unite their offspring. Alexis does not want to part with his little country girl, and goes to the Muromsky home in despair. He is informed that the father is away and demands to see the daughter, to tell her he will never be her husband. He is ushered into the presence of his pretty peasant, no longer in a *sarafan,* but wearing an elegant lace morning gown. Like Tatyana, when Onegin discovers her in the final canto of the poem, Liza is holding her lover's letter in her hand; but unlike Tatyana, she does not drive him away. She tells all, and the happy parents bless their children, whom chance has already united.

Chance also inspires Minsky the hussar, in *The Postmaster,* when, stopping at a post station, he notices Dunya, the postmaster's pretty daughter, and carries her off to St. Petersburg. Dunya, who goes with her abductor willingly, becomes an elegant, loved, happy young woman. Minsky, the carefree hussar who decides to kidnap her in a matter of hours and with no thought for the morrow, is rewarded for his rashness with lasting felicity. But the old postmaster, plodding, unimaginative and peace-loving, dissolves into despair and alcohol. He makes the long trip to St. Petersburg to find his daughter and try to bring her back. He locates her abductor and implores him to return Dunya, but the hussar gives him money instead. He learns his daughter's address and goes to see her. She is beautiful, like a princess in a fairy tale. But she faints at the sight of him, and he understands that he has lost her forever. How could she give up the lights and jewels and cozy apartment, and the man she loves, for a wooden cottage in the middle of nowhere, with only the wind to talk to? Foulmouthed travelers, coarse postilions, loneliness: They are no longer for her. She must remain where she is. The postmaster goes back to his station and soon dies of grief and vodka. A young woman, very beautiful, sometimes comes with her children to pray by the side of his grave. She weeps sincerely, but she is not sorry that she obeyed chance, in the person of the elegant, lighthearted traveler.

In this story, Don Juan-Minsky receives a visit from a stone guest, in the guise of the brokenhearted and outraged old postmaster, who, like the other stone guest come to claim his wife, comes to claim his daughter. But in real life, in everyday prose, as opposed to fairy tales and verse tragedies, the stone guests are always vanquished by the Don Juans.

Once again, the people whom the hero of *The Undertaker* summons to his banquet are "stone guests." But where Pushkin's treatment of the situation was tragic in the Don Juan play and realistic in *The Post-*

master, The Undertaker is pure farce. At a feast given by the German shoemaker Gottlieb Schultz, the guests, all local craftsmen, drink to the health of their clients. One calls out to the undertaker, "Come on, little father; let's have a toast to your cadavers." The undertaker, drunk, dignified and offended, announces, when he returns to his new home, that he is going to invite his customers to a housewarming; and that very night they turn up—from those longest dead, who are reduced to a few disjointed bones, to those newly laid in their graves, still wearing their beribboned bonnets and uniforms, but with unshaven beards. The party begins; sweating in terror, the undertaker barely has time to shake off his nightmare and wake with a start, to avoid suffering the fate of his customers.

The idea for this quick sketch was given to Pushkin by an undertaker's parlor located opposite the Goncharov home. When he wrote it, he was thinking both of death, so near at hand in the cholera-ravaged countryside, and of his fiancée, so far away in the big city filled with temptation.

Love, death and chance are thus the general themes of these prose tales and verse tragedies. The former, however, are written in a lighter vein and supplied with happy endings; they are variations on the same theme, in smaller scale. In Pushkin's "Publisher's Note," the tales are presented as the work of one Ivan Petrovich Belkin, a rural gentleman who supposedly made a hobby of writing down true stories told to him by his friends. Thus they bear at once the stamp of the "titular counselor," "lieutenant colonel," or "shop clerk" who is supposed to have told them to Belkin-Pushkin, and the stamp of Belkin-Pushkin himself, who consigned them to paper. There is a slight difference in tone in each story to account for this, which adds to the charm of the collection.

Pushkin had already given Russia a new poetry; with *The Tales of Belkin*, he opened the way to the prose writers of future generations. Pushkin's prose is even more lean and lively than his poetry. Short, nervous sentences, a deliberately poor vocabulary, a syntax of initially disconcerting simplicity. The pace of the tales is achieved through the judicious choice of verbs. In all his work, Pushkin sacrifices the modifier for the verb. Even his descriptions are full of motion, even his explanations are action—the story is actually alive and moving beneath its coating of words, advancing in rapid bounds, with only here and there an adjective, a metaphor, a detail, which stands out in almost blinding relief:

"His surroundings disappeared into a thick yellowish fog, out of which the white flakes whirled and spun."[9]

"The moon coming through the windows lit up their yellow and blue faces, their sunken mouths, dull, half-closed eyes, flattened noses."[10]

"A man of fifty, robust and vigorous, in a long green fitted coat, with three medals dangling from faded ribbons."[11]

In these deft recitals, the characters' personalities are indicated as succinctly as their dress and features. Pushkin refuses to "explain" his heroes, he lets events do it for him; as when Minsky hands the postmaster some paper ruble notes as the price of his daughter. Back in the street, the postmaster sheds tears of indignation and throws them away. Is he, then, a "noble father"? No; very humble. He knows the value of money. He repents of his action; it was really too lordly for a poor fellow like him—but the author is careful not to tell us all this. He merely says: "He crumpled up the notes, threw them down, stamped on them and walked away. . . . After a few steps, he stopped and paused . . . then turned back . . . but the notes were gone. A decently dressed young man, seeing him, ran over to a fiacre and jumped inside, calling to the driver, 'On the double!' "

This paragraph is a perfect example of Pushkinian psychology. The soul of the actor is illuminated by his acts. The character is drawn only from without; but in one or two well-chosen gestures and words, he reveals the very depths of his being. *The Tales of Belkin*—especially *The Postmaster*, with its mediocre, ignorant, contemptible hero—are the forerunners of the whole of Russian literature to come: the stories of Gogol, peopled by drab little civil servants, the anguished novels of Dostoevsky, the disenchanted idylls of Turgenev and the rest.

"They cannot be published under my name," Pushkin wrote to Pletnev on December 9, 1830; "Bulgarin would cover me in abuse."

Anonymity did not save him, however. Behind the mask of the late Ivan Petrovich Belkin, the *Northern Bee* recognized its archfoe: "There is not the slightest point to any of these stories. You read them: They are nice, they run along harmoniously, but when you have finished nothing remains in your memory but a vague notion of the plot."

In this instance, the public agreed. Pushkin's simplicity was too much for his readers, who had all been reared on decadent classicism or Teutonic Romanticism. It was too undecorated, too bare, too "conversational." It was not art.

Nearly half a century had to pass before people ceased regarding this quintessence of thought and image as a sign of poverty and began to detect its latent richness. "Have you read Pushkin's prose lately?" Tolstoy said in 1874. "Do me a favor, then, and read *The Tales of Belkin* again. Every author ought to study every word of them."

When Pushkin was asked the identity of the real author of the tales, he would answer: "Whoever he is, that is the way stories should be written—simply, briefly and precisely."

At Boldino, while he was working on *The Tales of Belkin,* the tragedies and the final chapters of *Eugene Onegin,* Pushkin also composed "thirty short poems" and "a short story in octaves." The latter was entitled *The Cottage at Kolomna,* and it is an echo of *The Tales of Belkin.* By virtue of its lowly and laughable heroes, the deliberate triviality of its plot, and its wealth of realistic detail, *The Cottage at Kolomna* may be seen as a bold attempt to expand the range of subjects susceptible to poetic treatment. The poem is a tour de force, intended to prove that anything can be a fit subject for a work of art. It bears out the process described in the poem already quoted:

I have watched the calming
Of the yearnings of my spring,
And into the poet's goblet poured
A goodly measure of pure water.

More than in the prose or verse tales and little tragedies, however, and more than in *Eugene Onegin,* it is in Pushkin's Boldino lyrics that we must look for the author's most private thoughts. Everything he wrote there expresses a single state of mind. Unity of time and place dictated unity of inspiration. The lyric poems form a sort of rhymed private diary, reflecting every rise and fall of his anguish and hopes. They invariably allude to death and love, and the whole confession is permeated by a sense of anxiety.

On the eve of his marriage to Natalya Goncharov, Pushkin turned back in his memory to the other women he had loved—how delightful they appeared now, those inscrutable, discreet creatures. How much more fondly he cherished them, now that they were no longer there to disappoint him by some vulgar word or gesture.

Amalia Riznich: He thought of her most of all—the lovely, pale, slender, ardent young woman he had courted in Odessa, who was banished to Italy by a jealous husband and died there of tuberculosis, friendless and uncared-for. Just as he was about to enfold in his arms the living, palpable Natalya, he dedicated some of his finest lines to a dead woman:

Your beauty, your many sufferings,
Are inside a funerary urn.
But the kisses you promised me?
I am waiting. You owe me them.[12]
Come back, O adorable phantom. . . .
I do not call you here
To punish those whose spite
Has struck you down, my friend,
Or to learn about the other world,
Or to relieve the jealousy
That clutches at me. But I want
To tell you it hurts, I love you still,
I am yours. . . . Come back! Come back![13]

All these women from the past came flooding back to Boldino, masking Natalya behind their drifting phantoms. It took a letter from Moscow to recall Pushkin to reality, and suddenly, reality frightened him:

The road is sad before me. Hard work and pain
Swell the stormy waves of the future.
And yet, I do not want to die, my friends,
No: I want to live, so I can think and suffer;
I believe I shall still know how to find some joy
Among so many griefs, worries and irritations;
I think my head will reel again from harmony,
I think I shall yet weep over another poem,
And perhaps, one day, in my sinking years,
Love will turn my way her parting smile.[14]

Pushkin had no illusions about his marriage; he was not sure he loved Natalya alone and forever, and he guessed that she cared little for him. But he thought she would grow used to him, submissively, would let him live in peace, and later, in his "sinking years," would finally come to understand him. That was all he hoped for: this small respite, this breath of tenderness in the clutter of worries, fatigues, failures and remorse. His work would console him for the rest. The joy of creation was the only reliable joy.

Why was he so absolutely bent on contracting a liaison from which he could hope so little return? The marriage was far from irrevocable, it could still be broken off. But in his heart Pushkin felt some grim necessity, as though he were being moved by a higher will. Even at night, the question tormented him. He sat up in bed, listening to the creaking of the old wooden house, the moan of the wind, the confident regularity of his watch. A dread premonition contracted his heart. The paper and pencil were there. He wrote:

I can sleep no more. It is dark.
Shadow and dreams all around me.
The steady ticktock of a watch
Beside my bed is the only sound:
The old women's mutter of the Parcae,
The palpitation of the night.
Life is like a scuttering mouse.
What is the purpose of this torment?
Is it a reproach, is it a lament?
What does this monotonous sound
Want of me? . . . Summons, or deadly omen?
I want to understand your language,
I seek the meaning of your speech. . . .[15]

In his sleigh, on the plains lashed by flurries of white and blue snow, Pushkin imagined he was being attacked by a swarm of devils. His future appeared before him in a gust of loathsome faces, crooked fingers and false voices:

> The clouds race past and veer.
> An invisible moon lights up
> The spinning snowflakes.
> Uneasy is the sky. Uneasy is the night.
> I go on, on across the empty plain,
> The sleigh bells jingle tirelessly,
> And an involuntary fear
> Rides beside me in the desert.
> Keep moving, driver! "Can't;
> You can see the horses are half dead."
> The gusts blind my eyes.
> Every road is buried:
> Not a trace, whatever you try.
> We've gone wrong. What can I do about it?
> Some demon must be leading us,
> Turning us in every direction. . . .
> In horrible, interminable lines,
> In the muffled play of the moon,
> The demons whirl at breakneck speed,
> Like leaves in November.
> How many? Where are they flying?
> Is it some sprite they are burying,
> Or a witch they are marrying?
> The clouds race past and veer.
> An invisible moon lights up
> The spinning snowflakes.
> Uneasy is the sky. Uneasy is the night.
> The demons fly in hundreds,
> At incalculable heights,
> They peep so sadly, and they shrill,
> And their voices weigh down my heart.[16]

The poet was going to see those demons again in Moscow: He knew it whenever he glorified the marriage of the pretty witch Natalya to Pushkin the traveler. He knew all the spite, and the arguments, and the disappointments that were awaiting him back there, the drawing-room enemies, the family enemies, the critical enemies—Nadezhdin, Bulgarin . . .

To the latter, Pushkin wanted to send one parting shot. Bulgarin disparaged his Negro ancestry and his pretensions to aristocracy? Bulgarin was trying to unite all the toadying courtiers in a fraternal campaign against the poet? So be it. Time would tell about that. But first: Where had they come from themselves, those eminent personages bloated with hauteur and imbecility? What were their credentials? Pushkin boldly replied:

My grandfather did not sell pancakes,*
He did not shine the tsar's boots,†
He did not sing as a sacristan,‡
He did not rise from serf to prince,*
And he was not a runaway soldier
From the powdered Austrian army.
So how could he be an aristocrat?
I, friends, am a petit bourgeois.[17]

Fierce as it is, this poem did not calm Pushkin's wrath; he was bubbling over with indignation, and went on: "I am a Russian gentleman, I knew my ancestors before I ever heard of Byron. If taking pride in an ancient lineage means that I am imitating the English poet, then the imitation is quite involuntary. But what does a lord's attachment to feudal prerogatives have in common with a disinterested veneration for an ancestry whose past renown can procure neither promotion nor protection in the present? Our ruling class today is chiefly composed of new men, newly ennobled by Russian tsars. Whatever my politics may be, I have never shared with anyone the democrat's hatred of nobility. To me the nobility has always seemed a natural and necessary class in any civilized state. A French or English erudite piously preserves every line by some old annalist who mentions the name of one of his ancestors, a noble knight slain in such-and-such a battle or returned from the Holy Lands in such-and-such a year; the Kalmuks have neither nobility nor history. It is only boorishness, cowardice and ignorance that do not respect the past, that wallow in the present. . . . Certainly, there are qualities greater than birth, I mean the qualities of character; but I have seen Suvorov's genealogy written by himself. Suvorov did not disdain his noble origins. . . ."

Pushkin knew that his poem *My Genealogy* and his article would make him more enemies. But what could he do? Swallow and be silent? That was not in his nature. Alone against a thousand, he would stand up to that league of courtiers, spies and plagiarists! And he was so tired! He so longed to be able to work in peace and quiet, far from the critics and the envious who were poisoning his existence. He did not ask for love: only a quiet life and studious solitude. He dedicated to his fiancée a poem of deep distress and humble supplication:

Quickly, quickly; my heart needs rest.
Day follows day, every hour takes away
A little of our life; and while we two
Dream of the future, death is already there!

* Which Prince Menshikov did, in the reign of Peter I.
† Which Count Kutaysov did in the reign of Paul I.
‡ Allusion to Count Razumovsky.
* Which Prince Bezborodko did during the reign of Catherine II.

No happiness for us on earth; but peace,
Freedom, to which I have so long aspired.
For so long a weary slave, I have dreamed of flight
To a haven of untroubled calm and work.

That haven of untroubled calm and work he was not going to find in Moscow or with Natalya. Yet he went on, hoping against hope.

It was time to think of the future. At Boldino, during those weeks of rain and snow, he wrote his poetic testament. He composed these lines of verse and prose in haste, like a man who knows he is dying. He had to reap that huge harvest of memories within him. Out of the child, the youth, the lover, the exile, out of all the people he had been, he had to extract and pass on this final testimony before embarking upon his new life. He felt lighter after making his confession. He could become another man. A married man, the head of a family. He, Pushkin. With a wife, children. Was it possible?

4. *The Wedding*

On December 5, 1830, braving all the quarantine barriers, Pushkin reached Moscow and went straight to the Goncharov home. Alas: Neither Natalya nor Mrs. Goncharov had changed in his absence. The maman was as suspicious, evil-tongued, rapacious and mule-headed as ever, and the daughter as beautiful and brainless. He immediately found himself swimming in the familiar waters of bickering, insinuation and precarious reconciliation. There was a strong aroma of tears, melissa cordial, clothes and incense. Mrs. Goncharov trotted the couple to church after church, concentrating on their dear heads the blessings of every saint in Moscow. Mrs. Goncharov, passing in front of dress shops, heaved heart-rending sighs. Mrs. Goncharov, her eyes welling tears, added up column after column of figures. And Pushkin was losing patience.

"I returned to find my mother-in-law up in arms against me, and had great difficulty in calming her," he wrote to Pletnev on December 9. To Alexeyev, on the twenty-sixth of the month: "I have let my whiskers grow long and cut my hair short, I have grown tame and soft, but that's nothing: I am engaged, my dear, engaged; and about to be married!"

Kiselev, one of Pushkin's friends, added a postscript to this letter *with the poet's consent*: "Pushkin is marrying Miss Goncharov, who is, *entre nous*, a soulless beauty, and I think he would not be sorry to break the contract."

Indeed, the poet was waxing increasingly tepid on the topic of marriage. "What interests me most right now," he wrote to Mrs. Khitrovo, "is what is happening in Europe." The quarrels of nations were decidedly preferable to the quarrels of Mrs. Goncharov. He followed every turn in the French revolutionary movement, accused Polignac of treason, admired the audacity of the young *députés* and prayed that Louis Philippe, the democrat, would not prove to be a "nonentity." But the political upheavals of far-off France were as nothing compared to the Polish insurrection. On the night of November 17 the rebels looted the Warsaw arsenal, and Grand Duke Constantine Pavlovich hastily removed himself from a capital bristling with barricades.

The Polish nationalists were rebelling against great Russia, and Western Europe was backing them. Even in Russia there were many liberals who thought that the dignity and courage of this people whose country had been reduced to the status of a colony deserved a better fate, and were wishing for their success. Pushkin, however, regarded the Polish revolt as a domestic quarrel to be stifled as quickly as possible in the interests of both parties. He maintained that Poland could not exist outside the Russian Empire, that Polish nationalism should become one with Russian nationalism. He wrote to Mrs. Khitrovo:

"What a year! What events! The news of the Polish insurrection has upset me dreadfully. . . . We can only pity the Poles. We are too powerful to hate them, and the coming war will be a war of extermination, or ought to be. There is always something morbid about the love of the fatherland in the Polish soul."[1]

"The answer to the Polish question is simple. Only a miracle can save the country, and miracles do not happen. . . . There is no need to whip the Russians into a frenzy against the Poles. Our opinion was formed and stated eighteen years ago. . . . The French have almost ceased to interest me. The revolution should be over now, but every day new seeds are sown. Their king with his umbrella is far too bourgeois. . . ."[2]

Pushkin saw the events in Poland as a prelude to a world war, and rejoiced in the thought that the catastrophe might delay or even prevent his marriage. He contemplated enlisting at once. When Nashchokin tried to dissuade him, Pushkin only laughed and hummed a little tune:

My dear fellow, don't get wed,
Buy yourself a charger instead.

He also said, remembering the fortuneteller who had predicted his death at the hands of a white man: "There is a man named Weisskopf [white head] among the Poles; he will surely kill me and then all the fortuneteller's predictions will have come true."

Pushkin had become so detached from Natalya that he even refused to celebrate New Year's Eve with her and went to the gypsies instead, where he grew drunk on their wine, songs, joys and sorrow. In a letter written in January 1831, he casually remarked: "Today and tomorrow I am on duty at my fiancée's."

Delvig, his best friend, died the same month. His death seemed so irrelevant, so unjust and senseless that Pushkin took it as a sign intended for himself. With Delvig, the last trace of his youth disappeared. God must want him to be alone to face his coming misfortunes, preordained for centuries. Alone, without witnesses, without friends or allies of any kind.

"No one in the world was dearer to me than Delvig," he wrote, "for of all my childhood friends, he alone endured. Our sparse flock huddled together around him. Losing him, we suddenly felt like orphans."

It was not Natalya who could replace Delvig. Natalya could not replace anything, understand anything or express anything by herself. And just then he had more need of understanding and consolation than ever before.

The first month of 1831 brought him nothing but grief: Delvig's death, the failure of *Boris Godunov.* The press rose in a body against his tragedy. True, he was expecting some protest from the idiots and the envious, but even so, it was hard to read that his work was "old-fashioned and shortsighted," had "absolutely no interest," and betrayed "an erroneous concept of historic and romantic drama." In its first issue (1831), the *Northern Mercury* published this epigram:

Pushkin tires us,
Pushkin bores us,
His lines are tedious,
His talent's burned out.
Now he's given the public
His grand *Godunov;*
What a poor present
To start our new year.

"People here are bemoaning my utter, utter downfall," Pushkin wrote to Pletnev on January 7, 1831. "They call my tragedy an imitation of Victor Hugo's *Cromwell;* they say that verse without rhyme is not verse; that it was most imprudent of my pretender to confide in Marya, that it was a very silly and irresponsible thing to do, and other remarks of equal profundity. . . ."

But the war would not come, the sky refused to fall and Pushkin did not dare, did not really want, to break off his marriage. He had gone too far to back out now without an imperative reason. He would have needed the thunder of battle, a lethal epidemic, a purifying conflagration, to justify his flight; but all he had to fight were journalists, all he had to mourn was the death of a friend and all he could complain about was the poor sale of a tragedy.

Mrs. Goncharov had set February 18 as the date for the nuptial blessing of her daughter and Mr. Pushkin. All right, then; February 18 it would be! But there was no money. Pushkin wrote to Pletnev; Pletnev sent a thousand rubles here, two thousand there, so much a line, so much a poem. "Money! Money! That's what I need. Send me money and I'll send thanks."[3] Pushkin sold his lines and poems to buy ribbons for his fiancée.

The poet turned his pockets inside out, brandished his last IOUs, bargained, begged, totted up columns and wrote down his totals with a flourish. According to his calculations, he was a rich man. According to those of Mrs. Goncharov and Natalya's aunts, he was a pauper. "I don't like living in Moscow. Here I do as the aunts say, not as I say." The coven of aunts, presided over by Mrs. Goncharov, had decreed that the trousseau would cost between eleven thousand and twelve thousand rubles at the very least. Pushkin was appalled: Why, twelve thousand rubles was a fortune! Was it possible, was it right, to spend so much on gewgaws? Mrs. Goncharov raised supercilious eyebrows at his vulgar indignation, and Natalya twisted her handkerchief. Nothing to do but give in. Pushkin mortgaged the land and the two hundred serfs his father had just given him, for thirty-eight thousand rubles. Of that amount, he gave eleven thousand to his future mother-in-law for the trousseau and ten thousand to his friend Nashchokin, who was momentarily low on funds, leaving seventeen thousand rubles for furniture and the rest. Mrs. Goncharov plunged into a mad whirl of shopping. She flew from dressmaker to dressmaker, perfumer to perfumer, bootmaker to bootmaker, feverishly fingered silks, laces, velvety suede, argued, ordered, bought and paid, paid, paid with her son-in-law's poetry and bequest. The eleven thousand rubles were gone in a flash—especially as Mrs. Goncharov had taken advantage of them to replenish her own wardrobe. Already overspent, the future mother-in-law pouted, sighed and prayed nervously in her little chapel.

"Now do you understand what a trousseau means and why I grow angry?" Pushkin wrote to Pletnev a few days before the wedding. "I have enough money to marry a wife without money, but I don't have enough to go into debt for my sweet spouse's rags. There's nothing to be done. We shall have to publish the short stories."

Only one week to go. Natalya was radiant, smiling, ravishing. Mrs. Goncharov was more frantic than if she herself were the bride. She fired her supreme shots at the poet, determined to squeeze the highest possible moral and fiscal return from him; she overwhelmed him with pious exhortations and financial exactions.

"Don't forget that it is my family you are entering!" she told Pushkin, who replied, "That is your daughter's business. It is she I am marrying, not you."

On February 10, 1831, he wrote to Krivtsov: "I am married, or as good as. I have long since thought of everything good you could tell me about celibacy and everything bad about marriage. I have coldly weighed the pros and cons of my decision. My youth was spent in a great clamor of sterility. Thus far I have not lived as ordinary people do. I have not known happiness. There is no happiness outside the ordinary.[4] I am over thirty. People usually marry at thirty; I am simply doing what everyone else does, and I do not suppose I shall repent of it. Besides: I am marrying without rapture, without any childish enchantment. I see the future with its morning face, in all its harsh nakedness. Trouble will not come as a surprise; I have made allowance for it in my budget. Joy will come as a surprise. I am in a rotten mood today. I shall end this letter because I don't want to transmit my gloom to you."

Thus, after his initial blaze of passion for the madonna, Pushkin found himself facing his betrothed with a heart full of dead embers, sad and cold. He was marrying "without rapture." Doing "what everyone else does." Trouble would not "come as a surprise." His cold lucidity and dejection mounted steadily. Forty-eight hours before the wedding, he went to the gypsies.

"Sing me something to bring me luck," he said to Tanya; "I'm getting married, you know."

Tanya took her guitar and intoned a song so mournful that Pushkin suddenly burst into sobs and buried his head in his hands. His friends rushed over.

"What's wrong, Pushkin?"

"Ah!" he said, "that song has finished me. It foretells some great sorrow, not joy."

On the eve of the wedding, Pushkin invited his friends to bury his bachelorhood with him. A dozen guests gathered around the table, all prepared to joke, laugh and drink, as is the custom on such occasions. But their host was so lugubrious that they hardly dared open their mouths. He recited some lines of farewell to his youth—as though he were taking leave of life itself, not just unmarried life; as though he were about to die, not acquire a wife. He was reading his last will and testament, uttering his final word: Tomorrow he would cease to exist. His listeners stared at one another in dismay and shook their heads. Then, with foggy brain and contracted throat, Pushkin left them to make his final visit to his fiancée.

The next day, February 18, 1831, the marriage of Alexander Sergeyevich Pushkin and Natalya Nikolayevna Goncharov was solemnized in the big Church of the Ascension at Nikitskaya Gate in Moscow. That morning Mrs. Goncharov sent a messenger to her future son-in-law to announce that she did not have enough money to hire a carriage and would have to call off the wedding. Pushkin dispatched the required sum. He did not want to be angry; he wanted to be happy—at least that day.

Invitations were checked at the door. Police directed the arrival and departure of the coaches. Inside the church, a large, elegant, malicious, whispering throng crowded into the nave. Natalya's entrance into the gilded cavern filled with wavering lights and incense was greeted by a rustle of admiration. The choir sang lustily. The bride came forward, gliding over the carpet, so light, so white, so beautiful that Pushkin was genuinely moved. He smiled broadly and drew himself up to his full height, for Natalya was taller than he. The ushers held the ceremonial crowns over their heads. The bearded, solemn priest intoned the words uniting them for life. The guests chattered in undertones, estimating the cost of the gowns and the probable consequences of this extravagant display.

Suddenly, during the exchange of rings, one of the circlets fell to the floor. Bending over to retrieve it, Pushkin knocked against the lectern and, according to one witness, the crucifix and Gospels dropped with a thud. Pushkin's candle went out. The poet stood up again, extremely pale, and simply murmured, "All the bad omens."

The newlyweds had rented an apartment in Moscow, on the second floor of the Khitrovos' house on the Arbat. The drawing room was papered with an extraordinary design, made to look like lilac velours with flowers in relief. Huge tile stoves mounted to the ceiling. The interior was pretentious, but untidy and not very clean: "Natalya Nikolayevna is disorderly and rather slovenly," noted Tumansky after lunching in the poet's apartment. "I need no other proof than the dirty napkins and tablecloth, and the motley assortment of furniture and china."

But on important occasions the house was given the full treatment, and Pushkin received his guests in style. Ten days after the wedding, he gave a reception described by Bulgakov, the postmaster general: "Yesterday Pushkin gave a magnificent ball. Both of them treated their guests admirably. She is exquisite, they behave like a pair of turtledoves. Pray God they stay that way! The supper was superb, everyone said how extraordinary it was that Pushkin, who has spent his whole life in taverns, should suddenly be able to command such a well-equipped establishment."

The first weeks of the honeymoon were conventionally happy. To affirm his independence, Pushkin went out with friends the day after the wedding, leaving Natalya to wait up all evening, weeping abundantly, alone and lost in the unfamiliar rooms. After that, he did not have the heart to continue a course of "training" as cruel as it was necessary. He never left his wife's side, accompanied her to every ball and rejoiced in her success. They were seen at masquerades, dinners, theaters, in the park. Pushkin had bought an elegant barouche in which Natalya sat like a queen, wearing her brand-new blue velvet pelisse.

"Pushkin is wonderfully attentive to his wife," wrote Bulgakov. "They make me think of Vulcan and Venus." A Miss Kashkina wrote that he reminded her of a pet monkey, sitting by the fair Natalya: "Since his marriage, he is a changed man, staid, sensible, adoring his wife. . . . Whenever I see him out with his gorgeous wife, I am involuntarily reminded of that highly witty and clever little animal whose name you can no doubt guess without my writing it."[5]

Natalya was, in fact, a modest, subdued and affectionate wife. Passionate she was not, but her mildness compensated for all other shortcomings. And Pushkin was so proud to find himself a respectable and respected husband that he quite forgot his somber forebodings. He who, two or three days before his marriage, claimed to be embarking upon it "without rapture" and because "everyone else does," was now writing: "I am married and happy. All I ask is that nothing in my life should change, for I shall know nothing better. This is all so new to me that I feel as though I were being reborn. The memory of Delvig is the only shadow in my serene existence."[6]

However, the couple's resources dwindled rapidly in the whirl of Muscovite festivities, and by March money was already running short.

"I do not intend to stay in Moscow," Pushkin wrote to Pletnev on March 26, 1831. "Do you know, I have a mad urge to go to Tsarskoye Selo? What a blessed idea! There I shall spend the entire summer and autumn in inspiration-giving solitude, close to the capital, in the circle of my cherished memories, and with all sorts of subsidiary advantages. . . . Thanks to my father, who made it possible for me to raise thirty-eight thousand rubles, I have managed to get married and set up some sort of household without going into debt. It is useless to count on my mother-in-law or my wife's grandfather, for their affairs are in a bad way and they cannot be trusted. For my part, at least, I have acted honestly and disinterestedly and in saying so I am neither boasting nor complaining, for my little wife is charming, and not only for her physical attributes; so I do not regard what I had to do as a sacrifice."

While Pushkin was asking Pletnev to find him an inexpensive home in Tsarskoye Selo, large enough to accommodate the two of them and three or four servants, Mrs. Goncharov was bludgeoning Natalya with complaints, prayers and solemn commandments. According to her, Pushkin was ruining Natalya's life with his avarice and obstinacy. He had money, that was certain. But he wanted to bury himself in Tsarskoye Selo deliberately, just to steal Natalya away from her mother's loving care and counsel. And Natalya, the silly goose, was letting him get away with it. She didn't grasp the fact that her great beauty gave her power over Pushkin. She didn't see how to extort the indispensable gowns, gifts and concessions from him. She didn't even know that divorce was a threat she could use to bring the half-witted poet to his knees. During her long seminars with her daughter Mrs. Goncharov explained, patiently and maliciously, all the advantages Natalya ought to be deriving from her situation. But Natalya was too young to understand; she simply wept. At last, hearing her sniffling, Pushkin burst into the room with a roar of profanity and threw his mother-in-law out the door. Driven to distraction by a series of increasingly violent scenes, he left Moscow on May 15 with his wife. He wrote to Mrs. Goncharov: "I have been compelled to leave Moscow in order to avoid further irritations which, in the long run, could have endangered more than my peace of mind: I was portrayed to my wife as an odious, grasping person, a vile usurer; she was told, 'You are a silly fool to allow your husband, etc. . . .' You will admit that was preaching divorce. A wife cannot decently permit herself to be told that her husband is a cad, and the duty of mine is to be content with what I allow myself. It is not for a girl of eighteen to govern a man of thirty-two. I have shown patience and tact, but both, it seems, are pure deceit. I love my peace of mind and shall take steps to safeguard it."[7]

From Moscow the Pushkins went to St. Petersburg, where the poet presented Natalya to his parents, his sister and a few friends. They all agreed that she was even lovelier than they had anticipated, and Pushkin more serious, happy and settled than they had dared to hope. Only young Countess Ficquelmont, after seeing them, predicted a tragic future for the couple. On May 25, 1831, she wrote to Prince Vyazemsky: "I find Pushkin even more likable than before. I think I see signs in him of a new and becoming gravity. His wife is a splendid creature, but her melancholy, meek expression seems somehow to presage misfortune. The faces of both husband and wife do not bespeak tranquillity or a happy confidence in the future; in Pushkin one observes all the signs of passion, and in his wife those of painful self-sacrifice."

After spending a fortnight at the Hotel Demuth, the Pushkins left St. Petersburg for Tsarskoye Selo.

5. *Tsarskoye Selo*

They moved into Kitaev's town house, where their furniture had already been sent from Moscow. It was an Empire house, large and quite pretty, with a bow front and white columns, but there were only six servants to take care of it.* There was also a little garden. The neighborhood was calm. Beyond it stretched the immense imperial park, an invitation to romantic promenades. To Pushkin, the slumbering town was a haven of peace and meditation. He was looking forward to a profitable holiday, far from the evil tongues and high cost of St. Petersburg and Moscow. He wrote to Nashchokin: "It now seems to me that I have organized everything for the best and can live in peace without a mother-in-law and without a carriage, hence without excessive expenditure and without gossip."[1]

Venevitinov wrote to Pogodin: "Apropos of Pushkin: He is living very nicely with his very nice wife; he loves her, he spoils her, and he engages in no debauchery."

At Tsarskoye, Pushkin returned to his studious childhood. He visited the imperial school, and was welcomed by a tribe of enthusiastic scholars. With them, he paced the corridors, poked his head into the study rooms, crossed the great hall and paid his respects to the walls and frescoes that had witnessed the dawn of his hopes. Surrounded by them, his thoughts turned to his own former schoolmates, so many of whom were dead, or deported, or buried in their bureaucratic cells. He inspected his old room, his cubicle, which now belonged to someone else. Staring at the ghost of a little, dark-skinned, tousled, wiry Pushkin reading poetry to the skeleton of the great Derzhavin in dress uniform, he suddenly felt very old.

He liked to stroll through the imperial park, too, searching for the

* In those days people with an income of seventeen thousand rubles kept as many as forty servants.

avenues, arbors and lakes of his past. The sentinels posted along the drives stood at attention as he passed.

"It's because I carry a cudgel, no doubt," he said with a smile.

His "little wife," affectionate and monotonous, awaited him at home, along with his work and his books. What more could he desire? At the end of June, however, the cholera epidemic reached St. Petersburg and Tsarskoye Selo was cordoned off. Food became scarce. Prices soared. "Cholera is all around us, and everything is becoming more and more expensive. Here I am with no carriage and no pastry for dessert," Pushkin wrote on June 26, "but the money keeps vanishing. Just think; since I left I have drunk one bottle of champagne, and I made that last for days!"[2]

Nothing had prepared Natalya to manage a household. The servants obeyed her unwillingly. The steward robbed her respectfully. The budget rose steadily. Pushkin was obliged to intervene in absurd altercations with the menials. Pushing aside his inexperienced wife, he checked accounts, detected frauds, discharged one lot of servants in tears and hired another lot as dishonest as the first. Meanwhile, Natalya's family showed no signs of coming to the couple's assistance. After the abortive attempt to convert the bronze statue of Catherine II into cash, the grandfather considered himself relieved of all further obligations to his granddaughter's husband. And Mrs. Goncharov deemed that she had done her duty, and no more than her duty, by borrowing eleven thousand rubles from her son-in-law to pay for her daughter's trousseau. "I have no news of my wife's affairs. Grandfather and mother-in-law are keeping still, only too pleased that God has sent their pretty little Natalya such a docile husband," Pushkin wrote crossly.

In mid-July the imperial court removed to Tsarskoye Selo, and he abandoned all thought of economy or solitude. Overnight, the town was transformed into a temporary capital, with its elegant crowds, its clutter of carriages, its palace intrigues and entertainments. Natalya was happy to see a little animation, while Pushkin cursed the quarantine for preventing him from fleeing to some more tranquil place. "Alexander," his sister Olga wrote, "has become as snappish as a woman in labor."[3] Everybody in Tsarskoye knew Pushkin and his madonna. The walks in the park and the shore of the lake were lined with people straining to catch a glimpse of the bewhiskered poet and his tall, radiant wife in her white gown and wide-brimmed hat, with a red shawl twisted over her shoulders. A small dog ran alongside the couple, yapping arrogantly.

Every morning Pushkin took an ice-cold bath before going up to his room to sprawl on a settee covered with books and papers. His wet hair curled fiercely. Despite the stifling heat in the room, he never unbuttoned his brown fitted coat. A little table stood within reach, and on it a jug of water, some ice and a jar of jam. From time to time, he would stop work to suck on a spoonful of marmalade, push back the papers and pencils, pace the floor as he recited aloud, walk out onto the balcony for a breath of air, yawn, leaf through a manuscript, sharpen a quill. Natalya would be in the little ground-floor salon with her embroidery, waiting for Pushkin to finish his work so he could take her for a walk in the park.

Zhukovsky, who had come to Tsarskoye Selo with the court, was a frequent visitor. He was mild-tempered, infinitely obliging and naïve. As a protégé of the tsar and a friend of the imperial family, he sincerely wanted to reconcile Pushkin with the regime and its representatives. Pushkin's marriage seemed a hopeful sign. He was settling down. He had a place to live. A man with a home and a wife is already half a monarchist.

"Pushkin lives nearby," Zhukovsky wrote to A. I. Turgenev, "and we see a lot of each other. Since you told me how I drool whenever I look at my wife, I cannot keep from seeing myself as an aged Great Dane. The old hound sits, half asleep, staring at the delectable morsels being devoured before his eyes, while two long rivulets of saliva run down either side of his muzzle. Pushkin's little wife is an adorable creature. I love to see them together. And I am increasingly happy to think of him married. His soul, his life, his poetry will benefit from this union."

In those days, Zhukovsky was also writing Russian tales in verse; the two poets compared their works, criticized, admired and corrected each other in an atmosphere of friendly emulation.

Another regular caller at the Pushkin home was one of the empress' maids of honor, the bright and witty Miss Rossetti. Miss Rossetti was a handsome girl of twenty-two, with a tiny waist and twinkling eyes in a fine-featured, dark-skinned face. She was exceptionally bright and learned, a passionate lover of poetry, politics and romantic entanglements, and she enlivened the drowsiest drawing rooms, inflamed the best-guarded hearts and left a trail of young bumpkins and middle-aged dignitaries in the wake of her flounced skirts. Zhukovsky called her a "celestial imp." Vyazemsky, Tumansky, Sobolevsky, Grand Duke Michael Pavlovich and the emperor himself were all in love with her.

Miss Rossetti first met Pushkin in St. Petersburg in 1828; at Tsarskoye Selo, their acquaintance warmed into a frank friendship. Every morning the "celestial imp" would come to the Kitaev house, to be met by Natalya in the little downstairs drawing room.

"You haven't come to see me, it's my husband you want to see," pouted Natalya.

"Of course it's your husband! Ask if he can receive me."

But Pushkin had already opened the door of his room and was happily calling out to his wife and friend to come up. Uncombed and damp-headed, he received them with shining eyes, amid a wild disarray of pens and paper testifying to his morning's work.

"I've prepared something to read to you," he would say.

"Well, read away, then."

Pushkin read. Miss Rossetti listened intently. Natalya could not conceive how such a pretty and jolly girl could pretend to find anything interesting about a story as insipid as *Tsar Saltan*. She wished she could be like Miss Rossetti and share in her husband's experiments, enthusiasms, hesitations. She wished she could criticize him, too, and hear him say: "You are the best critic of all; you simply say, 'That line is bad, I don't like it!' "

But really, she felt incapable of admiring this cadenced speech; it droned in her ears, it put her mind to sleep, sometimes it actually bored her. Probably, it required some special type of mentality actually to like the game of rhymes and words. What mattered most to Natalya was her house, her compliments, her gowns and her maman's letters. What mattered most to Pushkin was outside the visible world. He lived in a dream. And to join him in his dream was such a long and frustrating journey that it would be better not to try. But that Rossetti woman suited him so well, it was shocking! They had the same interests, the same excitements, the same language. They laughed about things Natalya didn't understand. They argued over books she hadn't read. They talked about writers and artists she had never heard of. They were like two disciples of the same religion, two children of the same family. And it was she, the wife, who felt like an intruder. Often and tearfully, Natalya would confess her jealousy to Miss Rossetti.

"There's no need for you to be jealous," the other woman told her. "Don't you see that Zhukovsky, Pushkin and Pletnev are all one to me? Don't you see that I am not at all in love with Pushkin and Pushkin isn't at all in love with me?"

"Yes, I know," Natalya answered, "but it makes me so angry to see him so cheerful when you are around, while he sits and yawns with me."[4]

One morning when Pushkin was reading his poetry to the two young women, Natalya turned away in exasperation and exclaimed, "Lord, how you can bore me with your poetry, Pushkin!"

"I do beg your pardon," he said, "but you don't know this one yet, I haven't read it to you before."

"This one or the others, it's all the same. You bore me with your poetry and that's all."

Embarrassed, Pushkin shrugged and tried to laugh it off.

"Natalya is a child," he said. "She has the terrible truthfulness of her age."

A few moments later, ashamed of her outburst, Natalya added: "Please. Go on reading. I can see you're dying to. I have to look at my dresses. Come to my room afterward and tell me what you think I ought to wear to the theater."[5]

Sometimes, Natalya would try to interest the poet, feigning a sudden passion for literature: "Why won't you read anything to me? Am I not able to understand? Don't you care about my opinion?"

"No, Natalya. Don't be offended, but it isn't for you; on the whole, it isn't for any woman."

"Oh, isn't Mademoiselle Rossetti a woman then, and a pretty one too?" Natalya snapped, with pink face and tear-filled eyes.

"To the rest of the world, yes," Pushkin said. "But to me she is a comrade, a friend, a good critic."[6]

With that, he left her and went off to his good critic.

"She [Natalya] didn't love him," a contemporary wrote, "and cared more for her social career than for his literary career."[7]

Miss Rossetti also noted in her memoirs: "What a child she is! She is so undeveloped that all she wants to hear about are my life at the Institute, my drive past the fair booths in the imperial coach on Shrove Tuesday, etc. . . . What a pity she is so uncultivated!"

Pushkin, for his part, later wrote that "her inexperience and lack of knowledge" made her "all the more precious" to him.

Thus, there was no intellectual affinity between the two. In not one of his letters did the poet tell Natalya of his literary projects, the books he was reading, the battles he was waging for his art. With his wife, he avoided the themes he would willingly expatiate upon to his friends. He probably knew that her reactions would have been irrelevant. For her, poetry was simply an easy way to gain access to people's homes and make money. She would have liked her husband to become an official poet, like Zhukovsky. And the court was at Tsarskoye Selo; it was an excellent opportunity.

One day the emperor and empress met Pushkin and his wife out walking in the park and stopped to talk to them. Nicholas knew Natalya from the Moscow parties at which he had admired her two years before; now he found her even more appetizing, and turned a few neat compliments with a twirl of his long mustache. The empress invited the young woman to court. Natalya melted with gratitude. Pushkin felt like a fool. The emperor inquired, "Why are you no longer in the service?"

"I am very ready to serve," Pushkin replied, "but literature is my only profession."

After a moment's thought, Nicholas said he would give him a position in the foreign ministry, with an annual salary of five thousand rubles. His job would be to study the documents in the Archives and write an official history of Peter the Great. He added, in French: "Since he is married and has no fortune, we'll have to keep his pot boiling for him."

Pushkin and his friends were amazed by this double mark of imperial approbation. The author, who was incapable of dissimulation, supposed that everyone else was the same, and that if the emperor were doing him a favor it was in recognition of his high merits. He saw himself reconciled with the court and Benkendorf, free to travel the world. He dreamed of a future as a true European. Natalya dreamed of new dresses. Both were wild with gratitude to their good sovereigns.

"The emperor and empress," Pushkin's sister wrote to her husband, "met Natalya and Alexander out walking. They stopped to talk to them and the empress told Natalya she would be very happy to become acquainted with her and a thousand other gracious and charming things. And so there: Now she will have to appear at court, even if she doesn't want to."[8]

If Natalya pretended to see her presentation at court as an irksome chore, it was only to please Pushkin, who was dreading the cost. And then, she thought it would be so distinguished and refined to appear as a retiring young woman dragged protesting from her obscurity and thrust into the limelight of society.

On August 29, 1831, Olga Pavlishchev wrote to her husband again: "My sister-in-law is delightful. . . . She is the wonder of all Tsarskoye, and the empress wants her to come to court; she is very upset about it, because she is no fool. . . . She is still somewhat timid, but that will pass, and she will make herself a place both at court and with the empress, as a beautiful, young and charming woman. . . .

"Physically, they [Pushkin and his wife] are perfect opposites: Vulcan and Venus. . . . Moreover, in my opinion there are other women just as pretty as she. . . ."[9]

Pushkin, in his innocence, wrote to his friend Nashchokin on July 21: "This autumn I shall begin a new literary occupation: I'm going to bury myself in the Archives, to which the tsar has given me access. He is being very gracious and kind to me. A little more and I shall become a favorite. . . ."

To Pletnev, the next day: "I am going to tell you a piece of news (but keep it a secret, for numerous reasons): The tsar has taken me into his service, but the service is neither as bureaucrat nor courtier nor soldier, no, he has given me a salary and opened the Archives to me, on the sole condition that I paw through a stack of documents and do nothing. Very nice of him, no? He said: 'Since he is married and has no fortune, we'll have to keep his pot boiling for him.' By God, he really is good to me!"

What Pushkin did not see was that the emperor was more interested in his pot than in him, and cared more about Pushkin's wife than his work.

He decided to take advantage of his sudden return to favor to launch a new offensive against the odious Bulgarin and his clique. Now that he was in the emperor's confidence again, he would apply for permission to found a review to replace Delvig's *Literary Gazette* (which became defunct in June 1831). The new periodical would be politically conservative and literarily radical; in Pushkin's view, it should have a wider readership than the other reviews in print, it should be more comprehensive, lively and free. No spies on the board of editors, only poets. No publicity in the columns, only respectful and honest criticism of books and events. Pushkin duly wrote to Benkendorf, mentioning in support of his application the fact that the emperor had already appointed him to write an official history of Peter the Great: "Periodicals in Russia are not echoes of individual political parties, which do not exist here. . . . Nevertheless, public opinion needs to be guided. I would edit a political and literary review with the greatest pleasure. . . . I dare not and would not pretend to claim the title of historiographer, which belongs to our unforgettable Karamzin, but I know that I shall one day carry out my intention of writing the life of Peter the Great and his descendants down to Peter III."

For all the eagerness of his appeal, the new "favorite" had to abandon his dream of a review: "Unnecessary," was the decision of the authorities. It was not the moment to found periodicals: The Polish conflict was at its apogee. The Russian army was painfully advancing toward Warsaw. In France, politicians were making impassioned speeches in favor of Poland. All Europe was seething with hatred of Russia. Pushkin took it as a personal affront. On this point the liberal, the "friend of December 14," sided with the conservative Zhukovsky. On August 26 (September 8 N.S.) Warsaw fell. French newspapers immediately began publishing such grief-stricken or vengeful outcries as:

> Noble heart! Warsaw! She has died for us!
> Died gun in hand, head unbowed! . . .
> May the hue of shame inflame our brow;
> You'd like to see the Russians coming; well, they'll come.

Pushkin replied with two poems, *Reply to the Slanderers of Russia* and *Anniversary of Borodino*, which appeared, in the company of similar efforts by Zhukovsky, in a pamphlet entitled *On the Capture of Warsaw.*

> Why are you buzzing, orators of the people?
> Why do you threaten Russia with anathema?
> What has so upset you? An uprising in Poland?
> Well, leave us alone: It's a quarrel between Slavs,
> An old, old fight, a domestic row. . . .
> Fate decided it long ago. You won't change anything. . . .

The *Reply to the Slanderers of Russia* was infused with such fanatical nationalism that Pushkin's friends were incensed by it. The Poles were fighting for democracy, and here was Pushkin dragging them through the mud. The nations of Europe were outraged by the barbarity of Nicholas I, and here was Pushkin, who had suffered so much at the hands of the imperialist regime, glorifying its conquests. Was that all it took to make him forget the Rights of Man: for Nicholas to appoint him historiographer and the empress to invite Natalya to court? Had he sold himself to the enemy? Was he a traitor?

Pushkin did not feel at all guilty. He did not see why he could not be a patriot and a republican at the same time, possessively loving the territorial integrity of Russia and criticizing the regime that was responsible for it. If that integrity were threatened, one had to think of the country first and its politics afterward; the liberal Poles were Poles first and liberals afterward, the Russian monarchists were Russians first and monarchists afterward, and when the fatherland was in danger, all hands must rally to its defense.

On September 15, 1831, Vyazemsky wrote in his notebook: "If there were any real freedom of the press here, Zhukovsky and Pushkin would never have dared to applaud Paskevich's victory—in the first place, because that type of enthusiasm has gone out of fashion, and in the second, because it is absurd to blench and swoon when a lion puts its paw on a mouse. . . . Why write nonsense, when it goes against one's conscience and is useless besides? . . ."

A. I. Turgenev wrote that Pushkin's poem proved him "a barbarian, as far as Poland was concerned." Viegel said that well-informed people in Moscow regarded Pushkin's latest efforts as "two huge blemishes upon his reputation as a poet."

Melgunov wrote: "Pushkin is now so repellent to me as a man that I will no longer respect him as a poet. The Pushkin of today has stopped short in mid-career; instead of meditating upon the features of Apollo, he is looking wildly around for some other god to take his offerings to. Pushkin has fallen, flat on his face."

All his liberal friends concurred in their contempt for this "barracks verse."

Pushkin sadly concluded: "Public opinion is no more, in Moscow; nowadays, the achievements and defeats of the fatherland leave the Russian heart untouched. It was sad to hear the Moscow aristocracy during the recent Polish insurrection, appalling to think of those subscribers to French newspapers coolly reading away, smiling smugly at the news of our misfortunes."

At Tsarskoye Selo, in addition to these ill-fated patriotic poems, Pushkin also wrote a short story (which he never finished) entitled

Roslavlev, the *Tale of the Pope and his Servant Balda*, and completed the wonderful *Legend of Tsar Saltan.*

In *Tsar Saltan*, Pushkin achieved the feat of putting the very words of his nanny Arina Rodionovna into utterly unforced rhythms and rhymes. The style was so unaffected, the material so commonplace, the phrases so familiar, that many critics mistook their purity for poverty.

"*Tsar Saltan* is a perfect Russian folk tale," wrote Baratynsky, "and that is the main thing the matter with it."

Komovsky said: "When you read Pushkin's legend, it is as though he were telling it to you aloud, in the Russian manner, to put you to sleep."

What Pushkin's contemporaries disliked about the poem was what later generations revered in it: its old-fashioned air, its innocence and simplicity. When Zhukovsky wrote his tales, he was still Zhukovsky. When Pushkin wrote his, he became Arina Rodionovna, and that is why the lines of *Tsar Saltan* still sing in the ears of Russian children, lulling them to sleep to the pink flicker of the vigil light, becoming part of the soothing little room, the warm silence, the gilding on the ikon and the picture book lying open on the floor. Thanks to *Tsar Saltan* and Pushkin's other tales, every one of us has had his Arina Rodionovna, leaning bent and wrinkled over his white infant's bed, filled with a murmur of soft words.

One of these eternal children, who was also a lover of legend, often came to call on Pushkin at Tsarskoye Selo. He was a sort of gnome, with the expressionless face, sharp nose, and huge, sad, glacial eyes of an owl. His name was Gogol. He wrote. And the stories he gave the poet to read enchanted him.

"I have just read *Evenings on a Farm*," Pushkin noted, "and am quite speechless. Now, there is real gaiety, sincere and spontaneous, without affectation or gimcrackery! And what poetry, too, in places! What sensitivity! It is all so new in our literature that I cannot believe my eyes."

The novice and the famous poet immediately became close associates, but there was never true friendship or camaraderie between them. Gogol looked up to Pushkin as a demigod, but grieved to see him so earthbound—Pushkin drank, he played cards, he loved women, he profaned. Poetry was not his only interest in life. He wrote, but he also lived. Gogol neglected life for art. He was a refugee from the material world, a stranger to common pleasures, he existed solely for the sake of his private spiritual visions. He seemed to have fallen from another planet. There was a smell of the grave about him.

"I don't know if anyone ever actually liked Gogol," Aksakov wrote. "I don't think so; it was impossible."

Pushkin did not like Gogol, but he recognized his talent, encouraged him, corrected him, taught him the resources of the language and even gave him the subjects for *Dead Souls* and *The Government Inspector*.

Later, he wrote numerous articles in praise of Gogol's work; but at Tsarskoye Selo his only contributions to journalism were two ferocious "stories" against Bulgarin. His new-found favor with Nicholas I—an ephemeral, summer-romance patronage—had incited him to renew his attack upon the *Northern Bee*.

Meanwhile, Natalya was presented to the empress. The ceremony took place on September 4. According to Olga Pavlishchev, the sovereign was literally enchanted with the young woman's beauty and sweetness. Pushkin did not know whether to rejoice at her triumph or moan at the additional expense it would entail.

"When I married, I counted on spending three times as much as before, but I find that it is more like ten times as much," he wrote to Nashchokin on October 7, 1831. "In Moscow they claim I am receiving a salary of ten thousand rubles, but so far I haven't seen a sign of it; if someone were to give me even four thousand, I would thank heaven."

After three months at Tsarskoye Selo, Pushkin was again floundering in a sea of unpaid bills, usurers' interest and private debts. His letters to his friends were strewn with acrobatic calculations. One note found among his papers, written in French to an unidentified person, merely says: "Honestly and truly, I haven't a cent. Be good enough to wait a day or two. Yours. A.P."

It was time to leave Tsarskoye Selo, and lay siege to the publishers in the capitals. In mid-October the Pushkins went to St. Petersburg.

They moved into an apartment on Galernaya Street. Natalya was pregnant. Pushkin had no money. They were deluged with invitations which it was impossible to refuse without incurring the displeasure of "aristocratic circles." Besides, Natalya's figure was still presentable, and she would have been heartbroken to miss a single occasion to show herself and please her public. One of her aunts, Katerina Zagryazhskaya, a maid of honor to the empress, took her beautiful niece under a jealously protective wing. She bought gowns for her, introduced her to the best homes, stage-managed her triumphs. One day Countess Nesselrode, the Foreign Minister's wife, took Natalya to an evening party at the Anichkov palace without Pushkin's knowledge. When he learned of her escapade he flew into a violent rage, insulted his wife, insulted Countess Nesselrode and concluded with the words: "I do not want my wife to appear in places where I do not go myself!"

Countess Nesselrode snorted at the vulgarity of this upstart Negroid pen-pusher. By insulting her, he had made himself another enemy—and a powerful one, for the Nesselrode clique was enormous.

Other enemies sprang up in the drawing rooms, day by day. Delvig had refused to print Pushkin's vindictive *My Genealogy* in his *Literary Gazette*, but copies of it were circulating in St. Petersburg and Moscow. A few representatives of the upper nobility took umbrage and spoke to the emperor. Pushkin was certain they must have distorted the facts, and immediately tried to justify himself by writing to the chief of the third section, on November 24: "About a year ago one of our periodicals published a satirical article about a certain man of letters who claimed to be of noble descent but was really only a member of the gentry. It went on to say that his mother was a mulattress whose father, a poor blackamoor, had been purchased by a sailor for a bottle of rum. Although Peter the Great bore little resemblance to a drunken deck hand, I was clearly the target of the article, as I am the only Russian man of letters to number a Negro among my ancestors. In view of the fact that this article appeared in an official gazette, that it carried its insolence to the point of alluding to my mother in a periodical which purports to be exclusively literary, and that our gazetteers do not fight duels, I considered it my duty to reply to the *anonymous* satirist, which I did with some asperity, in verse. I sent my reply to the late Delvig with the request that he put it in his paper. He tried to dissuade me, on the ground that it was ridiculous to defend oneself with pen and ink against attacks of this nature. . . . I conceded his point, and that was the end of the matter, except that a few copies of the reply went around—which did not displease me, since there was nothing in it which I wished to retract. I confess that I am attached to what are called prejudices: I mean to be as much of a gentleman as anyone on earth, although it is hardly a profitable calling; I also care a great deal about my ancestors' good name, since that is the only thing they have left me. . . ."[10]

On this letter Nicholas I penciled the following annotation: "You can tell Pushkin for me that I fully agree with his late friend Delvig: Abuse as base and vile as that addressed to him dishonors its author and not its victim; *scorn* is the only possible weapon against it, and that is what I would have chosen in his place. As for his poem: It has some wit, but is more spiteful than anything else, and for the honor of his pen, and more particularly for the justice of his cause, he would have done better not to allow it to circulate."[11]

In the quarrel with Bulgarin, Nicholas had deigned to incline in Pushkin's favor: a point for Pushkin. But it was scored less by the poet than by Natalya, whose appearance in the drawing rooms was greeted by a flattering murmur of affection. Her beauty, her modesty, her soulful expression were universally applauded. "His wife is beautiful, beautiful, beautiful," Countess Ficquelmont wrote, "but there is a pained expression on her brow which, in my opinion, augurs ill for the future."

"My sister-in-law is utterly charming," Olga Pavlishchev wrote, "pretty and quick-witted, and altogether a sweet and dear girl."[12]

And: "My sister-in-law is the most fashionable woman here. She frequents the best society and is commonly said to be the most beautiful of all; she has been nicknamed 'Psyche.'"[13]

In a letter dated November 17, 1831, Baron Serdobin wrote to Baron Vrevsky: "His wife has appeared in society, and been extremely well received; everyone admires her face and bearing, there is something rather appealing about her."

She "shone," she "sparkled," she was "the most beautiful," the "queen": Those were the expressions used by everyone who came in contact with Natalya.

She herself was becoming increasingly aware of her success, and determined to pursue a career so auspiciously commenced. Listening to the wind moan in the chimney, one November evening in 1831, Pushkin said: "God, how good it would be at Mikhailovskoye now! I never write as well as I do in the country, in the autumn. Why don't we go?"

Natalya dissolved in tears, and Pushkin promised to stay in town for the season—the emperor was counting on her. On November 14, 1831, Pushkin became officially attached to the foreign ministry; on December 6, he received the title of "titular counselor."

The titular counselor was in Moscow that day, however. Having found no money in St. Petersburg, he had decided to try elsewhere. He could pawn his wife's diamonds, or try a game of cards, or put the touch on a few charitable friends: He would see when he got there. A few days before setting out, he wrote to Nashchokin: "I am very anxious to come to Moscow. I am dying to talk to you and also have some business to settle, in particular my wife's diamonds, which I must at all costs salvage from my mother-in-law's estate. The grandfather [Natalya's] is a pig: He gives his third concubine in marriage with a dowry of ten thousand rubles, but he cannot repay my twelve thousand and gives nothing to his granddaughter. Natalya is pregnant, the child is due in May. This will have a considerable effect upon our standard of living, and I have to think about it all."

For Pushkin, Moscow was Nashchokin. He stayed at Nashchokin's home and spent his days and nights with Nashchokin. The house was a sort of grand bazaar, a meeting place for students, cardsharpers, officers, gypsies, violin players, usurers, spies and poets. They wandered in, talked, gambled, drank, ate, laughed, napped on the settees in a haze of smoke and noise, and went out again only to return two hours later. Nashchokin would be rich as Croesus one day, penniless the next. In a single evening he had been known to lose his cash, his gold watch, his table silver, his coach and horses and the coach and horses of his gypsy mistress Olga. A fortnight later Olga would be preening herself in a brand-new carriage and Nashchokin would be telling time by a watch that was even heavier and more intricately engraved than the last. When Pushkin wanted a private conversation with his friend, they would go to the Turkish baths, hire a cabin, undress and conduct their business in leisurely fashion, reclining like gods on clouds of drifting, downy steam.

"Just between us," Yazykov wrote to his brother on December 22, "Pushkin has not come to attend to literary business or any other business, but to play cards. He is keeping the lowest possible company, nothing but swindlers, buffoons and thieves. Every time he comes to Moscow it's the same thing; he lives more respectably in St. Petersburg. There is no truth, brother, in the old saying about marriage making a new man."

In fact, Pushkin no longer found any real pleasure in dissipation. He had hoped to divert himself in the company of the companions of his youth, and, with Nashchokin's help, to put his finances on a firmer footing. But all he could think of, in the din and laughter and shouting, was his wife and how sorry he was to have left her.

"I am bored here," he wrote Natalya. "Nashchokin is busy with his own affairs, his house is like a slum, it makes my head whirl. From morning to night it is filled with an unending procession of people of the most unlikely kinds: gamblers, retired hussars, students, lawyers, gypsies, spies, and, most of all, usurers. The door is wide open. Everybody needs him. Everyone shouts, smokes, eats, drinks, dances; there is not an inch of free space. What to do? He has neither money nor credit; time is passing and my affairs are in no better shape than before. It all drives me wild, of course. . . . Yesterday Nashchokin invited us to a gypsy evening; I have so lost the habit that my head is still aching from the shouting of the guests and the Bohemian songs. I am bored, angel. Farewell."

Pushkin may have been annoyed by Nashchokin's fecklessness, but Natalya's conduct worried him far more.

She was young, pretty and utterly naïve. She might accept improper invitations. She might let herself go too far in her flirtations. She was pregnant too. Was she taking care of herself, at least? Whenever he was not with her, he felt that waves of calamity must be rising to engulf her. His letters were filled with touching moral and medical exhortations. Two days after his arrival in Moscow, he wrote: "I hope to see you in two weeks' time. I am bored without you; also, I have been continually afraid for you from the moment I left. You won't want to stay home, you will go to the palace and have a miscarriage on the 105th step of the staircase. My soul, my little wife, my angel, do me this one favor: Walk two hours every day indoors, and be careful. Tell your brother to look after you and not to let you have your way about everything. If you go dancing, for the love of God, don't do anything except the quadrilles; write and tell me if the servants are too much of a nuisance and if you are able to manage them. . . ."

Two days later: "Moscow is still dancing, but so far I have not been to a single ball. I don't like Moscow. . . . I have not been to your old home yet . . . for if I went, I would have to pay a call on Nat.-Iv. [the mother-in-law] and endure the inevitable scene; she tells the whole town about my grasping avarice, but I want no more to do with her. I kiss you and implore you to walk back and forth in the drawing room; don't go to the palace and don't dance."

Again: "For pity's sake, don't lace yourself, don't sit with your legs folded underneath you, and don't become friendly with any countesses we don't speak to in public. I am not joking, I mean what I say, and I worry. . . . Don't go to the gallery [in the palace, reserved for those without personal invitations]. It is not your place."

Finally, on December 16: "My love, you are very sweet, you write often; there is just one problem, which is that your letters are hardly comforting: What is this *vertige*, fainting or vomiting? Have you seen the midwife? Have you been bled? I am horribly worried. The more I think about it, the more certain I am that it was foolish of me to go off and leave you. Without me, you will do something rash. You'll have a miscarriage before you're through. Why aren't you walking? You gave me your word you would walk two hours a day. That is not good of you. God knows if I shall ever come to the end of my business here, but I shall be back with you for the holidays. . . ."

Meanwhile, far from her husband, Natalya was having the time of her life. When she laced, she was still quite elegant, everybody told her so. The emperor himself whispered compliments in her ear when he danced with her—for she was dancing with the emperor! The tsar of all the Russias was pleased to take her in his arms and whirl her away to the beat of the music. She was dancing alone with the demigod of steely gaze and perfumed mustaches. For the length of a waltz, she was a queen. What were Pushkin's literary satisfactions compared with Natalya's rapturous pride at being singled out from all other women by Nicholas I?

When Pushkin returned for the Christmas holidays, he found his wife in excellent health despite her imprudences. "She dances at all the balls," he wrote Nashchokin on January 8, 1832, "flirts with the emperor, and jumps off the front steps. I shall have to take the little lady in hand."

But it was becoming increasingly difficult to take the little lady in hand. Her cajoling smile, her tender look unmanned Pushkin and all his arguments. If he went rushing about in search of money, it was in order to buy new gowns for her. He wrote more letters, trying to borrow twenty-five thousand rubles at an acceptable rate of interest. The bronze statue of Catherine II hove into view again: The hapless object, originally destined for the foundry, now became worthy of acquisition by the state.

"The statue proved to be a fine work of art," he wrote to Benkendorf, "and my conscience could not suffer its destruction for the sake of a few thousand rubles. If no private individual's fortune will allow him to purchase or preserve it, this fine statue might advantageously be placed in one of the institutions established by the empress, or at Tsarskoye Selo, where there is no effigy of her among the monuments she erected to the great men who served her. I should want twenty-five thousand rubles for it, which is a quarter of its cost."[14]

But the state stubbornly refused to buy the colossus. Pushkin would have to count on his work alone; and instead of working, he was escorting Natalya to balls and watching her dance and laugh with others while he, in his own words, "dozed" and "swallowed ices." "One can only see Pushkin at balls," wrote Gogol. "He will waste his whole life at them if some event—or better, some necessity—does not remove him to the country."

Toward March, the couple's "outings" became less frequent. Natalya's pregnancy was nearing its term. She felt heavy. Pushkin worried over her every breath. "To look at you, one would think it was you and not Natalya who was having the baby," his sister told him.

On May 19, 1832, the pains began. In the new apartment on Furstadtskaya Street, Pushkin's howls and sobs formed a counterpoint to Natalya's moans. He said the agony was unendurable, he would leave home for the birth of the next child. But when the last spasm was over, he was filled with joy at the sight of the dusky, wailing daughter who had just made her entrance into the world. His daughter. Marya Pushkin. He wrote to Princess Vyazemsky: "Can you imagine, my wife has had the tactlessness to produce a miniature lithograph of myself. I am brokenhearted in spite of my fatuity."[15]

As soon as she could, Natalya resumed her exhausting, empty social life. Motherhood had enhanced her beauty. Her Aunt Zagryazhskaya covered her with gifts. How happy Pushkin must be to have such a sought-after wife! Why on earth was he burying himself in those dusty old papers in the Archives, when he ought to be by her side night and day, to admire and divert her and gently descant upon his jealousy?

For Pushkin had gone back to work. In 1832 he wrote a draft of *Dubrovsky*, a large "social" novel, and *The Undine*, a verse drama. He also made another attempt to found a review:

"The object of the review will be to prove to the authorities that there are some honest men, not only literary scum," wrote Mukhanov.

"I want to break up a monopoly [Bulgarin's]," wrote Pushkin.

But permission was again refused, the monopoly was not broken up and the *Northern Bee* went on buzzing in his ears. Worse yet: Benkendorf, now aware of Pushkin's intentions, redoubled his vigilance and began to assail the poet with a stream of remonstrances and friendly advice. He rebuked him for publishing—*The Anchar* in particular—with the sole consent of the regular censor. In other words, under the imperial dispensation Pushkin was actually forced to pass two distinct censors, the regular one and that of Nicholas and Benkendorf.

"I had always understood," Pushkin wrote back, "that the unexpected *favor* granted to me did not deprive me of the *right* which the emperor grants to all his subjects, namely, the right to publish with the permission of the censor."

At last, early in the autumn of 1832, Pushkin received the five thousand rubles of his salary as titular counselor; but they did not begin to cover his expenses.

In September, weary of domestic complications, changes of cooks and chambermaids, wardrobe dramas and unpaid bills, Pushkin made another trip to Moscow. This time he visited the university with the Minister of Education, who stood before a class and announced, pointing to their professor: "There is the theory of art."

Turning to Pushkin, he added: "And here is art."

"Five feet away from me stood the genius, the pride and glory of Russia," one of the students wrote. "We devoured Pushkin with our eyes."

That same Pushkin, genius, glory and pride of Russia, was in the throes, just then, of the most prosaic of torments. What were the servants doing? Had Natalya engaged such-a-one? Was so-and-so still drinking? Should they hire a new cook? Was it good to give cream to a nursling? Above all, he was obsessed by petty jealousy; he could not control it. He did not really believe Natalya capable of unfaithfulness; but by taking too obvious a pleasure in the compliments of her dancing partners, by entertaining gentlemen in his absence, by smiling and dropping her gaze and playing with her fan, she might well ruin her reputation. Wholly absorbed by his anxieties, he sermonized her relentlessly in his letters. And by a simple epistolary process, she turned all his reproaches against him, accusing him of a thousand imaginary infidelities. In her, the gnawing doubt that was so acutely sincere in the poet became a pretext for coy fencing. She thought her allegations gave a frightfully romantic and piquant tone to her billets-doux. She made all sorts of cutting allusions, stirred up the past, exhumed memories of old liaisons. . . . Natalya's letters have not been preserved. But those of Pushkin give the exact tone of these domestic and amorous controversies:

"It worries me to think of the people I have left you with. Peter, that drunken lazybones . . . Irina Kuzminichna who makes war on you, Nenila Anufryevna who robs you! And little Marya? What is the news of her scrofula? . . . Ah, my little wife! What will become of you?"[16]

"What a sweet, good girl you are! What a long letter I have had from you, and so serious! Thank you, little wife. . . . You can make any arrangements you like with the cook provided that after lunching at home I am not obliged to dine at the club. . . . For the love of heaven, don't stuff little Marya full of cream and don't keep anointing her with unguents. . . . By the way, do be careful, aren't you pregnant again? If so, you must pay attention from the beginning. Don't ride; there are other ways to play the flirt."[17]

"Thank you for going to bed early. But you are wrong to embark upon a career of flirtation. You should not have invited Pushkin [a relative]; in the first place because he had never been to our home before, and in the second because, in spite of all my confidence in you, people must not be given food for scandal."[18]

"I was expecting a storm from you, because according to my calculations, you could not have had my last letter before Sunday; and instead, you are so sweet, so affectionate and nice that I am positively dazzled. What is the meaning of it? Have I become a cuckold? Take care! . . . You commit a sin by suspecting me of being unfaithful and running after my friends' wives. But oh, how I envy these friends whose wives are not angels of loveliness and madonnas, etc. Do you know the Russian song:

> "God spare me a wife who is too fair.
> Fair wife is asked too often to the feast!"[19]

"You are flirting with the entire diplomatic corps and you can still find something to complain about! Little woman, little woman! But never mind that. It seems to me you are soldiering valiantly on at home without me, changing servants, breaking carriages, checking accounts, milking wet nurses. . . . What a woman of action!"[20]

On October 13 Pushkin returned to St. Petersburg, his right leg racked by rheumatism, leaning on a cane, grouchy. His wife had danced too much, the servants had stolen too much. He scolded the former, discharged the latter and changed apartments. Along with his furniture and books, however, he moved the vexations and frustrations that were built into his fate into the new rooms on Gorokhovaya Street. The setting was different, life was the same.

"My life in St. Petersburg is like nothing. The cares of everyday existence keep me from being bored, but I do not have the bachelor's leisure that is so essential to an author. I rush about in society; my wife is extremely fashionable; all that requires money, but money comes from my work and work demands solitude."[21]

This was the letter of a disenchanted man. He could count on his wife's affection, no doubt; but could he count on her love?

"Pushkin is intoxicated with his wife," Shevyrev, a civil servant and journalist, wrote to Sobolevsky. Was Natalya "intoxicated" with Pushkin? He didn't think so. When they first became engaged, he had written: "I may hope she would come to care for me in the end, but I have nothing alluring to offer her; if she consents to marry me, I shall see it only as proof of the tranquil indifference of her heart."

Once married, he saw that he had been right. Natalya accepted his caresses with shrinking apathy. She obeyed his desire, offered her body, moaned a little because you were supposed to. But the creature Pushkin held in his arms and pinned down with his weight was too compliant. He was alone in his fervor. He told himself Natalya secretly held his past against him. He comforted himself with the thought that she refused herself out of pride, in order to be different from the other women he had possessed. He took upon himself the responsibility for her indifference.

In 1831 he wrote:

When I lock my arms about
Your long, elastic form,
And my mouth murmurs
Words of fever and desire,
Without an answer, you deliver
Your tense body into my hands,
But all you give me, my sweet friend,
Is a mistrustful smile,
Keeping stored in your memory
All the follies of my past;
Indifferent, inattentive,
Preoccupied, you listen,
And I curse all that made the pride
Of my criminal youth. . . .

At first, Pushkin tried to overcome Natalya's mistrust, passiveness and indifference. But his efforts to awaken a body hostile to his own remained humiliatingly in vain. Then he tried to pretend that he loved Natalya for her very coldness. One poem written in 1832 expresses Pushkin's amorous torments with distressing exactness:

No, I do not prize more active ecstasies,
The madness of the flesh, the wild embrace,
The sobs and screams of a young bacchante,
Who, writhing like a serpent in my arms,
By her fierce caress and vibrant kiss
Hastens the moment of the decisive spasm.

How much better you please me, my quiet friend,
What blessed torment I savor with you,
When, yielding at last to my long pleas,
You abandon yourself, unrapturously, tenderly,
So ashamed and cold, scarcely responding
To my inflamed transports you don't understand.
But little by little, as the heat spreads through you,
Unknown to yourself, you share my pleasure.

This confession defines Pushkin's relations with his wife in unambiguous terms: He had to plead patiently before she would yield to him, and when she did she was "ashamed and cold," merely turning over her body to be used by him. While he crushed her in his arms, she stared watchfully at his distorted features, his eyes widened in ecstasy, his lips whispering words she did not understand. At last, grudgingly, cross and disgusted, she felt the little thrill that was her delayed recompense. And that was all.

"Is it not terrible," the Pushkin scholar Bryusov wrote, "to think that Pushkin had to plead with his wife, begging for her caresses, that she gave herself to him 'unrapturously, tenderly,' that she 'scarcely responded' to his passion and only participated in the ultimate pleasure 'unknown to herself'?"

Lerner, another Pushkin scholar, wrote in reply: "In these lines Bryusov sees the proof of Natalya Nikolayevna's indifference to her husband. But the poem refers only to a sexual incompatibility between the two, and to the young woman's frigidity."

In reality, and despite Pushkin's naïve pretensions, Natalya remained intellectually as well as physically alien to him. Neither their souls nor their bodies lived in unison. And it was natural that Pushkin, who was disappointed by his wife's sexual incapacity no matter what he said to the contrary, should regret his old mistresses and be tempted to look elsewhere for a pleasure Natalya was unable to give him. In a third poem, written on October 27, 1832, Pushkin rationalized his mental infidelities as follows:

I must not, I dare not, I cannot
Fling myself madly into the fury of love.
Jealously I guard my peace of mind,
Forbid my heart to follow guilty whims.
No, enough of love. But why then
Do I sometimes stand and muse
When a girl happens past before my gaze;
She slips away—and is gone? Am I forbidden
To admire this maiden; gratified
And sorrowing, to follow her with my eyes;
To bless her for good fortune and joy,
And to wish her a happy future? . . .

These lines were intended for the young and pretty Countess Sollogub, on whom Pushkin was dancing attendance and of whom Natalya was fiercely jealous.

"Why bother to be jealous, little wife," Pushkin wrote in October 1833, "of Countess Sollogub? You are a beauty, a superb creature, she is only a shell."

But Pushkin had too much vitality and passion to content himself with blessing pretty girls and mentally wishing them all earthly joys. He was, on occasion, unfaithful to Natalya. In 1832 he took a fancy to Dolly Ficquelmont, Mrs. Khitrovo's daughter. As the wife of the Austrian ambassador to Russia, her social position was unassailable. She was handsome, intelligent and passionate. Seduced by Pushkin's singular charm, she confessed a reciprocal attraction and gave him a rendezvous in her home. At nightfall Pushkin slipped into the palace according to a prearranged route, entered the dark drawing room and stretched out on his stomach under a settee. In this position he waited several hours, blinking into the darkness, with aching back and cheek pressed against the chilly floor, which smelled of dust and beeswax. Gradually, his limbs grew numb, his head grew heavy, he began to be sorry he had come. But it was impossible to escape now; he might meet a servant in the corridors. At last, the sound of carriage wheels. A coach drew up before the door. On the other side of the wall, light, running feet. The door opened. Two footmen entered bearing torches. Slowly, Dolly followed them, accompanied by a maid of honor whom she casually dismissed. Alone in the room, she called out feebly: "Are you there?"

Pushkin struggled out of his hiding place and wrapped his arms around Dolly Ficquelmont, in her fairy-tale queen's ball gown and tiara. Together, smiling and weaving as they went, they entered the brocade-hung bedroom where, at last, the poet consoled himself for Natalya's "unrapturous" surrender. He consoled himself so thoroughly, in fact, that when he went to the window and drew back the curtain, he saw broad daylight outside. The lovers looked at each other in dismay. What to do? Pushkin huddled into his clothes. Dolly dabbed at her tear-filled eyes. When her lover was ready, she led him toward the glass-paneled doors into the hallway; but through the panes, she spied the Italian doorkeeper. Then, completely losing control, she swayed on her precious dancing pumps and announced that she was about to faint. Pushkin exhorted her to save her swooning until later, and help him out of the palace first. The poor woman pulled herself together and went back to fetch her austere French chambermaid, an aged expert in amorous camouflage and escape. She conducted Pushkin to the husband's rooms on the lower floor. Count Ficquelmont was still in his bed behind a screen. With thudding heart, holding his breath, Pushkin tiptoed into the room behind her. Suddenly a deep voice broke the silence: "Who's there?"

"It's I," the old woman answered, shoving Pushkin into the antechamber, where his presence was no longer compromising. Once in the street, he gratefully filled his lungs with the fresh morning air. The next day he gave the Italian doorkeeper a thousand gold rubles to buy his silence, and, no doubt, did not attempt to repeat such a costly and acrobatic feat. He found the whole incident so piquant and droll, however, that he related it to Nashchokin in detail.[22]

He also confided to Nashchokin that he was in love with the empress. This, of course, was a nonreciprocated passion, a purely abstract and theoretical infatuation, whose very absurdity delighted the poet. "The empress," wrote the Marquis de Custine, "has a most beguiling expression, and the sound of her voice is as gentle and penetrating as that of the emperor is naturally imperious. . . . Her tall, slender form has so regular a grace, her swift, light step is at the same time so noble; she has certain gestures of arm and hand, certain attitudes, a carriage of the head, which are unforgettable."

"Pushkin was terribly enamored of the empress," Nashchokin said; "he was in adoration before her and even felt a certain physical attraction to her."

In his private diary Pushkin wrote: "I love the empress inordinately." And he dedicated these lines to her:

> All in grace and harmony,
> The turbulent universe
> She rules, calm and modest,
> With triumphant beauty.
> She looks: beside her
> Neither rival nor friend;
> The tarnished throng of our beauties
> Pales in her light.

Another of Pushkin's ephemeral passions was Baroness Krüdner, pale, insipid and mild. At a ball given by the Ficquelmonts, he began besieging her with compliments and pleas, to Natalya's intense annoyance. Natalya went home without her husband. Pushkin rushed after her and found her in her room unhooking her gown.

"What's wrong? Why did you leave?" he asked.

In reply, Natalya looked him straight in the eye and suddenly struck him smartly on the cheek. Momentarily taken aback, Pushkin burst out laughing, kissed his wife and ran off to tell his friends that "the madonna had a surprisingly heavy hand."

But the "madonna" had nothing to begrudge the poet; her social success was becoming more firmly established every season. Young Count

Sollogub, who met her in 1833, wrote: "I fell desperately in love with her at first sight; it must be said that in those days there was not one youth in Petersburg who was not secretly sighing after Mrs. Pushkin; her luminous beauty, coupled with that magic name, turned every head; I knew very young men who honestly believed themselves in love with her although they had not met her, and sometimes had never even seen her."

As proof of his assertions, Count Sollogub related an incident he had witnessed at a ball given by the Buturlins. Little Peter Buturlin, then thirteen years old, was sitting next to Natalya in a window recess and speaking to her with great intensity. His young rooster's voice carried so well that Sollogub heard him utter the following engaging declaration: "Yes, Natalya Nikolayevna, you absolutely must listen to me. Do not be offended, but it is absolutely essential that I tell you right now that I love you, because, you see, it is already midnight and they will be coming any minute to fetch me and send me to bed."

Following his young subjects' example, the emperor, too, never tired of singing Natalya's praises. She arrived at one costume ball disguised as a priestess of the sun, whereupon Nicholas I, irremediably conquered, proclaimed her queen of the ball. The priestess of the sun was then five months pregnant. During Lent, a high fever endangered her life. Despite the young woman's "interesting condition," the physicians prescribed bleeding, which curious form of treatment she rather surprisingly survived.

For the summer, the Pushkins took a big country house at Chernaya Rechka, on the outskirts of St. Petersburg. While Natalya rested, Pushkin continued his work in the Archives, going and coming home on foot every day.

On July 6 Natalya gave birth to a little boy, Alexander. The confinement was arduous; the convalescent's body was covered with abscesses; but thanks to her robust constitution, she recovered, and when she was able to get out of bed and look at herself in the mirror again, she found to her joy that her beauty was not altered. Pushkin was very proud to be twice a father, but his responsibilities were growing at the same time as his family. Aunt Zagryazhskaya, Natalya's "sponsor" in society, did pay for part of her clothes, but the Pushkins' financial position was still extremely precarious. Somehow, he had to find some money.

Intense but unremunerative literary activity marked 1831, 1832 and the first half of 1833. Apart from *The Undine*, his unfinished play, Pushkin's verse output consisted chiefly of his *Imitations of the Ancients* and *Songs of the Eastern Slavs*. As he did not know Greek, Pushkin had recourse, for the former, to the French adaptations of Lefébure and Villebaune. He somehow succeeded in reading through the corrupt and halting French to the rough-and-ready mind of the original and its hammered, sprung prosody. Still more unlikely was the story of the *Songs of the Eastern Slavs.* In 1827 Prosper Mérimée brought out a clever parody of Slavic songs in Paris, under the title of *La Guzla, ou choix de poésies illyriques recueillies dans la Dalmatie, la Bosnie, la Croatie, et l'Herzégovine.* Mérimée's mystification was so skillfully contrived that it misled not only his French readers, but even such specialists in Slavic verse as Mickiewicz and Pushkin. Pushkin was delighted with the so-called Illyrian anthology, and translated the prose poems of *La Guzla* into Russian verse. But although he was guided by Mérimée's text, Pushkin departed widely from his model and intuitively recaptured the tone of the authentic Serbian songs. He instinctively discarded everything that was false, adulterated and Western in Mérimée's text; he unconsciously altered the lines of a humorous caricature to resemble the true face and soul of a country. Learning of Pushkin's mistake, Mérimée wrote to Sobolevsky on January 18, 1835: "Do apologize to Mr. Pushkin for me. I am both proud and ashamed of having taken him in." It was Pushkin, in fact, who "took in" Mérimée, by transforming his parodies into real poems.[23]

At this period of his life, however, Pushkin was mainly writing prose. He did some work on *Dubrovsky,* his social novel, and made notes for *The Queen of Spades,* but was almost wholly absorbed in his *History of Peter the Great.* In the imperial Archives he pored over secret documents and sank slowly through a cloud of dust into the dark past of his homeland. Having obtained permission to consult Voltaire's personal library, which was kept in the Hermitage, he experienced the unique satisfaction of working in the company of the ghosts of both his idols, Peter the Great and old Arouet. The pages of his manuscript are decorated with numerous sketches of Voltaire copied from Houdon's bust. While he was thus transcribing, analyzing and collating the correspondence and chronicles of the eighteenth century, however, other, less noble figures were burrowing into his mind. From Peter the Great, imperceptibly, he turned to Pugachev, the brigand-pretender who led an army of Ural Cossacks against Catherine II and finally had his head cut off after laying whole provinces waste. Pushkin decided to write a *History of Pugachev* too, and a novel, *The Captain's Daughter,* the action of which was to take place during the same period. But in order to accomplish these tasks, the one historical and the other fictional, he thought it essential to visit the scene of the insurrection and collect some oral testimony. Also, he knew that in the city of balls, masquerades, espionage and intrigue, he would never find the quiet he needed to write such a long work. Two weeks after the birth of his second child, Pushkin accordingly requested permission to examine the archives of the governments of Kazan and Orenburg. The emperor wished to know the motive for such a long trip, so Pushkin duly sent Mordvinov, the director of the chancellery of the third section and a close associate of Benkendorf's, a tongue-in-cheek note (dated July 30) setting forth his reasons for wanting to leave the capital:

"In the past two years I have occupied myself solely with historical research and have not written a single line of literature proper. It is absolutely essential that I spend two months in complete solitude, to rest from my arduous labors and to complete a book I began long ago and am counting upon to bring in a little of the money I so badly need. It mortifies me to have to waste time on such trivialities, but what else can I do? They alone give me the independence and the wherewithal to live, and keep my family, in St. Petersburg, where, thanks to the emperor, my occupations have a more serious purpose.

"His Majesty may wish to know what book it is I intend to finish in the country: it is a novel,† most of whose scenes take place in Orenburg and Kazan, which is why it is those two districts I want to visit. I repeat that I have no regular income apart from the salary generously allotted to me by His Majesty; and living in the capital is costly and adds to my expenses."

Nicholas I was persuaded by these sound considerations to authorize Pushkin's departure and order him to be kept under observation by the police while in Orenburg. With a four months' leave of absence, Pushkin set out from St. Petersburg on August 18, 1833. He was very happy to be getting away from the tedium of society in the capital, and very sad to be leaving his wife, so young, pretty and unworldly, in the clutches of a mob of servants and admirers.

† *The Captain's Daughter.*

6. The Bronze Horseman

Pushkin left St. Petersburg in a heavy storm. "The Neva was so high that the bridge had buckled," he wrote his wife a few days later. "They had put a rope across the road and the police were stopping all carriages. I almost turned back to Chernaya Rechka, but I managed to cross a little farther upstream, and left St. Petersburg. The weather was foul. The trees along the prospect in Tsarskoye Selo were falling over one after another. I counted fifty of them down. The puddles were being swept up by the wind. The marshes were boiling with white wavelets. . . ."

The next day the weather grew calmer and Pushkin continued his journey. On his way to Yaropolets, he stopped off at the Wulf estate to pay his respects to the scene of so many triumphs of his heedless bachelor days. But the haven of his former loves had changed enormously in a few short years. The Wulf-Osipov girls were gone; only the furniture greeted him, stiff and unfriendly, and the smell of all his country memories—old floors and sour apples. To allay Natalya's probable suspicions, he described his sentimental pilgrimage as follows: "Five years ago, Pavlovskoye, Malinniki, and Bernovo were full of lancers and young ladies, but the lancers are stationed elsewhere now and the young ladies have scattered to the four winds. The only old girl friend I met was the white mare I rode at Malinniki—but she too had changed, and no longer curvets and prances. At Malinniki, instead of the Annettes, Eufrasias, Sashas, Mashas and so forth, there is only the steward, whose name is Reichmann, and who gave me schnapps to drink. The Velyashev girl, of whom I sang in days gone by, is still around, but I shall not go to see her as I know you would dislike it. I have been eating preserves, and lost three rubles in four rubbers of whist."

At Yaropolets Pushkin saw his mother-in-law, who lived in a dilapidated but once magnificent old country house, and who welcomed him "with the greatest possible cordiality." She even allowed him to go through her library and select some thirty books which she was to send on to St. Petersburg together with some preserves and homemade liqueur. From Yaropolets, Pushkin went to Moscow, where he saw Sobolevsky, Nashchokin and Sudyenko. "I dined at Sudyenko's—a friend, a comrade of my bachelor days," Pushkin wrote to Natalya. "Now he too is married, he too has two children, he too has stopped playing cards, but he also has an income of 125,000 rubles, and for us, my angel, that is still to come. His wife is quiet and gentle; not a beauty. We dined together, just the three of us, very informally; I proposed a toast to your health* and we drank off a large glass of champagne without blinking. Then a soiree at Nashchokin's, and what a soiree! Champagne, Laffite, flaming punch and pineapples. . . . The next day . . . Nashchokin gave me a farewell dinner with sturgeon and punch, handed me into my barouche and I took to the highroad."

In his barouche on the highroad, Pushkin thought continually of his wife and children, imagining hosts of assorted perils looming over them. Debts, illness, the servants' insolence, the assaults of the young gallants, expenses: "I can imagine exactly what your first of the month is like. You are badgered for payments, Parasha, the cook, the coachman, the chemist, Mrs. Zischler, etc. . . . You work yourself into a state, you accuse me, and quite rightly too. . . ."

In Kazan, Pushkin questioned Pugachev's contemporaries, visited the neighborhood of the fortress and submitted to the blandishments of a provincial poetess "with waxen teeth and dirty fingernails," who read him two hundred lines at one go. In Simbirsk he watched a dancing lesson at the home of the governor of the town. The girls asked him to invite them to waltz, whereupon he drew a pistol from his pocket, laid it on the window ledge and gallantly proceeded to oblige. The young ladies were to cherish an imperishable memory of this great honor. At last, after a tiring and monotonous journey, he reached Orenburg on September 18, 1833. The day after his arrival, he wrote to his wife: "I am bored without you. If I weren't ashamed, I would come straight back without writing a line. But it is impossible, my angel. I've made my bed, I must lie in it; in other words, having left to write, I must write, novel after novel and poem after poem. Already, I can feel the madness coming over me. I compose even in the carriage, what will it be like when I'm in bed? One thing distresses me, and that is my servant, a species of Muscovite scribbler, stupid, bawling, drunk every second day, who eats my cold grouse, drinks my Madeira, ruins my books and calls me count at one posting house and general at the next. . . . Incidentally, how are you getting along with the household? I am afraid you don't have enough help; don't you want to hire some more? . . ."

* Natalya's feast day was August 26, her birthday August 17.

At Orenburg Pushkin met his comrade Dahl, a writer, specialist in folklore and lexicographer, who was employed as private secretary to the governor of the town. Dahl took Pushkin to see the historic village of Berda, Pugachev's ex-capital. He showed him the St. George bell tower on which Pugachev had mounted a pair of cannon, the remains of the trenches and the Zaouralsk wood, supposedly haunted by the dread pretender's ghost. He told him about Pugachev's golden palace, which was nothing but a thatched hut hung with copper sheeting, and about the Cossack chief's entrance into the village church: The crowd drew back in horror as he strode the length of the church, lowered himself majestically onto the altar and declared: "It's a long time since I've sat on a throne!"

Pushkin unearthed an ancient woman who had known Pugachev and remembered him. She showed the visitors where the golden palace had stood, the place where the bandit executed hostile inhabitants, the hills where, according to legend, Pugachev's vast treasure lay buried, sewn into a shirt and covered by a corpse in order to make treasure seekers think they had found an ordinary grave. The old woman quavered out a few songs, and Pushkin gave her a golden louis for her good memory. But the natives of Berda did not like the looks of this gold. After the tourists had gone, the Cossacks held a counsel and concluded that the attitude of this stranger who asked all sorts of questions about a brigand anathematized by the Church and who paid such a high price for his information was suspicious, to say the least. Wouldn't he be a successor to Pugachev, an enemy of imperial power and religion, the devil's henchman? Wouldn't the local authorities punish the old woman and all her family for even mentioning the blackguard's name?

"The next day," Dahl wrote, "the Cossacks hitched up a team and drove the old woman and her poor louis to town. They deposed as follows: 'Yesterday, an unknown master came to us, whose chief identifying marks are that he is short of stature and has curly black hair and a swarthy complexion. He encouraged people to start the Pugachev uprising again and distributed gold. He must be Antichrist, for he had claws instead of nails."[1]

It took the governor some time to tranquilize the old woman and her Cossack escort.

On September 20 Pushkin left Orenburg for Uralsk, where the Cossacks drank in his honor more than was good for them. From Uralsk he called in at the estate of his friend Yazykov, and went on to Boldino.

There, in his literary fortress, he intended to revise, classify and organize the impressions he had gathered on his journey. The long steppe, the dull sky, the puddles of water, the worm-eaten house were all unchanged; and, as on the first occasion, Pushkin burrowed delightedly into this gloomy solitude. Awake at seven, he drank his coffee and returned to bed, where he wrote and read until three in the afternoon. From three to five, he rode. At five, he bathed and ate something—baked potatoes and porridge. Then he returned to his room and read or made notes until nine. He grew a beard. He became a savage in a jungle of rhyme. But when inspiration flagged and the writing fever left him, his heart filled with regrets, anxieties and depression. At Boldino, as everywhere else, he thought of Natalya, and always with apprehension. His letters were all variations on the theme of jealousy. Pushkin was jealous of everyone who came near his wife, and most of all, of the tsar—for with all his pontificating about family tradition, Nicholas adored to flirt with the young women by whom he was surrounded.

"He carried on like a debutante," noted Pushkin's friend Miss Rossetti.

"Our master [the emperor] did not miss a single costume ball," Countess Nesselrode wrote to her son. "He stayed until three in the morning, walking about with ordinary persons. One of these common women, whose status was such that he need not trouble to be particular in his speech, told your uncle that the audacity of his allusions was unimaginable."

It was just those turns around the dance floor, those audacious allusions, those soldiers' compliments that Pushkin feared. Although he had faith in Natalya's basic virtue, the idea that the emperor might supplant him in his wife's imagination was intolerable. He felt ugly, defenseless and puny, alongside that colossus with the smooth Roman face and noble gaze and the tight-fitting uniform. All he possessed to ward off this omnipotent rival was his poetic genius. And Natalya was totally uninterested in poetry.

"Don't upset me," he wrote to her on October 11, 1833, "don't frighten me, keep well, take care of the children, and don't flirt with the tsar or Princess Lyubov's fiancé. I'm writing, I'm having enormous difficulties, I see no one. . . . Do you know what they say about me in the districts around here? This is how they think I write: 'Pushkin composes his poems with a bottle of the best liqueur in front of him; he gulps down one, two, three glasses, and begins to write.' Such is fame!"

Ten days later, the bell tolled again: "Yesterday I was so depressed that I don't recall ever feeling anything like it. I am happy to hear you are not pregnant and that nothing can prevent you from shining at the balls. . . . I don't forbid you to flirt altogether, but I do require you to know what you're doing and to be honorable and distinguished; of course, I am not speaking of the over-all respectability of your conduct, which has nothing to do with 'tone' but concerns something more basic. Who besides Ogarev is paying court to you? Send me a list, in alphabetical order. . . . As far as I am concerned, I can report that I am working slowly and with bad grace. The last few days I have had a headache and boredom has been gnawing at me. Now I feel better. I have started on a mass of things, but nothing really excites me. God knows what's going on inside me. I'm getting old, my mind is wearing out. I shall come to renew myself at your youth. . . ."

The next letter, dated October 30, 1833, expressed the same suspicion and depression, but more emphatically than ever before. Natalya had thought it would be clever to send her husband a list of her latest conquests—after all, he ought to be as proud of her success as she was. She mentioned names, quoted compliments, added up the waltzes, oglings, admonitory taps of her fan. Pushkin fumed to see how brainless and weak she was in his absence. He was coming to fear, to hate, Natalya's beauty.

"It seems to me you are becoming rather too flirtatious," he wrote. "Do take care: It's not for nothing that coquetry has gone out of fashion and is now seen as a mark of bad taste. It is senseless. You love it when men run after you, like dogs running after a bitch and sniffing at her behind with their tails in the air. Something to boast about, truly! You are not the only one who knows how to do it. Praskovya Petrovna can also train unmarried dandies to come to heel, all one needs to do is spread it about that one is that way inclined. That's the only secret of coquetry. Bring a trough to swine, they will feed. Why do you receive the men who flirt with you? You never know who might turn up. Read Izmailov's fable of *Thomas and Kuzma.* Thomas fed Kuzma on caviar and herring. When Kuzma asked for a drink, Thomas refused, so Kuzma thrashed Thomas like a common serf. The poet's moral to this story is, 'My beauties, do not offer herring if you will not give water afterward, for you may chance upon a Kuzma.' There. I ask you not to hold any of these luncheons in my house. And now, my angel, I kiss you as though nothing had happened, and thank you for writing so sincerely and in such detail on the subject of your dissipations. Enjoy yourself, my little wife, but not too much, and don't forget me. I can't wait to see you with your hair dressed à la Ninon, you must be wonderfully pretty. . . . Tell me what you're wearing to the balls—which must, from what you say, have already begun. Still, my angel, I do beseech you not to be a flirt. I am not jealous and I know you will not exceed the limits; but you know, too, how I loathe anything reminiscent of the Muscovite marriageables, anything that is vulgar or not *comme il faut*. If, when I get back, I find the least little change in your pleasant, natural, aristocratic bearing, I shall get a divorce, as the Lord is my witness, and will go for a soldier to drown my sorrows."

A week later, ashamed of having spoken so coarsely, Pushkin wrote a letter that was more gentle in tone, but still on the same subject: "My friend, my little wife, by the last post I sent you a letter that said things I don't very well remember. I think I was a little angry and my letter was rather harsh. I will repeat, more gently, that no good can come of coquetry: It offers some satisfactions, no doubt, but it rapidly deprives young women of the one asset without which there can be neither a happy family nor agreeable social relations, I mean respect. It is not right for you to rejoice in your conquests. The woman whose coiffure you have borrowed (N.B. You must be ravishing in it, I thought about it last night), Ninon, said, *'Il est écrit sur le coeur de tout homme: à la plus facile.'*† After that, just try to go on being proud of your triumphs over men's hearts. Think about it, and don't torment me needlessly. . . . My little wife, my little wife, I go out on the roads, I spend three months in a deserted steppe, I go to slanderous Moscow, which I abhor, and for whom do I do all this? For you, my little wife, so that you may rest easy, so that you may shine as brightly as you wish and as befits your age and beauty. Then do have some consideration for me. Don't add domestic complications and fits of jealousy to a poor man's other tribulations. . . . Not to mention the 'blessed state of ignorance,' on the subject of which I recently read a long dissertation in Brantôme. . . ."

What an army of reasons he marshaled to convince his little goose to give up her systematic flirtation! Pushkin treated her as though he were teaching a child—giving plenty of concrete examples, quoting fables, repeating the same rules ten times over, losing his temper, backtracking, slipping in a humorous remark to sugar-coat the pill. And when he wrote, "I shall bring back heaps of poems for you, but don't tell a soul," he knew full well that her first thought would be for the money they would earn.

Pushkin's second season at Boldino was as productive as the first. He was alternately drawn and held by prose and poetry, history and legend.

First he wrote his *Pugachev*, in a dry, cool, uncompromising style. This poet was also a stern historian. He based his work on authentic primary sources, would not be tempted by neat hypotheses and discreetly removed himself behind his heroes. Having lived through the rebellion of December 14 and so many other military or popular uprisings in Russia, the Pugachev incident naturally attracted him. He saw it as the first collision between two irreconcilable powers: imperialism with its bureaucrats, and the Russian mass, conscious of its strength and rights. In his notes, he wrote: "The entire population, the nobodies,

† "It is written on the heart of every male: to the most willing."

were for Pugachev. . . . Only the nobility were clearly committed to the authorities. At first, Pugachev and his partisans tried to win the nobles to their cause, but their interests were too opposed."

In the text itself: "In Moscow, Pugachev (after his capture) was met by a huge crowd, which had once awaited his coming so impatiently and was now pacified, but with difficulty, by the capture of the terrible bandit."

In fact, Pushkin showed exceptional daring throughout his historical essay. He ventured to say, for instance, that the rebels "adopted the surest and most effective means to their end," whereas the government "acted weakly, slowly and clumsily." Although he called Pugachev a bandit, an impostor and a drunkard, he also accused Catherine and her generals. He criticized the empress for entrusting the country's fate to foreigners like Reinsdorp, Karr and Freimann. . . . Through them, the poet was pointing at the Benkendorfs, Von Foks, Nesselrodes and the whole club of senior officials hailing from Courland, that bureaucratic freemasonry with the dubious names, that regiment of bodyguards of Nicholas I, who had no sympathy for Russia and defended their own interests at the expense of the nation's.

When Pushkin submitted the text to his imperial censor, Nicholas covered it with comments and corrections. In the first place, the essay could never be called the *History of Pugachev,* because impostors did not have "histories"; it would be the *History of the Pugachev Rebellion.* Then, there were various infelicitous turns of phrase that would have to be altered.

For instance, Pushkin had written that General Wallensterg's men, finding themselves surrounded by enemy fire, had "fled." Nicholas I peevishly amended this sentence to read: "His regiment became disorganized." Elsewhere, the author stated that Pugachev "promoted" one of his followers to the rank of colonel. Nicholas would not hear of promotion except in the regular army, so he crossed out "promoted" and wrote "named" instead. Similarly, the "famed rebel" became, under Nicholas' pencil, a plain "rebel." And so forth.

Duly revised, the work was published in December 1834. The public reacted coolly to these excessively gray and sober pages. They had expected a new Robin Hood, spicy and romantic. They wanted local color, wild night rides, cannon salvos, blood, shouting and gunsmoke, instead of which Pushkin offered them an objective reconstruction.

"Among the public," Pushkin wrote, "there is severe criticism of my *Pugachev,* and, what is worse, it is not selling."

In an article that remained without echo, however, Pogodin wrote: "Pushkin, who gave us a language of tragedy with *Boris Godunov,* has now dealt a deathblow to oratorical history, of which Karamzin was the first and last master, with his *Pugachev Rebellion*. . . . Pushkin has cleared a new path for us. Many readers, accustomed only to rhetoric, are misled by the style of the *Pugachev Rebellion*. Disconcerted by its apparent simplicity and facility, they do not give it the respect it deserves. Ah, if they but knew how difficult and how complicated it is to write simple, easy Russian, they would change their tune and begin to sing their admiration of the author, who is such a master of his style that he can do anything he likes with it. . . . This history reads like the most thrilling of novels, and, despite all its formal dryness, once you have picked it up it is impossible to put it down. . . . Such is the power of talent."

The *poetry* of the insurrection, which Pushkin deliberately neglected in his essay, he exploited in *The Bronze Horseman*, written at Boldino during the same period.

The Bronze Horseman is a poem of full maturity. It is the purest and most finished, and also the most profound and elusive of Pushkin's works. In it the threads of history and romance, realism and fantasy are wound together into a single skein. Only one of the poem's three heroes is human: Eugene, the little white-collar clerk. The second hero is the bronze equestrian statue of Peter the Great. The third is the Neva, which overflows its banks and floods the streets. Flesh, bronze and moving water. The superficial pretext for the poem is the St. Petersburg flood of November 7, 1824. Its deeper subject is the revolt of the individual against imperial authority, symbolized by the bronze horseman. Some of the sources of *The Bronze Horseman* are the *Exact Historical Account of the St. Petersburg Floods*, which appeared in 1826, some lines by Batyushkov, a poem by Mickiewicz entitled *To the Monument of Peter the Great*, Shevyrev's *Petrograd* and an anecdote telling how the statue of Peter the Great came down from its pedestal during the War of 1812 to inform Alexander I that his foreign policy was disastrous.

One cold November evening in 1827, Pushkin and Mickiewicz stood draped under a single cape in front of the monument of Peter the Great, arguing the merits of the man whose bronze gallop dominated the city. Perhaps, at that moment, Pushkin had a revelation of what later became his poem; perhaps it began ripening within him then. Six years later, at Boldino, it had grown to maturity.

The poem begins with a description of St. Petersburg, the city of granite and iron: new and rectilinear, severe and cold, like a surveyor's mind. From this vast bureaucratic anthill Pushkin singles out one ant: a poor, hard-working, colorless young man. He doesn't even have a face. He doesn't even have a last name. He is just Eugene. Eugene comes home, goes to bed and listens to the sounds of the city. The wind is howling.

The Neva is turbulent. If the bridges are carried away, Eugene will not be able to visit Parasha, his betrothed, for a day or two—for he has a betrothed, this infinitesimal, and pretensions to a snug little house, wifely affection, promotion in his job and progeny. When he wakes next morning, his fears have been far surpassed. The river has overflowed its banks, inundated the streets and drowned the squares under its muddy, growling waters.

Boats smash in the windowpanes,
Gardens are sucked beneath the water;
Whole houses, beams, roofs,
The treasures of miserly tradesmen,
The rags of lowly poverty,
Shards of bridges, coffins
From the sunken cemetery,
All drift slowly through the streets.

The imperial palace stands like an island of stone in the maddened sea of froth and waves. Little by little, however, the squall subsides and the waters recede; Eugene begs a boatman to ferry him across to the other shore, where his beloved Parasha dwells. There, the uprooted and shattered houses stand empty. Their gaping windows exhale an inimical silence. With a terrible foreboding, Eugene hurries through the ruins to his fiancée's house. He finds the place, but the cottage is gone. The river has swept everything away, killed everything in its path. Parasha is no more. Dazed with horror, Eugene wanders through the wasteland of sodden earth and splintered boards, all that remain of his love. His thoughts limp and falter in his brain. He staggers through the fog. He begins to laugh. He has gone mad.

For days, weeks, he roams the city, sleeping on the quays, living on charity, his mind in a perpetual tempest of wind, icy water and evil clouds. One evening he dozes off on the banks of the Neva. When he wakes, it is night. The rain is coming down in sheets. Sentinels cry out in the distance. Eugene stands up and begins to walk, aimlessly. All of a sudden, he finds himself on the great Senate Square. He sees the palace and its lions with upraised paws; in the center, the statue of Peter the Great rises out of its mist-shrouded rock, seated on the heavy, motionless, galloping bronze horse.

Then he recognized the place
Where the flood came pouring in,
Where the voracious water seethed.
The lions; the square; and Him,
Lifting his bronze head, up there,
Motionless in the mists,
The man whose fateful commandment
Built the city on the sea!

How awesome, in that darkness!
What thoughts move behind his iron brow?
What strange force lives within him?
And what fire in that horse!
Where are you riding your proud charger?
Where will you set your hoof?
O, powerful master of Destiny!
Just so, on the edge of the abyss,
Hauling on iron reins,
You pulled Russia onto its haunches.

Hypnotized by the mass of the bronze horseman, Eugene draws nearer. A dull rage is working in him. This bronze hero, who dared to build a city on the waves, who defied the unchained elements, who preferred glory to caution and reason, whose pride jeopardized the lives of so many human beings: Eugene holds him responsible for his misfortune.

His jaw like a vice, clenching his fists,
Shaken by bitter wrath,
"Hail, old miracle worker,"
He mutters, shuddering.
"Just you wait!" Then suddenly
He flees, begins to run: He thinks
The face of the dread tsar
Has turned, slowly, toward him,
Showing a quick flash of rage.
He races across the empty square,
And hears, close behind him,
A noise like a huge roll of thunder.
A heavy clang of galloping
Jars the hard paving stones.
Lit by the pallid moon,
Arms outstretched in space,
The bronze horseman follows
On his pounding, galloping horse.
All night long, wherever
The madman tries to hide,
On this side or that, behind him,
The bronze horseman gallops,
Battering the streets with heavy hoof.

In this poem, with its rare perfection of form, the human hero and the bronze hero have equal weight. Eugene, the nonentity-clerk, affronts the statue of bronze. The history of a people collides with the story of an individual. The infinitesimal joins the incommensurable. We know the anguish of the infinitesimal: The disaster of the flood is crystallized in his frail black silhouette. He has lost everything as a result of a decision made by somebody else. And when he sees the image of that somebody, he calls him to account. Eugene's bereavement gives

35. Katerina Goncharov, the poet's sister-in-law.
Painting by Henri Beltz (1840)

37. Alexandra Goncharov, portrait in pencil by Rait

36. Madame Khitrovo, lithograph of a water color by Hau

38. Count Benkendorf, from a lithograph by Pol

39. Nashchokin, pencil drawing by K. Maser

40. Smirnova-Rossetti, reproduction of a water color by Sokolov

41. Baron Heckeren, from a lithograph by Krieshuber (1843)

42. Idalya Poletika and her daughter, by Von Nef

43. Baron Georges d'Anthès de Heckeren

44. Katerina Ushakov

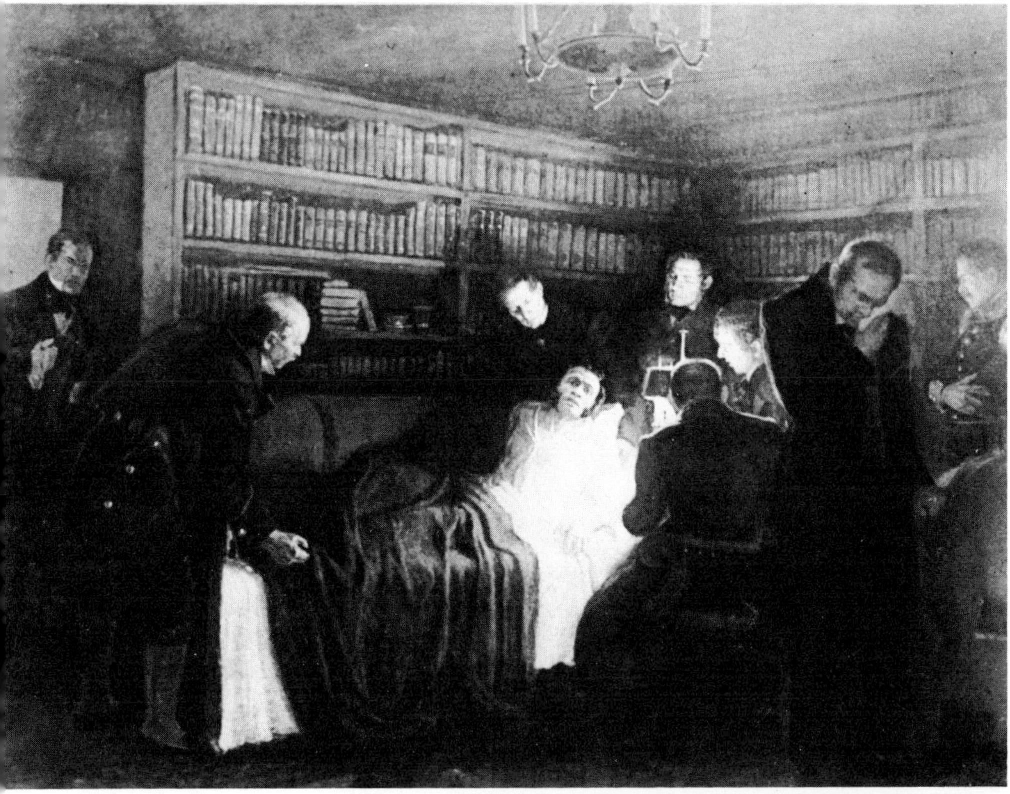

45. The death of the poet, painting by Stronk

46. Painting of "Pushkin in His Coffin"

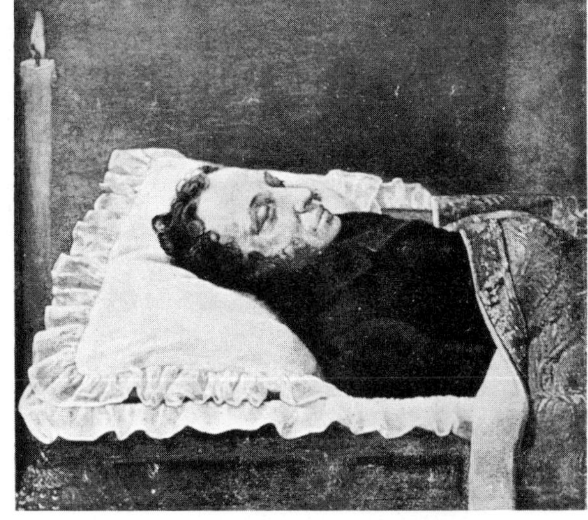

47. Statue of Pushkin sculpted by M. G. Manizer for the 150th anniversary of Pushkin's birth (1949)

him rights. For one split second, it makes him the equal of Peter the Great. Eugene speaks to Peter as one man to another. This moment is reminiscent of *The Anchar:*

> But a man of lofty mien
> Sends another to the anchar tree.

The Bronze Horseman is a transposition of *The Anchar*. Eugene is a man, Peter the Great was one too. Why should the will of one man command the happiness or misery of all? Why must Eugene pay for the potentate's mistakes? Someone else, unknown to him, disposed of his life and love. Someone else condemned him to his grief and madness. Someone else took his self away from him—out of pride, for the pleasure of opening "a window onto Europe," building a city on the water, flouting nature, the laws of architecture and the mind of God. And Eugene has to obey. His rebellion is instantly punished by the wrath of the monarch whose crashing gallop pursues him through the city.

Because there is no justice on earth. Because historical necessity takes priority over all. Because the rise of a nation implies the crushing of a million men like Eugene and a million women like Parasha. Peter the Great will be great, in spite of Eugene's insults and in spite of Parasha's death; Peter the Great does not even know they exist, Eugene and Parasha and their minute love. It is not only Eugene he pursues through street after street on his bronze horse: it is the whole race of Eugenes, the indignant ants, exasperated amoebae, mutineers present and to come. He will drive them all to exhaustion, to ultimate insanity. He will triumph over them on Senate Square, as he triumphed over the Decembrists posted around his statue in straight lines, as he triumphed over the flood whose waves broke against his rock. The revolt of men and elements cannot touch him. And just as Eugene is the incarnation of a million humans cruelly deprived of their chance in life, so the figure of Peter the Great is the incarnation of all tsars, past and future, of all the princes, despots and governors of the world.

The people need a leader. But the instant he is named, he ceases to be part of the people, ceases to be a citizen aware of the individual destinies of his brothers. He can no longer see except in hordes, he can no longer count except by provinces. His eyes leave the ground and soar to incalculable heights. For him, all faces here below are a pinkish sea, anonymous and docile, through which he cleaves his way toward what he believes to be the general good, often only to increase his own glory. He sacrifices masses of individual values, hopes, loves, talents, greeds, devotions, family names, Christian names, letters, pressed flowers, smiles. He grinds, stirs, scatters, collects, pummels, heats, pushes away and snatches back again. He is a great man; he is not, any more, a man.

And it is Eugene who is right. There will be no real equality and justice as long as Peter the Great sits on his bronze horse. And yet there have always had to be Peter the Greats to keep the world going, and there always will have to be. And until the night of time poor, demented, white-faced, wild-haired little men will shake their fists at bronze idols. In his *To the Monument of Peter the Great,* Mickiewicz wrote:

> But what do I see? Years go by, one by one,
> The tsar is still there, on his bronze horse . . .
> Like a cascade above the chasm,
> Frozen in mid-fall into the void.
> What will become of this petrified rush
> When, in the spring, from the top of a calm, clear sky
> The bright sun of freedom lights upon
> And warms that ice in the fire of its rays?

Pushkin was not thinking of the overthrow of the bronze horseman: If he went, another would come in his place. Total freedom was a snare and a delusion. Private will would always be subject to the whim of the one who personifies, or thinks he personifies, the will of all. The principle of authority was absurd, odious, harmful—but indispensable. Nicholas I alias Peter the Great and Pushkin alias Eugene were equally necessary to the stability of mankind.

That is the implicit meaning of the poem. It was the work of a revolutionary, to be sure, but of a revolutionary who had been disappointed by the failure of December 14, a revolutionary convinced of the futility of revolution, a revolutionary who had gone out of business. It was the Pushkin of thirty-three, judging the Pushkin of twenty-five.

In *The Bronze Horseman* the poet's thought is admirably served by its expression. Pushkin was never more master of his art; his choice of verb and adjective is unfaltering, his style changes from scene to scene and character to character. When Eugene is onstage, Pushkin adopts a familiar, pale, prosaic language and a verse scheme continually broken by enjambments. When it is the bronze horseman, his words ring like iron hoofs on stone. It is really as though the Eugene passages were written in cadenced prose and the Peter the Great passages in a succession of charging onomatopoeias. The furious gallop rings in the reader's ears as it rings in Eugene's. The reader understands and shares his madness, his head whirling in the mist and the clang of heavy iron.

The "Eugene rebellion," like the *Pugachev Rebellion,* was submitted to Nicholas I for approval, and aroused all the monarch's fastidious ire. Everywhere, he underlined "idol," "proud idol," in reference to Peter the Great. He rejected the expression:

> Hello there, you old miracle worker.

The lines:

> The man whose fateful commandment
> Built the city on the sea

suffered the same fate.

Censored too was the line in which Pushkin tells Peter the Great:

> You pulled Russia onto its haunches.

In the end, Nicholas forbade publication of the entire passage in which Eugene insults the statue and runs off through the city pursued by its gigantic tread.

"On the eleventh [of December 1833]," Pushkin wrote in his diary, "I received an invitation from Benkendorf to see him the following morning. I went. *The Bronze Horseman* was handed back to me with the emperor's annotations. Question marks everywhere. I had to make a good many changes, and to alter the terms of my contract with Smirdin."

Nicholas had guessed at another idea, more powerful and dangerous, behind the fable of the little clerk who was a victim of a flood. He started when he read Eugene's words to the bronze horseman, as though they had been addressed to himself. Pushkin could not alter the poem, and decided not to publish it; it was not printed until after his death, in a watered-down version by Zhukovsky.

Pushkin had suffered the same fate as Eugene. He had had to bow to the authority of the monarch. And he knew, now, that he would be hearing his master's ponderous gallop until he died. He would find no refuge from the pursuing idol. It would be everywhere he would be; and when, one day, he collapsed after all the shouting and fighting and running, he would find himself lying at its feet.

"I believe," Pushkin told Mrs. Smirnov, "that the dead can affect the thoughts of the living." All the while he was writing *The Bronze Horseman*, he was fascinated by the supernatural, by cabalism and madness. Eugene was a rebel madman. Hermann, the hero of *The Queen of Spades*, a short story in prose, is also a rebel madman. One challenges the emperor, the other challenges fate. Their parallel adventures take place in the same St. Petersburg of mystery, chill and fog. Both works are handled similarly, too, for both contain an element of the supernatural injected into a realistic psychological tale.

Hermann is a Russian officer of German origin. "He had powerful passions and a fiery imagination, but his strength of character had always preserved him from the usual errors of youth." He is a clearheaded, ambitious schemer, who never touches a card but is always present at his friends' noisy gatherings around the green table. "I cannot risk the essential in the hope of the superfluous," he says to those who urge him to bet. One such nocturnal session, however, is to decide his fate. That evening Tomsky, a card player, tells how, long ago, his grandmother learned an infallible combination from Count Saint-Germain. It involves three cards. But which three? Any player would pay dearly to know, but the old countess has sworn never to play again and will not disclose the miraculous combination that saved her from ruin and dishonor.

The story makes a deep impression on Hermann. He is poor. He needs money to live respectably in this luxurious city. "A sure win!" How idiotic that an old woman's stubbornness should prevent him from making all his dreams come true. After a night filled with weird visions, he determines to storm the grandmother's citadel.

The grandmother lives in a vast palace defended by an army of manservants and chambermaids. She is eighty-seven years old. "She was miserly," Pushkin wrote, "and indulged in the cold selfishness of old people who have ceased to love and detest the world of the present. She took part in every social event and dragged herself to every ball, where, painted and dressed in the old fashion, she sat in a corner, a hideous and essential ornament of the ballroom." With this rouged and crabbed monster lives a ward, Liza, an extremely pretty girl, shy, diffident and miserable. She is employed by the old woman as companion, reader and, above all, scapegoat. "If she were reading a novel aloud, the countess held her responsible for all the author's shortcomings. If she were accompanying the countess on a walk, the bad weather and revolting state of the pavement were attributed to her. . . . At the ball she never danced except when there was a partner short, and the ladies leaned on her arm whenever they needed to leave the room. . . ." It is through this unhappy and tenderhearted child that Hermann decides to seek access to the countess. He stations himself under Liza's window. He sends billets-doux to her through a seamstress. And Liza, dumfounded to think that anyone could actually be interested in her, eventually yields to Hermann's urgings and gives him a rendezvous inside the house. He is to come on an evening when Liza and the old woman are at an embassy ball, slip into the empty hall, cross the countess' room and go on into that of the girl. But the countess' room intrigues Hermann far more than Liza's. On the appointed day, after watching the old woman's solemn departure with her companion from a distance, he enters the palace and soon makes his way into a large room, dimly lit by a vigil lamp. He hides behind a screen and settles down to await the old woman's return.‡

‡ For this scene, Pushkin undoubtedly used his memories of his clandestine tryst with Dolly Ficquelmont.

At last she comes, accompanied by three servants, and drops exhausted into a huge armchair. Then the lugubrious toilette begins: "Her rose-bedecked bonnet was removed; her powdered wig was removed, revealing a pate covered with pure white stubble. Hairpins showered to the ground." At last the servants withdraw, taking their candles with them, and the countess is left alone in the room. "Her skin was yellow, her pendulous lips moved, she swayed from side to side." Then Hermann emerges from his hiding place and advances upon her: "I have no intention of harming you, I have come to beg a favor. . . . You are able, I know, to tell me three cards which . . ."

The old woman stares at him incredulously and does not even seem to hear his pleas. He loses patience and threatens her with a gun, whereupon the countess shakes her head, turns pale with terror and falls back in her armchair, dead.

Hermann flees without obtaining the secret. Three days later, he attends the funeral. As he comes up to the coffin it seems to him that the corpse winks at him. He goes home in a state of extreme agitation and throws himself down on his bed fully dressed. After a time, he hears someone walking, "shuffling softly in carpet slippers." The door opens and a woman enters, dressed in white. He recognizes the countess: "'I have come against my will,' she said in a firm voice. 'But I am commanded to grant your wish. Three, seven, ace will win, played in that order, but you will play only one card each night, and afterward you will never play again in your life. I forgive you my death on condition that you marry my ward Liza.'"

Having spoken, the vision disappears. Hermann, obsessed by the three magic cards, can hardly wait to test their power. He goes to a gaming club, bets on the three, and wins. The next day he comes back, bets everything he won the previous night on the seven, and wins again. The third day, he stakes all his winnings on the card he has chosen, an ace. The banker begins to cut. An ace comes up on the left.

"'The ace wins,' cried Hermann, and turned up his card.

"'Your queen is beaten. . . .'

"Hermann started: So it was, instead of an ace, he was holding a queen of spades. . . . At that instant it seemed to him that the queen winked and smiled at him. He was struck by an extraordinary likeness.

"'The old woman,' he cried out in horror."

Pushkin's short story ends with Hermann's committal to an asylum and Liza's marriage to "a very personable young man."

The whole story of *The Queen of Spades* is infused with mystery. The three fatal cards form a background of red, black and white against which the gambler's tale unwinds. Some have classed it as realistic, others as fantasy. For the former, Hermann merely makes a mistake when he chooses his third card, and bets on a queen, thinking he is betting on the ace. For the latter, he does bet on an ace, but the evil forces converging upon him change the ace into the queen of spades. Is it a player's error, or a punishment exacted by God? Are we on earth, or off to one side?

The real issue is elsewhere. In *The Queen of Spades* Pushkin was not relating either the adventure—ordinary enough, after all—of a player who mistakes one card for another, or the adventure of a player who tries to solve the enigmas of the occult by force. Instead, he was reverting to the theme of *Mozart and Salieri, The Covetous Knight, The Stone Guest* and so many other works written during his first stay at Boldino. Hermann is a Salieri, a hoarder, a laborious computer. He aspires to domesticate chance rather than submit to it, to transform a game into a mathematical operation; and he does not stop at crime in his efforts to obtain the infallible combination. Seated at the table afterward, still dazed by the murder and vision, he knows he is stronger than Providence. But once again, Providence crushes all who dream of dominating her. The only humans who conquer are those who surrender to her; it is only the "prodigals" who win. Hermann wants to be stronger than God, but God punishes him for building his shaky house of cards so high, and hurls him from the summit of that blasphemous edifice into nothingness, into madness.

In May 1831 Pushkin had written to Mrs. Khitrovo: "I beg you to send me the second volume of *The Red and the Black*. I adore it."[2] And indeed, Hermann is a true kinsman of Julien Sorel, a satanic opportunist, a monster of prediction, a miniature Napoleon. Both are gamblers seeking to master chance. Even the titles of the two works, *The Red and the Black* and *The Queen of Spades*, belong to the vocabulary of games of chance.

Another writer would have given this fantastic subject the full treatment, padding it out with resounding adjectives, making liberal allusion to the supernatural and sprinkling a good pinch of sulphur over all. Pushkin, on the contrary, sets out the drama in the flat light of day. His vocabulary is more bareboned than ever, his syntax more straightforward, making the contrast between the spare, lean language and the miraculous events all the more arresting. The less the author seems to be trying to intrigue us, the more we are intrigued, as though the mystery grew in defiance of the author's talent rather than because of it, as though we let ourselves be bewitched by him without his knowledge or ours, as though the game were lost by the author but won, in some inexplicable fashion, by the story. That is Pushkin's supreme merit: to shun the limelight for the sake of his creation. Here again, by giving the reader only the essence of his thought, he proves his supreme mastery. His prose, so clean and uncluttered, remains a model of the genre. The words of the short sentences, devoid of modifiers, all strain toward one strong verb. The story hurtles from one verb to the next, dry, precise, breathless, without any oratorical flourishes. There is nothing but sinew and muscle—the faster to run with, the faster to reach the end. What could be more convincing, and more simple, than this description of Hermann waiting outside the old woman's palace?

"The weather was foul. The wind howled, huge flakes of half-melted snow were falling. The street lights gave out a muffled glow, the streets were deserted. Now and then a sledge glided past, pulled by some emaciated nag, its driver looking out for a late fare. . . . At last, the countess' coach drew up. Hermann saw the old woman come out, all bent over, enveloped in a sable pelisse and held up by two footmen; immediately after her hurried Lizaveta Ivanovna with a light cloak over her shoulders and fresh flowers in her hair. The door banged and the coach rolled swiftly away over the wet snow. The hall porter closed the front door. The lights in the windows went out. Hermann paced back and forth in front of the deserted house."

When he came to describe the old woman's ghost, Pushkin was careful to resist the temptation of ghastly glimmers, fluorescences and clanking chains. At first, the apparition seems almost disappointingly drab:

"Just then, someone going past in the street outside glanced into the room and moved quickly on. Hermann paid no attention. A minute later, he heard his front door open. He thought it was his orderly, drunk as usual, coming back from some nocturnal prowl. But no; it was an unfamiliar step. Someone was walking, shuffling softly in carpet slippers. The door opened and a woman dressed in white came into the room. . . . Hermann recognized the countess."

In this paragraph of utter flatness and unrelieved gray, the eye is caught by two short phrases: "Someone was walking, shuffling softly in carpet slippers," and "a woman dressed in white came into the room." That's all there is to the ghost, a woman in white shuffling in her slippers. But her whiteness and her slippers are uncanny; accompanied by no supporting details, they take on enormous importance in our minds. They obsess us. Pushkin was right to rely upon his reader to build up a whole world behind a few well-chosen words.

This story, allegedly inspired by the adventures of the aged Princess Golitsyn, was received by critics and public alike with an enthusiasm to which Pushkin had grown unaccustomed in recent years.

"My *Queen of Spades* is having quite a vogue," he wrote. "Gamblers are all betting the three-seven-ace. The court has detected a similarity between my old countess and Princess Natalya Petrovna [Golitsyn], but I do not think it is held against me."

In addition to the *Pugachev Rebellion, The Bronze Horseman* and *The Queen of Spades,* Pushkin wrote two folk tales in verse at Boldino, *The Fisherman and the Fish* and *The Dead Princess and the Seven Knights.* He also began a translation of Shakespeare's *Measure for Measure,* but changed his mind halfway through it, and, starting with a free adaptation of the play, composed a long poem on the same theme, interspersed with dialogue, entitled *Angelo.*

Having completed his work, and becoming daily more worried, jealous and impatient, Pushkin began to think seriously of going back. He left Boldino on November 9, stopping first in Moscow. A police report of November 11 records that "throughout his stay, he was engaged exclusively in literary occupations, called upon none of the local gentry and received nobody."

In Moscow, Pushkin found Nashchokin divested of his burdensome gypsy mistress and engaged to a proper young lady. The young lady was presented to the poet, who pronounced her charming in every particular. It pleased him to see his friends "settling down" one after another, following his example. Despite a steady stream of invitations, he seldom went out, and declared that all he wanted was to sit by the fireside with his pipe and converse with friends. The real reason for his reluctance to appear in public, however, was that he had grown a fantastic, gleaming, frizzly beard and did not want to shave it off until he had shown it to his wife.

7. *Gentleman of the Chamber*

Pushkin returned to St. Petersburg on November 20, 1833, without telling Natalya he was coming. To his annoyance, he was informed that she was at a ball at the Karamzins'. Thither he betook himself, installed himself in his wife's carriage and ordered the footman to inform Mrs. Pushkin that she was urgently required to deal with a domestic crisis at home, expressly forbidding him to say that Pushkin himself was waiting in the coach. Natalya, who was dancing a mazurka with Prince Vyazemsky, was not at all anxious to leave. Hunched in the dark corner of the carriage, Pushkin fretted, looked at his watch, peered up at the windows, behind which he could see the dancers' silhouettes. At length Natalya appeared, an evening cape half covering her diaphanous pink gown. She was hurrying toward the coach when she suddenly noticed a little man with an immense black beard inside it, his white teeth gleaming in laughter as he watched her.

"I arrived home to find everything as usual," Pushkin wrote to Nashchokin a few days later. "My wife was at a ball, I went to fetch her, and carried her off like a hussar abducting a provincial maid. . . . In my absence, my finances have become still more entangled, but I hope to disentangle them now."

He really did make an effort to straighten out his finances, and to sell his autumn's output for the highest possible price. Smirdin, the publisher, was heard to complain uncharitably: "For three poems that will hardly fill three pages, Alexander Sergeyevich is asking fifteen thousand rubles!"

Smirdin also told how he had arranged to buy one of Pushkin's poems (*The Hussar*) for fifty gold rubles; when he went to collect the manuscript, however, Pushkin sent him to Natalya, who demanded a hundred gold rubles instead of fifty. Smirdin gallantly accepted. As he was leaving, Pushkin called him back to his study and said: "Well, now you see that the author's wife drives an even harder bargain than the author.

You have no choice but to comply; she needed a new ball gown and we have to raise the money somehow. . . ."

Thus, Pushkin worked to buy ball gowns for his wife, the ball gowns enhanced Natalya's dangerous beauty and the response to that dangerous beauty tormented Pushkin. It was a vicious circle. Pushkin was the artist of his own jealousy.

His contemporaries were familiar with his stormy temper and, according to their natures, laughed at or were alarmed by it. "One evening in November 1833, I was at the Odoevskys'," a contemporary[1] wrote. "Suddenly—I shall never forget it—a woman entered, slender as a palm tree, dressed in black satin to the throat. It was Pushkin's wife, the greatest beauty of the day. I had never seen such a figure or such bearing. Her features, of patrician regularity, reminded me of the Euterpe in the Louvre. Prince Gregory Volkonsky came up and whispered in my ear, 'It doesn't do to look at her too hard.'" Another witness said Natalya sometimes had to leave the ball in the midst of a dance, to humor her husband's whim.

A man named Kikin, "having invited the adorable Natalya Pushkin to dance, took intense pleasure in provoking the poet, who stood a few feet from the couple darting glances of hatred at him."[2]

But what were the Kikins and Lenzes, or any other transitory worshipers, compared to Pushkin's only true and lasting rival—Nicholas I?

Nicholas, long a slave to Natalya's beauty, expressed surprise at her poor attendance at court balls, and, upon inquiring into the reasons for it, was informed that protocol forbade Pushkin to accompany his wife to imperial receptions and he would not allow her to go without him.

Nicholas was struck by the logic of his reasoning. Pushkin had no official title at court? Well then, he would give him one; Natalya's beauty was certainly worth this small sacrifice. On December 31, 1833, His Imperial Majesty issued a decree to the court chancellery, which read as follows: "We have graciously bestowed the title of Gentleman of the Chamber of Our Court upon Alexander Pushkin, titular counselor in the foreign ministry."

The next day Pushkin wrote in his private diary: ". . . I have been named gentleman of the chamber (hardly appropriate, at my age). But the court wanted Natalya Nikolayevna to dance at the Anichkov palace, and so I shall now become the Russian Dangeau."*

Pushkin's enemies were already saying he had intrigued for the "honor." While the new gentleman of the chamber's resentment turned to white rage, a drawing of Pushkin kissing a key (emblem of chamber-

* The Marquis de Dangeau (1638–1720) was a diarist; his journals are a storehouse of facts about the reign of Louis XIV.

lains) went flying around the salons. For once, his wrath was justified: By tradition, the gentlemen of the chamber were aristocratic youths of eighteen, and it was an insult—possibly unintended, but nevertheless serious—to induct Pushkin into their adolescent, slim-waisted, babbling cohort. Even for Nicholas I, it was a crude affront to force Russia's greatest poet into a page-boy uniform. For leading a disastrous cavalry charge against the Decembrists, Orlov had been made a count. Did Pushkin merit less than a blundering officer? Why had Orlov been made a count and he only a gentleman of the chamber? What would people say when they saw him with his lined and wrinkled cheeks, decked out as a courtier in a short tunic, patent-leather boots and a plumed tricorne? There would be snickers and whispers everywhere he went! Pushkin imagined the whole scene of his humiliation. His shame and hatred and frustration rose to such a pitch that he cursed the emperor in the presence of Zhukovsky and his closest friends, and threatened to march off to the palace and refuse this latest "grace." His cheeks were burning, he was positively frothing at the mouth. He had to be taken to another room and doused with cold water.

At last, under considerable pressure from his friends, he resigned himself to this grotesque promotion—but he would not order a uniform, and N. M. Smirnov had to buy him one second-hand.

At first, Natalya was terrified by her husband's contempt for this mark of favor that would be so beneficial to her, but gradually her hopes rose. After an initial struggle, Pushkin accepted his bonds. He was tamed. He was broken.

"I must tell you the news," the poet's mother wrote on January 4, 1834; "Alexander has been named gentleman of the chamber. Natalya is delighted, because now he can go to court."[3]

A few days later, Mrs. Karamzin wrote: "Pushkin dreaded the teasing which he feared that his sudden appointment as gentleman of the chamber would provoke, but now he has calmed down and is going to the balls and delighting in the triumphs of his wife."

The emperor was very pleased with his latest gesture. In conversation with Princess Vyazemsky, he declared: "I hope Pushkin has taken his appointment in good part. So far, he has kept his word to me and I have been satisfied with him."[4]

Pushkin consigned this remark to his diary on January 7, 1834, and added: "The Grand Duke congratulated me at the theater today. 'Many thanks, Your Highness,' I replied; 'so far, everyone else has laughed at me, you are the first to congratulate me.' "

On January 17 another allusion to his new title: "The emperor has not spoken to me about my duties as a gentleman of the chamber, and I have not thanked him for the appointment."

And on January 26: "Last Tuesday I was summoned to the Anichkov palace. I went in uniform, and was informed that all the other guests were in evening dress. I left Natalya, came home and changed, and went to a party at Sergey Vasilyevich Saltykov's. This displeased the emperor, and he repeated several times, 'He might have taken the trouble to come back again. Scold him for me.' "[5]

"Thursday, I went to Prince Trubetskoy's. . . . The emperor turned up unexpectedly. He stayed half an hour and said to my wife, 'Is it boots or buttons that have been keeping your husband away recently?'[6] (He meant the buttons of my uniform.) Old Countess Bobrynsky apologized for me, saying the buttons had not been sewn on yet."

Later he wrote: "I am supposed to go to the palace tomorrow. I still don't have my uniform. Not for anything in the world will I be seen in the company of my fellow gentlemen of the chamber, all nurslings of eighteen. The tsar will be angry, but I can't help it."

Pushkin was incessantly preoccupied by this bizarre mark of favor. In the past, he had loved Nicholas and hated autocracy. Now, he hated both the man and the sovereign. Since he could not show his resentment openly, he indulged it by making a careful record in his private diary of every minute blunder committed by the emperor or his government.

"Three things are being justly condemned: 1. The appointment of Sukhozanet, a depraved pederast and inveterate gambler. . . . All the emperor sees in him is the campaign veteran, and he gives him one of the most important positions in the empire, like a sinecure at the Disabled Veterans' Hospital; 2. uniforms for women; 3. the extradition of guards officer Brinken, a Courland nobleman. Brinken was caught in the act of stealing. The sovereign did not send him before our courts, but decided to have him extradited so he could be judged by his peers in Courland. Why is that? Why this distinction between a German officer and any other servant of the state? Is it fitting for the sovereign to interfere in common court cases? Have our laws on theft been abolished?"

Elsewhere, on the famine: "The holiday festivities will cost half a million. What will the people who are dying of hunger have to say to that?"

Or, after the death of Kochubey: "Such is the penury of statesmen in Russia that they can find no one to replace a Kochubey."

He also recorded, with a sniff of satisfaction, every disparaging remark he heard about the emperor personally: "He contains a large portion of second lieutenant and a small portion of Peter the Great."[7]

Pushkin's relations with the emperor were aggravated by the fact that although he loathed Nicholas I, he could not survive without his help. For example, when the authorities forbade the publication of *The*

Bronze Horseman and Pushkin had to forfeit his contract with Smirdin, he applied to Benkendorf for a loan of twenty thousand rubles, payable in two years, to cover the cost of publishing *Pugachev*. By giving him the twenty thousand rubles, Nicholas was merely adding another turn of the screw.

Too good-natured to refuse his wife anything, too proud to play the clown, Pushkin dragged himself from ball to ball, swallowing his spite, gritting his teeth and making new enemies by the hundred. The "smart set" needled him relentlessly, knowing how much he disliked their little clique; and the large body of liberals began to turn away from him too, thinking he had sold out to the tsar. Refused on one hand and rejected on the other, Pushkin watched as a great block of isolation froze around him. But by a curious play of the scales, the more abandoned and alone he felt, the more popular and triumphant became Natalya. Was she blind to her husband's misery, or did she take it for poetic caprice? In any event, she never spared him a single dinner or ball. In January, at a ball at the Bobrynskys', she experienced the signal honor of dancing a quadrille with Nicholas I while her husband spooned sherbet in the corner. At supper she sat next to the emperor, who whispered sweet nothings to her in French between mouthfuls.

She would come home at four or five in the morning, lunch at eight in the evening, leap up from the table to dress and set off, with Pushkin in tow, for yet another imperial *divertissement*.

As Lent drew near, the court and aristocracy became possessed by a veritable frenzy, with balls, masquerades and suppers following each other at breakneck pace; sometimes there were two balls a day. Bulgakov's comment on the season of 1834 was: "What a carnival! Balls every day! Today the Shuvalovs', tomorrow the Lazarevs', then the French actresses are giving a benefit masquerade for some widow, everyone will be there; Wednesday we go to the Austrian embassy, Friday to Prince Volkonsky, Saturday there will be a costume ball for children at the palace, and Sunday, they say, a small private ball at the Anichkov palace."

Natalya, pregnant for the third time, would not listen to Pushkin's entreaties to forgo even a little of this pointless fatigue. Where her social career was at stake, she spared neither her health nor her husband's pocket.

On the Sunday before Lent, the Pushkins went to a grand ball at the palace. Natalya seemed more pale and listless than usual. After two rounds of a mazurka, she felt a pain in her stomach and ran to lie down in the empress' rooms while Pushkin called the coach. At home, she had a miscarriage. Pushkin's enemies immediately accused him of maltreating his wife. "Do you know," Sergey Lvovich wrote to Olga, "that when Natalya lost the baby they said it was because he beat her!"[8] Pushkin, however, knew that it was "they" themselves—society, the tsar—who were the cause of his latest misfortune.

"Just imagine," Pushkin wrote to Nashchokin early in March 1834, "my wife almost died a few days ago. This winter there has been a positive epidemic of balls. During Carnival there were often two a day. At last came the Sunday before Lent, and I heaved a sigh of relief, 'Thank God, the end of the balls!' My wife was at the palace. Suddenly I saw her looking ill. I rushed her home, and the moment we got there she had a miscarriage. Now (touch wood) she is well again, and is going to stay with her sisters in a village in Kaluga. . . . My financial position is now worse than ever, owing to the following incident: A few days ago, my father asked me to call on him. I arrived to find him in tears, my mother in bed, and the house in a dreadful state. 'What's going on?' 'They are going to seize the estate.' 'Well then, you must pay your debts right away.' 'My debts have been paid. Here's the steward's letter.' 'Then why the crisis?' 'We have nothing to live on between now and October.' 'Go to the country.' 'I can't afford to.'

"Now what? I shall have to take over the estate and give my father a pension. More debts, more worries! But it has to be done: I would have wanted to take care of my father in his old age anyway, and arrange something for my brother Leo. Another piece of news: Since January, I am a gentleman of the chamber. The emperor was thinking of my title, no doubt, and not of my age. . . ."

To provide for his lachrymose, puerile and ill-fated father, and to ensure a respectable future for his children, Pushkin decided, despite opposition from his wife, to assume responsibility for Boldino, which had been half ruined by mismanagement. As executor of the estate, he planned to give allowances to his father, brother and sister Olga.

Boldino brought him nothing but more problems and quarrels. His parents were grateful to him for taking a hand in their affairs, but Olga's husband, the petty and plaintive Pavlishchev, immediately began to hound him for money: "I was delighted to hear you were taking over the management of Sergey Lvovich's estate and intended to give something to us, even if it is only fifteen hundred rubles a year," he wrote. "But tell me when you expect to make the first payment."

Pushkin replied: "Until I have sorted out this very confused business, I can promise Olga nothing, and indeed I have promised nothing. I am not in a position to withhold anything from the income of an estate belonging to my father, and my own fortune will not permit me to give you any money of my own."

Pavlishchev's pleas became more insistent: "You don't have to pay my debts, but—is my wife Sergey Lvovich's daughter and my children his grandchildren, or not?"

Harassed by family affairs, court intrigues, the debts accumulated during the winter, Natalya's miscarriage and the fierce heckling of the journalists, Pushkin had a bilious attack. Early in April, he wrote to Pogodin: "I am writing a lot, for myself, but shall publish, against my will, for money; what pleasure can there be in exposing oneself to a public that does not understand one, just so that four imbeciles can insult one for the next six months in their reviews? . . . There was a time when literature was an honorable and aristocratic occupation. Now, it's a street bazaar."

On April 15 Pushkin sent his convalescent wife to her family's estate in Kaluga, and stayed on in St. Petersburg alone to make the arrangements for his management of Boldino, hurry along the publication of *Pugachev* and study a few more documents in the Archives in connection with his *Peter the Great*. Work on the latter, however, demanded a certain degree of peace and quiet—and in Nicholas I there was nothing of the sympathetic and discreet patron of the arts. To him, Pushkin was first a gentleman of the chamber, and only afterward a poet, and no elucubrations could excuse him from attendance at official ceremonies. Two days after Natalya's departure, the first warning arrived: "Upon returning from Tsarskoye Selo at 5 P.M.," Pushkin wrote, "I found two invitations to a ball on April 29, and an order to see Litta [Chief Gentleman of the Chamber] the next day; I guessed that I was going to be taken to task for failing to attend the official mass (in the palace). And so it was; that evening Zhukovsky dropped by to tell me the emperor was very cross because so many of the chamberlains and gentlemen of the chamber had been absent, and had ordered us to be informed of his displeasure. At the palace, Litta passionately declared: 'But there are fixed rules for the gentlemen of the court, fixed rules!'[9] To which Naryshkin retorted, 'You are mistaken, those are for the maids of honor.'[10] I sent a written excuse and did not go. They say we are going to have to march in pairs like convent girls. Just imagine me, with my gray beard, prancing along next to Bezobrazov or Reimars! Not likely! I would rather be whipped in public,[11] as M. Jourdain says."

On April 22 he wrote to Natalya again: "I reported sick, and now I am afraid to meet the tsar; I shall stay home for this whole round of festivities. I have no intention of taking an oath of fealty to the heir to the throne; his reign is yet to come, and I shall probably not live to see it. I have seen three emperors in my life; the first ordered me to take off my hat, and as I was too young to be scolded myself, he scolded my nurse instead.† The second was hardly an admirer of mine; and although the third has raised me to the exalted rank of gentleman of the chamber in my dotage, I have no great desire to exchange him for a fourth—let us

† He is referring to Paul I, who was supposed to have met him out walking with his nanny.

leave well enough alone. We must see how our Sashka [nickname for Alexander, here referring to Pushkin's son] will get on with his royal namesake;‡ I didn't at all, with mine. May God preserve him from following in my footsteps—writing verse and bickering with royalty! In poetry he cannot better his father, he will never break an ax with a horsewhip. . . . Enough joking, now. Let us talk seriously. . . . Go for walks, but not too far, and go to bed early. Don't let your father* come near the children, he may frighten them. . . . Don't read those nasty books in your father's library, either, while you are in the country; do not pervert your imagination, little wife. . . ."

Knowing that Natalya's only interest in life was in parties and gowns, he took pains to give her a report on all the events he refused to attend himself.

"Tomorrow there is another ball, to which I shall also not go," he wrote on April 28. "It has thrown everyone into a turmoil and made conversation all over town. There are to be eighteen hundred guests. On the basis of one carriage per minute, the arrival of the guests is calculated to last ten hours. So the carriages are going to come up by threes, which will require only one third as long."

On April 30: "Apparently it was possible to move [at the ball] after all, and there were tons of sherbet, which would have been just the thing for me. But I stood outside in the crowd, watching the whole town go by in their carriages. . . . I shall make inquiries about the ladies' gowns and describe them to you later."

The days passed, and in his solitude Pushkin's melancholy deepened: "My days are all the same. I dine at Dumé's at two, to avoid the bachelors, and spend my evenings at the club. . . ."

"The only benefit I derive from your absence is that I am not required to snore through balls and guzzle sherbet."

In answer to these mournful, impassioned missives, Natalya wrote sketchy little notes of which only one authentic example has been preserved, and even that is a postscript to a letter written by her mother. In her uncertain French, Mrs. Goncharov had told her son-in-law: "Although Natalya seems content to be with me, the void your absence causes in her is very easy to see."

To this well-meaning remark Natalya added a few lines in French, here reproduced verbatim:

"It is hard for me to bring myself to write, having nothing to say and having taken advantage of a recent opportunity to give you my news. Maman herself was going to put off her letter until the next post, however she was afraid you might worry to be so long without news of us,

‡ The heir apparent's name was also Alexander.

* Natalya's father was insane.

which is what made her decide to overcome the sleepiness and fatigue she is feeling, as am I, for we have been outdoors all day. You will see from Maman's letter that we are all keeping well, so I will not write anything on that subject, I will stop now and send kisses, I mean to write more at the first opportunity, and so farewell, keep well, and do not forget us.

Monday, May 14, 1834, *Yaropolets.*"

The script is docile and sloping, all the letters carefully formed. The words flow along, one after the other. But the content is stupefyingly vacuous. Not one personal thought, not one spontaneous impulse, not one detail. There is nothing to learn, nothing to respond to, in Natalya's lines to her husband. Natalya was writing under her mother's eye, of course; and she had a horror of public show of affection; and she was tired after being outdoors all day; and it would be unfair to judge her on such slender evidence. But one shudders to think that all of Natalya's letters may have been like this one, that for sole response to his ardor, Pushkin had to content himself with these tepid boarding-school natterings.

One of the letters quoted above—the one dated April 22, 1834, in which the poet derided the brotherhood of the gentlemen of the chamber and referred to the oath of fealty of the grand duke—was opened by Bulgakov, postmaster general of Moscow: Pushkin might be received at court, but the police had not forgotten him. Bulgakov duly passed the letter on to Benkendorf, who handed it to the emperor, who flew into a rage when he saw how Pushkin maligned the noble institution of the gentlemen of the chamber. That man was an incorrigible revolutionary and an ungrateful scoundrel. He, Nicholas I, tsar of all the Russias, had had the goodness to overlook this scribbler's liberal follies, to censor his poems with his own eyes, to raise him to a position of enviable dignity, and instead of thanking him, here he was daring to make jokes, at his expense, in a letter to his own wife! Zhukovsky got wind of the affair, and hastened to assure the monarch that such minor expressions of spite were of no consequence and that Pushkin's devotion to the emperor was profound and sincere. Nicholas let himself be persuaded, but privately, he marked Pushkin as an enemy.

When Pushkin learned how the police had violated the privacy of his correspondence, he nearly suffocated with rage. This last attack upon his freedom was more intolerable than all the rest. It was no longer enough for the emperor's spies to interfere with his writing, his movements and his dress. Now they were poking their dirty noses into the sanctuary of his private life. They were meddling with his love, taking notes on the secrets of his heart. House, bedroom and bed, everything belonged to them! There was no more privacy in Russia! The shame of it!

On May 10, 1834, he wrote in his diary: "The Moscow post opened one of my letters to Natalya Nikolayevna; reading in it an account of the oath-taking ceremony which was undoubtedly not drafted in the proper official style, the post transmitted it to the police. They, in turn, without pausing to consider the sense of my letter, presented it to the emperor, who, in his anger, also failed to grasp my meaning. Fortunately, the letter was shown to Zhukovsky, who explained, and everyone calmed down. The emperor desires me to speak of my appointment as gentleman of the chamber in tones of gratitude and humility only. What I say is: I may be his subject and even his slave, but I shall never be a lackey or a clown, not even for the King of Heaven! What staggering immorality reigns over the actions of our government. The police open a husband's letters to his wife and then present them to the tsar (who is a well-bred and honorable man), and the tsar is not even ashamed to be a party to this unconscionable prying and to condone machinations worthy of Vidocq and Bulgarin! Ah, it is hard to be an autocrat, no matter what they say."

Pushkin was a long time recovering from this incident. He wrote a letter to Natalya, knowing it was likely to be opened, in which he begged her to be careful of what she said, on account of a certain postmaster in Moscow, a dastard named Bulgakov who read other people's mail and prostituted his daughter. This letter never reached its destination. On May 18 Pushkin apologized for not having written recently, "but I was angry; not with you, with the others. One of my letters fell into the hands of the police, etc. No one must know what we say to each other; no one can come into our bedroom. Without privacy, there can be no family life."

Later: "I have not written lately because that swine of a post has given me such a cold shower that I did not have the heart to put pen to paper. The thought that somebody is spying on us, on you and me, drives me literally wild. . . . One can manage easily without political freedom, but life is impossible without the inviolability of the family. A prison camp is preferable by far. That was not meant for you. This is what is meant for you: Have you started your treatment with the iron-water baths? Has Masha [Pushkin's daughter] cut her next teeth, and how has she been with the first ones? . . . I went to visit Her Imperial Highness at Kamenny Ostrov, in that cheerful frame of mind in which you ordinarily see me when I don my flashing uniform. But she was so delightful that I quite forgot my absurd appearance and ill temper. . . . Do not be angry if my letters seem cool. It takes all my strength to stifle my anger and write to you at all."[12]

Elsewhere: "Do be careful. Your letters are probably being opened too—for reasons of state security!"[13]

Or: "Please, do not ask me for letters of tenderness and love. The thought that they are being opened and read by the post, police and so forth turns me to ice and I involuntarily become stiff and dreary."[14]

In his empty, hostile St. Petersburg, harassed by creditors and police, Pushkin thought seriously of resigning from his "position" as gentleman of the chamber and going to seek refuge in the country.

"With your permission," he wrote to Natalya, "it is necessary, I think, to resign and regretfully pack away my uniform which was so flattering to my vanity but in which I will unfortunately be unable to admire myself for long. You are young, but you are already a mother, and I am sure the duties of motherhood will be no more difficult for you to fulfill than were those of a respected and charming wife; dependency and confusion in one's affairs are terrible for a family, and no considerations of vanity can outweigh spiritual peace and ease."[15]

But Natalya either would not or could not understand the causes of this sour humor. She persisted in playing the coy mistress with a man who was worn out by worry and anxiety about the future. She complained that he knew too much about all the social events, and if he knew so much it must be because he was going out all the time, and if he were going out all the time he must be seeing other women and being unfaithful to her. She took his dread of unnecessary expenditure as a personal rebuff. Pushkin had to explain, to apologize: "I am feeling positively dismal. It is sad to be without you, and not even to be able to tell you what is on my mind. Do not be angry with me, little wife, do not misinterpret my lamentations. I have never dreamed of blaming you for my dependency. I had to marry you, because I would have been miserable for the rest of my life without you: But I ought not to have accepted any official position, and still less to have allowed myself to become bogged down in debt. Family obligations improve us, but those we contract for vanity or material need demean us. Now they are treating me like a flunky with whom they can do whatever they please. But disgrace is better than contempt. Like Lomonosov, I will not play the clown, not even for God. But none of this has anything to do with you: I alone am at fault, because of my naïveté—which is so great, despite my vast experience of the world, that it borders on idiocy. I cannot send you any money just now, I have had to pay for my parents' journey; they are fleecing me unmercifully. I believe I may take your advice and give up managing their farm before long. Let them ruin it as they please: Even so, it will give them enough to last them for the rest of their days, and we shall try to scrape together a little something for Sashka and Mashka. . . . St. Petersburg is empty; everybody is in the country. I sit in my room and write until four. I dine at Dumé's and am at the club in the evenings. That is my whole day. Just to distract myself, I tried playing cards at the club, but had to give it up. Gambling upsets both me and my liver."[16]

After paying for his parents' removal to the country, and despite his threats to give it up, Pushkin continued to manage the estate in order to subsidize his brother and sister, who were plaguing him with demands for money. He was also playing cards, in the hope that he might recoup his fortunes that way—sitting up night after night, losing his composure and, as always, his money, running up more debts and signing more pledges.

"We must plan for our children's future," he wrote to Natalya in the second half of June. "I now know that my father's estate is in the worst possible condition and can only be salvaged by a policy of rigorous economy. I am capable of making a lot of money, but we spend a great deal too. If I were to die today, what would become of you? . . . Petersburg is dreadfully dull. There is only one thing that keeps me here: the printers. And the mortgage on the estate too. But will it even be possible to mortgage it? How right you were to tell me I should not get involved in this and that nobody would thank me for it; it has turned my blood so sour that all the leeches in the house could not draw off the poison! You are entitled to be very angry with me, as far as money is concerned: I had some money—and lost it at cards. What to do? I was feeling so disgruntled that I had to do something to take my mind off my problems. It's all *his*† fault. God forgive him, he should have let me go on living my own life."

On June 25, 1834, after taking stock of all the troubles resulting from his fictitious post in the foreign ministry and his appointment as gentleman of the chamber, Pushkin girded up his loins, took pen and paper and wrote a letter to Count Benkendorf:

"Excellency: As family affairs require me to spend part of my time in Moscow and the country, I have no choice but to resign my position, and I beg Your Excellency to obtain permission for me to do so.

"As a final favor, may I ask that His Majesty's kind authorization to consult the Archives not be withdrawn. . . ."[17]

Now what had he done! In his unbelievable innocence, the poor fool probably imagined that Nicholas I would take his letter at face value and cheerfully agree that freedom was essential to the poet. It never occurred to him that his resignation might offend his "benefactor" and make him appear a renegade deserving of public opprobrium. When Zhukovsky learned what he had done, he threw up his hands in despair at this sacrilege and vowed to save the day; he saw it as his duty to reconcile the emperor and the author, immediately and at all costs. In the interests of Pushkin himself, of literature, of the whole civilized world,

† Nicholas I's, that is.

the great statesman and the great man of letters must become friends again.

"The emperor has spoken to me about you," he wrote to Pushkin on July 2. "If I had known what caused you to hand in your resignation I would have been able to explain it to him, but as I had no idea what prompted you to do this absurd thing, I could find nothing to say, except to ask if there were no way to save the situation. 'Why not?' was his reply; 'I have never forced anyone to remain against his will and I shall accept his resignation. But in that case, everything is finished between us. He may, however, take back his letter if he wishes.' I was truly touched by that. Do as you please; but in your place, I should not hesitate for one moment."

Shaken by Zhukovsky's charge of ingratitude and folly, Pushkin lost his head. Perhaps he was wrong to break with the government after all; perhaps his personal felicity and that of his family were only possible in an *entente cordiale* with the emperor. The next day, July 3, he wrote to Benkendorf again: "Excellency! I recently had the honor of writing to ask you for permission to resign from the service. It being improper of me to do so, I implore you to take no action on my request. I would rather be accounted inconsistent than ungrateful."[18]

That same day Pushkin received a stream of bitter reproach from Zhukovsky: "You are an utter imbecile, I am now convinced of it; and not only an imbecile, you are lacking in the most elementary decency: How could you fail to say a single word about this cunningly contrived scheme to me or Vyazemsky before putting it into action? I simply don't understand! It was lamentable, selfish, incommensurable stupidity on your part. This is what I would do now, if I were you (for if I were you I would have been stirred to the soul by the emperor's words): I would write directly to the emperor, in complete sincerity, accusing myself of being a stupid fool and explaining in so many words what caused me to behave like a stupid fool, and I would say it all with the expressions of gratitude our emperor so amply deserves. Write immediately, and send the letter through Benkendorf. I would never have thought there could be any hope of putting right what you have so heedlessly deigned to compromise. If you do not leap at this opportunity you are nothing but an animal that feeds on acorns and makes a grunting noise offensive to the ears of well-bred men. Joking aside: You would be doing something wrong and silly, ruining your entire life and fully justifying the complaints of your friends and yourself."

At the same time as Zhukovsky's letter, a brief note from Benkendorf arrived in reply to Pushkin's tender of resignation of June 25. In his bittersweet style, the chief of police, who had not yet received Pushkin's retraction of July 3, wrote: "His Majesty, not desiring to hold anyone against his will, has instructed me to inform the Vice-Chancellor that he accepts your resignation, and I shall do so. His Majesty has not deigned to accede to your request to make use of the imperial Archives after your resignation, for this privilege is given only to persons enjoying the special trust of the government."

By his ingratitude, it seemed, Pushkin had lost the government's "special trust." But when had he ever had it? He had been subject to police observation from the day Nicholas I came to the throne. Alarmed at the turn events were taking, the poet dashed off two more letters on July 4, one to Zhukovsky and the other to Benkendorf. To the former he said: "As soon as I received your first letter [of July 2], I wrote to Count Benkendorf asking him to take no action on my letter of resignation, as it was 'improper,' and saying 'I would rather be accounted inconsistent than ungrateful.' Thereupon, I received an official letter informing me that my resignation had been accepted and that I would no longer be able to use the Archives. Now I am more depressed than ever. I submitted my resignation in a moment of discouragement and resentment of everyone and everything. My family situation is very difficult, my own position is no laughing matter, some change in my way of life is absolutely necessary. I hadn't the courage to explain all that to Count Benkendorf, which is why my letter must have seemed dry, whereas in reality it was only foolish. . . ."

To Benkendorf, Pushkin wrote: "I am deeply pained to learn that my thoughtless action, the result of an acutely uncomfortable position and various trivial but irritating problems, should have been interpreted as an act of wild ingratitude and rebellion against the will of him who has hitherto been far more a benefactor than a sovereign to me. I await the final decision; but whatever it is, nothing will alter the sense of profound devotion and filial gratitude I cherish toward the tsar for his past kindness."

Benkendorf submitted this letter to Zhukovsky for his opinion before passing it on to the emperor. Zhukovsky judged it far too cold and unbending for someone as culpable as his friend; he asked Benkendorf to keep it, and wrote to Pushkin again, on July 6: "Really, I don't understand what is the matter with you. One is tempted to say you have become a raving idiot. You ought to be locked up in the yellow house or given a good thrashing to get your blood moving again. . . . Your last letter, asking for things to be left as they are, is so stuffy that the emperor might well take it as a fresh offense. Have you forgotten how to write? Do you think it is beneath your dignity to show some emotion to the emperor? Why are you trying to be subtle? Be simple. The emperor is displeased by your attitude, he sees it as ingratitude on your part. Until now he has liked you and wished you well. He shows every sign of being sorry to lose you. What is there to think about? Write what your heart dictates. . . ."

At this, Pushkin lost all patience. He was head over ears in debt, solitude was essential for his work, it had seemed to him that his obvious, natural course was to resign; and here they were calling him an ungrateful wretch, an enemy of the monarchy, a heartless, witless scoundrel.

"I don't know myself what is the matter with me," he wrote to Zhukovsky on July 6. "I hand in my resignation when circumstances make it necessary, when it becomes essential for the future of my family and my own peace of mind; what crime have I committed, and why am I taxed with ingratitude? The emperor sees my action as something expressing I don't know what. This being so, I withdraw my resignation and ask to be left as I am. Why do you say my letters are unfeeling? Why should I be flowing in tears? In my heart of hearts, I feel that I have done nothing to offend the sovereign; his anger pains me, but the more confused my situation becomes, the more cold and embarrassed my style will be, too. What am I supposed to do? Apologize? Gladly; but what for? I shall try to write a third letter."

Filled with shame, anguish and revulsion, Pushkin sat down and wrote his third letter to Benkendorf on July 6, 1834:

"Permit me to open my heart to you. In submitting my resignation, I was thinking only of my involved and embarrassing family situation. All I had in mind was the inconvenience of being absent so often while in service. By God and my soul, that was my only motive; I am deeply chagrined to see it so cruelly misinterpreted. The emperor has showered favors upon me from the moment I first came to his royal attention. I cannot recall some of them without emotion, so much loyalty and generosity did they express. He has always been my good angel, and if, in the course of these past eight years, I have ever chanced to murmur, there was never, I swear it, any bitterness in my sentiments toward him. And at this moment, it is not the thought of losing an omnipotent protector that fills me with sorrow, but that of leaving an impression in his mind which, happily, I have not deserved.

"I therefore repeat my most humble request that you take no further action on my thoughtless proposal."

Upon perusal of this last piece of homework, Benkendorf judged it sufficiently "flowing in tears" to be submitted to the royal eye.

"He shows every sign of being sorry to lose you," Zhukovsky had written. In fact, neither the tsar nor Benkendorf had ever dreamed of being "sorry"; but it seemed wiser to keep a dangerous fanatic like Pushkin on a short rein. In his report to the emperor, Benkendorf noted: "Herewith two letters from Pushkin, one to me and the other to Zhukovsky. Considering that he admits his act to have been mere foolishness and prefers to be regarded as inconsistent rather than ungrateful . . . I presume it will please Your Majesty to discount his first letter. We know the measure of the man: It is better for him to stay in service than to be abandoned to himself."

Nicholas I wrote his decision in the margin of the report: "I forgive him, but call him in and explain to him again how inconsistent his behavior has been and how much it nearly cost him. What may be forgiven in a scatterbrain of twenty cannot be excused in a married man of thirty-five with a family."

The crisis had lasted two weeks (from June 25 to July 8), during which Pushkin was too upset and sick at heart to write to his wife. He knew only too well that she would have sided with Nicholas against him.

"This last month has been very agitated," he wrote in his diary. "I nearly had a falling-out with the court. But now everything is all right again. However, I won't get away with it forever."

At last, on July 11, the storm was over and he could write to Natalya: "A short while ago I nearly came to grief, I was within an ace of quarreling with *him*. But then I became frightened and lost heart. If I break with this one, I shall never find another."

On July 13: "I must tell you my sorrow. Not long ago, in desperation, I submitted my resignation, but Zhukovsky gave me such a going-over and Benkendorf heaped such mountains of reproach upon my head that I took fright and begged them, for God's sake, not to accept it. You will be delighted, I daresay? Everything will come right in the end, if I can only live another twenty-five years, but if I drop dead within the next ten I don't see how you could manage, or what Mashka and, most of all, Sashka would have to say about it. For them, it would be scant comfort to know their papa died a clown and their maman was superbly adorable at the Anichkov balls. Oh well, there's no help for it. God is great. The main thing is that I *will not* be suspected of ingratitude: That is even worse than liberalism."

So Pushkin withdrew his resignation rather than be called ungrateful by the tsar and rather than upset his wife, for whom court balls were the only reason for existing. "You will be delighted, I daresay?" Lord, yes, she was delighted, all right! Now fully recovered from her miscarriage, she had resumed her campaign of flirtation in Kaluga. While Pushkin was telling her about his financial predicament, she was sending him a pair of scales to symbolize his alleged miserliness. While Pushkin, broken by the "filth of St. Petersburg," was struggling to resign and then apologizing and falling straight into the emperor's lap, she was giving him all the details of her Kaluga conquests and the physical attributes of some booby who was paying court to her. While Pushkin was anxiously asking how he was going to support his wife and children, she was telling him how she had decided to invite her two sisters to live with them in St. Petersburg, and was going to have them appointed maids of honor to the empress. To be sure, Katerina and Alexandra were perishing of boredom in the country with their shrewish bigot of a mother. To be sure, Natalya was very fond of her older sisters and suffered to see them so left out of things. But how could she fail to realize that Pushkin's resources would not allow him to provide for two young ladies with expensive tastes?

"What an idea, to want to get your sisters into the palace," he wrote on June 11, 1834. "In the first place, they will probably be refused; and in the second, even if they are accepted, just think a little of the flattering comments it will provoke in this pigsty of a St. Petersburg. You are too beautiful, my angel, to be a petitioner. Wait until you are a widow, until you grow old; then you can become a duenna and official matchmaker. My advice to you and your sisters is to keep far away from court, it isn't worth it. Besides, you are not rich, and you can't all be kept by Auntie [Zagryazhskaya]. . . . Good Lord, if the Zavodys [Mrs. Goncharov's estate] were mine, nothing could drag me to court. . . . I should live like a lord. But you women do not understand the joys of independence, you will sacrifice anything for the pleasure of hearing someone say that 'yesterday, Madame Whoosis was definitely the most beautiful and best-dressed woman at the ball.'[19] Farewell, Madame Whoosis."

A month later, on July 14, 1834, he wrote again: "You must have become more of a flirt than ever. . . . In reality, I don't even blame you for it, little wife. It is all in the order of things; you are young, so make the most of your youth; you are beautiful, so rule over hearts. . . . If you are really determined to bring your sisters here, we can't go on living at Olivier's, there isn't enough room. But is it *both* sisters you want to take under your wing? Do be careful, little wife. This is my opinion: The family should be together under one roof: husband, wife, and children while they are small, and parents if they are already old; otherwise, one is asking for no end of trouble and destroying all hope of peace in the family."

This time again, Pushkin had to give in, and rent a larger and more expensive apartment—that of the Vyazemskys, who were going abroad.

"How can you pretend to call yourselves workers and helpers?" he wrote to Natalya toward the end of July. "The only work you do is at balls, with your little feet, and the only help you give is when you help your husbands to spend their money. But even for that, I thank you. Do not be angry because I am still in the city. I am longing to come, but the state of my pocketbook will not permit it. I am working myself to death, proofreading the two volumes [of the *History of the Pugachev Rebellion*], taking notes, mortgaging the property."

By August 25 he had finished his proofreading and left St. Petersburg to join his wife on the Goncharov estate. "I fled St. Petersburg five days before the raising of the Alexander Column," he wrote in his diary, "in order to avoid having to attend the ceremony in the company of my fellow gentlemen of the chamber."

Seeing Natalya again was worth the wait. The moment he set eyes on her, he forgot all the grievances he had been pouring out in his letters. After a fortnight on the Goncharov estate, Natalya and her sisters began making preparations to return to the capital, while Pushkin hurried to Boldino, where the complicated affairs of the estate were calling him.

The poet's third stay at Boldino was taken up with business. He had too much on his mind, inspiration would not come. The only major piece of work he managed to complete was a verse tale, *The Golden Cockerel*. "The lines will not come to my head," he wrote Natalya toward the end of September, "and the novel [*The Captain's Daughter*] has not been recopied. I am reading Walter Scott and the Bible, and thinking of you all the time. Is Sashka well? Have you got rid of that nurse? And that cursed German woman? Did you get back all right? A thousand worries are plaguing me. I do not think I shall stay much longer at Boldino this year, but I will wait a little while in case inspiration should happen to strike. Otherwise, the will of the Lord be done, and en route!"

Pushkin reached St. Petersburg on October 18. He found Natalya pregnant for the fourth time, and more determined than ever to flirt and enjoy herself. The two sisters were there too.

"Why have you saddled yourself with those two girls?" Sobolevsky asked.

"Their mother has begun drinking from dawn to dusk," Pushkin replied, "and is sleeping with all the footmen."

And Pushkin's mother wrote to his sister Olga, on November 7, 1834: "Natalya is already pregnant again, her sisters are with her, and are going halves with them on a very beautiful house. He said it was a help financially, but he is not too happy about it because he does not like anything that interferes with his habits as lord of the manor."[20]

8. *Three Sisters*

It was not one woman but three, three sisters whom Pushkin now had to escort to the balls. The eldest, Katerina, "Koko" to her friends, "was rather like a gawky mare," one contemporary wrote, "or a floor mop, to make a comparison of somewhat Caucasian gallantry." Her portrait, at Soultz, belies this sweeping assertion: There she appears as a tall young woman with rounded shoulders, full bosom and slender waist. Black plaits frame a long, pale face. Her wide, dark, rather myopic eyes are wistful. Katerina was no beauty, but she did not lack appeal.

Her sister Alexandra, on the other hand, was a living caricature of Natalya. She was tall and well proportioned, like Natalya, but heavier, more fleshy; she had a soft, regular complexion, like Natalya, but with an unpleasant yellowish cast. Natalya squinted a little, which imparted a special charm to her gaze; Alexandra squinted a lot, which turned her lifeless features into a grotesque mask. "Pushkin's wife," wrote ex-Zizi Wulf (now Countess Vrevsky), "is ravishing in every sense of the word, but her sister Alexandra is so ugly that I burst out laughing afterward in the coach with my sister." The trio, of whom Natalya was the uncontested queen, lived in a continual whirl of gowns, perfumes, hair pieces, "Apollo knots" and sentimental confidences. For them, every outing was a memorable occasion; for Pushkin, a dreaded ordeal.

"Nevertheless, I did not go to the palace on December 6," he wrote in his diary. "I reported sick. The tsar wanted to send a courier for me, or Dr. Arendt [the court physician]."

However, he could not feign illness for every ball and ceremony. Nicholas would have been offended by such pusillanimity, and so would Natalya, no doubt. On December 16, 1834, thus, he duly prepared to obey an imperial summons to appear "at the Anichkov palace at half past eight in dress uniform, Natalya Nikolayevna in her ordinary attire."

"We arrived at nine," Pushkin wrote in his diary. "On the stairs I met old Countess Bobrynsky, who never tires of lying to get me out of trouble. She saw me with a feathered tricorne. (But now only round hats are worn to the Anichkov palace—an innovation.) There was already a crowd. The ball opened with a set of *contredanses*. The empress was in white, with a turquoise tiara. The emperor was wearing the uniform of the horse guards. The empress' looks have greatly improved. After scrutinizing my tricorne, Count Bobrynsky ordered them to find me a round hat. One was duly procured, so thick with hair oil that my gloves became impregnated with it and turned yellow."

Pushkin was increasingly preoccupied, silent and gloomy at these balls. He would stand in a window recess, his lips puffed out, his eyes glazed, apparently oblivious to the whirl of light skirts and epaulets around him. It was columns of figures, however, and not lines of poetry, that were running through his head. His wife was costing him a great deal of money, even with the help of Aunt Zagryazhskaya's generous contributions toward her niece's adornment. His parents, back from Mikhailovskoye, were bankrupt. Nadezhda Osipovna was ill, her doctor was urging her to see specialists, but there was no money for a consultation. Leo was piling up debts. Olga's husband was complaining that the promised allowance had not come. Alone, the poet struggled beneath this avalanche of trivialities while Natalya and his sisters-in-law danced. Mashka, their little daughter, was so accustomed to Parisian gowns and tiaraed coiffures that she burst into tears at the sight of her grandmother and refused to kiss her, because Nadezhda Osipovna was wearing "an ugly bonnet and an ugly dress." To feed and clothe his wife, children, sisters-in-law and parents, Pushkin slaved away at his interminable *History of Peter the Great*. On January 20, 1835, he wrote to Nashchokin: "No doubt you have seen my *Pugachev* on the book shelves, but I hope you did not buy it. The good Emelka [Pugachev's first name] has now become a model taxpayer and my infinitely divisible serf. He has brought in a fair sum of money, but since I have been living on credit for the last two years, my purse is still empty, it has all gone to pay my debts."

However, the sale of *Pugachev* fell off with alarming rapidity.

"Among the public," Pushkin noted, "there is severe criticism of my *Pugachev*. . . . Uvarov [the Minister of Education] is a scoundrel, he keeps shouting that my book is a disgusting piece of work. His *âme damnée*, that imbecile Dundukov [chairman of the board of censors], is pursuing me with his censors. He refuses to allow me to publish with the emperor's blessing alone. The tsar likes what I do, but his flunky does not. Uvarov, incidentally, is a master cur and a charlatan. His depravity is notorious. He is so craven that he has been errand boy for Kankrin's children [Kankrin was the Minister of Finance]. They say he began as a p——, then became a children's nurse, and ended up president of the Academy of Sciences, like Princess Dashkov and the Russian Academy. He has stolen firewood from the state, and has some explaining to do (he owns eleven thousand serfs) for employing state locksmiths on private business, etc."

Not content with recounting every detail of the turpitudes of Dundukov and Uvarov in his private diary, Pushkin assailed the pair with stinging epigrams. Whenever he detected moral corruption, stupidity or greed in an official, his caution forsook him. His past experience had taught him nothing. To relieve his spite, he simply *had* to undress his foe and give him a public scourging. His lines on Dundukov, a social upstart and noted pervert who had once had an affair with Uvarov and was now chairman of the board of censors and vice-president of the Academy of Sciences, gained instant fame:

Inside the Academy of Sciences
There sits one Prince Dunduk.
Honor so great, it is alleged,
Ill befits the said Dunduk.
How is it then that he there sits?
Because he has an ass.

Pushkin gave an even sharper tongue-lashing to Dundukov's protector Uvarov in his poem *On the Recovery of Lucullus.* At the time, Uvarov was impatiently awaiting the death of his brother-in-law, the multimillionaire Count Sheremetyev, who was ill with scarlet fever and had been given up by the doctors. Through his wife, Uvarov was the patient's direct heir. Counting on Sheremetyev's imminent demise, and eager to know the exact size of his fortune, he gave instructions that the unfortunate man's possessions were to be inventoried and his coffers sealed. But Sheremetyev unexpectedly recovered, and the fuming Uvarov became a general laughingstock.

Pushkin's *On the Recovery of Lucullus* was in reality nothing more than an epigram against the precipitous heir, in which the poet addressed himself to Lucullus-Sheremetyev:

Your heir, meanwhile,
Like raven after carrion,
Turned pale and shook with fever
By your bed. Already,
His greedy wax had sealed
Your strong-room locks,
He dreamed of golden mountains,
Paper dust heaps;
Said, "No more shall I
Be nursemaid to the great,
But shall be great myself,
My cellar filled with wine;

It will be easy to be good,
I need no longer fleece my wife,
Can forget to rob and sneak
My firewood from the state. . . ."

Despite its utterly transparent allusions, the censors, thrown off by the subtitle "imitated from the Latin," authorized publication of the poem, whereupon one Zhobar, who had been dismissed from the faculty of the University of Kazan by Uvarov, translated *Lucullus* into French and sent it to the minister (Uvarov) with a request that he accept the dedication and allow the piece to be published under his august name. Mr. Zhobar acidly commented to Pushkin: "Were His Excellency to deign to accept my proposal, I should soon—notwithstanding my ignorance and waywardness, which have been legally certified by his order—find myself a fellow of the Academy, a counselor of state, a grand cordon and all the rest, his whim sufficing nowadays to make and unmake all such notables, professors and people of worth. . . ."[1]

Meanwhile, Uvarov complained to Benkendorf and Benkendorf to the emperor. The chief of police summoned the poet and admonished him severely.

"But those lines are not intended for Uvarov," exclaimed Pushkin.

"For whom, then?"

"For yourself."

"Me?" Benkendorf boggled. "Here, let me see. . . . When did I ever steal firewood from the state?"

"Your answer," smiled Pushkin, "is proof, though, that Uvarov did. Why else would he think the poem was directed at him?"

This anecdote cannot be substantiated, but drafts of letters to Benkendorf have been found in which Pushkin was trying to establish his innocence. Neither the chief of police nor the emperor, however, could be deceived by such childish ruses. Sensing that he had gone too far again, Pushkin asked Mr. Zhobar to give up his idea of publishing the French version of the poem in Belgium.

"Its publication," the poet wrote, "has aroused the displeasure of someone whose good opinion I value, someone whom it would be ungrateful and mad of me to defy. Please be good enough, therefore, to exchange the satisfaction of seeing your work in print for that of doing a colleague a good turn."[2]

Pushkin's latest epigrams earned him a few more enemies, of course: Count Uvarov and Prince Dundukov now came to swell the ranks of the Nesselrodes, Bulgarins and others whom the poet had rashly offended. They pounced gleefully upon every derogatory remark made about Pushkin and his wife, they entangled him in a sticky web of spite, they chortled at his difficulties, they longed to see him undone.

Moreover, his position was giving his foes ample cause for rejoicing: On April 1 he borrowed 3500 rubles from a moneylender, leaving some family heirlooms as security. On April 15 the court of the fourth department ordered him to pay 1063 rubles and 33½ kopecks in back rent to one of his previous landlords, plus a fine of 106 rubles and 30 kopecks. To raise this amount, Pushkin had to sell some of his personal serfs at Boldino. At the end of April 1835 he wrote to his brother Leo, whose regiment was quartered at Tiflis: "Since the day I was rash enough to take over my father's affairs, I have not seen as much as 500 rubles; the loan of 13,000 has already been exceeded. . . . Your bill of exchange for 10,000 has been redeemed. . . . Not counting food, lodging and the tailor, which cost you nothing, you have thus received 1230 rubles. As my mother has been very ill, I am still handling the estate, although it makes me sick to do it, but I intend to hand over the reins at the first opportunity and shall try to get your share of the land and peasants for you then. After that, you will probably begin to take an interest in your own affairs and shed some of your laziness and that faculty you have of living with never a thought for the morrow. I have not paid your little gambling debts, because I was not going to look up your chums, it was for them to come to me."[3]

On May 2 he dealt with the importunities of his brother-in-law Pavlishchev: "These are the arrangements which I recently proposed to my father, and to which, thank God, he has consented: To Leo he gives half of Kistenovo [a hamlet attached to Boldino]; I cede my share to my sister (the income, of course), on condition that she use the income and pay the interest on the mortgage. I have written all of this to the steward. Papa keeps Boldino. . . . I want to leave St. Petersburg and live in the country; if only I can do so without causing displeasure."

Natalya was stoically enduring her pregnancy. Her time was near. But suddenly, Pushkin could not resist his longing for fresh air and solitude. By May 8 he had gone to Mikhailovskoye, Trigorskoye and Golubovo, where the young Baroness Vrevsky, formerly Zizi Wulf, now lived. "Lord, how good it is to be here!" he exclaimed to Mrs. Osipov; "often, back in St. Petersburg, I am unable to breathe for anguish!" Looking at the pretty Zizi, whom he had known when she was a mere slip of a lovestruck girl and who was now also in her fourth pregnancy, the memory of all that pointless agitation returned to plague him. "You were surprised to see Pushkin," Annette Wulf wrote to Zizi on May 24, "and say you cannot imagine why he came. But I think it was simply for the trip, and to see you and Maman and Trigorskoye, Golubovo and Mikhailovskoye, for I can't imagine any other plausible reason. Would he have made such a journey, at such a time, just to talk to Maman about the two thousand rubles he owes her?"[4]

After this gulp of fresh air, Pushkin hurried back to St. Petersburg to greet the arrival of his third child. He arrived on May 15, but Natalya had already given birth to a little boy, Gregory, three days before. Guilty, shamefaced and delighted, Pushkin rushed into the room where his wife lay resting. They both wept; Natalya was sick for a whole day from the excitement.

The arrival of this third child made Pushkin more determined than ever to resign from his post. But in view of the results of his previous attempt, he decided to proceed with more caution. He would not mention the word resignation, he would simply apply for a leave of absence from court for three or four years, motivated solely by financial considerations. The letter he wrote this time could not conceivably have been misconstrued:

"Count: It mortifies me to be forever importuning Your Excellency, but the indulgence and interest you have deigned to show me in the past must be blamed for my indiscretion. I have no fortune; neither I nor my wife has come into our inheritance. Thus far I have lived from the sale of my work. My only fixed income is the salary which the emperor has deigned to grant me. There is nothing humiliating, in my eyes, in selling one's work for money. But I am accustomed to independence, and it is quite impossible for me to write for money alone; the very idea reduces me to silence. Also, life in St. Petersburg is fearfully expensive. Hitherto, I have not worried unduly about my expenses: A political and literary periodical—a strictly commercial venture—would provide me with an immediate income of thirty thousand to forty thousand rubles. But the sheer labor of producing it is so repugnant to me that I have kept the idea as a last resort. Now I must reduce my expenses, which are only driving me deeper into debt and heading me toward a future of worry and financial embarrassment, if not actual poverty and despair. Three or four years of retirement in the country will enable me to return and resume those activities in St. Petersburg which I owe, as so much else, to His Majesty's kindness.

"The emperor has shown me every mark of favor; I should be heartbroken if His Majesty were to imagine any motive other than absolute necessity in my desire to leave St. Petersburg. The smallest sign of displeasure or suspicion would be enough to keep me where I am, for when all is said and done I would rather continue to struggle with my difficulties than lose the esteem of the man who has been my benefactor—not only as sovereign and not only out of a sense of duty and fairness, but out of unprompted, noble and generous benevolence."[5]

This letter put Benkendorf and the emperor in an embarrassing position; the tone was so meek that it would be difficult to find anything to take offense at. Nevertheless, it would be dangerous to give Pushkin his freedom. Nicholas inscribed his decision in the margin of the letter: "There is nothing to prevent him from going wherever he pleases, but I do not see how he intends to reconcile this with his duties here. Ask him if it is his resignation he wants, for he cannot be given such a prolonged leave of absence."

When he heard the emperor's decision, Pushkin thought he could outmaneuver him at last. In his letter he had not even mentioned resignation, it was the tsar who opened the door to salvation; he had only to take him at his word.

"His Majesty," he wrote to Benkendorf on July 4, "has deigned to note on the letter I sent Your Excellency that I could go to the country for several years only if I resigned from the service altogether. I place myself entirely in the sovereign's hands, asking only that His Majesty's decision not be a sign of my disgrace, and that I be allowed access to the Archives whenever circumstances permit me to return to Petersburg."

The poet thought he had won: After virtually offering him his resignation, Nicholas could not refuse it. But once again, he thought too soon.

Nicholas and Benkendorf were absolutely determined to keep Pushkin under their thumb. On the poet's latest letter, the emperor wrote another decision: "If he needs money, the emperor is ready to come to his assistance, he has only to ask; if he wishes to spend some time at home, he may have a leave of absence of four months."

Pushkin finally understood that the emperor would never let him go, however he pleaded and threatened. The monarch wanted him within reach and within sight. Him or Natalya? Both of them—Pushkin, the better to keep his eye on; Natalya, the better to flirt with. He had no choice but to bow his head and say thank you, again.

Frustrated and angry, Pushkin nevertheless decided to take up the offer. He wrote to Benkendorf explaining that his debts amounted to sixty thousand rubles, which was more than he could get from a moneylender. Allowing his jealousy to speak at last, he added: "Gratitude is not humiliating to me. . . . But I cannot conceal it from myself that I have absolutely no right to His Majesty's favors, and it is impossible for me to ask anything myself. It is therefore to you, Count, that I must appeal once again."[6]

If the emperor had been able to read between the lines, he would have guessed that Pushkin needed freedom even more than money, that it was Natalya's beauty, more than his straitened circumstances, that was driving him out of St. Petersburg. But the emperor guessed nothing, or chose to guess nothing, and offered the poet ten thousand rubles and six months' leave of absence.

After using lack of money as the motive for his original request, Pushkin could hardly refuse; but ten thousand rubles was almost an insult.

He needed at least thirty thousand to pay off even half his debts, and offered to repay the loan over six years, using his official salary of five thousand rubles.

The emperor readily agreed to this plan, but Pushkin still had to argue with the ministry of finance, which wanted to deduct half of the advance he had had for *Pugachev* (ten thousand rubles) from the thirty thousand; the negotiations dragged on until autumn.

The money was spent almost before it reached his hands, to pay off old bills and buy new dresses—for Natalya, recovered from her last confinement, was enjoying life to the full. She went riding in an elegant habit that fitted smoothly over the bust and was nipped in tightly at the waist. She appeared at balls with a train of young adorers at her heels. She went to bed late and rose even later. When Pushkin implored her to spend the autumn with him in quiet seclusion at Mikhailovskoye, she raised her voice, stamped her nervous foot, shed a tear or two, and he gave in again and set out, alone, with a leaden heart.

But once more, Mikhailovskoye accomplished its miracle of regeneration. Among the scenes of his early loves, he began to feel a hankering for a new affair—with anyone at all, just to pass the time. He started a halfhearted pursuit of Mrs. Osipov's youngest daughter Marya, who was then sixteen; but when he heard that her stepdaughter, whose favors he had shared with Alexis Wulf before her unhappy marriage in 1833, might be coming, he began to rejoice at the prospect of seeing her again, and giving her a practical demonstration of his ardor: "My angel," he wrote her in September, "you cannot imagine how I miss you, or how happy Eufrasia Nikolayevna [Zizi] made me when she told me you might be coming this way soon. Come, for the love of God! If only for the twenty-third. I have three baskets full of declarations, explanations and sundry other things for you. We can take advantage of our leisure to fall in love. . . ."

But Alexandra, also called Aline, also called Sashenka, did not come, which only added to Pushkin's melancholy.

Zizi wrote to her brother Alexis Wulf: "When he first arrived, our poet was very gay, laughing and bounding about as before, but now he seems to have sunk into a depression again. He was impatiently awaiting Sashenka's arrival—hoping, I think, to rekindle his own aging physical and emotional forces in the fire of her passionate temperament."

His amatory prospects thus thwarted, Pushkin expended his energy riding horseback, bathing, leaping over tables and digging up the flower borders in Zizi Vrevsky's garden. At Trigorskoye, Mrs. Osipov was ill, her elder daughter Annette was in mourning for cousin Netty, who had died in childbirth. At Golubovo, Zizi was surrounded by squabbling, screaming infants. All her husband knew how to do was play chess.

Pushkin was bored. Inspiration would not come. On September 14 he wrote to Natalya: "It has been a week since I left you, and already I am wondering why I went. I have not begun to write and do not know when I shall. On the other hand, I think of you continually and my thoughts bring me no comfort. What weather! I have spent the past three days outdoors, on foot and on horseback. I could go on like this all autumn, and if God does not send a good sharp frost, I may come back without having written a word. Today I saw the moon over my left shoulder, and began to worry about you. . . . Write as often as you can and tell me everything you are doing, so that I can know with whom you are flirting, where you are going, whether you are behaving yourself, and what you are talking about. . . ."

On September 21, having received no answer, he wrote again: "You cannot conceive how intensely one's imagination works when one is alone in a room or walking in the forest and there is no one to stop you from thinking, thinking, thinking yourself dizzy. What do I think about? This: How are we going to live? My father will leave me nothing, he is half ruined already; your family is in no better shape. The tsar will not let me live in the country or be a journalist. Write books for money? As God is my witness, I cannot do it. We have not one cent of certain income, and thirty thousand rubles of very certain expenditure. Everything rests on me and the aunt [Zagryazhskaya]. But neither she nor I will live forever. God only knows how it will end. For the moment, it is not very gay. . . . It is a gray day, autumn is beginning. Perhaps I shall sit down and write. . . . I am doing a lot of walking and riding, on decrepit old nags who are delighted to go out, because afterward they get some oats, a treat to which they have not been habituated. I eat oven-baked potatoes, like a Finn, and soft-boiled eggs, like Louis XVIII. That is dinner. I go to bed at nine, get up at seven. . . ."

On September 25, still no news from Natalya: "What is happening, little wife? It is already the twenty-fifth, and I have not had one word from you. I am angry and upset. . . . Are you well? And are you managing with the household, at least? And how are my little ones? Can you imagine, I still have not written a word, all because my mind is so unsettled. At Mikhailovskoye I found everything as before, except that my old nanny is gone* and a whole family of saplings have grown up around the venerable pines I knew so well; I look at them sourly, as sourly as I watch the young horse guards shining at balls at which I no longer dance. But there is no help for it: Everything I see tells me I am growing old, sometimes in pure peasant Russian. For example, yesterday I met a woman . . . and could not refrain from telling her that she had changed. And she ups and says to me, 'You too, my benefactor, have grown old

* Arina Rodionovna died in 1828.

and ugly.' I can but repeat the words of my departed nanny: 'Handsome I never was, but I was young once.'"

The day after he sent off this letter, Pushkin composed a verse transcription of it:

I have come back to see this plot of land
That sheltered me for two swift years of exile. . . .
It seems only yesterday, at nightfall, that
I stood here in this thicket. Here is the humble house
Where I lived with my poor nanny . . .
And here the wooded hill, where I often
Used to stand, motionless, staring at the lake
Whose mirror reminded me so sadly
Of other far-fled shores and other ripples. . . .

He also put the pine saplings crowding around their high-branched ancestors into his poem:

. . . I salute you, O people
Unknown and new, whose lingering, mighty growth
I shall not see, in the years
When you will pass my old companions by
And hide their tops from passing eyes.
When my grandson listens to your murmur
On his way home from some friendly encounter,
His heart full of mirth and happy plans,
He will walk past you, in the shadow of the night,
Perhaps he will remember me. . . .

The poem was never finished. Pushkin abandoned it, out of lassitude, out of boredom. His worries were holding down the tide of rhyme inside him. He no longer felt like a poet; he felt like a jealous husband, a landowner on the verge of ruin, a courtier in disgrace.

"The emperor promised me a review," he wrote to Natalya toward the end of September, "and has forbidden me to publish it; he compels me to live in St. Petersburg and does not give me the means to live by my work. I am wasting my time and energy, throwing away the money I earn by my labor, and I can expect nothing of the future. My father is frittering away the income from his property senselessly and without pleasure, your parents are losing everything. . . . What will become of us? God alone knows. In the morning, I do nothing. In the evening I go to Trigorskoye, snoop about in old books and munch walnuts. But I am not even thinking about writing, either poetry or prose. . . ."

At last, on October 2: "I began to write yesterday (touch wood). The weather is turning. Autumn has come in earnest. Perhaps inspiration will come too. I look out the window and say to myself, what joy, if all of a sudden a coach were to roll up in the courtyard, and Natalya were to be inside that coach! But no, my friend. Stay in St. Petersburg. I shall try to shorten my time here and come back to you sooner than I planned."

"I am writing in fits and starts," he wrote Pletnev. "For inspiration, some degree of mental peace is necessary, and I am not at all peaceful."

The autumn of 1835 was the least productive period in Pushkin's whole career. He labored vainly to begin a new chapter of *Eugene Onegin*, compose a few medieval scenes and get on with his *Egyptian Nights*, but he never had the energy to finish it. This work was based on a poem he had written in 1825, glorifying the amorous cruelties of Cleopatra as related by the very mediocre Latin author Aurelius Victor. After several attempts, he managed to insert the poem in a short story in prose, which is singular in more than one respect. It was supposed to draw a parallel between antiquity and modern times; but was it possible for nineteenth-century men to be enslaved by a modern-day Cleopatra? Was Cleopatra conceivable anywhere outside the Egyptian nights, with hordes of slaves and vials of scented unguents? In Pushkin's tale, a Russian poet named Charsky receives a visit from an Italian virtuoso, newly arrived in St. Petersburg to give a series of evening entertainments in the form of improvisations for the people of high society. After hearing a dazzlingly brilliant audition, Charsky decides to introduce the amazing Italian to a select group of acquaintances. An assemblage of elegant eminences crowds into the drawing room to hear this new rare bird. A young, serene beauty, the modern-day Cleopatra draws the theme for the improvisation from an urn: "Cleopatra and her lovers." Inspiration descends upon the Italian, transfiguring him. He moves toward the public, crosses his hands on his chest and relates in ringing verses the ecstasy of the men who consent to die in fair payment for one night in the queen's arms.

Pushkin's story breaks off after the Italian's monologue. His Italian was like the intense, magnificent Mickiewicz, whose improvisations were always so astonishing; Charsky was like Pushkin himself. Into him, Pushkin poured all his loathing of society. He wrote, thinking of himself: "His life might have been happy, except that he had the misfortune to write and publish poetry. The journalists called him 'poet,' the footmen said 'man of letters.' . . . The most galling misfortune for a poet, the most daunting, is this title, his appellation, whose indelible marks he bears forever. The public regard him as their property; to them he was born for their particular service and delectation. Should he come back from the country, the first person to see him asks, 'Haven't you created anything new?' Should he fall to musing over his precarious financial position or the illness of someone dear, he is instantly called to order by a sly smile and a trite exclamation: 'No doubt you are composing something?' Should he fall in love, his inamorata runs to buy an album at the English store and thrusts it out for him to fill with elegies. Should he go to call upon some neighbor whom he hardly knows to discuss some matter of importance, the other man immediately sends for his son and orders him to recite the lines of *Such-and-So*, whereupon the child emits a stream of the poet's own mutilated verse to delight his ears. . . ."

Elsewhere: "Charsky led a very dissipated life; he dragged himself to all the balls, overate at all the diplomatic dinners, and was as indispensable to every evening's entertainment as the sherbet. Yet he really was a poet, and that passion dominated all else in him. When the fit (or so he called his inspiration) was upon him, he shut himself into his study and wrote from morning till night."

At Mikhailovskoye the fit would not come upon Pushkin, and he did not shut himself into his study from morning till night. So, sweeping up his unfinished poems, unexpanded sketches and useless notes, he decided not to insist, and, since the country did not want him any more, to go back to St. Petersburg.

His arrival in the capital was dismal: He came home sick with frustration at having wasted his time and dreading to hear what new folly Natalya had committed, or that Sashka and Mashka were ill, only to be greeted by worse news: His mother was at death's door, and Pushkin's enemies were accusing Natalya of refusing hospitality to her. There Natalya was in her enormous house, they said, with all her sisters and expensive ball gowns, and yet she could not be bothered to take in her suffering, penniless, abandoned mother-in-law, and had let her go stay with a stranger!

Pushkin, however, defended his wife: "I found my mother at the last extremity," he wrote to Mrs. Osipov; "she had come from Pavlovsk to look for an apartment and had a sudden attack in the home of Mrs. Knyazhnin, where she was staying. Kauch and Spassky say there is no hope. To make my misery complete, I have the added tribulation of seeing my poor Natalya the butt of general spitefulness. Everybody is saying how shocking it is that she is so elegant when her father-in-law and mother-in-law don't have enough to eat and her mother-in-law is dying in a stranger's house. You know the truth. One cannot really say that a man with twelve hundred peasants is poverty-stricken. It's my father who has something and I who have nothing. In any event, it is nothing to do with Natalya, I am the one who has to answer for it. If my mother had come to stay with us, Natalya would naturally have welcomed her, but a chilly house full of young children and strangers is hardly the place for someone who is seriously ill. My mother is better off where she is. By the time I arrived, she had already moved; my father is in a truly pitiable condition, while I fret and worry and am completely numb. Believe me, my dear Mrs. Osipov, life, however *süsse Gewohn-*

heit† it may be, has a bitterness that makes it loathsome in the end, and the world is a nasty sea of mud."[7]

About the same time, Pushkin wrote to Nashchokin: "My family is multiplying, growing up, and making a fearful din all around me. It seems to me now that one is no longer entitled to complain of existence, and old age ceases to be the awful terror it was. Bachelors have a dreary time of it here below: They suffer to see the younger generation coming up; only a father can contemplate youth without envy. From this I conclude that we have done well to marry."

Pushkin loved his children—especially his son Sashka, of whom he was very proud. It saddened him to see his excessively young and flighty wife neglect her home for receptions and shopping sprees. In her absence, her sister Alexandra kept watch over the nest and cared for the fledglings. Natalya and Katerina came home only to sleep, eat and change, but Alexandra was always there, inspecting the wardrobes and linen, checking the accounts, giving orders to the servants and scolding the children.

She was a strong-minded, passionate woman, this tall sister with the ivory mask and the pronounced squint. She admired Pushkin, knew all his poems by heart, trembled at the sound of his footstep in his study and forgave all his outbursts. She had spent her entire childhood alone and was haunted by fantasies. She was a faded virgin, jealous of her sister, who so undeservedly shared the poet's bed. In her brother-in-law's presence, she became overexcited and tense. All her repressed affections, frustrated desires and rancid vestal reveries flowed out to Pushkin, and Pushkin was not insensitive to this late-blooming passion. Alexandra surrounded him with that feminine solicitude of which Natalya had always deprived him. Gradually, she came to "supplement" Natalya in his mind and heart: Natalya's body and Alexandra's soul blended into an indissoluble whole. Unconsciously, he began to love the two women at once. "He is openly carrying on with his sister-in-law," Annette Wulf wrote in February 1836, "and his wife has become a great flirt."[8] Princess Vyazemsky related how, on his deathbed, Pushkin handed her a gold chain, with the request that she give it to Alexandra. The children's maid claimed that the chain had belonged to Alexandra, and that the valet had found it in the poet's bed one day. "Explain it any way you like," the maid told the children; "in my opinion your aunt has done your maman a great wrong." In support of these allegations, certain phrases from Zhukovsky's notes on Pushkin's death may also be relevant:

> The revelations of Alexandra . . .
> The story of the bed.

† "Sweet habit" (German).

The devil . . . very good‡
You brought me luck.

Did "the revelations of Alexandra" relate to "the story of the bed," and was "the story of the bed" the same as that of the chain?*

Natalya, pregnant for the fifth time, was jealous of Alexandra. Alexandra was jealous of Natalya. The poet's mother was ill. He had written nothing that autumn. There was no money.

So, on February 1, 1836, he had to deposit 1200 rubles' worth of shawls, pearls and silver as security with a moneylender; and on March 13, to the same moneylender, he took 650 more rubles' worth of shawls, pearls and silver. On March 24, 1836, Belizar the bookseller demanded payment of 2172 rubles and 90 kopecks for books supplied in 1834 and 1835. Pushkin was in debt to everyone. He owed money to tradesmen, to officers, to his landlord, his tailor, his coachman, the druggist, the milkman, the baker, the bookbinder, the English store where his wife did her shopping, and to all of his servants. He wrote:

To the valet	100 rubles
To the first nanny	40
To the second nanny	60
To the first chambermaid	100
To the second and third chambermaids	40
To the fourth chambermaid	20
To the nurse	177
To the kitchen help	60
To the footman	90
To the cook	50
To the coachmen	20
To the floor waxer	15
To a table waiter	60
To the laundress	90

Etc.

One contemporary recalled seeing Pushkin whirl into Smirdin's bookshop shouting, "Money! Money! Money!" When his brother-in-law Pavlishchev dared to send another appeal for funds, the poet roared himself hoarse: "He yelled until his voice gave out," Olga Pavlishchev

‡ According to I. Borichevsky, the Pushkin scholar, this should read, "The devil is a good shot" (version (a) le gaillard . . . très bien; (b) le gaillard . . . tire bien).

* Most authorities now favor the existence of an actual liaison between the poet and Alexandra. In support of this thesis there is also a letter, written in French by an unknown woman to A. I. Turgenev, containing the passage: "Neither his [Pushkin's] past nor his present argues in his favor. My God, had he forgotten he was a husband and father?"

wrote to her husband, "about how he would give up everything he owned (including his wife, maybe) sooner than have anything to do with Boldino ever again."[9] His tantrums were becoming increasingly frequent. He was growing irritable, hypernervous, grouchy. He was seldom heard to laugh. In January 1836 he quarreled with a young admirer of his, Count Sollogub, and challenged him to a duel.

"I was at a reception, talking to Natalya Nikolayevna Pushkin," Sollogub wrote, "who thought it would be amusing to tease me about my romantic passion and the creature who had inspired it. I wanted to point out that she was no longer a child, and asked her a question: 'How long have you been married?' Later, we spoke of Lensky, a nice Polish chap who used to dance a splendid mazurka at St. Petersburg balls. It was all very innocent and without any hidden meanings. But the ladies standing by turned it into a calumny and claimed they heard me say that Natalya Nikolayevna fancied Lensky (which was false) and had allowed herself to forget her recent marriage more than she ought."

Friends having informed Pushkin of Sollogub's alleged offense, the poet issued a challenge to the young man in regulation form, through the intermediary of a man named Khlyustin, who was a friend of Leo Pushkin's and a disappointed suitor for the hand of Katerina Goncharov. By then, Sollogub had left St. Petersburg; he replied with a respectful written explanation. Pushkin would not accept it; he wanted satisfaction in blood. The affair dragged on until May 3, 1836, when the adversaries finally met in Moscow, were reconciled and became fast friends. But meanwhile, in February 1836, Khlyustin himself, the intermediary in the Pushkin-Sollogub affair, had incurred his principal's wrath by tactlessly quoting a particularly hostile article by Senkovsky in the poet's presence. "On February 4, 1836," he wrote to Pushkin, "I quoted a remark by Senkovsky to the effect that you had deceived the public. Instead of accepting my words as what they were—a quotation—you preferred to believe I was stating my own opinion in agreement with that of Mr. Senkovsky; in a sense, you mixed the two of us up together and cemented the alliance by saying, 'It makes me sad to see how these people can repeat the inanities of a tramp and pig like Senkovsky.' By 'these people' you meant me; the tone and vehemence of your voice left no doubt as to your meaning, even if the actual words were not specific."[10]

The poet answered the same day: "I can take no action on the statements of a Senkosvky, but I cannot ignore them when a man like you makes them his own. I shall accordingly instruct Mr. Sobolevsky to ask you on my behalf to be good enough either to retract what you said without delay, or to accord me the customary satisfaction."[11]

Still on February 4, another letter from Khlyustin to Pushkin: "I have the honor to inform you that it is impossible for me to retract anything

I said, having adequately explained my action in my previous letter. As regards the customary satisfaction to which you allude, I am at your service."[12]

The adversaries did not, however, reach the stage of the "customary satisfaction" and, after exchanging three sets of letters in one day, were reconciled.

Without pausing for breath, Pushkin flung himself into another quarrel of honor the very next day, February 5, 1836. He had been told that Prince Repnin had made some unflattering remarks about his poem *On the Recovery of Lucullus*, so he wrote to Repnin:

"To my regret, I find myself compelled to importune Your Excellency; but as a gentleman and father I must look to my honor and the name I shall leave to my children.

"I do not have the honor to be personally acquainted with Your Excellency. Not only have I never offended you, but for reasons of my own I have hitherto felt nothing but sincere respect and gratitude toward you. However, a man named Bogolubov has publicly repeated statements offensive to me as coming from you, and I would ask Your Excellency to be good enough to let me know the truth of the matter.

"I know better than anyone the distance separating us; but you, as a great lord and exponent of that ancient and authentic nobility to which I also belong, will clearly understand, I trust, the imperious necessity prompting this action on my part."[13]

On February 10, 1836, Prince Repnin replied: "I see Mr. Bogolubov only at the home of S. S. Uvarov. I have never had any relations with him and have never spoken of you in his presence. Moreover, having read your *Envoi to Lucullus* I must tell you frankly that your great talent would be a precious boon to the fatherland and bring personal glory to yourself, if only you will consent to sing of the faith and solidarity of Russia instead of indulging in personal attack."

"I cannot choose but agree with you," Pushkin replied; "Your Excellency's opinion of expressions of personal grievance is absolutely correct."

This matter went no further. But all these duels, planned and postponed, and these letters of insult and apology, bear sufficient witness to the poet's exaggerated susceptibility during 1836. On all sides, people were saying ugly things about him. On all sides, he felt hated, threatened, spurned.

Two months after his quarrel with Sollogub and one month after his exchanges with Khlyustin and Prince Repnin, fate struck again. Early in March, the doctors began to be seriously concerned by his mother's condition. She often lost consciousness, her heart was weak. Sergey Lvovich sat in her room weeping noisily, and his tears, wails and genuflections terrified the dying woman. Looking down at Nadezhda Osipovna's emaciated features, Pushkin suddenly felt the affection he had never been able to give her before. His long, faraway past was sinking into oblivion with this feeble, haggard, silent creature. Now that he was about to lose a mother, he suddenly understood the meaning of the word. Nadezhda Osipovna had been a poor mother, true enough—authoritarian, erratic, distant . . . but even a poor mother was better than none at all. He showered her with attentions and consideration, and spent what little money he had on doctors and drugs, while Nadezhda Osipovna readily acknowledged her past inadequacies and begged her son's forgiveness. "I met him at his parents' home, with his wife," Mrs. Kern wrote, "a few days before his mother's death. . . . They sat side by side on a little sofa against the wall. Nadezhda Osipovna was watching them tenderly, lovingly. Alexander Sergeyevich was holding the tip of his wife's boa in his hand and stroking it gently, as though to express his affection for his wife and his mother, but he never spoke. Natalya was wearing curlers in her hair, she was on her way to a ball."

Pushkin's mother died on March 29, 1836. He accompanied her body to the Holy Mountain cemetery near Mikhailovskoye, where she was inhumed, and reserved a plot for himself. "He was very depressed after the burial," Countess Vrevsky (Zizi Wulf) said. "He complained that fate had not spared him again this time—he had had so short a while to taste the blessings of a mother's love, which he had never known before."

In St. Petersburg his enemies said he had openly enjoyed himself at the funeral mass.

After burying his mother, Pushkin had to begin thinking of the impending birth of his fourth child. More expenses. More worries. And not a penny in the house to pay for the confinement, the doctors, the wet nurse. . . . Smirdin, the publisher and bookseller, offered Pushkin fifteen thousand rubles to give up his idea of a review and continue contributing to Smirdin's *Reading Library*. Pushkin would not be tempted: Only the review, he thought, could bring in the eighty thousand rubles a year he had to have. But the authorities had consistently refused permission to found it. In 1836 Pushkin tried again, and the miracle happened: It was authorized. The review would be a quarterly, to be called *The Contemporary*.

The first issue, which came out early in April 1836, was an attractive volume whose table of contents included *The Journey to Arzerum* and *The Covetous Knight*. Pushkin was delighted. On the strength of the vast sums to be earned by the review, Natalya rented a summer house twice as expensive as the last one. The only people who were not enthusiastic were the readers. The new magazine was judged dull and dry:

no society gossip, no views on ladies' fashion, not a single line of amusing or timely comment. Nothing but fine, firm prose and fine, sober poetry. Food for professors! Yet *The Contemporary* had secured the services of several important names: Zhukovsky, Gogol, Yazykov, Vyazemsky. To launch it, Pushkin gave up his own royalties; he worked for nothing, collected contributions, corrected proofs, supervised sales—although page layout, printing, distribution and bookkeeping were all minor matters, in his view. The censor, however, took pains to make sure that nothing would be done to smooth the path for the diabolical Pushkin. Underlings, terrified by the poet's reputation, picked over every paragraph with fastidious malice, sat on the galleys for weeks, imperturbably delayed the publication of every issue. Uvarov, Minister of the Interior, had not forgotten *On the Recovery of Lucullus*—"imitated from the Latin"—and exhorted his army of clericals to be doubly vigilant with *The Contemporary*. Story after story was rejected on the most spurious grounds. Benkendorf upbraided Pushkin for publishing an article by a cornet of the guards without first obtaining permission from the chief of police, his commanding officer. Uvarov wrote to the chairman of the board of censors: "It is not fitting for officials attached to my ministry to have anything to do with persons of such pernicious mentality as Pushkin." He was scolded by the third section for *receiving* a letter from Küchelbecker. Bulgarin and Senkovsky, the government spies, wrote: "The prince of thought has become the slave of the herd; the eagle has descended from the clouds to turn a treadmill."

And: "Pushkin has throttled his inspiration in order to grind out chronicles and polemics."

Revolted by the unending complaints and criticism, Pushkin was soon sorry he had ever heard of journalism.

"Cleaning out Russian literature," he wrote to his wife, "is like cleaning out the latrines; it is the job of the police. . . . The devil take them! My very blood is turning to bile."[14]

Elsewhere: "A ghastly shudder runs through me whenever I remember I am a journalist. In the days when I was still an honest man, the police were already after me, with their 'You have deceived . . .' and so forth. Now what will they do? Mordvinov [one of Benkendorf's associates] will look upon me as a Thadeus Bulgarin or a Nicholas Polevoy—as a spy: It was the devil who caused me to be born in Russia with a soul and talent! Very funny, you must admit!"[15]

At the end of April Pushkin settled his wife into the new country house and went to Moscow, where he hoped to do some work, find new contributors for *The Contemporary* and forget the gossip of the capital.

As always, he stayed with Nashchokin, who had mended his ways since his marriage. No more orgies at home, no more gypsy feasts and black-eyed singers: The only habit he had retained from his bachelor days was the English club, where he bet and lost considerable sums of an evening. Pushkin felt at home with the Nashchokins. His wife was gentle and pretty and reasonably cultivated. Nashchokin himself had put on weight since his marriage, but lost none of his conviviality. Pushkin turned down every other invitation, in order to stay home with his friends. He learned to play whist, rearranged Nashchokin's doll house, asked Vera Nashchokin to play him a waltz on her diminutive harpsichord. He forgot all about working in the Archives or writing poetry.

"I feel so happy with you! As though I had found my true family," he would say, sitting down beside Nashchokin and Vera on the Turkish sofa in the bedroom. He wore a red dressing gown with little green checks, his eyes were misty with contentment, he was gay, he was actually unwinding; but his anxiety returned as soon as he had been a few days without news of his wife. Vera Nashchokin said his love for Natalya was unusual, remarkable: He adored her, he trusted her; it was only that he dreaded the consequences of her excessive frivolity. "His wife was not a bad woman, but so superficial!" she wrote. "A breeze! A breeze! It is true, to me she always seemed totally insensitive!"

Strange rumors were filtering into Moscow. In the clubs and drawing rooms, people were saying that Nicholas I was becoming increasingly open in his flirtations, and had conceived a sudden passion for the pupils of the Academy of Dramatic Art.

"I am hearing reports about you, my soul," Pushkin wrote to Natalya on May 5, 1836; "although by the time they reach me they are muffled, of course, because the husband is always the last to know what his wife is doing; but it seems that your coyness and cruelty have driven *someone* to such a pitch of despair that he has had to hire a harem of pupils from the Drama Academy to console himself. That is not nice of you, my angel. Modesty is the fairest adornment of your sex. . . . How is your belly and how is your pocketbook? I am not sorry I came to Moscow, but I do miss St. Petersburg. Are you in the country? How did you manage with the landlord? How are the children? Oh, woe! I see I must have an income of eighty thousand rubles. And I will have it. It is not for nothing that I have launched into journalistic speculation."

Pushkin stayed less than three weeks in Moscow. On the eve of his departure, Nashchokin gave him a farewell supper. During the meal, the poet made an awkward gesture and spilled oil on the tablecloth—an evil omen.

"What an oaf!" Nashchokin cried. "You drop everything you touch."

"I take the consequences upon myself," Pushkin said. "It's nothing."

But he was visibly upset and would not leave the house before the last stroke of midnight, hoping the spell would be broken at the end of the day. He never saw Nashchokin again.

However, there was a new face awaiting him in the country villa. While Pushkin was galloping through the night toward the summer home at Kamenny Ostrov, Natalya was giving birth to their fourth child, a girl. Pushkin learned the news as he stepped over the threshold.

"In the doorway," he wrote to Nashchokin on May 27, 1836, "I was informed that Natalya Nikolayevna had given birth to a girl, Natalya, a few hours before. She was sleeping. The next day I went to congratulate her and, instead of a gold piece, gave her your necklace, with which she is delighted. Money! Money! I need it so desperately that I would go on screaming for it with a knife at my throat."

He was still hoping *The Contemporary* would produce this money; but until it did, he would have to borrow another 7060 rubles from a moneylender, leaving more shawls, silver and family jewels as pledges.

The second issue of the review came out in July, the third in October. The profits remained infinitesimal. On November 19, working day and night, Pushkin finished the novel on which he was counting to boost the sales of *The Contemporary*. It was *The Captain's Daughter*.

"In comparison with *The Captain's Daughter*," Gogol wrote, "all our other novels and short stories are like watered porridge. In it, purity and restraint reach such heights that reality itself seems artificial, a caricature. For the first time, we have truly Russian characters: a simple officer commanding a fort, his wife, a sergeant, the fort itself with its one lone cannon, the disorder of the period, the modest grandeur of ordinary people. Not only is it reality; it is even better."

Pushkin had already treated the Pugachev uprising as a historian; now, he approached it as novelist. Faces sprang up behind signatures, guns and cannon reared their muzzles behind outlines; the name of a town became a town, a military rank a heart and a uniform; a date a certain shade of blue in the sky, a powdery quality of the sand, a particular coolness of the air, a specific sense of contentment. The past slipped away from the dry ink and stood upright on the ground, flushed with energy, color and mass. In *The Captain's Daughter* Pushkin wrote a chronicle of Russian domestic life in the eighteenth century, with its background of peasants, its provincial garrisons, its clergy, gentry, bandits, aristocrats and Pugachev and Catherine II herself.

The plot of the story centers around the adventures of young Sergeant Grinev, relegated by his father's will to the little fort of Belogorsky, forty versts from Orenburg.

The journey is long. Snow is falling. On the road, Grinev meets a ragged peasant who guides him through the blizzard to the nearest inn.

In return, Grinev gives him his hareskin coat. The next day he goes on to Orenburg, and from there to Belogorsky. The fort is like some wretched hamlet, surrounded by a palisade and defended by one cast-iron cannon and a handful of disabled veterans in faded uniforms. It is commanded officially by Captain Mironov, and unofficially by his wife, Vasilyevna Egorovna, "who regarded all military business as her business and ran the fort the way she ran her home." Mironov drills his old soldiers, while Vasilyevna Egorovna supervises the morals of the garrison, metes out disciplinary measures and grants dispensations. This fatherly, phlegmatic captain and his bossy, homely, hearty matron have a daughter, Marya, with whom Sergeant Grinev hastens to fall in love. He even fights a duel to avenge her honor and is seriously injured, after which the girl nurses him so tenderly that he instantly makes up his mind to marry her. He writes to his parents, informing them that he has at last found the woman of his life. But old Grinev's reply dashes the novice's hopes. No consent, no blessing: He is dismissed as a bumbling greenhorn. At first, Grinev wants to brave the paternal wrath, but Marya will not marry him against his parents' will. The two young people are desperate; history pales before their personal dilemma.

But the world is still going round. Corresponding to the revolt of the young couple is the revolt of a region. The dread Pugachev has escaped from prison, set himself up as Tsar Peter III and begun inciting the Ural Cossacks to attack loyalist garrisons. After raiding and destroying a few nearby forts, the pirate's hordes begin to advance upon Belogorsky. Captain Mironov gives orders: Clean the cannon, double the sentries, send young Marya to Orenburg. Too late. The enemy are at the gate. It is an uneven fight: They do manage to fire their cannon, and they try to make a sortie against the swarm of Cossacks and Bashkirs armed with rifles and bows; but the rebels are soon overrunning the village. Pugachev enjoins the regular troops to swear allegiance to him. Mironov refuses and is hanged. The lieutenant repeats his captain's words and is hanged too. Mironov's wife insults the pretender and is struck down with one blow of a saber. Sergeant Grinev is likewise preparing to meet his maker when Pugachev, in a burst of unaccountable magnanimity, spares his life. After these summary executions, the remainder of the people file past their new chief, bowing low to the throne and kissing the crucifix with reverence.

Still dazed by his sudden reprieve, Grinev sets out to find Marya. He learns she is hidden in the home of the priest's wife. He also learns why Pugachev has spared him alone of all the garrison: The rebel chieftain is none other than the ragged peasant he met in the snowstorm, to whom he gave his hareskin coat. "I shall remember as long as I live," the muzhik had said as he took the coat from the hands of "His Honor."

Pugachev the pseudo tsar was keeping the promise of the muzhik. So, contrary to all appearances, some sense of nobility still slumbered within the bloodthirsty drunkard. The impostor summons Grinev and asks him to join his forces. Grinev loftily refuses to betray his empress, whereupon Pugachev gives him permission to leave the fort. Grinev bids farewell to the unhappy Marya, swearing to bring a regiment to deliver her. He goes straight to Orenburg and implores the commanding officer there to march on Pugachev and liberate Belogorsky, but the Orenburg staff officers favor a policy of defense, and calmly wait for Pugachev to besiege them—which he does, bringing famine in his wake. All the Orenburg garrison's sorties end in ignominious defeat. Then Grinev learns from a messenger that Marya has fallen into the clutches of a man named Shvabrin, a former officer of Mironov's who has gone over to Pugachev. Grinev resolves to return to Belogorsky alone, either to abduct his beloved or perish at her feet. Arrested on the road by a rebel patrol, he lets himself be taken to the false tsar and tells him of his apprehensions. Again, Pugachev indulges himself by allowing the enemy officer to go free. Grinev is embarrassed by the kindness of this monster who has been anathematized by the Church. "I am a gentleman and an officer," he tells Pugachev; "yesterday, I was fighting against you . . . today the happiness of my whole life depends upon you. . . ."

Pugachev orders Marya's release. Grinev and the girl leave the fort. His parents give refuge to their son's orphaned fiancée, while he goes back to fight Pugachev. But after the impostor has been defeated and taken prisoner, the investigating commission summons Grinev and charges him with having been in Pugachev's camp: More than once, Pugachev spared his life, he even invited him to his drunken orgies. That story of the hareskin coat is hardly credible. A criminal like Pugachev is incapable of gratitude. Grinev can only be a traitor in the renegade's pay. He merits an exemplary punishment: deportation to Siberia for life.

When she hears the verdict, Marya goes straight to St. Petersburg to appeal to the empress in person, and by doing so, saves her sergeant. The empress, whose understanding is broader than that of the judges, acknowledges Grinev's innocence, honesty, loyalty and courage, orders his release and promises the girl that in future she herself will be her guardian. The novel ends with Grinev's vindication, return and happy marriage to the captain's daughter.

Here again, as in *The Bronze Horseman*, Pushkin is relating the conjuncture of one story and history. The romance of Sergeant Grinev and the gentle Marya is set in an epic *décor*, and the deaths of Captain Mironov and his wife remain insignificant details in the official drama of Pugachev; but it is through such tiny deaths and commonplace romances that we come closest to the weighty events consigned to textbooks.

Pushkin's Pugachev is real because the poet sees him through the sensitivities of little people. He is real because he has been returned to his proper place in the group of anonymous silhouettes automatically discarded by historians. He is real because he is no longer alone at the head of a list of battles, generals and dates, but surrounded by all the people of his time who have come back to life around him.

Before Pushkin, literature had disdained unheroic destinies, ordinary bravery, commonplace calamity, and chosen its heroes among the resounding names and extraordinary personalities of the famous. Before Pushkin, "the hero" and "the people" were separated by an abyss. The hero was given all the advantages of individual attention and blazing lights; the people had to make do with the drab role of function. With Pushkin, the people emerged from the shadows. Thanks to Pushkin, a sergeant, a provincial captain, an orphan who was neither very bright nor very pretty, a thrifty housewife and a valet all receive the keys to the city of belles-lettres. Just as Pushkin had brought the people's speech into the vocabulary of poetry, he now brought the people themselves into the family of literary heroes. *The Captain's Daughter* is more than a skillful tale and a swift-moving story to read. It is a major innovation for its time. Tolstoy's *War and Peace* would not have seen the light of day if Pushkin had not written *The Captain's Daughter. War and Peace* is a master's orchestration of themes first stated in *The Captain's Daughter*. In Tolstoy, as in Pushkin, scenes of battle and camp alternate with scenes of love and domestic calm. The slender plot lines pick their way among the boulders of historic events. The frozen statues of official demigods (Napoleon, Alexander I, Kutuzov in Tolstoy; Catherine II and Pugachev in Pushkin) rise up to confront human forms of wonderful simplicity, and it is the walk-on parts, more than the leading roles, who bring the age to life.

But small as it is, Pushkin's novel embraces an even larger and more colorful universe than Tolstoy's whole vast canvas, for almost all the latter's characters are aristocrats or officers, whereas Pushkin teases out of the void individuals of every social class, servants, popes and brigands, undistinguished petty officers, hesitant old generals. Each of them, it is true, is given only a few lines of text; but their description, however cursory, is enough to stamp them indelibly on our minds. There they are, in two lines and three phrases. We know every inch of them. We can imagine their past and their future, we can invent hundreds of little incidents of which they might be the protagonists. For each of them, the poet has given the password that opens up the treasures of heart and body. Pushkin's whole *oeuvre* is made up of such passwords, such key words. We think we have read one line, but behind that line we have really read pages and pages of floating commentary. We think we have glimpsed a profile, an eye, a coattail, but behind those tiny details there is a whole man.

Here is Marya, the captain's daughter—uncomplicated, not especially pretty or particularly bright, but warmhearted and full of common sense. There is absolutely nothing outstanding about her. Average virtues, an average past. But what instinctive honor, what virile decisiveness spring suddenly to life in this slip of a girl. She would rather die than yield to Shvabrin. She boldly appeals to the empress to save her fiancé. And once the storm is over, she withdraws, goes back to the ranks of frugal housewives, placid spouses, attentive mothers. Her heroism is like the hidden heroism of Tatyana. Her figure rises above the whole herd of young Russian women invented by Tolstoy and Turgenev and others. She can be identified in a thousand. But where, when did Pushkin explain or describe her? Her fiancé, Grinev, is neither extremely handsome nor extremely enterprising: unsophisticated, a nice lad, loyal. He too seems a poor choice to honor with the prestige of the printed word. The fate of this very ordinary fellow, however, concerns us as intensely as that of Pugachev himself. Captain Mironov is an old, weary, lackadaisical soldier who allows his wife to run his garrison for him; but in the face of danger, he squares his shoulders and becomes the chief again quite naturally, dying a warrior's death for tsar and fatherland. And although Mironov's wife wears the trousers in time of peace, when the trumpet sounds she bows to him as protector of the threatened fort. Another example of the devotion of the meek is Grinev's manservant Savelich, ready to defy Pugachev in order to recover his master's hareskin coat or be killed in his master's place rather than face his parents' reproaches. And how much more alive and real than in any history book is Pugachev himself. Here, the man is a jumble of generosity, vainglory, foolishness, cunning and cruelty; all that historians can see in him is an unqualified scoundrel. To test his strength, he poses as a monarch; he assassinates and reprieves, condemns and pardons, swings from good to evil, acts irrationally and on impulse. Grinev has the good fortune to strike a responsive chord in him, providing him with an opportunity to savor the royal virtue of clemency. "I cannot define what I felt as I left this terrible man, a monster and villain to everyone on earth except me," Grinev says. "Why dissimulate? In that instant, I felt a strong bond of sympathy for him." Pushkin resisted the temptation to make Pugachev into a consummate brute and Grinev into a new Charlotte Corday. On several occasions, Pugachev forgets to be a swine and Grinev to be an officer. Despite the differences in their uniforms, rifles, convictions and destinies, they like each other. All the heroes of this tale are powerfully interconnected: They depend upon each other, upon the age they live in and the landscape they move in. They form a complete world of their own. Such little contretemps as these, such little eccentricities, little loyalties, aspirations and sorrows: it takes no more to make a great people. Russia is not Catherine II or Pugachev; Russia is Mironov, his wife, his daughter, Sergeant Grinev and the garrulous old manservant. It is of them Pushkin was thinking when he wrote, in Chapter XIII, "God forbid that we should ever see a Russian rebellion, senseless and merciless, again."

The Captain's Daughter is a masterpiece of both psychology and expression. The deftness of its conception is expressed with the same wonderful assurance of construction and vocabulary. The Russian language has produced nothing more finely wrought, more pure or finished than this seemingly linear, straightforward tale. As usual, Pushkin wrote in short sentences packed around one forceful verb, with no unnecessary epithets and few metaphors, and every one of those few ringing true. For instance, the helplessness of the little fort of Belogorsky in the face of Pugachev's hordes is expressed in a single image: "The next morning on her way back from mass, she [Mironov's wife] saw Ivan Ignatyich [the lieutenant] pulling out of the cannon's mouth the rags, stones, shavings, knucklebones and all sorts of rubbish which had been stuffed down it by the children."

Here is Pugachev, that prize Romantic figure: "He wore a red Cossack kaftan edged in braid. A high sable hat with gold tassels was pulled clear down to his glittering eyes. . . . The Cossack elders crowded around him. Father Gerasim, pale and trembling, stood by the steps with a crucifix in his hand and seemed to be silently imploring it for mercy for the victims."

Pushkin cuts out all the easy effects—such as a description of that floating gallows sailing down the Volga with its macabre cargo of the hanged. He deliberately chooses the hard way. He rubs down his prose, wears it away, aerates it to the point of transparency, to the ultimate resistance of the one right word. He makes of it that taut and slender thing in which no line or facet can be altered without shattering the whole.

Future generations hailed this novel as Pushkin's finest work; his contemporaries greeted it with reserve. Pushkin had become too great for his public.

The poetry he wrote in 1836 showed the extent of his proud isolation:

> To be dependent on a monarch, or the multitude . . .
> To me, one is no better than the other. I want to live
> My way, serve no one but myself and please no other,
> Not bend my mind, my honor, or my knee
> To any power or any livery. I want to go
> Here and there, wherever my fancy leads,

To admire the divine beauty of this world,
Tremble with ecstasy, happiness, and love
For the creations of art, for genius. . . .

This disgust with society, rank, livery and administrative intrigue followed the poet into the very cemeteries of the capital. His hatred pursued government officials and courtiers into the hereafter, into the ultimate putrefaction, the irreducible remnant, the dab of human liquid and the vermin. He snarled:

The grill and column and pretty tomb
That cover the city's stinking dead,
Piled side by side at the bottom of a swamp . . .

Inside the city of the dead, built of slimy stones and silence, Pushkin thought of his own end. He would not be buried here, among his enemies; he wanted to lie beside his mother, in the generous earth of the country. And he knew he would need no marble monument to remind people he had lived and written and had died singing to the deaf.

On August 21, 1836, two weeks after writing the poem on the cemetery, Pushkin completed it with his *Exegi monumentum:*

I have built for myself a spiritual monument.
The people's road will always pass that way,
For it rears its proud, rebellious brow
Higher than the Alexander Column.
No, I shall not die entirely! And my soul,
My lyre will outlive ashes and the void,
I shall be famed to the ends of the earth
As long as there is still one poet here.
My name will ring throughout all Russia,
Every tribe of the land will call to me,
The proud descendant of the Slav, the Finn,
The savage Tungunz, and the Kalmuk of the steppe.
I shall long be deemed congenial
For having taught my voice to sing
Of noble hearts, and freedom in a cruel age,
And for crying mercy upon those who failed. . . .
Be then docile, Muse, to the will of God;
Fear no offense, grasp for no crown,
Learn indifference to both praise and blame
And never stoop to strive with fools.

This funereal vanity, this premonition of death and apotheosis, preyed involuntarily on Pushkin's mind. He was thirty-six, and he thought he had come to the end of his road. He was thoroughly unhappy, demoralized, full of doubt, as though he had nothing more to hope from life. The poem he read at his classmates' annual reunion on October 19, 1836, bears witness to his dejection:

Time was, when our youthful feast
Glowed and hummed, bedecked with roses,
When the clink of glasses rang in answer to our songs,
And we sat in serried ranks. . . .
All that has changed. Our tumbling merriment
In time grew calmer, like ourselves. . . .
We laugh less now, at the end of every song,
We often sigh, and sometimes do not speak at all. . . .

The minutes of the meeting end with this paragraph: "Pushkin began to recite a poem on the twenty-fifth anniversary of the founding of the school, but could not remember all the lines and eventually confessed he had not finished it. He promised to do so, make a copy and append it to these minutes."

But Yakovlev, who was presiding, said Pushkin had not been able to continue because his eyes were blinded by tears.

PART VIII

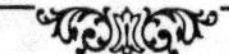

1. *D'Anthès*

Natalya's re-entry into society after her latest confinement was marked by fresh triumphs. The emperor was more eager than ever to dance and exchange pleasantries with her. He often rode his horse beneath her windows, spurring it to make it rear and curvet in elegant arabesques, arching his back and frowning sternly, and then would inquire in the evening, "How is it that your curtains are always closed?" It was whispered that Natalya's beauty gave him no peace.

In a book entitled *Nicholas I and Holy Russia*, a malicious Frenchman named Gallet de Kulture wrote: "The tsar was as autocratic in his loves as in every other aspect of his life. If he singled out a woman in the park or at the theater or a reception, the person who had attracted the god's attention was immediately observed and followed. If she were married, the husband—if single, the parents—were notified of the honor that had befallen them.

" 'And did the tsar never encounter any resistance in the object of his affection?' I inquired of the pretty, witty and virtuous woman who was giving me these details.

" 'Never,' she replied with an air of vast surprise. 'How could that be?' "

In reality, Nicholas I was not an ogre famished for fresh females. His authentic affairs were few; but he did love to please the ladies, and Natalya was just his "type." He told her so, no doubt, and she was proud of it, and that was the end of the matter.

The year 1836 brought the poet's wife another admirer of note, however. Baron Georges-Charles d'Anthès, a few months her junior, was as popular with the ladies as Natalya with the men.

He was born on February 5, 1812, at Soultz, in Alsace, where his family had been established for several generations.* In 1806 his father, Baron

* The D'Anthès family originated in Gotland. By 1529 they were established at Weinheim in the Palatinate, where several of its members served as municipal magis-

Joseph-Konrad, married Marie-Anne de Hatzfeld, niece of that Prince of Hatzfeld whose memory was made famous in the folk art of the Napoleonic era. Six children were born of this union. After doing reasonably well in his studies at the Collège de Fontaine in the Haut-Rhin, then at the Lycée Bourbon in Paris, Georges-Charles applied for admission to the military academy at Saint-Cyr and was accepted as No. 4 out of 180 applicants. His career was interrupted by the revolution of 1830. By tradition a legitimist, he joined the academy's regiments, which were defending the cause of Charles X in Paris, and even spent a few weeks with the partisans rallying around the Duchesse de Berry in the Vendée, but eventually, cursing Louis Philippe and all his clique, he made his way home to Soultz. Provincial isolation and inactivity soon began to weigh upon this active and undisciplined youth, however, and Georges-Charles decided to seek his fortune abroad. The D'Anthès family was large, its resources small. Through his relatives, he sought the patronage of the King of Prussia and Prince Wilhelm, the future William I. He aspired to make his career in the Prussian army and was keenly disappointed to hear that he would have to begin as a noncommissioned officer. "You may think," the ruler told him, "a king of Prussia can do whatever he pleases. Don't you believe it! Our military code is inflexible, no one can dispense you from the regulations. But what I cannot do myself, I can ask my son-in-law, the emperor of Russia, to do for you."[1]

Georges d'Anthès accordingly set out for Russia, where legitimists were always sure to carve a handsome niche for themselves in the army. The Prussian prince gave him letters of introduction which were sufficiently impressive to convince Count Adlerberg, a close associate of the tsar's and the head of the chancellery of the ministry of war. With this backing, Georges had no qualms about his military and social career.

On his journey across Germany, however, he acquired another powerful protector, in the person of the Netherlands ambassador to the Russian court. Their meeting took place in the autumn of 1833. The ambassador, Baron Heckeren (or, to be exact, Jacob Theodore Derk Borchard Anne, Baron van Heeckeren-Beverwaert), was returning to his post in St. Petersburg after a leave of absence. Passing through a little German town, the ambassador learned that a young, handsome Frenchman was languishing, ill and abandoned, in the only hotel. Heckeren paid a bedside call, talked to D'Anthès at length, found him nicely pathetic and offered him a place in his carriage, which D'Anthès gratefully

---

trates or "counsuls." Jean-Henri d'Anthès, born January 2, 1670, settled in the southern Alsatian highlands, where his father exploited forges at Belfort and owned silver mines at Giromagny. He managed the Oberbrüch forge himself, and founded a royal tin manufacture there. Ennobled in 1731, he died on November 11, 1733; in 1720 he acquired the property at Soultz which became the family's permanent residence.

accepted.[2] On October 11, 1833, the *St. Petersburg News* announced that the good ship *Nicholas I* had "docked at Kronstadt on October 8 after a seventy-eight-hour crossing, with forty-two passengers on board," among whom were the ambassador from Holland and Georges-Charles d'Anthès.

The man into whose care Georges d'Anthès had just committed himself was a singular individual. Baron Heckeren belonged to one of the oldest families of Holland. In his youth, during the reign of Napoleon I, he had served as a volunteer in the French navy. In 1815, after the recognition of the Kingdom of the Netherlands, he changed careers, trading the sea for diplomacy. He was appointed chargé d'affaires, then minister plenipotentiary of Holland in St. Petersburg, where he managed to become one of the most influential of the ambassadors accredited to the court of Russia.

A lithograph dating from 1843 shows him seated in an armchair, his chest paved with decorations and his back very stiff. He has a long, thin face with a sharp nose, sensual mouth and chin whiskers. The eyes are pale, the hands elegant. Refinement and restrained distinction emanate from the portrait. Heckeren's contemporaries appreciated the ambassador's caustic wit, but did not hesitate to qualify him as decadent and intriguing.

"Old Heckeren [he was forty-three when this was written] was a sly dog, more calculating than depraved," Prince Vyazemsky wrote.[3]

"Baron Heckeren," Princess Vyazemsky told Bartenyev, "was known for his immorality; he surrounded himself with shamefully depraved young men, lovers of scandal and intrigue."[4]

Smirnov spoke even more emphatically: "Heckeren was an evil, selfish man for whom the end justified any means. Known throughout St. Petersburg for his malicious tongue, he had already caused many people to quarrel and was held in utter contempt by all who had seen through him."[5]

Baron Tornau, who knew Heckeren later in Viennese diplomatic circles, accused him of having "a rather flexible concept of the truth" and being "a scandalmonger."

These unrelievedly negative views of Baron Heckeren were not recorded until after Pushkin's death, however, and are excessively biased. For the period prior to 1837 I have found only one item, in the archives of the foreign ministry in Paris. This is the opinion of M. de Barante, the French ambassador in St. Petersburg; it is dated October 8, 1836: "Baron Heckeren, the Netherlands minister, often speaks to me of the Belgian question. He is a man of wit, indulging in much unnecessary subtlety, whose words need never be credited with the least degree of sincerity." Viewed in the cool light of afterthought, these images combine and complete each other to present a fairly plausible likeness of a man of the world, cold, mocking, intelligent, whose very profession incited him to weave and unmask intrigues. Habituated to the complex moves of diplomacy, the baron approached the realm of personal relations with the same feints and gambits that were the tools of his trade in international affairs. He wove alliances, set up coalitions, upset balances, stirred and kneaded the drawing-room flock at will. "A little old man," Rossetti said of him, "forever smiling, uttering witticisms, and poking his finger into every pie."[6] The Netherlands government had a very high regard for the abilities of its "little old man," however, and the Russian government bestowed upon him the Order of St. Anne, First Class. To be sure, there was a voluminous "Heckeren" dossier in the foreign ministry in St. Petersburg, bristling with complaints lodged against the Dutch diplomat by the customs officials; but those were mere peccadilloes. Taking advantage of his position, the ambassador sent for "abusive quantities of goods" from abroad and brought them into the country duty-free: crystal vases, porcelain, silver, cheese, chocolates, perfume, anisette cordial, bed linen, furniture, *bibelots*—and all in commercial quantities. Every month, the packages became more numerous and the customs office's complaints more vehement;[7] but the foreign ministry would take no action on them, for Baron Heckeren was an intimate friend of the Foreign Minister himself, Count Nesselrode. Nesselrode liked Heckeren's wit, elegance and violently monarchist sympathies. He sensed in him a man of his own rank, of his breed, and accepted him as a member of that far-flung fraternity which, from the Faubourg Saint-Germain to Vienna and from Vienna to St. Petersburg, ran Europe according to Metternich. Nesselrode's contemporaries titled him "Austrian Minister of Russian Foreign Affairs."

Heckeren rapidly became a prominent figure with enviable connections. But although he lived openly, indeed conspicuously, his closest friends knew nothing of the private man. He never married. He is not known to have had any affair, however ephemeral, in St. Petersburg. Apparently, no woman ever crossed his path. It was as though he had decided to keep all dangerous passions at arm's length in the interests of his career, or had been rendered immune to the fair sex by some mysterious past sorrow. He lived on the surface. He economized his emotions. He avoided every form of commitment, out of skepticism or natural reserve.

But this all changed the day he met Georges-Charles d'Anthès. For Heckeren, the encounter was a revelation. For the first time in years he found himself drawn, vanquished, disarmed by a human being. He was alone in the world. He had no family. No deep friends. Suddenly, he became aware of the warmth and substance of which he had been voluntarily depriving himself. Georges d'Anthès, who had precipitated this sudden realization, was also its sole beneficiary. The Netherlands ambassador determined to be his patron, and did so with such devotion and intensity that his perplexed contemporaries tried to invent all kinds of hidden motives for his behavior. Some said D'Anthès was the ambassador's natural son, or his nephew, or even a bastard son of Charles X! Others said that Heckeren and D'Anthès were bound by an unnatural passion. Prince Trubetskoy, for example, a comrade in arms of D'Anthès and his advocate in all other respects, did not hesitate to say: "D'Anthès was guilty of a few pranks, but they were all quite innocent, the usual thing for youths of the day; in one respect, however, he was different, but we did not hear about that until long afterward. I don't know quite how to put it. . . . In those days, homosexuality was very common in society; and as D'Anthès was always running after women, he must have been the passive partner in his relations with Heckeren."[8]

Louis Metman, grandson of Georges-Charles d'Anthès, tried to account for the friendship between his grandfather and the ambassador in very different terms: "The bond of friendship that developed between two men of very different tastes and personalities may be very simply explained by the exclusively French education and upbringing they had shared, and a remote kinship such as may have existed between Baron Heckeren and one or another of the Rhine families to which Georges d'Anthès was connected through his father and mother."[9]

The bold assertions of Prince Trubetskoy and the feeble deprecations of Louis Metman are equally unjustified. If Baron Heckeren had been known as a homosexual, Pushkin would have been only too happy to add that charge to his list of accusations in his final letter of insult. But he made no allusion to any ambivalence in the relationship between D'Anthès and Heckeren. Even more significant is the fact that throughout the long and brilliant careers of both men, no such allegation was ever made about either of them, yet they spent their lives in the world of high diplomacy, politics and society, where idle minds seize upon the smallest symptom as proof positive, and hasten to ruin a reputation with it. Lastly, there are the letters from D'Anthès to Heckeren (quoted later in the book), in which the young man tells his protector of his unhappy love for a woman. "Be indulgent toward my new passion," he writes, "for I love you too with all my heart." The tone of his letters defines the relations between the two men. It would seem, when all is said and done, that Baron Heckeren was simply very repressed—emotionally retarded. He bravely forced his attraction to D'Anthès into a socially acceptable, abstract mold. He sublimated whatever ambiguity and frustration he may have felt, and encouraged his protégé in his pursuit of women, bitterly rejoicing in his conquests. Eluding the call of his instincts, he compelled himself to demand nothing in return for his fervor beyond the permission to guide, cherish, nourish and observe a youth whose affection flattered him. This fatherly concern was a more beneficial manifestation of an impulse which, if given free rein, would have been the talk of St. Petersburg, Vienna and Paris.

D'Anthès, in any event, never had occasion to repent of his decision. He arrived in St. Petersburg in October 1833, knowing no word of Russian and having no intention of learning a language he held in contempt. On February 14, 1834, he joined the army as cornet of the seventh reserve squadron of the horse guards. The recommendation of Wilhelm of Prussia had overcome every administrative obstacle. His entrance examination was reduced to a formality: On January 5, 1834, a few days before the examination, Count Adlerberg wrote to D'Anthès: "He [the examiner] has promised not to be hard, as you say."[10] Empress Alexandra Fyodorovna, as commander of the regiment of horse guards, allocated nearly ninety thousand rubles to outfit the new recruit. Two years later, he was promoted to the rank of lieutenant, with permission to retain his French nationality while serving in the Russian army.

Pushkin, as though visited by a premonition, wrote these few words in his diary on January 26, 1836: "Baron D'Anthès and the Marquis de Pina, two Chouans,† are to be taken directly into the guards as officers. There is some protest."

The new horse guardsman's military zeal was unobtrusive: He amassed a heap of disciplinary warnings with perfect aplomb, left the ranks ahead of his superiors, lit cigars when the company stood at ease after review, missed his fixed periods of duty, arrived late for roll call. The regiment's historiographer calculated that Baron D'Anthès received forty-four official reprimands during his brief sojourn in the army.

These venial sins did not impede his rise. He had "the suffrage of the heart." He was said to be "one of the most handsome men in the horse guards, and one of the most fashionable men in society." His comrades liked his company because he made them laugh. Grand Duke Michael Pavlovich admired his puns, his fine mustache and his dancing. Countess Musin-Pushchin, who was an aunt of his, was also well disposed toward him; Count Adlerberg encouraged him; Heckeren, Nesselrode and the rest of the international aristocracy were his patrons in society.

As time passed, the ambassador's affection began to assume more tangible form. The father of Georges d'Anthès, informed of this exceptional friendship, wrote to his son's protector from Soultz, on December 21, 1833: "I cannot find words to express my gratitude for your kindness

† A word originally used to refer to bands of French partisans who fought in the Revolution against the French Republic; it became an epithet for any French (although usually upper class and royalist).

to my son; I hope he will prove himself worthy of it. Your Excellency's letter has quite set my mind at rest, for I cannot deny that I was very worried about him. With his outspoken manner and nonchalance, I was afraid he might get into bad company, but thanks to you, who have been good enough to take him under your wing and treat him as a friend, my fears are altogether allayed. . . . I gratefully accept Your Excellency's proposal to cover the initial cost of fitting him out, and ask you to be good enough to write down the amount you have spent, so that I may repay you in due course."[11]

On March 12, 1834, a second letter from Georges's father to Heckeren: "Georges owes his future to you alone, Baron, and is well aware of it; he looks upon you as a father, and I hope he will prove worthy of it. . . . I have no anxiety about the fate of my son, and entrust him wholly to Your Excellency's care."[12]

In 1834 Baron Heckeren went to Alsace to meet the young man's family, and early in 1836 he decided to adopt Georges d'Anthès as his son and heir.

Contemporaries did not know what to make of this adoption of a man of twenty-four by a man of forty-five; Georges's father, however, seemed to find the baron's idea perfectly reasonable and gave his reasons, on February 15, 1836: "It is not without a keen sense of gratitude that I find myself having to speak to you of the proposal you have been good enough to make on several occasions, to adopt my son Georges-Charles d'Anthès as the heir to your name and fortune. . . . This generous action opens up a future to my son which I could never have offered him, and gratifies my fondest aspirations. Therefore, I ask you to put down my delay in adding my official consent to that already given by my heart solely to the ties that bind a father to his son. Now, having attentively observed the progress of the affection the boy has inspired in you . . . and seen with what solicitude you have undertaken to watch over him, satisfy his needs, and show an unremitting concern for him until this day, on which your protection leads him into a career in which he cannot fail to distinguish himself, I have told myself that this reward was surely your due and that my paternal affection for my child must yield to so much devotion and generosity. I accordingly hasten to inform you, Baron, that from this day forward I relinquish my paternal authority over Georges-Charles d'Anthès and authorize you to adopt him as your son, endorsing fully and in advance whatever steps you wish to take to make this action legally valid."

The adoption proceedings went on for three months. It was a delicate maneuver, for the French code of civil law, which was still in force in the Netherlands, prohibited adoption in such circumstances (Articles 343 and 345); but the Dutch bureaucrats found a verbal device to circumvent the problem. In its final form, the royal decree made no mention of adoption, which would have been illegal, and simply stated that D'Anthès and his descendants were entitled to bear the name of Heckeren. On May 22, 1836, Baron Heckeren triumphantly wrote to Nesselrode: "I have the honor to inform Your Excellency that I have legally adopted Baron Georges-Charles d'Anthès as my son and that by decision of His Majesty the King of the Netherlands, of May 5, 1836, the Supreme Court of Nobility of the Kingdom has recognized his right to bear my name, title and arms."[13]

So Georges-Charles moved from one family to another, to the satisfaction of both his fathers. As for the young man himself: This change of identity was the answer to his prayers. At one stroke, his fortune and his future were ensured. There was not one home whose doors were not flung open to him. The ladies went wild over the French Chouan who was now an officer in the Russian horse guards, the Georges d'Anthès who was now Georges d'Anthès de Heckeren.

And they had reason to: D'Anthès was tall, with a splendid chest, a full, rosy face, prominent eyes, an eager, appetizing mouth and blond, curly hair. A fine golden mustache curled over his upper lip. His laughter was arrogant, his voice pleasant, with a faint trace of an Alsatian accent. His gestures had a manly grace that sent the fair sex into raptures. Prince Trubetskoy said of him: "He was very handsome, and was ruined by his invariable success with the ladies; as a foreigner, he was able to treat them more lightly and with less diffidence than we Russians, and through being spoiled by them he became more demanding, more difficult, if you will, and more arrogant than is permissible in our society." "The women all fought over him," another contemporary wrote.

Two of the women who paled at the sight of the mettlesome horse guardsman were Natalya Pushkin and her sister Katerina Goncharov. The most fashionable woman and the most adulated officer in society were drawn together by virtue of being set apart from the rest. It was flattering for Natalya to be noticed by the first slayer of fair hearts. Besides, D'Anthès corresponded exactly to her concept of the ideal man. Pushkin was short, slight and drab. He disliked drawing-room society. He danced only to be polite. His conquests in the field of poetry did not alter the fact that as dancing partner and escort he made a poor showing. He lacked the uniform, the epaulets, the dashing mustache, the jingling spurs, the love of bright lights, music and beautiful gowns, the resounding name, the easy money and the light touch. And D'Anthès had them all. He was a male replica of Natalya. Like her, he lived in a perpetual whirl. Like her, he was in the pink of health, young, madcap and excitable. At his side, she felt like a woman. With his first glance, D'Anthès instilled in her that sweet confusion which Pushkin had never been able to awaken. Every time she saw him, Natalya realized more clearly all the good things she had missed by marrying the poet. But she did not dream of being unfaithful to her husband. On that point, she was essentially honest. She knew right from wrong; but between right and wrong, there were so many accommodating nuances! An honest woman could savor small pleasures without failing in her duty. A pure wife could venture to the very edge of sin without anyone having a right to censure her conduct. Pushkin himself had authorized "flirtation." Natalya was simply making use of that authorization a little, with the emperor; with D'Anthès, a lot. What was so scandalous in that?

Here and there, the memoirs of their contemporaries re-create the image of the couple, through a glimpse of their feelings or a detail of their dress. From writer to writer and page to page, these faded, precious illustrations take form, marking off the acts of the drama.

Here is D'Anthès at a ball in August 1835: "D'Anthès invited Mrs. Pushkin for a dance, I forget which. He was very showy, danced skillfully, chattered and entertained everyone, and thought himself the hero of the ball. He was powerfully built, of average height, solid, fair-haired; I was unfavorably impressed by his affectation and self-assurance, and compared him, I believe, to a stableboy."[14]

Here is Natalya on horseback, with Katerina and D'Anthès: "On the back of a tall, restive horse that kept impatiently pawing the ground swayed the graceful silhouette of a beauty: Pushkin's wife. Her sister and D'Anthès were with her. . . . The pretty woman gave her mount a cut of her whip and the little cavalcade cantered off down an avenue of birches. It was like a picture come to life."[15]

Elsewhere, we see Natalya after the ball: "The ball was over. Natalya Nikolayevna was waiting for her carriage, leaning against a column in the entrance hall in the midst of a group of young officers, mainly from the horse guards, who were assailing her with their compliments. A short distance away, Pushkin stood by another column, taking no part in the conversation and seeming to be lost in thought."[16]

At first flattered, then intrigued, then disturbed by the pressing attentions of D'Anthès, Natalya was finally unable to live without him. He contrived to find more and more occasions to meet her, at the homes of mutual friends, at the theater and the balls, in the park. Natalya's sister Katerina, who was hopelessly in love with the officer, was the inevitable witness to their encounters. Choking down her pride, stifling her jealousy, she humbly accepted the role of chaperon for the sole pleasure of seeing and speaking to D'Anthès.

Pushkin distastefully observed this game. He himself was being unfaithful to Natalya with her other sister Alexandra—out of inertia, perhaps, or vindictiveness. The atmosphere in the poet's home had become heavily erotic. Domestic quarrels followed in rapid succession, increasingly violent and fruitless. Natalya was infatuated with D'Anthès but resented Pushkin's attentions to her sister Alexandra. Pushkin resented Natalya's excessive kindness to D'Anthès. Katerina was jealous of Natalya, who had won D'Anthès and did not deserve him. This tangle of surreptitious intrigue, suspicion, clandestine bed-hopping, billets-doux, nagging, daydreaming, rendezvous and wrinkled skirts exasperated the poet. The youngsters wailed, the women wept, the doors slammed. And then hurry, hurry, we have to dress, a dash of cold water on the face, which dress to wear, how to do my hair, will the emperor be there tonight, and D'Anthès?

The winter of 1835–36 was the period of Pushkin's quarrels of honor and aborted duels with Sollogub, Khlyustin and Repnin. Natalya was pregnant again, but still too beautiful, too desirable. Money was scarce. Inspiration was growing scarcer.

Perpetually distracted by all this agitation, Pushkin had no time for work. He was becoming obsessed by his thoughts about women, and their immense, unfathomable, baneful significance. There was some enigma in these smooth, white, weak creatures who unleashed earthquakes with a sidelong glance or a wave of the wrist. A man's supreme goal and *raison d'être* was to serve women. Poetry was secondary. Genius was secondary.

To young Paul Vyazemsky, Pushkin spoke strange words. The boy wrote: "Pushkin worked on my mind systematically, trying to turn my attention to the fair sex and to convince me how important it was for a man to be able to win the favors of women. He taught me that the great problem of life was this: Everything that is done on earth is done in order to win the attention of women. . . . He was constantly giving me advice about how one should behave toward them, supplementing his lessons with cynical quotations from the works of Chamfort."

D'Anthès needed no advice: He had outstripped Pushkin. He was greater than Pushkin, because he had captured Natalya's heart. One day, Count A—— said, to him: "D'Anthès, I hear you are a Don Juan."

"Get married, Count," he answered, "and I shall prove it to you."

The more the poet thought about the situation, the more he thought it would be unwise to forbid Natalya to associate with the horse guardsman, for there is magic in forbidden love. Natalya must tire of D'Anthès and send him away of her own accord. Besides, she would never actually be unfaithful, Pushkin knew that. Therefore, he could simply compose himself to wait for the end of this absurd flirtation. Alexandra was there to console him.

But the days went by, and Natalya showed no signs of tiring of her rendezvous and little secrets. She was constantly receiving books and notes from D'Anthès, and answering them. Liza, her servant, was the messenger.

What was the exact nature of the feeling between Natalya and D'Anthès? Were they, as most of their contemporaries thought, simply indulging in a superficial flirtation, or was it something deeper? Initially, it would seem that it was only the titillations of coquetry that incited Natalya to respond to his advances, while he undoubtedly had no ambition beyond obtaining the favors of an elegant woman whose attention flattered him. But in the end, by meeting so often at balls and theaters and in the park, by seeing themselves continually reflected in each other's eyes, by feigning love, they were finally caught in their own snare. What began as an exercise in gallantry grew into a mutual passion, violent and desperate. After the beginning of 1836, Natalya was no longer merely enjoying the company of D'Anthès: She was suffering, probably for the first time in her life. Pushkin had married a bland, silly, affectionless child; D'Anthès conquered a woman. His entrance into her life matured her, as he himself intimates in a letter quoted in full further on: "This woman, who is generally supposed to have little intelligence—I don't know if love can give it, but it would be impossible to show more tact, grace and intelligence in a conversation than she did with me." With the aid of this new experience, Natalya was growing up; and D'Anthès, instead of shrewdly observing the progress of his spell, threw himself body and soul into her anguish. She was married. She wanted to be faithful. But she did not love Pushkin, she loved him and him alone. What to do? In his dilemma, D'Anthès looked for advice and assistance, and found no one to give it. His protector, Baron Heckeren, had left St. Petersburg a short time before and was traveling in France. Several times, D'Anthès resisted the temptation to confide the secrets of his troubled heart to the post. He feared a lecture from the cautious ambassador, who would certainly disapprove of such an irrational liaison. At last, at his wit's end, the horse guardsman wrote a letter to Heckeren, confessing his woeful predicament.

This highly significant document, whose existence was long unknown, is published here for the first time.

"Petersburg, January 20, 1836.

"My dear friend,

"I am very guilty for not answering immediately the two good and amusing letters you have written to me, but what with spending all night dancing, all morning at the riding school, and all afternoon asleep—that has been my life the past two weeks, and I can look forward to at least as much more of the same, and the worst of it all is that I am hopelessly in love! Yes, hopeless, for I don't know where to turn, I won't tell you her name because a letter can go astray, but remember the most exquisite creature in Petersburg and you will know who she is. And the awful part of the situation is that she loves me, too, and we cannot meet, so far it has been impossible, because the husband is disgustingly jealous: I am confiding in you as in my best friend, because I know you will share my suffering; but in God's name, not a word to anyone, or any questions to others about the women I am being seen with, you would ruin her without meaning to and I should be inconsolable. For, you see, I would do anything on earth for her, just to please her, for my life these past weeks has been pure hell. It is a terrible thing to love and not to be able to say so except between two *ritournelles* of a *contredanse*: It may be wrong of me to tell you all this, and you will say it is foolish nonsense, but my heart is so heavy and full that I must pour out a little of it. I am sure you will forgive me this folly, I don't deny it is folly, but I cannot talk myself out of it even though I badly need to, for this love is poisoning my whole existence: But do not worry, I am being careful and have been so careful that until now, the secret has been known only to the two of us (her name is the same as that of the lady who wrote to you about how she was desperate on my account and how the plague and the famine had destroyed her villages); now you must understand how it is possible to lose one's mind over such a creature—especially when she loves me too! I repeat again, not a word to Broge [or Brage?], because he is in correspondence with Petersburg and one word from him to his wife would ruin us both! God alone knows what might happen; so, my very dear friend, the four months you are still to be away will seem like centuries to me, for in my situation one absolutely needs someone one loves to confide in and turn to for strength. That is why I am not looking well these days, for otherwise I have never felt better, physically, in my life, but my head is in such a whirl that I cannot find an instant's repose day or night, that is what is making me look ill and sad, not my health. . . . Farewell, dear friend, be indulgent toward my new passion, for I love you too with all my heart."[17]

The letter is obviously sincere, and sheds considerable light upon the relationship between D'Anthès and Natalya, to the credit of both. In the past, historians have always condemned the young woman for being insensitive to her husband's torments and incapable of forgoing the trivial pleasures of flattery; and the young man as well, for callously provoking a domestic drama in order to add one more name to his list of conquests. Passion, however, in some degree justifies those it torments, and there was passion between D'Anthès and Natalya. She could tell herself as often as she liked that it would be wiser not to continue seeing her admirer: She was physically unable to live without his stimulating presence. D'Anthès could tell himself as often as he liked that his love could lead to nothing: He clung to his folly and reveled in his misery.

Carnival came, bringing its clamor and mad whirl of parties. Natalya and D'Anthès met almost daily, at balls and theaters and receptions. The memoirs of one contemporary, N. K. Merder, inform us that Princess Butereau gave a sensational ball on Wednesday, February 5, 1836, with a row of liveried footmen lining both sides of the grand staircase, rooms cluttered with rare flowers and enormous hothouse plants and an invisible orchestra playing waltzes. "The great hall, with its gilded white marble walls, seemed like the very temple of fire. It blazed," he wrote.

Among the crowd, N. K. Merder soon identified D'Anthès, his anxious, imploring eyes scanning the faces of the dancers; after a time, he left the room, but soon reappeared with Mrs. Pushkin at his side. Merder heard him murmur to Natalya: "Leave? You cannot really think of it, Madame? I do not believe so. That is not your intention."[18]

"They are madly in love," the diarist wrote. "After staying at the ball another half-hour, we turned to go: The baron was dancing a mazurka with Mrs. Pushkin. How happy they looked at that moment!"

At one of these balls, perhaps this one, D'Anthès threw caution to the winds and asked Natalya to be his mistress. This fact is also disclosed in a hitherto unpublished letter from Georges d'Anthès to the ambassador, preserved among the papers of the Heckeren d'Anthès family:

"*Petersburg, February* 14, 1836.

"My dear friend, Carnival is over, and part of my torment with it; really, I think I am a little more at ease now that I do not see her every day; and then, everybody else cannot come and hold her hand and waist and dance and talk to her as I do, but even more freely than I because they have nothing on their consciences. It's stupid to say, but so it is—a thing I would never have believed: It was jealousy that was keeping me so on edge all the time and making me so unhappy. And then we had a talk the last time I saw her, it was terrible but it has done me good. This woman, who is generally supposed to have little intelligence—I don't know if love can give it, but it would be impossible to show more tact, grace and intelligence in a conversation than she did with me, and it was a hard thing to do because what she was saying was nothing less than that she would not sacrifice her duty for a man she loved and who adored her; she portrayed her situation with such abandon, begged me to have pity on her with such innocence, that I was truly overpowered and could find no argument to make in return. If you knew how she consoled me, for she could easily see how I was suffering and how frightful my position was, and when she said, I love you as I have never loved, but never ask me for more than my heart, for all the rest does not belong to me and I can only be happy by respecting all my obligations, pity me and love me always as you do now, my love will be your reward; do you know, I think I would have fallen at her feet and kissed them if we had been alone, and I assure you that since that day my love for her has increased, but now it is not the same thing: I venerate her, I respect her, as one venerates and respects someone to whom your whole being is bound. But forgive me, my very dear friend, I begin my letter to you by talking about her: But she and I are one, for in speaking of her I speak of myself, and in your letters you say I do not tell you enough about myself. As I said before, I am better, much better, and I am beginning to breathe again, thank God, for my torment was unbearable before: To be cheerful and jolly in public, with people who were seeing me every day, while there was death in my heart, is a horrible position which I would not wish upon my cruelest enemy. . . ."

Thus, although Natalya was in love with D'Anthès, she would not be his mistress. What were her reasons? In the first place, she was five months pregnant at the time. It would be repugnant to her to yield to the young man when she was carrying that beginning of a new life inside her, and she was embarrassed and conscience-stricken by this mark her husband had left upon her body. She was afraid of disappointing D'Anthès, too. Did she tell him this, during their conversation? One sentence in the letter might imply that she did: "She portrayed her situation with such abandon . . ." But Natalya also told him, with a nobility that should at least partly redeem her in the eyes of her detractors; "I love you as I have never loved, but never ask me for more than my heart, for all the rest does not belong to me and I can only be happy by respecting all my obligations."

This fine declaration stirs an old memory. In the last chapter of *Eugene Onegin*, when Onegin, finding Tatyana married to an old general, implores her to be his, she says:

> Well: I know how you worship
> Pride and honor.
> I love you (why deny it?),
> But I am the wife of another man,
> And shall belong to no one but him.

Everyone Natalya knew admired this poem, among all of Pushkin's work, and spoke of Tatyana as the ideal Russian woman. She must have been affected to some extent by this fictional character. Placed by circumstance in Tatyana's position, she consciously decided to imitate her, or was unconsciously influenced by the moral of Pushkin's poem. In any case, Natalya's attitude was unexceptionable, and D'Anthès, who was not insensitive to grandeur, loved and esteemed her the more for it. Instead of chafing against her edict, he was actually relieved. But did it last?

The letter is dated February 14, 1836. What happened in the ensuing weeks? It might be argued, of course, that a woman's objections are never final and that Georges d'Anthès, desperately in love as he was, could not have failed to try again and obtain on the morrow what was refused the night before. This argument is weakened by one fact, however: As we have seen, Natalya was pregnant in February 1836, and it is unlikely that after resisting his pleas when her figure was still presentable, she would change her mind a few weeks later when, with her swelling belly, she might well disappoint a new lover. The child was born on May 23, 1836; according to the medical practice of the day, women remained in bed for twenty-one to twenty-five days after their delivery, and did not resume a normal life until three or four weeks after that. This means that Natalya would not have begun going out again until July.

When, at last, she did, she continued to see her horse guardsman, and to love and be loved by him, but her respect for her duty kept her on the near side of sin. Burning with useless desire, intoxicated with secret despair, the couple danced together, pressed together, sighed and suffered in vain. Natalya did not have the strength to break off; and D'Anthès may have thought he would eventually overcome her regrettable scruples.

For him, Pushkin was just another jealous husband; that this particular husband was a poet and a national glory, he neither knew nor cared. How could he? D'Anthès did not know Russian and was not interested in literature. In the circles he frequented, Pushkin was despised as a liberal and a nuisance. For him, nothing could outweigh the rare quality of his feeling for Natalya Pushkin. Nevertheless, he continued to obey her constant injunctions to be careful and discreet—but in vain, for however he might try to conceal his passion, it illuminated his countenance. Nasty rumors were already beginning to circulate in the drawing rooms on the subject of this enduring and brilliant liaison. Pushkin was already receiving anonymous letters of salacious purport, written in an elaborate script. One such missive was handed to him during a dinner at the Grech home, and he opened and read it immediately.

"That must be a fascinating letter," said the lady of the house, "to make Mr. Pushkin so forget his manners."

Pushkin paled, got up from the table and left the house without a word.

Other letters awaited him, under his napkin in the restaurant, inside his coat at the theater. Pushkin's friends tried to reason with Natalya:

"I love you like my own daughter," Princess Vyazemsky told her one day. "But think for one minute: How is this going to end?"

"I like to be with him," Natalya retorted. "I simply like him, that is all. Nothing more will happen between us than has happened these last two years."

What else could she say to Princess Vyazemsky? Could she confess that she was mad about D'Anthès? At all costs, the world must be made to believe that she was engaging in a frivolous flirtation and nothing more.

"If Natalya had not been so impenetrably stupid, if D'Anthès had not been so spoiled by his popularity, the whole business would have trailed away to nothing," Trubetskoy wrote. "At that time there was nothing between them except a few squeezes of the hand, caresses and kisses. Nothing more. In our day, that was perfectly normal."

This was not "perfectly normal." Natalya saw her husband's agony but did not know how to relieve it. The Pushkin household did not consist of a great genius consumed by jealousy on one side and a flighty little female indulging in criminal caprices on the other. The drama was double. Pushkin was suffering because he was unloved, Natalya because she could not openly love the man she wanted. It was not easy for her to resist temptation. To be worthy of the Tatyana of *Eugene Onegin* was no small order when the seducer was as young, handsome and headstrong as D'Anthès and the husband as querulous and ill-tempered as the poet. However, if contemporaries' statements are to be believed, Natalya did remain true to Pushkin—in body alone; but could she do more?

Pushkin was losing weight, his skin had taken on a yellowish tinge, he was becoming unbearably nervous. He could not keep up a conversation for any length of time. He could not stay seated at his desk. He jumped every time the bell rang. He opened his letters apprehensively. His children's wails sent him into tantrums. Sadly, he wrote: "Youth has no need to feel 'at home.' Maturity is terrified by solitude. Happy he who has found a true companion. Then, he must barricade himself inside *his house*. Ah, shall I soon be able to plant my flag in the country again? Fields, garden, peasants, books, poetry, family, love, etc. . . . religion and death."

Instead of his domestic seclusion, rural tranquillity, poetry and religion, however, Pushkin continued, perforce, to live in a dress shop and frequent glittering drawing rooms in which everyone hated the sight of him. His loathing for D'Anthès increased daily.

Writing to her brother Andrey about a party given on her birthday, September 17, 1836, Sofya Karamzin said: ". . . The ball was perfect in every way and very gay, judging from all the faces I saw, except that of Alexander Pushkin, forever mournful, preoccupied and anxious. His gloom quite put me out of sorts. His wandering, wild-animal, distracted eyes only came to rest—and then with frightening intensity—upon his wife and D'Anthès—who is carrying on as before, glued to the side of Katerina Goncharov and leering at Natalya from afar; he finally danced the mazurka with her, and it was pitiful to see Pushkin's face framed in the doorway across from them, silent, white, threatening. Lord, it's so stupid! When Countess Stroganov arrived I asked Alexander Pushkin to talk to her; he was just about to do so, all red in the face (you know how he loathes any form of servility), when I saw him stop short and turn angrily away. 'Well?' 'No, I won't go; there is that count already, sitting over there!' 'What count?' 'D'Anthès, Heckeren, I don't know.' "[19]

Out walking one day on the Nevsky Prospect, Paul Vyazemsky met the inevitable trio: Natalya, her sister Katerina and D'Anthès.

"Just then," Vyazemsky wrote, "Pushkin flashed past in front of us without turning, and vanished immediately into the crowd. The expression on his face was terrible. I saw it as a forewarning of the tragedy."

One evening at Prince Vyazemsky's home, Pushkin and D'Anthès exchanged some bitter remarks. Afterward, at the door, the footman called out: "Pushkin's carriage!"

"Which Pushkin?" another flunky called back.

"The man of letters!"

Pushkin felt all the contempt implied in that empty title. He was nothing but a little man of letters, lost in the great world. He was tolerated in society for the sake of his wife, not his talent.

"That ravishing creature," Korf wrote, "was interested in her husband's fame only to the extent that it made possible her social successes; she preferred the glitter of the ballroom to all the poetry in the world. But by a strange inconsistency, all the time she was reaping the benefits of Pushkin's literary fame, she was secretly ashamed that someone like herself, the very quintessence of a socialite, should be attached to a 'man of letters.' "

In the drawing rooms, they said Natalya had a "soul made of lace."

Pushkin forgave her everything, and laid all the blame on D'Anthès and Baron Heckeren—for Baron Heckeren had now returned, and was taking an active part in his adopted son's intrigues. From a distance, he had urged caution. At closer range, he took a more lenient view. Had the husband been anyone other than Pushkin and the wife anyone other than Natalya, the ambassador would assuredly have counseled D'Anthès to hold back. But Pushkin was the sworn enemy of the Nesselrodes and thereby of Heckeren himself, who was a close friend of the Foreign Minister's. By dishonoring Pushkin, D'Anthès would only be obliging the mandarins. He would earn the respect of all the people in power. He would move a step up the ladder. It was a question of his career. In mid-October, D'Anthès fell ill and was confined to his room, and Pushkin thought he could breathe easier; but in his absence, D'Anthès was replaced by Heckeren himself. He followed Natalya around, discoursing upon the insane passion she had inspired in his adopted son's breast, and insisting that Georges was capable of killing himself if she persisted in refusing him. At a ball given by the assembly of the nobility, he is even alleged to have suggested that she leave Pushkin and run away to live with D'Anthès abroad—a proposition which Natalya indignantly rejected.[20]

For the first time, she began to be frightened. She saw how far she had gone. She wanted to back out. But when D'Anthès reappeared, she did not have the strength to send him away.

Soon afterward, Count Adlerberg advised Grand Duke Michael, commander in chief of the horse guards, to send D'Anthès to the Caucasus in order to separate him from Natalya. But Grand Duke Michael was certainly not going to deprive the ladies of such a fine dancing partner: Life-of-the-party D'Anthès was far more essential to the court of Russia than Poet Pushkin.

Then, the Vyazemskys asked D'Anthès not to pay his addresses to Natalya in their house. He laughed and came back a few days later, at which Natalya seemed both terrified and delighted, but Princess Vyazemsky rebuked him sharply and forbade him the door.

Hearing of this latest impertinence, Pushkin began to think seriously of challenging him to a duel. He could see no other way out of this degrading situation. He was losing his footing in a swamp of calumny. *The Contemporary* was not selling. His debts were mounting steadily: 120,000 rubles already, in bills of exchange; and masses of *bibelots*, shawls—even the silver of his sister-in-law Alexandra and his friend Sobolevsky—had gone to the moneylender. And his father, and his sister Olga, and his brother Leo were all crying for money. He wrote to Yakovlev: "I am so guilty toward you that I will not even try to justify myself. The money came in and ran through my fingers; I paid other people's debts, redeemed other people's property and my own debts are still on my hands. The confusion in my affairs has rendered me temporarily insolvent, and I must ask you for another extension, until this autumn. . . ."[21]

To Pavlishchev: "My head is whirling!"[22]

About Leo: "I really cannot support the whole world."

To his father, on October 20, 1836: "I was hoping to go to Mikhailovskoye and could not. That has upset my plans for at least another year. In the country I would have worked, whereas here I do nothing but worry myself sick."[23]

Meanwhile, he rented an apartment on Admiral Street costing 4300 rubles a year. Brüllow, the painter, called on him in his new residence.

"His children were asleep," Brüllow said. "He woke them and presented them to me, one after the other, in his arms. It did not suit him somehow, it was like a travesty of domestic contentment. I could not refrain from asking, 'What devil ever drove you to get married?' He answered, 'I wanted to go abroad, but they wouldn't let me; I was in such a state that I did not know what to do, so I got married.' "

2. *The Anonymous Letters*

On November 4, 1836, Pushkin received several copies of an anonymous letter through the newly inaugurated St. Petersburg postal service:

"The Grand Crosses, Commanders and Chevaliers of the Most Serene Order of Cuckolds, meeting in plenary session under the presidency of H. E. D. L. Naryshkin, Venerable Grand Master of the Order, have unanimously elected Mr. Alexander Pushkin Coadjutant to the Grand Master of the Order of Cuckolds and historiographer of the Order.

"The Perpetual Secretary:

"Count J. Borch."[1]

The same day, Mrs. Khitrovo forwarded to the poet an envelope she had received in the mail, addressed to "Mr. Pushkin" and containing the same "diploma," written in the same hand. Lastly, Count Sollogub called at Pushkin's home and deposited on the poet's desk an envelope containing a text identical in every respect to the others.

"Pushkin was sitting in his study," Sollogub wrote. "He opened the letter and immediately said:

"'I know what it is. . . . It is an insult to my wife. Besides, you know I cannot be offended by an anonymous letter. If someone spits on my suit it is my valet's job, not mine, to wipe it off. My wife is an angel, no suspicion can touch her.'"

Although he greeted this nugget of filth with an affectation of serene contempt, Pushkin was in reality no longer able to control himself. He was shaking with impotent fury, reeling and shuddering as though he had been publicly whipped. Half the town had received copies of the "diploma." His wife was flouted, his name dragged through the mud. What face could he wear in public? How could he ever dare to write another poem? He wanted to smite the slanderer, denounce him, brand him, kill him.

But who was he?

After Sollogub left, Pushkin spread the anonymous letters in front of him and studied them carefully: luxurious paper, a disguised hand, a high-class, diplomatic style. He called his wife. He showed her the letters. Pale and stammering, Natalya, not daring to confess her love for D'Anthès, admitted only to inconsequential trifling and tried to throw the blame onto Heckeren, accusing him of upsetting and importuning her with his evil propositions. She was drenched in tears. She begged his forgiveness. Her only fault was her extreme thoughtlessness. Mollified, Pushkin sent her away. He was sure of her. But until he had utterly crushed *the other*, there could be no peace in his marriage. That same evening, he went to see Yakovlev, who was celebrating a birthday with some friends. When the dinner was over and the champagne was being poured, Pushkin pulled the "diploma" out of his pocket and said: "Look at this filth I have just received!"

Yakovlev, who was director of the imperial press in the second section, studied the letters and agreed that the paper was of foreign origin and could only have come from embassy stock, the import duty on such articles being prohibitively high. That was all Pushkin wanted to know. His suspicions were confirmed. For him, Heckeren was the author of the anonymous letter.

This hasty judgment now deserves amendment. Pushkin had rightly guessed the direction of the shot, but mistaken the identity of the man holding the gun. Such stationery could, in fact, be procured elsewhere than in an embassy. And Heckeren would not have risked writing the message himself. But the idea did come from the Nesselrode coterie of which Heckeren was a member, and which was violently hostile to the poet. The diplomas had been sent out as a favor to Heckeren and D'Anthès, and it was they alone who were supposed to benefit from them. What could have been the object of Heckeren's friends? By attacking Pushkin, they were inciting him to challenge D'Anthès to a duel—but D'Anthès was their pet, their protégé, their star, and they would not have wanted a hair of his head to be harmed. Some Pushkin experts maintain that it was Heckeren himself who wrote the letters, acting out of pure jealousy in the hope of compromising any future relationship between Natalya and his adopted son; but a second look at the diploma is enough to disprove this theory. In the text, Pushkin is elected "Coadjutant to the Grand Master of the Order of Cuckolds," the Venerable Grand Master being D. L. Naryshkin. Now, his name was not chosen by chance. Naryshkin was the husband of the beautiful Marya Antonovna, official mistress of Alexander I for fourteen years. Mrs. Naryshkin was held to be "a supernatural, unimaginable beauty"—like Natalya; and Mr. Naryshkin had been awarded compensation in the form of an annual salary of forty thousand assignation rubles from the emperor—like Pushkin; although the latter drew a paltry five thousand. By naming Pushkin coadjutant to Naryshkin, the author of the anonymous letter was insinuating that his wife occupied the same position in relation to Nicholas I as did Naryshkin's wife in relation to his predecessor, and that Pushkin, like Naryshkin, was receiving state money in payment for his (indirect) services.*

Thus, the letter was designed to direct Pushkin's suspicions to the emperor, who was openly and insistently flirting with Natalya. Fearing that D'Anthès had gone too far and was risking a scandal, the Nesselrode-Heckeren clique thought it would be a clever idea to shield the young man behind the unassailable figure of the monarch. In all likelihood, Heckeren and his cronies had not even told D'Anthès the details of the scheme. With his headstrong nature, he would never consent to be a party to such fiddling: They must save him in spite of himself. Anything would do, to transfer Pushkin's jealousy to some other object.

But whose hand had actually formed the disguised characters of the diploma? Pushkin's enemies were legion. Countess Nesselrode, Count Uvarov, Princess Byeloselskaya, Idalya Poletika, Prince Gagarin, Prince Dolgorukov, Prince Urusov. One can imagine the idea taking form in the Nesselrode drawing room, growing out of some remark made by Nesselrode himself, or Heckeren, or some other intimate of the group, such as, "It is very wrong of Pushkin to look such daggers at D'Anthès, when Nicholas I is after her just as much as he." Caught on the wing by some drawing-room habitué eager to curry favor with his hosts, the remark was instantly turned to account in the writing of the anonymous letter. There were so many depraved young wastrels hanging about the embassy and ministry salons! In all likelihood, it was one of them who, following explicit instructions or his own imagination, penned and dispatched the diplomas. In doing so, he knew he would be approved and shielded by powerful protectors; he would be doing a favor to Heckeren, and indirectly to Nesselrode. It would be remembered.†

* As for Count Borch, whose name appears at the bottom of the diploma: He was notorious for his marital irregularities. "His wife sleeps with the coachman and he with the whipper-in," Pushkin said. Lastly, the election of Pushkin as historiographer of the Order was an allusion to his work in the Archives.

† Recent graphological analyses have pointed to Prince Dolgorukov as the probable author of the diplomas. At that time he was twenty years old, and a member of the Nesselrode and Heckeren circle. He was undersized, his features were deformed, one of his legs was shorter than the other; and his ugliness, of which he was very conscious, had made him extremely spiteful. He was a notorious homosexual and had a morbid fondness for defamation. In 1843, using a pseudonym, he published a book in Paris in which he heaped abuse on his country's most ancient and noble families. In 1856 he sent a letter to M. C. Vorontsov, asking him for documents relating to the Vorontsov family tree; an unsigned note accompanied the letter, informing the prince that upon payment of fifty thousand silver rubles to Dolgorukov, his genealogy would be published exactly as he desired. Prince Vorontsov's son sued Dolgorukov in the French courts, which concluded, after analysis, that Dolgorukov had written the letter, and convicted him of attempted blackmail. In 1927, Shchegolov, a Russian Pushkin scholar, submitted the first anonymous letters for analysis and the ex-

Hence, although Baron Heckeren had not physically manufactured the letters, he was indirectly responsible for them, by virtue of having suggested or condoned the scheme. Pushkin would not be misled, however. He knew Natalya flirted with the emperor, but without exceeding the bounds of propriety. He saw more plainly than his first biographers that Heckeren alone had reason to point to Nicholas I as his wife's official lover.

"I made certain the anonymous letter was written by Mr. Heckeren," Pushkin later wrote to Benkendorf.

Prince Vyazemsky said: "From the instant he first received the anonymous letters, Pushkin suspected Heckeren senior of having written them, and he died with that idea. We were never able to ascertain the basis for his supposition and regarded it as unacceptable until after Pushkin's death, when a fortuitous discovery gave it a degree of probability."‡

In his memoirs, N. M. Smirnov wrote: "The one sure thing is that Heckeren was the author of the anonymous letters."

Nicholas himself was later to say to Grand Duke Michael Pavlovich: "This incident has caused a great deal of talk, in which the condemnation of Heckeren is the only correct and justified item."

Pushkin, convinced that he knew his man, determined to act quickly: parry to the right, parry to the left—first of all, break with the court, since it was his preposterous title as gentleman of the chamber and the salary he received from the emperor, coupled with Natalya's constant presence at palace balls, that had provided the pretext for the calumny. Next, strike Heckeren, in the person of his adopted son, since it was the two of them who were responsible for his humiliation.

On November 6, two days after receiving the anonymous letters, Pushkin wrote to Count Kankrin, the Minister of Finance:

"As a result of a ministerial arrangement with which Your Excellency is familiar, I am in receipt of (unsecured) loans from the ministry totaling 45,000 rubles, 25,000 of which I am to repay during the next five years.

"Wishing to clear this debt entirely and without delay, I see only one obstacle to my doing so, and that can easily be overcome, but only by you.

"I own 220 souls in the government of Nizhny Novgorod, 200 of which have been mortgaged for 40,000 rubles. According to the dispositions of my father, who gave me the property, I may not sell it during his lifetime, but I can mortgage it to the state or any individual.

---

pert's conclusions were categorical: Dolgorukov had written them. An expert may make a mistake, of course, but all that is known of Dolgorukov's life and personality adds credence to the accusation.

‡ It is not known to what this refers.

"Now, the state can call in debts outstanding without regard for private arrangements unless they have been endorsed by the sovereign.

"I would like to offer this property in payment of the 45,000 rubles mentioned above; it is certainly worth that amount, and probably more.

"I take the liberty of making one further request of Your Excellency, to which I attach great importance: In view of the fact that this matter is of no consequence and can be treated as a perfectly ordinary transaction, I would appeal to you not to bring it to the attention of His Majesty the emperor, who, in his generosity, will probably not wish to accept repayment (although, in itself, it is no burden to me), and may order the cancellation of the debt, which would put me in a most delicate and distressing position: In such a case I should be compelled to refuse the imperial favor, which might conceivably be construed as an act of insolence or vainglory or even ingratitude."

This totally unrealistic letter shows what a state the poet was in: In the first place, Pushkin could not dispose of Boldino, for his father had only given him a procuration. In the second, the state did not have the right, on its own initiative, to call in a loan granted by the emperor, which was to be reimbursed by annual deductions from the poet's salary. But Pushkin was making a last-ditch attempt to escape from St. Petersburg and the court and the drawing-room flirtations and the anonymous letters, all at once.

On the day before he sent this letter,* Pushkin challenged D'Anthès to a duel. D'Anthès was on duty with his regiment, so it was Heckeren who accepted the letter for him and realized to his dismay that instead of turning Pushkin against the emperor, their device had boomeranged into the laps of the real culprits. He had been trying to save his son, and here he had lost him for good. What to do now?

Later that day, the ambassador called on Pushkin and announced, in broken tones, that he accepted the challenge in Georges's name, but requested a delay of twenty-four hours to give Pushkin time to reflect. Pushkin consented. He felt vastly relieved, now that he had taken the fatal step. He joked easily with his wife, who knew nothing of his plan. If he survived, his honor would be avenged forever. If he were killed, his worries and shame and weariness would die with him. What more ideal solution could he hope for?

On November 6, when the twenty-four hours were up, Heckeren returned to find the poet obdurate.

At that, the baron lost his composure and began to weep; the thought that his son might be slain in a duel quite unmanned him. Pushkin was no mean adversary, and D'Anthès was so young. . . . To soften the poet's hard heart, Heckeren spoke of his old age, his fatherly affection,

* Upon which no action was taken.

the disastrous effects a duel would have upon his diplomatic career. He said D'Anthès had not been told of the challenge. He moaned: "I see the whole edifice of my hopes collapsing in the very instant of their fulfillment."

In the end, he begged for another extension—a week, this time.

Pushkin was touched by the man's desperation, his working features, his eyes bloodshot with sleeplessness.

"In these circumstances," he said, "it is not one week but two that I will give you, as well as my word to take no further action in the matter until the date of the duel has been set."

Zhukovsky, whom Heckeren had asked to witness the interview, was moved to tears.† Heckeren himself had hardly expected such magnanimity. What an innocent he was, this poet; now, there was still a chance to hush up the scandal.

After thanking Pushkin, the baron went to war. He expended a truly prodigious quantity of energy. The two "neutral powers" on whom he could rely were Aunt Zagryazhskaya and Zhukovsky. The following day, November 7, the latter called upon the former for a final consultation, then proceeded to Heckeren's home. The hapless Zhukovsky—innocent, loyal, bustling and muddled—talked himself hoarse in his efforts to defend contradictory causes. He desperately wanted to prevent a meeting between Pushkin and D'Anthès; and that day, Heckeren showed him the way out. In his notes, Zhukovsky wrote: "November 7. Heckeren's revelations. His son's love for Katerina (my mistake about the name). Prospect of kinship. Possible marriage. Gave my word. Thought to stop everything."

Heckeren had hit upon the most honorable solution possible. He swore to the tenderhearted Zhukovsky that D'Anthès was not in the least in love with Natalya, but with her older sister Katerina. The poet had been blinded by jealousy. He was going to fight a duel with his potential brother-in-law. He was going to destroy a long-premeditated alliance that had been progressing beautifully. Zhukovsky was aghast. Beaming and full of joy, he ran to tell Pushkin the glad tidings. Pushkin was less credulous. The poets' conversation was stormy. After a masterful exchange of insults, Zhukovsky noted: "The revelations. His fury."

To Pushkin, Heckeren's revelations were just a vile contrivance designed to wriggle out of the fight. He had no faith in any plans for marriage. He was sorry he had given the ambassador two weeks to maneuver in.

The next day, Heckeren went to moan to Aunt Zagryazhskaya while

† Earlier that day, Aunt Zagryazhskaya had sent her nephew to Tsarskoye Selo to fetch the poet, in the hope that he might be able to reconcile the parties.

Zhukovsky returned to Pushkin. "His tears," wrote Zhukovsky. Pushkin wept, all right, but he was still unconvinced.

At last, on November 9, D'Anthès returned from his regiment and learned the whole story. Pushkin had challenged him to a duel, and to avoid the duel he was going to have to marry this Katerina for whom he felt absolutely nothing. The officer's first reaction, no doubt, was indignation at Heckeren's cowardly manipulations. D'Anthès was courageous, he desired Natalya fiercely and he was not afraid to fight a duel with Pushkin; he also knew that if he refused and proposed to Katerina instead, he would be called a coward. But Heckeren did not look at it that way. A duel between Pushkin and D'Anthès meant the end of his diplomatic career. After all he had done for D'Anthès, he was entitled to ask this one small sacrifice in return. "He [D'Anthès], too, was probably entangled in his father's diabolical machinations; it was a sacrifice he was required to make," Vyazemsky wrote afterward to Grand Duke Michael.

But marrying Katerina would also bring him closer to Natalya. He would become her brother-in-law, he could meet her as often as he pleased and Pushkin would have nothing to say. And, after all, Katerina was not so bad as all that. Less pretty than her sister, but very tall and slender, with a fine pair of shoulders and dreamy dark eyes. She had charm. And a heart of gold. She would make an excellent housewife, an attentive companion, a good mother.

Heckeren's arguments, threats and pleas must have been convincing, for the uncertain and unhappy D'Anthès finally agreed to pretend to be in love with Katerina Goncharov.

Heckeren hastened to spread the news of this spontaneous passion all over town. According to the official version, D'Anthès had loved Katerina all along and had been wanting to marry her for ages, but his adoptive father had opposed the match on the grounds that it was not sufficiently advantageous to the brilliant young officer. Now that his son was accused of compromising a married woman, however, Heckeren would give his consent to the betrothal which the young couple had so devoutly desired from the beginning.

While he was orchestrating this impromptu wedding march, the Netherlands ambassador also advised Natalya to write a letter begging D'Anthès to refuse the duel. Having finally learned what was happening, Natalya would have no part of such a low trick. She watched in dumb amazement as the fruits of her fatal frivolity began to ripen. She saw her husband's honor and very life endangered by her fault. She imagined the worst, yet she still could not understand how the exchange of a few love notes and hasty kisses could stir up such a fuss. It was probably then, hoping to forestall suspicion in the future, that Natalya insisted upon being given written confirmation of her fidelity to Pushkin, signed by Georges d'Anthès himself. The ambassador made no difficulty about producing such a document, which would serve his son's interests and his own as well as those of Natalya. Thus, when he was subsequently accused of acting as pander and go-between to the young people, he was able to write to Nesselrode, without fear of contradiction: "Will it also be said that I ought to have used my authority over my son? Mrs. Pushkin might give a conclusive reply to this question as well, by producing a letter I required my son to write, addressed to her, in which he stated his determination to cease all pursuit of her. The bearer of this letter was myself, and I placed it in her hands. Mrs. Pushkin showed it to her husband and family as proof that she had never actually failed in her duty."[2]

In reality, Heckeren's attitude toward the frustrated romance of D'Anthès and Natalya was always dictated by circumstance. When he was far from St. Petersburg, he had urged the young man to exercise restraint. When he returned and saw how the Nesselrode clan were encouraging D'Anthès, he added his voice to the chorus of Pushkin's enemies. When he saw his adopted son languishing in the throes of his passion, he implored Natalya to yield to him. But Natalya had been difficult. To ease her conscience, she had confessed to Pushkin and aroused his jealousy; and Pushkin's fits of temper were reputed to be hair-raising. Whereupon, hearing the first note of warning, Heckeren had suggested or endorsed the idea of the anonymous letters. Alas, this latest stratagem had totally misfired. There was only one chance left: to allay Pushkin's suspicions, bring D'Anthès to reason, calm Natalya, smother their obsession under the weight of words. And in any case, his dissuasive efforts would be counted in his favor in the event of a catastrophe. This move did serve its purpose, moreover, by giving Heckeren another argument to use in his letter to Nesselrode: "She [Natalya] can confirm all that I repeated to her so many times in an attempt to make her realize the dangers of this liaison, to see the abyss yawning beneath her feet. If concern for her self-respect does not inhibit her, she will also say that in my conversation I carried frankness to the point of using terms which must have been wounding to her, but must also have opened her eyes; or such, at least, was my intention."[3]

This was all true. Heckeren did indeed explain to Natalya all the risks she was running by continuing to associate with D'Anthès. What he failed to say was that this became his policy only in the eleventh hour, and that in the days before the threat of open scandal he had sung a very different tune. Natalya, moreover, was so confused by these interminable and contradictory sermons in which her peace of mind was the pawn that she did not want to listen to anybody ever again, and Heckeren in particular disgusted and frightened her.

Not finding in Natalya the strong ally he had hoped for, Heckeren fell back on Aunt Zagryazhskaya and Zhukovsky, and Zhukovsky set out again to explain to Pushkin how D'Anthès was really and truly in love with Katerina and really and truly intended to marry her. But Pushkin, who knew the truth about D'Anthès' feeling for Natalya, found the joke none too funny, and maintained that after the duel was called off, D'Anthès would somehow manage to forget his promise of marriage. Zhukovsky implored Pushkin to meet D'Anthès. Pushkin adamantly refused.

"I cannot resign myself to regard the matter as closed," Zhukovsky wrote to Pushkin on November 9. "I have still given no answer to Heckeren senior; in my note I told him you were out when I came and that as I had not seen you I had nothing to tell him. So it is still possible to turn back. Your reply will finish everything, irrevocably. But in the name of God, change your mind. Make me happy by not committing this senseless crime and exposing your wife to public humiliation. . . ."

The next morning brought another letter from Zhukovsky:

"This morning I am going to tell Heckeren that I will not act as arbiter, because my conversation with you yesterday convinced me that arbitration is useless. . . . I consider it my sacred duty to attest that young Heckeren [D'Anthès] is just as eager to fight with you as you with him, and just as apprehensive as you lest the secret become known. You must do justice to the father too. He is desperate, but this is what he said to me: 'I am condemned to the guillotine; I appeal for grace; if I am refused, I shall have to mount the steps, and I shall mount, for I love my son's honor as much as his life.'[4]

"With this declaration ends the role I have so pitifully and uselessly played."

Zhukovsky having abandoned the field, Heckeren turned to Aunt Zagryazhskaya, and Aunt Zagryazhskaya reopened negotiations. The object, in short, was to obtain an official proposal of marriage from D'Anthès and an official retraction of the challenge to his future brother-in-law from Pushkin. Good; but the two sides could not agree upon the order of events. Heckeren, wishing to protect his son's self-esteem, demanded that Pushkin abandon the duel first, in a letter that made no mention of a marriage; D'Anthès would announce his intention to marry Katerina afterward. Pushkin, on the other hand, was willing to write a letter calling off the duel, but only as a consequence of an announcement of the impending marriage of D'Anthès and Katerina. In the end, they reached a compromise: Pushkin met Heckeren at the home of Aunt Zagryazhskaya. Aunt Zagryazhskaya swore by all that was holy that she was the sole instigator of the match between D'Anthès and Katerina. Pushkin heard her out with a sardonic smile. He was not deceived. But he was thinking with relish how ridiculous D'Anthès was going to appear, marrying Katerina to avoid a duel with a "man of letters." He was also thinking of Natalya's certain contempt for an officer who was so forward in the drawing room but could not be lured onto the field of honor. "A week from now," he told Princess Vyazemsky, "you will learn of a new and unique form of revenge; it will be full, complete; it will plunge the man into the mud; Raevsky's achievements were child's play in comparison with what I am about to do."[5]

Now he could savor his sweet revenge. In the presence of Heckeren and Zagryazhskaya, Pushkin finally consented to withdraw the challenge. It was all done with words: a verbal promise of marriage, a verbal retraction of the challenge. The matter seemed to be settled to everyone's satisfaction.

But D'Anthès, after initially giving in to Heckeren, suddenly rebelled. Every day the perfect grotesqueness of his position became more obvious to him. He was willing to make some sacrifice for his adoptive father's career or Natalya's honor and peace of mind—but not to the point of playing the coward. What would his comrades in the horse guards say? What would the ladies say? Pushkin's verbal retraction was unacceptable. He had to have a signed document in which there was no mention of Katerina. A sort of apology, on the lines of, "I made a mistake when I challenged you . . . A moment of aberration . . . Let us be friends again. . . ." Only then would D'Anthès resign himself to marrying Katerina, whose chief attraction was that she was Natalya's sister. Without a word to Heckeren, D'Anthès scribbled on a scrap of paper, "Marry or fight: As my honor forbids me to accept conditions, the sentence unfortunately compels me to do the latter. I shall continue to insist that this motive of marriage must not appear in the letter, because I have always reserved my right to propose after the duel, if it turned out in my favor. It must be understood that I am not asking for Mlle. Katerina's hand in order to give satisfaction to anyone or as a concession of any sort, but because I like her, it is my wish and has been decided by my will alone."[6]

Having set his ideas in order, D'Anthès wrote to Pushkin:

"Baron Heckeren has just informed me that he has been authorized by M—— to make it known that the reasons for which you challenged me no longer exist, and that I may accordingly regard your provocation as null and void.

"When you challenged me, without telling me why, I unhesitatingly accepted, for it was my duty on my honor to do so; but now that you say you have no further reason to desire a duel, I must know, before allowing you to take back your word, what has induced you to change your mind, as I had instructed no one to give you the explanations which I was intending to furnish myself. You will be the first to agree that before withdrawing, explanations must be given on either side, for the sake of our mutual respect hereafter."[7]

This letter sent Pushkin into a towering rage. "Letter from D'Anthès to Pushkin," Zhukovsky noted. "His fury." So now D'Anthès was trying to be clever! Well, the comedy had gone on long enough. A duel. And the quicker the better. Sollogub had offered to act as Pushkin's second. He would have to arrange that. Today was November 16. That evening there was a birthday dinner at the Karamzins', Sollogub would be there. "At dinner at Karamzins'," Sollogub wrote, "I was sitting next to Pushkin. During an animated conversation about nothing in particular he suddenly leaned over to me and said rapidly, 'Go to D'Archiac [D'Anthès' second] tomorrow. Settle the details of the duel. The bloodier the better. Do not consent to any explanations.' Having said this, he went on joking and chatting as before. I was stunned, but did not dare to object. There was a determination in Pushkin's voice that allowed of no argument."

Later that evening, Sollogub went to a party at the Ficquelmonts'. Most of the ladies were in mourning for Charles X. Natalya was not there. But Katerina, in a white gown, was in seventh heaven, sitting in a corner listening to the gallantries of D'Anthès. They looked like an engaged couple. Suddenly Pushkin arrived. "He seemed very disturbed," Sollogub wrote. "He forbade Katerina Nikolayevna to talk to D'Anthès and, I subsequently learned, said a few words to D'Anthès himself that were more than rude. I exchanged a look with D'Archiac, the young and elegant secretary at the French embassy, and we parted. . . ."

Fearing a scene, Sollogub drew D'Anthès out of Pushkin's hearing and bluntly asked: "What sort of man are you?"

"What a question!" exclaimed the other. "I am a man of honor, my dear fellow, and hope to prove it soon."

He added: "I have told D'Archiac everything, and will send either him or my father to you. . . ."

As D'Anthès was preparing to leave, Pushkin caught up with him on the stairs and snarled into his face: "You French are a fine lot! You all know how to speak Latin, but when it comes to the field you want to be thirty paces away to shoot. For us Russians, the rougher the duel, the better!"

Poor Sollogub did not close his eyes that night. "I saw the part I was playing in the eyes of all Russia," he wrote. "No Russian could have raised a hand against Pushkin. But a Frenchman had no cause to spare a Russian glory."

The next day, Sollogub called on D'Anthès, who burst out: "You all refuse to understand that I am going to marry Katerina. Pushkin has withdrawn his challenge, but I do not want people to think I am getting married in order to avoid the duel. Furthermore, I do not want any women's names mixed up in this business. My father has been opposed to my marriage for a year now."

From D'Anthès, Sollogub floundered through a violent snowstorm to Pushkin's house. Pushkin was beside himself.

"D'Anthès is a scoundrel," he shouted. "I told him yesterday that I spat upon him. Now go see D'Archiac and settle the details of the duel. You are my second, so I must tell you the cause of it. People in society are saying that D'Anthès is paying too much attention to my wife. Some say she likes him, others not. That is not the point; I do not want their names linked together. After I received the anonymous letters I challenged him, Heckeren asked for a fortnight, the time is almost up. D'Archiac has been here. Go to him."

And the good Sollogub rushed to D'Archiac. D'Archiac too had not slept a wink. Although he was not Russian, he was very conscious of the place Pushkin occupied in Russian literature, and his one desire was to go through the documents relating to the duel once more, carefully, in a spirit of conciliation. The two seconds accordingly bent their heads over the file, which included a copy of the anonymous letter, Pushkin's challenge and various notes from Heckeren and the poet.

D'Anthès was not present at the interview, but D'Archiac must have known that the horse guardsman was less eager to fight than to save face. They would make one last attempt, therefore, sacrificing his interests. Perhaps Pushkin would agree to state verbally, if not in writing, that D'Anthès' matrimonial plans could not be attributed to motives unworthy of a man of honor? And perhaps, this time, D'Anthès would be content with an oral declaration? Acting on D'Archiac's advice, Sollogub accordingly sent the following note to Pushkin:

"As you desired, I have been to see Mr. D'Archiac to settle the time and place. We decided on Saturday [November 21], as I am not free on Friday, early in the morning, near Pargolova, at ten paces. Mr. D'Archiac told me confidentially that Baron Heckeren [D'Anthès] was determined to announce his marriage plans, but had postponed the announcement in order not to appear to be trying to avoid the duel; he will not, therefore, declare his intentions until everything is settled between you, and until you have orally stated to myself or to Mr. D'Archiac that his matrimonial intentions cannot be imputed to motives unworthy of a man of honor.

"Not being authorized to commit you to an action which I wholeheartedly approve, I would beg you, in the name of your family, to consent to this arrangement which will reconcile the parties. Mr. D'Archiac and I can, of course, speak for Heckeren [D'Anthès]."[8]

This Pushkin considered satisfactory, and he wrote his answer to Sollogub: "I do not hesitate to write what I can say. I challenged Mr. Georges Heckeren to a duel and he accepted, without giving any explanation. It is I who now request the seconds to regard my challenge as null and void, having learned by hearsay that Mr. Georges Heckeren has decided to announce his intention to marry Miss Goncharov after the duel. I have no reason to impute his decision to motives unworthy of a man of courage. I would ask you, Count, to make whatever use you will of this letter."[9]

The letter bore no resemblance to the text D'Anthès had originally demanded: Contrary to his wishes, it gave his "intention to marry," learned "by hearsay," as the sole motive for calling off the duel. Pushkin's only concession was the phrase about "motives unworthy of a man of courage." But small as it was, it was enough, at least for D'Archiac. "That will do," he said when Sollogub handed him Pushkin's answer. He did not want to show it to D'Anthès, however, for fear of provoking another outburst, and simply informed him that the matter had been settled and congratulated him upon his forthcoming engagement. D'Anthès turned to Sollogub: "Go to Mr. Pushkin," he said, "and thank him for agreeing to end our quarrel. I hope in future we can act as brothers to each other."

D'Archiac offered to accompany Sollogub to Pushkin's house to confirm his principal's praiseworthy intentions. Before they got there, Pushkin received a little note from D'Anthès, ceremoniously asking for Katerina's hand in marriage. Pushkin was dining. He unfolded the note, glanced at it, paled slightly and said to Katerina, with an edge of sarcasm in his voice: "I congratulate you. You are engaged. D'Anthès is asking for your hand."

Katerina, who knew that she was a pawn in the parleys, threw down her napkin and ran to her room. Natalya followed. Pushkin turned to his guest Rossetti, who was watching the scene.

"What is your opinion of the fellow?" he asked.[10]

Suddenly they heard the bell in the entrance hall. It was D'Archiac and Sollogub. Pushkin went to meet them, livid and with quivering jaw. He listened in stony silence to the formal words of thanks transmitted by D'Archiac. Trying to be helpful, Sollogub added: "I took the liberty of promising that you would treat your brother-in-law as an acquaintance."

"That was wrong of you," barked Pushkin. "That will never be. There can never be anything in common between the house of Pushkin and that of D'Anthès."

Sollogub and D'Archiac exchanged dismayed looks. The poet could hardly breathe. At last he mastered himself and said, in a lower tone: "Besides, I have admitted and am ready to admit that D'Anthès has behaved as a man of honor."

"I ask for no more," D'Archiac hastened to reply.

And left the house.

Meanwhile, behind closed doors, Katerina and Natalya were arguing themselves to exhaustion, with flying locks and tear-filled eyes. Katerina had long nursed a forlorn and secret passion for D'Anthès, but had never imagined any greater happiness than to meet him in the park or at the theater. She had never dreamed she could play any role but that of a *suivante*, a chaperon at the meetings of Natalya and the horse guardsman. She would have been content to spend her whole life thus, in the service of her beloved. And suddenly, here was her beloved asking for her hand. She had been hearing about this engagement for days, but she had not believed in it. And then, this very day, at the dinner table, Pushkin had opened a letter and said, "I congratulate you," with that nasty, stupid smile on his face. She knew full well that D'Anthès was marrying her against his will, because circumstances forced him to. But he was marrying her. She would be his wife. That was all that mattered. She thought she must be dreaming. As in a dream, she listened to Natalya, who was talking to her softly, insistently. Natalya was saying that D'Anthès did not love her, that the marriage was an odious machination, that it could only lead to a life of shame and suspicion. . . .

"My feeling for him is so strong," Katerina sighed, "that in the end I shall win his heart, and if I have that happiness to look forward to, no suffering can frighten me."

Natalya kept at her, urging her to reconsider; then suddenly Katerina screamed, like a madwoman: "The truth is you don't want to give him up to me, you're afraid to give him up to me!"[11]

In the evening of that same eventful day, the engagement was officially announced at a ball given by S. V. Saltykov. Pushkin was there, but refused to speak to D'Anthès. He still did not believe the marriage would ever take place.

"I think he has a chest complaint," he told Sollogub. "You'll see, he will have to run off abroad to some spa! Do you want to bet there will not be a wedding?"

On November 19 Heckeren and D'Anthès called on Aunt Zagryazhskaya to make a formal offer for the hand of her niece. "Thank God, it seems to be over," Zagryazhskaya wrote to Zhukovsky. "The fiancé and his honorable papa came to me with their proposal. To make everything perfect, the eldest Goncharov boy arrived fifteen minutes earlier from Moscow bringing the paternal consent. So it is over and done with.

Today the fiancé is making his official application for permission to marry, and tomorrow the fiancée's will be submitted to the empress."

In society, the announcement of this improbable match fell like a brick into a frog pond. The "D'Anthès-Katerina" affair was on everyone's lips, in drawing rooms, antechambers, theaters and palaces, in letters and private diaries. People took sides, laughed or snorted, wrung their hands. Some held that D'Anthès' marriage to Katerina showed true devotion and chivalry on his part, since it would save his lady's honor (Natalya's). Others maintained that it was the act of a buffoon to prefer this trumped-up union to a conclusive explanation on the field of honor. The empress herself, intrigued by the latest turn of events, wrote to Baroness Tiesenhausen: "I should so much like you to tell me more about this strange marriage of D'Anthès. Is it possible that the match was forced by the anonymous letters? Or is it a noble sacrifice? In my opinion, the gesture is pointless because it comes too late."

Sofya Karamzin expressed the reaction of another level of society in a letter she wrote to her brother Andrey on November 20: "Who can look at an ordinary painting after seeing the madonna of Raphael? Well, a buyer has been found for the object in question, perhaps because its price is lower. Guess: Yes, you're right; D'Anthès, the young, the handsome, the insolent D'Anthès (now rich too), is marrying Katerina Goncharov, and I declare he looks perfectly content with the idea. In fact, he is in a positive fever of madness and high spirits; we see him here in the evenings, for he can only be with his fiancée in the mornings, at the home of her Aunt Zagryazhskaya; Pushkin will not receive him, on account of being so furious ever since that letter Arkady told you about. Natalya is all on edge, very tense, her voice is ready to break every time she speaks of her sister's marriage; Katerina is walking on air and says she still cannot believe she is not dreaming. People are asking questions, but as hardly anyone has heard about the letters, they usually find a very simple explanation for the marriage. Pushkin alone, with his distraught manner, the mysterious allusions he keeps making to everyone in sight, and his way of turning his back on D'Anthès in public and trying to avoid him, will arouse suspicion and conjecture in the end. Vyazemsky says, 'He looks as though he is annoyed on his wife's account that D'Anthès has stopped paying court to her.' "[12]

Nevertheless, Pushkin had emerged victorious from the first round. He had done better than kill D'Anthès, he had made him ridiculous.

The duel had been set for November 21; that day, instead of exchanging fire with D'Anthès, Pushkin was placidly seated at his desk writing two letters, which summarized recent events and accused Heckeren of being the author of the anonymous notes. The first was to Heckeren himself, the second to Benkendorf. Pushkin absolutely had to write that first letter. He had finished with D'Anthès, "the puppet," all right; but Heckeren, the man who pulled the strings, needed separate treatment. This canceled duel and last-minute marriage must not be allowed to give people the idea that Pushkin had been mistaken when he named the Netherlands ambassador as the cause of the whole affair. Through Heckeren, Pushkin was trying to get at the Nesselrodes, Uvarovs, Gagarins and Dolgorukovs, the whole "power elite" of the capital.

His epistle to Heckeren required several drafts, of which some shapeless fragments have been found and pieced together to provide a rough idea of the original text: "On November 2," Pushkin wrote, "you heard [from] your son a piece of news. . . . He told you [that I suspected the] truth, that my wife feared [a scandal, or some violence], and that she was being driven to distraction. [You then resolved to] strike a decisive blow. . . . I received three copies of the anon[ymous] letter, of the half score that were sent out. . . . [This anonymous letter] had been prepared so carelessly [that with] one glance I was on the [au]thor's trail. . . . I was sure of my quarry, [and] had no more worries on that score. In less than three days of research, I had learned the facts. If diplomacy is the art of finding out what other people are doing and thwarting all their plans, then you will do me the justice of admitting that you have been beaten at every point. Now I come to the object of my letter. You may wish to know what has prevented me from dishonoring you in the eyes of our court and your own. I shall tell you. I am good-natured and ingenuous . . . but I have a sensitive heart. . . . A duel is not enough for me . . . no, and whatever its [outcome] [I should not feel] sufficiently avenged by the —— of your son, or by the letter I now have the honor to be wr[iting to] you [and] a copy of which I am keeping for my [priva]te use. I want you yourself [to find] suffic[ient] reason why I should refrain from spitting in your f[ace], and should instead [b]ury every trace of this sordid affair, for I could easily turn it into a fine chapter in my history of cuckoldry."‡

Sollogub went to see Pushkin that day; the poet called him into the study and said, closing the door behind him: "I am going to read you my letter to Heckeren senior. With the son, everything has been settled. Now for the old boy."

"Thereupon," Sollogub wrote, "he read me the letter he had written to the Netherlands ambassador. His lips were trembling, his eyes were bloodshot, he was terrifying to behold, and it was then I understood the reality of his African ancestry. What could I say to such impassioned fury? I said nothing, although against my better judgment, and as this happened on a Saturday [Prince Odoevsky's at-home day], I went to Prince Odoevsky's house, where I met Zhukovsky and told him about it.

‡ The letters and words in brackets have been added by the author.

Zhukovsky was alarmed, and promised to intercept the letter. He managed to do so, and told me a few days later at the Karamzins' that he had taken care of the matter and that the letter would not be sent."

Pushkin consented to keep his letter, but with the intention of using it later if the occasion arose.

The second letter he wrote on November 21 was designed to inform Benkendorf of all that had transpired between Heckeren, D'Anthès and himself.

"On the morning of November 4," he wrote, "I received three copies of an anonymous letter that was an outrage to my honor and that of my wife. From the appearance of the paper, the style of the letter, and the manner in which it was written, I immediately suspected that it was composed by a foreigner, a man from the highest class of society, a diplomat. I made inquiries. I learned that seven or eight other persons had received copies of the letter that same day, sealed and addressed to me in an inner envelope. Most of the people receiving them suspected foul play and did not forward them.

"On the whole, people were incensed by such a cowardly and gratuitous insult; but while insisting that my wife's conduct was above reproach, they also said that the cause of the letter was the pressing attentions she was receiving from Mr. D'Anthès.

"In these circumstances it did not please me to have my wife's name linked with that of anyone. I informed Mr. D'Anthès accordingly. Baron Heckeren came to my home and accepted a duel on behalf of Mr. D'Anthès, asking me for a fortnight's grace.

"It so happened that during this interval Mr. D'Anthès fell in love with my sister-in-law, Miss Goncharov, and proposed to her. Having heard this unofficially, I sent word to Mr. D'Archiac (Mr. D'Anthès' second) that my challenge was to be withdrawn. Meanwhile, I learned beyond the shadow of a doubt that the anonymous letter had been written by Mr. Heckeren himself, and I believe it my duty to inform the government and public of that fact.

"As sole judge and guardian of my honor and that of my wife, and consequently asking no one else to give me justice or revenge, I cannot and shall not give proof of my allegations to anyone."[13]

After writing this letter, Pushkin thought better of sending it: It would be wiser to explain his position to the emperor and chief of police in person. He would ask for an audience, the cause warranted it. Two days later, at 3 P.M. on November 23, 1836, Pushkin, accompanied by Benkendorf, went to see Nicholas I. During his audience, Pushkin undoubtedly gave free rein to his eloquence, and Benkendorf and Nicholas equally undoubtedly acknowledged the justice of his cause but advised him to remain calm and do nothing.

Pushkin was finding it impossible to remain calm. He continued to search for some means of administering a crushing blow to Heckeren. His friends sadly observed that he was growing more irritable and touchy than ever.

"I was astonished," Princess Meshchersky (née Karamzin) wrote, "by Pushkin's feverish agitation. Every time he looked at the man . . . his face and whole body twitched and jerked."

Pushkin himself said: "I feel all the time as though I had a fever. . . . Everywhere I go I am cold, I cannot manage to get warm. Then, suddenly, I am stifling."

And yet, life went on—life: that is, work and borrowing money. Pushkin returned to the moneylender for another 1250 rubles, and collated the notes for a critical edition of the *Song of the Regiment of Igor*.

"He read me his notes," Turgenev wrote, "which were highly pertinent and humorous. Everything is based on his profound knowledge of idiom and the Russian language. . . ."

Elsewhere: "His wife is still beautiful, at the ball and at home, in her full black mantle. Her sister's fiancé is seriously ill. He does not associate with the Pushkins." On December 12, Georges d'Anthès had come down with catarrhal fever.

Pushkin had forbidden his door to Katerina's fiancé. He spent whole days in town, returning exhausted to lock himself into his study, where he was heard pacing up and down and muttering imprecations. Every time the bell rang, he rushed out and called to the servants: "If it's a letter by post, don't take it!" When he arrived too late, he would tear the envelope from the footman's hand and run to open it in his study. In the presence of his wife and friends, and even of Katerina, however, he kept his composure. Of the latter, he said: "My sister-in-law does not know any more what nationality she will be, Russian, French or Dutch."

He wrote to his father: "My sister-in-law Katerina is marrying Baron Heckeren, nephew [?] and adopted son of the ambassador of the King of Holland. He is a very handsome and fine fellow, very much in fashion, rich, and four years younger than his betrothed. Preparations for the trousseau are keeping my wife and her sisters fully occupied, but they are driving me wild because they have turned my home into a dress shop."[14]

Katerina, meanwhile, was miserable, living in a house in which everyone was hostile to her fiancé. She hated Pushkin for refusing to be reconciled with D'Anthès. She envied Natalya because D'Anthès was in love with her. She could not wait to get away from these odious rooms and vindictive people, and bask in the radiance of her handsome horse guardsman.

D'Anthès did his best to allay his fiancée's fears. Having agreed to this forced marriage, he meant to see it through like a man. Whatever his resentment of the girl who was coming between him and the object of his passion, he would not blame her for his misfortunes. Disarmed by Katerina's blind devotion and melancholy pliancy, he strove to feel compassion for her, he wrote her little notes of beguiling gentleness, tiny rectangles engraved with his crest and covered with his energetic script: "Arrange it so that we can be alone, not in the same room as your good aunt.* I have so many things to tell you—I want to talk to you about our future happiness—and they preclude the presence of witnesses. Let me believe you are truly happy, for I feel so happy myself, this morning. I could not talk to you, and yet my heart was full of sweet and tender thoughts for you, for I do love you, my dear Katerina, and will tell you so in my own words, with the sincerity which is the foundation of my character and which you will always find in me. . . ."[15]

And: "Please accept, dear friend, my most fervent wishes for your felicity, you will never be as happy as I should like, but rest assured that I shall always strive to make you so, insofar as it lies within my power; with the aid of our excellent friend† I shall succeed, I trust, for you are good and indulgent. And where I do not succeed, you will know, at least, that I tried, and will take that into account."[16]

But all Georges d'Anthès' honeyed words and oaths and abnegations could not reassure the doubting Katerina. She knew her fiancé's impulsive nature, she knew how much he admired and desired Natalya; however often he swore he would be true, she could not believe him. This passage from one of his letters to Katerina is particularly revealing: "No clouds on the horizon, banish all your fears, and above all never mistrust me; it little matters whom we may frequent, I see and shall always see no one but you; do not fret; I am yours. Katerina, you can trust me, my actions will prove it to you since you doubt my word."[17]

"My actions will prove it to you . . ." How could he be so sure? During their brief meetings at Aunt Zagryazhskaya's, Katerina anxiously scanned the polite mask and calm eyes of her fiancé for signs of his real thoughts. She had only one consolation: Natalya, at any rate, no longer loved him. There could be no doubt about that. She said so. She said it again and again. She even said it too often; her ostentatious contempt for D'Anthès infuriated Katerina. Everything was so complicated in that house. Everyone's nerves were on edge. Everyone's balance was so extraordinarily precarious. It was an artificial peace, stifling and ominous, that reigned among all these people who were being consumed by their passions. One look, one ill-timed word, and disaster would surely follow.

* Aunt Zagryazhskaya, at whose home the couple met.
† Baron Heckeren senior.

And Natalya was so clumsy. Now that she had seen the error of her ways at last, she had come back to her husband full of docility and affection, and that was all well and good. But to prove the full measure of her devotion, she conscientiously deposited every scrap of drawing-room gossip at his feet, driving him into frenzies. To him, the most innocuous remark was an attack upon his name, his wife's honor and the privacy of his home. He began to see that his "revenge" upon D'Anthès had been wasted effort. During a Christmas ball at one of the embassies, the poet entered a room decorated with stags' antlers and exclaimed, "Now, here is a room for married men, for husbands, people like me!"

On the day before New Year's Eve, there was a big reception at the Vyazemskys', attended by both Pushkin and Natalya and D'Anthès and Katerina. D'Anthès moved deliberately to Natalya's side and stayed there the whole evening. Pushkin was quivering with rage. "He looked so awful that if I had been his wife, I should have been afraid to go home with him," Countess Stroganov said.

And Sofya Karamzin, who was decidedly partial to D'Anthès, described the scene as follows: "Pushkin is continuing to behave in the most foolish and absurd manner possible; he snarls like a wildcat and gnashes his teeth every time he mentions the subject [of the marriage], which is something he does all too willingly, as he is always delighted to find a new listener. You should have seen how eagerly he related every obscure and half-imaginary detail of the whole mysterious saga to my sister Katerina, as though he were narrating a play or story that had nothing to do with him. He keeps insisting that he will never allow his wife to go to the wedding or entertain her sister afterward in their home. Yesterday I gave her a good talking-to, to encourage her to make him change his mind about this absurd prohibition, which would only set every tongue in town wagging again. Her own attitude is far from honest too, for as long as her husband is around she pretends not to see D'Anthès and snubs him, but as soon as he leaves she is up to her old tricks again, with the downcast eyes and the fluttery, nervous conversations, and D'Anthès plants himself in front of her, gazing endlessly into her eyes and seeming to forget the very existence of his fiancée, whose face changes and reveals all her jealousy. In a word, it is a never-ending comedy, with nobody knowing the real secret of the plot. . . ."[18]

D'Anthès and Katerina were married on January 10, 1837, in a double Russian Orthodox and Roman Catholic ceremony. Pushkin delegated his wife to represent him, and Natalya left immediately after the service.

The newlyweds moved into Baron Heckeren's residence on the Nevsky Prospect.

We can glean some idea of the first days of their marriage from a letter which Katerina wrote to her father-in-law Konrad d'Anthès:

"My happiness is complete," she said after the wedding; "I only hope my husband is as happy as I. I can promise you that my whole life's work will be to love him, to study his tastes so that I may conform to them and be able, one day, to offer you an image of shared felicity and domestic contentment. For the moment, I can only send you a most affectionate embrace, and pray that you will all give me your friendship."[19]

Katerina meant what she said. Georges d'Anthès made her happy. He felt affection and respect for her, if not love. He allowed her to worship him with the fond condescension of an overgrown boy who has been spoiled by too much female attention. And she—tender, wistful, resigned, infinitely obliging—palpitated with embarrassment and excitement at the thought that this man, the most handsome, the cleverest, the most gallant man on earth, was actually her husband and was going to make her a mother.

3. *The Challenge*

Acting on Heckeren's advice, D'Anthès tried to make it up with Pushkin after the wedding. He paid a courtesy call; Pushkin refused to see him. He wrote a letter; Pushkin tore it up. He wrote another letter; Pushkin decided to let Aunt Zagryazhskaya return it for him. Pushkin went to her home and, to his discomfiture, found himself face to face with Baron Heckeren's dry features, bald pate and unsettling smile. The baron was prepared to make any concession, utter any inanity; Pushkin thrust out D'Anthès' letter and curtly asked him to return it to its author, adding that he did not wish to receive any letters from D'Anthès, endure any visits from him or hear his name pronounced. Heckeren stiffened his little figure and declared that since the letter was addressed to Pushkin and not to him, he could not take it. Pushkin turned pale, his eyes danced.

"But you will take it, cur!" he shouted, and threw it in his face. Then he strode from the room, leaving the baron standing there, petrified with hatred and alarm.[1]

Baron Heckeren, no doubt, was unable to refrain from relating this incident to his adopted son, and Georges was justifiably incensed. It was not in his nature to receive an insult without returning it a hundredfold. For weeks now, he had been imposing a humiliating meekness upon himself for the sake of the baron, who lived in utter terror of a scandal. It was beyond his strength to keep it up any longer; and besides, it was useless. What good had it done them to dream up this marriage, just to avoid a duel? D'Anthès had tied himself for life to a creature who was perfectly pleasant, but whom he did not love. He had broken with Natalya, and was haunted by her memory. And now here was Pushkin, trying to play the hero. Was that what Baron Heckeren had been hoping to achieve for himself and his son? Challenged, the ambassador had to admit that his diplomacy had failed lamentably. They would have to change tactics.

Georges insisted: What he wanted was revenge, and right away. And after his initial fright at the young man's ferocity, Baron Heckeren began to think that perhaps in this affair the madmen were wiser than the sane. One thing was certain: There was no way to calm Pushkin's rage, he would be an implacable enemy of Heckeren and his kin forever. Even after the smothered duel, the improvised marriage and the conciliatory gestures, he remained aggressively adamant. If something were not done to stop that African, he would denounce the ambassador to the Russian court as the instigator of the anonymous letters. He would blacken the name of Heckeren, compromise the careers of both Heckerens. Anything rather than that.

The best course, then, would be to take the initiative—to fight back, cut him down, make him ridiculous, disarm him, do away with him, before he had time to publish his revelations. Thus, after entreating Pushkin to give up the duel, Heckeren turned coat again: Before, he had been restraining the hotheaded D'Anthès, now he resolved to urge him on. There was Katerina, of course, who would suffer, but she was used to suffering. A little more, a little less . . .

After making a superhuman effort to please his adoptive father and forget Natalya, Georges, at last given his head, bolted back to his passion. He would show the world he was not afraid of Pushkin. On he came, head high and eye agleam. In this melodramatic lighting, Natalya was too fascinating; really, he wanted her too badly, he could not live without her. Damn the consequences, for her, for Katerina, for the old baron and the jealous husband, damn the consequences for himself. Let the world come to an end, that woman was going to be his.

At the theater, the balls, everywhere, there was D'Anthès again, frantic, radiant, arrogant, a whirlwind at Natalya's side. He had never been in better form, gayer, more sure of his voice, his eye, the ring of his spurs and the wavy blondness of his hair. Katerina stonily looked on while her husband drank to Natalya's health, danced with Natalya, leaned over to whisper warm secrets smelling of scented mustaches and champagne into Natalya's ear. People began to whisper and exchange knowing looks: What a gorgeous scandal! After marrying the sister, he is still courting her! But, in short, it is starting all over again! Serves Pushkin right for his idiotic pride! That upstart! That epigram-writing revolutionary!

"The young man," Vyazemsky wrote, "continued to flaunt his passion for Mrs. Pushkin in front of his wife. The town gossips revived, the murderous eye of the public focused with renewed curiosity on the characters of the drama being enacted before it." N. M. Smirnov said: "He never ceased his pursuit of his sister-in-law. He made not even the slightest pretense; sometimes he seemed to be openly provoking the jealousy of the husband who had refused to be reconciled with him. Baron Heckeren was visibly encouraging him."

When Pushkin drew near the couple, D'Anthès drifted away with noble dignity, only to return the instant Natalya was alone. And Natalya, instead of repulsing him, stood there paralyzed and bewitched. All her good resolutions fled the moment she caught sight of him. She became strangely animated and intense. She began to live faster. For the space of an instant, she was happy. And anyway, wasn't he her own brother-in-law? How could it be wrong of her to talk to him? At night, to relieve her conscience, she would assiduously confess to Pushkin that D'Anthès was still pursuing her, after which she felt perfectly at peace: She was not deceiving her husband, and she was not having to forgo the pleasure of being adored.

Pushkin took her female cowardice for innocence. For him, Natalya was simply irresponsible—a big, scatterbrained girl, a flirt, but so sweet. He could not blame her for anything she did. It was the others who were to blame, for leading her astray. The others: that is, D'Anthès, who was deliberately provoking him, and Heckeren, who was plotting cathedrals of revenge. "She should have withdrawn from society," Prince Vyazemsky wrote, "and insisted that her husband do so too; but she had no character. She found herself virtually at the same point in her relationship with young Heckeren as before the marriage. There was nothing really culpable, but a great deal of thoughtlessness, and too much security."[2]

The emperor himself, meeting Natalya at a ball, counseled her to have a care for her reputation. Natalya repeated the sovereign's words to her husband, who was gratified and duly thanked Nicholas I for his concern.

"Could you expect anything else of me?" Nicholas inquired.

"Indeed I could expect something else of you," Pushkin replied; "to be quite frank, I expected that you were flirting with my wife too."

"At home, good humor and no strain," Zhukovsky noted; and it was true, Pushkin had such faith in Natalya that he almost felt sorry for her, rather than condemning her. But it was not enough for him to be sure of Natalya: He intended that the rest of the world should be sure of her too.

"Pushkin's friends," Vyazemsky wrote, "tried to calm him by telling him that since he was convinced of his wife's innocence and his conviction was shared by all his friends and all decent people in society, he was wrong to make such an issue of it; to which he would reply that it was not enough for himself and his friends to be convinced; he belonged to the nation and he wanted his name to be untainted wherever it was pronounced."[3]

He also said: "There are two kinds of cuckolds: Some are so in fact, and they have no uncertainties about their position; others are made so by public opinion, and their position is far more difficult; I am one of those."

Pushkin's thoughts were returning to the idea of a duel. He said so to Baroness Vrevsky (ex-Zizi Wulf), who was passing through St. Petersburg. She used his children as an argument to dissuade him. "The emperor knows all about the situation and has promised to look after them," Pushkin replied impatiently.

From force of habit, however, he went on planning for the future; he tried to do a little work on his *History of Peter the Great,* he talked of going to Mikhailovskoye. His face would clear and lighten for the length of a memory or thought, and then cloud over again, and he could think of nothing but D'Anthès and Heckeren and society and all those evil eyes fixed upon him, all those mealymouthed faces hooting with laughter at his squirming discomfort.

D'Anthès later testified in his official statement on February 26, 1837, that every time Pushkin saw Katerina with Mrs. Pushkin, "he would come up and stand beside her, and when she remarked upon it one day he said, 'I want to see how you are when you are together, what you look like when you are talking to each other.'" This occurred once at a ball given by the French ambassador; at supper the same evening, he went up to Katerina when D'Anthès was out of hearing and "asked her to drink his health. When she refused, he asked her again, and she refused again. Then he went away, saying, 'Take care, I shall bring you bad luck. . . .'"[4]

On January 21 Pushkin and Natalya went to a ball given by the Ficquelmonts. "There were crowds of people at the Ficquelmont ball," Durnovo wrote in his diary. "'La Londonderry' [the wife of an English general] was there with all her emeralds and heaps of diamonds. Mrs. Krudner is really very handsome, such gorgeous skin and fine features. Mrs. Pushkin wore her hair close to her head, with braids at the back. She was absolutely like a beautiful cameo."[5]

D'Anthès was also at the ball, in frantic pursuit of Natalya. The diary of one contemporary, N. K. Merder, contains the following entry for the same date:

"I did not dance at the ball, it was too crowded. . . . D'Anthès spent part of the evening nearby. He was conversing animatedly with some older lady. . . . I could not make out what she was saying, she was talking under her breath. But D'Anthès replied loudly, in tones of offended dignity: 'I understand, Madame, what it is that you wish me to understand, but the point is that I am not at all sure I have behaved foolishly.'

" 'Prove to the world that you can be a good husband . . . and that the rumors going around are unfounded!'

" 'I am very grateful to you, Madame, but the world must judge me as it can.' "[6]

Then D'Anthès returned to Natalya. Pushkin watched in silence; one witness said he was so utterly obsessed by his jealousy that he looked like "a monster." Natalya herself was afraid of him and said, "Every time he speaks to me, he makes me shiver."[7]

On January 23 there was a ball at the Vorontsovs'. D'Anthès contrived to be opposite Natalya for every *contredanse*. As they went in to supper he said to Katerina, "*Allons, ma légitime.*"*[8] Pushkin overheard the insolence, but controlled himself. Later, D'Anthès leaned toward Natalya and told her he had learned that his wife and sister-in-law had the same chiropodist.

"Now I know," he added mischievously, "that your corn is more beautiful than my wife's." Natalya paled a little at this tasteless jest; Pushkin saw, and immediately took her home. On the way, she repeated D'Anthès' pun.†[9]

The next day—Sunday, January 24—Pushkin borrowed another two thousand rubles and went to a concert at the Engelhardts'. "He was leaning against the doorjamb," I. S. Turgenev‡ wrote, "with his arms crossed on his broad chest, staring disgustedly at the crowd. I remember his small, swarthy face, his African lips, the gleam of his strong white teeth, his drooping side whiskers, his deep eyes muddied with liverish yellow, his high forehead and almost invisible eyebrows, and his bush of frizzled hair. He glanced at me; my rude stare must have made an unpleasant impression upon him. He shrugged—he seemed to be in a bad mood—and moved away."

That same day, after the concert, Pushkin and his wife spent a few hours at the Meshcherskys'. D'Anthès was there. Pushkin went off to play chess with the prince. To the young officer Rossetti, who came over to watch the game, he snapped: "Well? Have you been in the drawing room? *He* must be there, next to my wife, no?" And burst into laughter.

Sofya Karamzin was also there, and described the evening in a letter to her brother: "On Sunday there was a big reception at Katerina's [Meshchersky]; the Pushkins and Heckerens [D'Anthès and Katerina] were there, still playing their sentimental comedy for the world to admire. Pushkin gnashes his teeth and scowls like a wildcat. Natalya lowers

* "*Légitime*" means "lawfully wedded wife"; the term is somewhat sarcastic and disrespectful, and implies, among other things, that the wife is a nuisance anyway, or that she is a pitiable creature (i.e. there is a mistress).

† In French the phrase is "*. . . que votre cor est plus beau que celui de ma femme,*" *cor*=corn and *corps*=body being pronounced alike.

‡ The future novelist, then aged eighteen.

her gaze and blushes under the fervent and protracted stare of her brother-in-law; it is all beginning to be more than ordinarily immoral. Katerina aims a jealous lorgnette in their direction, and, just so that nobody will be left without a part to play, Alexandra flirts openly with Pushkin, who is seriously involved with her. He is jealous of his wife on principle, but with his sister-in-law—it is from the heart. . . ." This letter was written on January 27, while Pushkin was sitting in Wulf's sweetshop with Danzas, on his way to the duel.[10]

Later that evening, as Pushkin was leaving the theater with his wife, Heckeren senior came up to Natalya and whispered something in her ear. What exactly did he say? Was he pleading the cause of his adopted son or advising Natalya to be more circumspect? Natalya turned quickly away and rejoined her husband in the throng. But Pushkin had seen the exchange and was irritated by it.

On January 25 Pushkin went to call on the painter Brüllow, whose water colors and caricatures delighted him. Forgetting all his troubles, he laughed until he cried and begged the artist to give him one particularly successful drawing entitled "The Arrival at the Ball of the Ambassador from Smyrna." Brüllow refused, but promised to paint Pushkin's portrait, and arranged the first sitting for January 28.

While Pushkin sat there chuckling and trying to shake off his grief and humiliation, Natalya was dressing for a rendezvous. A friend of hers, Idalya Poletika—an illegitimate daughter of Count Stroganov's—had sent a note asking Natalya to call at her home on an urgent matter. Her husband was an officer in the regiment of horse guards, and she lived in an apartment in the barracks. She loathed Pushkin, who had rejected her advances in the past, and utterly adored D'Anthès. She may have been his mistress, or she may not; in any case, she was deeply concerned by anything touching the private life of the horse guardsman. To her, the intrigue between D'Anthès and Natalya was exalting and noble; but above all, she relished the thought that the union of these two young, handsome beings would make an eternal laughingstock of the horrid little poet with the long fingernails, the unkempt mane of hair and the grotesque vanity.

Upon entering Idalya's apartment, Natalya received a shock: D'Anthès was there. The hostess soon made some feeble excuse and disappeared. A man named Lanskoy was pacing back and forth in the street below: It was his job to stand lookout. Natalya saw that she had fallen into a trap. D'Anthès was already at her feet, entreating her to be his mistress, to leave Pushkin and run away with him abroad. He brandished a pistol and threatened to kill himself before her eyes if she would not yield to him. Alarmed and outraged, Natalya fluttered about the room crying that she would never surrender to blackmail and that this meeting would be their last. Hearing the noise, Idalya Poletika's daughter, who was not in the plot, rushed into the room, allowing Natalya to make her escape. They had not been alone more than a few minutes.[11]

That same day, Pushkin received an anonymous letter informing him that his wife had met D'Anthès alone in the home of a friend and that he was now, technically and irrefutably, a cuckold. Pushkin immediately asked Natalya where she had been, and Natalya, panic-stricken and in despair, told him all and wept copiously on his shoulder. It was too much. Pushkin decided to strike a final blow. He cared nothing about D'Anthès, who was an infatuated and irresponsible puppy; but Heckeren senior deserved to be punished. Pushkin instantly began a letter to the ambassador. In his fever, he put the wrong date at the top (he wrote January 26, which was the following day). It required several drafts to set his rage in order.

At last, he wrote out a fair copy and closed the envelope with his personal seal. Then he took Natalya to a party at the Vyazemskys', at which D'Anthès, Natalya and Katerina all feigned a brittle gaiety. Pushkin contemplated D'Anthès with lofty irony. He said to Princess Vyazemsky: "I do love to watch that man enjoying himself here, little suspecting what is waiting for him at home."

"What do you mean?" asked the princess. "Have you written a letter?"

Pushkin nodded.

"To his father," he said.

"Has it already been sent? Today?"

Pushkin rubbed his hands and nodded again, with an air of gleeful venom.

"Is it possible you are still thinking about that?" the princess exclaimed. "We thought it was all over."

Pushkin stiffened: "Do you take me for a coward? I told you I had finished with the young one, but the father is a different matter altogether. As I told you before, my revenge will give them something to talk about."[12]

That same day, January 25, 1837, while Georges d'Anthès was imploring Natalya to be his mistress and Pushkin was plotting his diabolical revenge, old Mrs. Goncharov, at Yaropolets, was writing a letter to her daughter Katerina. The words echo eerily in the charged atmosphere surrounding the newlyweds: "Thank you, dear Katerina, for giving me the details of your wedding. I congratulate you with all my heart on the fulfillment of your wishes, and can hope nothing better for you than that your present happiness should never fade: You tell me it is so great that you fear it cannot last; but since heaven in its mercy has granted it to you, enjoy it and give thanks. You tell me you do not know how to show your husband how grateful you are for the happiness he gives you;

an even temper and consideration will prove your devotion, and they are easily achieved when the heart is moved by genuine attachment. You praise the kindness of Baron Heckeren, your husband's uncle [?], according to what you and your brothers have told me; it is true that you must be filled with gratitude for all he is doing for you."[13]

Katerina's apprehensions were not as unfounded as her mother tried to make out. On Tuesday, January 26, the day after Mrs. Goncharov wrote her letter, Baron Heckeren found a communication in French, signed Pushkin, in his mail. It was the last straw:

"Baron, allow me to give you a summary of recent events. The conduct of your son has long been known to me, and could not leave me indifferent. I was content to remain an observer for a time, prepared to intervene when I should see fit. Then, an incident that would have been highly disagreeable at any other time came most opportunely to assist me: I received some anonymous letters. I saw that the moment had come, and seized it. You know the rest: I made your son look such a piteous fool that my wife, amazed at his cowardice and pettiness, could not refrain from laughing, and any emotion she may have felt before in response to this great, sublime passion, shriveled into the most tranquil contempt and highly merited disgust.

"I must admit, Baron, that your behavior throughout all this has not been altogether seemly. You, the representative of a crowned head, have played the fatherly role of pimp to your son. It appears that all his actions (and clumsy enough they were, too) have been guided by you. It is you, I suppose, who dictated the inanities he has been uttering and the simpering nonsense he has taken it upon himself to write. Like some obscene old harpy, you have been sidling up to my wife in corners to urge the suit of your bastard or so-called bastard; and when an attack of syphilis kept him indoors you said he was dying of love for her; you sniveled: Give me back my son.

"You must see, Baron, that after all this I really cannot allow my family to have any contact with yours. It was on that sole condition, moreover, that I agreed to take no further action in this foul business and to refrain from dishonoring you in the eyes of our court and your own, as I intended and had it in my power to do. It is of no concern to me that my wife continues to listen to your paternal exhortations. I cannot, however, tolerate that your son should presume to speak to her after his contemptible behavior, and still less to make barracks puns to her or pretend to be filled with adoration and frustrated passion, when he is nothing but a coward and a scoundrel. I am therefore obliged to turn to you and ask that you put a stop to these goings on if you wish to avoid another scandal, from which I, you may be sure, shall not draw back.

"I have the honor to be, Baron, your must humble and obedient servant, Alexander Pushkin."

How did Baron Heckeren react to this letter? He had been waiting for an outburst, and had in fact done everything possible to provoke it—and here were Pushkin's insults, the answer to his prayers. He himself would not fight a duel, he was too old, and the "representative of a crowned head." But D'Anthès would avenge the honor of his adoptive father.

True, Pushkin was a good shot, and it would be a considerable risk for D'Anthès to meet him. Nevertheless, Heckeren would not and could not back out now, however great his love for his son. He was staking everything on this last card. Either D'Anthès would kill Pushkin, and the odious pen-pusher would carry his hatred and his revelations into the grave; or Pushkin would kill D'Anthès, and for Heckeren that would be the same as being killed himself. What injustice could touch him after that? What lost career add one jot to his woe?

After consulting Count Stroganov, the arbiter of disputes among the aristocracy, Heckeren informed D'Anthès that he was being called upon to perform another deed of heroism in service to the cause. And D'Anthès, of course, wanted nothing better than a fight, which would efface the memory of his recent submission. The whole Nesselrode clan was behind him. He felt strong and eager for the fray. Heckeren wrote to Pushkin immediately:

"Sir, as I am unacquainted with your writing and signature I had recourse to the Vicomte d'Archiac, who will give this to you, to ascertain that the letter to which I am replying did come from you. Its contents so far exceed the limits of the possible that I will not deign to reply to it in detail. You appear to forget, sir, that it was you who withdrew the challenge you sent to Baron Georges Heckeren [D'Anthès], which he had accepted. Proof of what I say exists, written in your hand and preserved by the seconds. It remains only for me to warn you that M. D'Archiac's purpose in calling upon you is to determine the place in which you will meet Baron Georges Heckeren, and to notify you that there can be no delay.

"I shall subsequently teach you, sir, to respect the quality invested in me, which no act of yours can touch.

"I am, sir, your very humble servant, Baron Heckeren.

"Seen and approved by me,

"Baron Georges Heckeren."[14]

D'Archiac gave the letter to Pushkin, who accepted the challenge without looking at it. But when D'Archiac asked the name of his second, the poet replied that he had not yet discussed the matter with anyone. A little while later, D'Archiac sent the following note to Pushkin:

"The undersigned informs Mr. Pushkin that he will wait at home until eleven tonight, and after that at Countess Razumovsky's, for the person who is to act for him in this matter, which must be concluded tomorrow."[15]

Both Heckeren's letter and D'Archiac's note show what a terrible hurry the ambassador was in: "there can be no delay" . . . the "matter which must be concluded tomorrow." Heckeren's chief objective now was to silence Pushkin, and a few days, even a few hours, might be enough for the poet to reveal his tale of the anonymous diplomas. That he must never do.

Natalya knew nothing. In the presence of his family and friends, Pushkin affected a sort of impish lightheartedness which they found faintly alarming. At a dinner at Countess Rostopchin's, he had to go into the bathroom several times to plunge his head in a bucket of cold water. From there, he went to the Razumovsky ball, but without Natalya. The two Heckerens also forbore to appear. Pushkin danced, laughed with Turgenev, invited him to call the next day. During a pause in the dancing, D'Archiac came up to the poet and reminded him that he had still not given him the name of his second.

The truth was that Pushkin was reluctant to ask a compatriot to act for him, knowing that the poor man would probably be arrested and tried when the duel was over. Looking around the room, he saw Magenis, a counselor at the British embassy, and asked him to act. Magenis wanted to know the cause of the duel, but Pushkin would tell him nothing. With dignity, the Englishman declined. At the end of the evening Pushkin was still without a second, and the duel had to take place the following day at the latest.

A few of the pinnacles of society had already been secretly informed. The authorities too, of course, were fully aware of the meeting.

What did they do to prevent it?

Nicholas I asked Benkendorf to send his men to the scene before the duel took place. But Benkendorf did not share the emperor's views in this matter. On the eve of the duel he received a visit from Heckeren himself, Count Uvarov and Princess Byeloselskaya. Baron Heckeren explained all the reasons why it would be best to let matters take their course. Hadn't that tempestuous pseudo poet blackened enough paper and upset enough people already? If Pushkin were killed, there would be one less enemy of the aristocracy, monarchy and God in Russia. If he came out of it unscathed or only wounded, the authorities could convict and exile or imprison him, duels being illegal. Minister Uvarov and Princess Byeloselskaya urged Benkendorf to follow Heckeren's advice.

"Send your men somewhere else," Princess Byeloselskaya suggested.

And that is what Benkendorf decided to do.[16]

4. *On the Field of Honor*

The sun rose, that January 27, on a city of snow and slush. It was cold. The wind howled monotonously. The black, stiff, bent figures of the early risers scuttled down the leveled white avenues. Shopkeepers unfastened their wooden shutters. Concierges swept their doorsteps.

It was eight o'clock when Pushkin opened his eyes. He sprang out of bed, washed and dressed hurriedly and swallowed a cup of scalding tea. Natalya, Alexandra and the children were still asleep. He was the only member of the family awake, the only one to know he might die before nightfall. But the thought did not frighten him; in fact, he felt strangely cheerful and fit. He had suffered too much from all the gossip and anonymous letters, the provocations and delays, the reconciliations and pretense, to want anything except to have done with his enemies once and for all. Even death was better than a universe populated by Benkendorfs, Nicholases, Uvarovs, Bulgarins, D'Anthèses and Heckerens. There was Natalya, of course and the children and his work. What would they do without him? Well, they would go on living, like everybody else. . . . Besides, he was not going to die. God was just. He would not allow an uneducated stripling to assassinate the foremost poet of Russia. He would be laughing at his apprehensions, no doubt, by tomorrow, by tonight even. What he must do is act as though this morning were no different from any other morning. Work, the review, his mail.

Pushkin went into the room he used as a study. A large, light room, its walls enameled with books: crowded shelves, three luminous windows, a sofa covered in red, a table laden with papers, paintings on the wall, the smell of tobacco and ink. Pushkin smiled at the candid, familiar scene. This was his refuge, his den. He sat down in his armchair, dipped a pen in his bronze inkwell, jotted a few notes on a scrap of paper. Then he glanced through a *History in Tales* by Mrs. Ishimov. The book was written for children—simple, entertaining, skillful. One day Mashka and Sashka would spell it out; would he be there to listen to their halting efforts? Perhaps he had the curiosity to glance through a review. In the latest issue of the *Northern Bee,* one or two items must have caught his eye: Two officers had fought a duel at Strasbourg; the library of the Duchesse de Berry was to be sold at auction; the English ambassador was returning to his government. . . .

A duel, a dispersed library, an ambassador. . . . Everything brought him back to the question of his own life. The blood began mounting to his head. When would it end? Between 9 and 10 A.M., a note came from D'Archiac: "Sir, I return once more, and with insistence, to my request of yesterday evening. It is essential that I communicate with your second immediately. I shall be in my apartment until noon, and hope to receive a visit before then from whatever person you choose to send."[1]

That business of the second again! What a lot of fuss, just to kill a man. Pushkin crossly scribbled a draft, then carefully recopied it: "M. le vicomte, I am not at all anxious to inform every idler in Petersburg of the details of my private life, and I accordingly oppose all negotiations between seconds. You will see mine on the field, not before. As Mr. Heckeren [D'Anthès] is the challenger and offended party, he may choose one for me if he likes; I accept his choice in advance, be it his own lackey. As to the time and place, I am entirely at his orders. According to our Russian customs, that should suffice. Please understand that this is my last word, that I have nothing further to say on any subject relating to this matter, and that I shall not stir from my house except to go to the field."[2]

Having dispatched this note, Pushkin tried to return to work. There was the fifth issue of *The Contemporary* to prepare for the printers. He wanted it to include some scenes by the English author Barry Cornwall. Mrs. Ishimov, who was a contributor to *The Contemporary,* had undertaken to translate them, but he had still to select the passages. He stood up, took a book from the shelf and began turning the pages of Cornwall's *Dramatic Scenes.* He paused at two titles: *Amelia Wentworth* and *Ludovic Sforza.* The first was a study of jealousy, in which Gottfried Wentworth, enraged by his wife's excessive friendliness for a handsome youth, planned to banish the culprit or throw him into prison. He did not suspect his wife, he was sure of her fidelity; he only dreaded the suppositions and sneers of his entourage. The coincidence intrigued Pushkin. He too had no misgivings about Natalya. The second play, *Ludovic Sforza,* preached that revenge was the inalienable right of every individual. Here too, Pushkin felt an alliance with the violent, overproud and vindictive characters. He took a pencil and ticked off the titles of the two scenes in the table of contents.

Just then, there came a timid knock at the door; it was his valet, holding out an envelope from the French embassy. D'Archiac's reply. Lord, what a hurry they were in!

"Sir: You, having attacked the honor of Baron Georges Heckeren, owe him satisfaction. It is for you to procure your second. There can be no question of finding one for you. Baron Georges Heckeren is ready to go onto the field and insists that you conform to the rules at once. Any delay will be considered as a refusal on your part to give the satisfaction to which he is entitled and, by allowing the matter to become known, will prevent its conclusion.

"A meeting of the seconds is indispensable before the encounter; if you continue to refuse, it would become one of the conditions of Baron Georges Heckeren, all of which, as you told me yesterday and wrote today, you accept."[3]

Pushkin threw down the letter. A second. One more outsider in his private life. He would have to talk about all those things that were so hateful: his suspicions, his humiliation, his anger. Yet D'Anthès' condition was categorical; he had to have a second. But who? He would see about that later. Everything in its time, no? First, the letter to Mrs. Ishimov. Now, what was it about? Yes, Barry Cornwall's *Dramatic Scenes.* Pushkin ticked a few more titles and wrapped the book in heavy gray paper. Then he took his pen, dipped it in his inkwell again, and wrote to Mrs. Ishimov:

"I sincerely regret that I shall be unable to accept your invitation for today. In the meantime, I send you Barry Cornwall. At the end of the book you will find certain titles marked in pencil, translate them as best you can, I am sure you will do it very well. Today, I chanced to open your *History in Tales,* and involuntarily forgot myself reading it. That is the way to write!

"With deepest respect and devotion, I have the honor to remain, Madame, your humble servant,

"A. Pushkin."

After signing the letter, he read it through. Wasn't it strange: Here he was, about to go off and fight a duel, and his last thought was for this woman who made her living by the drudgery of translation. It could not have been better. Order. Neatness. Precision. Even in the face of death.

Past noon. Time to look for a second. Pushkin put on a fur coat and went into the street. First, he drove to the home of young Rossetti. Rossetti was out. Then, he thought of his old schoolmate Danzas. Danzas was a brash, idle officer, a lover of puns, women and good food. But he could count on his friendship and discretion.

"To Danzas!"

The sleigh lurched forward in a cloud of steam and jingling bells. Just as the horses started across Tsepnoy Bridge, Pushkin caught sight of Danzas in the crowd on the pavement. The horses stopped.

"Danzas! I was on my way to see you!" Pushkin called out. "Get in and come along with me to the French embassy; you can witness an explanation."

Danzas heaved himself into the sleigh and the team moved on toward the Great Milyonnaya. On the way, Pushkin spoke abundantly, but made no reference to the duel. At the French embassy, the two friends were met by D'Archiac. Pushkin turned to Danzas and spoke firmly: "Now, I want to tell you what has been going on."

He calmly related the sequence of events between himself, D'Anthès and Heckeren, and concluded: "Now, the only thing I have to say to you is that if this business is not concluded today, the first time I see either of the Heckerens I shall spit in his face."

Danzas and D'Archiac stood motionless and mute.

"Here is my second," Pushkin added, turning to Danzas. "Danzas, do you accept?"

Danzas could only nod; the responsibility which had suddenly been thrust upon him rendered him speechless. Pushkin made his exit, leaving the seconds to draw up the conditions of the duel.

By 2:30 P.M. D'Archiac and Danzas had agreed upon and duly written down the following provisions:

"Conditions of the duel between Baron Georges Heckeren and Mr. Pushkin:

"1. The two adversaries shall stand at a distance of twenty paces, each being five paces behind his barrier, and the barriers being placed ten paces apart;

"2. Each shall be armed with a pistol; at a given signal, they may move up to but not beyond the barrier, and fire;

"3. It shall further be stipulated that once a shot has been fired, neither adversary may alter his position, so that the person who shot first shall be exposed to his opponent's fire at the same distance;

"4. If both parties have fired without result, the procedure shall be repeated, with the adversaries being placed at the same distance of twenty paces and the barriers and other conditions remaining as before;

"5. The seconds must be the intermediaries in any communication between the principals on the field;

"6. The undersigned, witnesses invested with full powers therefore, undertake upon their honor to ensure the strict observance of the conditions set forth above, each for his principal.

"January 27, 1837, 2:30 P.M.

"[signed] Vicomte D'Archiac,
Attaché at the French Embassy.
Constantine Danzas
Lieutenant Colonel of Engineers."[4]

Bearing this document, Danzas went to Pushkin's home; the poet saw him from the window, ran to meet him, pushed him into his study and locked the door. He seemed to be in very high spirits. He was wearing his red dressing gown with the green checks. His eyes burned feverishly. Papers and books strewn over his desk showed that he had been working. Danzas conscientiously reported his conversation with D'Archiac, adding only that as Pushkin had addressed his letter of insult to Heckeren senior, it was with him he should be having the duel and not with the son. Pushkin did not answer. He simply wanted to get it over with. Danzas then suggested they meet in Wulf's sweetshop a little before 4 P.M. From there they would go to Chernaya Rechka, near the so-called commander's house, where the duel would take place around five. In the interim, Danzas had to go out and buy the pistols, which Pushkin had already selected in the shop of Kurakin the gunsmith, hire a two-horse sleigh and transact some private business.

After his friend's departure, Pushkin bathed, perfumed, changed his clothes and donned his best coat, humming as he dressed. At times it seemed to him that all his grievances and humiliations had disappeared and he was standing, pure and transparent, on the threshold of a new existence. He no longer thought about Natalya or the children. He had never been married. His silver watch ticked steadily in his pocket. The light was mellow where it struck the bindings of his books. Time was passing. Pushkin shrugged. En route! Calling his valet, he asked for an overcoat. He opened the door, shivered, turned back and exchanged it for a fur coat. He lived on the ground floor. Would he ever see this handsome entrance hall again, with its stone columns—cold, anonymous, formal? On his way out he passed the second-floor tenant, Lubyanovsky, and exchanged a friendly greeting. How absurd to die, after washing and dressing so carefully, winding and setting his watch, saying hello to a fellow tenant. Quickening his step, Pushkin turned into the Nevsky Prospect and entered Wulf's sweetshop, where Danzas was already waiting. It was nearly four o'clock. The friends ordered a lemonade. Pushkin emptied his glass, exchanged a look with Danzas, and they walked to the sleigh. The driver gave his team a cut of the whip, and they pulled away in the direction of Trinity Bridge.

The air was crystalline, shattering, cutting. The streets were full of people. Suddenly, on Palace Quay, Danzas saw Natalya in a sleigh. The teams passed. Husband and wife, a few feet apart. One movement, one smile, one cry and the catastrophe could be averted. Natalya was nearsighted, though; and Pushkin was looking the other way. Their horses bore them apart. The wind was blowing in from the sea. Behind the Neva rose the Petropavlovsk Fortress, squat and somber.

"You aren't taking me to the fortress?" Pushkin joked.

"No," said Danzas; "but the shortest route to Chernaya Rechka goes past it."

Danzas was still hoping the police would head them off, or some comrades would catch up to them, or someone would somehow prevent Pushkin from risking his life. He himself had no authority over the poet; he could only obey. Ah, let this duel not take place!

To attract the attention of people in the streets, Danzas took out the case he had bought at the gunsmith's and opened it wide on his knees. Two handsome pistols, long and gleaming, lay on the velvety surface of the box, surrounded by loading rod, hammer, powder flask and a few large lead balls. Danzas played with the pistols, weighed the shot in his hand. Friends of Pushkin hailed the sleigh as it went by. Danzas fumed impotently, unable to shout out to them that Pushkin was going to fight a duel and must be stopped. On Kamennostrovsky Prospect, two officers called out with a laugh: "Why are you going out to the slides at this hour? Everybody else is coming back!"

Pushkin laughed too. He appeared terrifyingly calm. His face was pale and drawn from the cold. Snowflakes melted in his bristling side whiskers. His breath steamed around his thick mauve lips.

Danzas and Pushkin reached the building known as the "commander's house" just as D'Anthès and D'Archiac were pulling up. The two seconds greeted each other politely and began to inspect the terrain. The snow was deep and soft. An icy breeze shook the undergrowth. Ravens flapped heavily past. The seconds selected a site some three hundred yards from the road, where a thick ring of bushes shielded a clearing from observers and the wind. But they sank up to their knees in the snow. Danzas and D'Archiac studiously began trampling it down—they looked like a pair of overgrown boys preparing a skating rink. They worked hard. Their faces were red. Pushkin sat on the ground, his back hunched, his body huddled into his bearskin coat. His little triangular face shone with curious intensity out of all that spiky fur. He observed the preparations intently. D'Anthès stood not far away. A beaver collar framed his pretty, arrogant face. His gaping overcoat showed a glimpse of the white uniform of the horse guards. Did Pushkin remember the prediction of the old German soothsayer who had warned him against "a white man," *weisser Mensch?* There he stood, the white man, and Pushkin was about to fight him. Or perhaps he was thinking of the duel between Eugene Onegin the dandy and Lensky the poet, in the same white setting, over the same nonsense of a woman's honor. The dandy had killed the poet.

> "Move forward."
> Coolly,
> With slow, deliberate steps,
> Not taking aim, the two have moved
> Four paces toward each other.

Four steps, four mortal steps.
But now, as he walks forward,
Unhurriedly, Eugene lifts his arm.
They walk. Five steps more.
Lensky takes aim too,
Squinting his left eye. Then,
Onegin fires. And the fatal
Hour has struck. The poet
Lets fall his pistol,
Claps one hand to his chest,
And drops . . .

All those omens! Imperceptibly, dusk was beginning to gather. They would have to hurry. And those seconds, stamping and trampling, measuring off the path of death with their great strides! Danzas called out to ask Pushkin if he were satisfied with the condition of the firing lane.

"I couldn't care less," Pushkin answered. "Just do it as quickly as you can."

The seconds laid their coats on the ground to mark the barriers. Then, with trembling, cold-stiffened fingers, they began loading the pistols.

"Haven't you finished yet?" Pushkin called.

Everything was ready. Danzas and D'Archiac placed the adversaries five paces behind each barrier and held out the loaded pistols. An endless silence stretched between the two men, who stood, face to face, each willing the other's death. Danzas waved his hat: the signal.

Pushkin walked swiftly to the barrier, raised his arm and began to aim. D'Anthès, seeing him, did not wait until he reached the barrier but jerked his pistol into the air. A shot rang out—dry, dumb. The smoke cleared. Pushkin had collapsed onto the coat marking the barrier. His face lay in the snow. He did not move. The seconds rushed over. Then he raised his frizzled head and his face appeared, gray and damp, like a lump of clay.

"I think my thigh is shattered," he murmured.

Meanwhile, D'Anthès was turning to leave his position; Pushkin cried out hoarsely: "Wait! I feel strong enough to take my shot!"

D'Anthès returned to his place and stood, in profile, his right arm folded across his chest to protect his heart. Pushkin glared at him. That man was going to die by his hand. Now.

He had let go of his pistol when he fell, and it had sunk deep in the snow. Danzas held out another. The poet grasped it with a steady hand. Half prone, his weight on his left arm, he aimed. He aimed a long time. Two minutes, they say. Then he fired.

The ball struck D'Anthès in the right arm, went through it, sheered off one of his brass buttons and broke two ribs. The wound was superficial, but the violence of the blow knocked him off his feet. Seeing him fall, Pushkin threw his gun in the air and cried: "Bravo!"

But a red soup was soaking into the snow around his abdomen. Pushkin fainted twice. When he came to, he asked weakly: "Did I kill him?"

"No," D'Archiac answered, "but you hit him."

"Strange," Pushkin said; "I thought it would have given me pleasure to kill him, but I see that it would not. Anyway, it doesn't matter, once we have recovered we shall have to start all over again."[5]

Pushkin was losing blood. The clothing over his stomach was sticky and heavy. It would be dangerous to carry him as far as the sleigh. Danzas and D'Archiac called the drivers and, with their help, tore apart the fence so that the horses could get into the clearing. Then, all together, they lifted the poet and laid him in the sleigh. The horses set out at a walk, with Danzas alongside. The path was full of ruts, the injured man lurched from side to side, his features wincing in spasms of silent pain. D'Anthès and D'Archiac followed. It was already dark. The chilly wind raised clouds of snow. Near the "commander's house" stood a closed carriage, sent by Baron Heckeren—just in case. D'Anthès and D'Archiac offered it to Danzas to convey Pushkin home, and Danzas was careful not to let Pushkin know to whom the vehicle belonged. He installed the poet inside it and sat down next to him, holding his head, supporting his body. Slowly, the horses moved off.

In the darkness, Danzas scrutinized the wounded man anxiously, tenderly. The poet's face was pale, drenched in sweat. His features were distorted by the effort to hide his agony. At times he tried to smile and jest; then the ravening pain would burrow into his guts again, his cheeks would swell with retching; then, humbly, he complained. He remembered someone named Shcherbatov who had been fatally injured in the abdomen in a duel with Dorokhov.

"I'm afraid. Haven't I been hit in the same place as Shcherbatov?" he asked.

Then he spoke of his duel with Zubov in Kishinev. And he recited all the precautions that must be taken in order not to frighten Natalya, who did not know about the duel. He tried to dictate a few instructions and domestic arrangements. His voice strangled in his throat. His breathing grew short. He wanted to vomit. He fainted. When he regained consciousness, he struggled to keep talking. The lurching of the carriage was weakening him dangerously. Blood was streaming from his clothes. They had to stop several times. At last, the city lights eased into view behind the frost-starred windows. Sleigh bells rang out merrily around the carriage. They could hear people laughing and talking in the streets. It was nearly six o'clock when the team halted in front of Pushkin's home. The poet asked Danzas to go in first to warn his wife and send the servants to carry him in. Danzas followed his instructions. While the alarmed servants were rushing out to the carriage, Danzas went into the dining room where the table was already laid for supper. The peaceful scene, the everyday silver and china, suddenly destroyed his self-possession. He crossed the drawing room unannounced and went up to Natalya and Alexandra. Both women instantly knew that something dreadful had happened. Before he could open his mouth, Natalya cried out and ran into the hall.

Meanwhile, Pushkin's servants were awkwardly removing their master from the carriage. The poet's valet took him in his arms and began walking toward the house. Pushkin saw the entrance again, with its arches and columns and the eight marble steps leading up to his apartment door. He remembered how it looked when he left. In less than two hours, everything had become very different. He murmured to his valet: "You are sad to be carrying me, aren't you?"

The man's eyes were filled with tears. In the entrance hall, Natalya flung herself at her husband. Livid, ugly, her hair in disorder, she screamed, she called out his name. He ordered her to leave. She did not answer; she had fainted.

Danzas and the manservant carried Pushkin into his study, lighted the lamp, stretched him on the sofa and began to undress him. The bearskin, the fine coat, the trousers, underclothes—there was blood on everything. On the surface of the flat, muscular abdomen there was a little black hole ringed with clots and boiling with red liquid. The ball had entered two inches above the pelvis. The bone must be fractured, the intestine perforated. Pushkin was shivering from head to foot. But he managed to wash himself, put on clean underclothes and lie down more comfortably. His wife tapped at the door; he called out: "Don't come in!"

He did not want her to see his wound. He would not let her come near him until his toilette was finished.

Meanwhile, Danzas had gone off in search of a doctor. He could find neither Spassky, the family doctor, nor Arendt, Solomon or Parson, the most highly reputed physicians in the capital. Not knowing where to turn next, Danzas went, on Mrs. Parson's advice, to the Foundling Hospital, where he found a Dr. Scholtz, who, being a specialist in the delivery of babies, could not pretend to treat Pushkin, but who promised to bring someone else immediately. Danzas went back to the house. Pushkin was still lying on his sofa. Natalya, white-faced and horror-stricken, sat meekly, holding his hand. Pletnev was also there. At seven o'clock Dr. Scholtz entered the poet's study with Dr. Zadler, who had just finished bandaging D'Anthès. The moment he saw them, Pushkin asked his wife and friends to leave him alone with them.

He would not allow Natalya to watch while they probed the wound.

After inspecting it, Zadler left to fetch his instruments. Alone with Scholtz, Pushkin roughly asked: "What do you think of it? When the shot was fired I felt a violent blow in my side and a burning around the kidneys. On the way home, I lost a lot of blood. Tell me the truth, how do you find the wound?"

"I cannot conceal the fact that it is dangerous."

"Answer me: fatal?"

"Duty compels me not to hide it from you. But we should wait to hear the opinion of Arendt and Solomon, who have been sent for."

While Scholtz changed his compress, Pushkin gritted his teeth, rubbing his forehead with the back of his hand, and murmured: "Thank you for telling me the truth. I have some matters to attend to. It seems I am losing a lot of blood?"

"Wouldn't you like to see your friends?" Scholtz asked.

"Farewell, my friends," Pushkin said with a look at his books. "Do you think I have less than an hour to live?"

"Oh, no! That is not why I said it; I only thought it would be nice for you to see one of your friends; Mr. Pletnev is here."

"Yes, but I would have liked to see Zhukovsky," Pushkin fretted. "Give me some water. I feel sick."[6]

Scholtz took his pulse—feeble, fluttering—and went out to prepare a cool drink. Arendt, Solomon and Zadler soon appeared, followed shortly by Spassky, the family doctor.

"Well, it's bad," Pushkin said as he held out his hand.

More softly, he added: "I ask you not to hold out any false hopes to my wife; do not conceal the truth from her; she is no actress, you know her well enough; she must know everything. As for me, you can do whatever you like with me; I consent to everything, I am ready for anything."

In compliance with the wishes of Pushkin's friends and family, Spassky spoke of his duty as a Christian.

"Call in the first priest you see, the nearest one," Pushkin said.

Suddenly recalling that N. I. Grech had lost a son a few days before, the poet, himself ready to die, sadly added: "If you see Grech, give him my regards and tell him I share his grief sincerely."

At eight o'clock Dr. Arendt returned to examine the patient again. Immediately afterward, the priest arrived. A lot of water had gone under the bridge since Pushkin composed *The Gabriliad*. . . . "Woe to the country that has turned its back on Christianity!" he had written as early as 1830. And a short while before the duel, he had been telling Pletnev about his new mystical conviction. It was very vague, to be sure, very far from any dogma, religion or church; he simply believed in God.

He saw the necessity for man to accept God. And in his way, perhaps, he even prayed. The anonymous priest who had to receive his submission needed no more. Pushkin confessed and took communion.

When the priest had gone, Pushkin asked Spassky: "What is my wife doing?"

"She is somewhat calmer now."

"Poor woman; even though she is innocent, she is going to bear the brunt of public malevolence, perhaps for a long time to come."

Just then, Dr. Arendt appeared and announced that he would have to report the matter to the emperor. Pushkin asked him to beg Nicholas I not to prosecute Danzas: "Intercede for Danzas, he has been a brother to me!"

Arendt left, promising to return at eleven. On his way out he said to Danzas, who was accompanying him: "Nasty business: He will die."

One by one, Pushkin's friends arrived: Zhukovsky, Vyazemsky, Meshchersky, Turgenev, Valuyev. Pushkin heard them walking and talking in the next room. They were all on the other shore. With every beat of his heart he was moving farther away from them. It was not so terrible to die. But this pain in his stomach was driving him insane. Were there really no drugs they could give him to ease it? What a round dance of doctors around his bed! It was like a comic ballet. Exit one, enter the next. Always with spectacles, fingers smelling of chemicals and disenchanted mouths.

At midnight Dr. Arendt came again. He brought Pushkin a note scribbled in pencil by Nicholas I. Pushkin glanced at the message and handed it back to the doctor, for the emperor had given instructions that the paper was to be returned after he read it.* Arendt listened to his breathing, inspected the bandage and advised them to continue as before. At last he went, leaving Pushkin to the care of his colleagues.

The pain became sharper. From time to time, he fainted. The instant he regained consciousness, he raised his head, listened, stared avidly about on all sides. Natalya, exhausted by emotion and tears, tried to creep up to his bed. But he did not want her to see his face distorted by his battle with death. He cried out: "My wife is there! . . . Send her away! . . ."

Then, when the pain subsided, he called for her. She bent her beautiful, weary face toward him. He looked at her—the queen of the ball, without powder or rouge, her hair hanging loose. He even felt a little sorry for her. He murmured: "Don't worry. . . . You are innocent of my death. . . . It has nothing to do with anyone except me. . . ."

* A Mr. Andreyev wrote in his diary that the emperor's message was: "As a Christian I forgive you. As a monarch I shall help you. As a man I pity you." Nothing is less certain, however, and the contents of the note, which was never recovered, are not known.

And sent her away with a weary motion of his hand.

Spassky asked if he did not have "certain arrangements" to make; he asked the doctor to take a sheet of paper written in his hand from the drawer and burn it in his presence. He would not hear of a will: "Everything to my wife and children," he said.

Later, he dictated to Danzas a list of his debts of which he had no written record; and, removing a ring from his finger, offered it to him as a keepsake. Deeply moved, Danzas said he intended to avenge him by challenging D'Anthès.

"No, no! Peace! Peace!" Pushkin sighed.

What were they doing, coming to talk to him about revenge and D'Anthès and Heckeren? They were so small, those men, beside the night that was playing with his body like a long, long wave. The ebb and flow of death made him dizzy. The shadow caught him up and released him, accepted and rejected him, sucked him in and cast him away.

Around 3 A.M. on January 28, a painful swelling began to distend the right side of his abdomen. The doctors decided to administer an enema, but the attempt proved disastrous. Pushkin could not lie on his side. The sacrum had been shattered. The tumefied rectum was so sensitive that the slightest pressure made him scream. The enema had no effect. Spassky sent for Dr. Arendt, who came immediately but could offer no suggestions to relieve Pushkin's agony.

By 4 A.M. it had become unbearable.

"It was literal torture," Spassky wrote. "Pushkin's face was unrecognizable. His expression had become haggard, his eyes seemed to be trying to leap from their sockets, his forehead was covered with cold sweat, his hands were icy, his pulse imperceptible. The patient was suffering atrociously. He showed extraordinary courage. Wanting to scream, he scarcely moaned—fearing, as he said, that his wife would hear and be alarmed.

"'Why this torture?' he said. 'Without that, I would have died in peace.'"

In the end, however, the pain was too much for him. He began to howl like a flayed animal. Dreadful convulsions strung his body like a bow. He rolled from side to side. He slid onto the floor. They had to pick him up, lay him out again, pull the sheets around him, wash the froth off his lips and the sweat from his cheeks. His wife had dropped asleep like a stone in the drawing room, her head against the partition. She awoke, half drugged, at the sound of Pushkin screaming. Alexandra and Princess Vyazemsky calmed her by telling her the noise came from the street.

Meanwhile, Pushkin had exhausted his strength and his will; he rang for the footman and ordered him to bring one of the drawers of his desk.

The footman obeyed; but knowing that the poet's pistols were in the drawer, he ran to warn Danzas, who came rushing into the room. Pushkin had already hid them under the blankets, and relinquished them unwillingly. He was so eager for death; why were the doctors, why were his own friends tormenting him like this instead of letting him go? Didn't they see there was no hope? Didn't they see he had already ceased to exist, there was nothing left of him but a little flesh, a little blood, a little spirit, just enough to suffer?

The night was ending. The city began to jerk itself awake. Church bells rang in the distance. Here, in the overheated room smelling of sweat and drugs and human pain, Pushkin begged them to let him go.

At dawn, the pain subsided slightly.

"My wife, call my wife," Pushkin said.

Natalya sped into the room, fell upon Pushkin's bloodless body, her fingers kneading his thin limbs, covering his cold hands with kisses. She had to be removed by force.

"Do you want to see your friends?" Spassky asked.

"Call them."

One by one, Zhukovsky, Vyelgorsky, Vyazemsky, Turgenev, Danzas, Mrs. Karamzin came up to the dying man's bed. Pushkin looked up into their tired faces, their anguished smiles, their moist eyes. He told himself that they, anyway, still cared about him. He would live on in their hearts, at least. He held out his hand to them.

"Farewell! Be happy," he murmured.

Then he motioned them to go away, and, weeping, they turned aside.

After his friends, Pushkin wanted to see his children. Alexandra brought them in, one by one. They were still full of sleep, pink and fresh, their hair tousled, their lips soft. They didn't understand. Later, later . . . Pushkin blessed each of them three times, laid the back of his hand against their small, unpracticed mouths, and ordered them to be put back to bed. He would not see them grow up, he would not teach them, he would not be proud of their achievements, alarmed by their follies, happy in their joy, miserable in their grief. . . . From this day on, he would be a portrait for them, a name on the back of a book, a date, a statue. . . .

There was light in the sky behind the window. At the back of the room, Natalya cried out: "He won't die, I feel sure he won't die! Something tells me he will live."

Spassky took Pushkin's hand and listened to his pulse. When he had finished, Pushkin grasped his own right wrist in his left hand, closed his eyes and calmly said: "Death is coming."

At noon, Dr. Arendt examined him again and ordered a few drops of opium.

"My God! My God! What is it?" whined Pushkin, clenching his fists.

Then he grew calmer. He began to feel better, as the opium eased his pain-racked body. And then, Zhukovsky had assured him that the tsar would take care of Natalya and the children. Good. The future was already being organized, without him. . . . In Pushkin's wallet, there were seventy-five rubles.

Around 1 P.M. Dr. Dahl, one of Pushkin's friends, arrived.

"I am glad to see you, not only as a doctor but as a colleague in the profession of literature," Pushkin said, adding: "It's bad, my friend."

Dahl sat down at his bedside.

Meanwhile, at Pushkin's request, Princess Dolgorukov had gone to the Heckerens to convey the poet's pardon. Katerina ran to meet her, crying: "Georges is out of danger!"

The princess told them of Pushkin's agony and said that he forgave them for his suffering and his death. Katerina began to weep. D'Anthès laughed lightly: "Well, I forgive him too."[7]

The afternoon was quiet. Toward evening, however, his pulse began to race, it rose to 120. His temperature went up. He felt oppressed, anxious. Twenty-five leeches were applied to his abdomen. He caught them himself with a steady hand and stuck them onto his skin.

"That's fine! That's perfect!" he muttered.

Then his temperature fell, the swelling went down again, his pulse rate became more regular. Hope revived throughout the house. In amazement, Pushkin clutched Dahl's hand and asked:

"Dahl! Tell me the truth. Am I going to die soon now?"

"We still have hope, Pushkin," Dahl said.

"Thank you," Pushkin sighed with a childish smile.

But immediately afterward, he shook his head and murmured: "What a pity neither Pushchin nor Malinovsky could be here! It would have been easier for me to die."

Evening came upon the city again. In the closed room, Pushkin was still alive. He drank cold water held out to him in a teaspoon. Sadly, he watched the night descend, the lights spring up in the windows. The lamps in his study were lit. Huge shadows leaned into the walls. Books and papers stood guard around his deathbed. He still had so much to say. So many thoughts, so many melodies had been haunting his mind on the eve of the duel. And he was going to take them all away with him into his grave. An unfinished poem lay on the desk. How did it go, now?

I have ripened for eternity,
And the torrent of my days
Has slowed . . .

The rest? He would not write it. Too bad.

"No, there is no place for me here below," he said. "I shall die, it seems to be necessary."

He wrung Dahl's hand in his.

Everything in the house was asleep. High in the sky, some great silent battle of clouds must be taking place. The quays of the Neva were deserted. On Senate Square, the bronze horseman was wearing a hat of snow. The rigid sentinels stood freezing. Somewhere, people were dancing. But his only world now was this room. His only pleasure, these few drops of cool water to drink. Sometimes, too, he asked for a piece of ice, and gently rubbed his temples with it or sucked on it. He removed and replaced the compresses on his stomach himself. He said: "Perfect. . . . That's excellent. . . ."

In fact, his pain had not been so great in the last few hours. But there was a sort of anguish stifling him. He felt as though he were being sucked into a black vacuum. He was losing his foothold. He was falling. And he fell so slowly, so sadly. . . .

"So sad!" he suddenly cried, clutching his head in his hands. "My heart is torn. Hold me up. . . . Turn me. . . . That's it. . . . That's right. . . . Now it's perfect. . . . That's far enough. . . . Good. . . . Stop, no more. . . . Now pull my arm. . . ."

He was so feeble, so gentle, so docile. Like a child. Standing guard over his infant's slumber, Dahl—a strange nanny with steel-rimmed spectacles and unshaven cheeks.

"Who is with my wife?" Pushkin asked.

"Many good people are sharing your sufferings," Dahl replied. "The hall and entrance have been filled all day."

"Well; thank you. . . . Still: Go tell my wife that I am better; otherwise they would make her believe things . . . No . . . I mustn't make a noise. . . . My wife will hear. . . . It would be ridiculous if this stupid thing got the best of me. . . . I don't want . . ."

The minutes fell, one by one, like the spokes of a turning wheel. Dahl's cool hand. Now, behind the closed shutters, the sour little pallor of morning. Another day to live. January 29.

Pushkin called his wife.

"Try to be forgotten," he told her gravely. "Go live in the country. Stay in mourning for two years, then remarry, but choose somebody decent."

He was already so far away that he could think of his wife's marriage without emotion. He held out a little cross on a gold chain to Princess Vyazemsky, and asked her to give it to Alexandra. When it was handed to her, Alexandra turned scarlet and ran to her room. Perhaps it was a souvenir of her liaison with the poet; perhaps, by giving her this token, Pushkin meant to say he had truly loved her. Love. Death. Doctors.

There they were again, around his bed, anxious and black as vultures. They shook their heads. They mouthed Latin formulas. As he turned to go, Arendt announced that Pushkin did not have more than two hours to live.

The news of his tragic end had already spread through the city. A throng of worshipers, friends and inquisitive strangers filled the antechamber, the stairway, the street outside. One little old man told his neighbors: "Lord! I can remember the death of Field Marshal Kutuzov! They didn't make such a fuss over him!"

As the dying man's room was next to the entrance hall, the main door had been barred and callers entered through the service door and assembled in the pantry. Only close friends were allowed inside the apartment. Soon they had to send for guards from the Preobazhensky regiment to keep order. Pushkin heard the noise of the crowd, beating at the walls of his retreat:

"How is he?"

"What does he say?"

"What about his wife?"

"Has he forgiven her?"

"Is there any hope?"

At noon Pushkin demanded a mirror and stared at his reflection for a long time: the angular face, the pinched nostrils, the blue lips. Then he gave a vague, discouraged wave of his hand, bidding farewell to his human face, to the skin, hair, eyes, teeth that had been his. Slowly, he disengaged himself. Only his mind was still watching his benumbed carcass. Then he felt a sudden, curious whim, the whim of a pleasure-loving, greedy, capricious little boy: He wanted some blackberries in syrup.

"Call my wife, she can feed me."

Kneeling at his side, Natalya helped him to swallow a few spoonfuls of blackberries. He chewed them slowly, earnestly. That was good. It reminded him of his childhood, Arina Rodionovna, Zakharovo, the tall trees, the preserves stewing outdoors in big copper kettles. Natalya leaned her cheek against her husband's forehead. Pushkin stroked her hair with a heavy hand.

"Now . . . now. . . . It's nothing," he said; "everything has turned out for the best. . . ."

Natalya left the room transfigured. She cried: "You'll see, he will live!"

All that was left in the world for Pushkin was the taste of blackberries, the smell of medicine. When that taste, that smell had gone, he would be dead. Already, he was beginning to rock, gently, on vague currents.

Already, he was rising above the city of noise and lights. He gripped Dahl's hand. He gasped: "All right, then! Lift me! Come on! Higher! Higher! Come on!"

Then he smiled: "I was dreaming that you and I were climbing up those books, those shelves, very high, and I was growing dizzy."

He sank into the fog again. Then he came back: "Is that really you?"

"Yes, my friend."

"It's funny, I couldn't recognize you. . . . All right, then, let's go, please, but together. . . ."

And he took wing, along the rows of books, the printed letters, the rows of rhymes. Everything he had written. The food he was leaving to his race: *Eugene Onegin, The Bronze Horseman, The Queen of Spades, Poltava, The Prisoner of the Caucasus.* . . . Wonderful rhymes sang in his ears. Was it really he who had invented them, long ago, in another life?

Onegin had killed the poet. Onegin had killed Pushkin!

Dead! Where now the upheavals,
The valorous young thrust . . .

There were other lines too:

No, I shall not die entirely! And my soul,
My lyre will outlive ashes and the void. . . .
My name will ring throughout all Russia,
Every tribe of the land will call to me,
The proud descendant of the Slav, the Finn,
The savage Tungunz, and the Kalmuk of the steppe. . . .

And:

Arise, prophet! Listen, behold!
Grow tall and full with my will. . . .

He had done good work. He had had a good life. But so short. Why had they not let him finish? The tsar, the court, Benkendorf, the Neva, Natalya, D'Anthès, Heckeren, honor, letters, blood. The blood that was rising in his mouth, choking him.

"I'm choking . . ."

A bitter hiccup unclenched his lips: "Close the shutters. . . . I want to sleep. . . ."

The old clock struck two. He opened his eyes again. Dahl and Spassky turned him onto his right side and placed a cushion behind his back.

"That's fine," he said.

He sighed deeply and added: "Life is over."

"Yes, it's over, we've finished turning you," said Dahl, who had not understood his words.

"I said life was over," Pushkin slowly explained. "I can't breathe . . . something is crushing me . . ."

His friends leaned over him. Zhukovsky, Dahl, Spassky, Vyelgorsky, Princess Vyazemsky, others. Pushkin stretched, relaxed. His breathing became regular. He was pale and cold.

He was turning out to sea.

Suddenly Dahl stood up and whispered: "Amen."

It was 2:45 P.M.

Pushkin died so quietly that no one but Dahl had seen him breathe his last.

A light hand closed the poet's eyes. The face was nothing now but a white wax object. The lips were creased in a sad smile. The women cried. The men lowered their heads.

Princess Vyazemsky went to Natalya. When she saw her, Natalya cried out: "Pushkin is dead? Tell me, tell me the truth! Is he dead? Is it all over?"

The princess nodded.

Natalya began to scream like a madwoman: "Poor Pushkin! Poor Pushkin! It's too horrible! No! No! It isn't true! I'll go to him!"

She rushed into the room, pushed the doctors aside, collapsed across the body, caressing, embracing, shaking it, calling out Pushkin's name. Her eyes were dry. Sobs split her breast. Violent convulsions snapped her spine.

"Pushkin, you're alive, you're alive! Forgive me, forgive me!" she kept crying.

She had to be carried to her room. She called for Danzas and fell to the floor at his feet. She thanked him. She said she was sorry. She kissed his hands. After Danzas left, Dr. Dahl came; she clutched at his sleeve and poured out, all in one breath: "I killed my husband. I am responsible for his death. But I swear before God that I am pure in heart and spirit."

She was delirious for hours, wrenched by terrible contractions that pulled her feet up to her neck. The doctors feared for her reason. Now it was her turn to suffer.

Back in the room with closed shutters, Pushkin, tiny and dry, lay between the walls of books. Zhukovsky came to sit beside him. He could not take his eyes from that pure, triumphant, pacified corpse, those hands abandoned after all their work and agitation, those lips closed after all their words, that forehead, smooth, hard and empty after all those thoughts. "His head was inclined slightly to one side," he wrote; "his hands, which had been twitching in nervous spasms a few minutes before, were relaxed, as though resting from some enormous labor. But I could not say in words what I felt looking at his face. He seemed to me at once so familiar and so new. His expression was not like sleep or rest. It did not show intelligence, as before; or even poetic exaltation. No; some profound, blinding idea had spread over his features, like the sign of a vision, some mysterious, perfect knowledge. Looking at him, I wanted to ask, 'What do you see, my friend?' And what would he have told me, if he could have come back to life in that moment? . . . Never had I seen on his face the expression of a thought so grave, so dignified, so victorious. . . ."

Dr. Dahl performed a rapid autopsy: "In the autopsy," he wrote, "I found the intestine highly inflamed over a surface the size of a half kopeck; the small intestine was affected by gangrene. That is probably where the ball entered. In the abdominal cavity there was not less than one pound of black, coagulated blood, presumably from the perforated femoral vein. On the right iliac crest, numerous small fragments of bone were found, and the top and lower part of the sacrum were completely shattered. From the course of the ball, it would appear that the injured man must have been turned somewhat to one side and that the shot was fired from above. The ball traversed the abdominal integument two inches above the right spina iliaca anterior superior, passed along the surface moving downward, and, upon encountering the resistance of the sacrum, fractured it and lodged nearby."

The friends washed the body, combed the poet's hair and dressed him for the vigil. They put on the "lucky" coat Nashchokin had lent him on that bright Easter seven years before, when he became engaged to Natalya. The secret police duly notified the emperor that Pushkin had been clothed in civilian dress, not in his official uniform of gentleman of the chamber. The emperor was vexed by this offense against etiquette perpetrated by a cadaver. He said, "That must have been one of Turgenev's or Prince Vyazemsky's bright ideas."

As a souvenir, his friends divided the seventy-five rubles in the poet's wallet. Then they picked up the little marionette's body—how light it had grown—and laid it on a table in the entrance hall. Following the emperor's orders, Zhukovsky sealed the study door with black wax. At 5 P.M. Halberg, the sculptor, molded a death mask. At 8 P.M. the first funeral mass was sung. In came the priests; flames blinked around the immortal profile, clouds of incense enveloped it, solemn voices commended it to God.

Natalya could be heard sobbing in the next room.

The first night, Danzas sat up with the body. Arrested after the duel, he had been allowed as a special favor to remain with Pushkin until the funeral.

The coffining took place the next morning. "I was holding his calves," Rossetti said, "thinking of his wiry, muscular frame, the long walks he used to force himself to take to build up his strength."

The coffin was lined with purple velvet; it sat in the center of the entrance hall on a dais two steps high, covered with a black cloth bordered in silver. The room was low-ceilinged, the walls ocher, the floor daubed with brown paint. The curtains were drawn. Sheets were hung over a mirror, a painting. In one corner squatted a fat buffet filled with china—smug, bourgeois, incongruous.

The corpse lay in its narrow boat, half-covered by a worn, gilded, green-tinged pall, holding a cracked ikon in its hands.

The head, slightly sunken between the shoulders, hardly made a dent in the big, ruffled pillow. A few tapers stuck into old candlesticks tied with crepe threw a ruddy, dancing glow on the last face of Alexander Sergeyevich Pushkin. Thick blue veins protruded at his temples. His heavy lips had frozen in a grimace of smiling scorn. His leaden eyelids had sunk into their sockets. His agony had hollowed his cheeks, pinched his nostrils, modeled his brow. Lying there, he looked as though he were floating, rudderless, downstream.

By the catafalque stood a footman in blue livery and brass buttons. From time to time, he sprinkled cologne over the dead man's face. It was hot. Servants were packing silver dishes into a chest. Crouching on a trunk, a painter sketched the poet's profile. And the silent, powerful crowd besieged the house.

A strange crowd, a strange public. Pushkin had never known it. He did not know what faces bent over his books from end to end of huge Russia. He said, "My readers . . ." He never saw them. Suddenly—the instant the beautiful voice that had sung to their loneliness and sorrow was stilled—they began emerging. They came forth and walked toward the silence, the absence that marked Pushkin's place. They came all the way to this hall. Fearfully, they looked down at their loss: a little man in a brown coat with bushy side whiskers. Oh, how he would have loved that crowd if he could have seen it. Not one hoary minister, not one effeminate aristocrat, not one diaphanous sophisticate, not one diplomat in squeaking pumps. People. Women in head scarves, old men with war medals, dazed children, gaunt students, common people in sheepskin jackets, bearded coachmen, paunchy merchants, soulful girls . . . Several thousand, at least. They rose from the paving stones of the capital. They swelled like a muttering tide, rising toward the house. Strangers: weeping, talking of killing D'Anthès "the assassin" and lynching "the bad surgeons." Two constables in tricornes stood guard in front of the house.

The main door of the apartment was still barred. The crowd came and went through the narrow, low service entrance, across which "Pushkin" had been scrawled in charcoal.

In the doorway, the pilgrims were met by a suffocating wave of heat and smells. Tapers, incense, cologne, medicine, sweat. The candle flames flickered. Masses of faces slid along the coffin. Lips stretched out toward the dead man's hands. One old man sobbed.

"You knew Pushkin personally, no doubt?" Prince Vyazemsky asked.

"No; but I am Russian," was the answer.

High society, however, pointedly shunned the poet in favor of the horse guardsman. The Netherlands embassy was thronged with distinguished visitors. A long line of carriages stretched before the residence. Count and Countess Nesselrode, Count and Countess Stroganov had become permanent fixtures in the Heckeren drawing room. There were expressions of compassion for poor, sweet Katerina, so sorely tried in the first days of her marriage, and of felicitation for D'Anthès, who had freed Russia of a notorious liberal.

"If anything can relieve my unhappiness," wrote Baron Heckeren senior, "it is the marks of concern I am receiving from the entire society of St. Petersburg."[8]

He also wrote:

"I am bound to say that public opinion expressed itself far more strongly than was expected on the occasion of Mr. Pushkin's death. However, it must be made clear that this opinion was not that of the upper class, which acknowledged that no reproach could be leveled against my son in this tragic circumstance; his behavior was in all respects that of a man of honor, showing more consideration, even, than is usual at his age, and than he would himself have shown, no doubt, in any other circumstance.

"The opinion to which I refer is that of the *third estate,* if that name can be given to the class in Russia which is intermediary between the nobility and senior officials and the mass of the population, who are totally unaffected by an event beyond their apprehension. It is composed of men of letters, artists, lesser civil servants, the merchant class, etc. Mr. Pushkin's death has revealed, or so the authorities seem to believe, the existence of a party of which he was the leader, perhaps only by virtue of his eminently Russian talent."[9]

Benkendorf was not expecting the wave of indignation that followed Pushkin's death.

"Good riddance," said Grand Duke Michael when he heard the news.

Not everyone, as it turned out, agreed with him. Zhukovsky and Count Orlov received anonymous letters demanding that the Heckerens be severely punished and their victim given a state burial.

"Your Excellency," one of them read, "in the name of your fatherland, in the name of the peace and prosperity of the empire, we ask you to explain to His Majesty that it is essential for him to bow to the common will; the advantages of adopting this attitude would be incalculable. Otherwise, we shall pay dearly for this affront to the people, and soon."

Informed of these ominous murmurs, Nicholas I overreacted. In an order to Benkendorf, he wrote: "Like you, I judge the matter worthy of attention; try to find out the author, and his trial will be brief."[10]

Was it so serious, then, to kill a poet? No; but there were politics in it: Pushkin was a force to be reckoned with, even in his grave. His eloquence had inflamed the multitude. Russia was delirious. Now, the police would have to make war on a ghost. It must be made illegal to mention his name, admire his poetry, muse over his books. They would have to launch a campaign—against tearful maidens, exalted students, flowers pressed between the pages of books, multicolored albums, hearts pierced by arrows, poetry, solitude, moonlight and breezes.

For a start, Benkendorf banned the first performance of *The Covetous Knight* and ordered the censors to suppress all obituary notices. By some miracle, one publication, and one only, managed to pay tribute to Pushkin: In its issue of January 30, 1837, the *Literary Supplement* of *The Russian Invalid* printed a notice framed in black and signed Kraevsky: "The sun of our poetry has set. Pushkin is dead, dead in his prime, in the prime of his magnificent career! We have no strength to say more; and besides, to what purpose? Every Russian heart knows the meaning of this irremediable loss, every Russian heart is rent by it. Pushkin! Our poet, our joy, the glory of our people! Is it really possible that we have no more Pushkin? We cannot accept the idea."

The next day Kraevsky was summoned by Prince Dundukov, chairman of the board of censors.

"I must inform you," that worthy said, "that the minister [Uvarov] is very, very displeased with you. What is the meaning of this article about Pushkin? What is this black border around the obituary of a man who had no official rank and no administrative position? Well; never mind that. But such words! 'The sun of our poetry!' Pray, why this honor? 'Pushkin died in the prime of his magnificent career!' What career? Sergey Semyonovich [Uvarov] very rightly said, 'Was Pushkin a general, a military chief, a minister, a statesman?' He died before he was forty. As Sergey Semyonovich pointed out, writing verse does not constitute a magnificent career. The minister has instructed me to admonish you severely and remind you that as an official of the ministry of education you must refrain from such effusions."

Minister Uvarov himself directed the administrator of the district of Moscow to see that the tone of all obituary notices was kept as moderate as possible. In St. Petersburg, Uvarov forbade university professors and students to leave their classes for the funeral.

The police were instructed to destroy all copies of a new portrait of Pushkin, edged in black and captioned, "The fire has gone out on the altar."

Despite these drastic measures, Pushkin's works were selling like hotcakes in Smirdin's bookshop. The latest edition of *Eugene Onegin* immediately became impossible to find. The shop took in the incredible sum of forty thousand rubles in two days.

Benkendorf did not like it. Hitherto, the Russian people had never wept or rejoiced except on order from the tsar. And here they were taking an initiative. Weeping without having been told to do so. Venturing to express their own opinion. It smelled of revolt. What would it be like on the day of the funeral?

Benkendorf's exact views on the subject were stated a few months later, in his *Report on Police Activities in 1837*: "At the beginning of the year," it says, "our celebrated poet Pushkin died of an injury received in a duel. Pushkin had a double personality: He was a great poet and a great liberal, the enemy of all authority. Despite the fact that he was shown every mark of favor and assistance by the emperor, he did not amend his ways, and only in the last years of his life did he consent to moderate the tone of his public pronouncements. These two sides of Pushkin's character determined the identity of his advocates. They formed a circle, composed of all the literary figures and liberals in society. Both groups reacted keenly, energetically to Pushkin's death; there was a remarkable congregation of mourners around his body; there was a move to give him a state burial; many people planned to follow the convoy to his place of burial in the government of Pskov; in Pskov, some are known to have attempted to unharness the horses and pull the wagon themselves. . . . It was difficult to decide whether these gestures were intended to honor Pushkin the liberal or Pushkin the poet. In this uncertainty, and taking into consideration the view of many right-minded people, i.e. that there was a danger that this so-called 'popular' expression of the grief of the crowd upon the poet's death might develop into a deplorable spectacle of triumph for the liberals, the executive office considered itself bound to adopt secret measures to suppress all honors. This was done."

Count Stroganov volunteered to pay for the funeral. Why he? No one knows. It was Stroganov who advised Heckeren to challenge Pushkin; he was indirectly responsible for his death. But he was also very rich, and Pushkin died leaving seventy-five rubles. So much for Stroganov. Announcements were sent out, in French and Russian, to friends and enemies, ministerial, military and diplomatic:

"Mrs. N. Pushkin, announcing with profound grief the death of her husband Alexander Pushkin, gentleman of the chamber of H.I.M., on the twenty-ninth of this month, requests the honor of your presence at the funeral service to be celebrated in the Cathedral of St. Isaac at the Admiralty, at 11 A.M. on February 1."

Stroganov asked the archbishop to officiate. The archbishop refused. They had to settle for three archimandrites. The body was to be transported from the house to the cathedral in the afternoon of January 31—but the police were worried by the size of the crowd, so the authorities ordered the coffin to be removed, not to St. Isaac's, but to a church on Stable Street, and at midnight, thus hoping to separate the people from their idol. On the evening of January 31, a few of the poet's close friends were sitting up with the body before it left home for the last time. Natalya, exhausted and half sick, was dozing fitfully in her room. Zhukovsky, Turgenev, Rossetti and Vyazemsky sat talking in undertones. Suddenly, the sound of boots, muffled commands. Guards were being stationed in the street. Police stumped up the stairs. General Dubelt appeared, with an escort of twenty officers, to remove the body. The poet's companions stood blankly by, aghast at this uniformed intrusion into a chamber of death. Again, Pushkin found himself confronting the braided officials of the regime; and again, he had to yield.

Without torches, in silence, like felons, the poet's "adepts" followed his mortal remains to the church. The police marched alongside, watching. The faithful lowered their heads in shame—not for themselves, but for Benkendorf and the tsar, for Russia.

"Against whom was this vast force, this machinery of war, being marshaled?" Vyazemsky wrote to Grand Duke Michael. "What could anyone fear of us? What intention, what ulterior motive could we have been imagined to possess, without taxing us with insanity or total knavery?"[11]

On February 1 many of the people who had received invitations went to St. Isaac's only to be met by closed doors. Meanwhile, the service was being held in the Stable Street church, witnessed only by persons in uniform or holding specially issued tickets. The little church was filled to overflowing with an apathetic crowd of epaulets, decorations, spurs and sabers, lorgnettes, high headdresses and white gloves. Courtiers, generals, ambassadors, princesses. Count Ficquelmont was there, and De Barante, the French ambassador—the only one who had seen fit to pay his respects to Pushkin in his coffin—and the hideous, livid Uvarov, squirming from the pricks of indigestion or conscience, and Count Orlov, Prince Trubetskoy, Count Stroganov, Sukhozanet, Adlerberg, Shypov . . . Among those absent were the ambassadors of England and Greece—diplomatically ill, perhaps; Baron Heckeren, who had not been invited; and Liebermann, the Prussian ambassador, who would have considered it degrading to attend the funeral of a "liberal."

The poet lay in his coffin in the midst of his enemies. They pressed in around him. They were all rejoicing in his downfall, but they were polite, so they crossed themselves, knelt and rose with deep sighs.

The dead man's appearance had altered. A blackish liquid had congealed at the corners of his mouth. His forehead seemed huge, taut, swollen to bursting point by some new thought. The light from the tapers danced in his close-curling hair. The mass was long and high. At last, the choir chanted: "Come, brethren, give the deceased your final kiss." Under cover of the rite of the last farewell, the inquisitive crowd surged toward the corpse. Souvenir hunters surreptitiously snipped locks of hair, pulled off buttons, tore away a fragment of coat.

Meanwhile, Pushkin's true friends, the people, the "third estate," were waiting for him in the square outside. They had been misinformed about the time and place of the mass. The temple doors had been closed to them. So they crowded together outside, quietly, patiently waiting to catch a last glimpse of the pallor of the face, a hand; then they could go, the memory rooted within them for the rest of their days.

The minutes passed. Silent and composed, the crowd prayed in its own fashion. At last, uniforms began bustling about on the steps of the church. A few black-clad footmen appeared. Behind them came the coffin. Friends and fellow authors carried Pushkin's body into an adjoining courtyard and lowered it into the burial vault, where it was to remain until leaving for Pskov. In the vault, a few ladies sat up with it that night, sniffling and exchanging sentimental reminiscences.

Natalya did not feel strong enough to undergo the ordeal of a voyage, and asked the emperor to let Danzas escort the body to its final resting place. Nicholas replied that he had already made an exception for Danzas, who was under arrest, by allowing him to remain at liberty so long, and he could not extend the privilege without breaking the law. He instructed Pushkin's old friend Turgenev to accompany the coffin—that same Turgenev who, twenty-five years earlier, had taken Pushkin for his first visit to the school at Tsarskoye Selo.

"On February 2," Turgenev wrote in his diary, "I decided to accept. I went to mass, where Count Stroganov presented me with a police officer. . . . I was not told our destination. Pushkin was nailed into his box. Vyazemsky [and Zhukovsky] put their gloves inside the coffin."

This odd act aroused the suspicions of the police. Why had these two men placed their gloves in the coffin? It must be some republican ritual, some treachery to the government! There would be no peace until that Pushkin was under a few feet of good, black earth. If only nothing happened on the trip. Benkendorf had stage-managed the proceedings with maniacal attention to detail. Everything was to take place at night. In secret. With police guards. A revolution can be ignited so quickly.

At midnight on February 3 three mysterious troikas drew up in front of the church. A police officer climbed into the first. The coffin, tied with stout rope and stout straps and covered with a tarpaulin, went into the second, along with Nikita Kozlov, Pushkin's old servant who had been with him from childhood and had followed him into exile; he crouched beside the coffin and never moved, despite snow, wind and cold, until the journey's end. Why the devil had that Frenchman killed his master?

Lastly, the portly Turgenev, representing Pushkin's family and friends, hoisted himself into the third troika.

The convoy set out in single file, the policeman in front, Turgenev behind, Pushkin in the middle. The night was cold and misty. The moon swam above a bluish, red-tinged froth of cloud. The snow gleamed. The horses galloped steadily, bearing their noble burden across the Russian plains. Eighty versts in one night. Police were posted at every station. They stood guard over the coffin while fresh horses were harnessed—torches, chilled hands, busy faces, icicle-hung mustaches, papers, stamps and seals, military salutes—an affair of state it was!

"My wife was on her way back from Mogilev," wrote Nikitenko, "and at one of the posting stations near St. Petersburg she saw an ordinary sleigh filled with straw. Under the straw was a coffin wrapped in a tarpaulin. Three policemen were bustling about the yard, shouting for fresh horses immediately, they had to get back on the road with their coffin.

" 'What is it?' my wife asked a peasant.

" 'God alone knows! It seems somebody named Pushkin has been killed, and now they're taking him away in a sledge as fast as they can, under a heap of straw, rolled up in a piece of canvas like a dog.' "

On they went, from station to station, policemen to policemen.

While Pushkin's body was being whisked away on this fantastic night ride, the querulous Pavlishchev, who did not know he was dead, was writing his last letter to the poet: "I knew you had no idea about managing property and that is why I could not believe you could try to falsify the accounts. . . . At whose expense? Your sister's? . . . You don't want to keep the property, God alone knows how you interpret my words. . . . I did not expect a refusal. . . . What am I to do now? . . ."

The body reached Pskov at 9 P.M. on February 4, just as Yakhontov, a chamberlain, arrived bearing a letter to the governor: "It is the will of His Majesty the Emperor that you forbid all special events, all receptions, in short, all ceremonies other than those normally performed in connection with the funeral of a gentleman, as dictated by the rites and customs of our religion. I should add that the funeral has already taken place here.

"Mordvinov. St. Petersburg, February 2, 1837."

The governor showed Turgenev this letter in confidence. At 1 A.M. the convoy set out again, bound for Trigorskoye by way of Ostrov; it arrived at three the following afternoon. The sledge bearing the coffin and Nikita Kozlov, escorted by a mounted constable, went on to Holy Mountain monastery. Mrs. Wulf-Osipov sent her peasants to dig the grave. Turgenev and his officer remained at Trigorskoye.

"We had tea," Turgenev wrote. "I put my officer to bed and sat up with the delightful ladies of the house, thinking about Pushkin and talking about Pushkin. I read their album, containing verses by him, Yazykov and others. I found some unpublished Pushkin. I was charmed by the daughter [Marya], we became friends."

In this warm, low house, the cult of Pushkin was still alive. Turgenev was introduced to the little long-handled silver jug in which Zizi used to make djonka for Pushkin, Yazykov and Wulf; the big table around which they all used to gather; the armchair in which Pushkin sat in front of the frost-covered window; the painting of the temptation of St. Anthony; the books he had handled. Sitting before the steaming samovar in the friendly old snowbound house, Turgenev, Mrs. Osipov and Marya recited their litany of the memories Pushkin had left them. They communed so completely with his thought, they loved him so fervently, that they would not have been surprised to see the door spring open and Pushkin himself come flying through it, radiant and laughing, with a red nose and chapped lips and snow on the tips of his boots.

But he did not come. He was dead. And death did not become him.

At six o'clock the following morning Turgenev and his policeman went to the monastery. They slipped on the ice-coated steps. A few vigil lights flickered behind the grilled chapel windows. A wretched little fire burned in the garden. The muzhiks were finishing the grave: a narrow slot, surrounded by rock-hard, root-filled clumps of earth. The priest raced through the mass, mumbling into his beard. Then Nikita Kozlov and the peasants from Mikhailovskoye lowered the coffin into the grave. They were crying. The red ball of the sun clambered up into a milky sky. Crosses on the monastery roof sparkled pink in its rays. The snow turned soft, sugary. Frail bells rang.

"I threw a handful of dirt into the grave," Turgenev wrote, "shed a few tears, and went back to Trigorskoye."

Pushkin was buried beside his mother and his maternal grandfather and grandmother Hannibal.

After the interment, Turgenev and Marya made a pilgrimage to Mikhailovskoye. The broad, white road was lined by tall trees vitrified in patterns of lace. The house sat humpbacked beneath the snow. Sniffling, the caretaker opened the poet's old room. A card table still stood by the window, and on it a china inkwell, a gnawed quill, a few books. In another room, the billiard table. How many tedious hours Pushkin had spent there, pushing the balls around and yawning. The cover was worn. It was cold in the room, damp ran down the walls. Turgenev and Marya shivered.

"Everything was empty. The caretaker and his wife were crying," Turgenev wrote.

He left the same day.

Pushkin stayed alone, in the earth. Snow was falling. The wind was howling. Monks scuttled along in the shadows. Hares bounded across the road. All the bad omens. But it no longer mattered.

Appendices

POST MORTEM

After Pushkin's death, Zhukovsky went to the emperor and asked him to assist the poet's destitute family. "For myself, Sire," he said, "I would request the same favor you granted me after Karamzin's death: Allow me, as on that occasion, to write a public decree embodying whatever measures you deign to adopt on Pushkin's behalf."

The emperor shrugged: "You must see that I am doing all I can for Pushkin and his family," he retorted, "and I agree to do whatever is necessary; but there is one matter on which I do not agree with you, namely, that you should write a manifesto as you did for Karamzin. There is a difference, after all. It was only with great difficulty, you know, that we brought him to die a Christian death, whereas Karamzin died like an angel."

To Dashkov, Nicholas was even more outspoken: "What an imbecile that Zhukovsky is! He wants me to give Pushkin's family the same pension as the Karamzins, and refuses to consider the fact that Karamzin was almost a saint, but what was Pushkin's life?"

Nevertheless, after refusing all official expressions of mourning for Pushkin's death, Nicholas I wrote out in his own hand the measures to be taken to assist his family, all of which had been requested by Zhukovsky:

"1. Pay his debts;

"2. Pay the mortgage on the father's estate;

"3. A pension to the widow and daughters until their marriage;

"4. The sons to enter the page corps, and 1500 rubles to outfit each when they enter the service;

"5. The works to be published by the state; profits to the widow and children;

"6. An immediate grant of 10,000 rubles."

Lastly, having instructed Zhukovsky to open Pushkin's study and go through his papers, the emperor approved the following additional provisions:

"1. Any papers which might be prejudicial to Pushkin's memory, to be destroyed;

"2. Letters to him from other persons, to be returned to their authors;

"3. Pushkin's own writings, together with those submitted to him for publication in *The Contemporary* and similar papers, to be preserved after cataloguing;

"4. Documents withdrawn from the State Archives and other official papers, to be returned to their rightful places."

When the Russian public learned of these generous provisions, they praised the ruler's delicacy and literary discrimination; but in reality, Nicholas I was only subsidizing Pushkin's family. He refused to honor a great national poet mourned throughout the country. He was not paying tribute to genius; he was giving alms to a poor widow and children.

On February 4 Nicholas wrote to Paskevich: "All is quiet here, and Pushkin's death alone has excited the public and stirred up all kinds of silly gossip. He died of a wound received in a duel resulting from an insolent and stupid provocation he had written himself. God be praised, he died a Christian."

"In Pushkin's loss I mourn only the author struck down in the full force of his talent; as a man, he was a worthless lot," Paskevich replied.

Nicholas I returned the observation: "I share your opinion of Pushkin entirely, and it may truly be said that we are mourning his future and not his past."

Bulgarin was jubilant: "Let us mourn the poet, and profoundly, but what a nasty beggar he was! He aped Byron and was shot down like a rabbit. His wife is utterly innocent. You knew what the man looked like. Could anybody love him when he was drunk?"[1]

Eugenius, the metropolitan himself, wrote on February 15: "And now the poet Pushkin has been killed in a duel. He was a good poet, but a bad son, a bad parent, a bad citizen."

Nicholas I and Benkendorf were even more suspicious of the bad son, bad parent and bad citizen now that he was in his grave. They instructed Zhukovsky to go through his papers; but they sent Police General Dubelt to oversee the work and make sure that the imperial instructions were faithfully executed. In addition, Zhukovsky was required to submit every single document and letter he found in Pushkin's study to Benkendorf before destroying it or returning it to its author. Zhukovsky was aghast. To examine these relics in the presence of a constable, to hand over the compromising remarks of Pushkin's friends —who were also his friends—to the police, to open up the poet's past to the eyes of the authorities: Why, that was spy's work! Nevertheless, the unhappy courtier had no choice but to submit to this supreme humiliation. "I must confess," he wrote to the emperor, "that my position was most painful. Of course I did not read any letters myself; I simply handed them to my collaborator, General Dubelt. But even so, it was painful for me to be an accomplice in this violation of privacy; letters from my own friends were opened before my eyes; I had to sit by and watch, fearing that those missives, written in the distant past at different periods of their authors' lives and in widely differing circumstances by people who were still alive, might, when placed side by side, lend themselves to a false interpretation of their authors' intentions. . . ."

If nothing else, this experience allowed Zhukovsky to understand at last the fatal role played by the government in the poet's undoing. He was horror-stricken to learn how implacable the emperor and Benkendorf had been. He had ordered Pushkin to resign himself to police surveillance, he had taken offense at the poet's slightest protest, he had called him "ungrateful" and "an imbecile" in his letters; now, he felt compelled to protest to Benkendorf himself, in the name of the most elementary sense of art and humanity. In a fine surge of bravery, Zhukovsky wrote a letter to the chief of police. He read it to Turgenev—and it became Turgenev's turn to advise him not to send it; at least, not then. Was it ever sent? The text is worth quoting:

"I have read all the letters Pushkin received from Your Excellency. They are all, I must say, inspired by a generous impulse. But my heart quailed when I read them. During the twelve years since the day the emperor so generously took Pushkin under his protection, the official attitude toward him never changed. In your eyes, he remained a sort of turbulent youth to whom one did not dare give any freedom, who had to be subjected to constant, agonizing surveillance. He wrote *Godunov, Poltava,* his *Odes to the slanderers of Russia* and on *The capture of Warsaw*; in other words, he did his best to prove his loyalty to the regime, but in judging him the authorities referred only to *Liberty* and *The Dagger,* which were written in 1820. In the Pushkin of thirty-six, they persisted in seeing the Pushkin of twenty-two. . . . From your position, you could not follow the transformation of his soul. But think for one moment how you would have felt, to find yourself caught in such a web in the middle of your life, to see your every action interpreted a priori, to be unable even to travel without exciting suspicion or calling forth rebuke. In your letters Pushkin was censured for going to Moscow, for taking a trip to Arzerum. What crime was there in that? Pushkin wanted to live in the country, to devote himself entirely to his writing; but he was not allowed to go, ostensibly because of his service, but in reality because he was not trusted. In what did his service consist? Solely on the fact that he was attached to the foreign ministry. What had he to do with a ministry? Pushkin's service was in his pen, his *Peter the Great,* his poems, his works that could have illustrated our glorious age. Service of this nature requires freedom and seclusion. What peace of mind could he have, with his bruised and ardent spirit and his domestic and financial problems, in a world in which nothing was ever kind to him, in which his pride was continually being injured by trivial incidents, in which he was ultimately destroyed by thousands of contemptible tales of pure malice to which he could make no reply? His Imperial Majesty set himself up as his censor. A supreme mark of favor, particularly precious as a proof of the sovereign's personal benevolence toward the poet. But I will frankly say that this favor put Pushkin in an extremely difficult position. Could he bother the emperor with every scrap of nonsense written for some review? To many of the emperor's remarks he had no possibility of giving an answer or explanation, for it was not the sovereign's business to hear it. . . . What then was Pushkin's real situation, under the weight of such restrictions? Was it not inevitable, with the intensity of feeling which was his by birth and without which he could never have become a poet, that he should give way to despair when he saw that neither time nor the change in his thinking could remove the shroud of prejudice that had fallen upon him forever, apparently annihilating all his chances for the future? I would make one final point: Pushkin was deprived of the joy of seeing Europe, which was essential to him as a writer. He sensed that Europe was forbidden to him, that he was not trusted. . . . But to fear that travel may be dangerous to a Russian only shows a great lack of trust in Russia. . . . Now you call him a demagogical writer; for which of his works have you bestowed this title upon him? The old or the new? And which works of his do you know, other than those brought to your attention by your agents and a few slanderous enemies? . . . He is a great national poet who, in his finest verse, expresses everything dearest to the Russian soul with rare felicity. With regard to his political opinions, I shall ask Your Excellency another question: Did you ever take the trouble to discuss any political subject with him? . . . Permit me to tell you what I think, in all honesty. By giving Pushkin his special protection, the emperor hoped to moderate his fervor and give his genius the freedom to develop fully; but you transformed that protection into surveillance, and surveillance, however discreet and well-meant, is torture."

Zhukovsky was not the only one to protest. All true lovers of literature condemned the government for allowing the duel to take place when the authorities had known both when and where it was to happen; for refusing the official honors to which Pushkin was entitled; for preventing the multitude from expressing their grief at his death; for smuggling his body away at night under police guard; and for treating Russia's greatest poet like a dangerous brigand to be buried in secret ignominy. On

January 28 and 29, while Pushkin was breathing his last, a new poet, the young ensign Lermontov, sat composing an anathema against society with tears in his eyes and rage in his breast. This poem was *On the Death of Pushkin*, and it earned him the enmity of Benkendorf, and exile:

You whose eager flock surrounds the throne,
You, the slayers of genius and freedom,
You hide in the shadow of the law;
But justice and truth, for you, are dead letters! . . .*

Ogarev, another writer, circulated a poem *To the Poet's Memory*:

His assassin? Still running free!
Proud and handsome and full of health.
Lightly he struts about,
And the whole sinister clique
Of scandalmongers of fashion
Thrives too. There is no revenge. . . .

A host of poems sprang out of nowhere, clandestine, anonymous, faltering or superb, by Polezhaev, Tyuchev, Guber, schoolboys, strangers. . . .

In Moscow, a boy of sixteen named Fyodor Mikhailovich Dostoevsky announced that he was going into mourning, as though Pushkin had been a member of his family.

From Italy, Gogol wrote to Pletnev: "No worse news could have come to me from Russia. With him goes the greatest joy of my life."

The young critic Belinsky said, in a letter dated February 4, 1837: "Poor Pushkin! What an end to his career! Lensky's death in *Onegin* was all too prophetic. . . . There was only one true poet in Russia, and even he was not allowed to finish his work. All his life he was misunderstood. Will he be seen more clearly now?"

Küchelbecker contributed a few ponderous lines, and Pushchin cried out from the oblivion of his exile: "I think that if this deplorable thing had happened in my presence and I had been in Danzas' place, the fatal ball would have entered my own breast."

Another old schoolmate, Matyushkin, wrote from Sebastopol on February 14: "Pushkin killed! Yakovlev, how could you allow this crime to be committed? What swine dared to raise a hand against him? Yakovlev, Yakovlev, how could you allow this crime to be committed?"

When Nashchokin heard the news, he fell ill and raved for days.

Even Sofya Karamzin, who had felt such disgust at the poet's behavior a few days earlier, suddenly sensed that she had misunderstood and misjudged him: "And I, who was prating away to you about this woeful tragedy last Wednesday, the very day, the very hour when it was coming

* Lermotnov was also killed in a duel, at the age of twenty-six. Cf. *The Strange Destiny of Lermontov*, by Henri Troyat (published in French by Plon).

to such a ghastly denouement! Poor, poor Pushkin! What he must have suffered those last three months since the anonymous letters—which were the outward pretext, anyway, for this calamity! . . ."[2]

Her brother Alexander took up his pen on March 13 and gave vent to his fury in seven full pages of script:

"When he first came here, D'Anthès was nothing, a mere boy; he was funny because he was so green, and then he had a little native wit, but apart from that, a complete blank, both morally and intellectually. If he had stayed that way, he would have been a jolly fellow and nothing more; and I should not have to blush as I do now to think that I ever associated with him. . . . Heckeren, being a man of considerable intelligence and the most consummate pig on whom the sun's rays ever shone, had little difficulty in gaining complete mastery over D'Anthès' mind and soul, seeing that he had far less than Heckeren of the former and of the latter, it may be, none at all. These two men, for whatever fiendish reasons they may have had, fastened themselves upon Mrs. Pushkin with such determination and perseverance that in less than a year, with the aid of her simplicity and the odious stupidity of her sister Katerina, they succeeded in driving her nearly insane and destroying every scrap of her reputation. At that point D'Anthès had a bad chest and was wasting away before our eyes, so old Heckeren told Mrs. Pushkin he was dying of love for her, implored her to save his son, threatened her with horrible vengeance, and two days later the anonymous letters arrived. (If Heckeren wrote them himself, it was an inexplicable absurdity on his part, yet people who must know what they are talking about say it is now virtually certain that he did.) Then came Mrs. Pushkin's confession to her husband, and the challenge, and Heckeren's marriage. Now it was the turn of the woman who had served so long as go-between to become a lover and a wife. She gained by it, of course; in fact, she is the only victor now, and has become so stupid with happiness that after destroying her sister's reputation and perhaps her sanity and killing her husband for her as well, on the day of her sister's departure she sent word that she was willing to forget and forgive! For a moment Pushkin too thought he had won—thought he had covered his enemy in ridicule and made him play the part of a coward. But Pushkin's hatred was too great, he had been swallowing his disgust for too long, he could not control himself and made no effort to do so. He took the whole town and every overcrowded drawing room in it to witness, he poured out his spite and hatred, he was unable to take advantage of his victory when he held it in his hands, he became almost ridiculous; and since he would not tell the reasons for his resentment we all said, 'Now what does he want? He must be mad! He's just showing off!' While D'Anthès, guided by his so-called father, bore himself with perfect circumspection and tried to win all Pushkin's friends to his side. He made more protestations of innocence than ever to our family. . . . He talked so convincingly of honor and nobility that I believed in his loyalty to Mrs. Pushkin, I believed in his love for Katerina Goncharov, I believed all that was most incredible rather than believe the truth. It was as though I were drugged, fascinated. . . . How Pushkin must have suffered, when I cordially shook hands with D'Anthès in front of him. Thus I too helped to rend his noble soul while it was already shuddering to see his enemy emerge all clean and shining from the mire. The genius, the glory of his country, the man whose ear was attuned only to applause, had been insulted by a foreign adventurer who was trying to stain his honor, and when he indignantly set the seal of infamy upon his enemy's brow, his own countrymen took up the adventurer's cause and blasphemed the great poet. No; it was not his countrymen who blasphemed, it was an ignominious coterie; but the poet in his outrage could not distinguish the baying of a pack of hounds from the great cry of the public to which he was so sensitive! . . . It was only after his death that I learned the whole truth about D'Anthès' behavior, and I have not seen him since. . . . Cry, O my most miserable country! You will not soon give birth to such another son! Being brought to bed of Pushkin has exhausted you. . . ."[3]

Pushkin's brother Leo was at the front in the Caucasus when the news reached him. He wanted to apply for a furlough to challenge D'Anthès and avenge the poet, but his friends talked him out of it. He wrote to his father: "If I had a hundred lives I would give them all to buy back my brother's. On the black day of his death I heard a thousand balls whistling around me, why was there not one to strike me down instead, a man of no account, weary of life, ready to throw it away for a song any time these last ten years?"[4]

Sergey Lvovich dragged himself from drawing room to drawing room, fat, deaf, drooling and tearful, descanting upon his despair to all the young ladies. Zhukovsky sent him an official letter on the heroic death of his son. The letter was intended for public consumption: It described Pushkin as a model subject, devoted body and soul to his emperor, the emperor as his understanding and compassionate father, and Natalya as a paragon of virtue. When people complained of this deformation of personalities and facts, Zhukovsky answered that he had done it for the sake of Pushkin's widow and children. His true feelings were embodied in his letter to Benkendorf.

That document, however, remained unknown to the public for many years, and it was the letter to Sergey Lvovich upon which diplomats, foreign journalists and Pushkin's first biographers based their comments —for Pushkin's death was reported to governments by their ambassadors and publicized in periodicals the world over. In this way, at least, the poet became a European figure—by his tragic death, if not by his work.

What became of the main characters in the drama—D'Anthès, Heckeren, Natalya, Katerina, Danzas? In view of the tide of public opinion, Nicholas I decided to take strong action against the "assassins" and in favor of the "victims." Besides, he did not share Benkendorf's indulgence toward D'Anthès and Heckeren. The emperor had certainly been suspicious of Pushkin, and was not heartbroken to be rid of him so cheaply; but the Heckerens had caused a court scandal. And the anonymous letters alluded to a liaison between himself and Natalya Pushkin. Both of them were foreigners, one the accredited representative of another power and the other permitted as a special favor to serve as an officer in the Russian army; but that only made their insolence more flagrant.

Vicomte d'Archiac, the French attaché, left Russia on February 2. D'Anthès and Danzas were committed for trial by court-martial. During the preliminary hearings, D'Anthès insisted that he had always behaved with perfect circumspection in his relations with Natalya and was innocent of all the crimes Pushkin had laid to his charge. He demanded a confrontation with Natalya. It was refused. He appealed to the innumerable friends of his adoptive father. In vain.

Then he said to Colonel Breven: "All the people to whom I have sent you for information turned their backs on me the moment the people began flocking to my adversary's house; they did it without thinking, and without making any attempt to separate the man from the talent. They have chosen to see me as the foreigner who killed their poet. . . ."[5]

The verdict was preceded by the following considerations: "Whereas the accused has made no definite admission of improper conduct toward Pushkin's wife or any intention to destroy the family harmony . . . whereas he has declared that his relations with her did not exceed the limits of social propriety . . . it should nevertheless be taken into consideration that the violent and insulting attacks [in Pushkin's letter to Heckeren] could not have been formulated without some foundation, which was, moreover, disclosed by Pushkin in his explanation to the seconds."

Danzas, charged with having failed to prevent the duel, received a token sentence of two months' guardhouse arrest. D'Anthès was demoted to the ranks and deported. "As to gentleman of the chamber Pushkin: Although his action is criminal on the same grounds as that of Heckeren and deserves the same penalty, no action is to be taken against him owing to his death."

So Russia's greatest poet died a convicted criminal and his grave was a malefactor's grave; but that is how his friend and protector Nicholas I had wanted it.

D'Anthès' friends and supporters lost no opportunity of telling him how thoroughly they approved his conduct. His regiment sent enthusiastic letters: "The instant I heard you were to go," Prince Alexander Kurakin wrote, "my only thought was to rush to the Admiralty guardhouse to embrace you; but it was already too late, you were far from us, and I had known nothing about it. May the knowledge of my sincere devotion give you happiness."[6]

Baratynsky: "Be assured that it is very much against my will that I have curtailed my visits to you, which were a source of pleasure to me and always seemed too brief; but I was finally forced to end them because of the severity of the guards officers. Imagine that twice I was ordered off the gallery on the pretext that that was not where I should be walking, and on two other occasions I asked to see you and was refused."

Idalya Poletika—who had, no doubt, been careful not to tell Katerina about the meeting between D'Anthès and Natalya in her apartment—sent the prisoner a message that was almost a love letter: "My poor friend, your imprisonment makes my heart bleed, I don't know what I would not give to come and gossip with you a little; it is as though all that has happened has taken place in a dream, but it was a bad dream, not to say a nightmare, since the result of it is that I can no longer see you. . . . My heart aches to think of poor Katerina, for she is having a dreadful time; you must make her forget all this when you are gone, she deserves it, you should give her a second honeymoon. Farewell, my good, my handsome prisoner, I do not despair of seeing you before you go. Yours with all my heart."[7]

A few days later, Georges d'Anthès sent Idalya a keepsake (probably a bracelet), whereupon she wrote again: "You have the gift of making me weep, but this time my tears were the salutary kind, for I could not have been more deeply touched by this souvenir, it will never leave my arm; but I resent your thinking, my friend, that I could ever forget that you existed after you have gone, that is a proof that you still do not know me, for if I ever love, I love well, and forever."[8]

Unlike Georges d'Anthès, and in spite of all her friends' encouragements, Katerina remained utterly prostrated. It little mattered to her that Pushkin was dead: Georges was wounded. Georges was suffering. Georges was going to be deported. Jealousy simmered within her, but she showed no outward sign of it. In this sentimental tragedy, she played the thankless part of the eternal martyr. There she stood, with mournful eyes and open arms, ready to understand and forgive.

At last, on March 19, Georges d'Anthès, chaperoned by a police officer, met his wife and adoptive father in the embassy for a final consultation. According to the official report, the interview lasted exactly one hour and was polite but heated. Countess Stroganov was present at the couple's leave-taking. That same day, *Private* Heckeren and a police escort set out for the frontier by sleigh.

"I met Heckeren sitting in a sleigh with a policeman," Turgenev wrote on March 19. "Another sleigh followed, with a police officer. The young man was wearing a cap and looked in very high spirits."

D'Anthès stopped in Berlin, to await the arrival of his wife and adoptive father.

Count Stroganov, who had, so to speak, sponsored first the duel and then the funeral, wrote to Baron Heckeren: "When your son Georges learns that I have the jar,† tell him, too, that his Uncle Stroganov is keeping it as monument, to remind him of the outstandingly noble and loyal conduct he displayed during his last month in Russia. If a duly punished criminal is an example to the masses, then an innocent man convicted without hope of redress is the concern of every honest man."[9]

Nevertheless, despite all the protestations of loyalty of the Stroganovs, Nesselrodes and other dignitaries, Baron Heckeren was expecting disgrace. The very next day after the duel, he began trying to justify himself to both the Russian authorities and the Netherlands Foreign Minister, Baron Verstolk van Soelen.

"His Majesty," he wrote to the latter, "will decide if he wishes to recall me or send me to another post in exchange for one of my colleagues. If I may be allowed to say anything with respect to a situation in which I am personally concerned, I would say that recall without reassignment would signify flagrant condemnation of my behavior, and I should be dismayed. Even in such a sorry plight, my conscience tells me that I would not deserve such a reproof, which would destroy in an instant my entire career in public life."[10]

He also wrote to the Prince of Orange: "I venture to believe that Your Royal Highness will approve my conduct, and that belief is the most precious balm to my pain in a circumstance in which my personal affections have been and still are seriously threatened, and my career upset at a time when I was least expecting it."[11]

To Nesselrode, Heckeren sent the letter referred to earlier, in which he called upon Mrs. Pushkin to vindicate him: "If Mrs. Pushkin's confirmation were not forthcoming, I would call to witness two ladies of the utmost distinction, to whom I confided all my fears and gave a day-by-day account of my efforts to break off this fatal liaison. . . . There is another charge, which it cannot be presumed that I would stoop to answer, and so it has not been stated in so many words; I mean

† A crystal vase given to Count Stroganov by Baron Heckeren.

the anonymous letters, with which my name has been linked. And in whose interests could this weapon, worthy of that most cowardly killer of all, the poisoner, be employed? Those of my son, of Mrs. Pushkin? . . . Then my son, too, might have been the author of these anonymous letters? As a means to win the lady, leaving her no choice but to fall into his arms? Such behavior would have been strangely at variance with the high sense of morality which led my son to jeopardize his future for the reputation of a woman he loved. . . . If all I have here set forth does not suffice to prove to Your Excellency the ignominy of the accusations against me, then, after handing in my letters of recall, I consent to remain in this country as a private citizen and submit my actions to the scrutiny of a public inquiry from which I stand only to benefit. . . . I trust, Count, that you will be good enough to show this letter to His Majesty."[12]

After sending this epistle to Nesselrode, Heckeren felt a twinge of remorse and, three days later, wrote to Count Orlov, the general aide-de-camp: "I do not think I have sufficiently absolved Mrs. Pushkin from all shadow of suspicion, and I believe I must assert, upon my honor, that she never forgot her duty in the course of her relationship with my son, and remained as pure in that respect as on the day when Mr. Pushkin gave her his name."[13]

His recall was inevitable, however; and Nicholas I's sudden aversion to him was becoming increasingly manifest.

"He behaved like an abject cur," Nicholas wrote to Grand Duke Michael. "He pandered for D'Anthès in Pushkin's absence and did all he could to force the poet's wife to yield to D'Anthès, who, according to him, was dying of love; this all came out when, after the first challenge—of D'Anthès by Pushkin—D'Anthès suddenly married Pushkin's sister-in-law. At that point Pushkin's wife, who was utterly innocent, told her husband of the infamous conduct of these two individuals."

One by one, alerted to the imperial attitude, the courtiers began drifting away from the ambassador. The man whose allies had been legion suddenly found himself alone, ignored and reviled. His government was asking him to leave St. Petersburg at once, and said nothing about a reassignment. He had to dispose of the contents of his house, make his arrangements for departure. He published an announcement for the sale of his possessions. His apartment began to resemble a furniture store, with price tags on all the tapestries, armchairs and *bibelots* and himself directing operations in the center of his wares. His successor, Gevers, had already arrived. After selling his goods and chattels, he applied for an official audience with Nicholas I. He wanted to tell the emperor that he was only taking a leave of absence for personal reasons.

The emperor refused to see him, and sent him a snuffbox—in diplomats' code, a sign of permanent separation.

Katerina, sickened by the attitude of the government and aristocracy, longed to flee this barbarous land as soon as possible. Aunt Zagryazhskaya had dropped her, the Stroganovs were prudently spacing their visits. She was pregnant, too, which made her nervous and irritable.

Nesselrode, once the all-powerful protector of both Heckeren and D'Anthés, also began skillfully edging away; in the circumstances, the Foreign Minister had no choice but to concur in the enlightened opinion of his sovereign. He wrote to Meyendorf, on December 28, 1840: "Heckeren is capable of anything; he is a man without honor or conscience. On the whole, he deserves no esteem and is undesirable among us. The king's greatest mistake was to give him an important post."

Natalya herself refused to see her sister. On February 16, 1837, Pushkin's widow left St. Petersburg, with Alexandra and the children, for Polotnyany Zavody, the Goncharov estate. She was exhausted, depressed and ill. She wanted to see no one. She wanted her very name to be forgotten. While she was beginning her long hibernation, Katerina and Baron Heckeren were making their final arrangements for departure, abandoning Russia never to return. They joined Georges d'Anthès in Germany, where, at Baden-Baden, the ex-horse guards officer was living the vain existence of a socialite. His tragic duel had earned him a kind of celebrity. He was sought after as an international star. The ladies were flattered to dance with him. "It was strange," wrote Karamzin's son, "to see D'Anthès leading the mazurkas and cotillions as before, with his old horse guards airs." Grand Duke Michael openly proclaimed his sympathy for Pushkin's victorious rival. After meeting him in Baden-Baden, he said to Countess Sollogub: "Guess whom I just saw? D'Anthès!"

"And were you disturbed by Pushkin's memory?"

"Not at all, he got what he deserved."

"What, then?"

"Well, but what a pity about D'Anthès! Just think, he was demoted!"

Other Russian tourists flocked around D'Anthès, clamoring for his friendship: Kiselev, Smirnov, Dolgorukov. . . . Old Heckeren played roulette. D'Anthès enjoyed himself. Katerina, deformed by her swelling belly, seldom went out. Before long, however, Katerina and D'Anthès left Baden-Baden and went to live with Georges's parents at Soultz, in Alsace, where, on October 19, 1837, Katerina gave birth to a little girl. On November 16 Mrs. Goncharov wrote to Georges d'Anthès: "Sir! It is with the keenest satisfaction that I learned the happy news of Katerina's delivery; I congratulate you wholeheartedly on this occasion, especially as the happiness you express seems so sincere that I was very touched by it. May your devotion to your wife remain ever the same."[14]

The letter from Georges d'Anthès to which this was a reply was, in effect, sincere. The young man's infatuation with Natalya, the duel and his deportation had been a severe test of his conscience. He wanted peace and quiet, he wanted to forget; and no one better than Katerina could help him to recover from his affliction. He began to discover his wife's qualities, and gratefully drew closer to her. Besides, Katerina looked a little like Natalya; the resemblance helped D'Anthès to transfer his affections from one to the other. A sort of slow fusion took place in his heart and mind. Natalya receded behind a curtain of flame and blood, Katerina moved into the foreground. He was happy with her.

Was Katerina happy with him? She still suspected him of thinking too much about the past, and she was still jealous of Natalya, no matter how many frontiers lay between them. But she was sure that time and emotional fatigue would smooth the last ripples of his passion. Several times, she wrote to Natalya, but in vain. On September 14, 1837, her brother Dmitry gave her his explanation of the situation: "Adulated as she was, Natalya cannot find much to amuse her in the monotony of Zavody, she is inclined to be sad and is often indisposed, which keeps her in her room instead of coming to dine with me. Her plans for the future? Nothing is settled, everything will depend on circumstances and our good aunt [Zagryazhskaya]. You ask me why she doesn't write; indeed, I do not know her reasons, but I suppose she has none except the fear of losing her dignity, or rather her name in society, by writing to you, and I don't imagine you will get any [letters] from her for some time. And after all, who knows which way the wind will blow?"[15]

Katerina's mother sent a similar message: "Natalya is with me, I have asked her why she does not write to you, but she pretends to be lazy. . . . It is true that her health has not been very good. . . . I am delighted, dear Katerina, that you continue to be so happy, it is a very great source of comfort to me to know that."[16]

After the birth of her first child, Katerina became more serene. She felt that her sufferings gave her some hold over her excessively young and handsome husband. But more than anything else, she wanted to give Georges a son, to carry on his name and race. She had a second daughter on April 5, 1839, and a third on April 3, 1840. She began to despair, she made barefoot pilgrimages to the miraculous chapel of Thierenbach, she even contemplated converting to the Roman Catholic faith. On December 26, 1842, D'Anthès wrote to her from Munich: "I am utterly forlorn at having left you, whom I love so much and whose pretty mouth I shall not be able to kiss for so long. . . . You will have this letter for the new year. . . . That day I shall make a wish that our future—as far as our personal happiness is concerned—may resemble our past."[17]

At last, on September 22, 1843, Katerina gave birth to a boy. Her dearest wish had come true, she could look forward to a future of uninterrupted domestic bliss. Everyone was so kind to her, her children were strong and handsome, her husband loved her more than ever, Baron Heckeren showered her with delicate attentions. But shortly after the baby was born, puerperal fever set in and the doctors despaired of her life. Katerina died on October 15, 1843.

Her husband was greatly afflicted by her death. Natalya, whom he had passionately desired, was inaccessible. Katerina, whom he had tenderly loved, expired in his arms. One after the other, the joys of his life had fled. Disappointed in love, Georges d'Anthès fell back on the family's traditional occupation, politics. His old companions in St. Petersburg would not have recognized, in this brusque and businesslike adult, the flashing horse guardsman who had been so much in love with Mrs. Pushkin and so ready to commit the wildest imprudences just to get the better of a jealous poet.

By 1845 Georges d'Anthès was a member of the Council of the Haut-Rhin. After the 1848 revolution and the fall of Louis Philippe, his electors sent him to the Constituent Assembly, then to the Legislative Assembly. On both occasions, D'Anthès opposed the introduction of republican institutions and voted consistently with the conservatives. But in 1850, casting off his family's legitimist tradition, he decided to back Prince Louis Napoleon.

Speaking to the Legislative Assembly on July 17, 1851, Victor Hugo depicted the perils into which the President-prince was leading the Republic. There was an uproar. The entire right shouted down the orator. In the minutes of the sitting, D'Anthès-Heckeren is recorded as having called out: "It should be permitted to boo, if people can applaud things like that. . . ."

And: "Let him go on, let him play his comedy!"

Later, in *Les Châtiments*, Victor Hugo made a violent attack upon the supporters of the Empire. In his poem *July 17, 1851: On Stepping Down from the Tribune*, he wrote:

These men who will die, a craven, uncouth horde,
Are mud already, before they turn to dust. . . ."

Among the partisans of the regime he mentioned D'Anthès-Heckeren: "Afterward senator of the Empire, with thirty thousand francs a year."

And so it was: After the *coup d'état* of December 2, D'Anthès was a member of the Constituent Assembly and Napoleon III sent him on a special mission to the courts of Vienna, Berlin and St. Petersburg. In Berlin, D'Anthès met Nicholas I again. Fifteen years had passed since Pushkin's death. Nicholas received the French representative graciously, recalled his period of service in the Russian army and assured him of his wholehearted sympathy for the new emperor. On his return, D'Anthès was rewarded with a seat in the Senate and an annual stipend of thirty thousand francs. He was forty years old, the youngest senator in France. In 1855 the Emperor of Austria awarded him the Grand Cordon of the Imperial Order of Franz Joseph. Baron Heckeren, who was then ambassador to Vienna, wrote his adopted son an effusive letter of congratulations: "There once were three emperors and a young Frenchman; one of these three mighty monarchs drove the young Frenchman out of his empire, in midwinter, in an open sledge, and wounded! The other two took it upon themselves to avenge the Frenchman; one made him a senator in his empire, and the other decorated him with the Grand Cordon which he himself devised as a reward for personal merit! That is the story of the ex-Russian private hustled off to the frontier. Georges, *we* are avenged!"[18]

Intelligent, enterprising and bold, Georges d'Anthés managed to promote the interests of both his constituents and himself. He brought the first railroad to Alsace, and became an associate of the Pereire brothers—high financiers with a long run of luck—in the founding of insurance companies, naval shipping firms and banks and export companies. He founded the Paris Gas Company and became its immutable director. In a letter to Panizzi dated February 28, 1861, Prosper Mérimée referred to one of D'Anthès' speeches in the Senate in the following terms: "After M. de Rochejacquelin came Mr. Heckeren, the one who killed Pushkin. He is a powerful man with a German accent, rough-mannered but quick, jovial, very crafty." On the strength of his connections with Baron Heckeren, the Netherlands ambassador to Vienna and his uncle, Count Hatzfeld, the Prussian ambassador to Paris, Georges d'Anthès became an unofficial adviser on foreign policy to the government of Napoleon III.

This rich, influential, highly esteemed personage, a stalwart, mustachioed gentleman, a commander of the Legion of Honor, ended his days in calm and dignity. He built a three-story house at No. 17 Avenue Montaigne in Paris, where he lived with his family. Every afternoon he was driven to the Cercle Impérial, of which he was a founding member, and he spent his evenings at home with his children, to whom he readily recounted his adventures at the court of Russia. "Several years ago," wrote Paul Hervieu, "around six o'clock every evening, I used to see a tall old gentleman of superb and solitary mien cross the club rooms where I went to read the papers. All I knew of him was that sixty years before, in the far-distant past, he had killed Pushkin in a duel. I observed his powerful air and aged gait with awe inspired by this ghost of a ghost. I said to myself, 'There goes the man who killed Pushkin, and Pushkin has immortalized him like the temple of Ephesus immortalized the man who destroyed it.' "

After the fall of the Empire, D'Anthès withdrew from public life and divided his time between Paris and Soultz. He died in 1895, at the age of eighty-three, surrounded by his children and grandchildren.

Baron Heckeren, his adoptive father, likewise prospered in all his days. Having contrived to get back into the good graces of the Prince of Orange, he was named ambassador to Vienna in 1842 and remained in that post for thirty-two years. On September 8, 1842, the Duchess of Dino wrote in her diary: "The appointment of Baron Heckeren as ambassador to Vienna has caused a great scandal in Holland and stirred up all the old, ugly rumors." Heckeren became *doyen* of the diplomatic corps before retiring to Paris in 1875, covered with honors, titles and decorations. He died in 1884 at the age of eighty-nine.

I have visited the cemetery at Soultz, looking toward the downy hump of the Ballon de Guebwiller. Behind a rust-eroded grill stand rows of stern, simple white marble tombstones, moss-stained and rain-washed. Baron Heckeren is buried there, with the D'Anthès family dead. Near him, beneath a slab identical in every respect to his own, Katerina, née Goncharov, sleeps her last sleep. Next to her, another marble slab, another name: Georges-Charles d'Anthès de Heckeren. All three lie here in the Alsatian soil, leagues away from the place where their destinies were decided. War has not disturbed the sober alignment of their tombs; but back in Russia, the bombs have uprooted the trees and shattered the stones that stood guard over the poet's resting place, as though God had not wanted him to rest ever, not even in death, not even in men's memories.

Natalya too began a new life after Pushkin's death.

Very soon (March 3, 1837), Katerina Andreyevna Karamzin, the historian's wife, passed a perceptive, tolerant judgment upon the widow of the poet: "The great and good Pushkin should have had a wife who understood him better, who had more in common with him. . . . Poor, poor Pushkin, victim of the frivolity, recklessness and lack of consideration of a young and beautiful woman who threw away his life, there can be no doubt about it, for the sake of a few hours of flirtation. Do not say I exaggerate, I am not blaming her; one does not blame children for the evil they do unwittingly, and because they have not learned to think."[19]

Natalya went first to Zavody, where it soon became apparent that she was not made for mourning. On April 8, 1837, only two months after the duel, Karamzin's son wrote to his mother: "It's strange, I was praying that she would get over it, but I did not imagine my prayers would be answered so soon."

Idalya Poletika wrote to Katerina on October 8 of that year: "I can tell you very little about Natalya; just now she is with your mother, then she is going back to your brother. Your aunt is leaving in a few weeks to spend part of the winter with her. They say she is still very low; I would like to believe it, for other people say she is bored and cannot wait to leave the country. . . ."

Idalya's hatred of Pushkin and his friends continued unabated after the poet's tragic death. She went on: "Yesterday I had the pleasure of dining with your aunt;‡ it is wonderful how that woman loves me, she gnashes her teeth whenever she has to speak,* while I honor her with a sublime indifference, that is the most I can do for her. That great rush to buy the works of the *deceased* has shrunk to a trickle; instead of bringing in 500,000 rubles, sales will not reach 200,000. That's always the way."[20]

In August 1837 Pushkin's father went to visit his daughter-in-law, but found Alexandra more melancholy than Natalya[21]—for Alexandra had loved both the man and the poet, whereas Natalya never loved the man and did not understand the poet. Her consciousness of her responsibility tormented her far more than her widowhood: She suffered less from being alone than from appearing to be indirectly to blame. But the days passed: Fresh air, long walks and good food restored peace to Natalya's soul and grace to her body.

After a year at Zavody, she returned to St. Petersburg with Alexandra and the children, and rented an apartment far from the center of town, on Apothecary Island. On January 30, 1838, the Comtesse de Circourt informed Katerina: "I learned of your sister's return through the Comtesse M——, I am sure she will marry again: Her children's future being provided for by the emperor, she does not suffer from the usual disadvantages of widows."[22]

Idalya Poletika wrote to Katerina: "I see your sisters quite often at the Stroganovs', but never here; Natalya hasn't the courage to come to my home.† We get along very well. She never speaks of the past: It does not exist between us, and thus, being very pleasant to each other, we talk a great deal about the weather, which, as you know, is seldom good in St. Petersburg. . . . Natalya is still beautiful, although she has lost

‡ Aunt Zagryazhskaya, who liked Pushkin, protected Natalya, and broke off relations with the D'Anthès family after the duel.

* Unlike Katerina, Aunt Zagryazhskaya presumably knew of Idalya Poletika's share in the responsibility for Pushkin's death.

† Another indication of Idalya Poletika's implication in the final events.

weight. On some days she looks particularly tired and low; two days ago, for example, I had dinner with her and the Maistres at the Stroganovs'. She seemed very anxious and upset, and when I asked her about it she told me it often happened. Her children are well, but the eldest daughter is a living image of the father, which is most unfortunate."[23]

A letter, dated April 10, 1839, unsigned but almost certainly written by some companion of Mrs. Goncharov at Polotnyany Zavody, supplemented the information given by Idalya Poletika: "Natalya goes out seldom if ever, has not been to court, but presented her respects to the emp. at her aunt's [Zagryazhskaya] one day when Her Majesty stopped in on her way to see Kuntuzov, a maid of honor who lives in the same house. The emp. was very pleasant to Natalya and asked to see her children and talked to them. It was New Year's Eve. The same day Alexandra received her monogram [insignia of maids of honor], at the request of the patron-aunt. Alexandra made her first appearance at court on Easter morning. She goes out, sometimes to balls or the theater, but Natalya does not go out at all."[24]

Natalya maintained her praiseworthy discretion for another two years. Early in 1841, however, when Pletnev asked her whether she thought of marrying again, she answered: "In the first place, I shall never remarry, and in the second, nobody would have me!"

"I advised her," Pletnev wrote to his friend Grot, "to settle for one or the other answer, for continuing to give both at once might cast doubts upon her sincerity; actually, I advised her to opt for the second part of her answer alone. But no, she insists on repeating the first as well, and occasionally adds that fate has willed it so."

"Of Natalya's two answers," Grot replied, "I would have preferred the one she chose first ["I shall never remarry"], but to my sorrow I gather from her conversation that the wound is already healed. God, is there nothing constant on this earth?"

On December 24, 1841, Natalya was in the English store buying decorations for her Christmas tree when the emperor came in to look for toys for his children. When he saw her, Nicholas came up and exchanged a few pleasantries. A little later, he told Aunt Zagryazhskaya that he hoped to see Natalya at court balls again. Ever obedient to the sovereign will, Natalya reappeared in society, where she was greeted with acclaim. Once again, she flew from ball to ball, play to play, changed her dress three times a day, gulped her food and fretted over the fine points of her coiffure or the qualities of her perfume. Forgotten, Pushkin; vanished, the poet's sighs; gone, the acrid smoke of gunfire. The music was still playing, the men still gallant and strong, the gowns elegant and expensive. And the face reflected in Natalya's mirror was a little more pale and thin than before, but mournfully and mysteriously beautiful. For a costume ball at the Anichkov palace, Aunt Zagryazhskaya presented her with a gown "in the Hebrew style," copied from an old painting of Rebecca. Natalya entered the grand ballroom in a long, clinging violet tunic with a white veil falling from her brow. The emperor was ecstatic: "Behold and admire!" he said to the empress.

The empress raised her lorgnette and mildly concurred.

"She is magnificent, truly magnificent! Her image should be preserved for future generations in that costume."

Nicholas I rubbed his hands with glee. Immediately after the ball, he summoned a court painter to make a water-color portrait of the new Rebecca.

"It seems that 'la Pushkin' is appearing at balls again," Dolly Ficquelmont wrote on January 17, 1843. "Don't you think she might have spared herself that; she was widowed in such atrocious circumstances, and was herself, however innocent, the cause!"[25]

The imperial indulgence was so marked that suitors began to reappear, for to marry a woman favored by the sovereign was to guarantee a brilliant career for oneself. Without being an accomplice, one could still be discreet. There was no shame for a husband if a lady of high society chose to divert herself with her monarch, and the tsar of all the Russias was no libertine, only somewhat fond of the ladies. He was not a collector of official mistresses, only of inconsequential flirtations: a dance, a little flattery, an ogle and a leer, a touch of the foot, a blush. . . . Nicholas I was a great amateur of such small change, and in return he handed out fine ranks, beautiful decorations and handsome, solid salaries—or so, at any rate, Major General Lanskoy must have reasoned.

In 1837, just before the duel, when D'Anthès and Natalya were alone in the apartment of Idalya Poletika, it was he who had stood guard outside the house. In 1844 he decided to take a more active hand in the destiny of this most interesting young woman. He was forty-five at the time, but still cut a fine figure in his uniform. He began to pay his addresses to Natalya. He proposed. Unfortunately, he was just another officer, conscientious and obscure, doomed to end his days in some provincial garrison. To marry him, Natalya would have to give up St. Petersburg, the Anichkov palace and the emperor, and go rot in a mudhole in darkest Russia. But Nicholas I was watching in the wings: Overnight, Lanskoy's merits received spectacular recognition. He, whom nothing had destined for distinction, found himself in charge of the regiment of horse guards, whose supreme commander was Nicholas I himself. He was given a luxurious apartment, paid for by the state. And the emperor insisted upon "sponsoring" his marriage to Natalya. Natalya wanted the ceremony to be private, however, to discourage evil tongues, so Nicholas I had to console himself by offering the bride a magnificent diamond clasp.

A few hours before his death Pushkin had said: "Try to be forgotten. Go live in the country. Stay in mourning for two years, then remarry, but choose somebody decent."

In short, that was exactly what Natalya had done.

When the Lanskoys' first child was born, Nicholas I was its godfather, and came to the baptism in person.

One day Natalya decided to give a small, private party for the officers of the regiment. Nicholas I summoned Lanskoy: "I hear there is going to be dancing at your place. I hope you won't forget to invite your chief?"

He came to the party, asked to see the nursery, patted and kissed his goddaughter under the gratified gaze of the couple. Later, on the twenty-fifth anniversary of the founding of the regiment, Lanskoy presented the emperor with an album containing the portraits of all the officers in the unit. But it was the emperor's desire—curious, to say the least—that the gracious features of Natalya should adorn the first page of the collection of military jaws, mustaches, epaulets and decorations. He commissioned another portrait of her from a miniaturist, which he had set in the golden cover of her watch.

Natalya was happy with Lanskoy—happier than with Pushkin, no doubt. Her later life was dignified and uneventful. She became a distinguished middle-aged lady with hard, faded features and huge, sad eyes. The couple spent a good deal of time abroad, in Paris and Nice. Natalya Nikolayevna died on November 26, 1863, at the age of fifty-one. She used to say to her children, "The memory of the dead is sacred, but I have a feeling that I shall have no peace, even in my grave."[26]

Alexandra, who had loved the poet so loyally, survived her sister by several years. In 1852, when she was forty, she married Baron Gustave Friesenhof, an official in the Austrian embassy, and died in 1868 or '70, it is thought.

Pushkin's brother Leo, ever jolly, bold, lazy and dissolute, made a modest career in the army, retired in 1842, married late and died childless in 1852.

Olga continued her obscure and dreary existence with the miserly Pavlishchev. At forty, she became seriously ill and spent her last days writing disenchanted verse.

Pushkin's father, Sergey Lvovich, became a licentious old buffoon. He was bloated, deaf, toothless and wheezed at every step. He drooled when he spoke. Liprandi's children called him "the samovar." On the top of his lumpy skull a few strands of hair, gummy with "fixative," curled in limp spirals. His only interest in life was females, particularly young ones, and more particularly the ones his son Alexander had loved before him. Involuntarily, he followed the poet's shifting memory from face to face: At Mikhailovskoye, he became enamored of Mrs. Osipov's youngest daughter Marya, wrote her letters in verse and finally proposed to her.

She, however, was in love with Leo Pushkin and refused the father. Sergey Lvovich was most offended: How could anyone prefer that harum-scarum Leo, that sword-brandisher, to him? In despair, he turned to Zizi Vrevsky, then to Anna Petrovna Kern, then to her daughter Katerina Kern. His passion for the latter was so consuming that he would pick up the cranberry skins she had spat out and rapturously chew them after her. He plied her with epistles in French, madrigals and lyric poems. He was growing increasingly hard of hearing, however, and could hardly climb a single step; but when he died, in 1849, he was still imploring Katerina Kern to marry him.

Pushkin's children led worthy, uneventful lives. One of his sons, both of whom were educated in the page corps, became a general (and died on the day war was declared in 1914), the other a government official (who died in 1905). Marya, his eldest daughter, was still alive during World War I; the younger girl, Natalya, first married the son of General Dubelt (who was in the service of Benkendorf; it was he who was assigned to "assist" Zhukovsky in making the inventory of Pushkin's papers), then the Duke of Nassau, whom she wed in Paris. Her daughter —Pushkin's granddaughter—married the grandson of Nicholas I, Grand Duke Michael Mikhailovich, thus concluding a new alliance between the Pushkin and Romanov families. Descendants of the poet are still living, in England, France, Belgium and Russia.

"No, I shall not die entirely," Pushkin wrote. And indeed, his posthumous career was far more brilliant than his earthly one. At his death, the enthusiasm of the multitudes was awakened. As early as 1838, an edition of his complete works was published—revised, expurgated and pruned by the cautious Zhukovsky.

In the 1840s the critic Belinsky launched a fervent campaign on the poet's behalf. Thanks to him, the public began to understand Pushkin better and appreciate his gifts more intelligently. He became part of the national heritage. He took his place in the hall of fame, with his inspired eye, his wind-blown side whiskers and his thick, sneering lips. From him welled rivers of legends, witticisms, secrets, swirls of strange and wonderful vapors. Gradually, he became a demigod. Annenkov and Bartenyev, the first Pushkin scholars, began the treasure hunt. Indefatigably, they retraced his every footstep, collected yellowed letters, exhumed manuscripts covered with notes and corrections, ambushed the poet's friends in their lairs, dogged them with questions, pushed, pried and insisted, wrung them dry and piously recorded their every utterance. Annenkov published the fruits of his labors in a volume entitled *Documents for the Biography of Pushkin,* which was used to introduce the 1855 edition of the complete works.

Simultaneously, the poet's contemporaries began to emerge from the shadows and publish their own memoirs, articles and notes. There was an avalanche of apocryphal stories, false reminiscences, dubious accounts. His true friends formed a united front against the impostors, and the impostors crumbled to dust.

Pushkin grew with the years. Every other writer claimed descent from him. Inexplicably, the whole of Russian literature proceeded from his genius. Poetry, novels, short stories, history, theater, criticism—he had opened up the whole gamut of literary endeavor to his countrymen. He was first in time, and first in quality. He was the source. Neither Gogol nor Tolstoy could have existed without him, for he made the Russian language; he prepared the ground for the growth of every genre.

In 1880 a Pushkin monument was unveiled in Moscow. On that occasion, Dostoevsky and Turgenev made speeches of such impassioned conviction that their listeners were moved to tears. Edition followed edition. Statues sprang up everywhere. Streets were named after the poet. Even the Revolution did not stem the miraculous tide of enthusiasm. On the contrary: The discovery of the secret archives of the third section brought new documents to light, which were immediately incorporated into subsequent biographies. An army of Pushkin experts began to tackle a vast range of projects. The specialists waded through tons of paper, scrutinized manuscripts, compared texts, counted the number of lines written each year, drew graphs, compiled statistics and flooded the market with their publications. They invented a veritable science of Pushkin. The exegesis of Pushkin became a profession, a special status, a title of nobility. Thanks to these scholars, no author of recent centuries in any other country has been the source of so much commentary as this most pure and uncomplicated of poets.

In France and elsewhere, however, Pushkin remained and still remains relatively unknown. Some have heard of him. Fewer have read him, despite all the efforts of Russian and foreign men of letters.

Gogol, Turgenev, Tolstoy, Dostoevsky and Chekhov have all conquered the Western world. The most Russian of the Russian authors have crossed the line of demarcation and influence. Pushkin alone remains a prisoner of his language. More than a century has gone by since his death, and no French, English or American publisher has risked an edition of his complete works. His foreign biographers are few, his foreign admirers sparse and uncertain. Yet whenever a European sets out to learn Russian, the first text his professor will ask him to ponder is an extract from the poems of Pushkin.[27] The reason for this is that the syntax, the logic, the general construction of the piece seem, at first glance, to be purely European, even French. "My friend," Pushkin wrote to Chaadaev in 1831, "I shall address you in the language of Europe, it is more familiar to me than our own." But in 1836 the same correspondent received the following declaration, also in French: "On my honor I swear to you that I would not wish another fatherland for anything on earth, or any other history than that of our ancestors as God has given it to us."

In his own words, then, Pushkin admitted that his verb was European, his meaning national. And how could it have been otherwise? He was born at the end of the eighteenth century and received a classical education; but his prodigious personality grew to maturity in the nineteenth century, the heyday of Romanticism and the dawn of realism.

In his childhood, he wrote French better than Russian and knew French literature better than his own. At Tsarskoye Selo, his schoolmates called him "the Frenchman," and the poetry he wrote was an imitation of Parny. Afterward, in St. Petersburg, he placed himself under the tutelage of the *encyclopédistes,* and nothing could be less Russian than his Russian poem *Ruslan and Ludmila.* But already, he was beginning to look for other idols. Why? Because although he admired the formal perfection of the classical authors, he was repelled by the abstract, impersonal emotions they expressed. Just as it seemed natural to him to distort reality when he was living among the artificial gardens of Tsarskoye Selo or the official drawing rooms of St. Petersburg, so it seemed absurd to him to sing of the heroes of mythology in the lands of his exile: How could he be satisfied by faded, fleshless, unsubstantial, odorless and voiceless fictions when the colossal architecture of the Caucasus was staring him in the face, and Circassian horsemen, armed to the teeth, were prowling the gorges? How could he prefer a bland, anonymous dryad to the girls he saw on the streets, or the Olympian mists to the season's actual storm? Far from the city, the physical presences of man and nature rudely imposed themselves upon his mind. He escaped from the impassioned algebra dear to Voltaire and Racine, and discovered the rich pleasure of saying what he saw and smelled, instead of repeating what others had seen and smelled for him.

But he was still too young to write without a model. His revolt against French classicism was not inspired by a desire for total freedom, but by a new subservience. He rejected his first masters, only to fall under the spell of Byron. He thought he had been liberated; he had simply changed jailers. That was the period of *The Prisoner of the Caucasus, The Fountain of Bakhchisarai, The Gypsies.* But although the protagonists of these long poems are strangely reminiscent of Byron's heroes, their settings owe nothing to any literary antecedent. Pushkin had still not freed his characters, but the world around them was a real world. One step more, and he would conquer his precursors and proclaim his true voice: In *Eugene Onegin*, there are Russian men and women, moving in a Russian setting and in a Russian manner; and every Russian can find something of himself in them. At Mikhailovskoye and Boldino, Pushkin underwent his final metamorphosis. Deliberately, he imposed a classical form upon his subjective passions. He wedded his respect for verbal precision to his urge to express unvarnished life—and the miracle happened. For it was a miracle: Love is there, and melancholy, and color, despair and joy, and every disorder of the human heart. But the language encasing them is stern and pure, and the classical balance in which they are poised has enabled them to endure.

Thus the superficial reader, attentive only to the poet's writing, may be disappointed by the remarkable spareness of his expression. He may accuse Pushkin of artificial classicism and deny his title of national poet. What repels the European, for example, is everything in his work that appears to be European, classical; for classical poetry demands a certain effort on the part of the uninitiated. Its appeal is not immediate, it charms in time.

Of a Russian poet, people demand Russian qualities. They expect to be physically and emotionally transported by their pilgrimage to the North. They revel at the thought of the strain this intellectual journey is going to place upon their minds. But at first glance, there is nothing Slavic about Pushkin. He is neither mystic, prophet nor revolutionary, neither chaotic nor profound. His universe is rational, his lyricism human, his aspirations short. What could be more disappointing to a reader in search of local color? For most, therefore, Pushkin will not be representative of his country in the way that Dostoevsky and Gogol are. When they want a gust of Russian air, they will seek it in the voluminous pages of the great nineteenth-century novelists, not in Pushkin's transparent lines. They tailor-make a Russia to fit their own specifications, a Russia of tawdry taverns, prisons and slums, inhabited by drunkards and epileptics and frosted with eternal snow. But the Russians, as connoisseurs, savor the Russianness of Pushkin's poetry, which foreigners are still unable to appreciate.

To his compatriots, and regardless of time, changing fashions and passing regimes, Pushkin's work remains the most masterful evocation of their cherished memories. In it they find an eternal image of their land—the simple line of the horizon, the long roads leading to the ends of the earth, the flight of sleighs over moon-soaked snow, the trembling of the sun through the leaves of lindens in provincial parks, the scent of tea and the laughter of girls. In it they also find the authentic spirit of the nation, which is not disenchanted and morbid, as too many foreigners tend to believe after reading the great novelists, but prodigiously gay, naïve and healthy. Pushkin's mind, unlike those of Dostoevsky, Chekhov, Gogol and Turgenev, is invigorating. His attitude to life is reminiscent of the masters of the Renaissance. His love of life awakens a desire to live. Pushkin loved life with frenzy, with recklessness. It was because he loved life so much that he died so soon.

"Russia without Pushkin," Gogol wrote; "how strange!" And Europe without Pushkin? For Russia, Pushkin is the first great European poet, who brought the universal themes of literature to his country. For Europe, Pushkin is the first great Russian poet, who brought his country out of the shadows and fashioned a symbol for it. For that reason, no effort should be spared to make him accessible to the foreign public. He belongs alongside Dante, Cervantes, Shakespeare, Racine, Corneille, Schiller, Goethe and Byron. Will a poet ever come who can help this Russian poet across the frontier?

Bibliography

So much has been written about Pushkin in Russia that a complete account of the books and articles dealing with the poet would fill a volume in itself; here I mention only those items I have used for this book. Works in French are starred.

PUSHKIN. *Complete Works* (edited by Annenkov in 7 vols., by Morozov in 7 vols., by Vengerov in 6 vols., by Tomashevsky in 1 large vol.).

—— *Correspondence* (edited by Saytov in 3 vols. and by Modzalevsky in 3 vols., appearing in 1935).

—— *Letters to Mrs. Khitrovo* (Leningrad, 1927).

—— *Letters to His Fiancée* (ed. MM. Hofmann and Serge Lifar, Paris, 1937).

—— *Pushkin's Diary* (ed. Modzalevsky, 1923).

—— *The Gabriliad* (ed. Tomashevsky).

—— *Eugene Onegin* (ed. Brodsky, 1937; M. Hofmann, 1937).

—— *Journey to Arzerum* (ed. MM. Hofmann and S. Lifar, Paris, 1935).

—— *Egyptian Nights* (ed. M. Hofmann, Paris, 1935).

ALAVERDOV. *Pushkin's Style and Language* (Moscow, 1937).

ANASTASIOS (Metropolitan). *Pushkin, Religion and the Orthodox Church* (Belgrade, 1939).

Anecdotes and Remarks on Alexander I (St. Petersburg, 1879).

Annals of the Pushkin Commission (*Vremennik*) (3 vols., 1935–37).

ANNENKOV, P.-V. *Documents for the Biography of Pushkin* (St. Petersburg, 1873).

—— *Pushkin in the Reign of Alexander* (St. Petersburg, 1874).

—— *Reminiscences and Criticism* (St. Petersburg, 1874).

Anthology (*Volume IV*) (published by the "Lenin Library"; 1939).

Anthology of Articles on Pushkin (published in Belgrade; 1937).

Nesselrode Archives.

Ostafyevo Archives (papers of the Vyazemsky family, 5 vols.).

Russian Archives (*Rusky Arkhiv*) (Bartenyev's periodical, 45 issues).

Vorontzov Archives.

ASHUKIN, N. *Pushkin Living* (Moscow, 1926).

* BAAK. *The Two Baron Heckerens.*
BARTENYEV. *Material for the Biography of Pushkin* (1855).
—— *For Use in the Biography of Pushkin* (1888).
—— *On Pushkin.*
—— *Accounts of Prince and Princess Vyazemsky.*
—— *Pushkin in the Words of His Friends* (ed. Tsyavlovsky, Moscow, 1925).
BELINSKY. *Articles on Pushkin* (1937).
BELYAEV and PLATONOV. *Pushkin's Last Apartment* (Leningrad, 1927).
BEM, A. *Articles on Pushkin* (1937).
BERG. *The Hamlet of Zakharovo* (*The Muscovite*, 1851, Nos. 9–10).
BLAGOVO. *Grandmother's Tales* (Moscow, 1885).
* BRIAN-CHANINOV. *History of Russia* (Fayard, 1929).
—— *Alexander I* (Grasset, 1934).
BRODSKY. A. S. *Pushkin* (biography; Moscow, 1937).
BURTSEV. *Study Pushkin!* (Paris, 1941).
—— *Chapters 8, 9 and 10 of Eugene Onegin* (Paris, 1937).
Chronicles of the National Museum of Literature (various studies on Pushkin; Moscow, 1936).
* CHULKOV. *The Last Autocrat Tsars* (Payot, 1928).
CUSTINE (de). *Russia in 1839* (Brussels, 1843).
DELVIG, Baron A.A. *Works* (St. Petersburg, 1895).
—— *Unpublished Poems* (1922).
DELVIG, Baron A.-I. *Recollections* (1913).
DMITRYEV. *A Glance at My Life* (Moscow, 1866).
Documents Relating to Pushkin in the Imperial Archives of the Ministry of Foreign Affairs (St. Petersburg, 1900).
Dossiers of the Court-Martial concerning Pushkin's Duel.
Dossiers of the Third Section Relating to Pushkin (St. Petersburg, 1906).
* FALLOUX, Comte de. *Memoirs of a Royalist* (Plon, 1888).
—— *Mme. Svechin* (Didier et Cie, 1865).
FOMIN. *Pushkiniana* (1911–17).
FRANK, S. *Pushkin as Political Thinker* (Belgrade, 1937).
GAEVSKY. *Pushkin at School* (*The Contemporary*, 1863, No. 7).
* GALLET DE KULTURE. *Tsar Nicholas and Holy Russia* (1857 edition).
GASTFREUND. *Pushkin's Schoolmates at Tsarskoye Selo* (3 vols., 1912).
GLADKY, A. *In Pushkin's Footsteps* (1931).
GROT, I.-K. *Pushkin, His Schoolmates and Teachers* (St. Petersburg, 1899).
GROT, K.-I. *Pushkin's School* (St. Petersburg, 1911).
HERSCHENSOHN, M.-O. *The Wisdom of Pushkin* (Moscow, 1919).
—— *Moscow in Griboedov's Day* (Moscow-Berlin, 1922).
—— *Images of the Past.*
HESSEN, C. *Pushkin in the Memoirs and Accounts of His Contemporaries* (Leningrad, 1936).
HINS, G.-K. *Pushkin and Russian Patriotism* (Kharbin, 1937).
HOFMANN, M.-L. *Pushkin, the Psychology of Creation* (Paris, 1928).
—— *Chapter One in the Science of Pushkin* (1922).

—— *Pushkin's Fiancée and Wife* (Paris, 1935).
* —— *Pushkin* (biography) (Payot, 1931).
—— *Pushkin as Don Juan* (Paris, 1935).
Illustrated Russian Review (special issue on Pushkin, February 6, 1937).
KAPNIST, Count P. *Regarding Pushkin's Expulsion from Odessa* (*Old Russia*, 1899).
KARAMZIN. *Letters to I.-I. Dmitryev.*
—— *Works and Unpublished Letters* (1862).
KHODASEVICH, V.-F. *On Pushkin.*
KIRPOTIN. *Pushkin* (Moscow, 1936).
KOTLYAREVSKY. *Pushkin* (Berlin, 1925).
KOZMAN. *Satire and Humor in Pushkin.*
* LACROIX, Frédéric. *Mysteries of Russia* (Pagnerre, 1845).
The Lenin Library Work on Pushkin (1934).
LERNER, N. *The Works and Days of Pushkin* (Moscow, 1903).
LEZHNEV, A. *Pushkin's Prose* (Moscow, 1937).
Literary Heritage (large volume of Pushkin lore, 1934).
LVOV, L. *Parisian Echoes in 1837* (relating to Pushkin; Paris, 1937).
MAYKOV. *Pushkin, Material and Historical Notes for Use in His Biography* (St. Petersburg, 1899).
MEREZHKOVSKY. *The Eternal Companions: Pushkin* (St. Petersburg, 1906).
* —— *The Enigma of Alexander I* (Calmann-Lévy, 1926).
* —— *The Death of Alexander I* (Calmann-Lévy, 1927).
METMAN, Louis. *Georges-Charles d'Anthès.*
* MILYUKOV. *Pushkin Living* (Paris).
—— *History of Russia* (with Seignobos and Eisenmann, 3 vols.; Leroux, 1932).
MODZALEVSKY. *Pushkin and Secret Surveillance* (1925).
—— *New Material Relating to Pushkin's Last Duel and Death* (pub. by Modzalevsky, Oxman and Tsyavlovsky, 1924).
—— *The Decembrists and Their Age* (1928).
—— *Pushkin's Manuscripts* (with Tomashevsky, 1937).
MYAKOTIN, V. *Pushkin and the Decembrists* (Prague, 1923).
NEGOVSKY, E. *Calendar of Pushkin's Days* (Kishinev, 1937).
NEVSOROV. *For Use in the Biography of Pushkin.*
Historical Notes (Moscow, 1937).
ONEGIN, A.-F. *Unpublished Writings by Pushkin* (1923).
On the Centenary of the Death of Pushkin (collection of writings; Moscow-Leningrad, 1938).
OVSYANIKO-KULIKOVSKY. *Pushkin.*
Past and Present (*Starina y novizna*); periodical.
PAVLISHCHEV, L. *Recollections of Pushkin* (1890).
* PERSKY, Sergey. *Three Wives* (Payot, 1929).
* PICCARD. *Alexander Pushkin* (biography; Editions de la Baconnière, Neuchâtel, 1939).
PIKSANOV. *Pushkin's Workroom* (1922).
* PLATONOV. *History of Russia* (Plon, 1929).

PLETNEV. *Zhukovsky's Life and Works* (1853).
POKROVSKY. *Pushkin, His Life and Works* (Moscow, 1916).
POLYAKOV. *Pushkin's Death in the Light of the New Documents* (St. Petersburg, 1922).
Pushkin and His Contemporaries (periodical anthology of Pushkin lore, fascicles 1 to 39).
Pushkin and His Period (Editions de la Russie illustrée; Paris, 1937).
Pushkin and Siberia (Irkutsk, 1937).
* *Pushkin Exhibition* (Paris, 1937).
Pushkin Memorial (Leningrad, 1937).
PUSHKIN, Basil Lvovich. *The Dangerous Neighbor.*
* PUTERMAN. *Pushkin* (texts compiled by Puterman; Editions sociales internationales; 1937).
Review: The Slavic World (February 1937).
Review of Comparative Literature (issue on Pushkin, January–March 1937).
ROSSETTI. *Stories About Pushkin* (Russian Archives, 1882).
ROZANOV, I. *The Pushkin Pleiad* (Moscow, 1923).
Russia and Pushkin (anthology of articles; Kharbin, 1937).
Russian Antiquity (*Ruskaya Starina*) (periodical–complete collection).
Russian Poets on Pushkin (anthology of poetry; St. Petersburg, 1899).
Russian Secret Societies in the Early Nineteenth Century (anthology).
SCHICK, A. *Pushkin's Odessa* (Paris, 1938).
—— *Pushkin Married* (Paris, 1936).
SHCHEGOLEV. *Pushkin's Last Duel and Death* (St. Petersburg, 1927 edition; enlarged and revised edition of 1936).
—— *Pushkin, Observations* (St. Petersburg, 1912).
* SHILDER. *History of Paul I in Anecdotes* (Calmann-Lévy, 1899).
—— *Emperor Alexander I, His Life and Reign* (St. Petersburg, 1904).
—— *Nicholas I* (2 vols., St. Petersburg, 1903).
SHIMAN. *Alexander I* (Moscow, 1909).
SHIROKY. *Pushkin's Villa at Tsarskoye Selo* (Leningrad, 1936).
SHKLOVSKY. *Remarks on Pushkin's Prose* (Moscow, 1937).
SHLYAPKIN. *For Use in the Biography of Pushkin* (St. Petersburg, 1899).
—— *Unpublished Pushkin Papers* (St. Petersburg, 1903).
SINYAVSKY and TSYAVLOVSKY. *Pushkin and the Press* (1914).
SMIRNOV, N.-M. *Recollections* (Russian Archives, 1882).
SMIRNOVA-ROSSETTI. *Notes* (St. Petersburg, 1895).
SOLLOGUB, Count V. A. *Recollections* (St. Petersburg, 1887).
—— *Yesterday and Today* (St. Petersburg, 1845).
* SONIS, Comte F. de. *Letters of Count and Countess Ficquelmont to Baroness Tiesenhausen* (Plon, 1911).
SREDIN. *Polotnyany Zavody* (archives of the Heckeren family).
STEIN, von. *Pushkin as Mystic* (Riga, 1931).
TOMASHEVSKY. *Pushkin: Current Problems in Historical and Literary Research* (Leningrad, 1925).
TROSHYN. *Pushkin and the Psychology of Creation.*

TSEITLIN, A. *Pushkin's Mastery* (Moscow, 1937).
—— *Pushkin* (anthology of articles; Moscow, 1937).
TSURIKOV. *Pushkin's Testament* (Belgrade, 1937).
TSYAVLOVSKY. *Pushkin's Moscow* (1937).
TSYAVLOVSKY, Modzalevsky, Sanger. *In Pushkin's Hand* (unpublished writings, 1935).
TURGENEV (archives of the brothers, 1911–13).
TYNYANOV. *Archaists and Innovators* (1929).
TYRKOVA-WILLIAMS. *Life of Pushkin* (Volume I, Paris, 1929).
VASILICH. *The Debacle of 1825.*
VERESAEV, V. *Pushkin in Life* (2 vols., 1936).
—— *Pushkin's Companions* (2 vols., 1937).
VIGEL. *Recollections* (Moscow, 1864).
* VOGUE, Vicomte E.-M. de. *The Russian Novel* (Paris, Plon, 1886).
VYAZEMSKY, Prince P.-A. *Works* (9 vols., 1878–84).
* WALICZEVSKY. *The Reign of Alexander I* (3 vols., Plon, 1923).
WEGNER, M. *Pushkin's Ancestors* (Moscow, 1937).
WULF, A. *Diary* (Moscow, 1929).
YARKHO, Romanovich and Lapchina. *Guide to the Metrics of Pushkin's Verse* (1934).
YAROSLAVSKY. *Pushkin's Atheism* (1937).
YATZEVICH. *St. Petersburg in Pushkin's Day* (Leningrad, 1931).
—— *Serfdom in St. Petersburg in Pushkin's Day* (Leningrad, 1937).
YENIKOLOPOV. *Pushkin in the Caucasus* (1938).
ZAMOTIN. *Pushkin* (Minsk, 1937).
ZAOERSKY. *Pushkin in the Reminiscences and Letters of His Contemporaries* (Moscow, 1910).
ZAVODCHIKOV. *The Sword* (Pushkin's political pamphlets and satires; 1927).
ZHIKHAREV. *Notes* (Moscow, 1890).
ZHUKOVSKY. *Complete Works* (3 vols., St. Petersburg, 1906).

To the above should be added fictionalized biographies such as those by I. Tynyanov (*Pushkin, Küchelbecker*), Zylov (*Pushkin's Return*), Novikov (*Pushkin at Mikhailovskoye*), Nazhyvin (*In Pushkin's Day*), etc.

Notes

PART I, CHAPTER 1

1. Memoirs of Father Georgel, quoted by the Comte de Falloux.
2. *Moscow News*, 1822, no. 72.
3. Blagov, *Tales My Grandmother Told*.
4. This account of the ideal housewife's day has been compiled from documents relating to Marya Ivanovna Rimsky-Korsakov (1765–1832), used by Herschensohn in his book *Moscow in Griboedov's Day*.
5. March 30, 1820.

PART I, CHAPTER 2

1. Sergey Lvovich protested fiercely against this version of the story, which he considered injurious to his father's memory. However, a document unearthed by Mr. Modzalevsky states that "for blows gratuitously inflicted upon the person of a Venetian in his employ, one Harlampius Mercadius, Pushkin was placed under arrest; but an order was issued by the sovereign and the said Pushkin was subsequently pardoned."
2. Count M. A. Korf.

PART I, CHAPTER 3

1. Pavlishchev, *Recollections*.
2. Told by the assistant of Pushkin's nanny.
3. Cf. Tynyanov, *Pushkin's Childhood*.
4. E. P. Yankova.
5. Draft of a poem.
6. Makarov.
7. Not published until 1822.
8. Written in French.
9. Pushchin, *Recollections of Pushkin*.

PART I, CHAPTER 4

1. Written in April 1812.
2. Written in 1809.
3. Related by K. A. Stork.

PART I, CHAPTER 5

1. Original in German.

PART I, CHAPTER 6

1. Written in 1815.
2. Written in 1829.

PART I, CHAPTER 7

1. Glinka, *Recollections.*
2. Letter, April 17, 1816.
3. In French in the original.

PART I, CHAPTER 8

1. Written in 1816.
2. Pushchin, *Recollections.* The emperor's last sentence is in French in the original.
3. Written in 1817.
4. "The Mustaches."
5. "Vadim."

PART II, CHAPTER 1

1. "I was bored all alone in Pskov. . . ." (Letter from Pushkin to Vyazemsky, September 1, 1817.)
2. Told by Gorchakov, as recorded by Bartenyev.
3. In French in the original.
4. Written in 1819.
5. "Can you imagine, in the days when we used to fight with the Germans at the Red Cabaret, we ourselves were never seriously hurt, and the Germans used to stand there and take it and not even fight back. . . ." (Letter from Pushkin to his wife, May 18, 1836.)
6. Kulikov.

PART II, CHAPTER 2

1. Count S. S. Uvarov.

2. *Envoi from Pushkin to Engelhardt.*
3. Annenkov and Bartenyev.
4. Shchegolev.
5. Letter to Mansurov, October 27, 1819.
6. Korsakov.

PART II, CHAPTER 3

1. Gribbe, *Reminiscences.*
2. Some scholars dispute his authorship.
3. Pushkin, *Imaginary Conversation with Alexander I.*
4. Yakushkin, *Memoirs.*
5. N. I. Pirogov.

PART II, CHAPTER 4

1. Poem dedicated to Gorchakov.
2. P. A. Katenev.
3. Pushchin, *Memoirs.*
4. The letter was written by Capo d'Istria, signed by Nesselrode, and approved by the emperor.

PART II, CHAPTER 5

1. *Neva Observer* (No. 7, 1820).
2. *European Herald* (or *Messenger*) (No. 11, 1820).
3. *Bacchic Chant.*

PART III, CHAPTER 1

1. Written in 1821.
2. Fadeev, *Recollections.*
3. Letter to his brother, September 24, 1820.
4. Ibid.
5. Dr. Rudykovsky, *Meeting with Pushkin.*
6. Ibid.
7. Letter, September 24, 1820.
8. Pushkin, *Journey to Arzerum.*
9. Draft of *Eugene Onegin.*
10. Letter of September 24, 1820.
11. Letter of December 1824.
12. Letter of September 24, 1820.
13. In French in the original.

PART III, CHAPTER 2

1. Letter to Gnedich, December 4, 1820.
2. A. M. Loboda.

3. Written in French.
4. Letter of April 29, 1822.
5. Letter of October 14, 1823.
6. Ibid.
7. Letter of February 6, 1823.
8. Dated May 15, 1821.

Part III, Chapter 3

1. Luginin (1822); his account was not published until 1934.
2. Letter to Vyazemsky, January 2, 1822.
3. Written in French.
4. Letter of June 1824.
5. Letter of July 21, 1822.
6. Letter of October 1822.
7. Letter in the beginning of 1823.
8. Letter of January 24, 1822.
9. Letter of September 26, 1822.
10. Letter of April 5, 1823.
11. Letter of June 13, 1823.
12. Letter of September 4, 1822.
13. Letter of December 8, 1823.
14. Dyditskaya.
15. *Russian Archives*, 1899, Vol. II, p. 343.

Part III, Chapter 4

1. As told by Urzul to Viegel.
2. Letter of November 11, 1823.
3. Draft of a letter to Bestuzhev, June 13, 1823.
4. Letter from Raevsky, March 10, 1825.
5. Letter to Chaadaev, March 7, 1825.
6. Written in French.
7. V. F. Raevsky, *Recollections*.
8. Letter of June 27, 1821.
9. Letter of June 21, 1822.
10. Letter of May 31, 1823.
11. Letter of June 1, 1823.
12. Letter to his brother, August 23, 1823.

Part IV, Chapter 1

1. Letter to Vyazemsky, October 14, 1823.
2. Letter to Delvig, November 16, 1823.
3. Letter to Turgenev, December 1, 1823.
4. Letter to A. I. Turgenev.
5. *Imaginary Conversation with Alexander I.*

6. Zelenetsky, based on the statements of an Odessa cab driver.
7. Written in French.
8. Letter to Grech, September 21, 1821.
9. Letter to Vyazemsky, 1823.
10. Letter to Bestuzhev, February 8, 1824.

Part IV, Chapter 2

1. Letter, in French, June 13, 1824.
2. Letter, in French, June 20, 1824.
3. Letter, in French, June 23, 1824.
4. Letter, in French, June 27, 1824.
5. Letter, in French, July 4, 1824.
6. Underlined in the original.
7. Letter, in French, July 11, 1824.
8. Letter, in French, July 27, 1824.
9. Original in French.

Part IV, Chapter 3

1. Original in French.
2. Original in French.
3. Original in French.
4. Original in French.
5. Original in French.
6. Original in French.
7. Original in French.
8. This letter was written in French, but has only been published in a Russian translation; consequently (before translation into English), the text given here may not be an exact replica of the original.
9. Letter, August 13, 1824.
10. The last sentence is in French in the original.
11. Potosky.

Part V, Chapter 1

1. Original in French.
2. Letter dated early October 1824.
3. Letters to Leo: October and November 1824; February, March, April 1825.
4. Letter to Pletnev, August 1825.
5. Letters, February, March, April 1825.

Part V, Chapter 2

1. Pushkin, *Observations.*
2. Letter, in French, to Princess Vyazemsky, dated mid-October 1824.

3. Letter, December 4, 1824.
4. Letter, late October 1824.
5. Original in French.
6. Original in French.
7. Original in French.
8. Original in French.
9. Letter, in French, July 21, 1825.
10. Letter, in French, July 25, 1825.
11. Letter, in French, August 14, 1825.
12. Letter, in French, August 14, 1825.
13. Letter, in French, mid-August 1825.
14. Letter, in French, August 28, 1825.

PART V, CHAPTER 3

1. *The Moscow Telegraph*, 1833, No. 2.
2. *Son of the Fatherland*, 1831, No. 20.
3. *Galatea*, 1839, No. 27.
4. Kamashev, *Son of the Fatherland*, 1831.
5. *The Telescope*, 1831, No. 2.
6. *Conversation*, 1831.
7. *Son of the Fatherland*, 1831.

PART V, CHAPTER 4

1. Letter to Pletnev, January 1826.
2. Letter to Delvig, mid-February 1826.
3. Letter to Delvig, February 20, 1826.
4. Letter, early March, 1826.
5. Letter, March 8, 1826.
6. Letter, mid-March 1826.
7. Letter, April 20, 1826.
8. Written in French.

PART VI, CHAPTER 1

1. This account of Pushkin's interview with the emperor is based on the following sources: as told by Pushkin's brother to N. I. Lorer; as told by Pushkin to Khomutova; Baron Korf's notes; a study by Grot.
2. N. V. Putyata, *Notebook*.
3. Countess E. P. Rostopchin.
4. Letter, in French, October 29, 1826.
5. Letter, in French, to Mrs. Osipov, September 15, 1826.
6. Written in French.
7. Bulletin of September 17, 1826, in French (with several mistakes).
8. Letter written in May 1826.

9. Letter, December 1, 1826.
10. Original in French.
11. Telepneva, *Journal*, June 22, 1827.
12. Original in French.

Part VI, Chapter 2

1. Original in French.
2. Report in French by Benkendorf to Nicholas I, July 12, 1827.
3. Report by Von Fok, October 1827.
4. Report by a secret agent, February 1828.
5. Original in French.
6. Letter to Pletnev, October 1829.
7. *Son of the Fatherland*, 1829.
8. *Northern Bee*, 1829.
9. Letter of November 26, 1828.
10. Letter, December 12, 1828.

Part VI, Chapter 3

1. Told by Kamenskaya, Mrs. Zakrevsky's niece.
2. Written in French.
3. N. M. Smirnov.
4. Letter, in French, dated late May 1830.
5. Ivanovsky, agent of the third section, *Recollections*.
6. Bulgakov, letter of March 21, 1829.
7. V. A. Ushakov, in the *Moscow Telegraph*, 1832.

Part VI, Chapter 4

1. Original in French.
2. Reminiscences of M. I. Pushchin, brother of the exiled Decembrist I. I. Pushchin.
3. N. I. Ushakov.
4. Hanheblov.
5. *The Journey to Arzerum.*
6. M. I. Pushchin, the Decembrist's brother.
7. Letter to Vyazemsky, August 30, 1829.
8. *The Journey to Arzerum.*

Part VII, Chapter 1

1. Letter, in French, April 1830.
2. Original in French.
3. Written in French.
4. Original in French.

Part VII, Chapter 2

1. Original in French.
2. By Delvig, in the *Literary Gazette.*
3. Original in French.
4. Original in French.
5. *Northern Bee,* No. 30, March 11, 1830.
6. Original in French.
7. In French in the original.
8. Original in French.
9. Original in French.
10. Written in French.
11. Written in French.
12. Letter, in French, May 1830.
13. Written in French.
14. Letter, in French, July 20, 1830.
15. Letter, in French, July 30, 1830.
16. Original in French.
17. Letter, in French, November 26, 1830.

Part VII, Chapter 3

1. Written in French.
2. Written in French.
3. Written in French.
4. Written in French.
5. Written in French.
6. Letter, in French, December 2, 1830.
7. Reminiscences of Nikitenko.
8. Letter from Mrs. Khitrovo, May 18, 1830.
9. *The Snowstorm.*
10. *The Undertaker.*
11. *The Postmaster.*
12. *For Your Distant Homeland Shores.*
13. *Incantation.*
14. *Elegy.*
15. *Lines Written During a Sleepless Night.*
16. *The Demons.*
17. *My Genealogy.*

Part VII, Chapter 4

1. Letter, in French, December 9, 1830.
2. Letter, in French, January 21, 1831.
3. Letter to Pletnev, January 13, 1831.

4. The sentence is in French in the original.
5. Letter, in French, from Miss Kashkina to Mrs. Osipov, April 25, 1831.
6. Letter to Pletnev, February 24, 1831.
7. Letter, in French, June 26, 1831.

Part VII, Chapter 5

1. Letter of June 1, 1831.
2. Letter to Nashchokin.
3. Letter, in French, July 30, 1831.
4. Miss Rossetti's memoirs.
5. This entire scene is described in Miss Rossetti's memoirs.
6. Based on statements by A. P. Arapov, Natalya's daughter by her second husband.
7. Polonsky.
8. Letter, July 26, 1831.
9. Written in French.
10. Original in French.
11. Written in French.
12. Written in French.
13. Written in French.
14. Written in French.
15. Letter, in French, June 4, 1832.
16. Letter of September 22, 1832.
17. Letter of September 25, 1832.
18. Letter of September 27, 1832.
19. Letter of September 28–30, 1832.
20. Letter of October 1–2, 1832.
21. Letter to Nashchokin, February 1833.
22. Told by Nashchokin to Bartenyev.
23. One contemporary Serbian critic has investigated the sources of *La Guzla,* and discovered among them an old Scottish ballad, an Italian legend, and one of the idylls of Theocritus.

Part VII, Chapter 6

1. Dahl, *Reminiscences.*
2. Written in French.

Part VII, Chapter 7

1. Lenz.
2. Marina, *A Nest of Aristocrats in the Arbat.*
3. Written in French.
4. Written in French.

5. Written in French.
6. Written in French.
7. Written in French.
8. Letter, in French, October 29, 1834.
9. Written in French.
10. Written in French.
11. Written in French.
12. Letter, June 3, 1834.
13. Letter, June 8, 1834.
14. Letter, June 30, 1834.
15. Letter, May 29, 1834.
16. Letter, June 8, 1834.
17. Original in French.
18. Original in French.
19. The last sentence in French.
20. Written in French.

Part VII, Chapter 8

1. Written in French.
2. Written in French.
3. Letter, in French.
4. Letter, in French.
5. Letter, June 1, 1835.
6. Letter, in French, July 22, 1835.
7. Letter, in French, October 1835.
8. Written in French.
9. Written in French.
10. Letter, in French.
11. Letter, in French.
12. Letter, in French.
13. Written in French.
14. Letter, May 5, 1836.
15. Letter, May 18, 1836.

Part VIII, Chapter 1

1. Comte de Falloux, *Memoirs of a Royalist.*
2. Cf. account of Mrs. Arapov.
3. Vyazemsky, *Complete Works,* p. 558.
4. Article in *Russian Archives,* 1888, Vol. II, p. 305.
5. Ibid., 1882, Vol. I, p. 234.
6. Ibid., 1882, Vol. I, p. 246.
7. Cf. the extracts from the Archives published by Grossman in *Annals,* No. 2, pp. 340–353.
8. *Account of the Relations Between Pushkin and D'Anthès,* 1887.

9. Louis Metman, *Study of the D'Anthès Family.*
10. Letter, in French, from the archives of Baron Heckeren d'Anthès.
11. Ibid.
12. Ibid.
13. Letter, in French.
14. Sukhotin, *Memoirs.*
15. Lenz, *Recollections.*
16. Kolmakov, *Recollections.*
17. This letter is preserved in the archives of Baron Heckeren d'Anthès.
18. Written in French.
19. This and six other letters quoted in subsequent chapters form part of a recently discovered group of sixty, written to Andrey Karamzin, the famous historian's son, by his mother Katerina Andreyevna, his older sister Sofya, and his brother Alexander. The correspondence was first published in 1956 in the Soviet review *Novy Mir* ("Some Karamzin Family Letters," ed. by N. Botashev with notes by I. Andronikov; cf. also *Pushkin in the Karamzin Letters,* published by the Academy of Sciences, Moscow-Leningrad, 1960).
20. See the account by Mrs. Arapov in *New Times,* No. 112, p. 416, and the statements by Gustave Friesenhof in *Red Neva,* No. 10, 1929.
21. Letter, July 9, 1836.
22. Letter, July 13, 1836.
23. Letter, in French.

Part VIII, Chapter 2

1. Written in French.
2. Letter of March 1, 1837.
3. Ibid.
4. Written in French.
5. Written in French.
6. Written in French.
7. Written in French.
8. Written in French.
9. Written in French.
10. Rossetti, *Memoirs.*
11. As told by Mrs. Arapov.
12. *Novy Mir,* "Some Karamzin Family Letters," ed. by N. Botashev, with notes by I. Andronikov, 1956. Cf. also *Pushkin in the Karamzin Letters,* published by the Academy of Sciences, Moscow-Leningrad, 1960.
13. The original of the letter is in French.
14. Letter, in French, late December 1836.
15. Letter from the archives of Baron Heckeren d'Anthès.
16. Ibid.
17. Ibid.
18. *Novy Mir,* "Some Karamzin Family Letters," ed. by N. Botashev,

with notes by I. Andronikov, 1956. Cf. also *Pushkin in the Karamzin Letters,* published by the Academy of Sciences, Moscow-Leningrad, 1960.

19. Letter, in French, from the archives of Baron Heckeren d'Anthès.

PART VIII, CHAPTER 3

1. According to Amosov.
2. Letter, in French, to Grand Duke Michael.
3. Ibid.
4. Written in French.
5. Written in French.
6. Written in French.
7. According to D'Anthès' testimony, February 26, 1837.
8. As told to Bartenyev by Princess Vyazemsky.
9. Quoted in a letter from Vyazemsky to Grand Duke Michael.
10. *Novy Mir,* "Some Karamzin Family Letters," ed. by N. Botashev, with notes by I. Andronikov, 1956. Cf. also *Pushkin in the Karamzin Letters,* published by the Academy of Sciences, Moscow-Leningrad, 1960.
11. According to the accounts of Mrs. Arapov, Baron Friesenhof and Princess Vyazemsky.
12. As told by Princess Vyazemsky.
13. Previously unpublished letter in French from the archives of Baron Heckeren d'Anthès.
14. Original in French.
15. Original in French.
16. Suvorin, *Diary,* p. 205.

PART VIII, CHAPTER 4

1. Written in French.
2. Written in French.
3. Written in French.
4. The original is in French.
5. Letter, in French, from Vyazemsky to Grand Duke Michael.
6. Dr. Scholtz's report.
7. As told by Princess Dolgorukov.
8. Letter, in French.
9. Letter, in French.
10. Original in French.
11. Letter, in French.

POST MORTEM

1. Letter, February 4, 1837.
2. Letter, January 30, 1837, in *Novy Mir,* "Some Karamzin Family Letters," ed. by N. Botashev, with notes by I. Andronikov, 1956. Cf. also *Push-*

kin in the Karamzin Letters, published by the Academy of Sciences, Moscow-Leningrad, 1960.

3. Ibid.
4. Letter, in French, March 19, 1837.
5. In French in the original.
6. Letter, in French, from the archives of Baron Heckeren d'Anthès.
7. Ibid., previously unpublished.
8. Ibid., previously unpublished.
9. Ibid.
10. Written in French.
11. Letter in French.
12. Letter, in French, March 1, 1837.
13. Previously unpublished letter, in French, from the archives of Baron Heckeren d'Anthès.
14. Ibid., previously unpublished.
15. Ibid.; the final sentence is in Russian.
16. Ibid.
17. Ibid.
18. Ibid., previously unpublished.
19. *Novy Mir*, "Some Karamzin Family Letters," ed. by N. Botashev, with notes by I. Andronikov, 1956. Cf. also *Pushkin in the Karamzin Letters*, published by the Academy of Sciences, Moscow-Leningrad, 1960.
20. Previously unpublished letter, in French, from the archives of Baron Heckeren d'Anthès.
21. Letter from Baroness Vrevsky to her brother, September 2, 1837.
22. Previously unpublished letter from the archives of Baron Heckeren d'Anthès.
23. Ibid.
24. Ibid., in French.
25. Letter, in French.
26. From an unpublished letter written by Alexandra Arapov née Lanskoy, to the son of Baron Georges-Charles d'Anthès.
27. Remark made by M. Jules Legras in *Le Monde slave.*

Index

P. refers to Alexander Pushkin. Pushkin's works are listed under the entry for Pushkin.

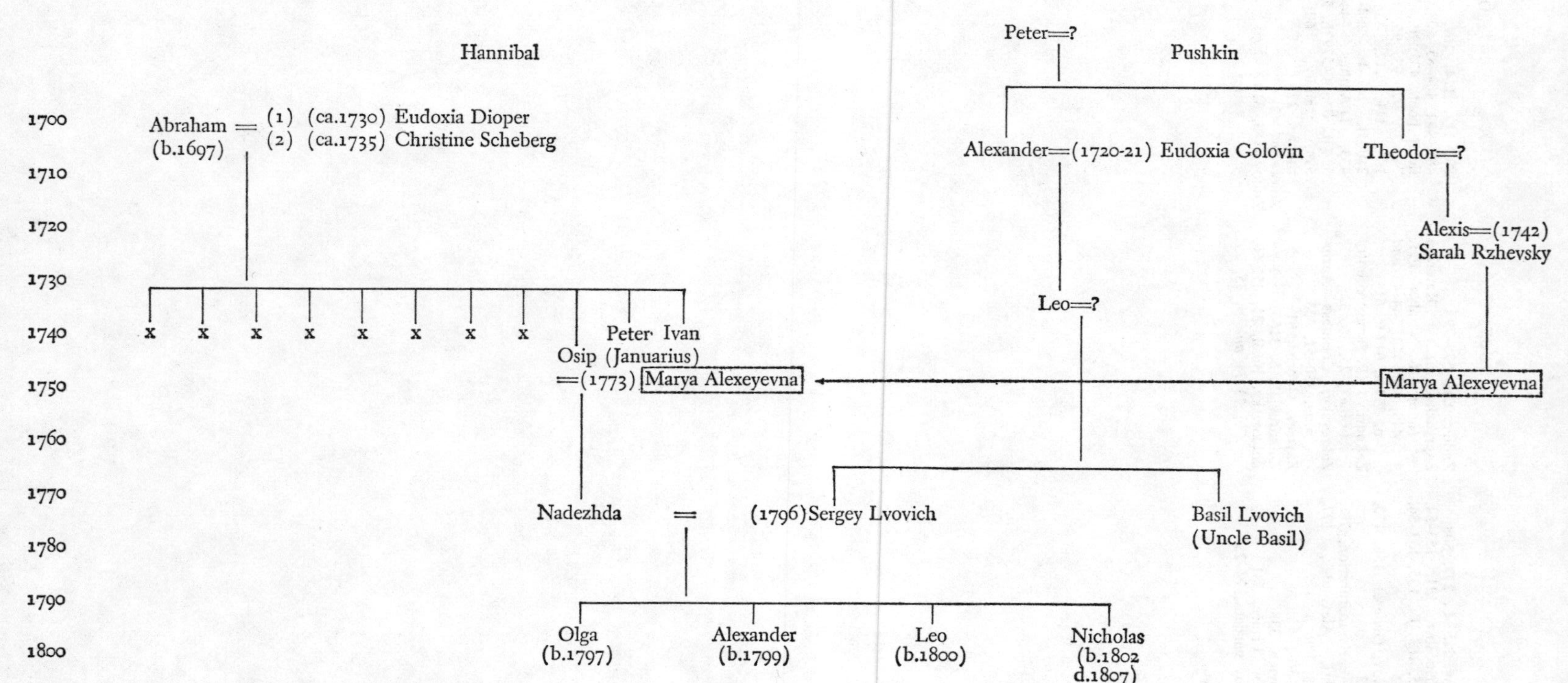

Hannibal
Pushkin
1700
1710
1720
1730
1740
1750
1760
1770
1780
1790
1800
Abraham = (1) (ca.1730) Eudoxia Dioper
(b.1697) (2) (ca.1735) Christine Scheberg
x x x x x x x x
Peter Ivan
Osip (Januarius)
=(1773) Marya Alexeyevna
Nadezhda = (1796) Sergey Lvovich
Olga (b.1797)
Alexander (b.1799)
Leo (b.1800)
Nicholas (b.1802 d.1807)
Peter=?
Alexander=(1720-21) Eudoxia Golovin
Theodor=?
Alexis=(1742) Sarah Rzhevsky
Leo=?
Marya Alexeyevna
Basil Lvovich (Uncle Basil)